Lecture Notes in Computer Science   11757

Commenced Publication in 1973
Founding and Former Series Editors:
Gerhard Goos, Juris Hartmanis, and Jan van Leeuwen

Formal Methods

Subline of Lectures Notes in Computer Science

More information about this series at http://www.springer.com/series/7408

Bernd Finkbeiner · Leonardo Mariani (Eds.)

Runtime Verification

19th International Conference, RV 2019
Porto, Portugal, October 8–11, 2019
Proceedings

Springer

Editors
Bernd Finkbeiner 🆔
Universität des Saarlandes
Saarbrücken, Germany

Leonardo Mariani 🆔
University of Milano Bicocca
Milan, Italy

ISSN 0302-9743   ISSN 1611-3349 (electronic)
Lecture Notes in Computer Science
ISBN 978-3-030-32078-2   ISBN 978-3-030-32079-9 (eBook)
https://doi.org/10.1007/978-3-030-32079-9

LNCS Sublibrary: SL2 – Programming and Software Engineering

This Springer imprint is published by the registered company Springer Nature Switzerland AG
The registered company address is: Gewerbestrasse 11, 6330 Cham, Switzerland

Preface

This volume contains the proceedings of the 19th International Conference on Runtime Verification (RV 2019), which was held during October 8–11, 2019, in Porto, Portugal, as part of the Third World Congress on Formal Methods (FM 2019).

The RV series consists of annual meetings that gather together scientists from both academia and industry interested in investigating novel lightweight formal methods to monitor, analyze, and guide the runtime behavior of software and hardware systems. Runtime verification techniques are crucial for system correctness, reliability, and robustness; they provide an additional level of rigor and effectiveness compared with conventional testing, and are generally more practical than exhaustive formal verification. Runtime verification can be used prior to deployment, for testing, verification, and debugging purposes, and after deployment for ensuring reliability, safety, and security and for providing fault containment and recovery as well as online system repair.

RV started in 2001 as an annual workshop and turned into a conference in 2010. The workshops were organized as satellite events of an established forum, including CAV and ETAPS. The proceedings of RV from 2001 to 2005 were published in the *Electronic Notes in Theoretical Computer Science*. Since 2006, the RV proceedings have been published in Springer's *Lecture Notes in Computer Science*. The previous RV conferences took place in Istanbul, Turkey (2012); Rennes, France (2013); Toronto, Canada (2014); Vienna, Austria (2015); Madrid, Spain (2016); Seattle, USA (2017); and Limassol, Cyprus (2018).

There were 38 submissions, 31 as regular contributions, two as short contributions, two as tool demonstration papers, and three as benchmark papers. Each benchmark paper was reviewed by three Program Committee members, submissions in the other categories were reviewed by four members. The committee decided to accept 19 papers, 14 regular papers, two short papers, two tool demonstration papers, and one benchmark paper. The evaluation and selection process involved thorough discussions among the members of the Program Committee and external reviewers through the EasyChair conference manager, before reaching a consensus on the final decisions. To complement the contributed papers, we included in the program three invited speakers covering both industry and academia:

- David Basin, ETH Zurich, Switzerland
- Akshay Rajhans, Mathworks, USA
- Sanjit A. Seshia, University of California, Berkeley, USA

The conference included four tutorials that took place on the first day. The following tutorials were selected to cover a breadth of topics relevant to RV:

- Christopher Hahn presented a tutorial on "Algorithms for Monitoring Hyperproperties"
- Georgios Fainekos, Bardh Hoxha, and Sriram Sankaranarayanan presented a tutorial on "Robustness of Specifications and its Applications to Falsification, Parameter Mining, and Runtime Monitoring with S-TaLiRo"
- Hazem Torfah presented a tutorial on "Stream-based Monitors for Real-time Properties"
- Yliès Falcone presented a tutorial "On the Runtime Enforcement of Timed Properties"

During a special award session at the conference, the 2019 RV Test of Time Award was given to Moonzoo Kim, Sampath Kannan, Insup Lee, and Oleg Sokolsky for their RV 2001 paper "Java-MaC: A Run-time Assurance Tool for Java Programs." The awardees gave a retrospective talk and an associated invited paper is included in the proceedings.

We would like to thank the authors of all submitted papers, the members of the Steering Committee, the Program Committee, and the external reviewers for their exhaustive task of reviewing and evaluating all submitted papers. We are grateful to José Nuno Oliveira, the general chair of FM 2019, and the entire Organizing Commmittee for their outstanding support. We highly appreciate the EasyChair system for the management of submissions. We acknowledge the great support from our sponsors, Runtime Verification Inc. and CPEC – TRR 248 (see perspicuous-computing.science).

August 2019   Bernd Finkbeiner
                                                               Leonardo Mariani

Organization

Program Committee

Wolfgang Ahrendt	Chalmers University of Technology, Sweden
Howard Barringer	The University of Manchester, UK
Ezio Bartocci	Vienna University of Technology, Austria
Andreas Bauer	KUKA, Germany
Eric Bodden	Paderborn University and Fraunhofer IEM, Germany
Borzoo Bonakdarpour	Iowa State University, USA
Christian Colombo	University of Malta, Malta
Ylies Falcone	University of Grenoble Alpes, France
Lu Feng	University of Virginia, USA
Bernd Finkbeiner	Saarland University, Germany
Adrian Francalanza	University of Malta, Malta
Luca Franceschini	University of Genoa, Italy
Radu Grosu	Stony Brook University, USA
Sylvain Hallé	Université du Québec à Chicoutimi, Canada
Klaus Havelund	Jet Propulsion Laboratory, USA
Catalin Hritcu	Inria, France
Felix Klaedtke	NEC Labs, Switzerland
Axel Legay	Université Catholique de Louvain, Belgium
David Lo	Singapore Management University, Singapore
Leonardo Mariani	University of Milano Bicocca, Italy
Viviana Mascardi	University of Genoa, Italy
Dejan Nickovic	Austrian Institute of Technology, Austria
Ayoub Nouri	Verimag, France
Gordon Pace	University of Malta, Malta
Doron Peled	Bar-Ilan University, Israel
Ka I. Pun	Western Norway University of Applied Sciences, Norway
Jorge A. Pérez	University of Groningen, The Netherlands
Giles Reger	The University of Manchester, UK
Grigore Rosu	University of Illinois at Urbana-Champaign, USA
Kristin Yvonne Rozier	Iowa State University, USA
Cesar Sanchez	IMDEA Software Institute, Spain
Gerardo Schneider	Chalmers—University of Gothenburg, Sweden
Nastaran Shafiei	University of York, UK
Julien Signoles	CEA LIST, France
Scott Smolka	Stony Brook University, USA
Oleg Sokolsky	University of Pennsylvania, USA
Bernhard Steffen	University of Dortmund, Germany

Scott Stoller   Stony Brook University, USA
Volker Stolz   Høgskulen på Vestlandet, Norway
Neil Walkinshaw   The University of Sheffield, UK
Chao Wang   University of Southern California, USA
Xiangyu Zhang   Purdue University, USA

Contents

A Retrospective Look at the Monitoring and Checking (MaC) Framework

Sampath Kannan[1], Moonzoo Kim[2], Insup Lee[1], Oleg Sokolsky[1(✉)],
and Mahesh Viswanathan[3]

[1] University of Pennsylvania, Philadelphia, USA
sokolsky@cis.upenn.edu
[2] KAIST, Daejeon, Republic of Korea
[3] University of Illinois, Urbana-Champaign, USA

Abstract. The Monitoring and Checking (MaC) project gave rise to
a framework for runtime monitoring with respect to formally specified
properties, which later came to be known as runtime verification. The
project also built a pioneering runtime verification tool, Java-MaC, that
was an instantiation of the approach to check properties of Java programs. In this retrospective, we discuss decisions made in the design
of the framework and summarize lessons learned in the course of the
project.

1 Introduction

Motivation. The idea for the MaC project came from the realization that static
verification of safety and security properties was difficult and run-time monitoring, which seemed more feasible and practical, lacked a formal framework.
Program checking [5] was a relatively new and rigorous framework at that time
for run-time verification of programs computing (terminating) functions computations. Our goal was to take ideas from program checking to create a formal
run-time monitoring framework that would apply universally, not just to function computations, but to arbitrary programs including reactive programs that
have an on-going interaction with an environment.

As a first instantiation of this goal we decided to look into run-time verification of sequential programs (e.g., C and single-threaded Java). We were
presented immediately with several challenges. Because program checking was
defined only for programs computing (terminating) functions, it could treat the
program being checked as a black box and check only its input-output behavior.
In contrast, we were interested in checking properties over program behavior
during execution. Since we were monitoring and checking stateful programs, our
monitors needed to keep track of the values of variables in the programs being
checked.

Next, in order to check the correctness of a program, one needs to have
a notion of correctness defined independently of the program. Program checking had been successfully used largely for functions whose correct behavior was

B. Finkbeiner and L. Mariani (Eds.): RV 2019, LNCS 11757, pp. 1–14, 2019.
https://doi.org/10.1007/978-3-030-32079-9_1

mathematically defined. Examples included functions in linear algebra such as matrix rank or matrix product, graph-theoretic functions such as graph isomorphism, and optimization problems such as linear programming. Not only did these functions have rigorous mathematical definitions of correctness, but they also admitted 'local' self-consistency conditions. For example if two graphs are not isomorphic, an isomorphic copy of one of them is not isomorphic to the other. To design a program checker, one proved the sufficiency of such local consistency checks for proving the correctness of these functions and then implemented a checker using local self-consistency checks.

Problems. In checking arbitrary programs, however, we would not have a simple exogenously-defined, mathematical notion of correctness. How then were we going to impose what correct behavior meant? For this we turned to formal methods, and specifically model checking, where such notions of correctness were defined using temporal logics such as CTL and LTL, and automata.

What makes a correctness specification in one of these formalisms truly different from a direct and step-by-step correctness specification of a program? For if the latter were the way correctness was specified, then the specification would be very specific to a particular implementation and programming language used to write the program. The key distinction between the specification and the program was the level of abstraction or detail. Correctness properties in temporal logic are generally specified in terms of permissible sequences of occurrences for certain high-level or abstract events, while the program's behavior depends on low-level details such as the values of variables and the changes to these values in the course of execution of the program.

Solutions. Regarding how we relate the detailed behavior of the program to the high-level events in the specification, which was a major design challenge, one of the important design decisions was to let the designer of the program specify these relationships, rather than seeking to automate the process of discovering them. Thus the programmer, who would be intimately familiar with the details of the program would identify the variables whose values and value changes would trigger high-level events. The programmer would also provide a logical specification of when a high-level event occurs. The MaC framework would provide the language for expressing these logical connections.

We had to decide how events would be expressed in terms of values of variables. We realized that, for example, an event could be triggered at the *instant* at which some variable changed its value, but only if it happened during the *duration* that another variable had a particular value. Thus, we needed primitive variables both for describing instantaneous changes and durations. The specific logic we used to combine these variables to describe events will be described in the sequel.

There were many other design decisions, some in setting up the conceptual framework, and some that arose when we implemented a system based on this framework. Again, we describe some of these choices in the sequel.

In the rest of this paper we describe the timeline of the MaC project, some of the detailed objectives of the project, and design decisions we made, and the impact the project has had.

Timeline of the MaC Project. The Monitoring and Checking (MaC) project started as part of ONR MURI funded during 1997–2002. Goals of the MURI project were to make advances in software verification with specific applications to cyber-security. One of the initial ideas was that the well-known program-checking hypothesis [5], namely that it is often more efficient to check the correctness of a result than actually generating the result, can be applied to program correctness verification. First publications of describing the framework architecture and design trade-offs appeared in 1998 [12] and 1999 [15, 17] and the initial version of the tool, Java-MaC, implementing the MaC framework for monitoring of Java programs, has been presented at the first workshop on Runtime Verification in 2001 [13]. Since then, several extensions to the monitoring language and tools have been incorporated, while keeping the architecture intact. As the most significant extensions, we mention the steering capability [14], parametric monitoring [24], and support for monitoring of timing and probabilistic properties [21]. The Java-MaC tool has been applied to a variety of case studies, including an artificial physics application [9], network protocol validation [4], and a control system application that provided a simplex architecture-like effect using steering [14]. A variant of the tool to generate monitors in C has been applied to monitor a robotic control system [25].

Objectives of the MaC Project. The MaC project has several distinct objectives from its inception:

- Understand requirements for formal specification to represent monitorable properties and choose or develop a suitable language;
- Understand requirements for a tool infrastructure for monitoring and checking of software systems with respect to formal properties and develop and architecture to help satisfy these requirements; and
- Develop a prototype tool for software monitoring and checking.

All of these objectives were achieved in the course of the project. In the rest of the paper we will discuss design decisions that were made in the process.

Overview of the MaC Architecture. A visual representation of the architecture for the MaC framework is shown in Fig. 1. The architecture has two tiers. The top tier represents design-time activity. The user specifies properties using the MaC languages. There is a clear separation between primitive events and conditions, defined directly in terms of observations on the system, and derived events and conditions, defined hierarchically in terms of simpler objects. This separation is also maintained at run time in the lower tier of the architecture diagram, where a component called monitor or event recognizer observes the execution and detects occurrence of primitive events and changes in the values of primitive conditions. The checker then operates on the stream of primitive events and determines whether the property is satisfied. The definitions of primitive events serve an additional purpose: they capture, which observations on the system are important for monitoring. This information is then used to instrument the system to provide required observations. Finally, the checker can raise alarms to notify system operators or provide feedback to the system through additional instrumentation or via an existing recovery interface.

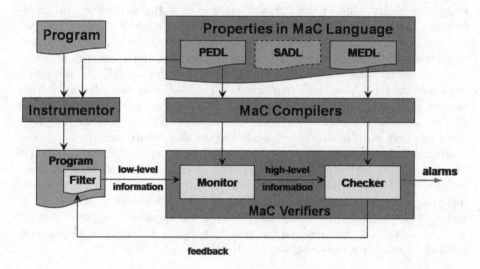

Fig. 1. Architecture of the MaC framework

2 MaC Design Highlights

In this sections, we take a closer look at components of the MaC framework and key design considerations for them. We consider property specification in the design-time layer of the framework, architecture of the run-time layer, and feedback capabilities.

2.1 Specification Languages and Their Semantics

Two-Tiered Specification. As mentioned above, the MaC framework includes two specification languages: Primitive Event Definition Language (PEDL) and Meta-Event Definition Language (MEDL). This approach allows for separation of concerns: behavior specification is expressed in MEDL, in terms of abstract notions such as events and conditions. Separately, primitive events and conditions are defined in PEDL in terms of program entities such as function calls and variable assignments. The PEDL language is by necessity specific to the system being monitored, since event definitions need to refer to system entities.

For example, in Java-MaC, an instantiation of the MaC framework for Java programs, PEDL expressions operate on method calls, updates to fields of an object, or local variables within a method. Objects are referenced using the "dot" notation familiar to Java programmers. By contrast, MEDL is intended to be system-independent.

A distinctive feature of MEDL is that it allows users to intermix two specification styles: a logical specification based on a past-time temporal logic and operational specification based on guarded commands over explicitly defined state variables. The interplay between the two specification styles is further discussed below.

Continuous-Time Semantics. MEDL specifications express properties of an executions at all time instances, not just instances where observations are available. This is in contrast to most RV approaches, where semantics of a specification are given in terms of a trace, i.e., samples of an execution captured by available observations. The consequence of defining semantics in terms of a given trace is that the question of whether we check the right trace is left out of the problem. To match MEDL specifications to program execution, the set of primitive events in a MEDL specification imposes requirements on what observations need to be extracted, and a PEDL specification describes how the extraction should be performed. We can easily check that every primitive event has a definition. If the right instrumentation technology is available, the PEDL specification also becomes the basis for automatic instrumentation.

Events and Conditions. The core of the MEDL language is the logic of events and conditions. Events and conditions are two distinct semantic entities in the logic. Events are instantaneous and signal changes in the state of the system. Typical examples of events are function calls and returns and assignment of values to variables. By contrast, conditions can be thought as predicates over the state of the system. Conditions evaluate to Boolean values and persist for a certain interval of time. Events and conditions as software specification devices have been around since the work of Parnas [1] and implemented in tools such as SCR* [11].

Most logics defined in the literature avoid making this distinction (e.g., duration calculus [30]) or concentrate on one or the other notion. State-based logics capture system properties in terms of states, while action-based logics concentrate on state changes. It is well-known that one specification style can be transformed into the other (see, e.g., [7]). In a monitoring setting, where properties are checked over a discrete trace, in which states are comprised of observations, it is indeed tempting to treat events as predicates. Such a predicate would be true in states where the event is observed and false everywhere else. Such a view would allow us to treat events and conditions uniformly. Nonetheless, we chose to treat events and conditions as semantically different kinds in the logic for the two reasons discussed below.

While, theoretically, it is sufficient to have either state-based or logic-based approach, they result in different specification styles. We believed that different kinds of system properties are more naturally specified using different styles. Moreover, it may be helpful to combine state-based and event-based reasoning, resulting in more compact and understandable specifications.

Second, we wanted to make claims about satisfaction of properties not just at instances when observations are available, but at all time instances. When we try to do this, we notice that conditions and events require very different reasoning. If, at a certain time point, there is no observation for an event, we conclude that the event is not occurring at that time point. By contrast, if there is no observation to evaluate the predicate of the condition, we conclude that the value of the predicate has not changed since the last time the predicate has been evaluated. If we tried to use the uniform representation of both events and conditions as predicates, as suggested above, we would not be able to properly choose the reasoning rule. To avoid this problem, we define separate semantic definitions for events and conditions.

The intuition presented above, treating conditions as abstractions of state and events as abstractions of state changes, allows us to define relationships between events and conditions. Each condition c, primitive or composite, gives rise to two events, $\mathsf{start}(c)$ and $\mathsf{end}(c)$. These events occur when c changes its value: $\mathsf{start}(c)$ occurs at the instance when the predicate defining c becomes true and $\mathsf{end}(c)$ occurs when the predicate defining c becomes false. Conversely, given two distinct event definitions e_1 and e_2, we can define the condition $[e_1, e_2)$, which is true at the current time if there has been an occurrence of e_1 in the past, but no occurrence of e_2 between that occurrence and the current moment. We refer to $[e_1, e_2)$ as the *interval* operator and note that it is similar to the *since* operator in past-time LTL.

The interval operator $[e_1, e_2)$ is the only temporal operator of the core logic of MEDL. From the discussion above, it is clear that it is a past-time temporal operator, with semantics given in terms of the prefix of the execution trace seen so far. This design decision was motivated by two considerations. First, we focused on detecting violations of safety properties and it is well known that if a safety property is violated, a violation is always exhibited by a finite prefix of an execution, so a past-time logic was deemed an appropriate specification approach. Second, a past-time approach allows us to avoid reasoning about future extensions of the current prefix and dealing with uncertainty about the future. In turn, this lack of uncertainty leads to more efficient checking algorithms. Processing a single observation takes time linear in the size of the formula and is independent of the length of the observed trace, which matches the complexity of checking past-time LTL [10]. The amount of space needed to represent the state of the monitor is also linear in the size of the formula and can be determined statically while generating the monitor.

Three-Valued Logic. Both specification languages of MaC framework are based on a three-valued logic to express *undefined* states of a target program in a compact manner. For example, a member variable v_j of an object o_i may not be visible until o_i is instantiated. In such situation, an expression e_k of behavioral specification like $\mathsf{o}_i.\mathsf{v}_j$ == 10 is undefined. This expression becomes defined only after o_i is instantiated. Similarly, this expression becomes undefined again if o_i is destructed. Thus, an expression of behavioral specification may change its definedness during the execution of a target program and three valued logic of PEDL/MEDL can conveniently describe such changes.

Monitor State and Guarded Commands with Auxiliary Variables. In addition to the logic of events and conditions, MEDL specifications can include guarded commands. Commands are sequences of expressions that update state variables of the monitor. We refer to these state variables as *auxiliary variables*, since they extend the state of the monitored system. Commands are triggered by occurrences of events defined in PEDL or MEDL. In turn, auxiliary variables can be used in predicates that define MEDL conditions and, ultimately, define new events. This creates a potential for infinite loops in monitor execution. MEDL semantics have been augmented to detect potential loops and reject such specifications as invalid.

2.2   Tool Architecture

Instrumentation vs. Virtual Machine. In order to support the continuous-time semantics defined above, instrumentation has to guarantee that no changes to monitored variables are missed. As a different method of extracting runtime information, we can utilize a monitoring and checking layer on top of a virtual machine such as JVM or LLVM virtual machine through debugging interfaces (e.g., The Java Virtual Machine Tools Interface (JVM TI)). Although a virtual machine-based approach can extract richer runtime information than the one extracted through target program instrumentation, it might be slower than the target program instrumentation. Also, at the time of developing Java-MaC (i.e., 1998–2000), JVM did not have "good" debugging interface, and thus, we determined that it would have required significantly more amount of effort to develop Java-MaC as a virtual machine layer than to develop Java-MaC as a framework to instrument a target program.

Bytecode-Level vs. Source-Level Instrumentation. To extract runtime information of a target program, a monitoring framework can instrument a target program either in a bytecode (i.e., executable binary) level or a sourcecode level. We decided to instrument a target program in a bytecode-level for the following reasons:

- *high applicability* (i.e., can be applied to almost all target programs).
- *fast setup* for runtime verification (i.e., no source code compilation required).
- *on-the-fly applicability to mobile applications* (e.g., Android applications) which are downloaded from app stores (e.g., Google playstore).

The weakness of bytecode level instrumentation is that it is difficult to directly obtain high-level runtime information from a target program execution. However, we believe that PEDL and MEDL scripts can enable reconstruction of high-level behavior of target program executions based on the low-level monitored data. In contrast, source-level instrumentation can be very complicated depending on the complexity of target source code, since the instrumentation should handle all possible complex statements of a target program.

Asynchronous vs. Synchronous Monitoring. Although MaC architecture can be applied to synchronous as well as asynchronous monitoring, our Java-MaC tool was designed to operate asynchronous monitors. The motivation for this design decision was to reduce timing overhead, i.e., disruption to the timing behavior of the system: instead of stopping the system while an observation is processed by the monitor, we send the observation to a stand-alone monitor, allowing the system to move along. Although the instrumentation to extract observation still needs to run as part of the system, checking of the property is performed elsewhere.

Checking of Timing Properties. When dealing with properties that specify quantitative timing behavior, the monitor needs to keep track of the progress of time. If an event e_2 should occur within a certain interval of time after an occurrence of e_1, the monitor needs to detect that the interval has expired. With the focus on asynchronous monitoring, timing properties present additional challenges in the MaC architecture, since the monitor clock may be different from the system clock. One can rely on timestamps of observations received from the system. Assuming in-order event delivery, once an observation with a sufficiently large timestamp is received, the monitor can conclude that e_2 did not occur in time. There may be a delay in detecting the violation, which may or may not be acceptable. However, if there is a possibility that observations will stop arriving if e_2 misses its deadline, then the violation will never be detected. In that case, the monitor would be required to track progress of time using its own clock, which requires additional assumptions about clock synchronization, delays in transmitting observations, etc. Extensions to the MEDL language and ways to provide guarantees of timely detection have been studied in [22].

2.3   Response

When a violation of a property is detected, it is not sufficient to just raise an alarm. Human operators may not be able to respond to an alarm fast enough, may not have sufficient situational awareness to choose an appropriate action to take, or may not have the right level of access to the running system. The MaC architecture allows the monitor to decide on the action and provides an interface to apply the action though the same instrumentation technology used to extract observations. We referred to this capability as *steering*. In response to an event raised by the monitor, a *steering action* can be performed to change the state of the running system or to invoke a recovery routine that may be provided by the system. A general theory of steering that would allow us to reason about the effects of monitor-triggered actions is not available. However, several case studies showed the utility of steering in situations where a high-level model of the system behavior is available. In particular, in [14], we developed a monitor-based implementation of Simplex architecture [23] and demonstrated its utility in a control system. In [9], a simulation-based study illustrated efficacy of steering in a distributed robotic application based on artificial physics.

3   Lessons Learned

After more than two decades of working on runtime verification problems, we can look back at the MaC framework and assess its vision and design through the prism of accumulated experience. We see two kinds of lessons that can be learned, as discussed in detail below. First, we can look at the impact of design decisions we have made and compare them with alternative decisions and possible extensions we did not pursue. Second, we can revisit our vision for how run-time verification would be applied and contrast it with emerging practical applications.

3.1   Reflections on MaC Design Decisions

Probably the most significant contribution of the MaC project was to perform an exploration of design choices in runtime verification, before settling on a particular set of decisions. We revisit some of these decisions below and briefly compare them with alternative approaches taken by the research community.

The Separation of MEDL and PEDL. Separation of event definition from the rest of the monitoring specification proved very useful and we believe it is one of the most important insights to come out of the MaC project. It allows to quickly adapt to changes both in properties to be checked and in system implementations. On the one hand, if a change to the property does not require any new primitive events, there is no impact on system instrumentation. However, if we are unable to represent the changed property with existing primitive events, we know that a new primitive event needs to be introduced, which in turn tells us exactly what new instrumentation is needed. On the other hand, if a system implementation is changed, we just need to update the definition of primitive events and the rest of the monitoring setup is not affected. In this way, primitive event definitions serve as a layer of abstraction, isolating checkers from the system itself to the extent possible. In the case of software monitoring, primitive event definitions are relatively straightforward and are defined in terms of function calls and returns and state updates. However, in many situations where direct observation is more difficult, in particular in cyber-physical systems where continuous environments need to be monitored. Here, event detectors need to deal with noisy observations, for example, using statistical techniques. In such cases, a clear separation between properties, checked in a conventional way using logics, and statistics-based detection of primitive events is even more useful. Preliminary investigation of such a setting has been explored in [20].

At the same time, it gradually became clear that separation between primitive events and the rest of the event and conditions used within the monitor may be rather arbitrary. In fact, a complex system may benefit from multiple levels of abstraction, where events and conditions on one level are defined in terms of events and conditions at levels below. This insight became one of the foundations in our follow-up work on modular runtime verification systems [29].

MEDL vs. LTL, Past Time vs. Future Time. Many people prefer to work with familiar temporal logics like LTL. Since LTL is a future-time logic that has its semantics over infinite traces, runtime verification requires additional machinery to reason about all possible extensions of the currently observed prefix. Elegant approaches have emerged after the conclusion of the MaC project, e.g., [2], which is based on three-valued semantics of LTL. In addition, such an approach allows us to easily decide when it is possible to turn the monitor off because the outcome of checking will not change in any future extension of the trace, something that is not always easy to do with past-time formulas.

Monitorability. Our approach in the MaC framework was to view runtime verification as an approach to detect *violations* of specifications. This means that *monitorable* properties would have to be safety properties, that have finite witnesses demonstrating their violation. Further, any checking framework can only detect safety properties whose set of violating prefixes is a recursive set. It turns out that the MEDL language (and its translation to automata) is as powerful as one can hope for—the MaC framework can detect violations of all safety properties whose set of violating prefixes are decidable [26]. Since this initial work on understanding the expressiveness of what can and cannot be monitored, subsequent work has identified richer notions. In this work, one views runtime verification as not just an approach to detect specification violations, but also as a means to establish that an observed execution is guaranteed to meet its specification for all future extensions of the observed prefix [2]. Such properties (i.e., those that can be affirmed) need to be such that a witnessing finite prefix of an execution guarantees their satisfaction; these are the class of *guarantee* or *co-safety* properties. The notion of monitorable properties has been further extended in [18].

Temporal Logic vs. Abstract Commands. The mixture of temporal logic constructs and guarded commands in the monitoring language makes the approach more expressive, but complicates semantics due to the presence of potentially circular dependencies. State of the monitor is now spread between explicitly introduced state variables and values of conditions defined in the logical part of the language. Understanding the property being checked may now require more effort by the user.

Synchronous vs. Asynchronous Monitoring. The focus of Java-MaC on asynchronous monitoring turned out to be one of the design decisions that, in retrospect, was not completely justified. Support for synchronous monitoring turned out to be useful in many situations, in particular for security properties as well as checking timing properties in real-time. Moreover, case studies suggest that asynchronous monitoring may not always reduce timing overhead. With asynchronous monitoring, instrumentation probes do not perform checking directly, but instead have to deliver collected observations to the monitor. When the monitor is running in a separate process or on a remote computing node, the overhead of buffering and transmitting observations often turns out to be higher than performing checks synchronously within the instrumentation probe. To the best of our knowledge, there has been no systematic exploration of the trade-off between synchronous and asynchronous deployment of monitors. Preliminary results are available in [28].

Randomization. As mentioned in the introduction, the original motivation for the work in the MaC project, was to extend ideas from program checking [5] to checking reactive program computations. In the context of program checking, randomization is often critical to obtain effective checkers. Does the same apply in the context of runtime verification of reactive programs? More recent work has tried to exploit randomization in the context of runtime verification [6,16], including identifying the theoretical limits and expressiveness of such checkers [6].

3.2   Applications of Runtime Verification in Safety-Critical Systems

Recurrent questions about runtime verification technologies concern which properties it makes sense to check at run time and why they were not verified at design time. As part of our original motivation for the MaC project, our answer to these questions was that properties come from system requirements, but they could not be formally verified at design time because state of the art in formal verification did not scale sufficiently well. For a safety-critical system this vision seems insufficient. Discovering a violation of a safety property during a mission does not improve safety, as it may be too late to react to an alarm. Therefore, more realistic approaches need to be applied to make sure that runtime verification improves safety assurance. Without trying to be exhaustive, we consider three such approaches below.

Predictive Monitoring. While discovering a safety violation after it occurs may not be acceptable, discovering that a violation is imminent would be very desirable. To achieve this capability would requires us to predict likely executions in the future for a limited horizon. Such prediction may be difficult for software executions. However, for cyber-physical systems, where an accurate model of system may be available, model-based predictions are able to achieve this goal. The challenge is to keep the approach computationally feasible, due to inherent uncertainties in the model and noisy observations. A promising approach [27], based on ideas from Gaussian process regression theory, appears to be efficient enough to be applied on small robotic platforms.

Monitoring-Based Adaptation. Finally, an important use case is when the outcome of monitoring is used to take action aimed at helping the system recover from the problem or adapt to a new situation. These actions can take different forms. In our early work, we showed that the well-known control-theoretic approach based on Simplex architecture [23] can be implemented in a monitored setting [14]. This case targets faults in controllers, where the checker monitors boundaries of the safety envelope of the system and triggers a switch to a safety controller, which may have worse performance but is trusted to keep the system safe. This approach relies on careful control-theoretic analysis of the system dynamics and targets a limited case when the source of the fault is assumed to be known and the action is pre-determined. In more general scenarios, several alternative approaches have been considered. One approach is to avoid diagnosing the problem, concentrating instead on ensuring that observable behavior is acceptable. This approach came to be known as runtime enforcement. Rather than altering the state of system components to allow them to return to correct operation, runtime enforcement concentrates on making sure that observable behavior is safe. Runtime enforcement actions involve delaying, suppressing, or modifying observations in other ways. A different approach is to diagnose the problem and localize the fault by collecting additional information and invoke an appropriate existing recovery procedure or applying a change directly to the internal state of a faulty component. Providing guarantees in the latter approach may be difficult and requires an accurate model of system components. A detailed survey of state of the art is given in [8].

Monitoring of Assumptions. In open systems that have to operate in environments that are not sufficiently known, verification is typically performed with respect to assumptions about the environment. In this case, it is important to detect that some of the assumptions are violated at run time. We note that a violation of the assumption does not necessarily indicate an immediate problem. The system may still be able to successfully operate in the new environment. However, some of the design-time guarantees may not hold any more and system operators should pay additional attention to the situation.

In some approaches, most notably in assume-guarantee frameworks for reactive systems [3], assumptions – just like guarantees – can be naturally expressed in specification languages such as LTL or MEDL. In many other cases, assumptions take drastically different forms. For example, in control systems, assumptions are often made about the levels of noise in sensor streams. Similarly, learning-based systems rely on assumptions about training data, in particular that training data are assumed to be drawn from the same distribution as inputs encountered at run time. Detecting violations of such assumptions require statistical techniques. While there is much literature on statistical execution monitoring in process control and robotics (see, e.g., [19]), treatment of statistical monitoring tends to be much less formal than logic-based monitoring. Much work remains to be done to determine monitorability conditions for statistical monitoring and develop specification languages with formal semantics.

Acknowledgement. We would like to thank Dr. Ralph Wachter who provided and encouraged us with research funding and freedom to explore and develop the MaC framework when he was at the ONR. We also would like to thank other participants of the ONR MURI project: Andre Scedrov, John Mitchell, Ronitt Rubinfeld, Cynthia Dwork, for all the fruitful discussions. Recent extensions of our monitoring and checking approach have been funded by the DARPA Assured Autonomy program under contract FA8750-18-C-0090, and by the ONR contract N68335-19-C-0200. One of the authors of the first MaC paper [12], Hanêne Ben-Abdallah, participated in the project as a summer visitor in 1998.

References

1. Alspaugh, T.A., Faulk, S.R., Britton, K.H., Parker, R.A., Parnas, D.L., Shore, J.E.: Software requirements for the A7-E aircraft. Technical report NRL Memorandum Report 3876, Naval Research Laboratory, August 1992
2. Bauer, A., Leucker, M., Schallhart, C.: Runtime verification for LTL and TLTL. ACM Trans. Softw. Eng. Methodol. **20**, 14:1–14:64 (2010)
3. Benveniste, A., Caillaud, B., Ferrari, A., Mangeruca, L., Passerone, R., Sofronis, C.: Multiple viewpoint contract-based specification and design. In: de Boer, F.S., Bonsangue, M.M., Graf, S., de Roever, W.-P. (eds.) FMCO 2007. LNCS, vol. 5382, pp. 200–225. Springer, Heidelberg (2008). https://doi.org/10.1007/978-3-540-92188-2_9
4. Bhargavan, K., et al.: Verisim: formal analysis of network simulations. IEEE Trans. Software Eng. **28**(2), 129–145 (2002). https://doi.org/10.1109/32.988495
5. Blum, M., Kannan, S.: Designing programs that check their work. J. ACM **42**, 269–291 (1995)
6. Chadha, R., Sistla, A.P., Viswanathan, M.: On the expressiveness and complexity of randomization in finite state monitors. J. ACM **56**(5), 26:1–26:44 (2009)
7. De Nicola, R., Vaandrager, F.: Action versus state based logics for transition systems. In: Guessarian, I. (ed.) LITP 1990. LNCS, vol. 469, pp. 407–419. Springer, Heidelberg (1990). https://doi.org/10.1007/3-540-53479-2_17
8. Falcone, Y., Mariani, L., Rollet, A., Saha, S.: Runtime failure prevention and reaction. In: Bartocci, E., Falcone, Y. (eds.) Lectures on Runtime Verification. LNCS, vol. 10457, pp. 103–134. Springer, Cham (2018). https://doi.org/10.1007/978-3-319-75632-5_4
9. Gordon, D., Spears, W., Sokolsky, O., Lee, I.: Distributed spatial control and global monitoring of mobile agents. In: Proceedings of the IEEE International Conference on Information, Intelligence, and Systems, November 1999
10. Havelund, K., Roşu, G.: Synthesizing monitors for safety properties. In: Katoen, J.-P., Stevens, P. (eds.) TACAS 2002. LNCS, vol. 2280, pp. 342–356. Springer, Heidelberg (2002). https://doi.org/10.1007/3-540-46002-0_24
11. Heitmeyer, C.L.: Software cost reduction. In: Marciniak, J.J. (ed.) Encyclopedia of Software Engineering. Wiley, New York (2002)
12. Lee, I., Ben-Abdallah, H., Kannan, S., Kim, M., Sokolsky, O.: A monitoring and checking framework for run-time correctness assurance. In: Proceedings of the Korea-U.S. Technical Conference on Strategic Technologies, October 1998
13. Kim, M., Kannan, S., Lee, I., Sokolsky, O., Viswanathan, M.: Java-MaC: a run-time assurance tool for Java programs. In: Proceedings of Workshop on Runtime Verification (RV 2001). Electronic Notes in Theoretical Computer Science, vol. 55, July 2001
14. Kim, M., Lee, I., Sammapun, U., Shin, J., Sokolsky, O.: Monitoring, checking, and steering of real-time systems. In: 2nd Workshop on Run-time Verification, July 2002

15. Kim, M., Viswanathan, M., Ben-Abdallah, H., Kannan, S., Lee, I., Sokolsky, O.: Formally specified monitoring of temporal properties. In: Proceedings of the European Conference on Real-Time Systems (ECRTS 1999), pp. 114–121, June 1999

16. Kini, D., Viswanathan, M.: Probabilistic automata for safety LTL specifications. In: McMillan, K.L., Rival, X. (eds.) VMCAI 2014. LNCS, vol. 8318, pp. 118–136. Springer, Heidelberg (2014). https://doi.org/10.1007/978-3-642-54013-4_7

17. Lee, I., Kannan, S., Kim, M., Sokolsky, O., Viswanathan, M.: Runtime assurance based on formal specifications. In: Proceedings of the International Conference on Parallel and Distributed Processing Techniques and Applications, June 1999

18. Peled, D., Havelund, K.: Refining the safety–liveness classification of temporal properties according to monitorability. In: Margaria, T., Graf, S., Larsen, K.G. (eds.) Models, Mindsets, Meta: The What, the How, and the Why Not?. LNCS, vol. 11200, pp. 218–234. Springer, Cham (2019). https://doi.org/10.1007/978-3-030-22348-9_14

19. Pettersson, O.: Execution monitoring in robotics: a survey. Robot. Auton. Syst. **53**(2), 73–88 (2005)

20. Roohi, N., Kaur, R., Weimer, J., Sokolsky, O., Lee, I.: Parameter invariant monitoring for signal temporal logic. In: Proceedings of the 21st International Conference on Hybrid Systems: Computation and Control, pp. 187–196 (2018)

21. Sammapun, U., Lee, I., Sokolsky, O., Regehr, J.: Statistical runtime checking of probabilistic properties. In: Sokolsky, O., Taşıran, S. (eds.) RV 2007. LNCS, vol. 4839, pp. 164–175. Springer, Heidelberg (2007). https://doi.org/10.1007/978-3-540-77395-5_14

22. Sammapun, U.: Monitoring and checking of real-time and probabilistic properties. Ph.D. thesis, University of Pennsylvania (2007)

23. Sha, L.: Using simplicity to control complexity. IEEE Softw. **18**(4), 20–28 (2001)

24. Sokolsky, O., Sammapun, U., Lee, I., Kim, J.: Run-time checking of dynamic properties. In: Proceeding of the 5th International Workshop on Runtime Verification (RV 2005), Edinburgh, Scotland, UK, July 2005

25. Tan, L., Kim, J., Sokolsky, O., Lee, I.: Model-based testing and monitoring for hybrid embedded systems. In: Proceedings of the 2004 IEEE International Conference on Information Reuse and Integration (IRI 2004), pp. 487–492, November 2004

26. Viswanathan, M., Kim, M.: Foundations for the run-time monitoring of reactive systems – *Fundamentals of the MaC Language*. In: Liu, Z., Araki, K. (eds.) ICTAC 2004. LNCS, vol. 3407, pp. 543–556. Springer, Heidelberg (2005). https://doi.org/10.1007/978-3-540-31862-0_38

27. Yel, E., Bezzo, N.: Fast run-time monitoring, replanning, and recovery for safe autonomous system operations. In: Proceedings of the IEEE International Conference on Intelligent Robots and Systems (IROS), November 2019, to appear

28. Zhang, T., Eakman, G., Lee, I., Sokolsky, O.: Overhead-aware deployment of runtime monitors. In: Finkbeiner, B., Mariani, L. (eds.) RV 2019. LNCS, vol. 11757, pp. 375–381. Springer, Cham (2019)

29. Zhang, T., Eakman, G., Lee, I., Sokolsky, O.: Flexible monitor deployment for runtime verification of large scale software. In: Margaria, T., Steffen, B. (eds.) ISoLA 2018. LNCS, vol. 11247, pp. 42–50. Springer, Cham (2018). https://doi.org/10.1007/978-3-030-03427-6_6

30. Zhou, C., Hansen, M.R.: Duration Calculus. Springer, Heidelberg (2004). https://doi.org/10.1007/978-3-662-06784-0

Introspective Environment Modeling

Sanjit A. Seshia$^{(\boxtimes)}$

University of California at Berkeley, Berkeley, USA
sseshia@berkeley.edu

Abstract. Autonomous systems often operate in complex environments which can beextremely difficult to model manually at design time. The set of agents and objects in the environment can be hard to predict, let alone their behavior. We present the idea of *introspective environment modeling*, in which one algorithmically synthesizes, by introspecting on the system, assumptions on the environment under which the system can guarantee correct operation and which can be efficiently monitored at run time. We formalize the problem, illustrate it with examples, and describe an approach to solving a simplified version of the problem in the context of temporal logic planning. We conclude with an outlook to future work.

1 Introduction

Autonomous systems, especially those based on artificial intelligence (AI) and machine learning (ML), are increasingly being used in a variety of application domains including healthcare, transportation, finance, industrial automation, etc. This growing societal-scale impact has brought with it a set of risks and concerns about the dependability and safety of AI-based systems including about errors in AI software, faults, cyber-attacks, and failures of human-robot interaction. In a previous article [13], the author defined *"Verified AI"* as the goal of designing AI-based systems that have strong, ideally provable, assurances of correctness with respect to mathematically-specified requirements. That article lays out five major challenges to applying formal methods for achieving this goal, and proposes principles towards overcoming those challenges. One of those challenges is that of *modeling the environment* of an AI-based autonomous system.

The environments in which AI-based autonomous systems operate can be very complex, with considerable uncertainty even about how many and which agents are in the environment (both human and robotic), let alone about their intentions and behaviors. As an example, consider the difficulty in modeling urban traffic environments in which an autonomous car must operate. Indeed, AI/ML is often introduced into these systems precisely to deal with such complexity and uncertainty! From a formal methods perspective, this makes it very hard to create realistic environment models with respect to which one can perform verification or synthesis.

A particularly vexing problem for environment modeling is to deal with *unknown variables* of the environment. In the traditional success stories for formal verification, such as verifying cache coherence protocols or device drivers, the *interface variables* between the system S and its environment E are well-defined. The environment can

© Springer Nature Switzerland AG 2019
B. Finkbeiner and L. Mariani (Eds.): RV 2019, LNCS 11757, pp. 15–26, 2019.
https://doi.org/10.1007/978-3-030-32079-9_2

only influence the system through this interface. However, for AI-based systems such as an autonomous vehicle, it may be impossible to precisely define all the variables (features) of the environment. Even in restricted scenarios where the environment variables (agents) are known, there is a striking lack of information, especially at design time, about their behaviors. Additionally, modeling sensors such as LiDAR (Light Detection and Ranging) that represent the interface to the environment is in itself a technical challenge.

In this paper, we present *introspective environment modeling* (IEM), an idea introduced in [13] to address this challenge. The central idea in this approach is to *introspect on the system in order to model the environment*. In other words, analyze the system's behavior and its sensing interface to the environment to extract a representation of environments in which correct operation is guaranteed. A key underlying computational problem is to *algorithmically identify assumptions* that the system makes about the environment that are sufficient to guarantee the satisfaction of the specifications. In general, we want to generate the weakest set of assumptions on the environment of the AI-based autonomous system. These assumptions form critical components of an assurance case for the safety and correctness of the autonomous system, since they precisely pinpoint weak points of the system. Moreover, the assumptions identified must be *efficiently monitorable at run time*: one must be able to monitor at run time whether they are true or false, and ideally to also be able to predict whether they are likely to be violated in advance, with sufficient lead time. Additionally, in situations where human operators may be involved, one would want the assumptions to be translatable into an explanation that is *human understandable*, so that the autonomous system can "explain" to the human why it may not be able to satisfy the specification (this information can be used offline for debugging/repair or online for control). We illustrate our ideas with examples drawn from the domain of autonomous driving, and more generally, for autonomous cyber-physical systems (CPS) and robotics.

Related Work: The topic of environment modeling, also termed as "world modeling", has been much studied in the literature in formal methods, AI, and related areas. We do not attempt to cover the vast literature here, focusing instead on algorithmic methods and other closely related papers. A common approach in the AI literature is to have a probabilistic model of the world and maintain a belief distribution over possible worlds which can be updated at run time. However, the model (or model structure) is typically created manually and not algorithmically. Some world models can be monitored at run time and updated online; this has been demonstrated, e.g., in the case of autonomous vehicles [14]. In the formal methods literature, the inspiration for IEM comes from the work on automated generation of environment assumptions. Closely related work includes that of Chatterjee et al. [4] on finding minimal environment assumptions, the work of Li et al. [10] on the first counterstrategy-guided approach to inductive synthesis of environment assumptions, and the subsequent work by Alur et al. [3]. However, none of these works focused on generating environment models that could be efficiently monitored at run time. To our knowledge, our prior work [11] is the first to place this requirement and show how to mine assumptions that can be efficiently monitored at run time during the controller synthesis process. All of the above work on assumption mining is for discrete systems/models. Later Ghosh et al. [9] showed how to algorithmically repair specifications, including environment assumptions, for receding horizon model predictive control for cyber-physical systems, but this work assumes knowledge of the structure of the environment model. In a more recent paper, Ghosh et al. [8] show how to close the gap between a high-level mathematical model of a system and its environment and a simulatable or executable model. Focusing on reach-avoid objectives, this work also assumes knowledge of the environment model structure, but shows how to adapt the environment model to account for behavioral discrepancies between the two models. Damm and Finkbeiner [5] present an approach to representing and analyzing the "perimeter" of the world model, which captures the environment variables that can be modeled and restricted via environment assumptions. They provide a notion of an optimal world model with respect to the specification and class of system strategies based on the idea of dominant strategies; such a notion of optimality could be useful in IEM as well.

The rest of the paper is organized as follows. In Sect. 2, we explain the idea of introspective environment modeling using an illustrative example, and formalize it. Section 3 shows how traditional controller synthesis from linear temporal logic (LTL) can be extended to perform IEM. We conclude in Sect. 4 with a discussion of future work.

2   Introspective Environment Modeling: The Idea

We now present the basic idea of introspective environment modeling (IEM). We start in Sect. 2.1 with a discussion of the problem, and then illustrate it with an example in Sect. 2.2. We conclude in Sect. 2.3 with a formalization of the IEM problem.

2.1   Problem Setup

Consider the standard picture of a closed system as shown in Fig. 1, where a system S interfaces to an environment E through sensors and actuators. Let x_S denote the state variables of S, x_E denote the state variables of E, y denote the inputs to S as output from its sensors, and z denote the outputs from S as generated by its actuators. The variables x_E represent the state of the agents and objects in the environment.

The challenge that IEM seeks to address is the lack of information about the environment E and its behavior. More specifically, there are three kinds of uncertainty about the environment:

1. *Uncertainty about Parameters:* The variables x_E are known and the dynamical model of E indicating how x_E changes is known too, but values of parameters in the dynamical model of E are not known.
2. *Uncertainty about Dynamics:* Variables x_E are known, but the dynamical model of E governing their evolution is not known.
3. *Uncertainty about Variables:* Even the agents in E and the variables x_E are not completely known, let alone the dynamics of E.

There are a variety of techniques available to deal with uncertainty about parameters, including using system identification or machine learning methods to estimate parameter values or ranges. The second and third type of uncertainty are much harder to handle and are the primary subject of this paper. We next introduce a simple example to illustrate the main ideas.

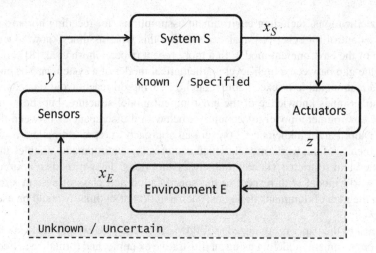

Fig. 1. System S and environment E in a closed loop.

2.2 Illustrative Example

Consider the traffic scenario depicted in Fig. 2 on an arterial road with a top speed of 45 mph (about 20 m/s). The blue car is an autonomous vehicle (AV) travelling at 20 m/s with no vehicles or obstructions initially in the lane in front of it. On the right (slow) lane is a slow-moving line of (orange) cars. The AV is equipped with a LiDAR sensor that allows it to detect objects around it to a range of 300 m [2], which is sufficient to cover the entire road scene shown in the figure. The LiDAR sensor allows the AV to estimate the position and velocity of each of the five cars A–E in the right lane; we assume for simplicity that the sensor's estimate is perfect. The challenge is that each of these five cars might suddenly decide to change to the left lane in which the AV is travelling, and the AV must avoid a collision. What assumptions on the environment (cars A–E) guarantee the safety of the AV in this scenario? Under those assumptions, what actions must the AV take to avoid a collision?

To answer these questions, first, we must formalize the notion of safety. Suppose that the true safety property is to guarantee that *the distance between the AV and any environment object is always greater than zero.* Such a property is expressible in a standard specification language such as linear temporal logic and its extensions for CPS such as metric temporal logic and signal temporal logic, as follows:

$$\text{G} \left[\bigwedge_{o \in Obj} dist(\mathbf{x}_{AV}, \mathbf{x}_o) > 0 \right]$$

One challenge with specifying such a property is that not all the environment objects (the set Obj) are known, and therefore, such a property cannot be guaranteed to hold at run time. Therefore, we suggest to specify a weaker property that can be monitored by available sensors. This requires the property to be based on the sensor model and be time-bounded, i.e., expressed over a finite window of time over which the environment

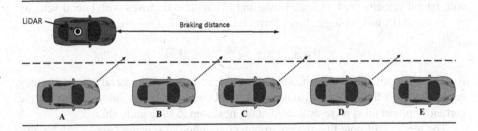

Fig. 2. Autonomous vehicle scenario illustrating IEM. The blue car at the top is an autonomous vehicle travelling from left to right, while the orange cars are in a slow-moving lane from which they may possibly change lane (Color figure online).

can be monitored with sufficient accuracy. For the example in Fig. 2, the absence-of-collision property will need to be revised on two counts: (1) to objects detectable by available sensors, and (ii) a finite window of time. This revised property can be formulated as follows:

$$G_{[0,\tau]} \left[\bigwedge_{o \in ObjSens(t)} dist(\mathbf{x}_{AV}, \mathbf{x}_o) > 0 \right]$$

where τ is a (typically short) time bound and $ObjSens(t)$ is the set of objects that are sensed by available sensors at the current time instant t. Using this alternate specification is sound only if it implies the original property over the $[0, \tau]$ interval. In this case, since we assume that the LiDAR range covers the entire scene, $ObjSens$ equals Obj.

While designing the controller for the AV, we have no knowledge of the exact number of environment agents (vehicles) or how they will behave. In the context of this example, the idea of IEM is as follows: given a strategy for the AV (based on its controller, sensors, etc.), extract an assumption on the environment E that guarantees the property of interest. As mentioned earlier, the AV is travelling at a velocity of 20 m/s. A typical braking distance from that speed on modern automobiles is about 24–48 m depending on road surfaces; we assume it to be 40 m for this example, which gives the AV 2 s to come to a complete stop. Typical lane widths in the United States are about 3 m [1]. Thus, assuming that the environment car starts in the middle of its lane, and vehicles are no more than 2 m wide, it would need to move with a lateral velocity of at least 1 m/s to cause a collision, provided it ends in the portion of the left lane overlapping with the braking distance.

Let us assume that the AV samples sensors periodically at (small) intervals of time Δ (of the order of a few milliseconds), and the control strategy executes instantaneously after the current sensor sample is received. Further, assume that at the current time step, the AV's strategy is to drive straight at 20 m/s and brake to stop within 2 s when it detects an object moving into its path. In this case, we set $\tau = 2$ to be the time bound within which the AV can come to a complete stop. Then, the AV can avoid a collision provided the following conditions hold on the environment agents: (1) Vehicle A moves with lateral velocity v_A less than 1 m/s, and (2) Vehicle B moves with lateral velocity v_B less than 0.5 m/s. In logic, this is expressed as the following predicate:

$$\mathsf{G}_{[0,\Delta]}\,(v_A < 1) \wedge (v_B < 0.5)$$

It can avoid a collision with vehicles C, D, and E no matter their lateral velocity as they are further than the braking distance. Note that these conditions are evaluated at the current step, and must be re-evaluated at the next step Δ time units later.

The reader will note that the environment assumption specified above can be efficiently monitored provided the estimation of velocities v_A and v_B is performed efficiently over a small window of sensor samples. If the assumption is broken, mitigating actions must be taken, such as moving to a degraded mode of operation with a weaker specification guaranteed. However, we also note that the process of coming up with these assumptions involved somewhat tedious manual reasoning, even for a small example like the one in this section with perfect LiDAR. Ideally, we need algorithmic methods to generate the environment assumptions automatically. Further, it would be best to co-synthesize those assumptions along with a strategy for the system (AV) to execute. We will discuss these in Sect. 3 after formalizing the IEM problem in Sect. 2.3.

2.3   Formalization

This section formalizes the IEM problem.

Consider Fig. 1. We model the system S as a transition system $(\mathcal{X}_S, \mathcal{X}_S^0, \mathcal{Y}_S, \mathcal{Z}_S, \delta_S, \rho_S)$ where $\mathcal{X}_S$ is the set of states, $\mathcal{X}_S^0$ is the set of initial states, $\mathcal{Y}_S$ is the set of inputs to S from its sensors, $\mathcal{Z}_S$ is the set of outputs generated by S via its actuators, $\delta_S \subseteq \mathcal{X}_S \times \mathcal{Y}_S \times \mathcal{X}_S$ is the transition relation, and $\rho_S \subseteq \mathcal{X}_S \times \mathcal{Y}_S \times \mathcal{Z}_S$ is the output relation. As before, we will denote a system state by x_S; this will also denote the variables used to model a system state. We model S as a non-deterministic system rather than as a stochastic system, but the core problem formulation carries over to other formalisms. We assume that a non-zero amount of time elapses between transitions and between outputs; for convenience we will assume this to be Δ time units as in the preceding section.

So far the formal model is fairly standard. Next, we consider the environment. As discussed earlier, the environment states and model are unknown. Let us denote the unknown set of environment states by $\mathcal{X}_E$, and the variables representing an environment state by x_E. We will assume that x_E is also unknown.

The sensor model is a crucial component of the overall formal model. If $\mathcal{X}_E$ is known, the sensor model can be formalized as a non-deterministic map Σ from $\mathcal{X}_E$ to $\mathcal{Y}_S$, where Σ maps an environment state x_E to a vector of sensor values $y \in \mathcal{Y}_S$. However, if we do not know $\mathcal{X}_E$ then the sensor model captures the sequences of sensor values in $\mathcal{Y}_S$ that are feasible. In other words, in this case we define Σ as the set of all sensor value sequences, a subset of $\mathcal{Y}_S^\omega$, that can be physically generated by the sensors in some environment. We say *an environment is consistent with* Σ if it only produces sensor value sequences in Σ.

The desired specification, denoted by Φ^*, is a function of x_S and x_E. For example, this can be a temporal property indicating that an AV maintains a minimum safety distance from any objects in the environment. However, since we do not know x_E, we instead have an alternative specification Φ which is a function of x_S, y and z. The following property must hold between these specifications:

Proposition 1. *Given specifications Φ and Φ^*, and a sensor model Σ, for all environments consistent with Σ, if a system satisfies Φ, it also satisfies Φ^*.*

We are now ready to define the introspective environment modeling problem formally.

Problem 1. Given a system S, a sensor model Σ, a specification Φ, generate an environment assumption $\Psi(x_S, y, z)$ such that S satisfies the specification $(\Psi \implies \Phi)$ in environments consistent with Σ.

Two other important aspects of the IEM problem are:

1. The environment assumptions Ψ must be *efficiently monitorable at run time*. More specifically, the environment assumption should be evaluated in sub-linear time and space (in the length of the trace), and ideally in constant time and space.
2. When Ψ does not hold and Φ is violated, the violation of Ψ should occur well in advance of the violation of Φ so that S can take mitigating actions, such as moving into a degraded mode of operation where it satisfies a weaker specification.

Note that S is not required to satisfy Φ when the environment assumption Ψ is violated. However, we want S to be "aware of its assumptions": the violation of Ψ should be detected by S and it should take actions that preserve a core (safety) specification.

In the following section, we present an approach to solving the IEM problem for a simple case where the world is modeled using propositional temporal logic and the controller for S is synthesized using standard game-theoretic approaches to reactive synthesis from temporal logic.

3   IEM for Synthesis from Temporal Logic

We now discuss how the IEM problem can be tackled in the context of synthesis of controllers from temporal logic specifications. The basic idea was presented in our prior work on synthesis for human-in-the-loop systems such as semi-autonomous vehicles [11]. Concretely, we consider the setting where a specification is given in linear temporal logic (LTL) in the GR(1) fragment [12], and one seeks to synthesize a controller so as to satisfy that specification in an adversarial environment. In GR(1), the specification is of the form $\varphi_a \implies \varphi_g$, where φ_a and φ_g are conjunctions of specific LTL formula types capturing safety and fairness properties, where φ_a represents the assumptions and φ_g represents guarantees. While typically the entire LTL specification is given as input, for the variant of the problem we consider, the guarantees are given, but the assumptions about the environment may be absent or only partial.

For this section, we consider S to be a finite-state transducer (FST) whose inputs $\mathcal{Y}_S$ are valuations to a set of Boolean input propositions and outputs $\mathcal{Z}_S$ are assignments to a set of Boolean output propositions. The sensor model Σ defines the sequences of input propositions that are physically feasible in some environment. The specification Φ is a GR(1) formula of the form $\varphi_a \implies \varphi_g$, where φ_a may be **true**. We wish to solve the IEM problem, i.e., to synthesize an environment assumption Ψ that implies Φ and additionally satisfies the following criteria: (1) it is efficiently monitorable at run-time; (2) it is *prescient*, meaning that S gets at least T time units to take mitigating actions before the property is violated, and (3) it is the weakest environment assumption satisfying the above properties (for some reasonable definition of "weakest").

We next present a motivating example to illustrate this variant of the IEM problem. Then we present the algorithmic approach to synthesize Ψ. Finally, we conclude by discussing some sample results. The material in this section is substantially borrowed from the author's prior work [11].

3.1   Example

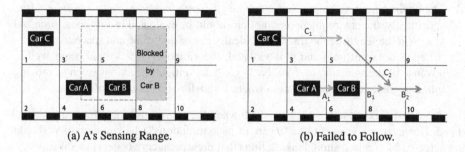

(a) A's Sensing Range.   (b) Failed to Follow.

Fig. 3. Controller synthesis – Car A following Car B

Consider the example in Fig. 3. Car A is a semi-autonomous vehicle, car B and C are two other cars on the road. We assume that the road has been divided into discretized regions that encode all the legal transitions for the vehicles on the map, similar to the discretization used in LTL synthesis for robotics and CPS, such as the work on receding horizon temporal logic planning [15]. The objective of car A is to *follow* car B. Car B and C are part of the *environment*. The notion of following can be stated as follows. We assume that car A is equipped with sensors that allows it to see two squares ahead of itself if its view is not obstructed, as indicated by the enclosed region by blue dashed lines in Fig. 3a. In this case, car B is blocking the view of car A, and thus car A can only see regions 3, 4, 5 and 6. Car A is said to be able to *follow* car B if it can always move to a position where it can see car B. Furthermore, we assume that at each step cars A and C can move at most 2 squares forward, but car B can move at most 1 square ahead, since otherwise car B can out-run or out-maneuver car A.

Given this objective, and additional safety rules such as cars not crashing into one another, our goal is to automatically synthesize a controller for car A such that:

- car A follows car B whenever possible;
- and in situations where the objective may not be achievable, *switches control* to the human driver while allowing *sufficient time* for the driver to respond and take control.

In general, it is not always possible to come up with a fully automatic controller that satisfies all requirements. Figure 3b illustrates such a scenario where car C blocks the view as well as the movement path of car A after two time steps. The brown arrows indicate the movements of the three cars in the first time step, and the blue arrows indicate the movements of car B and C in the second time step. Positions of a car X at time step t is indicated by X_t. In this failure scenario, the autonomous vehicle needs to notify the human driver since it has lost track of car B.

The IEM problem, for this example, is to *identify the environment assumptions that we need to monitor* and when they may fail, notify the driver sufficiently in advance so that the driver can take mitigating actions. In the next section, we give a brief overview of how such assumptions can be co-synthesized along with a controller.

3.2   IEM for LTL Synthesis

Our approach to solve Problem 1 is based on extending the standard game-theoretic approach to LTL synthesis, where one must solve a two-player zero-sum game between S and E. We begin with the specification Φ and check whether it is realizable (i.e. a finite-state controller can be synthesized from it). If so, no environment assumptions are needed, i.e., $\Psi = \textbf{true}$, and we are done.

The more likely case is that Φ is unrealizable. In this case, we need to synthesize assumptions so that the resulting specification becomes realizable. For this, we follow a *counterstrategy-guided approach* to environment assumption synthesis similar to that proposed first by Li et al. [10]. A counterstrategy is a winning strategy for the environment E to force violation of Φ. The approach is based on analyzing a data structure called the *counterstrategy graph* that summarizes all possible ways for the environment to force a violation of the system guarantees. It comprises the following steps:

1. *Identify Class of Assumptions:* Fix a class of environment assumptions that is efficiently monitorable. We use a class of LTL formulas of the form $\bigwedge_i(\mathsf{G}(a_i \rightarrow \neg \mathsf{X}\, b_i))$, where a_i is a Boolean formula describing a set of assignments over variables in (y, z), and b_i is a Boolean formula describing a set of assignments over variables in y. This is a property over a pair of consecutive states. The template and the approach can be extended to properties involving over a window of size k for a constant k.
2. *Transform Counterstrategy Graph:* Analyze the counterstrategy graph to find nodes that correspond to violations of safety properties, and cycles that correspond to violations of liveness properties. Transform the graph into a condensed directed acyclic graph (DAG) by contracting strongly connected components. Identify *error nodes* — nodes in this DAG that correspond to property violations. A cut in this DAG that separates nodes corresponding to start states from the error nodes corresponds to an environment assumption – a constraint one can place on the environment to eliminate the property violations.
3. *Extract Environment Assumption from Min-Cuts:* Assign weights to the edges in the graph so as to capture the penalty of reporting an environment assumption (and transferring control from the controller S to a higher level, supervisory controller such as a human operator). We consider all cuts in the graph that are at least T edges (steps) away from any error node in order to report an environment assumption

violation T time steps in advance of a potential property violation. Thus, we find a min-cut in the counterstrategy graph at least T steps away from an error node. Each edge in the cut provides one of the conjuncts in the template formula $\bigwedge_i (G(a_i \to \neg X\, b_i))$.

Further details of this approach are available in [11]. We demonstrate its working on the simple example in the following section.

3.3 Results

We now describe the operation of the approach on the car-following example introduced in Sect. 3.1. We denote the positions of cars A, B, C by p_A, p_B, p_C respectively; these variables indicate the rectangular regions where the cars are located at the current instant. Φ is of the form $\phi_S \implies \phi_E$ where each of the ϕ_i's are conjunctions of properties. We list some of these below:

- Any position can be occupied by at most one car at a time (i.e., no collisions):

$$G\big(p_A = x \to (p_B \neq x \land p_C \neq x)\big)$$

  where x denotes a position on the discretized space. The cases for B and C are similar, but they are part of ψ_E.
- Car A is required to follow car B:

$$G\big((v_{AB} = \textbf{true} \land p_A = x) \to X(v_{AB} = \textbf{true})\big)$$

  where $v_{AB} = \textbf{true}$ iff car A can see car B.
- Two cars cannot cross each other if they are right next to each other. For example, when $p_C = 5$, $p_A = 6$ and $p'_C = 8$ (in the next cycle), $p'_A \neq 7$. In LTL,

$$G\big(((p_C = 5) \land (p_A = 6) \land (Xp_C = 8)) \to (X(p_A \neq 7))\big)$$

The other specifications can be found in the supplementary material of Ref. [11]. Observe that car C can in fact force a violation of the system guarantees in one step under two situations – when $p_C = 5, p_B = 8$ and $p_A = 4$, or $p_C = 5, p_B = 8$ and $p_A = 6$. Both are situations where car C is blocking the view of car A, causing it to lose track of car B. The second failure scenario is illustrated in Fig. 3b.

Applying our algorithm to this (unrealizable) specification with $T = 1$, we obtain the following assumption Ψ.

$$\Psi = G\big(((p_A = 4) \land (p_B = 6) \land (p_C = 1)) \to \neg X((p_B = 8) \land (p_C = 5))\big) \bigwedge$$

$$G\big(((p_A = 4) \land (p_B = 6) \land (p_C = 1)) \to \neg X((p_B = 6) \land (p_C = 3))\big) \bigwedge$$

$$G\big(((p_A = 4) \land (p_B = 6) \land (p_C = 1)) \to \neg X((p_B = 6) \land (p_C = 5))\big)$$

Note how Ψ reports a violation at least $T = 1$ time steps ahead of a potential property failure. Also, Ψ corresponds to three possible evolutions of the environment from the initial state. In general, Ψ can be a conjunction of conditions at different time steps as E and S progress.

These results indicate the feasibility of an algorithmic approach to generating environment assumptions for temporal logic based planning. However, there are also several limitations. First, it is hard to scale this explicit graph-based approach to large state spaces and specifications. Second, it is only applicable to problems where a discretization of the state space is meaningful for planning in the real world. Recent work on repair of specifications for receding horizon control for real-time temporal logics over continuous signals [9] provides a starting point, although those methods need to be extended to handle highly adversarial environments. Third, the sensor model is highly simplified. Nevertheless, a counterstrategy-based approach provides a first step to producing environment models in the form of logical specifications (assumptions) that are usable for controller synthesis, efficiently monitorable at run time, and provide time for taking mitigating actions when the assumptions are violated.

4 Conclusion

We presented the idea of introspective environment modeling (IEM) as a way of dealing with the challenge of modeling unknown and uncertain environments of autonomous systems. The central idea is to introspect on the working of the system in order to capture a set of environment assumptions that is sufficient to guarantee correct operation and which is also efficiently monitorable at run time. We formalized the IEM problem and described an algorithmic approach to solving it for a simplified setting of temporal logic planning.

Much more remains to be done to solve the IEM problem in practice. First, the algorithmic approach presented in Sect. 3 must be extended from the discrete setting to cyber-physical systems. The scalability challenge must be addressed, moving from the explicit graph-theoretic method of Sect. 3 to one that scales to high-dimensional spaces involving both discrete and continuous variables, likely requiring symbolic methods. A particularly important problem is to devise realistic sensor models that capture the noise and errors that arise in real-world sensors; while this is challenging, we believe this is an easier modeling problem as the number of sensor types is much less than the number of possible environments. Approaches to extract the weakest environment assumptions that are also efficiently monitorable at run time must be investigated further. It would also be useful to explore formalisms to capture environment assumptions beyond temporal logic, and the use of IEM for stochastic environment models, represented, e.g., using probabilistic programming languages [7]. Finally, we believe the extracted assumptions and the sensor model could be valuable in building an assurance case for autonomous systems, especially when combined with techniques for run-time assurance (e.g., [6]).

Acknowledgments. I gratefully acknowledge the contributions of students and other collaborators in the work that this article draws from. This work was supported in part by NSF grants 1545126 (VeHICaL) and 1646208, the DARPA Assured Autonomy program, the iCyPhy center, and Berkeley Deep Drive.

References

1. Typical lane widths. https://en.wikipedia.org/wiki/Lane#Lane_width
2. Velodyne Lidar: Products. https://velodynelidar.com/products.html
3. Alur, R., Moarref, S., Topcu, U.: Counter-strategy guided refinement of GR(1) temporal logic specifications. In: Proceedings of the 13th Conference on Formal Methods in Computer-Aided Design (FMCAD2013), pp. 26–33 (2013)
4. Chatterjee, K., Henzinger, T.A., Jobstmann, B.: Environment assumptions for synthesis. In: van Breugel, F., Chechik, M. (eds.) CONCUR 2008. LNCS, vol. 5201, pp. 147–161. Springer, Heidelberg (2008). https://doi.org/10.1007/978-3-540-85361-9_14
5. Damm, W., Finkbeiner, B.: Does it pay to extend the perimeter of a world model? In: Butler, M., Schulte, W. (eds.) FM 2011. LNCS, vol. 6664, pp. 12–26. Springer, Heidelberg (2011). https://doi.org/10.1007/978-3-642-21437-0_4
6. Desai, A., Ghosh, S., Seshia, S.A., Shankar, N., Tiwari, A:. A runtime assurance framework for programming safe robotics systems. In: IEEE/IFIP International Conference on Dependable Systems and Networks (DSN), June 2019
7. Fremont, D.J., Dreossi, T., Ghosh, S., Yue, X., Sangiovanni-Vincentelli, A.L., Seshia, S.A.: Scenic: a language for scenario specification and scene generation. In: Proceedings of the 40th annual ACM SIGPLAN conference on Programming Language Design and Implementation (PLDI), June 2019
8. Ghosh, S., Bansal, S., Sangiovanni-Vincentelli, A., Seshia, S.A., Tomlin, C.J.: A new simulation metric to determine safe environments and controllers for systems with unknown dynamics. In: Proceedings of the 12th International Conference on Hybrid Systems: Computation and Control (HSCC), pp. 185–196, April 2019
9. Ghosh, S., et al.: Diagnosis and repair for synthesis from signal temporal logic specifications. In: Proceedings of the 9th International Conference on Hybrid Systems: Computation and Control (HSCC), April 2016
10. Li, W., Dworkin, L., Seshia, S.A.: Mining assumptions for synthesis. In: Proceedings of the Ninth ACM/IEEE International Conference on Formal Methods and Models for Codesign (MEMOCODE), pp. 43–50, July 2011
11. Li, W., Sadigh, D., Shankar Sastry, S., Seshia, S.A.: Synthesis for human-in-the-loop control systems. In: Proceedings of the 20th International Conference on Tools and Algorithms for the Construction and Analysis of Systems (TACAS), pp. 470–484, April 2014
12. Piterman, N., Pnueli, A., Sa'ar, Y.: Synthesis of reactive(1) designs. In: Emerson, E.A., Namjoshi, K.S. (eds.) VMCAI 2006. LNCS, vol. 3855, pp. 364–380. Springer, Heidelberg (2005). https://doi.org/10.1007/11609773_24
13. Seshia, S.A., Sadigh, D., Shankar Sastry, S.: Towards Verified Artificial Intelligence. ArXiv e-prints, July 2016
14. Urmson, C., Baker, C., Dolan, J., Rybski, P., Salesky, B., Whittaker, W., Ferguson, D., Darms, M.: Autonomous driving in traffic: boss and the urban challenge. AI Magazi $30(2)$, 17–17 (2009)
15. Wongpiromsarn, T., et al.: Receding horizon temporal logic planning. IEEE Trans. Autom. Control $57(11)$, 2817–2830 (2012)

Robustness of Specifications and Its Applications to Falsification, Parameter Mining, and Runtime Monitoring with S-TaLiRo

Georgios Fainekos[1], Bardh Hoxha[2], and Sriram Sankaranarayanan[3(✉)]

[1] Arizona State University, Tempe, AZ, USA
fainekos@asu.edu
[2] Southern Illinois University, Carbondale, IL, USA
bhoxha@cs.siu.edu
[3] University of Colorado, Boulder, CO, USA
srirams@colorado.edu

Abstract. Logical specifications have enabled formal methods by carefully describing what is correct, desired or expected of a given system. They have been widely used in runtime monitoring and applied to domains ranging from medical devices to information security. In this tutorial, we will present the theory and application of robustness of logical specifications. Rather than evaluate logical formulas to Boolean valuations, robustness interpretations attempt to provide numerical valuations that provide degrees of satisfaction, in addition to true/false valuations to models. Such a valuation can help us distinguish between behaviors that "barely" satisfy a specification to those that satisfy it in a robust manner. We will present and compare various notions of robustness in this tutorial, centered primarily around applications to safety-critical Cyber-Physical Systems (CPS). We will also present key ways in which the robustness notions can be applied to problems such as runtime monitoring, falsification search for finding counterexamples, and mining design parameters for synthesis.

1 Introduction

Embedding computers in physical engineered systems has created new opportunities and at the same time major challenges. A prime example is the recent Boeing 737 MAX 8. Improving the efficiency of an existing and proven airframe led to a new design which could become unstable at higher angles-of-attack. In turn, the Maneuvering Characteristics Augmentation System (MCAS) was developed to restrict pilot inputs and protect the system from entering potentially unsafe operating regions. However, the system was not properly developed and/or tested, which led to two tragic airplane crashes with devastating human losses. In light of these accidents, further scrutiny and investigation revealed a number of software related issues [31]. Unfortunately, software related issues

B. Finkbeiner and L. Mariani (Eds.): RV 2019, LNCS 11757, pp. 27–47, 2019.
https://doi.org/10.1007/978-3-030-32079-9_3

are not only troubling the aerospace industry, but also the autonomous vehicle industry [39], and they have been a long term issue in the medical device [45] and automotive [35] industries.

One of the main challenges on which the prior software related issues can be attributed to is that Cyber-Physical Systems (CPS) are inherently more complex than traditional computer systems. In general, the primary reason for the higher complexity is that the software or hardware interactions with the physical world cannot be abstracted away in order to use classical Boolean-based design frameworks and tools. In turn, this means that traditional software testing methods cannot be directly utilized for testing CPS software.

A decade ago, we recognized the limitations of traditional software testing methods in the context of CPS and we proposed a search based testing method explicitly targeted on testing CPS [43]. The framework proposed in [43] – sometimes also termed requirements guided falsification – falls under the broader class of search-based testing methods [36]. In brief, requirements guided falsification for CPS uses formal requirements (specifications) in temporal logic in order to guide the search for system trajectories (traces) which demonstrate that the requirement does not hold on that system (in other words the specification is falsified). In [43], the search is guided by the robustness with which a trajectory satisfies the formal requirement [27]. The robustness concept [27] captures how well a trajectory satisfies a formal requirement. Namely, the robustness measure provides a bound on how large disturbances a system trajectory can tolerate before it does not satisfy the requirement any more. Our robustness guided falsification is leveraging this property to identify regions in the search space which are more promising for the existence of falsifying system behaviors. In other words, our method is based on the principle that falsifying behaviors are more likely to exist in the neighborhood of low robustness behaviors.

Despite the apparent simplicity of robustness guided testing for CPS, the framework has been successfully utilized for a range of applications from medical devices [12] to Unmanned Aerial Vehicles (UAV) [47] and Automated Driving Systems (ADS) [46]. In addition, there is a growing community working on CPS falsification problems, e.g., see the ARCH falsification competition [19,24].

This paper provides a tutorial on the software tool S-TaLiRo [7], which started as an open source project [44] for the methods developed in [27] and [43]. Even though the temporal logic robustness computation engine [25,27] is implemented in C, S-TaLiRo is primarily a Matlab toolbox. The tutorial provides a quick overview of the S-TaLiRo support for temporal logic robustness computation [26], falsification [1,42], parameter mining [33], and runtime monitoring [17]. For other S-TaLiRo features such as conformance testing [3], elicitation and debugging of formal specifications [18,34], and robustness-guided analysis of stochastic systems [2] we refer the reader to the respective publications. The paper concludes with some current research trends.

Beyond S-TaLiRo: This paper accompanies a tutorial on S-TaLiRo and its applications. Whereas, S-TaLiRo remains one of the many tools in this space, there are many other tools that use temporal logic robustness for monitoring, falsification, requirements mining and parameter mining [10, 36]. A detailed report on current tools and their performance on benchmark problems is available from the latest ARCH competition report on falsification tools [24]. Besides commercial tools such as the Simulink (tm) design verifier toolbox in Matlab [40] and Reactis tester (tm) [8], falsification techniques have been explored by academic tools such as Breach [21], Falstar [50] and Falsify [5], in addition to S-TaLiRo. A recent in-depth survey on runtime monitoring provides an in-depth introduction to the specification formalisms such as Signal Temporal Logic (STL) and the use of robustness for runtime monitoring, falsification and parameter mining [10]. Other recent surveys focus broadly on modeling, specification and verification techniques for Cyber-Physical Systems [14].

2   Systems and Signals

In S-TaLiRo, we treat a CPS as an input-output map. Namely, for a system Σ, the set of *initial operating conditions* X_0 and *input signals* $\mathbf{U} \subseteq U^N$, are mapped to *output signals* Y^N and *timing* (or *sampling*) functions $\mathfrak{T} \subseteq \mathbb{R}_+^N$. The set U is closed and bounded and contains the possible input values at each point in time (input space). Here, Y is the set of output values (output space), $\mathbb{R}$ is the set of real numbers and, $\mathbb{R}_+$ the set of positive reals. The set $N \subseteq \mathbb{N}$, where $\mathbb{N}$ is the set of natural numbers, is used as a set of indexes for the finite representation (simulations) of system behavior.

A system Σ can be viewed as a function $\Delta_\Sigma : X_0 \times \mathbf{U} \rightarrow Y^N \times \mathfrak{T}$ which takes as an input an initial condition $x_0 \in X_0$ and an input signal $u \in \mathbf{U}$ and it produces as output a signal $\mathbf{y} : N \rightarrow Y$ (also referred to as *trajectory*) and a timing function $\tau : N \rightarrow \mathbb{R}_+$. The only restriction on the timing function τ is that it must be a monotonic function, i.e., $\tau(i) < \tau(j)$ for $i < j$. The pair $\mu = (\mathbf{y}, \tau)$ is usually referred to as a *timed state sequence*, which is a widely accepted model for reasoning about real-time systems [6].

The set of all timed state sequences of a system Σ will be denoted by $\mathcal{L}(\Sigma)$. That is, $\mathcal{L}(\Sigma) = \{(\mathbf{y}, \tau) \mid \exists x_0 \in X_0 . \exists u \in \mathbf{U} . (\mathbf{y}, \tau) = \Delta_\Sigma(x_0, u)\}$.

2.1   Input Signals

We assume that the input signals, if any, must be parameterizable using a finite number of parameters. This assumption enables us to define a search problem of finite dimensionality. In S-TaLiRo, the input signals are parameterized using m number of control points. The control points vector $\vec{\lambda}$ and the timing vector $\vec{t}$, in conjunction with an interpolation function $\mathfrak{U}$, define the input signal u. Namely, at time t, $u(t) = \mathfrak{U}(\vec{\lambda}, \vec{t})(t)$.

The practitioner may choose different interpolation functions depending on the system and application. Example functions, as shown in Fig. 1, include linear, piecewise constant, splines, piecewise cubic interpolation, etc. If timing control points are not included, the state control points will be distributed equidistantly with respect to time with a chosen interpolation function. Otherwise, the timing

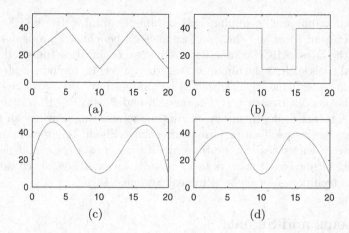

Fig. 1. Signal generation with state control points $\vec{\lambda} = [20, 40, 10, 40, 10]$ and equidistant timing control points $\vec{t} = [0, 5, 10, 15, 20]$ with various interpolation functions. (a) Linear, (b) Piecewise constant, (c) Spline, (d) Piecewise cubic interpolation.

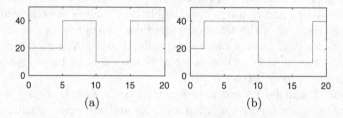

Fig. 2. Signal generation with state control points $\vec{\lambda} = [20, 40, 10, 40, 10]$ and piecewise constant interpolation. (a) With no timing control points, (b) With timing control points $\vec{t} = [0, 2, 10, 18, 20]$.

of the state control points is defined by the timing vector $\vec{t}$. The timing option is illustrated in Fig. 2. Choosing the appropriate number of control points and interpolation functions is application dependent. Timing should be included in the search space whenever the system should be tested under conditions where the input variation could be high in a very short period of time. By including timing between control points in the search space, one may be able to produce behaviors such as jerking behavior for the gas and brake throttle of an automotive vehicle. Note that in this framework, for systems with multiple inputs, each input can have a different number of control points and interpolation function. This enables the practitioner to define a wide array of input signals.

2.2　Automotive Transmission (AT)

As a running example, we consider an Automatic Transmission model that is widely used as a benchmark for CPS testing and verification [1,19,20,24,33].

We modify the original Simulink model provided by Mathworks[1] slightly to enable input and output interaction with Matlab scripts and S-TaLiRo. The input space of the model is the throttle schedule $u \in [0, 100]$. The physical component of the model has two continuous state variables x which are also its outputs $\mathbf{y}$: the speed of the engine ω (RPM) and the speed of the vehicle v. The output space is $Y = \mathbb{R}^2$ with $\mathbf{y}(i) = [\omega(i) \ v(i)]^T$ for all i in the simulation time. The vehicle is at rest at time 0. The model contains a Stateflow chart with two concurrently executing Finite State Machines (FSM) with 4 and 3 states, respectively. The FSM models the logic that controls the switching between the gears in the transmission system. We remark that the system is deterministic, i.e., under the same input signal u, we will observe the same output signal $\mathbf{y}$. For a more detailed presentation of this model see [32].

3   Metric Temporal Logic

Metric Temporal Logic (MTL) is an extension of Linear Temporal Logic that enables the definition of timing intervals for temporal operators. It was introduced in [37] to reason over quantitative timing properties of Boolean signals.

In addition to propositional logic operators such as conjunction ($\wedge$), disjunction ($\vee$) and negation ($\neg$), MTL supports temporal operators such as next ($\bigcirc$), weak next ($\ominus$), until ($\mathcal{U}_I$), release ($\mathcal{R}_I$), always ($\square_I$) and eventually ($\diamond_I$).

Definition 1 (MTL Syntax). *MTL syntax is defined by the grammar:*

$$\phi ::= \top \mid p \mid \neg\phi \mid \phi_1 \vee \phi_2 \mid \bigcirc \phi \mid \phi_1 \mathcal{U}_I \phi_2 \tag{1}$$

where $p \in AP$ with AP being the set of atomic propositions, and $\top$ is True ($\bot = \neg\top$ is False). Also, I is a nonsingular interval of the positive reals.

MTL enables the formalization of complex requirements with respect to both state and time as presented in Table 1.

In S-TaLiRo, the user defines a specification as a string where the temporal operators $\bigcirc$, $\square$ and $\diamond$ are represented as X, [ ] and <>, respectively.

The atomic propositions in our case label subsets of the output space Y. In other words, each atomic proposition is a shorthand for an arithmetic expression of the form $p \equiv g(y) \leq c$, where $g : Y \to \mathbb{R}$ and $c \in \mathbb{R}$. We define an observation map $O : AP \to 2^Y$ such that for each $p \in AP$ the corresponding set is $O(p) = \{y \mid g(y) \leq c\} \subseteq Y$. Examples of MTL specifications for our running example AT can be found on Table 2.

3.1   Parametric Metric Temporal Logic

MTL specifications may also be parameterized and presented as templates, where one or more state or timing parameters are left as variables. The syntax of parametric MTL is defined as follows (see [9,33] for more details):

---

[1] Simulink model discussed at: http://www.mathworks.com/help/simulink/examples/modeling-an-automatic-transmission-controller.html.

Table 1. Specifications in MTL and natural language.

Specification	Natural language
Safety ($\Box_{[0,\theta]}\phi$)	ϕ should always hold from time 0 to θ
Liveness ($\Diamond_{[0,\theta]}\phi$)	ϕ should hold at some point from 0 to θ (or now)
Coverage ($\Diamond\phi_1 \wedge \Diamond\phi_2 \ldots \wedge \Diamond\phi_n$)	ϕ_1 through ϕ_n should hold at some point in the future (or now), not necessarily in order or at the same time
Stabilization ($\Diamond\Box\phi$)	At some point in the future (or now), ϕ should always hold
Recurrence ($\Box\Diamond\phi$)	At every point in time, ϕ should hold at some point in the future (or now)
Reactive Response ($\Box(\phi \rightarrow \psi)$)	At every point in time, if ϕ holds then ψ should hold

Definition 2 (Syntax of Parametric MTL). *Let $\vec{\theta} = [\theta_1 \ldots \theta_n]$ be a vector of parameters. The set of all well-formed Parametric MTL (PMTL) formulas is the set of all well-formed MTL formulas where for all i, θ_i either appears in an arithmetic expression, i.e., $p[\theta_i] \equiv g(y) \leq \theta_i$, or in the timing constraint of a temporal operator, i.e., $\mathcal{I}[\theta_i]$.*

We will denote a PMTL formula ϕ with parameters $\vec{\theta}$ by $\phi[\vec{\theta}]$. Given a vector of parameters $\vec{\theta} \in \Theta$, then the formula $\phi[\vec{\theta}]$ is an MTL formula. There is an implicit mapping from the vector of parameters $\vec{\theta}$ to the corresponding arithmetic expressions and temporal operators in the MTL formula. Once a parameter valuation is defined, a PMTL formula is transformed into an MTL formula.

4   Robustness of Metric Temporal Logic Formulas

Once system specifications are defined in MTL, we can utilize the theory of the robustness of MTL to determine whether a particular behavior satisfies or falsifies (does not satisfy) the specification. Furthermore, we can quantify how "close" that particular behavior is to falsification. A positive robustness value indicates that the specification is satisfied and a negative robustness value indicates that the specification is falsified.

Using a metric d [28], we can define the distance of a point $x \in X$ from a set $S \subseteq X$ as follows:

Definition 3 (Signed Distance). *Let $x \in X$ be a point, $S \subseteq X$ be a set and d be a metric on X. Then, we define the Signed Distance from x to S to be*

$$\mathbf{Dist}_d(x, S) := \begin{cases} -\min\{d(x, y) \mid y \in S\} & \text{if } x \notin S \\ \min\{d(x, y) \mid y \in X \backslash S\} & \text{if } x \in S \end{cases}$$

Table 2. Various specifications for the AT model [32].

	Natural Language	MTL
ψ_1	It is not the case that eventually, the vehicle will be in fourth gear and the speed of the vehicle is less than 50	$\psi_1 = \neg\Diamond(g_4 \rightarrow (v < 50))$
ψ_2	There should be no transition from gear two to gear one and back to gear two in less than 2.5 s	$\Box((g_2 \wedge \bigcirc g_1) \rightarrow \Box_{(0,2.5]}\neg g_2)$
ψ_3	After shifting into gear one, there should be no shift from gear one to any other gear within 2.5 s	$\Box((\neg g_1 \wedge \bigcirc g_1) \rightarrow \Box_{(0,2.5]}g_1)$
ψ_4	When shifting into any gear, there should be no shift from that gear to any other gear within 2.5 s	$\wedge_{i=1}^{4}\Box((\neg g_i \wedge \bigcirc g_i) \rightarrow \Box_{(0,2.5]}g_i)$
ψ_5	If engine speed is always less than $\bar{\omega}$, then vehicle speed can not exceed $\bar{v}$ in less than T sec	$\neg(\Diamond_{[0,T]}(v > \bar{v}) \wedge \Box(\omega < \bar{\omega}))$ or $\Box(\omega < \bar{\omega}) \rightarrow \Diamond_{[0,T]}(v > \bar{v})$
ψ_6	Within T sec the vehicle speed is above $\bar{v}$ and from that point on the engine speed is always less than $\bar{\omega}$	$\Diamond_{[0,T]}((v \geq \bar{v}) \wedge \Box(\omega < \bar{\omega}))$
ψ_7	A gear increase from first to fourth in under 10 s, ending in an RPM above $\bar{\omega}$ within 2 s of that, should result in a vehicle speed above $\bar{v}$	$((g_1 \; \mathcal{U} \; g_2 \; \mathcal{U} \; g_3 \; \mathcal{U} \; g_4) \wedge \Diamond_{[0,10]}(g_4 \wedge \Diamond_{[0,2]}(\omega \geq \bar{\omega}))) \rightarrow \Diamond_{[0,10]}(g_4 \wedge \bigcirc(g_4 \; \mathcal{U}_{[0,1]} \; (v \geq \bar{v})))$

ω: Engine rotation speed, v: vehicle velocity, g_i : gear i. Recommended values:
$\bar{\omega}$: 4500, 5000, 5200, 5500 RPM; $\bar{v}$: 120, 160, 170, 200 mph; T : 4, 8, 10, 20 s
$\Box$: Always, $\Diamond$: Eventually, $\mathcal{U}$: Until, $\bigcirc$: Next

MTL formulas are interpreted over timed state sequences μ. We let the valuation function be the depth (or the distance) of the current point of the signal $\mathbf{y}(i)$ in the set $O(p)$ labeled by the atomic proposition p. This robustness estimate over a single point can be extended to all points on a trajectory by applying a series of min and max operations over time. This is referred to as the robustness estimate and is formally presented in Definition 4. The robustness estimate defines how much of a perturbation a signal can tolerate without changing the Boolean truth value of the specification.

For the purposes of the following discussion, we use the notation $[\![\phi]\!]$ to denote the robustness estimate with which the timed state sequence μ satisfies the specification ϕ. Formally, the valuation function for a given formula ϕ is $[\![\phi]\!] : Y^N \times \mathfrak{T} \times N \rightarrow \overline{\mathbb{R}}$. In the definition below, we also use the following notation: for $Q \subseteq R$, the *preimage* of Q under τ is defined as: $\tau^{-1}(Q) := \{i \in N \mid \tau(i) \in Q\}$. Also, given an $\alpha \in \mathbb{R}$ and $I = \langle l, u \rangle$, we define the timing interval shift operation as $\alpha + I = \langle \alpha + l, \alpha + u \rangle$. Here, $\langle$ and $\rangle$ are used to denote brackets or parentheses for closed and open intervals.

Definition 4 (Robustness Estimate [28]). *Let $\mu = (\mathbf{y}, \tau) \in Y^{[0,T]}$, and $i, j, k \in N$, then the robustness estimate of any formula MTL formula is defined as:*

$$[\![\top]\!](\mu, i) := +\infty$$
$$[\![p]\!](\mu, i) := \mathbf{Dist}_d(\mathbf{y}(i), O(p))$$
$$[\![\neg \phi]\!](\mu, i) := -[\![\phi]\!](\mu, i)$$
$$[\![\phi_1 \vee \phi_2]\!](\mu, i) := \max([\![\phi_1]\!](\mu, i), [\![\phi_2]\!](\mu, i))$$
$$[\![\bigcirc \phi]\!](\mu, i) := \begin{cases} [\![\phi]\!](\mu, i+1) & \text{if } i+1 \in N \\ -\infty & \text{otherwise} \end{cases}$$
$$[\![\phi_1 \, \mathcal{U}_I \, \phi_2]\!](\mu, i) := \max_{j \in \tau^{-1}(\tau(i)+I)} \left(\min([\![\phi_2]\!](\mu, j), \min_{i \le k < j} [\![\phi_1]\!](\mu, k)) \right)$$

When $i = 0$, then we write $[\![\phi]\!](\mu)$. With $[\![\phi]\!](\Sigma)$, We denote the system robustness as the minimum robustness over all system behaviors.

$$[\![\phi]\!](\Sigma) = \min_{\mu \in \mathcal{L}(\Sigma)} [\![\phi]\!](\mu) \tag{2}$$

In S-TaLiRo, the robustness of an MTL formula with respect to a timed state sequence is computed using two algorithms. The first algorithm, *dp_taliro* [25], uses a dynamic programming algorithm to compute the robustness in segments, iteratively. The second algorithm, *fw_taliro* [28], uses formula rewriting techniques. This approach maintains a state of the formula with respect to time, however, at a significant computation cost. If we consider the robustness estimate over systems, the resulting robustness landscape can be both nonlinear and non-convex. An example of the robustness landscape for an MTL specification is illustrated in Fig. 3.

We note that a similar notion of robustness is presented in [22] for Signal Temporal Logic (STL) formulas [41]. While between the two approaches the robust interpretation (semantics) for predicates of the form $x < a$ is identical, the two approaches differ over arbitrary predicates of form $f(x) < 0$. Using the notion of robustness in Definition 4, predicates of the form $f(x) < 0$ are interpreted as the signed distance of the current point x from the set $\{x \mid f(x) < 0\}$. On the other hand, predicates of the form $f(x) < 0$ are not directly supported by the theory as introduced in [22]. If the robustness of $f(x) < 0$ is simply defined as $f(x)$, then the robustness estimate is not guaranteed to define a robustness tube within which all other trajectories satisfy the same property. Nevertheless, for both semantics, positive robustness implies Boolean satisfaction, while negative robustness implies falsification.

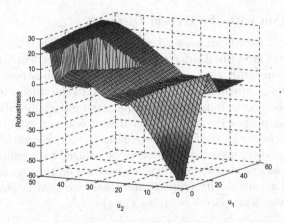

Fig. 3. Robustness estimate landscape for the AT model and specification $\phi_{AT} = \neg(\Diamond_{[0,30]}(v > 100) \wedge \Box(\omega \le 4500)) \wedge \neg\Diamond_{[10,40]}\Box_{[0,5]}(60 < v \le 80) \wedge \neg\Diamond_{[50,60]}\Box_{[0,3]}(v \le 60)$. The input signal to the system is generated by linearly interpolating control points u_1, u_2 at time 0 and 60, respectively, for the throttle input u. That is, $u(t) = \frac{60-t}{60}u_1 + \frac{t}{60}u_2$.

5   Falsification with S-TaLiRo

The problem of determining whether a CPS Σ satisfies a specification ϕ is an undecidable problem, i.e. there is no general algorithm that terminates and returns whether $\Sigma \models \phi$. Therefore, it is not possible to determine exactly the minimum robustness over all system behaviors. However, by repeatedly testing the system, we can check whether a behavior that does not satisfy the specification exists. In other words, we try to find a counter-example or falsifying example that proves that the system does not satisfy the specification within a set number of tests. The MTL falsification problem is presented as follows:

Problem 1 (MTL Falsification). *Given an MTL formula ϕ and a system Σ, find initial conditions and input signals such that, when given to Σ, generate a trajectory that does not satisfy ϕ. Formally, find $x_0 \in X_0$, $u \in \mathbf{U}$, where $\mu = \Delta_\Sigma(x_0, u)$ and $[\![\phi]\!](\mu) < 0$ (or with Boolean semantics $\mu \not\models \phi$).*

In S-TaLiRo [7,44], this is defined as an optimization problem that uses the notion of MTL robustness to guide the search. To solve this problem, an automated test case generation framework is utilized (see Fig. 4). S-TaLiRo takes as input a model, an MTL specification and a well-defined search space over the system inputs and initial conditions. Then, a stochastic optimization algorithm generates a point x_0 for the initial conditions and input signal u. These are given to the system model which generate an execution trace (output trajectory and timing function). By analyzing the execution trace, a robustness value is computed. This is then used by the stochastic optimization algorithm to select the next sample until a falsifying trajectory is generated or the maximum number of test is reached. The algorithm will return the least robust system behavior with the corresponding input signal and initial conditions.

5.1   Falsification with the Hybrid Distance

For falsification of specifications such as $\psi_1 = \neg\Diamond(g_4 \rightarrow (v < 50))$ over the AT model, where there is an implication relation and the antecedent is over a discrete mode of the system rather than a continuous state, the robustness estimate from Definition 4 does not provide sufficient information to the stochastic optimizer to find a falsifying behavior. In fact, the formula may be trivially satisfied since the search space that pushes the system to gear four is never explored. Therefore, the antecedent is false and the formula evaluates to true. For such specifications, in S-TaLiRo, a hybrid distance metric may be utilized to attempt falsification. In this case, we assume that the user has information on the logical modes of the model including a connectivity graph G and transition guards. Now, the output space becomes a hybrid space $Y = \{g_1, g_2, g_3, g_4\} \times \mathbb{R}^2$.

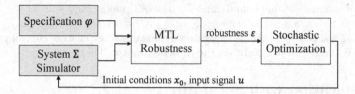

Fig. 4. The falsification framework in S-TaLiRo. Once a system Σ, initial conditions x_0, and input signals u are given, an output trajectory $\mathbf{y}$ is generated. The output trajectory $\mathbf{y}$ is then analyzed with respect to a specification and a robustness estimate ε is produced. This robustness estimate is then used by the stochastic optimizer to generate a new initial condition and input signal with the goal of minimizing the system robustness.

The hybrid distance metric is defined as a piecewise function. In the case when the current mode of the system is not in the mode where the specification can be falsified, then the hybrid distance is composed of two components. The first contains the number of hops/transitions from the current mode to the mode where falsification may occur. The second component is the continuous distance to the guard transition in the shortest path to the falsifying mode. In the case where falsification may occur in the current mode, the hybrid distance metric is the robustness estimate from Definition 4. For a detailed, formal presentation of the hybrid distance see [1].

In Fig. 5, we illustrate the robustness landscape from Definition 4 and the hybrid distance. While one is flat, offering little information to the stochastic optimizer, the other one has a gradient that leads to falsification. Note that the hybrid distance there is mapped to a real value using a weighting function that emphasizes the number of hops to the mode where falsification may occur.

6   Parameter Mining

Parameter mining refers to the process of determining parameter valuations for parametric MTL formulas for which the specification is falsified. The parameter

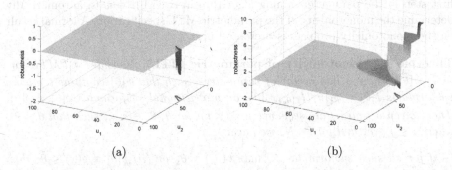

Fig. 5. Robustness landscape for the specification $\psi_1 = \neg\Diamond(g_4 \rightarrow (v < 50))$ over the AT model using the (a) euclidean robustness estimate and (b) hybrid robustness estimate.

mining problem can be viewed as an extension of the falsification problem, where not only are we interested in finding falsifying behaviors for a specific parameter valuation of a parametric MTL formula, but we are interested in finding falsifying behaviors for a range of parameter valuations. In other words, we answer the question of what parameter ranges cause falsification.

Our high-level goal is to explore and infer properties that a system does not satisfy. We assume that the system designer has partial understanding about the properties that the system satisfies (or does not satisfy) and would like to be able to determine these properties precisely. The practical benefits of this method are twofold. One, it allows for the analysis and development of specifications. In many cases, system requirements are not well formalized by the initial system design stages. Two, it allows for the analysis and exploration of system behavior. If a specification can be falsified, then it is natural to inquire for the range of parameter values that cause falsification. That is, in many cases, the system design may not be modified, but the guarantees provided should be updated.

The parameter mining problem is formally defined as follows.

Problem 2 (MTL Parameter Mining). *Given a parametric MTL formula* $\phi[\vec{\theta}]$ *with a vector of m unknown parameters* $\vec{\theta} \in \Theta = [\underaccent{\bar}{\vec{\theta}}, \bar{\vec{\theta}}]$ *and a system* Σ, *find the set* $\Psi = \{\vec{\theta}^* \in \Theta \mid \Sigma$ *does not satisfy* $\phi[\vec{\theta}^*]\}$.

That is, the solution to Problem 2 is the set Ψ such that for any parameter $\vec{\theta}^*$ in Ψ the specification $\phi[\vec{\theta}^*]$ does not hold on system Σ. In other words, it is the set of parameter valuations for which the system is falsified. In the following, we refer to Ψ as the parameter falsification domain.

6.1 Monotonicity of Parametric MTL

In S-TaLiRo, we solve this problem for a class of monotonic parametric MTL specifications. For these specifications, as you increase the parameter valuation, the robustness of the system is either non-increasing or non-decreasing. The first step in the parameter mining algorithm in S-TALIRO is to automatically determine the monotonicity of the parametric MTL specification. A formal result on the monotonicity problem is presented next.

Theorem 1 (Monotonicity of parametric MTL). *Consider a PMTL formula $\psi[\vec{\theta}]$, where $\vec{\theta}$ is a vector of parameters, such that $\psi[\vec{\theta}]$ contains temporal subformulas $\phi[\vec{\theta}] = \phi_1[\vec{\theta}]\mathcal{U}_{I[\theta_s]}\phi_2[\vec{\theta}]$, or propositional subformulas $\phi[\vec{\theta}] = p[\vec{\theta}]$. Then, given a timed state sequence $\mu = (\mathbf{y}, \tau)$, for $\vec{\theta}, \vec{\theta}' \in \overline{\mathbb{R}}_{\geq 0}^{n}$, such that $\vec{\theta} \leq \vec{\theta}'$, where $1 \leq j \leq n$, and for $i \in N$, we have:*

- *if for all such subformulas (i) $\max I(\theta_s) = \theta_s$ or (ii) $p[\vec{\theta}] \equiv g(x) \leq \vec{\theta}$, then $[\![\phi[\vec{\theta}]]\!](\mu, i) \leq [\![\phi[\vec{\theta}']]\!](\mu, i)$, i.e., function $[\![\phi[\vec{\theta}]]\!](\mu, i)$ is non-decreasing with respect to $\vec{\theta}$,*
- *if for all such subformulas (i) $\min I(\theta_s) = \theta_s$ or (ii) $p[\vec{\theta}] \equiv g(x) \geq \vec{\theta}$, then $[\![\phi[\vec{\theta}]]\!](\mu, i) \geq [\![\phi[\vec{\theta}']]\!](\mu, i)$, i.e., function $[\![\phi[\vec{\theta}]]\!](\mu, i)$ is non-increasing with respect to $\vec{\theta}$.*

Consider the parametric MTL formula $\phi[\theta] = \square_{[0,\theta]}p$ where $p \equiv (\omega \leq 3250)$. The function $[\![\phi[\theta]]\!](\mu)$ is non-increasing with respect to θ [9,33]. Intuitively, this relationship holds since by extending the value of θ in $\phi[\theta]$, it becomes just as or more difficult to satisfy the specification. In Fig. 6, this is illustrated using a single output trajectory over the AT model. However, using Theorem 1, we know that the monotonicity of the specification holds over all system behaviors.

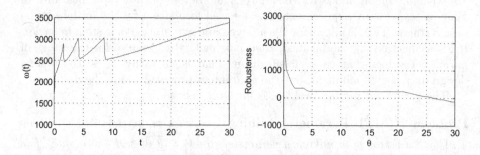

Fig. 6. Left: An output trajectory of the AT model for engine speed $\omega(t)$ for constant input throttle $u(t) = 50$; Right: corresponding robustness estimate of the specification $\square_{[0,\theta]}(\omega \leq 3250)$ with respect to θ.

6.2   Robustness-Guided Parameter Mining

To solve the parameter mining problem, we utilize the theory of robustness of MTL specifications to pose it as an optimization problem.

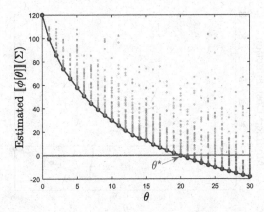

Fig. 7. Estimate of the robustness landscape for specification $\phi[\theta] = \square_{[0,\theta]}(v < 120)$ over the AT model. The figure is generated by running a falsification algorithm for parameter valuations 0 to 30. The red line drawn at 0 marks the boundary between satisfaction and falsification. The green (red) dots represent trajectories over different input signals that satisfied (falsified) the specification. (Color figure online)

In Fig. 7, the estimated robustness landscape over parameter valuations is presented for the specification $\phi[\theta] = \square_{[0,\theta]}(v < 120)$. The graph was generated by conducting falsification at parameter valuations 0 to 30. For each parameter valuation, 100 tests are conducted (hence estimated). Although we cannot calculate the exact robustness landscape, from Theorem 1, we know that the monotonicity of the specification is non-increasing. By increasing the value of θ you extend the time bounds for which $(v < 120)$ has to hold, and therefore the robustness cannot increase. Of particular interest is the parameter valuation where the robustness line intersects with 0, that is, the point where the specification switches from satisfied to falsified. Formally, in order to solve Problem 2, we solve the following optimization problem:

$$\text{optimize} \quad f(\vec{\theta}) \tag{3}$$
$$\text{subject to} \quad \vec{\theta} \in \Theta \text{ and } [\![\phi[\vec{\theta}]\!]](\Sigma) = \min_{\mu \in \mathcal{L}_\tau(\Sigma)} [\![\phi[\vec{\theta}]\!]](\mu) \leq 0$$

where $f : \mathbb{R}^n \to \mathbb{R}$ is a non-increasing ($\geq$) or a non-decreasing ($\leq$) function.

The function $[\![\phi[\vec{\theta}]\!]](\Sigma)$, which is the robustness of the system for a parameter valuation over all system behaviors, cannot be computed using reachability analysis algorithms nor is known in closed form for the systems we are considering. Therefore, we have to compute an under-approximation of Θ^*. We reformulate an optimization problem that can be solved using stochastic optimization methods. In particular, we reformulate the optimization problem (3) into a new one where the constraints due to the specification are incorporated into the cost function:

$$\text{optimize}_{\vec{\theta} \in \Theta} \left(f(\vec{\theta}) + \begin{cases} \gamma \pm [\![\phi[\vec{\theta}]\!]](\Sigma) & \text{if } [\![\phi[\vec{\theta}]\!]](\Sigma) \geq 0 \\ 0 & \text{otherwise} \end{cases} \right) \tag{4}$$

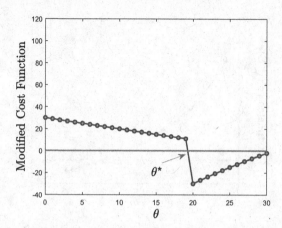

Fig. 8. The modified cost function for parameter mining for the specification $\phi[\theta] = \square_{[0,\theta]}(v < 120)$ over the AT model. The solution to the optimization problem in Eq. (4) returns θ^*

where the sign ($\pm$) and the parameter γ depend on whether the problem is a maximization or a minimization problem. The parameter γ must be properly chosen so that the solution of the problem in Eq. (4) is in Θ if and only if $[\![\phi[\vec{\theta}]]\!](\Sigma) \leq 0$. Therefore, if the problem in Eq. (3) is feasible, then the optimal points of Eqs. (3) and (4) are the same. For more details on Eq. (4), see [33] (Fig. 8).

For specifications with more than one parameter, the robustness landscape over the parameters forms a Pareto front. One inefficient and potentially misleading approach for generating the parameter falsification domain is by running a falsification algorithm for a set number of parameter valuations. For example, consider the parameter falsification domain in Fig. 9 (Left) for specification $\phi[\vec{\theta}] = \neg(\Diamond_{[0,\theta_1]} \wedge \square(\omega < \theta_2))$. The figure was generated by running the falsification algorithm for 200 iterations for every green/red dot. This approach is computationally very expensive and this specific example took 52 h to compute on a computer with an I7 4770k CPU and 16 GB of RAM. Furthermore, this approach may be misleading. It is possible that for a particular parameter valuation, falsification fails when in fact there exists falsifying behavior. For example, in Fig. 9 (Left), the green dot for the parameter valuation [36,4360], i.e. specification $\phi[36, 4360] = \neg(\Diamond_{[0,36]} \wedge \square(\omega < 4360))$, has falsifying behavior. We know this since there exists falsifying behavior for the red dot for parameter valuation [34,4190]. From Theorem 1, we know that the specification has a non-increasing robustness with respect to parameters. We say that the parameter valuation [34,4190] dominates [36,4360] in terms of falsification because if there exists a trajectory μ such that $\mu \not\models \phi[34, 4190]$ then $\mu \not\models \phi[36, 4360]$.

In S-TaLiRo, we provide two efficient approaches to explore the parameter falsification domain iteratively. The Robustness-Guided Parameter Falsification Domain Algorithm (RGDA) and the Structured Parameter Falsification Domain

Algorithm (SDA). In RGDA, parameters weights are utilized to guide the search towards unexplored areas of the parameter falsification domain. In SDA, the search is finely structured and does not depend on randomized weights. For details and analysis on the two algorithms, see [33]. The parameter falsification domain in Fig. 9 (Right) was computed with the RGDA algorithm with 100 iterations in 52 min.

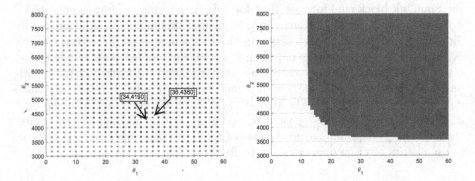

Fig. 9. The parameter falsification domain Ψ for the specification $\phi[\vec{\theta}] = \neg(\Diamond_{[0,\theta_1]} \wedge \Box(\omega < \theta_2))$ over the AT model for parameter valuations 0 to 60 for θ_1 and 3000 to 8000 for θ_2. Left: The figure is generated by running the falsification algorithm with 100 iterations for each dot in the figure. The green (red) dots represent the minimum robustness over 100 iterations that satisfied (falsified) the specification. Right: The figure is generated using the RGDA algorithm. The red area represents the parameter falsification domain, i.e. parameter valuations for which the specification is falsified. (Color figure online)

7   Runtime Monitoring

The discussion so far was primarily concerned with applications of offline monitoring of temporal logic robustness. However, many applications require *online* or *runtime* monitoring of robustness. In offline monitoring, the whole system trace is available offline for analysis, which means that it is possible to move forward and backward in time in order to compute its robustness with respect to a given specification. On the other hand, in runtime verification, the data become available during system execution.

Therefore, it is not clear that future time formal languages can always capture requirements in a meaningful way. For example, let us consider the future tense requirement that "*the RPM can remain higher than 2000 for more than 5 sec only when the vehicle is in gear 4.*" Formally, the requirement is $\varphi = \Box(\neg g_4 \rightarrow \Diamond_{[0,5]}(\omega < 2000))$ which is equivalent to $\Box(g_4 \vee \Diamond_{[0,5]}(\omega < 2000))$. If at time t the gearbox is not in the fourth gear, then we can only know at time $t + 5$ if the requirement was violated. From a requirements perspective, it is desirable to check at time t if the requirement is satisfied or violated. In other words, we may want to monitor an invariant like *"at least once in the past 5 seconds, either the system was in gear four or the RPM was below 2000."* The past tense requirement would guarantee that at time t we have not observed an interval that the RPM was above 2000 and the system was not in gear four.

In [17], we developed a Simulink block in S-TALIRO which can perform runtime robustness monitoring for past-future time MTL specifications. Namely, the Simulink block enables past time formula monitoring on data generated by a model or by a physical system interfaced with Simulink. In addition, if the Simulink model contains a prediction model with a prediction finite-time horizon h, then the user can express requirements with unbounded past and bounded future time horizon. In more detail, we have extended the syntax of MTL with past time operators such as "the previous sample satisfies ϕ ($\odot\phi$), "ϕ_1 since ϕ_2" ($\phi_1 \mathcal{S} \phi_2$), "sometime in the past ϕ" ($\Diamond\phi \equiv \top \mathcal{S}\phi$), and "always in the past ϕ" ($\Box\phi \equiv \neg\Diamond\neg\phi$). All these past-time operators can be additionally restricted though timing constraints as in the case of the future time operators. Details on the semantics of these operators can be found in [17].

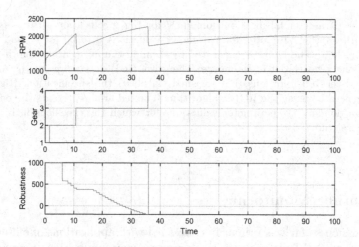

Fig. 10. S-TALIRO runtime monitoring on the automatic transition demo.

Figure 10 presents the output of the S-TALIRO Simulink monitoring block when applied to the Simulink automatic transmission model. For this demonstration, the throttle input has been set to a constant value of 20 while the brake input to a constant value of 0. The invariant checked is for the specification $\varphi = \Diamond_{[0,5]}(g_4 \lor (\omega < 2000))$ and its robustness is plotted in Fig. 10. Notice that about time 21.6 the RPM exceed the 2000 threshold while the gear is still in three. The instantaneous robustness value of φ drops below zero 5 s later as expected. When the system switches into gear four, the robustness of φ immediately becomes positive again. We remark that the robustness value of predicates with Boolean interpretation, e.g., *gear* = 4, must be mapped to some arbitrary large value within Simulink. Formalization of the robust interpretation of such predicates through hybrid distances (see Sect. 5.1) is not straightforward in Simulink, but potentially using input-output types [29] the process can become more systematic.

8   Future Directions

We will now turn our attention to problems surrounding learning-enabled and autonomous systems, which will form an important application area for many of the techniques detailed thus far. Autonomous systems such as self-driving cars are increasingly common on our streets. They rely heavily on machine learning components such as neural networks for detecting other vehicles, obstacles, pedestrians, traffic signals and signs from a combination of image and LiDAR data [38]. Besides perception, neural networks are also increasingly used as controllers that directly output steering and throttle commands to the vehicle [11]. Numerous accidents involving autonomous vehicles motivate the need for ensuring the safety of these systems [39]. At the same time, the key challenge lies in the lack of detailed component-wise specifications for the neural networks. In fact, most specifications are "end-to-end" high level specifications such as "the vehicle should brake if it detects a pedestrian in front".

Falsification approaches are increasingly being used to tackle the issue of missing specifications by using generative models tied in with rendering tools that can create realistic inputs to these systems with known "ground truth". Falsification tools including S-TALIRo have been employed directly to find corner cases that can cause these systems to potentially fail [4,23,30,46]. However, the key challenges posed by these applications are numerous:

(a) Falsification techniques have been designed primarily for control systems. The use of neural networks poses many challenges requiring a better formulation of the robustness concept that encompasses the robustness of classifiers as well as better stochastic search techniques [48]. Regarding the former, some first steps have been taken in [16] by defining a new formal logic for perception systems.

(b) Simply providing a falsifying scenario does not solve the issue of designing safe systems. Unlike human designed components, it is nearly impossible to localize failures to a bad value of a parameter or incorrect logic in software. Often neural networks have to be retrained. This requires us to consider a family of falsifying scenarios that can provide new training data for retraining the network to hopefully correct the underlying issue. Preliminary approaches have been proposed that involve repeated application of falsification search and retraining [13,49]. However, a lot of open challenges remain before this problem can be considered satisfactorily resolved.

(c) The problem of helping developers understand *root causes* for falsification is yet another important future challenge in this area. Current approaches for understanding root causes are at their infancy [15]. Ideas from other fields such as explainable machine learning and natural language processing are needed to tackle the challenge of producing human understandable explanations of failures.

9   Conclusions

Robustness of temporal logic specification provides a systematic way of defining real-valued semantics to denote the degree of satisfaction of a specification by a trace of the system. Starting from robustness, we present important applications including falsification, parameter mining, runtime monitoring and safe autonomy. This area continues to be active with new challenges arising from the rapid emergence of learning-enabled autonomous systems. Future work in this area will continue to draw upon ideas from diverse areas including machine learning, robotics, natural language processing and human factors.

Acknowledgments. GF acknowledges support from NSF award 1350420. SS acknowledges support from NSF award numbers 1646556, 1815983 and the Air Force Research Laboratory (AFRL). All opinions expressed are those of the authors and not necessarily of the US NSF or AFRL.

References

1. Abbas, H., Fainekos, G.E., Sankaranarayanan, S., Ivancic, F., Gupta, A.: Probabilistic temporal logic falsification of cyber-physical systems. ACM Transactions on Embedded Computing Systems **12**(s2) (2013)
2. Abbas, H., Hoxha, B., Fainekos, G., Ueda, K.: Robustness-guided temporal logic testing and verification for stochastic cyber-physical systems. In: IEEE 4th Annual International Conference on Cyber Technology in Automation, Control, and Intelligent Systems (CYBER) (2014)
3. Abbas, H., Mittelmann, H., Fainekos, G.: Formal property verification in a conformance testing framework. In: 12th ACM-IEEE International Conference on Formal Methods and Models for System Design (2014)
4. Abbas, H., O'Kelly, M., Rodionova, A., Mangharam, R.: Safe at any speed: a simulation-based test harness for autonomous vehicles. In: CyPhy 2017 (2017)
5. Akazaki, T., Liu, S., Yamagata, Y., Duan, Y., Hao, J.: Falsification of cyber-physical systems using deep reinforcement learning. In: Havelund, K., Peleska, J., Roscoe, B., de Vink, E. (eds.) FM 2018. LNCS, vol. 10951, pp. 456–465. Springer, Cham (2018). https://doi.org/10.1007/978-3-319-95582-7_27
6. Alur, R., Courcoubetis, C., Dill, D.: Model-checking for real-time systems. In: Mitchell, J. (ed.) 5th Annual IEEE Symposium on Logic in Computer Science (LICS), pp. 414–425. IEEE Computer Society Press, June 1990
7. Annpureddy, Y., Liu, C., Fainekos, G., Sankaranarayanan, S.: S-TaLiRo: a tool for temporal logic falsification for hybrid systems. In: Abdulla, P.A., Leino, K.R.M. (eds.) TACAS 2011. LNCS, vol. 6605, pp. 254–257. Springer, Heidelberg (2011). https://doi.org/10.1007/978-3-642-19835-9_21
8. Anonymous: Model-based testing and validation of control software with Reactis (2003). http://www.reactive-systems.com/papers/bcsf.pdf

9. Asarin, E., Donzé, A., Maler, O., Nickovic, D.: Parametric identification of temporal properties. In: Khurshid, S., Sen, K. (eds.) RV 2011. LNCS, vol. 7186, pp. 147–160. Springer, Heidelberg (2012). https://doi.org/10.1007/978-3-642-29860-8_12

10. Bartocci, E., et al.: Specification-based monitoring of cyber-physical systems: a survey on theory, tools and applications. In: Bartocci, E., Falcone, Y. (eds.) Lectures on Runtime Verification. LNCS, vol. 10457, pp. 135–175. Springer, Cham (2018). https://doi.org/10.1007/978-3-319-75632-5_5

11. Bojarski, M., Testa, D.D., Dworakowski, D., et al.: End to end learning for self-driving cars. CoRR abs/1604.07316 (2016)

12. Cameron, F., Fainekos, G., Maahs, D.M., Sankaranarayanan, S.: Towards a verified artificial pancreas: challenges and solutions for runtime verification. In: Bartocci, E., Majumdar, R. (eds.) RV 2015. LNCS, vol. 9333, pp. 3–17. Springer, Cham (2015). https://doi.org/10.1007/978-3-319-23820-3_1

13. Claviere, A., Dutta, S., Sankaranarayanan, S.: Trajectory tracking control for robotic vehicles using counterexample guided training of neural networks. In: ICAPS, pp. 680–688. AAAI Press (2019)

14. Deshmukh, J.V., Sankaranarayanan, S.: Formal techniques for verification and testing of cyber-physical systems. In: Al Faruque, M.A., Canedo, A. (eds.) Design Automation of Cyber-Physical Systems, pp. 69–105. Springer, Cham (2019). https://doi.org/10.1007/978-3-030-13050-3_4

15. Diwakaran, R.D., Sankaranarayanan, S., Trivedi, A.: Analyzing neighborhoods of falsifying traces in cyber-physical systems. In: International Conference on Cyber-Physical Systems (ICCPS), pp. 109–119. ACM Press (2017)

16. Dokhanchi, A., Amor, H.B., Deshmukh, J.V., Fainekos, G.: Evaluating perception systems for autonomous vehicles using quality temporal logic. In: Colombo, C., Leucker, M. (eds.) RV 2018. LNCS, vol. 11237, pp. 409–416. Springer, Cham (2018). https://doi.org/10.1007/978-3-030-03769-7_23

17. Dokhanchi, A., Hoxha, B., Fainekos, G.: On-line monitoring for temporal logic robustness. In: Bonakdarpour, B., Smolka, S.A. (eds.) RV 2014. LNCS, vol. 8734, pp. 231–246. Springer, Cham (2014). https://doi.org/10.1007/978-3-319-11164-3_19

18. Dokhanchi, A., Hoxha, B., Fainekos, G.: Formal requirement debugging for testing and verification of cyber-physical systems. ACM Trans. Embed. Comput. Syst. (TECS) 17(2), 34 (2018)

19. Dokhanchi, A., et al.: ARCH-COMP18 category report: results on the falsification benchmarks. In: ARCH@ ADHS, pp. 104–109 (2018)

20. Dokhanchi, A., Zutshi, A., Sriniva, R.T., Sankaranarayanan, S., Fainekos, G.: Requirements driven falsification with coverage metrics. In: Proceedings of the 12th International Conference on Embedded Software, pp. 31–40. IEEE Press (2015)

21. Donzé, A.: Breach, a toolbox for verification and parameter synthesis of hybrid systems. In: Touili, T., Cook, B., Jackson, P. (eds.) CAV 2010. LNCS, vol. 6174, pp. 167–170. Springer, Heidelberg (2010). https://doi.org/10.1007/978-3-642-14295-6_17

22. Donzé, A., Maler, O.: Robust satisfaction of temporal logic over real-valued signals. In: Chatterjee, K., Henzinger, T.A. (eds.) FORMATS 2010. LNCS, vol. 6246, pp. 92–106. Springer, Heidelberg (2010). https://doi.org/10.1007/978-3-642-15297-9_9

23. Dreossi, T., Ghosh, S., Sangiovanni-Vincentelli, A., Seshia, S.A.: Systematic testing of convolutional neural networks for autonomous driving (2017). Reliable Machine Learning in the Wild (RMLW) workshop

24. Ernst, G., Arcaini, P., Donze, A., Fainekos, G., Mathesen, L., Pedrielli, G., Yaghoubi, S., Yamagata, Y., Zhang, Z.: ARCH-COMP 2019 category report: falsification. EPiC Ser. Comput. **61**, 129–140 (2019)

25. Fainekos, G., Sankaranarayanan, S., Ueda, K., Yazarel, H.: Verification of automotive control applications using s-TaLiRo. In: Proceedings of the American Control Conference (2012)

26. Fainekos, G.E., Girard, A., Kress-Gazit, H., Pappas, G.J.: Temporal logic motion planning for dynamic robots. Automatica **45**(2), 343–352 (2009)

27. Fainekos, G.E., Pappas, G.J.: Robustness of temporal logic specifications. In: Havelund, K., Núñez, M., Roşu, G., Wolff, B. (eds.) FATES/RV -2006. LNCS, vol. 4262, pp. 178–192. Springer, Heidelberg (2006). https://doi.org/10.1007/11940197_12

28. Fainekos, G.E., Pappas, G.J.: Robustness of temporal logic specifications for continuous-time signals. Theoret. Comput. Sci. **410**(42), 4262–4291 (2009)

29. Ferrère, T., Nickovic, D., Donzé, A., Ito, H., Kapinski, J.: Interface-aware signal temporal logic. In: 22nd ACM International Conference on Hybrid Systems: Computation and Control, pp. 57–66 (2019)

30. Fremont, D.J., Dreossi, T., Ghosh, S., Yue, X., Sangiovanni-Vincentelli, A.L., Seshia, S.A.: Scenic: a language for scenario specification and scene generation. In: PLDI, pp. 63–78 (2019)

31. Gregg, A., MacMillan, D.: Airlines cancel thousands of flights as Boeing works to fix 737 max software problems. The Washington Post July 14 (2019)

32. Hoxha, B., Abbas, H., Fainekos, G.: Benchmarks for temporal logic requirements for automotive systems. In: Workshop on Applied Verification for Continuous and Hybrid Systems (2014)

33. Hoxha, B., Dokhanchi, A., Fainekos, G.: Mining parametric temporal logic properties in model based design for cyber-physical systems. Int. J. Softw. Tools Technol. Transfer **20**, 79–93 (2018)

34. Hoxha, B., Mavridis, N., Fainekos, G.: VISPEC: a graphical tool for elicitation of MTL requirements. In: IEEE/RSJ IROS (2015)

35. Johnson, T.T., Gannamaraju, R., Fischmeister, S.: A survey of electrical and electronic (E/E) notifications for motor vehicles. In: ESV 2015 (2015)

36. Kapinski, J., Deshmukh, J.V., Jin, X., Ito, H., Butts, K.: Simulation-based approaches for verification of embedded control systems: an overview of traditional and advanced modeling, testing, and verification techniques. IEEE Control Syst. **36**(6), 45–64 (2016)

37. Koymans, R.: Specifying real-time properties with metric temporal logic. Real Time Syst. **2**(4), 255–299 (1990)

38. LeCun, Y., Kavukcuoglu, K., Farabet, C.: Convolutional networks and applications in vision. In: Proceedings of 2010 IEEE International Symposium on Circuits and Systems, pp. 253–256, May 2010

39. Lee, T.B.: Report: software bug led to death in Uber's self-driving crash. Ars Technica May 07 (2018)

40. Leitner, F., Leue, S.: Simulink design verifier vs. SPIN - a comparative case study (short paper). In: Formal Methods for Industrial Critical Systems (2008)

41. Maler, O., Nickovic, D.: Monitoring temporal properties of continuous signals. In: Lakhnech, Y., Yovine, S. (eds.) FORMATS/FTRTFT -2004. LNCS, vol. 3253, pp. 152–166. Springer, Heidelberg (2004). https://doi.org/10.1007/978-3-540-30206-3_12

42. Mathesen, L., Yaghoubi, S., Pedrielli, G., Fainekos, G.: Falsification of cyber-physical systems with robustness uncertainty quantification through stochastic optimization with adaptive restart. In: IEEE CASE (2019)

43. Nghiem, T., Sankaranarayanan, S., Fainekos, G.E., Ivancic, F., Gupta, A., Pappas, G.J.: Monte-Carlo techniques for falsification of temporal properties of non-linear hybrid systems. In: Proceedings of the 13th ACM International Conference on Hybrid Systems: Computation and Control, pp. 211–220. ACM Press (2010)

44. S-TaLiRo Tools. https://sites.google.com/a/asu.edu/s-taliro/

45. Sandler, K., et al.: Killed by code: software transparency in implantable medical devices. Technical report, Software Freedom Law Center (2010)

46. Tuncali, C.E., Fainekos, G., Ito, H., Kapinski, J.: Simulation-based adversarial test generation for autonomous vehicles with machine learning components. In: IEEE Intelligent Vehicles Symposium (IV) (2018)

47. Tuncali, C.E., Hoxha, B., Ding, G., Fainekos, G., Sankaranarayanan, S.: Experience report: application of falsification methods on the UxAS system. In: Dutle, A., Muñoz, C., Narkawicz, A. (eds.) NFM 2018. LNCS, vol. 10811, pp. 452–459. Springer, Cham (2018). https://doi.org/10.1007/978-3-319-77935-5_30

48. Yaghoubi, S., Fainekos, G.: Gray-box adversarial testing for control systems with machine learning components. In: ACM International Conference on Hybrid Systems: Computation and Control (HSCC) (2019)

49. Yaghoubi, S., Fainekos, G.: Worst-case satisfaction of STL specifications using feedforward neural network controllers: a Lagrange multipliers approach. In: International Conference on Embedded Software (EMSOFT) (2019)

50. Zhang, Z., Ernst, G., Sedwards, S., Arcaini, P.: Two-layered falsification of hybrid systems guided by Monte Carlo tree search. IEEE Trans. CADIntegr. Circ.Syst. **37**(11), 2894–2905 (2018)

On the Runtime Enforcement
of Timed Properties

Yliès Falcone[1（✉）] and Srinivas Pinisetty[2]

[1] Univ. Grenoble Alpes, Inria, CNRS, Grenoble INP, LIG, 38000 Grenoble, France
`ylies.falcone@univ-grenoble-alpes.fr`
[2] School of Electrical Sciences, IIT Bhubaneswar, Bhubaneswar, India
`spinisetty@iitbbs.ac.in`

Abstract. Runtime enforcement refers to the theories, techniques, and tools for enforcing correct behavior of systems at runtime. We are interested in such behaviors described by specifications that feature timing constraints formalized in what is generally referred to as timed properties. This tutorial presents a gentle introduction to runtime enforcement (of timed properties). First, we present a taxonomy of the main principles and concepts involved in runtime enforcement. Then, we give a brief overview of a line of research on theoretical runtime enforcement where timed properties are described by timed automata and feature uncontrollable events. Then, we mention some tools capable of runtime enforcement, and we present the TiPEX tool dedicated to timed properties. Finally, we present some open challenges and avenues for future work.

Runtime Enforcement (RE) is a discipline of computer science concerned with enforcing the expected behavior of a system at runtime. Runtime enforcement extends the traditional runtime verification [12–14,42,43] problem by dealing with the situations where the system deviates from its expected behavior. While runtime verification monitors are execution observers, runtime enforcers are execution modifiers.

Foundations for runtime enforcement were pioneered by Schneider in [98] and by Rinard in [95] for the specific case of real-time systems. There are several tutorials and overviews on runtime enforcement for untimed systems [39,47,59], but none on the enforcement of timed properties (for real-time systems).

In this tutorial, we focus on runtime enforcing behavior described by a timed property. Timed properties account for physical time. They allow expressing constraints on the time that should elapse between (sequences of) events, which is useful for real-time systems when specifying timing constraints between statements, their scheduling policies, the completion of tasks, etc. [5,7,88,101,102].

This work is supported by the French national program "Programme Investissements d'Avenir IRT Nanoelec" (ANR-10-AIRT-05).

ⓒ Springer Nature Switzerland AG 2019
B. Finkbeiner and L. Mariani (Eds.): RV 2019, LNCS 11757, pp. 48–69, 2019.
https://doi.org/10.1007/978-3-030-32079-9_4

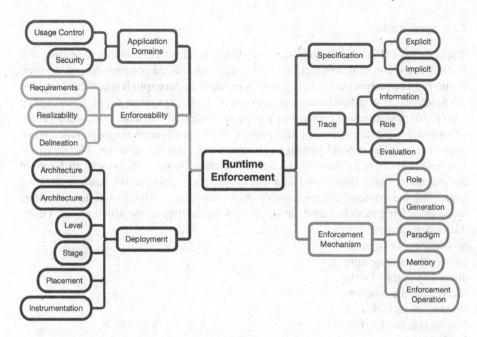

Fig. 1. Taxonomy of concepts in runtime enforcement.

This tutorial comprises four stages:

1. the presentation of a taxonomy of concepts and principles in RE (Sect. 1);
2. the presentation of a framework for the RE of timed properties where specifications are described by timed automata (preliminary concepts are recalled in Sect. 2, the framework is overviewed in Sect. 3, and presented in more details in Sect. 4);
3. the demonstration of the TiPEX [82] tool implementing the framework (Sect. 5);
4. the description of some avenues for future work (Sect. 6).

1   Principles and Concepts in Runtime Enforcement

In the first stage of the tutorial, we discuss a *taxonomy* of the main concepts and principles in runtime enforcement (see Fig. 1). We refer to this taxonomy as the *RE taxonomy*. The RE taxonomy builds upon, specializes, and extends the taxonomy of runtime verification [45] (RV taxonomy). In particular, the RE taxonomy shares the notions of **specification**, **trace**, and **deployment** with the RV taxonomy. We briefly review and customize these for runtime enforcement in the following for the sake of completeness. The RE taxonomy considers the additional **enforceability** and **enforcement mechanism** parts. We also present some **application domains** where the RE principles were used.

1.1 Specification

A specification (Fig. 2) describes (some of) the intended system behavior to be enforced. It usually relies on some abstraction of the actual and detailed system behavior. A specification can be categorized as being explicit or implicit. An **explicit** specification makes the functional or non-functional requirements of the target system explicit. An explicit specification is expressed by the user using a specification language (e.g., some variant of temporal logic or extension of automata). Such specification language relies on an operational or denotational paradigm to express the intended behavior. The specification language offers modalities which allow referring to the past, present, or future of the execution. Other dimensions of a specification are related to the features allowing expressing the expected behavior with more or less details. The *time* dimension refers to the underlying model of time, being either a logical time or the actual physical time. The *data* dimension refers to whether the specification allows reasoning about any form of data involved in the program (values of variables or function parameters). An **implicit** specification is related to the semantics of the programming language of the target application system, or its programming or memory models. Implicit specifications generally capture a collection of errors that should not appear at runtime because they could lead to unpredictable behavior. Implicit

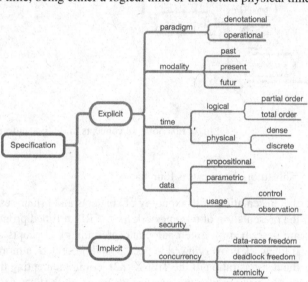

Fig. 2. Taxonomy - specification.

specifications include security concerns (see also Sect. 1.6) such as memory safety [10,105] where some form of memory access errors should be avoided (e.g., use after free, null pointer dereference, overflow) and the integrity of the execution (of the data, data flow, or control flow). They also include absence of concurrency errors [69] such as deadlocks, data races, and atomicity violations.

1.2 Trace

Depending on the target system and specification being enforced, the considered notion of trace can contain several sorts of **information** (Fig. 3): input/output from the system, events or sample states from the system, or signals. The notion of trace can play up to three different **roles**: it can be the mathematical *model* of a specification (when a set of traces defines the specification), the sequence of pieces of information from the system which is *input* to the enforcement mechanism, or the

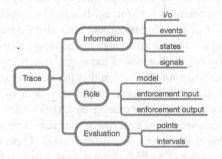

Fig. 3. Taxonomy - trace.

sequence of pieces of information enforced on the system which is *output* from the enforcement mechanism. In the two latter cases, the observation and imposition of the trace is influenced by the sampling on the system state, which can be triggered according to events or time. Moreover, the trace can contain more or less precise information depending on the points of control and observation provided by instrumentation. Such information can be gathered by **evaluating/abstracting** the system state at points of intervals of physical time. We refer to [74, 90] for more details on the concept of trace.

1.3 Enforcement Mechanism

An enforcement mechanism (EM, Fig. 4) is a mechanism in charge of enforcing the desired specification, be it either a mathematical model of the expected-behavior transformation or its realization by algorithms or routines. It is referred to by several names in the literature, e.g., enforcement monitor, reference monitor, enforcer, and enforcement mechanism. Several models of enforcement mechanisms were proposed: security automata [98], edit-automata [68] (and its variants [19]), generalized enforcement monitors [48], iteration suppression automata [21], delayers [83], delayers with suppression [44], sanitizers [104],

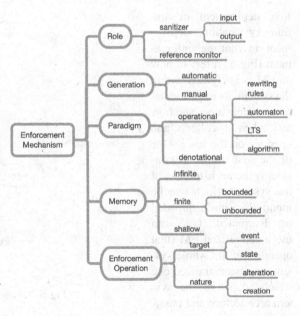

Fig. 4. Taxonomy - enforcement mechanism.

shields [63], safety shields [107], shields for burst errors [107], and safety guards [108]. An EM reads a trace produced by the target system and produces a new trace where the specification is enforced. It acts like a "filter" on traces. This conceptualization of an EM as a(n) (input/output) filter abstracts away from its actual **role**, which can be an input sanitizer (filtering out the inputs to the target system), an output sanitizer (filtering out the outputs of the target system), or a reference monitor (granting or denying permission to the action that the system executes). An EM can be **generated** automatically from the specification (it is said to be synthesized) or programmed manually. Automatically generating an EM provides more confidence and binds it to the specification used to generate it, whereas manual generation permits programming an EM and makes room for customization. There exist several **paradigms** for describing the behavior of an EM: denotational, when an EM is seen as a mathematical function with the set of traces as domain and codomain; or operational, when the computation steps for an EM are detailed (e.g., rewriting rules, automaton, labeled transition system - LTS, or algorithm). To transform the trace, an EM can use some internal **memory** to store information from the execution. Such memory can be assumed infinite, finite, or shallow when it cannot record multiple occurrences of the same piece of information. Moreover, using data from the input trace and this memory, **enforcement operations** in an EM may transform the trace. Examples of enforcement operations include terminating the underlying target system, preventing an action from executing or altering it, executing new actions, etc.

1.4 Deployment

Like deployment in runtime verification, deployment in runtime enforcement (Fig. 5) refers to how an EM is integrated within the system: its implementation, organization, and how and when it collects and operates on the trace. One of the first things to consider is the **architecture** of the system, which can be monolithic, multi-threaded or distributed. One can use a centralized EM (that operates on the whole system) or a decentralized one which adapts to the system architecture and possibly use existing communication mediums for decentralized EMs to communicate. An EM itself can be deployed at several **levels**: software, operating system or virtual

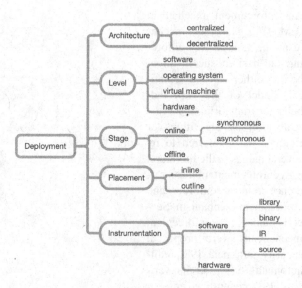

Fig. 5. Taxonomy - deployment.

machine, or hardware. The higher the level (in terms of abstraction), the more the mechanism has access to semantic information about the target system, while lower-level deployment provides the enforcement device with finer-grain observation and control capabilities on the target system. The **stage** refers to *when* an EM operates, either *offline* (after the execution) or *online* (during the execution, synchronously or asynchronously). Offline runtime enforcement (and verification) is conceptually simpler since an EM has access to the complete trace (in e.g., a log) and can thus perform arbitrary enforcement operations. On the contrary, in online enforcement, an EM only knows the execution history and decisions have to be made while considering all possible future behaviors. The **placement** refers to *where* an EM operates, either *inline* or *outline*, within or outside the existing address space of the initial system. The deployment parameters are constrained by the **instrumentation** (technique) used to augment the initial system to include an EM. Instrumentation can be software-based or hardware-based depending on the implementation of the target system. In the case of software-based instrumentation, it can operate at the level of the source (language) of the application system, its intermediate representation (IR), the binary, or using library interposition. Hardware-based instrumentation [8,9,75,99] can be for instance realized by observing and controlling the system through a JTAG port and using dedicated hardware (e.g., an FPGA).

Deployment Challenges. Deploying an EM with the appropriate parameters raises several challenges and issues. From a bird-eye view, the challenges revolve around ensuring that an EM does not "conflict with the initial system". We discuss this around two questions. First, *how to implement the "reference logic" where the enforcement mechanism takes important decisions regarding the system execution?* In the case where an EM is a sanitizer, deployment should ensure that all the relevant inputs or outputs go through the enforcement device. In the case where an EM is a reference monitor, the reference logic should ensure that the application actions get executed only if the monitor authorizes it. In security-sensitive or safety-critical applications, users of an enforcement framework may demand formal guarantees. There are some approaches to certify runtime verification mechanisms [3,23,33] and some to verify edit-automata [94], but more research endeavors are needed in these directions. Second, *how to preserve the integrity of the application?* As an EM modifies the behavior of the application, it should not alter its functioning by avoiding crashes, preserving its semantics, and not deteriorating its performance. For instance, consider the case where an EM intervenes by forbidding the access to some resource or an action to execute (denying it or postponing it). In case of online monitoring, an EM should be aware of the application semantics and more particularly of its control and data flows. In case of outline monitoring, there should be some signaling mechanism already planned in the application or added through instrumentation.

1.5 Enforceability

Enforceability (Fig. 6) refers
to the concept of determining the specification behavior that can effectively be
enforced on systems. EMs
should follow some **requirements** on how they correct
the behavior of systems. For
instance, *soundness* refers
to the fact that what is output by an EM should com-
ply with the specification

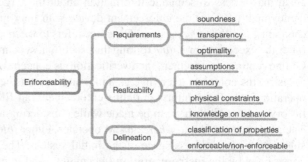

Fig. 6. Taxonomy - enforceability.

while *transparency* refers to the fact that the modification to the initial system behavior
should be minimal. Additional constraints such as *optimality* can be introduced to several possible modifications that a monitor can make, according to some desired quality
of service. Additionally, distances or pre-orders can be defined over valid traces for the
same purpose [20,58]. When it is possible to obtain an EM that enforces a property
while complying with the requirements, the property is said to be *enforceable*, and *non-
enforceable* otherwise. Enforceability of a specification is also influenced by the **realizability** of EMs. For this, assumptions are made on the feasibility of some operations of
an EM. An example is when an EM memorizes input events from the target system, it
should not prevent the system from functioning. Another example is when enforcing a
timed specification, as the time that elapses between events matters for the satisfaction
of the specification, there are assumptions to be made or guarantees to be ensured on
the computation time performed by EMs (e.g., the computation time of an EM should
be negligible) or on the system communication (e.g., communication overhead or reliability). Moreover, the amount of memory that an EM disposes influences how much
from the execution history it can record or events it can store, and thus the enforceable
properties [50,106]. Furthermore, importantly in a timed context, physical constraints
should be taken into consideration: in the online enforcement of a specification, events
cannot be released by an EM before being received. The realizability of EMs can benefit from knowledge on the possible system behavior. Such knowledge can come from
a (possibly partial) model of the system or static analysis. Knowledge permits upgrad-
ing an EM with predictive abilities [86] and it can thus enforce more specifications
(see also [11,85,110] for predictive runtime verification frameworks). Another concern
with enforceability is to **delineate** the sets of enforceable and non-enforceable specifications. Characterizing the set of enforceable specifications allows identifying the
(possibly syntactically characterized) fragments of a specification language that can be
enforced. For this, one can rely on existing classical classifications of properties, such
as the safety-liveness "dichotomy" [4,66,103] or the safety-progress hierarchy [27,71]
classifications. There exist several delineations of enforceable/non-enforceable properties based on different assumptions and EMs; see e.g., [26,48,58,68,98].

1.6   Application Domains

Application domains (Fig. 7) refers to the domains where the principles of runtime enforcement are applied. We briefly refer to some applications of runtime enforcement in categories: usage control and security/privacy, and memory safety. We do not further elaborate the taxonomy for application domains since classifying security domains is subject

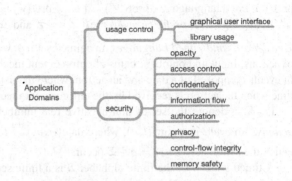

Fig. 7. Taxonomy - application domains.

to interpretation and most implementations of EMs for security address several flavors of security. Regarding applications for **usage control**, runtime enforcement was applied to enforce usage control policies in [73], enforcement of the usage of the Android library in [41], disabling Android advertisements in [36]. Regarding applications in the domain of **security**, runtime enforcement was applied to enforce the opacity of secrets in [46,55,109], access control policies in [76–78], confidentiality in [28,53], information-flow policies [28,49,64,64], security and authorization policies in [22,38], privacy policies in [28,56,65], control-flow integrity in [2,34,52,57,62], and memory safety in [24,25,35,100].

2   Real-Time Systems and Specifications with Time Constraints

The correctness of real-time systems depends not only on the logical result of the computation but also on the time at which the results are produced. Such systems are specified with requirements with precise constraints on the time that should elapse between actions and events. Formalization of a requirement with time constraints is referred to as a timed property. Timed automata is a formal model used to define timed properties. A timed automaton [6] is a finite automaton extended with a finite set of real valued clocks. It is one of the most studied models for modeling and verifying real-time systems with many algorithms and tools. In this section, we present the preliminaries required to formally define timed requirements and executions (traces) of a system.

2.1   Preliminaries and Notations

Untimed Concepts. Let Σ denote a finite alphabet. A (finite) word over Σ is a finite sequence of elements of Σ. The *length* of a word w is the number of elements in it and is denoted by $|w|$. The empty word over Σ is denoted by ε_Σ, or ε when clear from the context. The set of all (resp. non-empty) words over Σ is denoted by Σ^* (respectively Σ^+). The *concatenation* of two words w and w' is denoted by $w \cdot w'$. A word w' is a *prefix* of a word w, noted $w' \preccurlyeq w$, whenever there exists a word w'' such that $w = w' \cdot w''$, and $w' \prec w$ if additionally $w' \neq w$; conversely w is said to be an *extension* of w'.

A *language* over Σ is a subset of Σ^*. The *set of prefixes* of a word w is denoted by pref(w). For a language $\mathscr{L}$, pref($\mathscr{L}$) $\overset{\text{def}}{=} \bigcup_{w \in \mathscr{L}}$ pref(w) is the set of prefixes of words in $\mathscr{L}$. A language $\mathscr{L}$ is *prefix-closed* if pref($\mathscr{L}$) $= \mathscr{L}$ and *extension-closed* if $\mathscr{L} \cdot \Sigma^* = \mathscr{L}$.

Timed Words and Timed Languages. In a timed setting, we consider the occurrence time of actions. Input and output streams of enforcement mechanisms are seen as sequences of events composed of a date and an action, where the date is interpreted as the absolute time when the action is received by the enforcement mechanism.

Let $\mathbb{R}_{\geq 0}$ denote the set of non-negative real numbers, and Σ a finite alphabet of *actions*. An *event* is a pair (t,a), where date$((t,a)) \overset{\text{def}}{=} t \in \mathbb{R}_{\geq 0}$ is the absolute time at which the action act$((t,a)) \overset{\text{def}}{=} a \in \Sigma$ occurs.

A timed word over the finite alphabet Σ is a finite sequence of events $\sigma = (t_1,a_1) \cdot (t_2,a_2) \cdots (t_n,a_n)$, for some $n \in \mathbb{N}$, where $(t_i)_{i \in [1,n]}$ is a non-decreasing sequence in $\mathbb{R}_{\geq 0}$.

The set of timed words over Σ is denoted by tw(Σ). A *timed language* is any set $\mathscr{L} \subseteq$ tw(Σ). Even though the alphabet ($\mathbb{R}_{\geq 0} \times \Sigma$) is infinite in this case, previous untimed notions and notations (related to length, prefix etc.) extend to timed words.

When concatenating two timed words, one should ensure that the result is a timed word, i.e., dates should be non-decreasing. This is ensured if the ending date of the first timed word does not exceed the starting date of the second one. Formally, let $\sigma = (t_1,a_1) \cdots (t_n,a_n)$ and $\sigma' = (t_1',a_1') \cdots (t_m',a_m')$ be two timed words with end(σ) $\leq$ start(σ'), their concatenation is $\sigma \cdot \sigma' \overset{\text{def}}{=} (t_1,a_1) \cdots (t_n,a_n) \cdot (t_1',a_1') \cdots (t_m',a_m')$. By convention $\sigma \cdot \varepsilon \overset{\text{def}}{=} \varepsilon \cdot \sigma \overset{\text{def}}{=} \sigma$. Concatenation is undefined otherwise.

2.2 Timed Automata

A timed automaton [6] (TA) is a finite automaton extended with a finite set of real-valued clocks. Intuitively, a clock is a variable whose value evolves with the passing of physical time. Let $X = \{x_1, \ldots, x_k\}$ be a finite set of *clocks*. A *clock valuation* for X is an element of $\mathbb{R}_{\geq 0}^X$, that is a function from X to $\mathbb{R}_{\geq 0}$. For $\chi \in \mathbb{R}_{\geq 0}^X$ and $\delta \in \mathbb{R}_{\geq 0}$, $\chi + \delta$ is the valuation assigning $\chi(x) + \delta$ to each clock x of X. Given a set of clocks $X' \subseteq X$, $\chi[X' \leftarrow 0]$ is the clock valuation χ where all clocks in X' are assigned to 0. $\mathscr{G}(X)$ denotes the set of *guards*, i.e., clock constraints defined as Boolean combinations of simple constraints of the form $x \bowtie c$ with $x \in X$, $c \in \mathbb{N}$ and $\bowtie \in \{<, \leq, =, \geq, >\}$. Given $g \in \mathscr{G}(X)$ and $\chi \in \mathbb{R}_{\geq 0}^X$, we write $\chi \models g$ when g holds according to χ. A (semantic) state is a pair composed of a location and a clock valuation.

Instead of presenting the formal definitions, we introduce TAs on an example. The timed automaton in Fig. 8 formalizes the requirement *"In every 10 time units (tu), there cannot be more than 1 alloc action"*. The set of locations is $L = \{l_0, l_1, l_2\}$, l_0 is the initial location, l_0 and l_1 are accepting locations, and l_2 is a non-accepting location. The set of actions is $\Sigma = \{alloc, rel\}$. There are transitions between locations upon actions. A

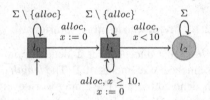

Fig. 8. Example of TA.

finite set of real-valued clocks is used to model realtime behavior, set $X = \{x\}$ in the example. On the transitions, there are (i) guards with constraints on clock values (such as $x < 10$ on the transition between l_1 and l_2 in the example), and (ii) assignment to clocks. Upon the first occurrence of action *alloc*, the automaton moves from l_0 to l_1, and 0 is assigned to clock x. In location l_1, if action *alloc* is received, and if the value of x is greater than or equal to 10, then the automaton remains in l_1, resetting the value of clock x to 0. It moves to location l_2 otherwise.

2.3   Partitioning the States of a Timed Automaton

Given a TA with semantic states Q and accepting semantic states Q_F, following [42], we can define a partition of Q with four subsets *good* (G), *currently good* (G^c), *currently bad* (B^c) and *bad* (B), based on whether a state is accepting or not, and whether accepting or non-accepting states are reachable or not. This partitioning is useful for runtime verification and enforcement. An enforcement device makes decisions by checking the reachable subsets. For example, if all the reachable states belong to the subset B, then it is impossible to correct the input sequence anymore (in the future). If the current state belongs to the subset G, then any sequence will lead to a state belonging to the same subset and thus the enforcement device can be turned off. This partition is also useful to classify timed properties and for the synthesis of enforcement devices.

Formally, Q is partitioned into $Q = G^c \cup G \cup B^c \cup B$, where $Q_F = G^c \cup G$ and $Q \setminus Q_F = B^c \cup B$, and:

- $G^c = Q_F \cap \mathrm{pre}^*(Q \setminus Q_F)$ is the set of *currently good* states, that is the subset of accepting states from which non-accepting states are reachable;
- $G = Q_F \setminus G^c = Q_F \setminus \mathrm{pre}^*(Q \setminus Q_F)$ is the set of *good* states, that is the subset of accepting states from which only accepting states are reachable;
- $B^c = (Q \setminus Q_F) \cap \mathrm{pre}^*(Q_F)$ is the set of *currently bad* states, that is the subset of non-accepting states from which accepting states are reachable;
- $B = (Q \setminus Q_F) \setminus \mathrm{pre}^*(Q_F)$ is the set of *bad* states, that is the subset of non-accepting states from which only non-accepting states are reachable.

where, for a subset P of Q, $\mathrm{pre}^*(P)$ denotes the set of states from which set P is reachable.

It is well known that reachability of a set of locations is decidable using the classical zone (or region) symbolic representation (see [18]). As Q_F corresponds to all states with location in F, the partition can then be symbolically computed on the zone graph.

2.4   Classification of Timed Properties

A timed property is defined by a timed language $\varphi \subseteq \mathrm{tw}(\Sigma)$ that can be recognized by a timed automaton. That is, the set of regular timed properties are considered. Given a timed word $\sigma \in \mathrm{tw}(\Sigma)$, we say that σ satisfies φ (noted $\sigma \models \varphi$) if $\sigma \in \varphi$.

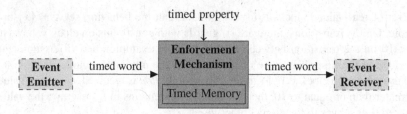

Fig. 9. RE of a timed property. The enforcement mechanism (EM) is synthesized from a timed property. At runtime, the EM is placed between an event emitter (EE) and event receiver (ER); it receives as input a timed word from the EE and produces as output a timed word for the ER.

Definition 1 (Regular, safety, and co-safety properties)

- *Regular timed properties are the properties that can be defined by languages accepted by a TA.*
- *Safety timed properties are the non-empty prefix-closed regular timed properties.*
- *Co-safety timed properties are the non-universal[1] extension-closed regular timed properties.*

As in the untimed case, safety (resp. co-safety) properties state that "nothing bad should ever happen" (resp. "something good should happen within a finite amount of time").

3 Overview of RE Approaches for Timed Properties

In this section, we overview some formal approaches [44,80,81,83,84,91–93] to the runtime enforcement of timed properties described by timed automata (TA). Properties can feature uncontrollable events which can be only seen by the enforcement mechanism (EM) and cannot be acted upon. The runtime enforcement problem is conceptualized as illustrated in Fig. 9: an EM reads as input a timed word and should transform and output it so that it complies with a timed property used to obtain the EM, using a timed memory which accounts for the physical time during which elements have been stored. In all the following frameworks, EMs are described with two paradigms: a denotational one where EMs are seen as functions through their input/output behavior, and two operational ones: input/output labeled transition systems and algorithms. These approaches differ either in the supported classes of properties for which EMs can be synthesized and the enforcement operations of the enforcement mechanism.

Runtime Enforcement of Timed Properties [84] *(for Safety and Co-safety Properties).* In [84] the first steps to runtime enforcement of (continuous) timed safety and co-safety properties was introduced. EMs were endowed only with an enforcement operation allowing to delaying events to satisfy the required property. For this purpose, the EM stores some actions for a certain time period computed when they are received. Requirements over the EMs ensured that their outputs not only satisfy the required property, but also with the shortest delay according to the current satisfaction of the property.

---

[1] The universal property over $\mathbb{R}_{\geq 0} \times \Sigma$ is $\mathrm{tw}(\Sigma)$.

Runtime Enforcement of Regular Timed Properties [81,83]. The approach in [81,83] generalizes [84] and synthesizes EMs for any regular timed property. It allows considering interesting properties of systems belonging to a larger class specifying some form of transactional behavior. The difficulty that arises is that the EMs should consider the alternation between currently satisfying and not satisfying the property[2]. The unique enforcement operation is still delaying events as in [84].

Runtime Enforcement of Regular Timed Properties by Suppressing and Delaying Events [44]. The approach in [44] considers events composed of actions with absolute occurrence dates, and allows increasing the dates (while allowing reducing delays between events in memory). Moreover, suppressing events is also introduced. An event is suppressed if it is not possible to satisfy the property by delaying, whatever are the future continuations of the input sequence (i.e., the underlying TA can only reach non-accepting states from which no accepting state can be reached). In Sect. 4, we overview this framework.

Runtime Enforcement of Parametric Timed Properties with Practical Applications [80]. The framework in [80] makes one step towards practical runtime enforcement by considering event-based specifications where (i) time between events matters and (ii) events carry data values ([54]) from the monitored system. It defines how to enforce parametric timed specifications which are useful to model requirements from some application domains such as network security which have constraints both on time and data. For this, it introduces the model of Parametrized Timed Automata with Variables (PTAVs). PTAVs extend TAs with session parameters, internal and external variables. The framework presents how to synthesize EMs as in [44,83] from PTAVs and shows the usefulness of enforcing such expressive specifications on application scenarios.

Enforcement of Timed Properties with Uncontrollable Events [91,92]. The approach in [91,92] presents a framework for enforcing regular untimed and timed properties with uncontrollable events. An EM cannot delay nor intercept an uncontrollable event. To cope with uncontrollable events, the notion of transparency should be weakened to the so-called notion of compliance. Informally, compliance means that the order of controllable events should be maintained by the EM, while uncontrollable events should be released as output soon after they are received.

Runtime Enforcement of Cyber-Physical Systems [87]. In synchronous reactive systems, terminating the system or delaying the reaction is not feasible. Thus, the approaches in [44,80,81,83,91,92] are not suitable for such systems. The approach in [87] introduces a framework for synchronous reactive systems with bidirectional synchronous EMs. While the framework considers similar notions of soundness, and transparency, it also introduces the so-called additional requirements of causality and instantaneity which are specific to synchronous executions. Moreover, the framework considers properties expressed using a variant of Discrete Timed Automata (DTA).

---

[2] Indeed, in safety (resp. co-safety) (timed) automaton, there are only good, currently good, and bad states (resp. bad, currently bad, and good states), and thus the strategies for the EM is simpler: avoiding the bad states (resp. reaching a good state) [42].

4 A Framework for the Runtime Enforcement of Timed Properties

In this section, we present a framework for the runtime enforcement of timed properties described by timed automata [44]. Most of the material comes from [44,79].

4.1 Overview

Given some timed property φ and an input timed word σ, the EM outputs a timed word o that satisfies φ. The considered EMs are *time retardants*, i.e., their main enforcement operation consists in delaying the received events[3]. In addition to introducing additional delays (increasing dates), for the EM and system to continue executing, the EM can suppress events when no delaying is appropriate. However, it can not change the order of events. The EM may also reduce delays between events stored in its memory.

To ease the design and implementation of EMs in a timed context, they are described at three levels of abstraction: *enforcement functions*, *enforcement monitors*, and *enforcement algorithms*; all of which can be deployed to operate online. EMs should abide to some requirements, namely the physical constraint, soundness, transparency.

- The *physical constraint* says that the output produced for an extension σ' of an input word σ extends the output produced for σ. This stems from the fact that, over time the enforcement function outputs a continuously growing sequence of events. The output for a given input can only be modified by appending new events (with greater dates).
- *Soundness* says that the output either satisfies property φ, or is empty. This allows to output nothing if there is no way to satisfy φ. Note that, together with the physical constraint, this implies that no event can be appended to the output before being sure that the property will be eventually satisfied with subsequent output events.
- *Transparency* says that the output is a delayed subsequence of the input σ; that is with increased dates, preserved order, and possibly suppressed events.

Notice that for any input σ, releasing ε as output would satisfy soundness, transparency, and the physical constraint. We want to suppress an event or to introduce additional delay only when necessary. Additionally, EMs should also respect optimality requirements:

- *Streaming behavior and deciding to output as soon as possible.* Since an EM does not know the entire input sequence, for efficiency reasons, the output should be built incrementally in a streaming fashion. EMs should take decision to release input events as soon as possible. The EM should wait to receive more events, only when there is no possibility to correct the input.

---

[3] Several application domains have requirements, where the required timing constraints can be satisfied by increasing dates of some actions [67].

- *Optimal suppression.* Suppressing events should occur only when necessary, i.e., when, upon the reception of a new event, there is no possibility to satisfy the property, whatever is the continuation of the input.
- *Optimal dates.* Choosing/increasing dates should be done in way that dates are optimal with respect to the current situation, releasing here as output as soon as possible.

The enforcement function $E_\varphi : \mathrm{tw}(\Sigma) \to \mathrm{tw}(\Sigma)$ for a property φ defines how an input stream σ is transformed into an output stream. An enforcement monitor (see [44]) is a more concrete view and defines the operational behavior of the EM over time as a timed labeled transition system. An enforcement algorithm realises enforcement monitor in pseudo code with two concurrent processes and a shared buffer At an abstract level, one process stores the received events in the shared buffer and computes their releasing date. The other process scrutinizes the shared buffer and releases the event at their releasing dates. In [44], we formally prove that enforcement functions respect the requirements, that enforcement monitors realizes enforcement functions, that enforcement algorithms implements enforcement monitors, and that all description of EMs can be optimized for the particular case of timed safety properties.

4.2 Intuition on an Example

We provide some intuition on the expected behavior of EMs. Consider two processes that access to and operate on a shared resource. Each process i (with $i \in \{1,2\}$) has three interactions with the resource: acquisition (acq_i), release (rel_i), and a specific operation (op_i). Both processes can also execute a common action op. System initialization is denoted by action $init$. In the following, variable t keeps track of the evolution of time.

Consider one specification, referred to as S_1, of the shared resource (Fig. 10): "*Operations op_1 and op_2 should execute in a transactional manner. Both actions should be executed, in any order, and any transaction should contain one occurrence of op_1 and op_2. Each transaction should complete within 10 tu. Between operations op_1 and op_2, occurrences of operation op can occur. There is at least 2 tu between any two occurrences of any operation.*"

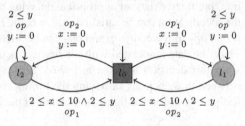

Fig. 10. TA defining property S_1.

Figure 11 illustrates the behavior of an EM and how it transforms an input timed word (red) to a correct output timed word (blue) satisfying S_1; actions are in abscissa and occurrence dates in ordinate. Note, the satisfaction of the property is not represented in the figure. The input sequence is $\sigma = (2, op_1) \cdot (3, op_1) \cdot (3.5, op) \cdot (6, op_2)$. At $t = 2$, the EM can not output action op_1 because this action alone does not satisfy the specification (and the EM does not yet know the next events i.e., actions and dates). If the next action was op_2, then, at the date of its reception, the EM could output action op_1 followed by op_2, as it could choose dates for both actions in order to satisfy the timing constraints. At $t = 3$ the EM receives a second op_1 action. Clearly, there is no possible date for these two op_1 actions to satisfy the specification, and no continuation could solve the situation. The EM thus suppresses the second op_1 action, since this action is the one that prevents satisfiability in the future. At $t = 3.5$, when the EM receives action op, the input sequence still does not satisfy the specifica-

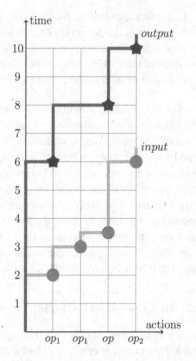

Fig. 11. Illustration of the behavior of an EM enforcing S_1. (Color figure online)

tion, but there exists an appropriate delaying of such action so that with future events, the specification can be satisfied. At $t = 6$, the EM receives action op_2, it can decide that action op_1 followed by op and op_2 can be released as output with appropriate delaying. Thus, the date associated with the first op_1 action is set to 6 (the earliest possible date, since this decision is taken at $t = 6$), 8 for action op (since 2 is the minimal delay between those actions satisfying the timing constraint), and 10 for action op_2. Henceforth, as shown in the figure, the output of the EM for σ is $(6, op_1) \cdot (8, op) \cdot (10, op_2)$.

5   Tool Implementations

Any tool for runtime verification [13] can perform basic enforcement by terminating the execution of programs violating their specification. There are, however, several runtime verification tools that go further and feature their own enforcement operations, for instance Java-MOP and EnforceMOP [70] with handlers, LARVA [31] with compensations [32]. There are also numerous tools in the security domain enforcing (implicit) specifications related to the security of the monitored applications (memory safety, control-flow integrity, etc.); see [104] for a recent overview.

To the best of our knowledge, there are two tools dedicated to the runtime enforcement of timed properties: TiPEX [82] and GREP [93]. TiPEX implements the framework presented in Sect. 4 and provides additional features to synthesize timed automata and check the class of a timed automaton as per Definition. 1. A detailed description of the TiPEX tool with some examples is provided in [82]. TiPEX can be downloaded from [97]. GREP [93] follows the same objectives as TiPEX but is based on game theory to synthesize the enforcement mechanisms. GREP also handles uncontrollable events.

6   Open Challenges and Avenues for Future Work

We conclude this tutorial by proposing some future research directions.

Enforcement Monitoring for Systems with Limited Memory. An enforcement mechanism basically acts as a filter storing the input events in its memory, until it is certain that the underlying property will be satisfied. As was the case with untimed properties [16,17,50,106], defining enforcement mechanisms and new enforcement strategies should be defined when there are bounds on memory usage or limited resources. Delineating the subset of enforceable timed properties for which effective enforcement mechanisms can be obtained is also a subject for future work.

Predictive Runtime Enforcement. Predictive runtime enforcement considers the case where knowledge about the event emitter is available [86]. When the enforcement mechanism knows the set of input sequences that it may receive, then it may anticipate decisions of releasing events as output without storing them in memory nor waiting for future events, e.g., when it knows that all the possible continuations of the input it has observed will not violate the property. Predictive runtime enforcement of timed properties poses several difficulties and challenges that have to be further explored [85,86].

Realizing Requirements Automatically. In current research efforts, enforcement mechanisms are seen as modules outside the system, which take as input a stream of events (output of the system being monitored) and verify or correct this stream according to the property. For a better adoption of runtime enforcement theories and tools, one direction is to define methods and instrumentation techniques so that enforcement mechanisms can realize the requirements (which could not be integrated in the initial application. For this, one can imagine enforcement monitors (realizing some requirements) integrated as another layer on top of the core functionality or with libraries, inspiring from aspect-oriented programming [60,61] and acceptability-oriented computing [95].

Decentralized Runtime Enforcement. Decentralized runtime verification approaches [15,29,37,40] allow decentralizing the monitoring mechanism on the components of a system (see [51] for an overview). Such approaches deal with the situations where it is not desired to impose a central observation point in the system. Frameworks for decentralized runtime enforcement (of timed properties) have yet to be defined and will permit enforcing properties on distributed systems. For this purpose, one can inspire from generalized consensus to help enforcement mechanisms forge a collective decisions when applying enforcement operations to the system.

Acknowledgment. The authors thank Frédéric Desprez, Antoine El-Hokayem, Raphaël Jakse, Ali Kassem, and the reviewers for their comments on a preliminary version of this tutorial. The framework for runtime enforcement of timed properties reported in Sect. 2 to Sect. 5 is based upon joint research efforts with colleagues and friends: Jean-Claude Fernandez, Thierry Jéron, Hervé Marchand, Laurent Mounier, Omer Nguena-Timo, Matthieu Renard, and Antoine Rollet.

References

1. Proceedings of the 5th Annual Symposium on Logic in Computer Science (LICS 1990). IEEE Computer Society (1990)
2. Abadi, M., Budiu, M., Erlingsson, Ú., Ligatti, J.: Control-flow integrity principles, implementations, and applications. ACM Trans. Inf. Syst. Secur. **13**(1), 4:1–4:40 (2009)
3. Aktug, I., Dam, M., Gurov, D.: Provably correct runtime monitoring. J. Log. Algebr. Program. **78**(5), 304–339 (2009)
4. Alpern, B., Schneider, F.B.: Defining liveness. Inf. Process. Lett. **21**(4), 181–185 (1985)
5. Alur, R., Courcoubetis, C., Dill, D.L.: Model-checking for real-time systems. In: Proceedings of the 5th Annual Symposium on Logic in Computer Science (LICS 1990) [1], pp. 414–425 (1990)
6. Alur, R., Dill, D.L.: A theory of timed automata. Theoret. Comput. Sci. **126**, 183–235 (1994)
7. Alur, R., Henzinger, T.A.: Real-time logics: complexity and expressiveness. In: Proceedings of the Fifth Annual Symposium on Logic in Computer Science (LICS 1990) [1], pp. 390–401 (1990)
8. Amiar, A., Delahaye, M., Falcone, Y., du Bousquet, L.: Compressing microcontroller execution traces to assist system analysis. In: Schirner, G., Götz, M., Rettberg, A., Zanella, M.C., Rammig, F.J. (eds.) IESS 2013. IFIP AICT, vol. 403, pp. 139–150. Springer, Heidelberg (2013). https://doi.org/10.1007/978-3-642-38853-8_13
9. Amiar, A., Delahaye, M., Falcone, Y., du Bousquet, L.: Fault localization in embedded software based on a single cyclic trace. In: IEEE 24th International Symposium on Software Reliability Engineering, ISSRE 2013, pp. 148–157. IEEE Computer Society (2013)
10. Azevedo de Amorim, A., Hriţcu, C., Pierce, B.C.: The meaning of memory safety. In: Bauer, L., Küsters, R. (eds.) POST 2018. LNCS, vol. 10804, pp. 79–105. Springer, Cham (2018). https://doi.org/10.1007/978-3-319-89722-6_4
11. Babaee, R., Gurfinkel, A., Fischmeister, S.: Predictive run-time verification of discrete-time reachability properties in black-box systems using trace-level abstraction and statistical learning. In: Colombo and Leucker [30], pp. 187–204
12. Bartocci, E., Falcone, Y. (eds.): Lectures on Runtime Verification - Introductory and Advanced Topics. LNCS, vol. 10457. Springer, Cham (2018). https://doi.org/10.1007/978-3-319-75632-5
13. Bartocci, E., et al.: First international competition on runtime verification: rules, benchmarks, tools, and final results of CRV 2014. STTT **21**(1), 31–70 (2019)
14. Bartocci, E., Falcone, Y., Francalanza, A., Reger, G.: Introduction to runtime verification. In: Bartocci and Falcone [12], pp. 1–33
15. Bauer, A., Falcone, Y.: Decentralised LTL monitoring. Form. Meth. Syst. Des. **48**(1–2), 46–93 (2016)
16. Beauquier, D., Cohen, J., Lanotte, R.: Security policies enforcement using finite edit automata. Electr. Notes Theor. Comput. Sci. **229**(3), 19–35 (2009)
17. Beauquier, D., Cohen, J., Lanotte, R.: Security policies enforcement using finite and push-down edit automata. Int. J. Inf. Sec. **12**(4), 319–336 (2013)

18. Bengtsson, J., Yi, W.: Timed automata: semantics, algorithms and tools. In: Desel, J., Reisig, W., Rozenberg, G. (eds.) ACPN 2003. LNCS, vol. 3098, pp. 87–124. Springer, Heidelberg (2004). https://doi.org/10.1007/978-3-540-27755-2_3

19. Bielova, N., Massacci, F.: Do you really mean what you actually enforced? In: Degano, P., Guttman, J., Martinelli, F. (eds.) FAST 2008. LNCS, vol. 5491, pp. 287–301. Springer, Heidelberg (2009). https://doi.org/10.1007/978-3-642-01465-9_19

20. Bielova, N., Massacci, F.: Predictability of enforcement. In: Erlingsson, Ú., Wieringa, R., Zannone, N. (eds.) ESSoS 2011. LNCS, vol. 6542, pp. 73–86. Springer, Heidelberg (2011). https://doi.org/10.1007/978-3-642-19125-1_6

21. Bielova, N., Massacci, F.: Iterative enforcement by suppression: towards practical enforcement theories. J. Comput. Secur. **20**(1), 51–79 (2012)

22. Birgisson, A., Dhawan, M., Erlingsson, Ú., Ganapathy, V., Iftode, L.: Enforcing authorization policies using transactional memory introspection. In: Ning, P., Syverson, P.F., Jha, S. (eds.) Proceedings of the 2008 ACM Conference on Computer and Communications Security, CCS 2008, pp. 223–234. ACM (2008)

23. Blech, J.O., Falcone, Y., Becker, K.: Towards certified runtime verification. In: Aoki, T., Taguchi, K. (eds.) ICFEM 2012. LNCS, vol. 7635, pp. 494–509. Springer, Heidelberg (2012). https://doi.org/10.1007/978-3-642-34281-3_34

24. Bruening, D., Zhao, Q.: Practical memory checking with Dr. memory. In: Proceedings of the CGO 2011, The 9th International Symposium on Code Generation and Optimization, pp. 213–223. IEEE Computer Society (2011)

25. Bruening, D., Zhao, Q.: Using Dr. Fuzz, Dr. Memory, and custom dynamic tools for secure development. In: IEEE Cybersecurity Development, SecDev 2016, Boston, MA, USA, 3–4 November 2016, p. 158. IEEE Computer Society (2016)

26. Chabot, H., Khoury, R., Tawbi, N.: Extending the enforcement power of truncation monitors using static analysis. Comput. Secur. **30**(4), 194–207 (2011)

27. Chang, E., Manna, Z., Pnueli, A.: Characterization of temporal property classes. In: Kuich, W. (ed.) ICALP 1992. LNCS, vol. 623, pp. 474–486. Springer, Heidelberg (1992). https://doi.org/10.1007/3-540-55719-9_97

28. Chong, S., Vikram, K., Myers, A.C.: SIF: enforcing confidentiality and integrity in web applications. In: Provos, N. (ed.) Proceedings of the 16th USENIX Security Symposium. USENIX Association (2007)

29. Colombo, C., Falcone, Y.: Organising LTL monitors over distributed systems with a global clock. Form. Meth. Syst. Des. **49**(1–2), 109–158 (2016)

30. Colombo, C., Leucker, M. (eds.): RV 2018. LNCS, vol. 11237. Springer, Cham (2018). https://doi.org/10.1007/978-3-030-03769-7

31. Colombo, C., Pace, G.: Runtime verification using LARVA. In: Reger, G., Havelund, K. (eds.) RV-CuBES 2017. An International Workshop on Competitions, Usability, Benchmarks, Evaluation, and Standardisation for Runtime Verification Tools. Kalpa Publications in Computing, vol. 3, pp. 55–63. EasyChair (2017)

32. Colombo, C., Pace, G.J.: Recovery within long-running transactions. ACM Comput. Surv. **45**(3), 28:1–28:35 (2013)

33. Dam, M., Jacobs, B., Lundblad, A., Piessens, F.: Provably correct inline monitoring for multithreaded java-like programs. J. Comput. Secur. **18**(1), 37–59 (2010)

34. Davi, L., Sadeghi, A., Winandy, M.: ROPdefender: a detection tool to defend against return-oriented programming attacks. In: Cheung, B.S.N., Hui, L.C.K., Sandhu, R.S., Wong, D.S. (eds.) Proceedings of the 6th ACM Symposium on Information, Computer and Communications Security, ASIACCS 2011, pp. 40–51. ACM (2011)

35. Duck, G.J., Yap, R.H.C., Cavallaro, L.: Stack bounds protection with low fat pointers. In: 24th Annual Network and Distributed System Security Symposium, NDSS 2017. The Internet Society (2017)

36. El-Harake, K., Falcone, Y., Jerad, W., Langet, M., Mamlouk, M.: Blocking advertisements on android devices using monitoring techniques. In: Margaria, T., Steffen, B. (eds.) ISoLA 2014, Part II. LNCS, vol. 8803, pp. 239–253. Springer, Heidelberg (2014). https://doi.org/10.1007/978-3-662-45231-8_17

37. El-Hokayem, A., Falcone, Y.: THEMIS: a tool for decentralized monitoring algorithms. In: Bultan, T., Sen, K. (eds.) Proceedings of the 26th ACM SIGSOFT International Symposium on Software Testing and Analysis, pp. 372–375. ACM (2017)

38. Erlingsson, Ú., Schneider, F.B.: SASI enforcement of security policies: a retrospective. In: Kienzle, D.M., Zurko, M.E., Greenwald, S.J., Serbau, C. (eds.) Proceedings of the 1999 Workshop on New Security Paradigms, pp. 87–95. ACM (1999)

39. Falcone, Y.: You should better enforce than verify. In: Barringer, H., et al. (eds.) RV 2010. LNCS, vol. 6418, pp. 89–105. Springer, Heidelberg (2010). https://doi.org/10.1007/978-3-642-16612-9_9

40. Falcone, Y., Cornebize, T., Fernandez, J.-C.: Efficient and generalized decentralized monitoring of regular languages. In: Ábrahám, E., Palamidessi, C. (eds.) FORTE 2014. LNCS, vol. 8461, pp. 66–83. Springer, Heidelberg (2014). https://doi.org/10.1007/978-3-662-43613-4_5

41. Falcone, Y., Currea, S., Jaber, M.: Runtime verification and enforcement for Android applications with RV-Droid. In: Qadeer and Tasiran [89], pp. 88–95

42. Falcone, Y., Fernandez, J., Mounier, L.: What can you verify and enforce at runtime? STTT **14**(3), 349–382 (2012)

43. Falcone, Y., Havelund, K., Reger, G.: A tutorial on runtime verification. In: Broy, M., Peled, D.A., Kalus, G. (eds.) Engineering Dependable Software Systems. NATO Science for Peace and Security Series D: Information and Communication Security, vol. 34, pp. 141–175. IOS Press (2013)

44. Falcone, Y., Jéron, T., Marchand, H., Pinisetty, S.: Runtime enforcement of regular timed properties by suppressing and delaying events. Sci. Comput. Program. **123**, 2–41 (2016)

45. Falcone, Y., Krstic, S., Reger, G., Traytel, D.: A taxonomy for classifying runtime verification tools. In: Colombo and Leucker [30], pp. 241–262

46. Falcone, Y., Marchand, H.: Enforcement and validation (at runtime) of various notions of opacity. Discrete Event Dyn. Syst. **25**(4), 531–570 (2015)

47. Falcone, Y., Mariani, L., Rollet, A., Saha, S.: Runtime failure prevention and reaction. In: Bartocci and Falcone [12], pp. 103–134

48. Falcone, Y., Mounier, L., Fernandez, J., Richier, J.: Runtime enforcement monitors: composition, synthesis, and enforcement abilities. Form. Meth. Syst. Des. **38**(3), 223–262 (2011)

49. Ferraiuolo, A., Zhao, M., Myers, A.C., Suh, G.E.: HyperFlow: a processor architecture for nonmalleable, timing-safe information flow security. In: Lie, D., Mannan, M., Backes, M., Wang, X. (eds.) Proceedings of the 2018 ACM SIGSAC Conference on Computer and Communications Security, CCS 2018, pp. 1583–1600. ACM (2018)

50. Fong, P.W.L.: Access control by tracking shallow execution history. In: 2004 IEEE Symposium on Security and Privacy (S&P 2004), pp. 43–55. IEEE Computer Society (2004)

51. Francalanza, A., Pérez, J.A., Sánchez, C.: Runtime verification for decentralised and distributed systems. In: Bartocci and Falcone [12], pp. 176–210

52. Göktas, E., Athanasopoulos, E., Bos, H., Portokalidis, G.: Out of control: overcoming control-flow integrity. In: 2014 IEEE Symposium on Security and Privacy, SP 2014, pp. 575–589. IEEE Computer Society (2014)

53. Hallé, S., Khoury, R., Betti, Q., El-Hokayem, A., Falcone, Y.: Decentralized enforcement of document lifecycle constraints. Inf. Syst. **74**(Part), 117–135 (2018)

54. Havelund, K., Reger, G., Thoma, D., Zalinescu, E.: Monitoring events that carry data. In: Bartocci and Falcone [12], pp. 61–102

55. Ji, Y., Wu, Y., Lafortune, S.: Enforcement of opacity by public and private insertion functions. Automatica **93**, 369–378 (2018)
56. Johansen, H.D., Birrell, E., van Renesse, R., Schneider, F.B., Stenhaug, M., Johansen, D.: Enforcing privacy policies with meta-code. In: Kono, K., Shinagawa, T. (eds.) Proceedings of the 6th Asia-Pacific Workshop on Systems, APSys 2015, pp. 16:1–16:7. ACM (2015). https://doi.org/10.1145/2797022
57. Kayaalp, M., Ozsoy, M., Abu-Ghazaleh, N.B., Ponomarev, D.: Branch regulation: low-overhead protection from code reuse attacks. In: 39th International Symposium on Computer Architecture (ISCA 2012), pp. 94–105. IEEE Computer Society (2012)
58. Khoury, R., Tawbi, N.: Corrective enforcement: a new paradigm of security policy enforcement by monitors. ACM Trans. Inf. Syst. Secur. **15**(2), 10:1–10:27 (2012)
59. Khoury, R., Tawbi, N.: Which security policies are enforceable by runtime monitors? A survey. Comput. Sci. Rev. **6**(1), 27–45 (2012)
60. Kiczales, G.: Aspect-oriented programming. In: Roman et al. [96], p. 730
61. Kiczales, G., Mezini, M.: Aspect-oriented programming and modular reasoning. In: Roman et al. [96], pp. 49–58
62. Kiriansky, V., Bruening, D., Amarasinghe, S.P.: Secure execution via program shepherding. In: Boneh, D. (ed.) Proceedings of the 11th USENIX Security Symposium, pp. 191–206. USENIX (2002)
63. Könighofer, B., et al.: Shield synthesis. Form. Meth. Syst. Des. **51**(2), 332–361 (2017)
64. Kozyri, E., Arden, O., Myers, A.C., Schneider, F.B.: JRIF: reactive information flow control for Java. In: Guttman, J.D., Landwehr, C.E., Meseguer, J., Pavlovic, D. (eds.) Foundations of Security, Protocols, and Equational Reasoning. LNCS, vol. 11565, pp. 70–88. Springer, Cham (2019). https://doi.org/10.1007/978-3-030-19052-1_7
65. Kumar, A., Ligatti, J., Tu, Y.-C.: Query monitoring and analysis for database privacy - a security automata model approach. In: Wang, J., et al. (eds.) WISE 2015, Part II. LNCS, vol. 9419, pp. 458–472. Springer, Cham (2015). https://doi.org/10.1007/978-3-319-26187-4_42
66. Lamport, L.: Proving the correctness of multiprocess programs. IEEE Trans. Softw. Eng. **3**(2), 125–143 (1977)
67. Lesage, J., Faure, J., Cury, J.E.R., Lennartson, B. (eds.): 12th International Workshop on Discrete Event Systems, WODES 2014. International Federation of Automatic Control (2014)
68. Ligatti, J., Bauer, L., Walker, D.: Run-time enforcement of nonsafety policies. ACM Trans. Inf. Syst. Secur. **12**(3), 19:1–19:41 (2009)
69. Lourenço, J.M., Fiedor, J., Krena, B., Vojnar, T.: Discovering concurrency errors. In: Bartocci and Falcone [12], pp. 34–60
70. Luo, Q., Rosu, G.: EnforceMOP: a runtime property enforcement system for multithreaded programs. In: Pezzè, M., Harman, M. (eds.) International Symposium on Software Testing and Analysis, ISSTA, pp. 156–166. ACM (2013)
71. Manna, Z., Pnueli, A.: The Temporal Logic of Reactive and Concurrent Systems - Specification. Springer, New York (1992). https://doi.org/10.1007/978-1-4612-0931-7
72. Margaria, T., Steffen, B. (eds.): ISoLA 2016, Part II. LNCS, vol. 9953. Springer, Cham (2016). https://doi.org/10.1007/978-3-319-47169-3
73. Martinelli, F., Matteucci, I., Mori, P., Saracino, A.: Enforcement of U-XACML history-based usage control policy. In: Barthe, G., Markatos, E., Samarati, P. (eds.) STM 2016. LNCS, vol. 9871, pp. 64–81. Springer, Cham (2016). https://doi.org/10.1007/978-3-319-46598-2_5
74. Meredith, P.O., Jin, D., Griffith, D., Chen, F., Rosu, G.: An overview of the MOP runtime verification framework. STTT **14**(3), 249–289 (2012)

75. Nguyen, T., Bartocci, E., Nickovic, D., Grosu, R., Jaksic, S., Selyunin, K.: The HARMO-NIA project: hardware monitoring for automotive systems-of-systems. In: Margaria and Steffen [72], pp. 371–379
76. Pavlich-Mariscal, J.A., Demurjian, S.A., Michel, L.D.: A framework of composable access control definition, enforcement and assurance. In: Bastarrica, M.C., Solar, M. (eds.) XXVII International Conference of the Chilean Computer Science Society (SCCC 2008), pp. 13–22. IEEE Computer Society (2008)
77. Pavlich-Mariscal, J.A., Demurjian, S.A., Michel, L.D.: A framework for security assurance of access control enforcement code. Comput. Secur. **29**(7), 770–784 (2010)
78. Pavlich-Mariscal, J., Michel, L., Demurjian, S.: A formal enforcement framework for role-based access control using aspect-oriented programming. In: Briand, L., Williams, C. (eds.) MODELS 2005. LNCS, vol. 3713, pp. 537–552. Springer, Heidelberg (2005). https://doi.org/10.1007/11557432_41
79. Pinisetty, S.: Runtime enforcement of timed properties. (Enforcement à l'éxécution de propriétés temporisées). Ph.D. thesis, University of Rennes 1, France (2015)
80. Pinisetty, S., Falcone, Y., Jéron, T., Marchand, H.: Runtime enforcement of parametric timed properties with practical applications. In: Lesage et al. [67], pp. 420–427
81. Pinisetty, S., Falcone, Y., Jéron, T., Marchand, H.: Runtime enforcement of regular timed properties. In: Cho, Y., Shin, S.Y., Kim, S., Hung, C., Hong, J. (eds.) Symposium on Applied Computing, SAC 2014, pp. 1279–1286. ACM (2014)
82. Pinisetty, S., Falcone, Y., Jéron, T., Marchand, H.: TiPEX: a tool chain for timed property enforcement during execution. In: Bartocci, E., Majumdar, R. (eds.) RV 2015. LNCS, vol. 9333, pp. 306–320. Springer, Cham (2015). https://doi.org/10.1007/978-3-319-23820-3_22
83. Pinisetty, S., Falcone, Y., Jéron, T., Marchand, H., Rollet, A., Nguena-Timo, O.: Runtime enforcement of timed properties revisited. Form. Meth. Syst. Des. **45**(3), 381–422 (2014)
84. Pinisetty, S., Falcone, Y., Jéron, T., Marchand, H., Rollet, A., Nguena-Timo, O.L.: Runtime enforcement of timed properties. In: Qadeer and Tasiran [89], pp. 229–244
85. Pinisetty, S., Jéron, T., Tripakis, S., Falcone, Y., Marchand, H., Preoteasa, V.: Predictive runtime verification of timed properties. J. Syst. Softw. **132**, 353–365 (2017)
86. Pinisetty, S., Preoteasa, V., Tripakis, S., Jéron, T., Falcone, Y., Marchand, H.: Predictive runtime enforcement. Form. Meth. Syst. Des. **51**(1), 154–199 (2017)
87. Pinisetty, S., Roop, P.S., Smyth, S., Allen, N., Tripakis, S., Hanxleden, R.V.: Runtime enforcement of cyber-physical systems. ACM Trans. Embed. Comput. Syst. **16**(5s), 178:1–178:25 (2017)
88. Pnueli, A.: Embedded systems: challenges in specification and verification. In: Sangiovanni-Vincentelli, A., Sifakis, J. (eds.) EMSOFT 2002. LNCS, vol. 2491, pp. 1–14. Springer, Heidelberg (2002). https://doi.org/10.1007/3-540-45828-X_1
89. Qadeer, S., Tasiran, S. (eds.): RV 2012. LNCS, vol. 7687. Springer, Heidelberg (2013). https://doi.org/10.1007/978-3-642-35632-2
90. Reger, G., Havelund, K.: What is a trace? A runtime verification perspective. In: Margaria and Steffen [72], pp. 339–355
91. Renard, M., Falcone, Y., Rollet, A., Jéron, T., Marchand, H.: Optimal enforcement of (timed) properties with uncontrollable events. Math. Struct. Comput. Sci. **29**(1), 169–214 (2019)
92. Renard, M., Falcone, Y., Rollet, A., Pinisetty, S., Jéron, T., Marchand, H.: Enforcement of (timed) properties with uncontrollable events. In: Leucker, M., Rueda, C., Valencia, F.D. (eds.) ICTAC 2015. LNCS, vol. 9399, pp. 542–560. Springer, Cham (2015). https://doi.org/10.1007/978-3-319-25150-9_31
93. Renard, M., Rollet, A., Falcone, Y.: Runtime enforcement using büchi games. In: Erdogmus, H., Havelund, K. (eds.) Proceedings of the 24th ACM SIGSOFT International SPIN Symposium on Model Checking of Software, pp. 70–79. ACM (2017)

94. Riganelli, O., Micucci, D., Mariani, L., Falcone, Y.: Verifying policy enforcers. In: Lahiri, S., Reger, G. (eds.) RV 2017. LNCS, vol. 10548, pp. 241–258. Springer, Cham (2017). https://doi.org/10.1007/978-3-319-67531-2_15

95. Rinard, M.C.: Acceptability-oriented computing. In: Crocker, R., Steele Jr., G.L., Gabriel, R.P. (eds.) Companion of the 18th Annual ACM SIGPLAN Conference on Object-Oriented Programming, Systems, Languages, and Applications, OOPSLA 2003, pp. 221–239. ACM (2003)

96. Roman, G., Griswold, W.G., Nuseibeh, B. (eds.): 27th International Conference on Software Engineering (ICSE 2005). ACM (2005)

97. Pinisetty, S., et al.: TiPEX website (2015). https://srinivaspinisetty.github.io/Timed-Enforcement-Tools/

98. Schneider, F.B.: Enforceable security policies. ACM Trans. Inf. Syst. Secur. **3**(1), 30–50 (2000)

99. Selyunin, K., Nguyen, T., Bartocci, E., Nickovic, D., Grosu, R.: Monitoring of MTL specifications with IBM's spiking-neuron model. In: Fanucci, L., Teich, J. (eds.) 2016 Design, Automation & Test in Europe Conference & Exhibition, DATE 2016, pp. 924–929. IEEE (2016)

100. Seward, J., Nethercote, N.: Using valgrind to detect undefined value errors with bit-precision. In: Proceedings of the 2005 USENIX Annual Technical Conference, pp. 17–30. USENIX (2005)

101. Sifakis, J.: Modeling real-time systems. In: Proceedings of the 25th IEEE Real-Time Systems Symposium (RTSS 2004), pp. 5–6. IEEE Computer Society (2004)

102. Sifakis, J., Tripakis, S., Yovine, S.: Building models of real-time systems from application software. Proc. IEEE **91**(1), 100–111 (2003)

103. Sistla, A.P.: Safety, liveness and fairness in temporal logic. Formal Asp. Comput. **6**(5), 495–512 (1994)

104. Song, D., Lettner, J., Rajasekaran, P., Na, Y., Volckaert, S., Larsen, P., Franz, M.: SoK: sanitizing for security. CoRR abs/1806.04355 (2018)

105. Szekeres, L., Payer, M., Wei, T., Song, D.: SoK: eternal war in memory. In: 2013 IEEE Symposium on Security and Privacy, SP 2013, pp. 48–62. IEEE Computer Society (2013)

106. Talhi, C., Tawbi, N., Debbabi, M.: Execution monitoring enforcement under memory-limitation constraints. Inf. Comput. **206**(2–4), 158–184 (2008)

107. Wu, M., Zeng, H., Wang, C.: Synthesizing runtime enforcer of safety properties under burst error. In: Rayadurgam, S., Tkachuk, O. (eds.) NFM 2016. LNCS, vol. 9690, pp. 65–81. Springer, Cham (2016). https://doi.org/10.1007/978-3-319-40648-0_6

108. Wu, M., Zeng, H., Wang, C., Yu, H.: Safety guard: runtime enforcement for safety-critical cyber-physical systems: invited. In: Proceedings of the 54th Annual Design Automation Conference, pp. 84:1–84:6. ACM (2017)

109. Yin, X., Lafortune, S.: A new approach for synthesizing opacity-enforcing supervisors for partially-observed discrete-event systems. In: American Control Conference, ACC 2015, pp. 377–383. IEEE (2015)

110. Zhang, X., Leucker, M., Dong, W.: Runtime verification with predictive semantics. In: Goodloe, A.E., Person, S. (eds.) NFM 2012. LNCS, vol. 7226, pp. 418–432. Springer, Heidelberg (2012). https://doi.org/10.1007/978-3-642-28891-3_37

Algorithms for Monitoring Hyperproperties

Christopher Hahn$^{(\boxtimes)}$

Saarland University, Saarbrücken, Germany
`hahn@react.uni-saarland.de`

Abstract. Hyperproperties relate multiple computation traces to each other and thus pose a serious challenge to monitoring algorithms. Observational determinism, for example, is a hyperproperty which states that private data should not influence the observable behavior of a system. Standard trace monitoring techniques are not applicable to such properties. In this tutorial, we summarize recent algorithmic advances in monitoring hyperproperties from logical specifications. We classify current approaches into two classes: combinatorial approaches and constraint-based approaches. We summarize current optimization techniques for keeping the execution trace storage and algorithmic workload as low as possible and also report on experiments run on the combinatorial as well as the constraint-based monitoring algorithms.

Keywords: Hyperproperties · HyperLTL · Information-flow · Monitoring · Runtime verification

1 Introduction

Hyperproperties [12] relate multiple computation traces to each other. Information-flow control is a prominent application area. Observational determinism, for example, is a hyperproperty which states that two executions agree on the observable output whenever they agree on the observable input, i.e., private data does not influence the observable behavior of the system. Standard trace monitoring techniques are not applicable to such properties: For example, a violation of observational determinism cannot be determined by analyzing executions in isolation, because each new execution must be compared to executions already seen so far. This results in a challenging problem: A naive monitor would store all traces and, thus, run inevitably out of memory. So how do we *efficiently* store, process and compare every executions seen so far? In this paper, we will

This work was partially supported by the German Research Foundation (DFG) as part of the Collaborative Research Center "Methods and Tools for Understanding and Controlling Privacy" (CRC 1223) and the Collaborative Research Center "Foundations of Perspicuous Software Systems" (TRR 248, 389792660), and by the European Research Council (ERC) Grant OSARES (No. 683300).

B. Finkbeiner and L. Mariani (Eds.): RV 2019, LNCS 11757, pp. 70–90, 2019.
https://doi.org/10.1007/978-3-030-32079-9_5

give an overview on the significant algorithmic advances [1,7–9,23,24,31] that have been made in monitoring hyperproperties.

Monitoring hyperproperties requires, in general, extensions of trace property monitoring in three orthogonal dimensions: (1) how the *set* of execution traces is obtained and presented to the monitor, (2) how hyperproperties can be rigorously specified formally and (3) how algorithms process multiple traces at once without an explosion of the running time or storage consumption.

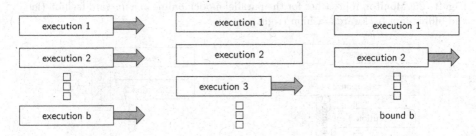

Fig. 1. Input Models: The parallel model (left), the unbounded sequential model (middle), and the bounded sequential model (right).

Input Model. There are three different straight-forward input models [25]: (1) The *parallel* model, where a *fixed* number of system executions is processed in parallel. (2) The *unbounded sequential* model, where an a-priori unbounded number of system executions are processed sequentially, and (3) The *bounded sequential model* where the traces are processed sequentially and the number of incoming executions is *bounded* (see Fig. 1). Choosing a suitable input model for the system under consideration is crucial: The choice of the model has significant impact on the monitorability and, especially, on the monitoring algorithms (Figs. 2 and 3). If, for example, the number of traces is a-priori bounded, offline monitoring becomes an efficient option. If, however, violations must be detected during runtime, algorithms must be specifically designed and optimized to reduce trace storage and algorithmic workload.

Hyper Logical Specifications. Hyperlogics are obtained by either (1) extending linear-time temporal and branching-time temporal logics with explicit trace quantification [11] or (2) by equipping first-order and second-order logics with the *equal-level predicate* [29,39]. There are several extensions of logics for trace properties to hyperlogics (see [13] for a recently initiated study of the hierarchy of hyperlogics). HyperLTL [11] is the most studied hyperlogic, which extends linear-time temporal logic (LTL) with a trace quantification prefix. Let $Out, In \subseteq AP$ denote all observable output and input propositions respectively. For example, the HyperLTL formula

$$\forall \pi. \forall \pi'. \left(\bigwedge_{o \in Out} o_\pi \leftrightarrow o_{\pi'} \right) \mathcal{W} \left(\bigvee_{i \in In} i_\pi \not\leftrightarrow i_{\pi'} \right) \tag{1}$$

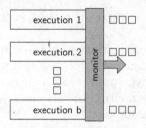
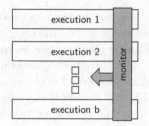
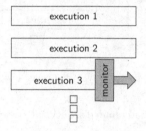
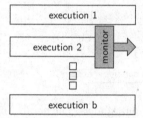

Fig. 2. [25] Monitor approaches for the parallel model: online in a forward fashion (left) and offline in a backwards fashion (right).

Fig. 3. [25] Monitor approaches for the sequential models: an unbounded number of traces (left) and bounded number of traces (right) are processed sequentially.

expresses observational determinism, i.e., that *all pairs* of traces must agree on the observable values at all times or until the inputs differ. With this added dimension, hyperlogics can relate traces or paths to each other, which makes it possible to express hyperproperties, such as information-flow control policies rigorously and succinctly.

Algorithms. Current monitoring approaches can be classified into two classes: (1) algorithms that rely on combinatorial constructions, for example, on multiple instantiations of automaton constructions and (2) constraint-based algorithms that translate the monitoring requirements into Boolean constraints and, for example, apply rewriting techniques, which rely on SAT or SMT solving. Both types of monitoring techniques require heavy optimization, in order to make the monitoring problem of hyperproperties feasible. The bottleneck in combinatorial approaches is that a monitor needs to store, in the worst case, every observation seen so far. Optimizing the trace storage is therefore crucial. We describe a trace storage minimization algorithm that prunes redundant traces to circumvent this problem. Constraint-based approaches on the other hand, suffer from growing constraints, such that naive implementations push SAT and SMT solvers quickly to their limits. Keeping the constraint system as small as possible is therefore crucial. We report an optimization technique that stores formulas and their corresponding variables in a tree structure, such that conjunct splitting becomes possible. The algorithms reported in this paper in detail, i.e., [25,31], have been implemented in the state-of-the-art monitoring tool for temporal hyperproperties, called RVHyper [24].

Structure. The remainder of this paper is structured as follows. We will report related work in Sect. 2 and give necessary preliminaries in Sect. 3. We classify current monitoring approaches into two classes in Sect. 4 and go exemplary into detail in [25, 31]. We will summarize the optimization efforts that have been implemented in RVHyper in Sect. 5. In Sect. 6, we will report a summary of the experimental results that have been done over the last couple of years on RVHyper before concluding in Sect. 7.

2   Related Work

HyperLTL was introduced to model check security properties of reactive systems [11, 26, 27]. The satisfiability problem [19, 20, 22] and the realizability problem [21] of HyperLTL has been considered as well. For one of its predecessors, SecLTL [16], there has been a proposal for a white box monitoring approach [17] based on alternating automata. The problem of monitoring HyperLTL [6] was considered in an combinatorial approach in [1, 25] and in a constraint-based approach in [9, 31].

Runtime verification of HyperLTL formulas was first considered for (co-)k-safety hyperproperties [1]. In the same paper, the notion of monitorability for HyperLTL was introduced. The authors have also identified syntactic classes of HyperLTL formulas that are monitorable and they proposed a combinatorial monitoring algorithm based on a progression logic expressing trace interdependencies and the composition of an LTL_3 monitor.

Another combinatorial and automata-based approach for monitoring HyperLTL formulas was proposed in [23]. Given a HyperLTL specification, the algorithm starts by creating a deterministic monitor automaton. For every incoming trace it then checks that all combinations with the already seen traces are accepted by the automaton to minimize the number of stored traces, a language-inclusion-based algorithm is proposed, which allows for pruning traces with redundant information. Furthermore, a method to reduce the number of combination of traces which have to get checked by analyzing the specification for relations such as reflexivity, symmetry, and transitivity with a HyperLTL-SAT solver [19, 22], is proposed. The algorithm is implemented in the tool RVHyper [24], which was used to monitor information-flow policies and to detect spurious dependencies in hardware designs.

A first constraint-based approach for HyperLTL is outlined in [9]. The idea is to identify a set of propositions of interest and aggregate constraints such that inconsistencies in the constraints indicate a violation of the HyperLTL formula. While the paper describes the building blocks for such a monitoring approach with a number of examples, we have, unfortunately, not been successful in applying the algorithm to other hyperproperties of interest, such as observational determinism.

A sound constraint-based algorithm for HyperLTL formulas in the $\forall^2$ fragment is proposed in [31]. The basic idea is to rewrite incoming events and a given HyperLTL formula into a Boolean constraint system, which is unsatisfiable if a violation occurs. The constraint system is built incrementally: the algorithm starts by encoding constraints that represent the LTL constraints, which result from rewriting the event into the formula, and encode the remaining HyperLTL constraints as variables. Those variables will be defined incrementally when more events of the trace become available.

In [7], the authors study the complexity of monitoring hyperproperties. They show that the form and size of the input, as well as the formula have a significant impact on the feasibility of the monitoring process. They differentiate between several input forms and study their complexity: a set of linear traces, tree-shaped Kripke structures, and acyclic Kripke structures. For acyclic structures and alternation-free HyperLTL formulas, the problems complexity gets as low as NC.

In [8], the authors discuss examples where static analysis can be combined with runtime verification techniques to monitor HyperLTL formulas beyond the alternation-free fragment. They discuss the challenges in monitoring formulas beyond this fragment and lay the foundations towards a general method.

For certain information flow policies, like non-interference and some extensions, dynamic enforcement mechanisms have been proposed. Techniques for the enforcement of information flow policies include tracking dependencies at the hardware level [37], language-based monitors [2,3,5,36,40], and abstraction-based dependency tracking [10,30,32]. Secure multi-execution [15] is a technique that can enforce non-interference by executing a program multiple times in different security levels. To enforce non-interference, the inputs are replaced by default values whenever a program tries to read from a higher security level.

3   Preliminaries

Since hyperproperties relate multiple computation traces to each other, standard trace property specification logics like linear-time temporal logic (LTL) [34] cannot be used to express them. In this section, we will give a quick overview on how classic logics can be extended to obtain hyperlogics. We define HyperLTL, which is the, so far, most studied hyperlogic. We furthermore give the finite trace semantics of HyperLTL and define monitorability for the different input models.

3.1   Logics for Hyperproperties

Two extensions for obtaining hyperlogics are studied in the literature so far: (1) extending temporal trace logics, like LTL [34] and CTL* [18], with *explicit trace quantification* or (2) extending first-order and second-order logics with the *equal-level predicate* [29,39]. An extensive expressiveness study of such hyperlogics has been initiated recently [13] and the hierarchy of linear-time hyperlogics is depicted in Fig. 4.

For example, HyperLTL extends LTL with trace quantification and trace variables. The formula

$$\forall \pi. \forall \pi'. \; \Box \bigwedge_{a \in AP} a_\pi \leftrightarrow a_{\pi'} \tag{2}$$

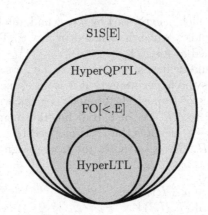

Fig. 4. The hierarchy of linear-time hyperlogics [13].

expresses that *all pairs* of traces must agree on the values of the atomic propositions (given as a set AP) at all times.

The other technique for obtaining hyperlogics consists of adding the equal-level predicate E, which relates the same time points on different traces. The HyperLTL formula (2), for example, is equivalent to the FO[$<, E$] formula

$$\forall x. \forall y.\ E(x, y) \rightarrow \bigwedge_{a \in AP} (P_a(x) \leftrightarrow P_a(y)).$$

Solving the runtime verification problem for logics beyond HyperLTL is still open. Current monitoring approaches focus on the, so far, best understood temporal hyperlogic HyperLTL, which we will define in the following.

3.2 HyperLTL

Let AP be a set of *atomic propositions*. A *trace* t is an infinite sequence over subsets of the atomic propositions. We define the set of traces $TR := (2^{AP})^\omega$. A subset $T \subseteq TR$ is called a *trace property*. A *hyperproperty* H is a set of trace properties, i.e., $H \subseteq \mathcal{P}(\Sigma^\omega)$. We use the following notation to manipulate traces: let $t \in TR$ be a trace and $i \in \mathbb{N}$ be a natural number. $t[i]$ denotes the i-th element of t. Therefore, $t[0]$ represents the starting element of the trace. Let $j \in \mathbb{N}$ and $j \geq i$. $t[i, j]$ denotes the sequence $t[i]\ t[i+1]\ldots t[j-1]\ t[j]$. $t[i, \infty]$ denotes the infinite suffix of t starting at position i. Let $\mathcal{V}$ be an infinite supply of trace variables.

The syntax of HyperLTL is given by the following grammar:

$$\varphi ::= \forall \pi. \varphi \mid \exists \pi. \varphi \mid \psi \ , \text{ and}$$
$$\psi ::= a_\pi \mid \neg \psi \mid \psi \vee \psi \mid \bigcirc \psi \mid \psi \mathcal{U} \psi \ ,$$

where $a \in AP$ is an atomic proposition and $\pi \in \mathcal{V}$ is a trace variable. The quantification over traces makes it possible to express properties like "on all traces ψ must hold", which is expressed by $\forall \pi.\ \psi$ and, dually, that "there exists a trace such that ψ holds", which is denoted by $\exists \pi.\ \psi$. The derived operators $\Diamond, \Box$, and $\mathcal{W}$ are defined as for LTL.

A HyperLTL formula defines a *hyperproperty*, i.e., a set of sets of traces. A set T of traces satisfies the hyperproperty if it is an element of this set of sets. Formally, the semantics of HyperLTL formulas is given with respect to a *trace assignment* Π from $\mathcal{V}$ to TR, i.e., a partial function mapping trace variables to actual traces. $\Pi[\pi \mapsto t]$ denotes that π is mapped to t, with everything else mapped according to Π. $\Pi[i, \infty]$ denotes the trace assignment that is equal to $\Pi(\pi)[i, \infty]$ for all π.

$$
\begin{aligned}
&(T, \Pi, i) \vDash a_\pi && \text{if } a \in \Pi(\pi)[i] \\
&(T, \Pi, i) \vDash \neg\varphi && \text{if } (T, \Pi, i) \nvDash \varphi \\
&(T, \Pi, i) \vDash \varphi \vee \psi && \text{if } (T, \Pi, i) \vDash \varphi \text{ or } (T, \Pi, i) \vDash \psi \\
&(T, \Pi, i) \vDash \bigcirc\varphi && \text{if } (T, \Pi, i+1) \vDash \varphi \\
&(T, \Pi, i) \vDash \varphi\,\mathcal{U}\,\psi && \text{if } \exists j \geq i.\,(T, \Pi, j) \vDash \psi \wedge \forall i \leq k < j.\,(T, \Pi, k) \vDash \varphi \\
&(T, \Pi, i) \vDash \exists \pi.\varphi && \text{if there is some } t \in T \text{ such that } (T, \Pi[\pi \mapsto t], i) \vDash \varphi \\
&(T, \Pi, i) \vDash \forall \pi.\varphi && \text{if for all } t \in T \text{ it holds that } (T, \Pi[\pi \mapsto t], i) \vDash \varphi\ .
\end{aligned}
$$

3.3   Finite Trace Semantics

We recap the finite trace semantics for HyperLTL [9,31]. Let $\Pi_{fin} \colon \mathcal{V} \to \Sigma^+$ be a partial function mapping trace variables to finite traces. We define $\epsilon[0]$ as the empty set. By slight abuse of notation, we write $t \in \Pi_{fin}$ to access traces t in the image of Π_{fin}. The satisfaction of a HyperLTL formula φ over a finite trace assignment Π_{fin} and a set of finite traces T, denoted by $(T, \Pi_{fin}, i) \vDash \varphi$, is defined as follows:

$$
\begin{aligned}
&(T, \Pi_{fin}, i) \vDash a_\pi && \text{if } a \in \Pi_{fin}(\pi)[i] \\
&(T, \Pi_{fin}, i) \vDash \neg\varphi && \text{if } (T, \Pi_{fin}, i) \nvDash \varphi \\
&(T, \Pi_{fin}, i) \vDash \varphi \vee \psi && \text{if } (T, \Pi_{fin}, i) \vDash \varphi \text{ or } (T, \Pi_{fin}, i) \vDash \psi \\
&(T, \Pi_{fin}, i) \vDash \bigcirc\varphi && \text{if } \forall t \in \Pi_{fin}.\,|t| > i+1 \text{ and } (T, \Pi_{fin}, i+1) \vDash_T \varphi \\
&(T, \Pi_{fin}, i) \vDash \varphi\,\mathcal{U}\,\psi && \text{if } \exists j \geq i \text{ with } j < \min_{t \in \Pi_{fin}} |t| \text{ such that } (T, \Pi_{fin}, j) \vDash \psi \\
& && \quad \wedge\, \forall k \geq i \text{ with } k < j \text{ it holds that } (T, \Pi_{fin}, k) \vDash \varphi \\
&(T, \Pi_{fin}, i) \vDash \exists \pi.\varphi && \text{if there is some } t \in T \text{ such that } (T, \Pi_{fin}[\pi \mapsto t], i) \vDash \varphi \\
&(T, \Pi_{fin}, i) \vDash \forall \pi.\varphi && \text{if for all } t \in T \text{ such that } (T, \Pi_{fin}[\pi \mapsto t], i) \vDash \varphi
\end{aligned}
$$

3.4   Monitorability of HyperLTL Specifications

We recap the monitorability definitions for trace properties [35] and hyperproperties [1,25]. Let $L \subseteq \Sigma^\omega$. We distinguish *good* and *bad* prefixes: $good(L) := \{u \in \Sigma^* \mid \forall v \in \Sigma^\omega.\ uv \in L\}$ and $bad(L) := \{u \in \Sigma^* \mid \forall v \in \Sigma^\omega.\ uv \notin L\}$, respectively. A trace language L is *monitorable* if every prefix has a (finite) continuation that is either good or bad, formally, $\forall u \in \Sigma^*.\ \exists v \in \Sigma^*.\ uv \in good(L) \vee uv \in bad(L)$.

Theorem 1 ([4]). *Deciding whether an LTL formula φ is monitorable is* PSPACE-*complete.*

Let $H \subseteq \mathcal{P}(\Sigma^\omega)$ be a hyperproperty. We say that a finite set of prefix traces is *good* if every continuation, i.e., a (possibly infinite) set of infinite traces, is contained in H. The set of *good* and *bad prefix traces* is then formally defined as $good(H) := \{U \in \mathcal{P}^*(\Sigma^*) \mid \forall V \in \mathcal{P}(\Sigma^\omega). U \preceq V \Rightarrow V \in H\}$ and $bad(H) := \{U \in \mathcal{P}^*(\Sigma^*) \mid \forall V \in \mathcal{P}(\Sigma^\omega). U \preceq V \Rightarrow V \notin H\}$.

Unbounded Sequential Model. A hyperproperty H is *monitorable* in the unbounded input model if every finite prefix set has a good or bad continuation, formally,

$$\forall U \in \mathcal{P}^*(\Sigma^*). \exists V \in \mathcal{P}^*(\Sigma^*). U \preceq V \wedge \big(V \in good(H) \vee V \in bad(H)\big) .$$

Theorem 2 ([25]). *Given an alternation-free HyperLTL formula φ. Deciding whether φ is monitorable in the unbounded sequential model is* PSPACE*-complete.*

Theorem 3 ([25]). *Deciding whether a HyperLTL formula φ is monitorable in the unbounded sequential model is undecidable.*

Bounded Sequential Model. We give the adapted definition of monitorability and a characterization for alternation-free HyperLTL. A hyperproperty H is *monitorable* in the bounded input model for some bound $b > 0$ if

$$\forall U \in \mathcal{P}^{\leq b}(\Sigma^*). \exists V \in \mathcal{P}^b(\Sigma^*). U \preceq V \wedge (V \in good^b(H) \vee V \in bad^b(H)) ,$$

where $good^b(H) := \{U \in \mathcal{P}^b(\Sigma^*) \mid \forall V \in \mathcal{P}^b(\Sigma^\omega). U \preceq V \Rightarrow V \in H\}$ and $bad(H) := \{U \in \mathcal{P}^b(\Sigma^*) \mid \forall V \in \mathcal{P}^b(\Sigma^\omega). U \preceq V \Rightarrow V \notin H\}$.

Theorem 4 ([25]). *Deciding whether a HyperLTL formula φ is monitorable in the bounded sequential model is undecidable.*

Parallel Model. Lastly, we consider the parallel model, were b traces are given simultaneously. This model is with respect to monitorability a special case of the bounded model. A hyperproperty H is *monitorable* in the fixed size input model if for a given bound b

$$\forall U \in \mathcal{P}^b(\Sigma^*). \exists V \in \mathcal{P}^b(\Sigma^*). U \preceq V \wedge (V \in good^b(H) \vee V \in bad^b(H)) .$$

Theorem 5 ([25]). *Deciding whether a HyperLTL formula φ is monitorable in the parallel model is undecidable.*

4   Algorithms for Monitoring Hyperproperties

We classify the current state-of-the art monitoring algorithms for hyperproperties into two approaches: *combinatorial* approaches [1,23,25] and *constraint-based* approaches [9,31].

As *combinatorial* approaches we understand algorithms that construct monitors by explicitly iterating over each (necessary) combination of traces for monitoring them. For example, consider a trace set T of already monitored traces

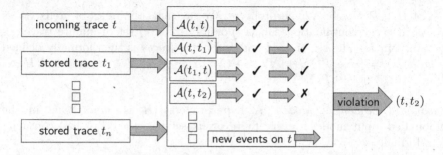

Fig. 5. A combinatorial approach to monitoring hyperproperties [23,25]: a monitoring template $\mathcal{A}$, constructed from a given HyperLTL formula φ, is initiated with combinations from the new incoming trace t and stored traces $\{t_1, \ldots, t_n\}$. The monitors progress with new events on t, in this case, until a violation is found for trace t and t_2.

and a fresh incoming trace t. A combinatorial monitor would construct each pair $T \times \{t\}$ and check whether the hyperproperty holds on such a trace tuple. The monitor, in the worst case, therefore has to store each incoming trace seen so far. This is currently done by explicit automata constructions, but other methods, such as SAT-solvers could be plugged into such combinatorial approaches as well. In Sect. 4.1, we will investigate one such approach [25] in detail, which is the algorithmic foundation for the combinatorial algorithm implemented in the current state-of-the-art monitoring tool RVHyper [24].

The *constraint-based* approaches try to avoid the storing of explicit traces by translating the monitoring task into a constraint system. This is currently implemented by rewriting approaches that translate the requirements that a current trace imposes on future traces into the formula. For example, a hyperproperty φ under consideration and a new event e_t on a trace t will be translated into $\varphi[e_t]$ and used as the new specification when monitoring new events on possibly new traces. Such a rewritten formula can then, together with the trace under consideration, be translated into an constraint system, which is fed, for example, into a SAT-solver. In Sect. 4.2, we will investigate a recently introduced [31] constraint-based algorithm for $\forall^2$ HyperLTL formulas in detail.

4.1 Combinatorial Approaches

Intuition. We describe the automaton-based combinatorial approach introduced in [23,25] in detail. The basic architecture of the algorithm is depicted in Fig. 5. Let a trace set $T := \{t_1, \ldots, t_n\}$ of already seen traces and a fresh trace t, which is processed online, be given. From a $\forall^*$ HyperLTL formula, a monitor *template* $\mathcal{A}$ is automatically constructed, which runs over two execution traces. This template is then initialized with every combination between t and T. A violation will be reported when one of the automaton instantiations ends up in a rejecting state.

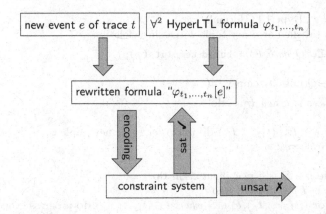

Fig. 6. A constraint-based approach to monitoring hyperproperties [31]: a fresh trace t, and a HyperLTL formula $\varphi_{t_1,\dots,t_n}$, which has already been rewritten with respect to seen traces $t_1,\dots t_n$, will be rewritten to a formula representing the requirements that are posed on future traces. The rewritten formula will be translated into a constraint system, which is satisfiable if the new event complies with the formula $\varphi_{t_1,\dots,t_n}$ and unsatisfiable if there is a violation.

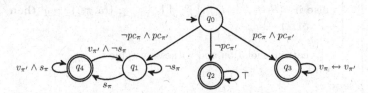

Fig. 7. [23,25] Visualization of the monitor template for Formula 3.

Example 1 (Conference Management System [23,25]). Consider a conference management system, where we distinguish two types of traces, *author traces* and *program committee member traces*. The latter starts with proposition pc. Based on these traces, we want to verify that no paper submission is lost, i.e., that every submission (proposition s) is visible (proposition v) to every program committee member in the following step. When comparing two PC traces, we require that they agree on proposition v. The monitor template for the following HyperLTL formalization is depicted in Fig. 7.

$$\forall\pi.\forall\pi'.\left((\neg pc_\pi \wedge pc_{\pi'}) \to \bigcirc\square(s_\pi \to \bigcirc v_{\pi'})\right)\wedge\left((pc_\pi \wedge pc_{\pi'}) \to \bigcirc\square(v_\pi \leftrightarrow v_{\pi'})\right) \quad (3)$$

Algorithm. Formally, a deterministic monitor template $\mathcal{M} = (\Sigma, Q, \delta, q_0, F)$ [23,25] is a tuple of a finite alphabet $\Sigma = \mathcal{P}(\text{AP} \times \mathcal{V})$, a non-empty set of states Q, a partial transition function $\delta : Q \times \Sigma \hookrightarrow Q$, a designated initial state $q_0 \in Q$, and a set of accepting states $F \subseteq Q$. The instantiated automaton runs in parallel over traces in $\mathcal{P}(\text{AP})^*$, thus we define a run with respect to a n-ary tuple $N \in (\mathcal{P}(\text{AP})^*)^n$ of finite traces. A run of N is a sequence of states

input : $\forall^n$ HyperLTL formula φ
output: satisfied or n-ary tuple witnessing violation

$\mathcal{M}_\varphi = (\Sigma_\mathcal{V}, Q, q_0, \delta, F) = $ `build_template`(φ);
$T \leftarrow \emptyset$;
$S : T^n \rightarrow Q$ initially empty;

while *there is a new trace* **do**
$\quad$ $t \leftarrow \epsilon$;
$\quad$ **for** $t \in ((T \cup \{t\})^n \setminus T^n)$ **do** init S for every new tuple t
$\quad\quad |$ $S(t) = q_0$;
$\quad$ **end**
$\quad$ **while** $p \in \Sigma$ *is a new input event* **do**
$\quad\quad$ $t \leftarrow t\,p$ $\quad$ append p to t;
$\quad\quad$ **for** $((t_1, \ldots, t_n), q) \in S$ where $t \in (t_1, \ldots, t_n)$ **do** progress every state
$\quad\quad$ in S
$\quad\quad\quad$ **if** $\exists t' \in \{t_1, \ldots, t_n\}.\,|t'| < |t|$ **then** some trace ended
$\quad\quad\quad\quad$ **if** $S((t_1, \ldots, t_n)) \in F$ **then**
$\quad\quad\quad\quad\quad |$ remove $(t_1, \ldots, t_n)$ from S and **continue**;
$\quad\quad\quad\quad$ **else**
$\quad\quad\quad\quad\quad |$ **return** violation and witnessing tuple t;
$\quad\quad\quad\quad$ **end**
$\quad\quad\quad$ **else if** $\delta(S((t_1, \ldots, t_n)), \bigcup_{i=1}^n \bigcup_{a \in t_i[|t|-1]} \{(a, \pi_i)\}) = q'$ **then**
$\quad\quad\quad\quad |$ $S(N) \leftarrow q'$;
$\quad\quad\quad$ **else**
$\quad\quad\quad\quad |$ **return** violation and witnessing tuple t;
$\quad\quad\quad$ **end**
$\quad\quad$ **end**
$\quad$ **end**
$\quad$ $T = T \cup \{t\}$;
end
return satisfied;

Fig. 8. [25] Evaluation algorithm for monitoring $\forall^n$ HyperLTL formulas in the unbounded sequential model.

$q_0 q_1 \cdots q_m \in Q^*$, where m is the length of the smallest trace in N, starting in the initial state q_0 such that for all i with $0 \leq i < m$ it holds that

$$\delta\left(q_i, \bigcup_{j=1}^n \bigcup_{a \in N(j)(i)} \{(a, \pi_j)\}\right) = q_{i+1} .$$

A tuple N is accepted, if there is a run on $\mathcal{M}$ that ends in an accepting state.

The algorithm for monitoring $\forall^n$ HyperLTL formulas in the unbounded sequential model is given in Fig. 8. The algorithm proceeds as follows. A monitoring template is constructed a-priori from the specification (in doubly-exponential time in the size of the formula [14,38]) and the trace set T is initially empty. For each new trace, we proceed with the incoming events on this trace. The automaton

```
input  : HyperLTL formula Q^n.ψ
          trace set T ⊆ P*(Σ*)
output: satisfied or violation
```

$\mathcal{A}_\psi = (\Sigma_\mathcal{V}, Q, q_0, \delta, F) = \text{build\_alternating\_automaton}(\psi);$

if $\bigdiamond\limits_{t_1 \in T} \cdots \bigdiamond\limits_{t_n \in T} . \text{LTL\_backwards\_algorithm}(\mathcal{A}_\psi, (t_1, t_2, \ldots, t_n))$ **then**

| **return** satisfied;

else

| **return** violation;

end

Fig. 9. [25] Offline backwards algorithm for the parallel model, where $\Diamond_i := \wedge$ if the i-th quantifier in φ is a universal quantifier and $\vee$ otherwise.

template will then be initialized by each combination between t and traces in T, i.e. $S(t) = q_0$. Each initialized monitor progresses with new input events p until a violation is found, in which case the witnessing tuple t is returned, or a trace ends, in which case this monitor is discarded if no violation occurred. If no violation occurred, and all trace combinations have been monitored, the current trace t is added to the traces that have been seen already, i.e., T.

While the online monitoring algorithms in the bounded sequential and parallel input model can be seen as special cases of the above described algorithm, traces can be processed efficiently in a backwards fashion when considering *offline* monitoring. The algorithm depicted in Fig. 9 exploits the backwards algorithm based on alternating automata [28].

4.2   Constraint-Based Approaches

Intuition. We describe the constraint-based monitoring algorithm for $\forall^2$ HyperLTL formulas introduced in [31] in detail. The basic architecture of the algorithm is depicted in Fig. 6. The basic idea is that a formula and an event on a trace will be rewritten into a new formula, which represents the requirements posed on future traces.

Example 2 (Observational Determinism [31]). Assume the event $\{in, out\}$ while monitoring observational determinism: $((out_\pi \leftrightarrow out_{\pi'}) \mathcal{W} (in_\pi \leftrightarrow in_{\pi'}))$. The formula is rewritten by applying the standard expansion laws and inserting $\{in, out\}$ for the atomic propositions indexed by the trace variable π: $\neg in \vee out \wedge \bigcirc((out_\pi \leftrightarrow out_{\pi'}) \mathcal{W} (in_\pi \leftrightarrow in_{\pi'}))$. Based on this, a Boolean constraint system is built incrementally: one starts by encoding the constraints corresponding to the LTL part $\neg in \vee out$ and encodes the HyperLTL part as variables. Those variables will then be defined incrementally when more elements of the trace become available. A violation will be reported when the constraint system becomes unsatisfiable.

Input $: \forall \pi, \pi'. \varphi, T \subseteq \Sigma^+$
Output: *violation* or *no violation*

$\psi := \mathbf{nnf}(\hat{\varphi})$
$C := \top$
foreach $t \in T$ **do**
    $C_t := v_{\psi,0}$
    $t_{enc} := \top$
    while $e_i := getNextEvent(t)$ **do**
        $t_{enc} := t_{enc} \wedge \mathbf{encoding}(e_i)$
        foreach $v_{\phi,i} \in C_t$ **do**
            $c := \psi[\pi, e_i, i]$
            $C_t := C_t \wedge (v_{\phi,i} \to c)$
        end
        if $\neg sat(C \wedge C_t \wedge t_{enc})$ **then**
            return *violation*
        end
    end
    foreach $v^+_{\phi,i+1} \in C_t$ **do**
        $C_t := C_t \wedge v^+_{\phi,i+1}$
    end
    foreach $v^-_{\phi,i+1} \in C_t$ **do**
        $C_t := C_t \wedge \neg v^-_{\phi,i+1}$
    end
    $C := C \wedge C_t$
end
return *no violation*

Fig. 10. [31] Constraint-based algorithm for monitoring $\forall^2$HyperLTL formulas.

Algorithm. We define the operation $\varphi[\pi, e, i]$ (taken from [31]), where $e \in \Sigma$ is an event and i is the current position in the trace, as follows: $\varphi[\pi, e, i]$ transforms φ into a propositional formula, where the variables are either indexed atomic propositions p_i for $p \in AP$, or a variable $v^-_{\varphi',i+1}$ and $v^+_{\varphi',i+1}$ that act as placeholders until new information about the trace comes in. Whenever the next event e' occurs, the variables are defined with the result of $\varphi'[\pi, e', i+1]$. If the trace ends, the variables are set to *true* and *false* for v^+ and v^-, respectively. In Fig. 11, we define $\varphi[\pi, e, i]$ of a $\forall^2$HyperLTL formula $\forall \pi, \pi'. \varphi$ in NNF, event $e \in \Sigma$, and $i \geq 0$ recursively on the structure of the body φ. We write $v_{\varphi,i}$ to denote either $v^-_{\varphi,i}$ or $v^+_{\varphi,i}$.

The algorithm for monitoring $\forall^2$ HyperLTL formulas with the constraint-based approach is given in Fig. 10. We continue with the explanation of the algorithm (taken from [31]): ψ is the negation normal form of the symmetric closure of the original formula. We build two constraint systems: C containing constraints of previous traces and C_t (built incrementally) containing the constraints for the current trace t. Consequently, we initialize C with $\top$ and C_t with $v_{\psi,0}$. If the trace ends, we define the remaining v variables according to their

$$a_\pi[\pi, e, i] \quad := \begin{cases} \top & \text{if } a \in e \\ \bot & \text{otherwise} \end{cases} \qquad (\neg a_\pi)[\pi, e, i] \quad := \begin{cases} \top & \text{if } a \notin e \\ \bot & \text{otherwise} \end{cases}$$

$$a_{\pi'}[\pi, e, i] \quad := a_i \qquad\qquad\qquad\qquad (\neg a_{\pi'})[\pi, e, i] \quad := \neg a_i$$

$$(\varphi \vee \psi)[\pi, e, i] := \varphi[\pi, e, i] \vee \psi[\pi, e, i] \qquad (\varphi \wedge \psi)[\pi, e, i] := \varphi[\pi, e, i] \wedge \psi[\pi, e, i]$$

$$(\bigcirc \varphi)[\pi, e, i] \quad := v^-_{\varphi, i+1} \qquad\qquad\qquad (\bigcirc_w \varphi)[\pi, e, i] \quad := v^+_{\varphi, i+1}$$

$$(\varphi \, \mathcal{U} \, \psi)[\pi, e, i] := \psi[\pi, e, i] \vee (\varphi[\pi, e, i] \wedge v^-_{\varphi \, \mathcal{U} \, \psi, i+1})$$

$$(\varphi \, \mathcal{R} \, \psi)[\pi, e, i] := \psi[\pi, e, i] \wedge (\varphi[\pi, e, i] \vee v^+_{\varphi \, \mathcal{R} \, \psi, i+1})$$

Fig. 11. [31] Recursive definition of the rewrite operation.

polarities and add C_t to C. For each new event e_i in the trace t, and each "open" constraint in C_t corresponding to step i, i.e., $v_{\phi,i} \in C_t$, we rewrite the formula ϕ and define $v_{\phi,i}$ with the rewriting result, which, potentially introduced new open constraints $v_{\phi',i+1}$ for the next step $i + 1$. The constraint encoding of the current trace is aggregated in constraint t_{enc}. If the constraint system given the encoding of the current trace turns out to be unsatisfiable, a violation to the specification is detected, which is then returned.

5 Optimizations

Both monitoring approaches rely heavily on optimization techniques to become feasible in practice. Naive implementations, that blindly store all traces seen so far or consider the same constraints multiple times, will run out of memory quickly or will take unfeasibly long. We present several techniques that significantly speed up the monitoring process.

5.1 Specification Analysis

We can analyze the specification and determine if it is symmetric, transitive, or reflexive. Formally, we define symmetry of a HyperLTL formulas as follows (reflexivity and transitivity is discussed in detail in [25]).

Definition 1 ([25]). *Let ψ be the quantifier-free part of some HyperLTL formula φ over trace variables $\mathcal{V}$. We say φ is invariant under trace variable permutation $\sigma : \mathcal{V} \to \mathcal{V}$, if for any set of traces $T \subseteq \Sigma^\omega$ and any assignment $\Pi : \mathcal{V} \to T$, $(\emptyset, \Pi, 0) \vDash \psi \Leftrightarrow (\emptyset, \Pi \circ \sigma, 0) \vDash \psi$. We say φ is symmetric, if it is invariant under every trace variable permutation in $\mathcal{V}$.*

Observational determinism, for example, is symmetric. To illustrate the impact of this observation, consider again Fig. 5. Symmetry means that one of the automaton instantiation $\mathcal{A}[t, t_i]$ or $\mathcal{A}[t_i, t]$ can be omitted for each $i \leq n$, resulting in an reduction of half the monitor instantiations.

A HyperLTL formula can be checked for symmetry, transitivity and reflexivity fully automatically and a-priori to the monitoring task with a satisfiability solver for hyperproperties, such as EAHyper [22]. Such a check, for example for observational determinism, is performed in under a second.

5.2   Trace Analysis

Keeping the set of stored traces minimal is crucial for a combinatorial approach to monitoring hyperproperties: We explain a method that checks whether a trace t poses strictly stronger requirements on future traces than another trace t'. In this case, t' could be safely discarded without losing the ability to detect every violation of the hyperproperty.

Definition 2 ([25]). *Given a HyperLTL formula φ, a trace set T and an arbitrary $t \in \Sigma^\omega$, we say that t is (T, φ)-redundant if T is a model of φ if and only if $T \cup \{t\}$ is a model of φ as well, formally*

$$\forall T' \supseteq T. T' \in \mathcal{H}(\varphi) \Leftrightarrow T' \cup \{t\} \in \mathcal{H}(\varphi) \ .$$

Example 3 ([31]). Consider the monitoring of the HyperLTL formula $\forall \pi, \pi'. \Box(a_\pi \rightarrow \neg b_{\pi'})$, which states that globally if a occurs on any trace π, then b is not allowed to hold on any trace π', on the following incoming traces:

| {a} | {} | {} | {} | $\neg b$ is enforced on the 1st pos. | (4) |

| {a} | {a} | {} | {} | $\neg b$ is enforced on the 1st and 2nd pos. | (5) |

| {a} | {} | {a} | {} | $\neg b$ is enforced on the 1st and 3rd pos. | (6) |

In this example, the requirements of the first trace are dominated by the requirements of the second trace, namely that b is not allowed to hold on the first and second position of new incoming traces. Hence, the first trace must not be stored any longer to detect a violation.

5.3   Tree Maintaining Formulas and Conjunct Splitting

For constraint-based approaches, a valuable optimization is to store formulas and their corresponding variables in a tree structure, such that a node corresponds to an already seen rewrite. If a rewrite is already present in the tree, there is no need to create any new constraints. By splitting conjuncts in HyperLTL formulas, we can avoid introducing unnecessary nodes in the tree.

Example 4 ([31]). Consider $\forall \pi, \pi'. \varphi$ with $\varphi = \Box((a_\pi \leftrightarrow a'_\pi) \vee (b_\pi \leftrightarrow b'_\pi))$, which demands that on all executions on each position at least on of propositions a or b agree in its evaluation. Consider the two traces $t_1 = \{a\}\{a\}\{a\}$, $t_2 = \{a\}\{a, b\}\{a\}$ that satisfy the specification. As both traces feature the same first event, they also share the same rewrite result for the first position. Interestingly, on the second position, we get $(a \vee \neg b) \wedge s_\varphi$ for t_1 and $(a \vee b) \wedge s_\varphi$

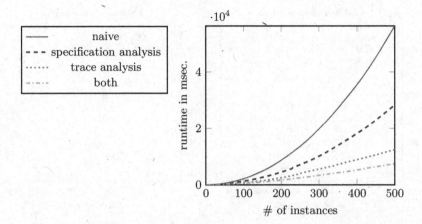

Fig. 12. [23,25] Hamming-distance preserving encoder: runtime comparison of the naive monitoring approach with different optimizations and the combination thereof.

Table 1. [31] Average results of BDD and SAT based constraint-based algorithms compared to the combinatorial algorithm on traces generated from circuit instances. Every instance was run 10 times.

Instance	# traces	Length	Time combinatorial	Time SAT	Time BDD
XOR1	19	5	12 ms	47 ms	49 ms
XOR2	1000	5	16913 ms	996 ms	1666 ms
Counter1	961	20	9610 ms	8274 ms	303 ms
Counter2	1353	20	19041 ms	13772 ms	437 ms
MUX1	1000	5	14924 ms	693 ms	647 ms
MUX2	80	5	121 ms	79 ms	81 ms

for t_2 as the rewrite results. While these constraints are no longer equal, by the nature of invariants, both feature the same subterm on the right hand side of the conjunction. We split the resulting constraint on its syntactic structure, such that we would no longer have to introduce a branch in the tree.

6   Experimental Results

The presented algorithms and optimizations implemented in RVHyper [24] were extensively evaluated over the last years [23–25,31].

A first benchmark that shows the impact of the trace and specification analysis is the following: it is monitored whether an encoder preserves a Hamming-distance of 2 [25], which can be encoded as a universally quantified HyperLTL formula [11]: $\forall \pi \pi'.(\Diamond(I_\pi \leftrightarrow\!\!\!/ \ I_{\pi'}) \rightarrow ((O_\pi \leftrightarrow O_{\pi'})\mathcal{U}((O_\pi \leftrightarrow\!\!\!/ \ O_{\pi'}) \wedge \bigcirc((O_\pi \leftrightarrow O_{\pi'})\mathcal{U}(O_\pi \leftrightarrow\!\!\!/ \ O_{\pi'})))))$. In Fig. 12 a comparison between the naive monitoring

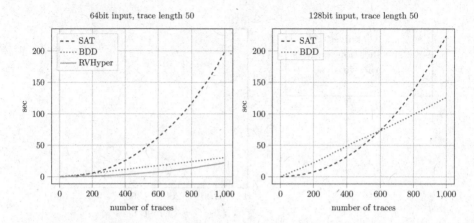

Fig. 13. [31] Runtime comparison between the combinatorial algorithm and the constraint-based algorithm implemented in RVHyper on a non-interference specification with traces of varying input size.

approach and the monitor using specification analysis and trace analysis, as well as a combination thereof is depicted. Traces were built randomly, where the corresponding bit on each position had a 1% chance of being flipped.

A second benchmark was introduced in [24] with the idea to detect spurious dependencies in hardware design. Traces were generated from circuit instances and then monitored whether input variables influence out variables. The property was specified as the following HyperLTL formula: $\forall \pi_1 \forall \pi_2.\,(o_{\pi_1} \leftrightarrow o_{\pi_2})\,\mathcal{W}(\bar{i}_{\pi_1} \leftrightarrow \bar{i}_{\pi_2})$, where $\bar{i}$ denotes all inputs except i. The results are depicted in Table 1.

The next benchmark [31] considers non-interference [33], which is an important information flow policy demanding that an observer of a system cannot infer any high security input of a system by observing only low security input and output. Reformulated we could also say that all low security outputs o^{low} have to be equal on all system executions as long as the low security inputs i^{low} of those executions are the same: $\forall \pi, \pi'.\,(o_{\pi}^{low} \leftrightarrow o_{\pi'}^{low})\,\mathcal{W}(i_{\pi}^{low} \leftrightarrow i_{\pi'}^{low})$. The results of the experiments are depicted in Fig. 13. For 64 bit inputs, the BDD implementation performs well when compared to the combinatorial approach, which statically constructs a monitor automaton. For 128 bit inputs, it was not possible to construct the automaton for the combinatorial approach in reasonable time.

The last benchmark considers *guarded invariants*, which express a certain invariant relation between two traces, which are, additionally, guarded by a precondition. Figure 14 shows the results of monitoring an arbitrary invariant $P : \Sigma \to \mathbb{B}$ of the following form: $\forall \pi, \pi'.\,\Diamond(\bigvee_{i \in I} i_{\pi} \leftrightarrow i_{\pi'}) \to \Box(P(\pi) \leftrightarrow P(\pi'))$. The constraint-based approach significantly outperforms combinatorial approaches on this benchmark as the conjunct splitting optimization synergizes well with current SAT-solver implementations.

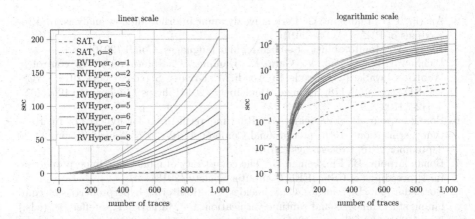

Fig. 14. [31] Runtime comparison between the combinatorial approach and the constraint-based monitor on the guarded invariant benchmark with trace lengths 20, 20 bit input size.

7 Conclusion

We classified current monitoring approaches into *combinatorial* and *constraint-based* algorithms and explained their basic architecture. We have gone into detail into two of these approaches and summarized current optimization technique making the monitoring of hyperproperties feasible in practice.

Future work consists of implementing and adapting more optimization techniques for constraint-based and combinatorial approaches. It would also be interesting to plug SAT and SMT solvers into combinatorial monitoring approaches, instead of using automata. Furthermore, considering the monitoring problem of specifications given in HyperQPTL, i.e., the extension of HyperLTL with quantification over propositions, is not studied yet. This problem is particularly interesting and challenging since HyperQPTL allows for a true combination of ω-regular properties and hyperproperties.

Acknowledgements. This paper is based on a tutorial that will be given at the 19th International Conference on Runtime Verification. The work summarized here has previously appeared in various publications [23–25,31]. The author is particularly grateful to his coauthors Bernd Finkbeiner, Marvin Stenger, and Leander Tentrup and, furthermore, to Maximilian Schwenger for his valuable comments on an earlier version of this paper.

References

1. Agrawal, S., Bonakdarpour, B.: Runtime verification of k-safety hyperproperties in HyperLTL. In: Proceedings of CSF. IEEE Computer Society (2016)
2. Askarov, A., Sabelfeld, A.: Tight enforcement of information-release policies for dynamic languages. In: Proceedings of CSF. IEEE Computer Society (2009)

3. Austin, T.H., Flanagan, C.: Permissive dynamic information flow analysis. In: Proceedings of PLAS. ACM (2010)
4. Bauer, A.: Monitorability of omega-regular languages. CoRR (2010)
5. Bichhawat, A., Rajani, V., Garg, D., Hammer, C.: Information flow control in WebKit's JavaScript bytecode. In: Abadi, M., Kremer, S. (eds.) POST 2014. LNCS, vol. 8414, pp. 159–178. Springer, Heidelberg (2014). https://doi.org/10.1007/978-3-642-54792-8_9
6. Bonakdarpour, B., Finkbeiner, B.: Runtime verification for hyperLTL. In: Runtime Verification - 16th International Conference, RV 2016, Madrid, Spain, 23–30 September 2016, Proceedings (2016)
7. Bonakdarpour, B., Finkbeiner, B.: The complexity of monitoring hyperproperties. In: Proceedings of CSF. IEEE Computer Society (2018)
8. Bonakdarpour, B., Sanchez, C., Schneider, G.: Monitoring hyperproperties by combining static analysis and runtime verification. In: Margaria, T., Steffen, B. (eds.) ISoLA 2018. LNCS, vol. 11245, pp. 8–27. Springer, Cham (2018). https://doi.org/10.1007/978-3-030-03421-4_2
9. Brett, N., Siddique, U., Bonakdarpour, B.: Rewriting-based runtime verification for alternation-free hyperLTL. In: Legay, A., Margaria, T. (eds.) TACAS 2017. LNCS, vol. 10206, pp. 77–93. Springer, Heidelberg (2017). https://doi.org/10.1007/978-3-662-54580-5_5
10. Chudnov, A., Kuan, G., Naumann, D.A.: Information flow monitoring as abstract interpretation for relational logic. In: Proceedings of CSF. IEEE Computer Society (2014)
11. Clarkson, M.R., Finkbeiner, B., Koleini, M., Micinski, K.K., Rabe, M.N., Sánchez, C.: Temporal logics for hyperproperties. In: Abadi, M., Kremer, S. (eds.) POST 2014. LNCS, vol. 8414, pp. 265–284. Springer, Heidelberg (2014). https://doi.org/10.1007/978-3-642-54792-8_15
12. Clarkson, M.R., Schneider, F.B.: Hyperproperties. J. Comput. Secur. **18**(6), 1157–1210 (2010)
13. Coenen, N., Finkbeiner, B., Hahn, C., Hofmann, J.: The hierarchy of hyperlogics. In: Proceedings of LICS (2019, to appear)
14. d'Amorim, M., Roşu, G.: Efficient monitoring of ω-languages. In: Etessami, K., Rajamani, S.K. (eds.) CAV 2005. LNCS, vol. 3576, pp. 364–378. Springer, Heidelberg (2005). https://doi.org/10.1007/11513988_36
15. Devriese, D., Piessens, F.: Noninterference through secure multi-execution. In: Proceedings of SP. IEEE Computer Society (2010)
16. Dimitrova, R., Finkbeiner, B., Kovács, M., Rabe, M.N., Seidl, H.: Model checking information flow in reactive systems. In: Kuncak, V., Rybalchenko, A. (eds.) VMCAI 2012. LNCS, vol. 7148, pp. 169–185. Springer, Heidelberg (2012). https://doi.org/10.1007/978-3-642-27940-9_12
17. Dimitrova, R., Finkbeiner, B., Rabe, M.N.: Monitoring temporal information flow. In: Margaria, T., Steffen, B. (eds.) ISoLA 2012. LNCS, vol. 7609, pp. 342–357. Springer, Heidelberg (2012). https://doi.org/10.1007/978-3-642-34026-0_26
18. Emerson, E.A., Halpern, J.Y.: "Sometimes" and "not never" revisited: on branching versus linear time temporal logic. J. ACM **33**(1), 151–178 (1986)
19. Finkbeiner, B., Hahn, C.: Deciding hyperproperties. In: Proceedings of CONCUR, LIPIcs. Schloss Dagstuhl - Leibniz-Zentrum fuer Informatik (2016)
20. Finkbeiner, B., Hahn, C., Hans, T.: MGHYPER: checking satisfiability of hyperLTL formulas beyond the ∃*∀* fragment. In: Lahiri, S.K., Wang, C. (eds.) ATVA 2018. LNCS, vol. 11138, pp. 521–527. Springer, Cham (2018). https://doi.org/10.1007/978-3-030-01090-4_31

21. Finkbeiner, B., Hahn, C., Lukert, P., Stenger, M., Tentrup, L.: Synthesizing reactive systems from hyperproperties. In: Chockler, H., Weissenbacher, G. (eds.) CAV 2018. LNCS, vol. 10981, pp. 289–306. Springer, Cham (2018). https://doi.org/10.1007/978-3-319-96145-3_16

22. Finkbeiner, B., Hahn, C., Stenger, M.: EAHyper: satisfiability, implication, and equivalence checking of hyperproperties. In: Majumdar, R., Kunčak, V. (eds.) CAV 2017. LNCS, vol. 10427, pp. 564–570. Springer, Cham (2017). https://doi.org/10.1007/978-3-319-63390-9_29

23. Finkbeiner, B., Hahn, C., Stenger, M., Tentrup, L.: Monitoring hyperproperties. In: Lahiri, S., Reger, G. (eds.) RV 2017. LNCS, vol. 10548, pp. 190–207. Springer, Cham (2017). https://doi.org/10.1007/978-3-319-67531-2_12

24. Finkbeiner, B., Hahn, C., Stenger, M., Tentrup, L.: RVHyper: a runtime verification tool for temporal hyperproperties. In: Beyer, D., Huisman, M. (eds.) TACAS 2018. LNCS, vol. 10806, pp. 194–200. Springer, Cham (2018). https://doi.org/10.1007/978-3-319-89963-3_11

25. Finkbeiner, B., Hahn, C., Stenger, M., Tentrup, L.: Monitoring hyperproperties. In: Formal Methods in System Design (2019)

26. Finkbeiner, B., Hahn, C., Torfah, H.: Model checking quantitative hyperproperties. In: Chockler, H., Weissenbacher, G. (eds.) CAV 2018. LNCS, vol. 10981, pp. 144–163. Springer, Cham (2018). https://doi.org/10.1007/978-3-319-96145-3_8

27. Finkbeiner, B., Rabe, M.N., Sánchez, C.: Algorithms for model checking hyperLTL and hyperCTL*. In: Kroening, D., Păsăreanu, C.S. (eds.) CAV 2015. LNCS, vol. 9206, pp. 30–48. Springer, Cham (2015). https://doi.org/10.1007/978-3-319-21690-4_3

28. Finkbeiner, B., Sipma, H.: Checking finite traces using alternating automata. Formal Methods Syst. Des. **24**(2), 101–127 (2004)

29. Finkbeiner, B., Zimmermann, M.: The first-order logic of hyperproperties. In: 34th Symposium on Theoretical Aspects of Computer Science, STACS 2017, 8–11 March 2017, Hannover, Germany (2017)

30. Le Guernic, G., Banerjee, A., Jensen, T., Schmidt, D.A.: Automata-based confidentiality monitoring. In: Okada, M., Satoh, I. (eds.) ASIAN 2006. LNCS, vol. 4435, pp. 75–89. Springer, Heidelberg (2007). https://doi.org/10.1007/978-3-540-77505-8_7

31. Hahn, C., Stenger, M., Tentrup, L.: Constraint-based monitoring of hyperproperties. In: Vojnar, T., Zhang, L. (eds.) TACAS 2019. LNCS, vol. 11428, pp. 115–131. Springer, Cham (2019). https://doi.org/10.1007/978-3-030-17465-1_7

32. Kovács, M., Seidl, H.: Runtime enforcement of information flow security in tree manipulating processes. In: Barthe, G., Livshits, B., Scandariato, R. (eds.) ESSoS 2012. LNCS, vol. 7159, pp. 46–59. Springer, Heidelberg (2012). https://doi.org/10.1007/978-3-642-28166-2_6

33. McLean, J.: Proving noninterference and functional correctness using traces. J. Comput. Secur. **1**(1), 37–57 (1992)

34. Pnueli, A.: The temporal logic of programs. In: Proceedings of FOCS. IEEE Computer Society (1977)

35. Pnueli, A., Zaks, A.: PSL model checking and run-time verification via testers. In: Misra, J., Nipkow, T., Sekerinski, E. (eds.) FM 2006. LNCS, vol. 4085, pp. 573–586. Springer, Heidelberg (2006). https://doi.org/10.1007/11813040_38

36. Sabelfeld, A., Myers, A.C.: Language-based information-flow security. IEEE J. Sel. Areas Commun. **21**(1), 5–19 (2003)

37. Suh, G.E., Lee, J.W., Zhang, D., Devadas, S.: Secure program execution via dynamic information flow tracking. In: Proceedings of ASPLOS. ACM (2004)

38. Tabakov, D., Rozier, K.Y., Vardi, M.Y.: Optimized temporal monitors for SystemC. Formal Methods Syst. Des. **41**(3), 236–268 (2012)
39. Thomas. Path logics with synchronization. In: Perspectives in Concurrency Theory (2009)
40. Vanhoef, M., De Groef, W., Devriese, D., Piessens, F., Rezk, T.: Stateful declassification policies for event-driven programs. In: Proceedings of CSF. IEEE Computer Society (2014)

Stream-Based Monitors
for Real-Time Properties

Hazem Torfah[✉]

Reactive Systems Group, Saarland University, Saarbrücken, Germany
torfah@react.uni-saarland.de

Abstract. In stream-based runtime monitoring, streams of data, called input streams, which involve data collected from the system at runtime, are translated into new streams of data, called output streams, which define statistical measures and verdicts on the system based on the input data. The advantage of this setup is an easy-to-use and modular way for specifying monitors with rich verdicts, provided with formal guarantees on the complexity of the monitor.

In this tutorial, we give an overview of the different classes of stream specification languages, in particular those with real-time features. With the help of the real-time stream specification language RTLOLA, we illustrate which features are necessary for the definition of the various types of real-time properties and we discuss how these features need to be implemented in order to guarantee memory efficient and reliable monitors.

To demonstrate the expressive power of the different classes of stream specification languages and the complexity of the different features, we use a series of examples based on our experience with monitoring problems from the areas of unmanned aerial systems and telecommunication networks.

Keywords: Stream-based monitoring · Real-time properties · Stream specification languages

1 Introduction

The online monitoring of real-time data streams has recently gained a great deal of attention, especially with the growing levels of autonomy and connectivity in modern real-time systems [1,7–9,14,17,28,30]. Runtime monitors are essential for evaluating the performance and for assessing the health of a running system, and are integral for the detection of malfunctions and consequently for deploying the necessary counter measures when these malfunctions occur at runtime.

This work was partially supported by the German Research Foundation (DFG) as part of the Collaborative Research Center "Foundations of Perspicuous Software Systems" (TRR 248, 389792660), and by the European Research Council (ERC) Grant OSARES (No. 683300).

B. Finkbeiner and L. Mariani (Eds.): RV 2019, LNCS 11757, pp. 91–110, 2019.
https://doi.org/10.1007/978-3-030-32079-9_6

Fig. 1. Spectrum of specification languages and tradeoffs in implementing monitors for real-time properties.

The integration of monitoring components into real-time systems demands the construction of monitors that are (1) *efficient*: using an on-board monitor that consumes a large amount of memory is bound to eventually disrupt the normal operation of the system, and (2) *reliable*: in the case of any malfunction or abnormality in one of the system's components, the monitor needs to provide, as early as possible, a correct assessment for deploying the right fallback procedure.

Monitors for real-time properties can be defined using a variety of languages, ranging over a spectrum that spans from formal languages with strong guarantees, such as temporal logics (e.g. [2,25,29]), to very expressive languages that allow for the definition of monitors with rich verdicts, such as scripting and programming languages. Moving from one end of the spectrum to the other, there is always a trade-off between the expressivity of a language and the guarantees it provides on the constructed monitors (Fig. 1). Monitors specified in temporal logics come with formal complexity guarantees, involving bounds on the maximum memory consumption of the monitor at runtime. Furthermore, temporal logics have the big advantage of allowing for the automatic construction of monitors from their specifications, and the guarantee that these monitors fulfill these specifications. A disadvantage of temporal logics is, however, that they are limited to describing monitors with simple boolean verdicts, which do not always suffice for the definition of monitors for practical real-world monitoring problems, where more involved computations over more complex datatypes are needed. Programming languages on the other hand allow for the implementation of such complex computations. This comes at the cost of losing formal guarantees on the constructed monitors, and also on their reliability, as there is no guarantee on the soundness of the manually implemented monitor.

In general, different monitoring applications require different approaches to constructing monitors. In modern real-time systems, monitors are required to perform complex arithmetic computations, but at the same time perform these computations with respect to the limited resources available on the platform they are running on. To implement such monitors for real-time properties, we need specification languages that are expressive enough, and, at the same time, provide certain guarantees on the complexity of the constructed monitor.

In this tutorial, we show how stream specification languages with real-time features can be used for the specification of runtime monitors for real-time properties. Stream specification languages allow for the definition of stream-based monitors, where input streams, containing data collected at runtime, such as sensor readings, or network traffic, are translated into output streams, containing aggregate statistics, threshold assertions and other logical conditions. The advantage of this setup is that it combines features from both sides of the specification language spectrum: the great expressiveness of programming languages on one hand, and the ability to compute a-priori formal guarantees on the monitor, as in the case for temporal logics, on the other hand.

We give an overview of the different types of real-time stream specification languages and illustrate, using the stream specification language RTLOLA [14, 15], the different features needed for expressing monitors for real-time properties. We further show how these features need to be implemented in order to obtain memory efficient and reliable monitors. To demonstrate the expressive power of stream specification languages in general and RTLOLA in particular, we will rely on examples from real-world monitoring problems from the area of unmanned aerial vehicles, which we have been investigating in close collaboration with the German Aerospace Center (DLR) [1], and from our experience with problems from the field of network monitoring [13].

This tutorial is structured as follows. In Sect. 2, we give an introduction to stream specification languages and show the different classes of these languages, according to their underlying computational model (synchronous vs. asynchronous), and the ways streams are accessed in the language (discrete-time vs. real-time access). In Sect. 3, we show the advantage of adding parameterization to stream specification languages and briefly explain the challenges in monitoring parameterized stream specifications. Section 4 shows how real-time stream specification languages subsume real-time logics like STL [25], and the role of parameterization in encoding STL formulas in stream specification languages like RTLOLA. In Sect. 5, we give an overview of the various monitoring approaches for real-time properties. Finally, in Sect. 6, we conclude our survey with a brief discussion on the usage of stream-based languages in practice, and mention some works that have been done along this line.

2 Stream Specification Languages

A stream-based specification defines a runtime monitor by describing the relation between the values of input streams, entering the monitor, and the values of the output streams, computed by the monitor. For example, if an input stream contains the elevation values measured by an altimeter in some aerial vehicle, the monitor could compute the output stream that determines whether the measured elevations are below a certain altitude. In a telecommunication network, we may deploy a monitor that checks the frequency at which data is received on a node in the network over a period of time. The input stream to this monitor is the stream of data packets entering the node, and the output stream of the monitor is a stream of values where each value defines the number of packets that entered the network, for example, in the last second.

Stream specification languages are classified according to the type of monitors they can describe (Fig. 2). The distinction depends, in general, on *which* values are allowed to be used in the definition of the output stream, and *when* the values of an output stream are computed. With respect to what values can be used in the definition of streams, we can distinguish between languages that allow for the definition of *rule-based* monitors, or *memoryless* monitors, i.e., monitors which do not need to memorize any previous stream values to compute the new values, and languages that allow for the definition of *state-based* monitors, i.e., monitors that can maintain a memory of previous values that were computed by the monitor. In state-based monitors, we further distinguish between how previous values of streams are accessed in the stream definition. Stream accesses can be either in *discrete-time*, i.e., in the definition of the output stream, concrete previous values of other streams were accessed. A stream access can also be a *real-time* access, i.e., the output stream has access to the values of another stream that occurred over a certain period of time.

In addition to maintaining the necessary memory of values for the computation of output streams, we also have to specify when the values of an output stream are to be computed. Values of an output stream can, for example, be computed every time the monitor receives a new input value, or at certain fixed points or periods of time. The computation models for stream-based monitors can be categorized according to when input data arrives into the monitor and whether the computation of output values depends on the arrival times of input data. In general, we can distinguish between the *synchronous* and the *asynchronous* computation models. In the synchronous model, new data on different input streams arrive at the same time, and the values of output streams are computed with every arrival of new input data. A prominent example of monitoring problems with a synchronous computation model are network monitoring problems where the monitoring task is defined over the individual packets arriving to a node in the network. In the asynchronous computation model, input data on different input streams may arrive at different times and the values of the output streams may be computed independently of the arrival of input values. Such a computation model can be found in any cyber-physical system with different sensors that function at different rates.

In the following we will elaborate on each of these notions with the help the stream specification language RTLOLA [14]. RTLOLA is a state-based asynchronous stream specification language with real-time features that allows for the definition of monitors for real-time properties over rich datatypes. An RTLOLA specification defines a typed set of output streams given as a set of typed stream equations that map output stream names to expressions over input streams and other streams defined by the specification[1].

2.1   A Classification of Stream Specification Languages

Rule-Based vs. State-Based Specifications. We distinguish between two types of stream specification languages with respect to whether the computation of an output stream depends on previously computed values. *Rule-based*

---

[1] For the complete syntax of RTLOLA we refer the reader to www.stream-lab.org.

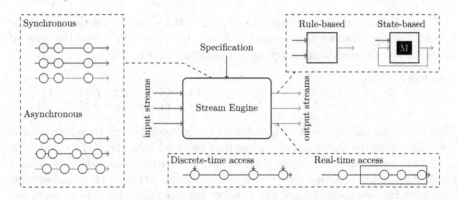

Fig. 2. Classification of stream specification languages.

languages are those specification languages that allow for the definition of memoryless monitors, i.e., computing the value of an output stream depends only on the current values of input streams and are independent from any history of values that have been computed up to that moment[2]. Monitors specified in a rule-based stream specification language are also known as stateless monitors and are very common in network intrusion detection [19,24].

An example of a rule-based stream-based monitor is given by the RTLOLA specification

```
input packet: IPv4
output empty_UDP: Bool := packet.isUDP() & packet.isEmpty()
```

Every time a data packet is received on the input stream `packet`, which represents the stream of packet traffic in some node in a network, a new event is computed for the output stream `empty_UDP`. If the packet is a UDP packet and has an empty payload, then the newly computed value of `empty_UDP` is true, otherwise it is false.

Another example of a rule-based stream definition is given by the following specification. Assume we want to monitor the vertical geofencing boundaries of a flying drone. A monitor for this task can be defined by the specification

```
input altimeter: UInt32
output too_low: Bool := altimeter < 100
```

For each value received from the altimeter, a new output value for the stream `too_low` is computed that registers whether the drone is flying below 100 ft.

Rule-based specification languages are easy to use and allow for the construction of simple and efficient monitors. They are, however, not suited for specifying complex monitoring tasks that need to maintain a state.

---

[2] The term memoryless here does not consider the memory needed to perform an operation on the current values of input streams in order to compute the value of the output stream, but refers the number of previous values that need to be stored to compute the current output value.

Consider for example a monitor that extends the vertical geofencing monitor by additionally counting the number of times the drone flew below the allowed height. A stream specification for such a monitor looks as follows

```
output count: UInt32 := if too_low
                        then count.offset(by: -1) + 1
                        else count.offset(by: -1)
```

The output stream represents a counter that is increased every time a new value is received from the altimeter, and when that value is below 100 ft. The new value of the stream count thus depends on its last computed value, which is defined in the RTLOLA specification by the expression count.offset(-1). To implement a monitor for this specification, the monitor needs to store the last value of the output stream in order to compute its new value.

Monitors that need to maintain a state can be defined using *state-based* specification languages like RTLOLA. State-based stream specification languages are powerful languages that combine the ease-of-use of rule-based specification languages with the expressive power of programming languages, when equipped with the right datatypes. State-based languages are common in state-based intrusion detection [12,27], or in developing mission control and flight managing tasks in UAVs [1].

Discrete-Time vs. Real-Time Stream Access. In state-based approaches a monitor may compute a value of an output stream depending on a history of values received on or computed over other streams, including the own history of the output stream. In the following we distinguish between the different types of stream access.

Accessing the values of other streams can be done in a discrete manner, i.e., the value of an output stream depends on certain previous values of some other stream. For example, in the stream count, the value of the stream depends on its own lastly computed value. A stream may also depend on the last n values of a stream, for example, when we want to compute a discrete sliding window over events. If we want to check whether the drone has been flying below the minimum altitude during the last three values received from the altimeter, we can define such a monitor using the following specification

```
output last_three: Bool :=
            too_low
        & too_low.offset(by: -1).defaults(to: false)
        & too_low.offset(by: -2).defaults(to: false)
```

Here, we access the current and, using the offset operator, the last and the before the last value of the stream too_low.

When using offset expressions to access previous values of a stream, we need to make sure that such values actually exist. A new value for the stream last_three is computed whenever a new value is computed for too_low. At the beginning of the monitoring process, the monitor may not have computed three values for too_low yet, because we have not received the necessary number of readings from the altimeter. Assume that we have received the first value over the input `altimeter`. Then, the values `too_low.offset(-1)` and `too_low.offset` `(-2)` are not yet defined. To still be able to evaluate the stream `last_three`, we need to divert to a fixed default value given in the specification above by the expression `defaults(to: false)`. This expression returns the value false when the stream expressions `too_low.offset(-1)` or `too_low.offset(-2)` are not defined.

Discrete offset expressions can also be used to access future values of streams. Consider for example a monitor that checks whether a drone reaches a specific waypoint with GPS coordinates (a, b), a geographic location the drone is commanded to fly to. A specification for such monitor is given as follows

```
input gps: (Float64,Float64)      // (latitude, longitude)
output reached_wp: Bool :=
            gps == (a,b) |
            reached_wp.offset(by: 1).defaults(to:false)
```

The monitor checks whether the current GPS coordinates match the targeted waypoint and if not repeats the check for the next received GPS value. In general, most of the monitors defined by stream specifications with future offsets can be defined with stream specifications with only past offsets. The future offsets are nevertheless convenient for encoding specifications given as formulas in temporal logics. One has to be careful however in using future offsets, as they introduce the possibility of defining ill-formed specifications, when they contain zero circular offset dependencies [9, 33].

An output stream may also depend on the values that occurred in a certain time interval. Real-time stream access can be achieved using real-time sliding windows, where an aggregation of events is computed over a fixed period of time. Consider for example a monitor that checks whether packets are received in large bursts. The specification of such a monitor can be given by the RTLOLA specification

```
input packet: IPv4
output burst: Bool :=
    packet.aggregate(over: 10sec, using: count)
    > threshold
```

For each new event received on the input stream `packet`, the monitor checks whether more than `threshold` many packets have been received over the input stream in the last 10 s.

Sliding windows can be implemented in two versions, *forward* and *backward* sliding windows. A backward sliding window of duration d is interpreted as in the last specification where the aggregate is defined over the values of the interval of d seconds until the last value arrived. Forward sliding windows consider the values in the period of length d starting with the time at which the last value arrived. Forward sliding windows are necessary for the specification of monitors that check timeouts. For example, to check whether the drone reaches a certain height h within d seconds we can specify the following monitor

```
input gps: (Float64,Float64)
input coordinate: (Float64,Float64)

output too_slow: Bool :=
    gps.aggregate(over: +2min, using: exists(coordinates))
```

where `exists(coordinates)` is syntactic sugar for an aggregation function that checks whether we received a value on the stream `coordinates` during a window of two minutes. Backward windows cannot be used to specify such monitoring tasks, at least not accurately, as they might miss some values (we explain this below). Backward sliding windows nevertheless come with the advantage that their computation does not have to be delayed as for the case of forward sliding windows, because they only rely on the events that have already been observed by the monitor. In general, one may use backward sliding windows to perform timeout checks, if the computational model of the specification language also allows to evaluate output streams at certain rates, as we will see later. This may come however at the cost of missing some windows, if the granularity in which the stream is computed is not small enough. We explain this with the help of the following example. Assume we want to check that there are no windows with a duration of one second that have events with values less than 3. A specification for such a monitor looks as follows

```
input x: UInt32
output y: UInt32 :=
                if x.aggregate(over: 1sec, using: max) <= 2
                then y.offset(by: -1).defaults(to: 0) + 1
                else y.offset(by: -1).defaults(to: 0)
```

Assume that we receive events 5, 4, 2, 2 on the stream x at times 0.1, 0.2, 0.6, and 1.4 s. A backward window approach will count 1 window with a maximum number of 2, namely when evaluating the stream at the arrival of the fourth event. A forward approach will count 2 windows when evaluated for the third an the fourth event. With the right rate, nevertheless, we can count the right number of windows, for example, if the output stream is computed every 0.5 s.

Synchronous vs. Asynchronous Computation Models. The evaluation of an output stream may depend on the values of several input streams. The computation of an output stream may thus depend on the arrival times of the input values. In general, we distinguish two computation models, the *synchronous* model and the *asynchronous* model.

In the synchronous model, events on all input streams arrive to the monitor at the same time. Output streams are evaluated with the arrival of new inputs values and thus are also evaluated simultaneously. Examples of systems with synchronous models are synchronous circuits and networks [9,13].

In the asynchronous model, the arrival times of inputs may vary from one input stream to another, and the computation of output streams does not necessarily depend on the arrival times of input values. In a cyber-physical system, for example, sensors may function at different frequencies, and thus data from these sensors arrive at different not necessarily synchronized rates. Computing the values of output streams may respect the arrival times of input values, or could completely be decoupled from them. In general, we distinguish two types of output streams with respect to their dependency on the rate in which input values reach the monitor, namely, *time-triggered* and *event-triggered* streams.

Time-Triggered Streams. In time-triggered output streams, values are computed at determined times, which are independent of the arrival of input values. These determined times can be periodic or dynamically determined. In periodic output streams, a new output is computed at a fixed frequency. Periodic monitors are associated with tasks for validating sensor frequencies in cyber-physical systems. For example, a monitor for checking whether a GPS sensor is delivering data in the right frequency can be specified as follows

```
input gps: (Float64,Float64)

output gps_glitch: UInt32 @ 1Hz:=
            gps.aggregate(over: 2sec, using: count)

trigger gps_glitch < 10 "GPS sensor: frequency < 5Hz"
```

The stream `gps` is an input stream that represents the values received from the GPS module and is expected to deliver data with a frequency greater than or equal to 5Hz. To check whether this data is delivered with the expected frequency, we define the output stream `gps_glitch`. A new value for the output stream `gps_glitch` is computed every second (the expression `@ 1Hz`), and at each time, it evaluates to the number of values received from the GPS module over a time window of two seconds, i.e., it computes the number of events received via the input stream `gps` (the expression `using: count`) over the last two seconds (the expression `over: 2sec`). The stream `trigger gps_glitch < 10` defines an assertion that evaluates to true when the value of `gps_glitch` is less than 10 (`trigger` is a special keyword adapted from the language LOLA [9] that raises an alarm and outputs a message in case the assertion is true).

Dynamically evaluated output streams allow further to use a function defined over streams to determine when to compute the next value of an output stream. An example of such a function is one that allows for the specification of streams where the output stream is delayed 5 s after `gps` received a new value[3]

```
output gps_glitch: UInt32 @ gps + 5 :=
            gps.aggregate(over: 2sec, using: count)
```

Event-Triggered Streams. In an event-triggered output stream, a new value is computed for this stream depending on the arrival times of new input events. An example of an event-triggered output stream is one where we extend our GPS

---

[3] The version of RTLola that is currently implemented in StreamLAB [14] does not allow for activation conditions with delay, but the implementation of such conditions is planned for the near future. Striver [17] and TeSSLa [8] have a native delay operator.

specification with a definition of an output stream that counts the number of glitches observed

```
output num_glitches: UInt32 :=
  if gps_glitch
    then num_glitched.offset(by: -1).defaults(to:0) + 1
    else num_glitches.offset(by: -1).defaults(to:0)
```

The specification defines a monitor that, with each new value computed for the stream gps_glitch, computes the number of glitches seen so far. This means that the pace in which num_glitches is computed is equal to the pace of gps_glitch.

If the output stream is defined over more than one input stream, then the new value of the output stream can be computed in different ways. In some cases it makes sense to use a hold semantics, where with each arrival of a new event on some input stream, the value of the output stream is computed with the latest values of all input streams. This is typical for monitors over piecewise constant signals. Piecewise constant signals can be represented as discrete signals where every change in the signal is a new event. In the continuous world, an operation over two piecewise constant signals result in a new piecewise constant signal that in each' point evaluates to the operation on the values of the two signals at that point. For example, if we have two signals $a : \mathbb{R}_{\geq 0} \to \mathbb{R}$ and $b : \mathbb{R}_{\geq 0} \to \mathbb{R}$, then the signal representing the sum of a and b, is a signal $s(t) = a(t) + b(t)$. To monitor whether the sum exceeds any threshold we construct the signal s and check if the value of s is larger than the threshold. Over the discrete representation, a monitor is given by the specification

```
input a: UInt32, b : UInt32
output exceededThreshold: Bool @ (a|b)
:= a.hold() + b.hold() > c
```

This output stream is evaluated every time a or b receives a new value. If a has a new value and b does not, then the value of the output stream is computed using the new value of a and the last received value of b. This is determined by the use of the access via the zero-order hold operator hold() which returns the last computed value of a stream. The condition a|b is called the activation condition. If the activation condition is empty then the stream is only computed if all values arrive at the same time.

Another advantage of the activation condition and the hold semantics is that in the case where the values of sensors arrive with slight delays, we can use the activation condition to evaluate the stream when the later value arrives and the hold operator to use the last value of the other sensor. Consider the following specification

```
input gps: (Float64,Float64)
input height: Float64
output too_low:Bool @ gps := if zone(gps)
  then (height.hold().defaults(to: 300)) < 300
  else false
```

where the function `zone` is some function that determines whether the drone is in an inhabited area. The output stream is evaluated every time the GPS sensor delivers a new value. The value of the stream `too_low` is determined using the last value of `height`.

2.2 Memory Analysis

To compute memory bounds on a monitor specified in RTLOLA, we need to analyze the stream accesses in the monitor's specification. For output streams that only use offset expressions to access other streams, memory bounds can be computed in the same way as for LOLA [9,33]. To give an idea on how these bounds are computed, we describe the process using the following examples.

Consider again the RTLOLA specification

```
output last_three: Bool :=
            too_low.offset
          & too_low.offset(by: -1).defaults(to: false)
          & too_low.offset(by: -2).defaults(to: false)
```

To evaluate an event of the output event `last_three`, we need the last three values of the streams `too_low`. This means that the monitor requires two memory units, where the last and the value before the last are saved, in order to be able to compute the values for the stream `last_three`.

Consider further the specification

```
input gps: (Float64,Float64)       // (latitude, longitude)
output reached_wp: bool :=
            gps == (a,b) |
            reached_wp.offset(by: 1).defaults(to:false)
```

To compute a value for the output stream `reached_wp`, the monitor checks whether the drone has reached the designated waypoint `(a,b)`, otherwise it will wait for the next values received from the GPS sensor to compute the current value of `reach_wp`. If the waypoint `(a,b)` is not reached, computing a value for `reached_wp` remains pending. This means that the monitor needs to save all unresolved values for `reached_wp` until the coordinates `(a,b)` are reached. In the hypothetical case that the drone will never reach these coordinates, the monitor needs to memorize an infinite number of unresolved values for `reached_wp`, which results in problems when the monitor is only offered a limited amount of memory to compute its streams.

The memory bounds can be automatically computed by constructing the annotated dependency graph of a specification [9]. The dependency graphs for the specifications above are depicted in Fig. 3. A RTLOLA specification is called efficiently computable, if we can determine memory bounds on the monitor specified by the specification. This is the case when the dependency graph of a specification does not contain any positive cycles. If an RTLOLA specification is efficiently computable, then we can compute the memory bounds for a stream by computing the maximum of the maximum added positive weights on a path

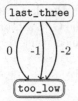

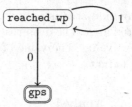

(a) An annotated dependency graph for the stream `last_three`. A monitor for `last_three` needs to save the last two events of `too_low`.

(b) An annotated dependency graph for the stream `reached_wp`. A monitor for `reached_wp` needs to save a possibly infinite number of unresolved expressions of itself.

Fig. 3. Annotated dependency graphs for the RTLOLA specifications of the streams `last_three` and `reached_wp`.

starting from the stream's node, or the maximum absolute value of the negative weights on edges exiting the node.

For specifications with sliding windows, and in the case of input streams with variable arrival rates, it is in general not possible to compute memory bounds on the monitors implementing these specifications. The reason for this lies in the fact that the number of events that may occur in a period of time might be arbitrary large. Nevertheless, in most cases the rates in which input data arrives on a an input stream are bounded by some frequency. If we do not know this frequency, we can still compute sliding windows efficiently by using periodic time-triggered streams. We use the following example to demonstrate how computing aggregates over sliding windows can be done with bounded memory[4]. Consider the specification

```
input packet: IPv4
output burst: Bool @ 1Hz:=
     packet.aggregate(over: 5 sec, using: count)
```

Instead of counting the number of packets that arrive within a window every time the sliding window needs to be evaluated, we split the window into intervals, called panes, and count the number of events in each pane [23]. When we compute the aggregate for a new window, we reuse the values of the panes that overlap with the new window to compute the new aggregate. Figure 4 illustrates the computation of the sliding window for our specification above. The memory needed for computing the aggregate count over the sliding window is bounded by five memory units that save the aggregate for each of the five one-second panes. Each second the window moves by one second to the right. To compute the aggregate over the new window, we just need to remove the value of the first pane form the value of the last window and add the value of a new pane that includes all events that arrived within the last second. The first pane of the last

---

[4] For more on the implementation of sliding windows we refer the reader to [5,14,23].

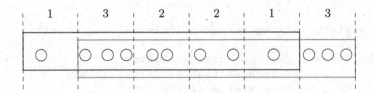

Fig. 4. Efficient computation of the aggregate count over a sliding window over 10 s that is computed in periods of one second. The value of the new window is equal to $9 - 1 + 3$, where 9 is the value of the aggregation over the last window.

window can be removed from memory and the value of the new pane is saved instead.

Splitting windows into panes showed to be very useful in practice [7,14]. However, it can only be applied to aggregation functions that fulfill certain properties [14]. The approach would for example not work for aggregation functions such as the median. Nevertheless, from our experience most aggregation functions used in practice can be efficiently solved by this approach. These include aggregation function such as count, sum, max, min and integral.

3   Parameterized Stream Specifications

In many cases, the same monitoring task has to be performed for multiple sets of data. For example, in an online platform with a large user base, we might want to compute the same statistics over the different user groups of the platform, distinguished by age, gender, or geographic location. To compute the statistic for each group we can define an output stream for each user group, but this results in unnecessary redundant stream definitions. The redundancy can be avoided by defining one stream using appropriate datatypes such as sets, maps, etc. This, however, may result in incomprehensible specifications and cumbersome extra work for managing the complex datatypes. Furthermore, when the statistics need to be computed separately for each individual user, writing different stream definitions for each user is not feasible and managing the computation in one stream results in a large overhead caused by updating the complex datatypes.

To overcome this problem, we can define parameterized monitoring templates, from which new monitors can be instantiated every time we want to perform the monitoring task for a specific user. Parameterized stream specifications allow for the dynamic construction of streams, when these streams are needed, and that run on their own individual pace.

Consider, for example, the following parameterized RTLOLA specification for monitoring the log-in's of users to some online platform

```
input user_activity: UInt32

output timeout(id: UInt32): Bool @ 1min
close timeout(id)
```

```
:=
user_activity.aggregate(over: 10min, using: count(id)) == 0

output logout: UInt32 @ user_activity :=
              if timeout(user_activity).hold()
              then user_activity
              else -1
```

The specification defines an output stream template timeout with one parameter id of type UInt32. An instance of the template timeout is a stream timeout(x) for a concrete value x of type UInt32. At the beginning, there are no instances for the template timeout, and instances for a concrete value x are only created when they are called by the stream logout. Every time a new user id is observed on the input stream user_activity, the stream logout calls the value of the instance timeout(user_activity). If the instance has not been created yet, then a new instance with the current value of user_activity is created and evaluated according to the expression of timeout with respect to the new parameter value. Here, the new instance evaluates to true, if the user with the id user_activity has not been active in the last 10 min. If the instance already exists, then logout is evaluated according to the last value computed for the instance. If a user with id x has not been active for more than 10 min, the instance timeout(x) is terminated, as defined by the termination expression close: timeout(id).

Memory bounds for parameterized stream specifications can be computed in the same way as for non-parameterized ones, with the significant difference, that the memory bounds determine the size of memory needed to compute each instance. The number of instances created by the monitor, and the number of instances that are active simultaneously depends highly on the application. In general, the number is limited, as most created streams define simple monitoring tasks that reach a verdict quickly. In the case, where the monitor is forced to produce a large number of instances at once, it is recommended to force the termination of instances after a period of time.

4 Embedding Real-Time Logics in RTLOLA Using Parameterized Specifications

Stream specification languages like LOLA that provide operators for referencing values in the future subsume temporal logics like LTL [9]. LTL is a linear-time logic that allows us to define properties over traces using boolean and temporal operators. Temporal operators in LTL are used to reason about time and are given by the operator "next" ($\bigcirc\varphi$), that states that a certain property φ must hold in the next step, and the operator "until" ($\varphi\,\mathcal{U}\,\psi$) that states that a property φ must hold until another property ψ is satisfied. The temporal operators can be specified in RTLOLA by the following stream specifications

```
output next: Bool := phi.offset(1).defaults(to: true)
```

```
output until: Bool :=
          psi |
          (phi & until.offset(1).defaults(to: false))
```

where phi and psi are stream definitions for the formulas φ and ψ.

For real-time logics like STL [25], the offset operator does not suffice as we need to check the values of signals at certain points in time. In the following we show how we can use parameterized RTLOLA specifications to encode STL specifications over piece-wise constant signals. The next definition gives a short recap on the syntax of STL.

Definition 1 (Signal Temporal Logic [25]). *An STL formula φ over signals $x_1, \ldots, x_m \in \mathbb{R}_{\geq 0} \to \mathbb{R}$ is given by the grammar*

$$\varphi = \mu \mid \neg\varphi \mid \varphi \vee \varphi \mid \varphi\,\mathcal{U}_{[a,b]}\,\varphi$$

where μ is a predicate from $\mathbb{R} \to \mathbb{B}$ with $\mu(t) = f(x_1[t], \ldots, x_m[t]) > 0$ for some function $f : \mathbb{R}^m \to \mathbb{R}$.

Given piecewise-constant signals $x_1, \ldots, x_m$, an STL formula φ, and predicates $\mu_1, \ldots, \mu_n$ we can encode the monitoring problem for φ in RTLOLA using the following recursively defined translations:

- x_i for $1 \leq x \leq m$:

```
input x_i: Float64
```

where x_i receives a new event every time the signal x_i changes its value.

- μ_j for $1 \leq j \leq n$:

```
output mu_j(t: Time): Bool @ any :=
             f(x_1.hold(),...,x_m.hold())>0
```

where f is an operation that defines the value of f. The stream template mu_j defines streams that represents the values of the expression f(x_1,...,x_m) starting at time t. Once a stream has be created, it is evaluated every time one of the streams x_i receives a new value (abbreviated by the word any).

- $\neg\varphi$:

```
output nphi(t: Time): Bool := !phi(t)
```

The stream computes the negated values of the stream phi(t), and is evaluated at the pace of phi.

– $\varphi_1 \vee \varphi_2$:

```
output orphi1phi2(t: Time): Bool @ any
:= phi1(t).hold() | phi2(t).hold()
```

The stream computes the disjunction of the streams phi1 and phi2.

– $\varphi_1 \mathcal{U}_{[a,b]} \varphi_2$. For such a formula, we need to check whether the formula φ_2 is true at some point $t \in [a, b]$, and the formula φ_1 must hold up to the point t. If φ_2 is also an until formula defined for some interval $[c, d]$ then the validity of φ_2 must then be checked relative to the time t. This is encoded in RTLOLA as follows.

```
output unitlphi1phi2(t: Time) : Bool @ (t+b)| any
close: time == b | !unitlphi1phi2(t)
:=
if time <= t+a
  then
    phi1<time>.hold() & unitlphi1phi2[a,b](t).offset(1)
  else
    if time < t+b
    then
      phi1(time).hold() &
      (phi2(time).hold() |
        unitlphi1phi2[a,b](t).offset(1))
    else
      phi1(time).hold() & phi2(time).hold()

trigger unitlphi1phi2[a,b](0)
```

The complete STL formula must hold at time 0. Therefore we check the value of the formula by calling the stream unitlphi1phi2[a,b](0). An instance unitlphi1phi2(x) is evaluated whenever a value of one of its substreams is computed or when reaching the time mark $x + b$. The evaluation at $x + b$ is necessary for the case that none of the signals change their values up to that point. At every evaluation point of unitlphi1phi2(x), we check in which time interval we are. If the current time is smaller than $x + a$, then we check that the value of phi1(x) is true. If this is the case, we check the validity of the right formula in the designated future interval $[a, b]$ by calling unitlphi1phi2 [a,b].offset(1). If we arrive at the time interval $[x + a, x + b]$ we check again whether the left formula still holds, and whether the right formula holds. If we exceed the time $x + b$ and the right formula has not been true yet then the stream is evaluated to false.

At each time t, where the instance is evaluated, new instances with parameter instantiation t are created for the subformulas. All instances are terminated once their intervals are exceeded.

Remark 1. Formulas in STL can also be encoded without the usage of parameterized stream definition, if the stream specification language allows for the definition of activation conditions where the evaluation of a stream can be set to certain points in time. Such activation conditions can be defined in languages like Striver [17].

5   Bibliographic Remarks

Most of the early work on formal runtime monitoring was based on temporal logics [11,16,18,21]. The approaches vary between inline methods that realize a formal specification as assertions added to the code to be monitored [18], or outline approaches that separate the implementation of the monitor from the one of the system under investigation [16]. Based on these approaches and with the rise of real-time temporal logics such as MTL [20] and STL [25], a series of works introduced new algorithms and tools for the monitoring of real-time properties described in one of the previous logics [3,4,6,10,26,32].

The stream-based approach to monitoring was pioneered by the specification language LOLA [9,33], a descriptive language, that can express both past and future properties. The main feature of LOLA is that upper bounds on the memory required for monitoring can be computed statically. RTLOLA extends LOLA with real-time features, such as sliding windows and time-triggered stream definitions, and allows for the definition of monitors with an asynchronous computation model. RTLOLA adapts the memory analysis techniques provided by LOLA, and extends those techniques for determining memory bounds for the new real-time features added to the language.

Further real-time stream specification languages based on LOLA were introduced with the languages TeSSLa and Striver. TeSSLa [22] allows for monitoring piece-wise constant signals where streams can emit events at different speeds with arbitrary latencies. TeSSLa has a native delay operator that allows for the definition of future times in which streams shall be computed. The version of RTLola that is currently implemented in the tool StreamLAB [14] does not yet have such a delay operator. On the other hand, TeSSLa does not have native support for real-time features such as the definition of sliding windows. Striver, is a stream specification language that allows the definition of involved activation conditions, that especially allow for the definition of timeout specifications. Using a tagging mechanism and the delay operator in Striver, one can define forward sliding windows. There is however no native operator in the language for the definition of sliding windows, for which built-in efficient algorithms are implemented, as in the case of RTLOLA.

Further stream-based specification languages with real-time features include the languages Copilot [28], which allow for the definition of monitors based on the synchronous computation model. Prominent specification languages specialized for specifying monitors for network intrusion detection include the frameworks Bro [27] and snort [31].

6   Conclusion

In this tutorial, we gave an overview of the different classes of stream specification languages for specifying monitors for real-time properties, and demonstrated, with the help of the stream specification languages RTLOLA, which features allow for the definition of monitors for the different types of real-time properties. We further discussed the construction of memory efficient monitors and showed how memory bounds can be computed for monitors written in the stream specification language RTLOLA. Finally we discussed parametric extensions to stream specification languages and showed that real-time logics such as STL are subsumed by RTLOLA with parameterization.

From our experience, stream specification languages like RTLOLA are well received by practitioners [1,34,35]. The outline monitoring approach given by stream-based monitors allows for the separation between the monitoring component and the system under scrutiny, which has the advantage of not interfering with the functionality of the system. Furthermore, stream specification languages provide a specification framework that is simple to use, easy to understand and one that combines features of high expressive scripting languages that are used in industry with important features of formal languages such as computing memory bounds.

Acknowledgements. I would like to thank Bernd Finkbeiner, Norine Coenen, Christopher Hahn, Maximilian Schwenger and Leander Tentrup for their valuable feedback and comments.

References

1. Adolf, F.-M., Faymonville, P., Finkbeiner, B., Schirmer, S., Torens, C.: Stream runtime monitoring on UAS. In: Lahiri, S., Reger, G. (eds.) RV 2017. LNCS, vol. 10548, pp. 33–49. Springer, Cham (2017). https://doi.org/10.1007/978-3-319-67531-2_3
2. Alur, R., Henzinger, T.A.: Logics and models of real time: a survey. In: de Bakker, J.W., Huizing, C., de Roever, W.P., Rozenberg, G. (eds.) REX 1991. LNCS, vol. 600, pp. 74–106. Springer, Heidelberg (1992). https://doi.org/10.1007/BFb0031988. http://dl.acm.org/citation.cfm?id=648143.749966
3. Basin, D., Klaedtke, F., Müller, S., Zălinescu, E.: Monitoring metric first-order temporal properties. J. ACM **62**(2), 15:1–15:45 (2015). https://doi.org/10.1145/2699444
4. Basin, D., Harvan, M., Klaedtke, F., Zălinescu, E.: MONPOLY: monitoring usage-control policies. In: Khurshid, S., Sen, K. (eds.) RV 2011. LNCS, vol. 7186, pp. 360–364. Springer, Heidelberg (2012). https://doi.org/10.1007/978-3-642-29860-8_27
5. Basin, D.A., Klaedtke, F., Marinovic, S., Zalinescu, E.: Monitoring of temporal first-order properties with aggregations. Formal Methods Syst. Des. **46**(3), 262–285 (2015). https://doi.org/10.1007/s10703-015-0222-7
6. Basin, D.A., Krstic, S., Traytel, D.: AERIAL: Almost event-rate independent algorithms for monitoring metric regular properties. In: RV-CuBES. Kalpa Publications in Computing, vol. 3, pp. 29–36. EasyChair (2017)

7. Baumeister, J., Finkbeiner, B., Schwenger, M., Torfah, H.: FPGA stream-monitoring of real-time properties. In: ESWEEK-TECS special issue, International Conference on Embedded Software EMSOFT 2019, New York, USA, October 13–18 (2019)
8. Convent, L., Hungerecker, S., Leucker, M., Scheffel, T., Schmitz, M., Thoma, D.: TeSSLa: temporal stream-based specification language. In: Massoni, T., Mousavi, M.R. (eds.) SBMF 2018. LNCS, vol. 11254, pp. 144–162. Springer, Cham (2018). https://doi.org/10.1007/978-3-030-03044-5_10
9. D'Angelo, B., et al.: LOLA: runtime monitoring of synchronous systems. In: 12th International Symposium on Temporal Representation and Reasoning (TIME 2005), pp. 166–174. IEEE Computer Society Press, June 2005
10. Deshmukh, J.V., Donzé, A., Ghosh, S., Jin, X., Juniwal, G., Seshia, S.A.: Robust online monitoring of signal temporal logic. In: Bartocci, E., Majumdar, R. (eds.) RV 2015. LNCS, vol. 9333, pp. 55–70. Springer, Cham (2015). https://doi.org/10.1007/978-3-319-23820-3_4
11. Drusinsky, D.: The temporal rover and the ATG rover. In: Havelund, K., Penix, J., Visser, W. (eds.) SPIN 2000. LNCS, vol. 1885, pp. 323–330. Springer, Heidelberg (2000). https://doi.org/10.1007/10722468_19. http://dl.acm.org/citation.cfm?id=645880.672089
12. Eckmann, S.T., Vigna, G., Kemmerer, R.A.: STATL: an attack language for state-based intrusion detection. J. Comput. Secur. 10(1–2), 71–103 (2002). http://dl.acm.org/citation.cfm?id=597917.597921
13. Faymonville, P., Finkbeiner, B., Schirmer, S., Torfah, H.: A stream-based specification language for network monitoring. In: Falcone, Y., Sánchez, C. (eds.) RV 2016. LNCS, vol. 10012, pp. 152–168. Springer, Cham (2016). https://doi.org/10.1007/978-3-319-46982-9_10
14. Faymonville, P., Finkbeiner, B., Schledjewski, M., Schwenger, M., Stenger, M., Tentrup, L., Torfah, H.: StreamLAB: stream-based monitoring of cyber-physical systems. In: Dillig, I., Tasiran, S. (eds.) CAV 2019. LNCS, vol. 11561, pp. 421–431. Springer, Cham (2019). https://doi.org/10.1007/978-3-030-25540-4_24
15. Faymonville, P., Finkbeiner, B., Schwenger, M., Torfah, H.: Real-time stream-based monitoring. ArXiv abs/1711.03829 (2017)
16. Finkbeiner, B., Sipma, H.: Checking finite traces using alternating automata. Form. Methods Syst. Des. 24(2), 101–127 (2004). https://doi.org/10.1023/B:FORM.0000017718.28096.48
17. Gorostiaga, F., Sánchez, C.: Striver: stream runtime verification for real-time event-streams. In: Colombo, C., Leucker, M. (eds.) RV 2018. LNCS, vol. 11237, pp. 282–298. Springer, Cham (2018). https://doi.org/10.1007/978-3-030-03769-7_16
18. Havelund, K., Roşu, G.: Synthesizing monitors for safety properties. In: Katoen, J.-P., Stevens, P. (eds.) TACAS 2002. LNCS, vol. 2280, pp. 342–356. Springer, Heidelberg (2002). https://doi.org/10.1007/3-540-46002-0_24. http://dl.acm.org/citation.cfm?id=646486.694486
19. Hindy, H., et al.: A taxonomy and survey of intrusion detection system design techniques, network threats and datasets. ArXiv abs/1806.03517 (2018)
20. Koymans, R.: Specifying real-time properties with metric temporal logic. Real-Time Syst. 2(4), 255–299 (1990). https://doi.org/10.1007/BF01995674
21. Lee, I., Kannan, S., Kim, M., Sokolsky, O., Viswanathan, M.: Runtime assurance based on formal specifications. In: Proceedings of the International Conference on Parallel and Distributed Processing Techniques and Applications (1999)

22. Leucker, M., Sánchez, C., Scheffel, T., Schmitz, M., Schramm, A.: TeSSLa: runtime verification of non-synchronized real-time streams. In: Proceedings of the 33rd Annual ACM Symposium on Applied Computing, SAC 2018, pp. 1925–1933. ACM, New York, NY, USA (2018). https://doi.org/10.1145/3167132.3167338

23. Li, J., Maier, D., Tufte, K., Papadimos, V., Tucker, P.A.: No pane, no gain: efficient evaluation of sliding-window aggregates over data streams. SIGMOD Rec. **34**(1), 39–44 (2005). https://doi.org/10.1145/1058150.1058158

24. Liao, H.J., Lin, C.H.R., Lin, Y.C., Tung, K.Y.: Intrusion detection system: a comprehensive review. J. Netw. Comput. Appl. **36**(1), 16–24 (2013). https://doi.org/10.1016/j.jnca.2012.09.004

25. Maler, O., Nickovic, D.: Monitoring temporal properties of continuous signals. In: Lakhnech, Y., Yovine, S. (eds.) FORMATS/FTRTFT -2004. LNCS, vol. 3253, pp. 152–166. Springer, Heidelberg (2004). https://doi.org/10.1007/978-3-540-30206-3_12

26. Nickovic, D., Maler, O.: AMT: a property-based monitoring tool for analog systems. In: Raskin, J.-F., Thiagarajan, P.S. (eds.) FORMATS 2007. LNCS, vol. 4763, pp. 304–319. Springer, Heidelberg (2007). https://doi.org/10.1007/978-3-540-75454-1_22

27. Paxson, V.: Bro: a system for detecting network intruders in real-time. In: Proceedings of the 7th Conference on USENIX Security Symposium, SSYM 1998, vol. 7, p. 3. USENIX Association, Berkeley, CA, USA (1998). http://dl.acm.org/citation.cfm?id=1267549.1267552

28. Pike, L., Goodloe, A., Morisset, R., Niller, S.: Copilot: a hard real-time runtime monitor. In: Barringer, H., Falcone, Y., Finkbeiner, B., Havelund, K., Lee, I., Pace, G., Roşu, G., Sokolsky, O., Tillmann, N. (eds.) RV 2010. LNCS, vol. 6418, pp. 345–359. Springer, Heidelberg (2010). https://doi.org/10.1007/978-3-642-16612-9_26

29. Pnueli, A.: The temporal logic of programs. In: Proceedings of the 18th Annual Symposium on Foundations of Computer Science, SFCS 1977, pp. 46–57. IEEE Computer Society, Washington, DC, USA (1977). https://doi.org/10.1109/SFCS.1977.32

30. Reinbacher, T., Rozier, K.Y., Schumann, J.: Temporal-logic based runtime observer pairs for system health management of real-time systems. In: Ábrahám, E., Havelund, K. (eds.) TACAS 2014. LNCS, vol. 8413, pp. 357–372. Springer, Heidelberg (2014). https://doi.org/10.1007/978-3-642-54862-8_24

31. Roesch, M.: Snort - lightweight intrusion detection for networks. In: Proceedings of the 13th USENIX Conference on System Administration, LISA 1999, pp. 229–238. USENIX Association, Berkeley, CA, USA (1999). http://dl.acm.org/citation.cfm?id=1039834.1039864

32. Rozier, K.Y., Schumann, J.: R2U2: tool overview. In: RV-CuBES. Kalpa Publications in Computing, vol. 3, pp. 138–156. EasyChair (2017)

33. Sánchez, C.: Online and offline stream runtime verification of synchronous systems. In: Colombo, C., Leucker, M. (eds.) RV 2018. LNCS, vol. 11237, pp. 138–163. Springer, Cham (2018). https://doi.org/10.1007/978-3-030-03769-7_9

34. Schirmer, S., Benders, S.: Using runtime monitoring to enhance offline analysis. In: Proceedings of the Workshops of the Software Engineering Conference 2019, Stuttgart, Germany, 19 February 2019, pp. 83–86 (2019). http://ceur-ws.org/Vol-2308/aviose2019paper05.pdf

35. Torens, C., Adolf, F., Faymonville, P., Schirmer, S.: Towards intelligent system health management using runtime monitoring. In: AIAA Information Systems-AIAA Infotech @ Aerospace. American Institute of Aeronautics and Astronautics (AIAA), January 2017. https://doi.org/10.2514/6.2017-0419

Accelerated Learning of Predictive Runtime Monitors for Rare Failure

Reza Babaee$^{(\boxtimes)}$, Vijay Ganesh, and Sean Sedwards

Electrical and Computer Engineering, University of Waterloo, Waterloo, Canada
{rbabaeec,vijay.ganesh,sean.sedwards}@uwaterloo.ca

Abstract. Predictive runtime verification estimates the probability of a future event by monitoring the executions of a system. In this paper we use Discrete-Time Markov Chains (DTMC) as predictive models that are trained from many execution samples demonstrating a rare event: an event that occurs with very low probability. More specifically, we propose a method of grammar inference by which a DTMC is learned with far fewer samples than normal sample distribution. We exploit the concept of *importance sampling*, and use a mixture of samples, generated from the original system distribution and distributions that are suitably modified to produce more failures. Using the *likelihood ratios* of the various samples, we ensure the final trained model is faithful to the original distribution. In this way we construct accurate predictive models with orders of magnitude fewer samples. We demonstrate the gains of our approach on a file transmission protocol case study from the literature, and highlight future directions.

1 Introduction

In conventional Runtime Verification (RV) [22], a *monitor* observes a finite prefix of an execution of a system and checks it against a given property specified in some form of temporal logic. The monitor accepts (or rejects) the prefix if all infinite extensions of the prefix belong (resp. do not belong) to the set of infinite paths satisfying the property [6]. Otherwise, the monitor outputs *unknown* until the property is either satisfied or falsified [5]. RV is an effective means of monitoring and analyzing black-box systems [23,33] as well as when there exists a compact executable description of a system whose state space is intractable [20]. The scope of the current paper is the latter.

In contrast to traditional RV, *predictive* RV [2] uses a model to predict extensions of an observed prefix of an execution of a system. The model is trained by observing previous execution samples that demonstrate the relevant behaviour. The trained model is then used to construct a predictive monitor, which estimates at runtime the probability of a future failure.

The challenge we address in this paper is when failure is *rare*, i.e., when it has low probability. This is generally the case in real-world applications, where failure is usually designed to be very rare (e.g., the violation of a safety property [35]). Training an accurate prediction model for rare events therefore poses problems

© Springer Nature Switzerland AG 2019
B. Finkbeiner and L. Mariani (Eds.): RV 2019, LNCS 11757, pp. 111–128, 2019.
https://doi.org/10.1007/978-3-030-32079-9_7

for conventional statistical learning, precisely because they occur very rarely, requiring many and/or long traces to adequately characterize the rare event.

To construct our predictive monitor we use *grammar inference* [12], which can produce accurate probabilistic models from observed executions of a system. In [8] the authors propose the ALERGIA algorithm to learn a probabilistic automaton that reproduces the grammar observed in a set of stochastically-generated traces of the language. The idea is to first construct a *Frequency Prefix Tree Acceptor* (FPTA) from the samples and to label its edges with the frequencies that the corresponding prefixes are observed. According to a metric of compatibility based on these frequencies, using the Hoeffding bound [13], nodes in the tree are then folded and merged into one another to form an automaton. To construct models suitable for verification, the AALERGIA algorithm of [24] adopts a different metric, based on Angluin's bound [1], and uses a Bayesian Information Criterion to select the best model.

To address the problem of predicting rare events, we adapt the above approaches and propose a solution that adopts notions from *importance sampling* [29, 30] (IS) to accelerate the learning of an accurate model of rare failures. IS is a standard technique by which a measure of an "inconvenient" probabilistic distribution is estimated by sampling from a "convenient" (IS) distribution over the same sample space. Typically, the inconvenience arises because the measure of interest is a rare event and the convenient distribution makes the rare event more likely. Samples are drawn from the IS distribution and compensated on the fly to give an accurate estimate of the rare event, but with fewer samples.

Optimizing the system distribution for a rare event can make normal behaviour rare, with the corresponding parts of the state space poorly covered by simulations, and consequently increasing the number of false positives by the monitor. To construct a good predictive model that adequately covers all the relevant parts of the state space, it may be necessary to use samples from more than one distribution, e.g., from the original system distribution as well as the distribution that favours the rare event. Our approach therefore allows arbitrarily many simulations from arbitrarily many distributions to be combined in a training set, using their *likelihood ratios* [30, Ch. 5] to ensure their correct contribution to the final model.

Our approach assumes that the monitored system has inputs or accessible parameters that allow its behaviour to be modified, and that there is a well-defined likelihood ratio between its behaviour before and after modification. Systems of this nature are common in the Statistical Model Checking (SMC) literature (see e.g., [18]), noting that SMC does not inherently provide means of predictive verification. With the above assumption, it is possible, within the context of RV, to optimize the parameters of the system with respect to the rare event, without access to the explicit representation of the state space. E.g., starting with randomly chosen parameters and knowing how the parameters affect the likelihood ratio, it is possible to find optimal parameters using an iterative algorithm based on cross-entropy minimization [14,18]. It is also possible to create effective IS distributions using heuristics, e.g., by locally balancing the transition probabilities from all states or by increasing the probabilities of specific critical transitions. Further discussion of IS distributions, however, is beyond the scope of the current work, so in what follows we assume that such a distribution has been obtained and that sample traces can be drawn from it.

Summary of Contributions:

- Given a training set assembled from samples of various distributions that cover the normal and rare behaviour, we propose an approach to construct a Weighted Prefix Tree Acceptor (WPTA) based on the likelihood ratio of each sample.
- We adapt standard grammar inference algorithms, e.g., A(A)LERGIA, to build a discrete-time Markov Chain (DTMC) from the WPTA, to act as a predictive model.
- We demonstrate our approach on a file transmission protocol [11], predicting the failure of a sender to report a successful transmission.

2 Preliminaries

In this section we briefly introduce definitions and notations. A probability distribution over a finite set S is a function $P : S \to [0,1]$ such that $\sum_{s \in S} P(s) = 1$. We use u and w to, respectively, denote a finite and an infinite path. We use Σ^* and Σ^ω to denote the set of finite and infinite paths over the finite alphabet Σ.

Definition 1 (FPTA). *A Frequency Prefix Tree Acceptor (FPTA) is a tuple $\mathcal{A} : (Q, \Sigma, Fr_I, \delta, Fr_F, Fr_T)$, where Q is a non-empty finite set of states, Σ is a non-empty finite alphabet, $Fr_I : Q \to \mathbb{N}$ is the initial frequency of the state(s), $\delta : Q \times \Sigma \to Q$ is the transition function, $Fr_F : Q \to \mathbb{N}$ is the final frequency of the state(s), and $Fr_T : Q \times \Sigma \times Q \to \mathbb{N}$ is the transition frequency function between two states.*

Definition 2 (PFA). *A Probabilistic Finite Automaton (PFA) is a tuple $\mathcal{A} : (Q, \Sigma, \pi, \delta, \mathbf{P}_T, \mathbf{P}_F)$, where Q is a non-empty finite set of states, Σ is a non-empty finite alphabet, $\pi : Q \to [0,1]$ is the initial probability distribution over Q, $\delta : Q \times \Sigma \to Q$ is the transition function that maps the state-symbol pair to another state, $\mathbf{P}_T : Q \times \Sigma \to [0,1]$ is the transition probability distribution, and $\mathbf{P}_F : Q \to [0,1]$ is the final probability distribution, such that for any $q \in Q$, $\mathbf{P}_T(q, \cdot) + \mathbf{P}_F(q)$ is a probability distribution.*

Definition 3 (DTMC). *A Discrete-Time Markov Chain (DTMC) is a tuple $\mathcal{M} : (S, \Sigma, \pi, \mathbf{P}, L)$, where S is a non-empty finite set of states, Σ is a non-empty finite alphabet, $\pi : S \to [0,1]$ is the initial probability distribution over S, $\mathbf{P} : S \times S \to [0,1]$ is the transition probability, such that for any $s \in S$, $\mathbf{P}(s, \cdot)$ is a probability distribution, and $L : S \to \Sigma$ is the labeling function.*

Let $\mathcal{M}$ be a DTMC. The sequence $\sigma_0 \sigma_1 \ldots$ is an execution path on $\mathcal{M}$ iff $\mathbf{P}(s_i, s_{i+1}) > 0$, where $L(s_i) = \sigma_i, i \geq 0$. An execution path can be finite or infinite. The probability measure of a finite path u on $\mathcal{M}$ is defined as

$Pr_{\mathcal{M}}(u) = \prod_{i \in [0,n]} \mathbf{P}(s_i, s_{i+1})$. The probability distribution over the infinite executions, $Pr_{\mathcal{M}}(w), w \in \Sigma^{\omega}$, is defined using the probability measure over the cylinder sets with the prefixes of w obtained from $\mathcal{M}$ [20].

3 Importance Sampling

In this section we briefly introduce the concepts of importance sampling (IS) that are necessary for the sequel.

Given a stochastic system with distribution $F \colon \Sigma^* \to [0,1]$, from which we may draw random samples $u \in \Sigma^*$ according to F, denoted $u \sim F$, and an indicator function $\mathbf{1}_{\varphi} \colon \Sigma^* \to \{0,1\}$ that returns 1 iff u satisfies some property φ, then the probability of satisfying φ under F, denoted $\mathrm{P}_F(\varphi)$, can be estimated using the standard Monte Carlo (MC) estimator,

$$\mathrm{P}_F(\varphi) \approx \frac{1}{N} \sum_{i=1}^{N} \mathbf{1}_{\varphi}(u_i), \text{ with } u_i \sim F. \tag{1}$$

$N \in \mathbb{N}$ *independent and identically distributed* (*iid*) samples, $u_1, \ldots, u_N$, are drawn at random according to F and evaluated with respect to φ. The proportion of samples that satisfy φ is an unbiased estimate of $\mathrm{P}_F(\varphi)$.

If satisfying φ is a rare event under F, i.e., $\mathrm{P}_F(\varphi) \ll 1$, the number of samples must be set very large to estimate $\mathrm{P}_F(\varphi)$ with low *relative* error [30, Chap. 1]. The intuition of this is given by the fact that N must be greater than or equal to $1/\mathrm{P}_F(\varphi)$ to expect to see at least one sample that satisfies φ.

Given another distribution, $G \colon \Sigma^* \to [0,1]$, such that $\mathbf{1}_{\varphi}F$ is *absolutely continuous* with respect to G, $\mathrm{P}_F(\varphi)$ can be estimated using the importance sampling estimator,

$$\mathrm{P}_F(\varphi) \approx \frac{1}{N} \sum_{i=1}^{N} \mathbf{1}_{\varphi}(u_i) \frac{F(u_i)}{G(u_i)}, \text{ with } u_i \sim G. \tag{2}$$

N samples are drawn according to G and the proportion that satisfy φ is compensated by the *likelihood ratio*, F/G. Absolute continuity of $\mathbf{1}_{\varphi}F$ with respect to G requires that for all $u \in \Sigma^*$, $G(u) = 0 \implies \mathbf{1}_{\varphi}(u)F(u) = 0$. This guarantees that (2) is always well defined. If φ is not a rare event under G, (2) will typically converge faster than (1). Under these circumstances, the IS estimator (2) is said to have lower variance than the standard MC estimator (1). Equation (2) is the basis of Statistical Model Checking (SMC) tools that use IS [7,15].

We call F the original distribution and G the IS distribution, using these symbols as synonyms for the explicit terms in the remainder of this section. Later, we also use the terms MC and IS to distinguish simulations or models generated from the original and importance sampling distributions, respectively.

In the present context, we assume that F and G are members of a family of distributions generated by two DTMCs, having different sets of transition probabilities over a common set of states and transitions. We can thus talk

(a) Reference DTMC with low error rate.

trace	freq.	trace	freq.
i, s	20	i, m	10
i, s, s	15	i, m, m	2
i, s, s, s	15	i, m, s	2
i, s, s, s, s	15	i, m, s, s	4
i, s, s, s, s, s	15	i, m, s, s, s	2

(b) Training set randomly generated from the model in Fig. 1(a).

Fig. 1. Running example.

about the likelihood ratio of a trace as well as of an individual transition, which is defined as the ratio of the transition's probability under F divided by its probability under G. Absolute continuity implies that every zero probability transition in G corresponds to a zero probability transition in F or a transition that does not occur in a trace that satisfies φ.

4   Running Example

Figure 1 describes the running example used throughout the paper. Figure 1(a) depicts a DTMC, $\mathcal{M}$, with four states, labelled i, m, e and s representing the *initial, middle, error,* and *success* states, respectively.

The training dataset, $\mathcal{D}$, contains samples that are randomly generated from $\mathcal{M}$. Each sample $u \in \mathcal{D}$ is a finite prefix of a random infinite path $w \in \Sigma^\omega$ representing a random variable from the distribution $Pr_\mathcal{M}$. The length of the samples is positive, unbounded, and selected randomly and independently of the sample itself. That is, the execution ends at a time independent of the behaviour of the system, with some fixed probability greater than zero [24].

Figure 1(b) shows a training set containing 100 samples from the DTMC in Fig. 1(a). The probability of *eventually* error from the initial state is less than 0.01, explaining why there is no instance in the samples. For the sake of illustration, we assume that this error is a rare event.

5   Training on Rare-Event Samples

Inferring the probabilistic languages of infinite strings from a set of samples is defined as obtaining the probability distribution over Σ^ω. The state-merging algorithms [8,24] are shown to be effective in learning probabilistic finite automata [12], which in turn, can be converted to DTMC [24]. Although we use the ALERGIA algorithm [12] to explain our approach; in principle it will work with any learning algorithm that uses an FPTA in its learning process (e.g., [25]).

1 ALERGIA(Sample dataset $\mathcal{D}, \alpha > 0$)
    output: PFA $\mathcal{A}$
2 **begin**
3      $\mathcal{A} \leftarrow$ BUILDFPTA($\mathcal{D}$)
4   RED $\leftarrow \{q_\epsilon\}$
5   BLUE $\leftarrow \{q_a : a \in \Sigma \cap \text{PREF}(\mathcal{D})\}$
6   **while** BLUE $\neq \emptyset$ **do**
7          $q_b \leftarrow$ SELECTBLUESTATE
8          $merge \leftarrow$ **false**
9   **foreach** $q_r \in$ RED **do**
10   **if** COMPATIBILITYTEST(q_b, q_r, α) **then**
11                 $\mathcal{A} \leftarrow$ STOCHASTICMERGE($\mathcal{A}, q_r, q_b$)
12                 $merge \leftarrow$ **true**
13   **break**
14   **if** $\neg merge$ **then**
15   RED $\leftarrow$ RED $\cup\{q_b\}$
16   BLUE $\leftarrow \{q_{ua} \mid q_u \in$ RED$, a \in \Sigma, ua \in$ PREF($\mathcal{D}$)$\}\backslash$RED
17     $\mathcal{A} \leftarrow$ NORMALIZEFPTA($\mathcal{A}$)
18   **return** $\mathcal{A}$

Algorithm 1: Generating a PFA from a set of *iid* samples.

Algorithm 1 demonstrates the main steps of ALERGIA, adapted from [24] and [8]. The algorithm starts by building the Frequency Prefix Tree Acceptor (FPTA) (line **3**). The tree is essentially a representation of the training dataset, such that each node represents a prefix that appeared in the dataset with its frequency, i.e., the number of times the prefix appeared in the training data (see Fig. 2(a)).

After building the FPTA, the algorithm initializes and maintains two sets of nodes: RED and BLUE. The *red* nodes have already been merged and will form part of the final automaton. The *blue* nodes are the candidates to be merged with a *red* node. The set RED is initialized with q_ϵ (line **4**), i.e., the initial node in the FPTA that represents the empty string (no prefix). The set BLUE is initialized with all the nodes connected to q_ϵ, which represent prefixes of length one (line **5**). We use PREF($\mathcal{D}$) to denote the set of all prefixes in the dataset $\mathcal{D}$.

The main while loop (lines **6–16**) selects a *blue* node and tests it against all the *red* nodes (lines **9–13**) for compatibility (line **10**). To be faithful to the sample data, as in [24] we assume that the compatibility test is performed on the original FPTA, rather than the intermediate automaton. The parameter $\alpha > 1$ is used for the compatibility criterion [24], which is based on Angluin's bound and the learning by enumeration principle [1]. If the two nodes are compatible, they are merged, with all the frequencies of the *blue* node and its descendants recursively added to the *red* node and its descendants (procedure STOCHASTICMERGE in line **11**).

If there is no compatible *red* node with a given *blue* node, then the *blue* node is promoted to a *red* node (line **15**). In either case, BLUE is updated in line **16** according to its declarative definition: all the successors of *red* nodes that are not themselves *red*.

```
1  PFA2DTMC(𝒜 : (Q, Σ, π_𝒜, δ, 𝐏_T, 𝐏_F))
   output: 𝑀 : (S, Σ, π_𝑀, 𝐏, L)
2  begin
3  │   S ← {}
4  │   foreach a ∈ Σ where δ(q_0, a) exists do
5  │   │   q ← δ(q_0, a)
6  │   │   S ← S ∪ {q}
7  │   │   π_𝑀(q) ← 𝐏_T(q_0, a)
8  │   └   L(q) ← a
9  │   foreach a ∈ Σ and q ∈ S, where δ(q, a) exists do
10 │   │   q' ← δ(q, a)
11 │   │   S ← S ∪ {q'}
12 │   │   𝐏(q, q') ← 𝐏_T(q, a)/(1 − 𝐏_F(q, a))
13 │   └   L(q') ← a
14 │   if δ(q, a) does not exist ∀a ∈ Σ then
15 │   └   𝐏(q, q) ← 1
16 └   return 𝑀
```

Algorithm 2: Constructing a DTMC from a PFA.

The output of Algorithm 1 is a PFA, which is essentially the transformation of the FPTA by normalizing all the frequencies to obtain the probability distributions for the transitions (line **12**).

Algorithm 2 constructs a DTMC from the trained PFA. Constructing the states of the DTMC begins by iterating all the successor states of q_0 in the PFA, i.e., the state representing the empty string. Notice that since we assume the length of the samples is positive, there is no empty string (ϵ) in the dataset. The for loop in lines **4–8** sets the initial probability distribution of the underlying DTMC, which is obtained from the transition from q_0 to the other states using each alphabet symbol a (line **7**). Those states are added to the set of states of the DTMC (line **6**), and labelled with a (line **8**).

The for loop in lines **9–13** computes the transition probability distribution of the DTMC for each pair (q, a). Notice that each state in the DTMC is also in the PFA, hence, $q \in S$ and $\delta(q, a)$ is well defined. In line **12** we normalize the transition probability by dividing it by the complement of the final probability distribution in the PFA (see Definition. 2). To generate a distribution over Σ^ω, if a state in the PFA does not have any outgoing transition, we turn it into an absorbing state in the DTMC by adding a self loop (lines **14–15**).

Figure 2(a) depicts the FPTA obtained from the training sample in Fig. 1(b), with Table 1 showing the prefix and final frequency (*fin. freq.*) associated with each state of the FPTA. The final frequency is obtained by counting the traces that are equal to the prefix that each state represents. Figure 2(b) shows the outcome of merging the states of the FPTA and turning the resulting PFA into a DTMC.

Table 1. The prefixes and their final frequencies associated with each state of the FPTA in Fig. 1(a).

state	prefix	fin. freq.	state	prefix	fin. freq.
q_0	ϵ	0	q_1	i	0
q_2	i, m	10	q_3	i, s	20
q_4	i, m, m	2	q_5	i, m, s	2
q_6	i, s, s	15	q_7	i, m, s, s	4
q_8	i, s, s, s	15	q_9	i, m, s, s, s	2
q_{10}	i, s, s, s, s	15	q_{11}	i, s, s, s, s, s	15

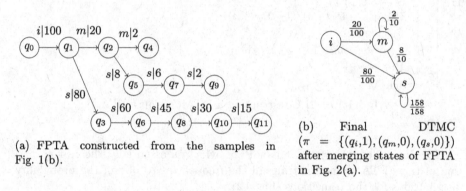

(a) FPTA constructed from the samples in Fig. 1(b).

(b) Final DTMC ($\pi = \{(q_i,1), (q_m,0), (q_s,0)\}$) after merging states of FPTA in Fig. 2(a).

Fig. 2. Training DTMC using normal samples.

5.1   Generating Rare-Event Samples from an IS Distribution

Drawing samples from the original distribution may result in a model that either does not contain any of the required structure, or estimates the probability with large errors, due to a low number of samples that exhibit the rare event.

In this section we present our modification of ALERGIA, which incorporates importance sampling such that, without increasing the sample complexity [31], i.e., the size of the training set, a DTMC is trained with reduced error for predicting the occurrence of a rare event.

We modify building the FPTA (the function BUILDFPTA in Algorithm 1), to adjust the probabilities of the final PTA with respect to the sample distribution generated by the importance sampling.

To achieve this goal, first we use the notion of likelihood ratio (LR) that is obtained by the importance sampling for each sample. The LR is effectively the inverse of the bias introduced in the transition probabilities of the model by the importance sampling distribution to increase the probability of the rare events (see Sect. 3). Let $F(u)$ be the probability measure of the path u under the original distribution F, and $G(u)$ be the probability measure of the same path under the importance sampling distribution, G. Then the likelihood ratio of u is defined as follows:

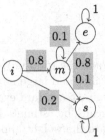

trace	freq.	LR	trace	freq.	LR
i,s	10	4	i,m	20	1/4
i,s,s	2	4	i,m,m	6	2/5
i,s,s,s	3	4	i,m,e	16	1/80
i,s,s,s,s	5	4	i,m,e,e	10	1/80
i,m,s	2	2	i,m,e,e,e	16	1/80
i,m,s,s	4	2	i,m,e,e,e,e	6	1/80

(a) DTMC of Fig. 1(a) modified to produce more errors.

(b) Importance sampling traces, generated by DTMC of Fig. 3(a).

Fig. 3. Importance sampling model with corresponding traces and their LR.

$$LR(u) = \frac{F(u)}{G(u)} \tag{3}$$

Figure 3(a) displays the modified version of the model in Fig. 1(a) obtained by an importance sampling distribution that increases the probability of *eventually error* to ≈ 0.8 (the changed transition probabilities are shaded). Samples randomly generated from this model, with the likelihood ratio for each sample, are shown in Fig. 3(b). The *LR* for each training sample is computed using (3). For example, $LR(i,m,e)$ is $\frac{0.2\times0.04}{0.8\times0.8} = 1/80$.

5.2   Weighted Prefix Tree Acceptor

We define the notion of Weighted Prefix Tree Acceptor (WPTA) to obtain an automaton as the representation of the samples with different likelihood ratios. A WPTA is similar to an FPTA except that instead of integer frequency counts, fractional numbers are used as weights.

Definition 4 (WPTA). *A Weighted Prefix Tree Acceptor (WPTA) is a tuple* $\mathcal{A} : (Q, \Sigma, W_I, \delta, W_F, W_T)$, *where Q is a non-empty finite set of states, Σ is a non-empty finite alphabet, $Fr_I : Q \to \mathbb{R}$ is the initial weighted frequency of the state(s), $\delta : Q \times \Sigma \to Q$ is the transition function, $Fr_F : Q \to \mathbb{R}$ is the final weighted frequency of the state(s), and $Fr_T : Q \times \Sigma \times Q \to \mathbb{R}$ is the transition weighted frequency function between two states.*

Let original distribution $F : \Sigma^* \to [0,1]$ be absolutely continuous with respect to importance sampling distributions $G_1, \ldots, G_n$, with $G_i : \Sigma^* \to [0,1]$ for $i \in \{1, \ldots, n\}$. Then let $N_1, \ldots, N_n$ be the number of samples drawn at random using $G_1, \ldots, G_n$, respectively.

When constructing our WPTA, we add a weight to each frequency count along the trace. If p_i denotes the probability measure of some property under F and $\overline{w}_i$ is the expected weight applied to traces drawn using G_i, then we require that in the limit of large $N_1, \ldots, N_n$,

$$p_i = \frac{N_i \overline{w}_i}{\sum_{j=1}^n N_j \overline{w}_j}. \tag{4}$$

That is, we expect the normalized total frequency to equal the total measure of probability, which follows from the laws of total probability and large numbers. Given that the properties of interest in the present context are rare events of a complex system, in practice the values of p_i will typically be estimated using rare event SMC. In order to derive a formula to calculate the weight applied to an individual simulation trace, in what follows we do not consider the potential statistical errors arising from finite sampling.

Re-arranging (4) for $\overline{w}_i$ gives $\overline{w}_i = \frac{p_i \sum_{j \in \{1,\dots,n\} \setminus \{i\}} N_j \overline{w}_j}{N_i(1-p_i)}$, however there is no unique solution because the numerator on the right hand side contains all the other unknown weights. To sufficiently constrain (4), we set $\sum_{j=1}^n N_j \overline{w}_j = \sum_{j=1}^n N_j$. Hence, the expected weight for samples from G_i is given by $\overline{w}_i = \frac{p_i \sum_{j=1}^n N_j}{N_i}$. The actual weight used for simulation trace $u \sim G_i$ is dependent on its likelihood ratio and is thus given by

$$w_i = \frac{F(u)}{G_i(u)} \frac{\sum_{j=1}^n N_j}{N_i}. \tag{5}$$

The relative values of the set of weights calculated by (5) are unique up to a positive scaling factor. This scaling factor may be important when deciding when nodes are compatible for merging, since metrics such as the Hoeffding bound, used in [8], and the Angluin bound, used in [24], are sensitive to the absolute value. The results presented in Sect. 6 are based on models created using the values calculated directly by (5), however it can be argued that IS achieves performance that is only possible with many more samples using MC, so the weights should be normalized with respect to the probabilities of the rare properties. For example, the weights could be scaled such that the expected weight associated to the lowest probability is equal to 1. Since the scaling factor is related to the specific learning algorithm being used, further discussion is beyond the scope of the present work.

5.3   WPTA Construction from a Single Distribution

In this section we describe the steps of the algorithm to build a WPTA. To simplify the algorithm description, in the remainder of this section we assume that the samples are drawn from a single distribution, therefore the weights defined in (3) become the likelihood ratio for each sample. In the case of multiple distributions it is straightforward to adjust the weights according to the number of samples generated from each distribution and use (5) instead.

Algorithm 3 builds the WPTA from the importance sampling samples, where the frequencies are multiplied by the likelihood ratio of each sample. The input is a dataset which contains samples, denoted by u, their frequency, denoted by $freq$, and their likelihood ratio, denoted by LR, provided by importance

```
1  BUILDWPTA(Sample dataset D, LR)
   output: WPTA A
2  begin
3  |    A ← (Q, Σ, W_I, δ, W_F, W_T)
4  |    Q ← {q_u|u ∈ PREF(D)} ∪ {q_ε}
5  |    W_I(q_ε) ← Σ_{∀u∈D}(u.freq) × LR(u)
6  |    forall the ua ∈ PREF(D) do
7  |    |    δ(q_u, a) ← q_ua
8  |    |_   W_T(q_u, a, q_ua) ← ua.freq × LR(ua)
9  |    forall the u ∈ D do
10 |    |_   W_F(q_u) ← u.freq × LR(u)
11 |_   return A
```

Algorithm 3: Building WPTA from the samples obtained by importance sampling.

sampling. Line **4** initializes the states of the WPTA with all the prefixes that exist in the dataset, with an additional state $q_ε$ that represents the empty prefix that is used as the initial state, whose initial weighted frequency is equal to the sum of the weights of the entire dataset (line **5**). The remaining states have the initial weighted frequency equal to zero. For each $ua ∈ \text{PREF}(D)$, where $a ∈ Σ$, the for loop in lines **6–8** sets the transition function between the states q_u and q_{ua}, and its transition weighted frequency by multiplying the frequency of ua in the dataset to its LR (lines **7–8**). The final weighted frequency is obtained as the product of the frequency of each sample and its likelihood ratio (line **10**).

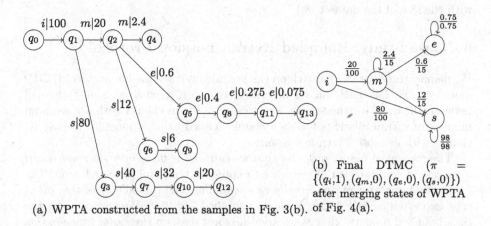

(a) WPTA constructed from the samples in Fig. 3(b).

(b) Final DTMC ($π = \{(q_i,1), (q_m,0), (q_e,0), (q_s,0)\}$) after merging states of WPTA of Fig. 4(a).

Fig. 4. Training DTMC using samples from IS.

Figure 4(a) illustrates the WPTA obtained from the IS samples shown in Fig. 3(b). Table 2 shows the final weighted frequencies of each state of the WPTA, which are used to judge compatibility when merging to obtain the final PFA. Figure 2(b) is the DTMC after converting the resulting PFA.

Table 2. The prefixes and their final weighted frequencies associated with each state of the WPTA in Fig. 4(a).

state	prefix	fin. Wfreq.	state	prefix	fin. Wfreq.
q_0	ϵ	0	q_1	i	0
q_2	i, m	5	q_3	i, s	40
q_4	i, m, m	2.4	q_5	i, m, e	0.2
q_6	i, m, s	4	q_7	i, s, s	8
q_8	i, m, e, e	0.125	q_9	i, m, s, s	8
q_{10}	i, s, s, s	12	q_{11}	i, m, e, e, e	0.2
q_{12}	i, s, s, s, s	20	q_{13}	i, m, e, e, e, e	0.075

Correctness & Complexity. Note that the weights in a WPTA are $LR(u) \times \overline{G}(u)$, where $\overline{G}(u)$ is the empirical probability of u according to the distribution G. Using (3), it is trivial to observe that the weights are essentially giving the same empirical probability distribution that the FPTA provides, i.e., F. Therefore, the correctness of our approach for predicting the failure, expressed as a reachability property, is implied by the convergence analysis of the compatibility test on an FPTA in the large sample limit (see e.g., Theorem 2 in [24]). The time complexity of building a WPTA has the additional multiplication operations to compute the weights. The order of the merging and the training in general would remain cubic with the size of the dataset [8].

6   Case Study: Bounded Retransmission Protocol

We demonstrate our IS approach on the bounded retransmission protocol (BRP) model of [9]. The BRP model describes a sender, a receiver, and a channel between them, which the sender uses to send a file in chunks with a maximum number of retransmissions for each chunk defined as a parameter. We use 64 chunks with at most 2 retransmissions.

The rare-event failure property that we consider is *the sender does not report a successful transmission* [9], which we express in temporal logic as F *error*. The F temporal operator means F*inally* or *eventually*. The probability of this property, expressed as $\Pr(F\ error)$, is approximately 1.7×10^{-4}. We also consider the time-bounded property that *the sender does not report a successful transmission within k steps*, expressed as $F_{\leq k}$ *error*.

The learned models of the BRP using IS and standard MC were constructed from simulation traces generated by PLASMA [15], according to the algorithms defined in Sect. 5. The resulting models were then checked with respect to the above properties using PRISM [21]. The results are illustrated in Figs. 5 and 6.

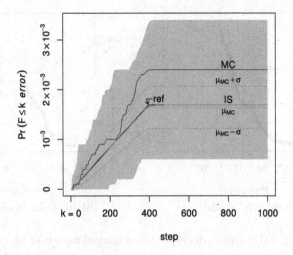

Fig. 5. Predictive performance of a typical 10^3-trace IS model of BRP (labelled IS) vs. that of 1000 10^4-trace MC models (shaded area). The reference performance is labelled ref. The performance of an example MC model is labelled MC.

Using standard MC simulation of the original distribution of the BRP model, we constructed 1000 learned models, each using a training set of 10^4 independently sampled traces. These training sets included between 6 and 34 traces that satisfy the property. Since the performances of different models generated by IS are visually indistinguishable, for comparison we trained just a single IS model, using a training set of only 10^3 sampled traces. The IS training set comprised 500 traces that satisfy the property, selected from simulations of an IS distribution over the original BRP model, and 500 traces that do not satisfy the property, selected from simulations of the original distribution of the BRP model. By combining these traces in accordance with (5), the resulting IS distribution adequately covers the parts of the state space related to both satisfying and not satisfying the property.

The results for the MC models are represented as a shaded area that encloses the minimum and maximum probabilities recorded for each value of k. To give a better intuition of the distribution of these results, we plot lines representing the empirical mean (μ_{MC}) and empirical mean ± 1 standard deviation ($\mu_{MC} \pm \sigma$). We also plot the performance of a typical MC model (labelled MC), where each apparent step in the curve corresponds to one of the 24 traces that satisfy the property in its training data.

The results for the IS model are almost coincident with the reference curve (ref), calculated by evaluating the property with respect to the original model of the system. The small difference at around k = 400 arises due to the learned models using an abstraction based on only two variables in the original system.

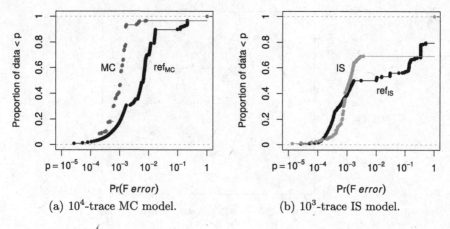

(a) 10^4-trace MC model.   (b) 10^3-trace IS model.

Fig. 6. Prediction distributions of learned models of BRP.

The results presented in Fig. 5 are with respect to a property in a single initial state. To judge the performance of our approach in constructing a typical failure monitor, we consider the predictive accuracy of *all* the states in learned models using MC and IS, with respect to probability $Pr(F\ error)$. As in the previous experiments, we constructed an MC model using 10^4 traces and an IS model using 10^3 traces. To eliminate an obvious source of discrepancy, we generated multiple sets of 10^4 MC traces and selected a set with exactly 17 traces that satisfy the property. This ensures that the MC model is based on approximately the same probability as the IS model.

Each training set contains a different randomly selected set of concrete states in the original model. Hence, even though we use the same merging compatibility parameter for both sets ($\alpha = 10$), the two learned models are different. Also, since we use abstraction, each learned model state maps to a different set of concrete states in the original model. Hence, for every state in each learned model, we calculate the probability of the property in the learned model and, for comparison, calculate the probability of the property with respect to its associated set of concrete states in the original model.

The results of our calculations are two pairs of sets of probabilities, which we visualize as cumulative distributions in Fig. 6(a) and (b). In this form, the maximum vertical distance between the curves in each pair is a measure of similarity of the two distributions (the Kolmogorov-Smirnov (K-S) statistic [19]). The K-S statistic for the MC model is 0.63, while that of the IS model is 0.19. As expected, the IS model significantly outperforms the MC model, despite the IS model being trained with an order of magnitude fewer training samples and hand-selecting a good MC training set.

7 Related Work

This paper continues the previous line of work on the predictive RV framework [2], where the monitor finitely extends the prefix based on a prediction model that is trained on the set of *iid* sample traces. This gives the monitor the ability to detect a monitorable [10] property's satisfaction or violation before its occurrence. Abstraction to the observation space is used in [3] to reduce the size of the prediction model, which directly impacts both the size and the performance of the monitor.

The present work's focus is on training a prediction model using rare-event samples. Importance sampling is used in the context of reinforcement learning [32] to estimate the optimal policy in an unknown partially observable Markov decision process [26–28]. Our technique uses the state-merging method as a form of supervised learning to build a DTMC for a rare event. The authors of [34] introduce a genetic algorithm to predict rare events in event sequences. Their approach is based on identifying temporal and sequential patterns through the mutation and crossover operators. Our approach instead uses importance sampling to identify the rare-event samples, and diversifies them by adding other (importance) sampling distributions. Our purpose is to construct the underlying model that captures the probabilities of a rare event.

In the context of statistical model checking (SMC), importance sampling [14, 18] and importance *splitting* [16,17] have already been used to mitigate the joint problems of intractable state space and rare events. SMC is essentially runtime verification of an accurate existing model that is deliberately not constructed in its entirety. Rare event SMC is therefore not inherently predictive, so not immediately applicable in the current context.

8 Conclusion

In this paper we have presented an accelerated-learning technique to create accurate predictive runtime monitors for rare events. We use importance sampling to generate samples with more failure instances, so that the part of the model responsible for failure is adequately covered. We also use regular Monte Carlo simulation of the original system so that we have sufficient training samples to cover the rest of the model. We then use the likelihood ratios of the samples to construct a probabilistic automaton to represent the true distribution of the model. Finally, the prediction model is used in building a monitor for predictive runtime verification [2]. To evaluate our approach, we applied it to the file retransmission protocol case study, demonstrating the efficacy of our method in using far fewer samples while achieving greater accuracy compared to previous approaches.

In line with previous work [3], we propose to explore importance sampling with abstraction, which is necessary when the state space is intractable. We have already demonstrated in our experiments that this combination works, but obtaining a good abstraction of a complex system may be challenging. Drawing on experience with parametrized importance sampling [14,18], we speculate to exploit cross entropy minimization or the coupling method [4] to find both good importance sampling distributions and good abstractions.

Acknowledgment. This work is partly supported by the Japanese Science and Technology agency (JST) ERATO project JPMJER1603: HASUO Metamathematics for Systems Design.

References

1. Angluin, D.: Identifying languages from stochastic examples. Technical report YALEU/ DCS/RR-614, Yale University, Department of Computer Science, New Haven, CT (1988)
2. Babaee, R., Gurfinkel, A., Fischmeister, S.: *Prevent*: a predictive run-time verification framework using statistical learning. In: Johnsen, E.B., Schaefer, I. (eds.) SEFM 2018. LNCS, vol. 10886, pp. 205–220. Springer, Cham (2018). https://doi.org/10.1007/978-3-319-92970-5_13
3. Babaee, R., Gurfinkel, A., Fischmeister, S.: Predictive run-time verification of discrete-time reachability properties in black-box systems using trace-level abstraction and statistical learning. In: Colombo, C., Leucker, M. (eds.) RV 2018. LNCS, vol. 11237, pp. 187–204. Springer, Cham (2018). https://doi.org/10.1007/978-3-030-03769-7_11
4. Barbot, B., Haddad, S., Picaronny, C.: Coupling and importance sampling for statistical model checking. In: Flanagan, C., König, B. (eds.) TACAS 2012. LNCS, vol. 7214, pp. 331–346. Springer, Heidelberg (2012). https://doi.org/10.1007/978-3-642-28756-5_23
5. Bauer, A., Leucker, M., Schallhart, C.: The good, the bad, and the ugly, but how ugly is ugly? In: Sokolsky, O., Taşıran, S. (eds.) RV 2007. LNCS, vol. 4839, pp. 126–138. Springer, Heidelberg (2007). https://doi.org/10.1007/978-3-540-77395-5_11
6. Bauer, A., Leucker, M., Schallhart, C.: Comparing LTL semantics for runtime verification. J. Log. Comput. **20**(3), 651–674 (2010)
7. Boyer, B., Corre, K., Legay, A., Sedwards, S.: PLASMA-lab: a flexible, distributable statistical model checking library. In: Joshi, K., Siegle, M., Stoelinga, M., D'Argenio, P.R. (eds.) QEST 2013. LNCS, vol. 8054, pp. 160–164. Springer, Heidelberg (2013). https://doi.org/10.1007/978-3-642-40196-1_12
8. Carrasco, R.C., Oncina, J.: Learning stochastic regular grammars by means of a state merging method. In: Carrasco, R.C., Oncina, J. (eds.) ICGI 1994. LNCS, vol. 862, pp. 139–152. Springer, Heidelberg (1994). https://doi.org/10.1007/3-540-58473-0_144
9. D'Argenio, P.R., Jeannet, B., Jensen, H.E., Larsen, K.G.: Reachability analysis of probabilistic systems by successive refinements. In: de Alfaro, L., Gilmore, S. (eds.) PAPM-PROBMIV 2001. LNCS, vol. 2165, pp. 39–56. Springer, Heidelberg (2001). https://doi.org/10.1007/3-540-44804-7_3
10. Falcone, Y., Fernandez, J.-C., Mounier, L.: Runtime verification of safety-progress properties. In: Bensalem, S., Peled, D.A. (eds.) RV 2009. LNCS, vol. 5779, pp. 40–59. Springer, Heidelberg (2009). https://doi.org/10.1007/978-3-642-04694-0_4
11. Helmink, L., Sellink, M.P.A., Vaandrager, F.W.: Proof-checking a data link protocol. In: Barendregt, H., Nipkow, T. (eds.) TYPES 1993. LNCS, vol. 806, pp. 127–165. Springer, Heidelberg (1994). https://doi.org/10.1007/3-540-58085-9_75

12. De la Higuera, C.: Grammatical Inference: Learning Automata and Grammars. Cambridge University Press, Cambridge (2010)

13. Hoeffding, W.: Probability inequalities for sums of bounded random variables. J. Am. Stat. Assoc. **58**(301), 13–30 (1963)

14. Jegourel, C., Legay, A., Sedwards, S.: Cross-entropy optimisation of importance sampling parameters for statistical model checking. In: Madhusudan, P., Seshia, S.A. (eds.) CAV 2012. LNCS, vol. 7358, pp. 327–342. Springer, Heidelberg (2012). https://doi.org/10.1007/978-3-642-31424-7_26

15. Jegourel, C., Legay, A., Sedwards, S.: A platform for high performance statistical model checking – PLASMA. In: Flanagan, C., König, B. (eds.) TACAS 2012. LNCS, vol. 7214, pp. 498–503. Springer, Heidelberg (2012). https://doi.org/10.1007/978-3-642-28756-5_37

16. Jegourel, C., Legay, A., Sedwards, S.: Importance splitting for statistical model checking rare properties. In: Sharygina, N., Veith, H. (eds.) CAV 2013. LNCS, vol. 8044, pp. 576–591. Springer, Heidelberg (2013). https://doi.org/10.1007/978-3-642-39799-8_38

17. Jegourel, C., Legay, A., Sedwards, S.: An effective heuristic for adaptive importance splitting in statistical model checking. In: Margaria, T., Steffen, B. (eds.) ISoLA 2014. LNCS, vol. 8803, pp. 143–159. Springer, Heidelberg (2014). https://doi.org/10.1007/978-3-662-45231-8_11

18. Jegourel, C., Legay, A., Sedwards, S.: Command-based importance sampling for statistical model checking. Theoret. Comput. Sci. **649**, 1–24 (2016)

19. Kolmogoroff, A.: Confidence limits for an unknown distribution function. Ann. Math. Stat. **12**(4), 461–463 (1941)

20. Kwiatkowska, M., Norman, G., Parker, D.: Stochastic model checking. In: Bernardo, M., Hillston, J. (eds.) SFM 2007. LNCS, vol. 4486, pp. 220–270. Springer, Heidelberg (2007). https://doi.org/10.1007/978-3-540-72522-0_6

21. Kwiatkowska, M., Norman, G., Parker, D.: PRISM 4.0: verification of probabilistic real-time systems. In: Gopalakrishnan, G., Qadeer, S. (eds.) CAV 2011. LNCS, vol. 6806, pp. 585–591. Springer, Heidelberg (2011). https://doi.org/10.1007/978-3-642-22110-1_47

22. Leucker, M., Schallhart, C.: A brief account of runtime verification. J. Logic Algebraic Program. **78**(5), 293–303 (2009)

23. Maler, O.: Some thoughts on runtime verification. In: Falcone, Y., Sánchez, C. (eds.) RV 2016. LNCS, vol. 10012, pp. 3–14. Springer, Cham (2016). https://doi.org/10.1007/978-3-319-46982-9_1

24. Mao, H., et al.: Learning probabilistic automata for model checking. In: Proceedings of the 8th International Conference on Quantitative Evaluation of SysTems (QEST), pp. 111–120. IEEE, September 2011

25. Mediouni, B.L., Nouri, A., Bozga, M., Bensalem, S.: Improved learning for stochastic timed models by state-merging algorithms. In: Barrett, C., Davies, M., Kahsai, T. (eds.) NFM 2017. LNCS, vol. 10227, pp. 178–193. Springer, Cham (2017). https://doi.org/10.1007/978-3-319-57288-8_13

26. Peshkin, L., Meuleau, N., Kaelbling, L.P.: Learning policies with external memory. In: Proceedings of the 16th International Conference on Machine Learning (ICML). pp. 307–314. Morgan Kaufmann (1999)

27. Peshkin, L., Shelton, C.R.: Learning from scarce experience. In: Proceedings of the 19th International Conference on Machine Learning (ICML), pp. 498–505. Morgan Kaufmann (2002)

28. Precup, D., Sutton, R.S., Dasgupta, S.: Off-policy temporal difference learning with function approximation. In: Proceedings of the 18th International Conference on Machine Learning (ICML), pp. 417–424. Morgan Kaufmann (2001)
29. Rubino, G., Tuffin, B.: Rare Event Simulation Using Monte Carlo Methods. Wiley, Hoboken (2009)
30. Rubinstein, R.Y., Kroese, D.P.: Simulation and the Monte Carlo Method, 2nd edn. Wiley, Hoboken (2007)
31. Russell, S.J., Norvig, P.: Artificial Intelligence - A Modern Approach (3. internat. ed.). Pearson Education, London (2010)
32. Shelton, C.R.: Importance sampling for reinforcement learning with multiple objectives. Ph.D. thesis, Massachusetts Institute of Technology, Cambridge, MA, USA (2001)
33. Sistla, A.P., Žefran, M., Feng, Y.: Monitorability of stochastic dynamical systems. In: Gopalakrishnan, G., Qadeer, S. (eds.) CAV 2011. LNCS, vol. 6806, pp. 720–736. Springer, Heidelberg (2011). https://doi.org/10.1007/978-3-642-22110-1_58
34. Weiss, G.M., Hirsh, H.: Learning to predict rare events in event sequences. In: Proceedings of the 4th International Conference on Knowledge Discovery and Data Mining (KDD-98), pp. 359–363. AAAI Press (1998)
35. Zuliani, P., Baier, C., Clarke, E.M.: Rare-event verification for stochastic hybrid systems. In: Hybrid Systems: Computation and Control (HSCC), pp. 217–226. ACM (2012)

Neural Predictive Monitoring

Luca Bortolussi[1,4], Francesca Cairoli[1(✉)], Nicola Paoletti[2], Scott A. Smolka[3], and Scott D. Stoller[3]

[1] Department of Mathematics and Geosciences, Università di Trieste, Trieste, Italy
FRANCESCA.CAIROLI@PHD.UNITS.IT
[2] Department of Computer Science, Royal Holloway,
University of London, Egham, UK
[3] Department of Computer Science, Stony Brook University, Stony Brook, USA
[4] Modelling and Simulation Group, Saarland University, Saarbrücken, Germany

Abstract. Neural State Classification (NSC) is a recently proposed method for runtime predictive monitoring of Hybrid Automata (HA) using deep neural networks (DNNs). NSC trains a DNN as an approximate *reachability predictor* that labels a given HA state x as *positive* if an unsafe state is reachable from x within a given time bound, and labels x as *negative* otherwise. NSC predictors have very high accuracy, yet are prone to prediction errors that can negatively impact reliability. To overcome this limitation, we present *Neural Predictive Monitoring* (NPM), a technique based on NSC and *conformal prediction* that complements NSC predictions with statistically sound estimates of uncertainty. This yields principled criteria for the rejection of predictions likely to be incorrect, without knowing the true reachability values. We also present an active learning method that significantly reduces both the NSC predictor's error rate and the percentage of rejected predictions. Our approach is highly efficient, with computation times on the order of milliseconds, and effective, managing in our experimental evaluation to successfully reject almost all incorrect predictions.

1 Introduction

Hybrid systems are a central model for many safety-critical, cyber-physical system applications [2]. Their verification typically amounts to solving a hybrid automata (HA) reachability checking problem [14]: given a model $\mathcal{M}$ of the system expressed as an HA and a set of unsafe states U, check whether U is reached in any (time-bounded) path from a set of initial states of $\mathcal{M}$. Due to its high computational cost, reachability checking is usually limited to design-time (offline) analysis.

Our focus is on the online analysis of hybrid systems and, in particular, on the *predictive monitoring* (PM) problem [10]; i.e., the problem of predicting, *at runtime*, whether or not an unsafe state can be reached from the current system state within a given time bound. PM is at the core of architectures for runtime safety assurance such as Simplex [26], where the system switches to a safe fallback mode whenever PM indicates the potential for an imminent failure.

B. Finkbeiner and L. Mariani (Eds.): RV 2019, LNCS 11757, pp. 129–147, 2019.
https://doi.org/10.1007/978-3-030-32079-9_8

In such approaches, PM is invoked periodically and frequently, and thus reachability needs be determined rapidly, from a single state (the current system state), and typically for short time horizons. This is in contrast with offline reachability checking, where long or unbounded time horizons and sizable regions of initial states are typically considered. PM also differs from traditional runtime verification in that PM is *preemptive*: it detects potential safety violations before they occur, not when or after they occur.

Any solution to the PM problem involves a tradeoff between two main requirements: *accuracy* of the reachability prediction, and computational *efficiency*, as the analysis must execute within strict real-time constraints and typically with limited hardware resources. In this work, we present *Neural Predictive Monitoring* (NPM), a machine learning-based approach to PM that provides *high efficiency and accuracy*, and crucially, *statistical guarantees on the prediction error*.

NPM builds on *Neural State Classification* (NSC) [21], a recently proposed method for approximate HA reachability checking using deep neural networks (DNNs). NSC works by training DNNs as state classifiers using examples computed with an oracle (an HA model checker). For any state x of the HA, such a classifier labels x as *positive* if an unsafe state is reachable from x within a given time bound; otherwise, x is labeled as *negative*. Executing a neural state classifier corresponds to computing the output of a DNN for a single input, and thus is extremely efficient. NSC has also demonstrated very high accuracy in reachability predictions, owing to the powerful approximation capabilities of DNNs. Some classification errors are, however, unavoidable, the most important being *false negatives*, in which positive states are misclassified as negative. Such errors may compromise the safety of the system.

NPM overcomes this problem by extending NSC with rigorous methods for quantifying the uncertainty of NSC predictions. NPM can consequently identify and reject predictions that are likely to produce classification errors. For this purpose, we investigate the use of *Conformal Prediction* (CP) [27], a method that provides statistical guarantees on the predictions of machine-learning models. Importantly, CP requires only very mild assumptions on the data[1], which makes it suitable for state classification of HA models.

Figure 1 provides an overview of the NPM approach. We sample from a distribution of HA states to generate a training set Z_t and a calibration set Z_c. An HA reachability oracle (a model checker or, for deterministic systems, a simulator) is used to label sampled states as positive or negative. A neural state classifier h (i.e., a DNN-based binary classifier) is derived from Z_t via supervised learning.

We use CP to estimate two statistically sound measures of prediction uncertainty, *confidence* and *credibility*. Informally, the confidence of a prediction is the probability that a reachability prediction for an HA state s corresponds to the

---

[1] The only assumption is exchangeability, a weaker version of the independent and identically distributed assumption.

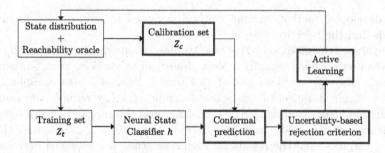

Fig. 1. Overview of the NPM framework. Double-bordered components denote extensions to the method of [21]. Training of the neural state classifier h and retraining via active learning are performed offline. The only components used at runtime are the classifier h and the rejection criterion.

true reachability value of s. Credibility quantifies how likely a given state is to belong to the same distribution of the training data.

Using confidence and credibility, we derive criteria for anomaly detection, that is, for rejecting NSC predictions that are likely to be erroneous. The rejection criterion is based on identifying, via support vector classification, confidence and credibility thresholds that optimally separate incorrect and correct predictions. The key advantage of such an approach is that predictions are rejected on rigorous statistical grounds. Furthermore, computation of CP-based confidence and credibility is very efficient (approximately 1 ms in our experiments), which makes our NPM method suitable for online analysis and PM.

Finally, our approach includes an active learning strategy to improve the reliability of the state classifier h. The idea is to employ the CP-based rejection criterion to identify HA states for which h yields uncertain predictions, and augment the training and calibration sets with those states. We then train a new state classifier with the augmented dataset, thus ensuring improved accuracy on the HA states where h performed poorly, and in turn, a reduced rejection rate. As opposed to simple random sampling of the state distribution, an advantage of our active learning strategy is its parsimony: by focusing on the states with uncertain predictions, it requires a significantly smaller number of additional re-training samples to achieve a given reduction in rejection rate, and thus significantly reduces the cost of re-training. The active learning procedure can be iterated, as shown in Fig. 1. We stress that these re-training iterations are part of the training process, which is performed offline and hence does not affect runtime performance.

In summary, the main contributions of this paper are the following:

- We develop Neural Predictive Monitoring, a framework for runtime predictive monitoring of hybrid automata that extends neural state classification with conformal prediction.
- We derive statistically sound and optimal criteria for rejecting unreliable NSC predictions, which leverage CP-based measures of prediction uncertainty.

- We develop an active learning method designed to reduce both prediction errors and the rejection rate.
- We evaluate the method on five case studies, demonstrating that our optimal rejection criteria successfully rejects almost all prediction errors (missing an average of only 1.4 errors out of 49.4 over a total of 50,000 samples), and that a single iteration of our active learning strategy reduces the range of prediction errors from 15.2–82 to 3.8–22.8, and the range of overall rejection rates from 3.46%–9.88% to 0.51%–2.74%. The ranges are taken over the set of case studies, and the results for each case study are averaged over 5 runs.

2   Problem Formulation

We describe the predictive monitoring problem for hybrid automata reachability and the related problem of finding an optimal criterion for rejecting erroneous reachability predictions. We assume that the reader is familiar with the definitions of HA and HA reachability. These definitions can be found in e.g. [21].

Problem 1 (Predictive monitoring for HA reachability). Given an HA $\mathcal{M}$ with state space X, time bound T, and set of unsafe states $U \subset X$, find a *predictor* h^*, i.e., a function $h^* : X \rightarrow \{0,1\}$ such that for all $x \in X$, $h^*(x) = 1$ if $\mathcal{M} \models \mathsf{Reach}(U, x, T)$, i.e., if it is possible for $\mathcal{M}$, starting in x, to reach a state in U within time T; $h^*(x) = 0$ otherwise.

A state $x \in X$ is called *positive* if $\mathcal{M} \models \mathsf{Reach}(U, x, T)$. Otherwise, x is *negative*.

The neural state classification method of [21] provides an approximate solution to the above PM problem[2], a solution based on deep neural networks (DNNs). NSC assumes a distribution $\mathcal{X}$ of HA states and derives a DNN-based reachability predictor h using supervised learning, where the training inputs are sampled according to $\mathcal{X}$ and labeled using a reachability oracle. Being an approximate solution, h can commit prediction errors: a state $x \in X$ is a *false positive* (FP) if $h(x) = 1$ but $\mathcal{M} \not\models \mathsf{Reach}(U, x, T)$; x is a *false negative* (FN) if $h(x) = 0$ but $\mathcal{M} \models \mathsf{Reach}(U, x, T)$. These errors are respectively denoted by predicates $fn(x)$ and $fp(x)$. Predicate $pe(x) = fn(x) \vee fp(x)$ denotes a generic prediction error.

A central objective of this work is to derive, given a predictor h, a rejection criterion R able to identify states x that are wrongly classified by h. Importantly, for runtime applicability, R should not require knowing the true reachability value of x, as computing it would be too costly at runtime. Further, R should be optimal, that is, it should ensure minimal probability of rejection errors w.r.t. the state distribution $\mathcal{X}$.

Problem 2. Given an approximate reachability predictor h, a state distribution $\mathcal{X} : X \rightarrow [0, 1]$, and $e \in \{pe, fn, fp\}$, find an optimal rejection rule $R : X \rightarrow \{0, 1\}$, i.e., such that it minimizes the probability $P_{x \sim \mathcal{X}}(e(x) \neq R(x))$.

---

[2] In [21], the PM problem is called "state classification problem", and its solution a "state classifier".

Note that Problem 2 requires specifying the kind of prediction errors to reject. Indeed, depending on the application at hand, one might desire to reject only a specific kind of errors. For instance, in safety-critical applications, FNs are the most critical errors while FPs are less important.

As we will explain in Sect. 4, our solution to Problem 2 will consists in identifying optimal rejection thresholds for confidence and credibility, two statistically sound measures of prediction uncertainty based on CP. The statistical guarantees of our approach derive from using these uncertainty measures as the basis of the rejection criterion.

3   Conformal Prediction for Classification

Conformal Prediction (CP) associates measures of reliability to any traditional supervised learning problem. It is a very general approach that can be applied across all existing classification and regression methods [5]. Since we are interested in the analysis of the DNN-based state classifiers of NSC, we present the theoretical foundations of CP in relation to a generic classification problem.

Let X be the input space, $Y = \{y^1, \ldots, y^c\}$ be the set of labels (or classes), and define $Z = X \times Y$. The classification model is represented as a function $h : X \to [0,1]^c$ mapping inputs into a vector of class likelihoods, such that the class predicted by h corresponds to the class with the highest likelihood. In the context of PM of HA reachability, X is the HA state space, $Y = \{0,1\}$ ($c = 2$) indicates the possible reachability values, and h is the predictor[3].

Let us introduce some notation: for a generic input x_i, we denote with y_i the true label of x_i and with $\hat{y}_i$ the label predicted by h. Test points, whose true labels are unknown, are denoted by x_*.

The CP algorithm outputs *prediction regions*, instead of single point predictions: given a significance level $\varepsilon \in (0,1)$ and a test point x_i, its prediction region, $\Gamma_i^\varepsilon \subseteq Y$, is a set of labels guaranteed to contain the true label y_i with probability $1 - \varepsilon$. The main ingredients of CP are: a *nonconformity function* $f : Z \to \mathbb{R}$, a set of labelled examples $Z' \subseteq Z$, a classification model h trained on a subset of Z', and a statistical test. The nonconformity function $f(z)$ measures the "strangeness" of an example $z_i = (x_i, y_i)$, i.e., the deviation between the label y_i and the corresponding prediction $h(x_i)$.

3.1   CP Algorithm for Classification

Given a set of examples $Z' \subseteq Z$, a test input $x_* \in X$, and a significance level $\varepsilon \in [0,1]$, CP computes a prediction region Γ_*^ε for x_* as follows.

1. Divide Z' into a training set Z_t, and calibration set Z_c. Let $q = |Z_c|$ be the size of the calibration set.
2. Train a model h using Z_t.

---

[3] We will interchangeably use the term "predictor" for the function returning a vector of class likelihoods, and for the function returning the class with highest likelihood.

3. Define a nonconformity function $f((x_i, y_i)) = \Delta(h(x_i), y_i)$, i.e., choose a metric Δ to measure the distance between $h(x_i)$ and y_i (see Sect. 3.2).
4. Apply $f(z)$ to each example z in Z_c and sort the resulting nonconformity scores $\{\alpha = f(z) \mid z \in Z_c\}$ in descending order: $\alpha_1 \geq \cdots \geq \alpha_q$.
5. Compute the nonconformity scores $\alpha_*^j = f((x_*, y^j))$ for the test input x_* and each possible label $j \in \{1, \ldots, c\}$. Then, compute the smoothed p-value

$$p_*^j = \frac{|\{z_i \in Z_c : \alpha_i > \alpha_*^j\}|}{q+1} + \theta \frac{|\{z_i \in Z_c : \alpha_i = \alpha_*^j\}| + 1}{q+1}, \tag{1}$$

where $\theta \in \mathcal{U}[0, 1]$ is a tie-breaking random variable. Note that p_*^j represents the portion of calibration examples that are at least as nonconforming as the tentatively labelled test example (x_*, y^j).
6. Return the prediction region

$$\Gamma_*^\varepsilon = \{y^j \in Y : p_*^j > \varepsilon\}. \tag{2}$$

together with a vector of p-values, one for each class.

Note that in this approach, called inductive CP [19], steps 1–4 are performed only once, while Steps 5–6 are performed for every test point x_*.

The rationale is to use a statistical test, more precisely the Neyman-Pearson theory for hypothesis testing and confidence intervals [15], to check if (x_*, y^j) is particularly nonconforming compared to the calibration examples. The unknown distribution of $f(z)$, referred to as $\mathcal{Q}$, is estimated applying f to all calibration examples. Then the scores α_*^j are computed for every possible label y^j in order to test for the null hypothesis $\alpha_*^j \sim \mathcal{Q}$. The null hypothesis is rejected if the p-value associated to α_*^j is smaller than the significance level ε. If a label is rejected, meaning if it appears unlikely that $f((x_*, y^j)) \sim \mathcal{Q}$, we do not include this label in Γ_*^ε. Therefore, given ε, the prediction region contains only those labels for which we could not reject the null hypothesis.

3.2 Nonconformity Function

A nonconformity function is well-defined if it assigns low scores to correct predictions and high scores to wrong predictions. A natural choice for f, based on the underlying model h, is $f(z) = \Delta(h(x_i), y_i)$, where Δ is a suitable distance[4]. Recall that, for an input $x \in X$, the output of h is a vector of class likelihoods, which we denote by $h(x) = [P_h(y_1|x), \ldots, P_h(y_c|x)]$. In classification problems, a common well-defined nonconformity function is obtained by defining Δ as

$$\Delta(h(x_i), y_i) = 1 - P_h(y_i|x_i), \tag{3}$$

where $P_h(y_i|x_i)$ is the likelihood of class y_i when the model h is applied on x_i. If h correctly predicts y_i for input x_i, the corresponding likelihood $P_h(y_i|x_i)$ is

---

[4] The choice of Δ is not very important, as long as it is symmetric.

high (the highest among all classes) and the resulting nonconformity score is low. The opposite holds when h does not predict y_i. The nonconformity measure chosen for our experiments, Eq. 3, preserves the ordering of the class likelihoods predicted by h.

3.3   Confidence and Credibility

Observe that, for significance levels $\varepsilon_1 \geq \varepsilon_2$, the corresponding prediction regions are such that $\Gamma^{\varepsilon_1} \subseteq \Gamma^{\varepsilon_2}$. It follows that, given an input x_*, if ε is lower than all its p-values, i.e. $\varepsilon < \min_{j=1,\ldots,c} p_*^j$, then the region Γ_*^ε contains all the labels. As ε increases, fewer and fewer classes will have a p-value higher than ε. That is, the region shrinks as ε increases. In particular, Γ_*^ε is empty when $\varepsilon \geq \max_{j=1,\ldots,c} p_*^j$.

The *confidence* of a point $x_* \in X$, $1-\gamma_*$, measures how likely is our prediction for x_* compared to all other possible classifications (according to the calibration set). It is computed as one minus the smallest value of ε for which the conformal region is a single label, i.e. the second largest p-value γ_*:

$$1 - \gamma_* = \sup\{1 - \varepsilon : |\Gamma_*^\varepsilon| = 1\}.$$

The *credibility*, c_*, indicates how suitable the training data are to classify that specific example. In practice, it is the smallest ε for which the prediction region is empty, i.e. the highest p-value according to the calibration set, which corresponds to the p-value of the predicted class:

$$c_* = \inf\{\varepsilon : |\Gamma_*^\varepsilon| = 0\}.$$

Note that if $\gamma_* \leq \varepsilon$, then the corresponding prediction region Γ_*^ε contains at most one class. If both $\gamma_* \leq \varepsilon$ and $c_* > \varepsilon$ hold, then the prediction region contains *exactly* one class, i.e., the one predicted by h. In other words, the interval $[\gamma_*, c_*)$ contains all the ε values for which we are sure that $\Gamma_*^\varepsilon = \{\hat{y}_*\}$. It follows that the higher $1 - \gamma_*$ and c_* are, the more reliable the prediction $\hat{y}_*$ is, because we have an expanded range $[\gamma_*, c_*)$ of significance values by which $\hat{y}_*$ is valid. Indeed, in the extreme scenario where $c_* = 1$ and $\gamma_* = 0$, then $\Gamma_*^\varepsilon = \{\hat{y}_*\}$ for any value of ϵ. This is why, as we will explain in the next section, our uncertainty-based rejection criterion relies on excluding points with low values of $1 - \gamma_*$ and c_*. We stress, in particular, the following statistical guarantee: the probability that the true prediction for x_* is exactly $\hat{y}_*$ is at most $1 - \gamma_*$.

In binary classification problems, each point x_* has only two p-values, one for each class, which coincide with c_* (p-value of the predicted class) and γ_* (p-value of the other class).

4   Uncertainty-Based Rejection Criteria

Confidence and credibility measure how much a prediction can be trusted. Our goal is to leverage these two measures of uncertainty to identify a criterion to detect errors of the reachability predictor. The criterion is also required to distinguish between false-negative and false-positives errors.

The rationale is that every new input x is required to have values of confidence, $1 - \gamma$, and credibility, c, sufficiently high in order for the classification to be accepted. However, determining optimal thresholds is a non-trivial task.

In order to automatically identify optimal thresholds, we proceed with an additional supervised learning approach. For this purpose, we introduce a *cross-validation strategy* to compute values of confidence and credibility, using Z_c as validation set. The cross-validation strategy consists of removing the j-th score, α_j, in order to compute γ_j and c_j, i.e. the p-values at $x_j \in X_c$, where $X_c = \{x \mid (x, y) \in Z_c\}$. In this way, we can compute confidence, $1 - \gamma$, and credibility, c, for every point in the calibration set.

We now state our supervised learning approach to derive the optimal rejection thresholds. Starting from the calibration set, we construct two training datasets, $\mathcal{D}_c^{fn}$ and $\mathcal{D}_c^{fp}$, which will be used to learn thresholds specific to FN and FP errors, respectively. The inputs of dataset $\mathcal{D}_c^{fn}$ ($\mathcal{D}_c^{fp}$) are the confidence and credibility values of the calibration points, and these inputs are labelled with 1 or 0 depending on whether the classifier h makes a FN (FP) error on the corresponding calibration point. Formally,

$$\mathcal{D}_c^{fn} = \{((\gamma_j, c_j), l_j) \mid x_j \in X_c, l_j = I(\hat{y}_j = 0 \land y_j = 1)\}$$
$$\mathcal{D}_c^{fp} = \{((\gamma_j, c_j), l_j) \mid x_j \in X_c, l_j = I(\hat{y}_j = 1 \land y_j = 0)\},$$

where $I(pred)$ equals 1 if predicate $pred$ is true and equals 0 otherwise.

For simplicity, let us now focus on one of the two cases, $\mathcal{D}_c^{fn}$. Analogous reasoning applies to $\mathcal{D}_c^{fp}$. We seek to find confidence and credibility values that optimally separate the points in $\mathcal{D}_c^{fn}$ in relation to their classes, that is, separate points yielding FN errors from those that do not. We solve this problem by learning two linear Support Vector Classifiers (l-SVCs), trained on pairs $(1 - \gamma, l)$ and (c, l), respectively. In this way, we identify individual confidence and credibility thresholds, denoted by $1 - \gamma_\tau^{fn}$ and c_τ^{fn}, respectively[5]. Given a test point x_* with predicted label $\hat{y}_*$, confidence $1 - \gamma_*$ and credibility c^*, the learned thresholds establish two rejection criteria: one for confidence, $R_\gamma^{fn}(x_*) = (1 - \gamma_* < 1 - \gamma_\tau^{fn})$, and one for credibility, $R_c^{fn}(x_*) = (c_* < c_\tau^{fn})$.

Proposition 1. *Both R_γ^{fn} (R_γ^{fp}) and R_c^{fn} (R_c^{fp}) are the best approximate solutions of Problem 2, i.e., they are such that the probability of wrongly rejecting or accepting a FN (FP) prediction is minimal.*

Proof (Sketch). A SVC finds the maximum-margin hyper-plane that separates the classes, i.e. it maximizes the distance between the hyper-plane and the nearest point from either group. In general the larger the margin, the lower the generalization error. If the classes overlap the exact separation of the training data can lead to poor generalization. The SVC allows some of the training points

---

[5] As opposed to learning a linear combination of confidence and credibility, which is less interpretable.

to be misclassified, with a penalty that increases linearly with the distance from that boundary. The optimization goal is to maximize the margin, while penalizing points that lie on the wrong side of the hyper-plane (see Chapter 7 of [7] for a complete treatment). Therefore, the learned hyperplane optimally separates erroneous from non-erroneous predictions, that is, the probability, over the calibration set, that a prediction is wrongly rejected or wrongly accepted is minimal and so is the generalization error. Since we are cross-validating, i.e. we are approximating a sample from the data distribution, then the criterion is optimal for any input test point. $\qquad\square$

The final rejection criterion is a conservative combination of the four rejection criteria. A test point x_* is rejected if:

$$R(x_*) = \left(1 - \gamma_* < \max(1 - \gamma_\tau^{fn}, 1 - \gamma_\tau^{fp})\right) \vee \left(c_* < \max(c_\tau^{fn}, c_\tau^{fp})\right). \quad (4)$$

Alternatively, one can implement rejection criteria specific to FN (FP) errors by using only the thresholds $1 - \gamma_\tau^{fn}$ and c_τ^{fn} ($1 - \gamma_\tau^{fp}$ and c_τ^{fp}).

Tuning of SVC hyperparameters. In NSC, we deal with high-accuracy state classifiers. This implies that the datasets $\mathcal{D}_c^e$, with $e \in \{fp, fn\}$, are highly unbalanced, as they contain more examples of correct classifications (label 0) than of classification errors (label 1). In binary classification problems, such as our l-SVCs, accuracy can be misleading with imbalanced datasets, as any model that "blindly" assigns the label of the most frequent class to any input will have high accuracy.

A simple method to handle imbalanced classes in SVC is to design an empirical penalty matrix $\mathcal{P}_e$, which assigns different error penalties by class [6]. In particular, the (i, j)-th entry of $\mathcal{P}_e$ gives the penalty for classifying an instance of class i as class j. Of course, when $i = j$, the penalty is null. The penalty matrix for dataset $\mathcal{D}_c^e$ is defined as

$$\mathcal{P}_e = \begin{bmatrix} 0 & \frac{q}{2r_e(q-n_e)} \\ \frac{r_e q}{2n_e} & 0 \end{bmatrix}, \quad (5)$$

where n_e is the number of points belonging to class 1 in dataset $\mathcal{D}_c^e$, and r_e is a parameter influencing how many errors of type e we are willing to accept. The term $\frac{r_e q}{2n_e}$, which represents the penalty for wrongly classifying an error of type e as correct, increases as n_e decreases. Note that, when $r_e = 1$ and the dataset is perfectly balanced ($q = 2n_e$), the penalties are equals: $\frac{r_e q}{2n_e} = \frac{q}{2r_e(q-n_e)} = 1$. Further, if $r_e > 1$, the penalty term increases, leading to more strict rejection thresholds and higher overall rejection rates. On the contrary, if $r_e < 1$, the penalty decreases, leading to possibly miss some errors of type e.

5   Active Learning

Recall that we are dealing with two combined learning problems: learning a prediction rule (i.e., a state classifier) using the training set Z_t, and learning a rejection rule using the calibration sets D_c^{fn} and D_c^{fp}. As the accuracy of a classifier increases with the quality and the quantity of observed data, adding samples to Z_t will generate a more accurate predictor, and similarly, adding samples to D_c^{fn} and D_c^{fp} will lead to more precise rejection thresholds. Ideally, one wants to maximize accuracy while using the least possible amount of additional samples, because obtaining labeled data is expensive (in NSC, labelling each sample entails solving a reachability checking problem), and the size of the datasets affect the complexity and the dimension of the problem. Therefore, to improve the accuracy of our learning models efficiently, we need a strategy to identify the most "informative" additional samples.

Our solution is *uncertainty sampling-based active learning*, where the retraining points are derived by first sampling a large pool of unlabeled data, and then considering only those points where the current predictor h is still uncertain. We develop an efficient query strategy that leverages the CP-based measures of uncertainty, and in particular, the rejection rule of Sect. 4, since rejected points are indeed the most uncertain ones. The proposed active learning method should reduce both the overall number of false-positive and false-negative predictions and the overall rejection rate.

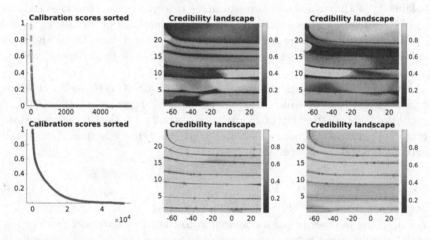

Fig. 2. Spiking Neuron: calibration scores (first column) and credibility landscapes using the initial calibration set Z_c (top line) versus the query set Z_Q (bottom line). The landscapes are obtained for different instances of the predictor h, trained on the same dataset Z_t.

5.1 Refining the Query Strategy

Sensitivity of the uncertainty measures. The distribution of calibration scores depends both on the case study at hand and on the trained classifier. If such a classifier h has high accuracy, then most of the calibration scores $\alpha_1, \ldots, \alpha_q$ will be close to zero. Each p-value p_*^j of an unseen test point x_* counts the number of calibration scores greater than α_*^j, the non-conformity score for label j at x_*. Credibility, which is the p-value associated with the class predicted by h, is expected to have a small score and therefore a high p-value. On the contrary, γ, which is the p-value associated to the other (non-predicted) class, is expected to have a larger score. However, given the high accuracy of h, the number of calibration scores significantly greater than zero is very small. Therefore, the fraction of calibration scores determining γ is not very sensitive to changes in the value of α_*, which is determined by $h(x_*)$. On the contrary, credibility is extremely sensitive to small changes in α_*. In general, the sensitivity of confidence with respect to α_* increases as the accuracy of h decreases, and vice versa for credibility. Figure 2 shows the credibility landscapes for two different training instances of model h on the same training set for a concrete case study. We observe that even if regions where misclassifications take place are always assigned low credibility values, outside those regions credibility values are subject to high variance.

This sensitivity results in a over-conservative rejection criterion, leading to a high rejection rate and in turn, to an inefficient query strategy. However, if we enrich the calibration set using additional samples with non-zero α-scores, we can reduce such sensitivity, thereby making credibility more robust with respect to retraining. This process is illustrated in Fig. 2, where the additional non-zero α-scores (bottom) lead to a more robust credibility landscape, where low-credibility regions are now more tightly centred around areas of misclassification.

Since samples with uncertain predictions will have non-zero α-scores[6], we will use the original rejection rule to enrich the calibration set, thereby deriving a refined rejection rule and in turn, a refined and more effective query strategy for active learning. Notice that, once the model h has been retrained we must accordingly retrain the rejection rule as well, since values of confidence and credibility depend on the predictions of h.

5.2   Active Learning Algorithm

The active learning is divided in two phases. In the first phase, we refine the query strategy: we use the current rejection rule to select a batch of uncertain points, temporarily add these points to the calibration set, and obtain an updated rejection rule, which represents our query strategy.

In the second phase, using the refined query strategy, we sample another batch of points, divide it in two groups, and use them to augment training and calibration sets, respectively. The resulting predictor h_a, trained on the augmented set, is expected to be more accurate then h. Further, h_a is used to update the α-scores and the values of confidence and credibility for the augmented calibration set. This results in an updated rejection rule, for which a lower rejection rate is expected.

---

[6] Note indeed that the α-score of a sample (x_i, y_i) is zero only if h both correctly predicts y_i and the corresponding class likelihood $P_h(y_i \mid x_i)$ is 1.

We now describe in details our uncertainty sampling-based active learning algorithm, which given an initial training set Z_t, a prediction rule h trained on Z_t, an initial calibration set Z_c, a rejection rule R trained on Z_c using some rejection ratios r_{fn} and r_{fp}, computes an enhanced predictor h_a and enhanced rejection rule R_a as follows.

1. **Refining the query strategy:**
   - Randomly select a large number of input points, compute their confidence and credibility using h, and identify the subset Q of points rejected based on R.
   - Invoke the reachability oracle to label the points in Q and define a query set Z_Q by adding these points to Z_c.
   - Obtain an updated rejection rule R_Q from Z_Q using the method of Sect. 4 with rejection ratios r_{fn} and r_{fp}.

2. **Active phase:**
   - Randomly select a large number of input points, compute their confidence and credibility using h, and identify the subset A of points rejected based on R_Q.
   - Invoke the reachability oracle to label the points in A, divide the data into two groups and add them respectively to Z_t and Z_c, obtaining an augmented training set, Z_t^a, and an augmented calibration set, Z_c^a.
   - Train a new predictor h_a from Z_t^a.
   - Train new detection thresholds using the method of Sect. 4, with rejection ratios r_{fn} and r_{fp}, and obtain the enhanced rejection rule R_a.

Note that the above algorithm can be iterated, using Z_t^a, Z_c^a, h_a, and R_a as new inputs.

It is important to observe that, in order for the active learning algorithm to preserve the statistical soundness of conformal prediction, the augmented training and calibration sets Z_t^a and Z_c^a must be sampled from the same distribution. This is guaranteed by the fact that, in the active learning phase, we add new points to both the training and the calibration dataset, and these points are sampled from the same distribution (in particular, we apply the same random sampling method and same rejection criterion). The only caveat is ensuring that the ratio between the number of samples in Z_c and Z_t is preserved on the augmented datasets.

6   Experimental Results

In order to experimentally evaluate the proposed method, both the initial approach and the active learning approach have been applied to hybrid systems with varying degrees of complexity. We consider three deterministic case studies: the spiking neuron [21], which is a two-dimensional model with non-linear dynamics, the artificial pancreas (AP) [18], which is a nine-dimensional non-linear model, and the helicopter [21], a linear model with 29 variables. In addition, we analyze two non-deterministic models with non-linear dynamics: a cruise controller [21], whose input space has four dimensions, and a triple water tank (WT) [1], which is a three-dimensional model. For the AP model, the unsafe set U corresponds to hypoglycemia states, i.e., $U = BG \leq 3.9$ mmol/L, where BG is the blood glucose variable. The state distribution considers uniformly distributed values of plasma glucose and insulin. The insulin control input is fixed to the basal value. The time bound is $T = 240$. For the WT model, U is given by states where the water level of any of the tanks falls outside a given safe interval I, i.e., $U = \vee_{i=1}^{3} x_i \notin I$, where x_i is the water level of tank i. The state distribution considers water levels uniformly distributed within the safe interval. The time bound is $T = 1$. Details on the other case studies are available in Appendix D of [20].

Experimental settings. The entire pipeline is implemented in MATLAB. Motivated by the results presented in [21], we define the state classifier as a sigmoid DNN. Each case study shares the same DNN architecture: 3 hidden layers, each consisting of 10 neurons with the Tan-Sigmoid activation function and an output layer with 1 neuron with the Log-Sigmoid activation function. In particular, the output of the DNN, which is our model h, is the likelihood of class 1, i.e., the likelihood that the hybrid automaton state is positive. Training is performed using MATLAB's `train` function, with the Levenberg-Marquardt backpropagation algorithm optimizing the mean square error loss function, and the Nguyen-Widrow initialization method for the NN layers. Training the DNNs takes from 2 to 39 s. For every model we generate an initial dataset Z' of 20,000 samples and a test set Z_{test} of 10,000 samples. The helicopter model is the only exception, where, due to the higher dimensionality, a dataset of 100,000 samples is used. The training and calibration sets are two subsets of Z' extracted as follows: a sample $z \in Z'$ has probability 0.7 of falling into Z_t and probability 0.3 of falling into Z_c. We used the dReal solver [13] as reachability oracle to label the datasets for the non-deterministic case studies. For deterministic ones, we used an HA simulator implemented in MATLAB.

Computational performance. We want our method to be capable of working at runtime, which means it must be extremely fast in making predictions and deciding whether to trust them. We must clarify that the time required to train the method does not affect its runtime efficiency, as it is performed in advance only once. Learning the rejection criteria, which is also performed offline, requires the following steps: (i) train the state classifier, (ii) generate the datasets $\mathcal{D}_c^{fp/fn}$, which requires computing the p-values for each point in Z_c, and (iii) train four l-SVCs. Executing the entire pipeline takes around 10 s, if $|Z'| = 20K$, and around 80 s if $|Z'| = 100K$. Nonetheless, given a new input x_*, it takes from 0.3 up to 2 ms to evaluate the rejection criterion. This evaluation time does not depend on the dimension of the hybrid system, but it is affected by the size of the calibration set Z_c. Refining the uncertainty measures leads to an increase in the size of Z_c. Hence the aim of active learning is to improve the performance while keeping the technique as efficient as possible. Instead of adding random samples to Z_c, our active learning approach adds only samples that are extremely informative and brings a consistent improvement in the precision of the uncertainty measures. It carries two additional training costs: the time needed to compute confidence and credibility for a large pool of data, and the time the oracle needs to compute labels for the uncertain points. The latter dominates, especially for non-deterministic systems, since their oracles are more expensive. Therefore, if the rejection rate is relatively high and we consider a large pool of points, which allows for a good exploration, the procedure may be long. However, this time spent to optimally tune the performance improves the run-time behaviour of our method. This is another good reason to improve the query strategy before proceeding with the active learning approach. The time required to refine the query strategy depends on the size of the pool of data, the higher the initial rejection rate, the higher the number of queries. However, the pool has to be large in order to find significant instances. Adding observations about uncertain samples results in a more precise rejection rule with a lower rejection rate. Therefore, points selected with the refined query strategy are fewer and more informative.

Experiments. We compare our uncertainty-based query strategy with a random sampling strategy. Both strategies add the same number of samples to Z_t and the same number of samples to Z_c. However, in the first case, referred to as active approach, these samples are selected according to the refined query strategy, whereas in the second case, referred to as passive approach, they are randomly sampled following a uniform distribution, the same distribution used to generate the initial datasets.

The duration of the active learning phase depends on the sizes of the sample pools. In our study, the pool used to refine the query strategy contains $100,000$ samples ($250,000$ for the helicopter), whereas the pool used for the active learning phase contains $200,000$ samples ($500,000$ for the helicopter). In particular, one iteration of the active learning procedure took around 10 min for the spiking neuron and the artificial pancreas, the simplest deterministic models, and around 70 min for the helicopter, due to the larger pools. For the non-deterministic models (triple water tank and cruise controller), it took around 2.25 h. This time is expected to decrease for subsequent iterations, as the rejection rate will be lower (leading to fewer retraining samples). Note that retraining is performed offline and does not affect runtime performance of our approach.

Tables 1 and 2 present the experimental performance of the rejection criterion obtained using the original method in Sect. 4 and the refined rejection criteria obtained using the active and passive approaches. All results are averaged over 5 runs; in each run, we resample Z_t and Z_c from Z' and retrain the DNN. Table 1 shows the performance obtained using the initial rejection rule on the test set Z_{test}. The accuracy of the NSC, averaged over the five case studies, is 99.5832%. The rejection criterion recognizes well almost all the errors (with average accuracy over the accepted predictions of 99.9956%), but the overall rejection rate is around 5%, a non-negligible amount. We see from Table 2 that the passive learning approach provides little improvement: the overall number of errors is similar to the initial one and the rejection rate is still relatively large. Table 2 also shows that the active approach provides much more significant improvements: the overall rejection rate and the number of errors made by the NSC fall dramatically, while preserving the ability of recognizing almost all of the errors, both false positives and false negatives, made by the predictor (average accuracy over the accepted predictions of 99.9992%). The overall rejection rates span between 3.46% and 9.88% when the initial rejection rule is applied. In contrast, the active learning approach achieves rejection rates between 0.51% and 2.74%. The overall number of errors reduces as well: the range of false-negative errors reduces from 7–33.2 to 1.8–11.6, while the range of false-positive errors reduces from 8.2–48.8 to 2–11.2.

In our analysis, parameters r_{fp} and r_{fn} are set to one, i.e., they do not influence the selection of rejection thresholds. If false negatives have severe consequences, one can design a stricter policy by assigning r_{fn} a value greater than one. On the contrary, we can relax the policy on false positives, assigning to r_{fp} a value smaller than one, and thus reducing the overall rejection rate. In general, it may be wise to first improve the performance of the predictor in recognizing both types of errors via active learning, and then decide to reduce the overall rejection rate by allowing some false positives.

Table 1. Performance of the initial rejection criterion on the test set. Results are averaged over 5 runs. Accuracy is the percentage of points in the test set that are correctly predicted. The **fp** and **fn** columns show the ratio of false positives and false negatives, respectively, recognized by each criteria. The last column shows the percentage of point rejected over the entire test set.

| Model | INITIAL | | | |
	accuracy	fp	fn	rej. rate
Spiking Neuron (SN)	99.582%	24.4/24.6	17.2/17.2	5.68%
Artificial Pancreas (AP)	99.488%	30.4/30.6	20.6/20.6	6.23%
Helicopter (HE)	99.180%	47.4/48.8	33/33.2	9.88%
Water Tank (WT)	99.818%	8.6/8.6	9.6/9.6	5.97%
Cruise Controller (CC)	99.848%	8.2/8.2	7/7	3.46%

Table 2. Performance of rejection criteria obtained by refining the initial rejection criterion using the passive and active approaches. Results are averaged over 5 runs. Most of the columns have the same meaning as in Table 1. "# samples" is the number of samples added globally to Z_t and Z_c.

| Model | # samples | PASSIVE | | | ACTIVE | | | |
		fp	fn	rej. rate	accuracy	fp	fn	rej. rate
SN	5748.2	18.2/18.2	10.6/10.8	3.91%	99.918%	2.8/2.8	5.4/5.4	1.16%
AP	6081.8	23/23.4	19.4/19.4	5.94%	99.892%	6.2/6.2	4.4/4.6	1.02%
HE	22014.6	31.4/31.6	26/26.6	7.21%	99.772%	11.2/11.2	10.4/11.6	2.74%
WT	4130.2	8.4/8.4	10.2/10.4	4.43%	99.962%	2.8/2.8	1/1	0.70%
CC	2280.6	6/6	6/6	5.15%	99.962%	2/2	1.8/1.8	0.51%

7   Related Work

A number of methods have been proposed for online reachability analysis that rely on separating the reachability computation into distinct offline and online phases. However, these methods are limited to restricted classes of models [10], or require handcrafted optimization of the HA's derivatives [4], or are efficient only for low-dimensional systems and simple dynamics [25].

In contrast, NSC [21] is based on learning DNN-based classifiers, is fully automated and has negligible computational cost at runtime. In [11,24], similar techniques are introduced for neural approximation of Hamilton-Jacobi (HJ) reachability. Our methods for prediction rejection and active learning are independent of the class of systems and the machine-learning approximation of reachability, and thus can also be applied to neural approximations of HJ reachability.

The work of [3] addresses the predictive monitoring problem for stochastic black-box systems, where a Markov model is inferred offline from observed traces and used to construct a predictive runtime monitor for probabilistic reachability checking. In contrast to NSC, this method focuses on discrete-space models, which allows the predictor to be represented as a look-up table (as opposed to a neural network).

In [22], a method is presented for predictive monitoring of STL specifications with probabilistic guarantees. These guarantees derive from computing prediction intervals of ARMA/ARIMA models learned from observed traces. Similarly, we use CP which also can derive prediction intervals with probabilistic guarantees, with the difference that CP supports any class of prediction models (including auto-regressive ones).

A related approach to NSC is smoothed model checking [9], where Gaussian processes [23] are used to approximate the satisfaction function of stochastic models, i.e., mapping model parameters into the satisfaction probability of a specification. Smoothed model checking leverages Bayesian statistics to quantify prediction uncertainty, but faces scalability issues as the dimension of the system increases. In contrast, computing our measure of prediction reliability is very efficient, because it is nearly equivalent to executing the underlying predictor.[7] In Bayesian approaches to uncertainty estimation, one often does not know the true prior distribution, which is thus often chosen arbitrarily. However, if the prior is incorrect, the resulting uncertainty measures have no theoretical base. The CP framework that we use is instead distribution-free and provides uncertainty information based only on the standard i.i.d. or exchangeability assumption. Avoiding Bayesian assumptions makes CP conclusions more robust to different underlying data distributions, which is also shown experimentally in [17].

A basic application of conformal predictors in active learning is presented in [16]. Our approach introduces three important improvements: a more flexible and meaningful combination of confidence and credibility values, automated

---

[7] Evaluating our rejection criterion reduces to computing two p-values (confidence and credibility). Each p-value is derived by computing a nonconformity score, which requires one execution of the underlying predictor h, and one search over the array of calibration scores.

learning of rejection thresholds (which are instead fixed in [16]), and refinement of the query strategy.

In [8], we presented a preliminary version of this approach. The present paper greatly extends and improves that work by including an automated and optimal method to select rejection thresholds, the active learning method, and an evaluation on larger HA benchmarks.

8 Conclusion

We have presented Neural Predictive Monitoring, a technique for providing statistical guarantees on the prediction reliability of neural network-based state classifiers used for runtime reachability prediction. To this purpose, we have introduced statistically rigorous measures that quantify the prediction uncertainty of a state classifier. We have employed these uncertainty measures to derive conservative rejection criteria that identify, with minimal error, those predictions that can lead to safety-critical state classification errors. We have further designed an active learning strategy that, leveraging such uncertainty-based rejection criteria, allow to increase the accuracy of the reachability predictor and reduce the overall rejection rate.

The strengths of our NPM technique are its effectiveness in identifying and rejecting prediction errors and its computational efficiency, which is not directly affected by the complexity of the system under analysis (but only by the complexity of the underlying learning problem and classifier). As future work, we plan to extend our approach to predict quantitative measures of property satisfaction (like the robust STL semantics [12]), which will require us to develop a regression framework for NPM.

Acknowledgements. This material is based on work supported in part by NSF Grants CCF-1414078, CCF-1918225, CPS-1446832, and IIS-1447549.

References

1. dReal - Networked Water Tank Controllers (2017). http://dreal.github.io/benchmarks/networks/water/
2. Alur, R.: Formal verification of hybrid systems. In: Proceedings of the Ninth ACM International Conference on Embedded Software (EMSOFT), pp. 273–278, October 2011
3. Babaee, R., Gurfinkel, A., Fischmeister, S.: Predictive run-time verification of discrete-time reachability properties in black-box systems using trace-level abstraction and statistical learning. In: Colombo, C., Leucker, M. (eds.) RV 2018. LNCS, vol. 11237, pp. 187–204. Springer, Cham (2018). https://doi.org/10.1007/978-3-030-03769-7_11
4. Bak, S., Johnson, T.T., Caccamo, M., Sha, L.: Real-time reachability for verified simplex design. In: Real-Time Systems Symposium (RTSS), 2014 IEEE, pp. 138–148. IEEE (2014)

5. Balasubramanian, V., Ho, S.S., Vovk, V.: Conformal prediction for reliable machine learning: theory, adaptations and applications. Newnes (2014)
6. Batuwita, R., Palade, V.: Class imbalance learning methods for support vector machines (2013)
7. Bishop, C.M.: Pattern Recognition and Machine Learning. Information Science and Statistics. Springer, New York (2006)
8. Bortolussi, L., Cairoli, F., Paoletti, N., Stoller, S.D.: Conformal predictions for hybrid system state classification. In: From Reactive Systems to Cyber-Physical Systems, to appear (2019)
9. Bortolussi, L., Milios, D., Sanguinetti, G.: Smoothed model checking for uncertain continuous-time Markov chains. Inf. Comput. **247**, 235–253 (2016)
10. Chen, X., Sankaranarayanan, S.: Model predictive real-time monitoring of linear systems. In: Real-Time Systems Symposium (RTSS), 2017 IEEE, pp. 297–306. IEEE (2017)
11. Djeridane, B., Lygeros, J.: Neural approximation of PDE solutions: an application to reachability computations. In: Proceedings of the 45th IEEE Conference on Decision and Control, pp. 3034–3039. IEEE (2006)
12. Donzé, A., Maler, O.: Robust satisfaction of temporal logic over real-valued signals. In: Chatterjee, K., Henzinger, T.A. (eds.) FORMATS 2010. LNCS, vol. 6246, pp. 92–106. Springer, Heidelberg (2010). https://doi.org/10.1007/978-3-642-15297-9_9
13. Gao, S., Kong, S., Clarke, E.M.: dReal: an SMT solver for nonlinear theories over the reals. In: Bonacina, M.P. (ed.) CADE 2013. LNCS (LNAI), vol. 7898, pp. 208–214. Springer, Heidelberg (2013). https://doi.org/10.1007/978-3-642-38574-2_14
14. Henzinger, T.A., Kopke, P.W., Puri, A., Varaiya, P.: What's decidable about hybrid automata? J. Comput. Syst. Sci. **57**(1), 94–124 (1998)
15. Lehmann, E.L., Romano, J.P.: Testing Statistical Hypotheses. Springer Texts in Statistics. Springer, New York (2006)
16. Makili, L.E., Sánchez, J.A.V., Dormido-Canto, S.: Active learning using conformal predictors: application to image classification. Fusion Sci. Technol. **62**(2), 347–355 (2012)
17. Melluish, T., Saunders, C., Nouretdinov, I., Vovk, V.: The typicalness framework: a comparison with the bayesian approach. University of London, Royal Holloway (2001)
18. Paoletti, N., Liu, K.S., Smolka, S.A., Lin, S.: Data-driven robust control for type 1 diabetes under meal and exercise uncertainties. In: Feret, J., Koeppl, H. (eds.) CMSB 2017. LNCS, vol. 10545, pp. 214–232. Springer, Cham (2017). https://doi.org/10.1007/978-3-319-67471-1_13
19. Papadopoulos, H.: Inductive conformal prediction: Theory and application to neural networks. In: Tools in artificial intelligence. InTech (2008)
20. Phan, D., Paoletti, N., Zhang, T., Grosu, R., Smolka, S.A., Stoller, S.D.: Neural state classification for hybrid systems. ArXiv e-prints, July 2018
21. Phan, D., Paoletti, N., Zhang, T., Grosu, R., Smolka, S.A., Stoller, S.D.: Neural state classification for hybrid systems. In: Lahiri, S.K., Wang, C. (eds.) ATVA 2018. LNCS, vol. 11138, pp. 422–440. Springer, Cham (2018). https://doi.org/10.1007/978-3-030-01090-4_25
22. Qin, X., Deshmukh, J.V.: Predictive monitoring for signal temporal logic with probabilistic guarantees. In: Proceedings of the 22nd ACM International Conference on Hybrid Systems: Computation and Control, pp. 266–267. ACM (2019)
23. Rasmussen, C.E., Williams, C.K.: Gaussian Processes for Machine Learning, vol. 1. MIT press, Cambridge (2006)

24. Royo, V.R., Fridovich-Keil, D., Herbert, S., Tomlin, C.J.: Classification-based approximate reachability with guarantees applied to safe trajectory tracking. arXiv preprint arXiv:1803.03237 (2018)
25. Sauter, G., Dierks, H., Fränzle, M., Hansen, M.R.: Lightweight hybrid model checking facilitating online prediction of temporal properties. In: Proceedings of the 21st Nordic Workshop on Programming Theory, pp. 20–22 (2009)
26. Sha, L.: Using simplicity to control complexity. IEEE Softw. **4**, 20–28 (2001)
27. Vovk, V., Gammerman, A., Shafer, G.: Algorithmic learning in a random world. Springer, Heidelberg (2005)

Comparing Controlled System Synthesis and Suppression Enforcement

Luca Aceto[1,2], Ian Cassar[2,3(✉)], Adrian Francalanza[3], and Anna Ingólfsdóttir[2]

[1] Gran Sasso Science Institute, L'Aquila, Italy
[2] School of Computer Science, Reykjavík University, Reykjavík, Iceland
[3] Department of Computer Science, University of Malta, Msida, Malta
`ian.cassar.10@um.edu.mt`

Abstract. Runtime enforcement and control system synthesis are two verification techniques that automate the process of transforming an erroneous system into a valid one. As both techniques can modify the behaviour of a system to prevent erroneous executions, they are both ideal for ensuring safety. In this paper, we investigate the interplay between these two techniques and identify control system synthesis as being the static counterpart to suppression-based runtime enforcement, in the context of safety properties.

1 Introduction

Our increasing reliance on software systems is inherently raising the demand for ensuring their reliability and correctness. Several verification techniques help facilitate this task by automating the process of deducing whether the system under scrutiny (SuS) satisfies a predefined set of correctness properties. Properties are either verified pre-deployment (statically), as in the case of model checking (MC) [7,12], or post-deployment (dynamically), as per runtime verification (RV) [11,20,27]. In both cases, any error discovered during the verification serves as guidance for identifying the invalid parts of the system that require adjustment.

Other techniques, such as *runtime enforcement* (RE), additionally attempt to automatically transform the invalid system into a valid one. Runtime enforcement [5,15,26,28] adopts an intrusive monitoring approach by which every observable action executed by the SuS is scrutinized and modified as necessary by a monitor at runtime. Monitors in RE may be described in various ways, such as: transducers [5,8,32], shields [26] and security automata [17,28,34]. They may opt to *replace* the invalid actions by valid ones, or completely *suppress* them,

This work was partly supported by the projects "TheoFoMon: Theoretical Foundations for Monitorability" (nr. 163406-051) and "Developing Theoretical Foundations for Runtime Enforcement" (nr. 184776-051) of the Icelandic Research Fund, by the EU H2020 RISE programme under the Marie Skłodowska-Curie grant agreement nr. 778233, and by the Endeavour Scholarship Scheme (Malta), part-financed by the European Social Fund (ESF) - Operational Programme II – Cohesion Policy 2014–2020.

© Springer Nature Switzerland AG 2019
B. Finkbeiner and L. Mariani (Eds.): RV 2019, LNCS 11757, pp. 148–164, 2019.
https://doi.org/10.1007/978-3-030-32079-9_9

thus rendering them immaterial to the environment interacting with the SuS; in certain cases, monitors can even *insert* actions that may directly affect the environment. Different enforcement strategies are applied depending on the property that needs to be enforced.

A great deal of effort [4, 13, 22, 23, 25] has been made to study the interplay between static and dynamic techniques, particularly to understand how the two can be used in unison to minimise their respective weaknesses. It is well established that runtime verification is the *dynamic counterpart* of model checking, which means that a subset of the properties verifiable using MC can also be verified dynamically via RV. In fact, multi-pronged verification approaches often use RV in conjunction with MC. Particularly, MC is used to statically verify the parts of the SuS which cannot be verified dynamically (*e.g.*, inaccessible code, performance constraints, *etc.*), while RV is then used to verify other parts dynamically in order to minimise the state explosion problem inherent to MC.

It is however unclear as to which technique can be considered as the *static counterpart* to runtime enforcement. Identifying such a technique enables the possibility of adopting a multi-pronged enforcement approach. One possible candidate is *controlled system synthesis* (CSS) [9, 14, 24, 30]: it analyses the state space of the SuS and reformulates it pre-deployment by *removing* the system's ability to execute erroneous behaviour. As a result, a restricted (yet valid) version of the SuS is produced; this is known as a *controlled system*.

The primary aim of both RE and CSS is to force the resulting monitored/controlled system adheres to the respective property − this is known as *soundness* in RE and *validity* in CSS. Further guarantees are also generally required to ensure minimal disruption to valid systems − this is ensured via *transparency* in RE and *maximal expressiveness* in CSS. As both techniques may adjust systems by omitting their invalid behaviours, they are ideal for ensuring *safety*. These observations, along with other commonalities, hint at the existence of a relationship between runtime enforcement and controlled system synthesis, in the context of safety properties.

In this paper we conduct a preliminary investigation on the interplay between the above mentioned two techniques with the aim of establishing a static counterpart for runtime enforcement. We intend to identify a set of properties that can be enforced either dynamically, via runtime enforcement, or statically via controlled system synthesis. In this first attempt, we however limit ourselves to study this relationship in the context of *safety properties*. As a vehicle for this comparison, we choose the recent work on CSS by van Hulst *et al.* [24], and compare it to our previous work, presented in [5], on enforcing safety properties via action suppressions. We chose these two bodies of work as they are accurate representations of the two techniques. Moreover, they share a number of commonalities including their choice of specification language, modelling of systems, *etc.* To further simplify our comparison, we formulate both techniques in a core common setting and show that there are subtle differences between them even in that scenario. Specifically, we identify a common core within the work presented in [5, 24] by:

- working with respect to the Safe Hennessy Milner Logic with invariance (sHML$_{inv}$), that is, the *intersection* of the logics used by both works, namely, the Safe Hennessy Milner Logic with recursion (sHML) in [5] and the Hennessy Milner Logic with invariance and reachability (HML$_{inv}^{reach}$) in [24],
- removing constructs and aspects that are supported by one technique and not by the other, and by
- taking into account the assumptions considered in both bodies of work.

To our knowledge, no one has yet attempted to identify a static counterpart to RE, and an insightful comparison of RE and CSS has not yet been conducted. As part of our main contributions, we thus show that:

(i) The monitored system obtained from instrumenting a suppression monitor derived from a formula, and the controlled version of the same system (by the same formula), need not be observationally equivalent, Theorem 2.
(ii) In spite of (i) we prove that both of the obtained systems are *trace (language) equivalent*, that is, they can execute the same set of traces, Theorem 3.
(iii) When restricted to safety properties, controlled system synthesis is the *static counterpart* (Definition 3) to runtime enforcement, Theorem 4.

Although (i) entails that an external observer can still tell the difference between these two resultant systems [1], knowing (ii) suffices to deduce (iii) since it is well known that trace equivalent systems satisfy the exact same set of safety properties, Theorem 1.

Structure of the Paper. Section 2 provides the necessary preliminary material describing how we model systems as labelled transition systems and properties via the chosen logic. In Sect. 3 we give an overview of the equalized and simplified versions of the enforcement model presented in [5] and the controlled system synthesis rules of [24]. Section 4 then compares the differences and similarities between the two models, followed by our first contribution which *disproves* the observational equivalence of the two techniques. Section 5 then presents our second set of contributions consisting of a mapping function that derives enforcement monitors from logic formulas, and the proof that the obtained monitored and controlled versions of a given system are *trace equivalent*. This allows us to establish that controlled system synthesis is the *static counterpart* to enforcement when it comes to safety properties. Section 6 overviews related work, and Sect. 7 concludes.

2   Preliminaries

The Model: We assume systems described as *labelled transition systems* (LTSs), which are triples $\langle \text{SYS}, \text{ACT} \cup \{\tau\}, \rightarrow \rangle$ defining a set of *system states*, $s, r, q \in \text{SYS}$, a finite set of *observable actions*, $\alpha, \beta \in \text{ACT}$, and a distinguished silent action $\tau \notin \text{ACT}$, along with a *transition* relation, $\longrightarrow \subseteq (\text{SYS} \times \text{ACT} \cup \{\tau\} \times \text{SYS})$. We let $\mu \in \text{ACT} \cup \{\tau\}$ and write $s \xrightarrow{\mu} r$ in lieu of $(s, \mu, r) \in \rightarrow$. We use $s \xRightarrow{\alpha} r$ to denote

Syntax

$$\varphi, \psi \in \text{sHML} ::= \text{tt (truth)} \quad | \quad \text{ff (falsehood)} \quad | \quad \varphi \wedge \psi \text{ (conjunction)}$$
$$| \ [\alpha]\varphi \text{ (necessity)} \ | \ \max X.\varphi \text{ (greatest fp.)} \ | \ X \text{ (fp. variable)}$$

Semantics

$$\llbracket \text{tt}, \rho \rrbracket \stackrel{\text{def}}{=} \text{Sys} \qquad\qquad \llbracket [\alpha]\varphi, \rho \rrbracket \stackrel{\text{def}}{=} \{s \mid \forall r \cdot s \text{ if } s \stackrel{\alpha}{\Rightarrow} r \text{ then } r \in \llbracket \varphi, \rho \rrbracket \}$$

$$\llbracket \text{ff}, \rho \rrbracket \stackrel{\text{def}}{=} \emptyset \qquad\qquad\quad \llbracket \varphi \wedge \psi, \rho \rrbracket \stackrel{\text{def}}{=} \llbracket \varphi, \rho \rrbracket \cap \llbracket \psi, \rho \rrbracket$$

$$\llbracket X, \rho \rrbracket \stackrel{\text{def}}{=} \rho(X) \qquad\quad \llbracket \max X.\varphi, \rho \rrbracket \stackrel{\text{def}}{=} \bigcup \{S \mid S \subseteq \llbracket \varphi, \rho[X \mapsto S] \rrbracket \}$$

We also encode $\Box \varphi$ as $\max X.\varphi \wedge \bigwedge_{\beta \in \text{Act}} [\beta]X$ where X is a fresh variable.

Fig. 1. The syntax and semantics for sHML.

weak transitions representing $s(\stackrel{\tau}{\longrightarrow})^* \cdot \stackrel{\alpha}{\longrightarrow} r$ and refer to r as an α-derivative of s. Traces $t, u \in \text{Act}^*$ range over (finite) sequences of observable actions, and we write $s \stackrel{t}{\Rightarrow} r$ for a sequence of weak transitions $s \stackrel{\alpha_1}{\Longrightarrow} \ldots \stackrel{\alpha_n}{\Longrightarrow} r$ where $t = \alpha_1, \ldots, \alpha_n$ for some $n \geq 0$; when $n = 0$, t is the empty trace ε and $s \stackrel{\varepsilon}{\Rightarrow} r$ means $s \stackrel{\tau}{\longrightarrow}^* r$. For each $\mu \in \text{Act} \cup \{\tau\}$, the notation $\hat{\mu}$ stands for ε if $\mu = \tau$ and for μ otherwise. We write $traces(s)$ for the set of traces executable from system state s, that is, $t \in traces(s)$ iff $s \stackrel{t}{\Rightarrow} r$ for some r. We use the syntax of the regular fragment of CCS [29] to concisely describe LTSs in our examples. We also assume the classic notions for *trace (language) equivalence* and *observational equivalence*, that is, weak bisimilarity [29,33].

Definition 1 (Trace Equivalence). *Two LTS system states s and r are trace equivalent iff they produce the same set of traces, i.e., $traces(s) = traces(r)$.* □

Definition 2 (Observational Equivalence). *A relation $\mathcal{R}$ over a set of system states is a weak bisimulation iff whenever $(s, r) \in \mathcal{R}$ for every action μ, the following transfer properties are satisfied:*

- *$s \stackrel{\mu}{\longrightarrow} s'$ implies there exists a transition $r \stackrel{\hat{\mu}}{\Rightarrow} r'$ such that $(s', r') \in \mathcal{R}$; and*
- *$r \stackrel{\mu}{\longrightarrow} r'$ implies there exists a transition $s \stackrel{\hat{\mu}}{\Rightarrow} s'$ such that $(s', r') \in \mathcal{R}$.*

Two system states s and r are observationally equivalent, denoted by $s \approx r$, iff there exists a weak bisimulation that relates them. □

The Logic: The safety logic sHML [6,7] is defined as the set of formulas generated by the grammar of Fig. 1. It assumes a countably infinite set of logical variables $X, Y \in \text{LVar}$ and provides the standard constructs of truth, tt, falsehood, ff, and conjunctions, $\varphi \wedge \psi$. As a shorthand, we occasionally denote conjunctions as $\bigwedge_{i \in I} \varphi_i$, where I is a finite set of indices, and when $I = \emptyset$, $\bigwedge_{i \in \emptyset} \varphi_i$ is equivalent to tt. The logic is also equipped with the *necessity (universal) modality*, $[\alpha]\varphi$, and allows for defining recursive properties using greatest fixpoints, $\max X.\varphi$, which bind free occurrences of X in φ. We additionally encode the *invariance* *operator*, $\Box \varphi$, requiring φ to be satisfied by every reachable system state, as the recursive property, $\max X.\varphi \wedge \bigwedge_{\beta \in \text{ACT}} [\beta]X$, where X is not free in φ.

Formulas in sHML are interpreted over the system powerset domain where $S \in \mathcal{P}(\text{SYS})$. The semantic definition of Fig. 1, $[\![\varphi, \rho]\!]$, is given for *both* open and closed formulas. It employs a valuation from logical variables to sets of states, $\rho \in (\text{LVAR} \to \mathcal{P}(\text{SYS}))$, which permits an inductive definition on the structure of the formulas; $\rho' = \rho[X \mapsto S]$ denotes a valuation where $\rho'(X) = S$ and $\rho'(Y) = \rho(Y)$ for all other $Y \neq X$. We assume *closed* formulas, *i.e.*, without free logical variables, and write $[\![\varphi]\!]$ in lieu of $[\![\varphi, \rho]\!]$ since the interpretation of a closed formula φ is independent of the valuation ρ. A system (state) s *satisfies* formula φ whenever $s \in [\![\varphi]\!]$.

It is a well known fact that trace equivalent systems satisfy the same set of safety properties. As the (recursion-free) subset of sHML characterises regular safety properties [21], this means that systems sharing the same traces also satisfy the same sHML formulas.

Theorem 1. *Let s and r be system states in an LTS. Then $traces(s) = traces(r)$ iff s and r satisfy exactly the same sHML formulas.* $\Box$

Example 1. Consider two systems (a good system, $s_{\mathbf{g}}$, and a bad one, $s_{\mathbf{b}}$) implementing a server that repeatedly accepts *requests* and *answers* them in response, and that only terminates upon accepting a *close* request. Whereas $s_{\mathbf{g}}$ outputs a *single* answer (ans) for every request (req), $s_{\mathbf{b}}$ occasionally produces *multiple* answers for a given request (see the underlined branch in the description of $s_{\mathbf{b}}$ below). Both systems terminate with cls.

$$s_{\mathbf{g}} = \text{rec } x.(\text{req.ans.}x + \text{cls.nil})$$
$$s_{\mathbf{b}} = \text{rec } x.(\text{req.}(\text{ans.}x + \underline{\text{ans.}(\text{ans.}x + \text{cls.nil})}) + \text{cls.nil})$$

We can specify that a request followed by two consecutive answers indicates invalid behaviour via the sHML formula φ_0.

$$\varphi_0 \stackrel{\text{def}}{=} \Box [\text{ans}][\text{ans}]\text{ff}$$
$$\stackrel{\text{def}}{=} \max X.[\text{ans}][\text{ans}]\text{ff} \wedge \bigwedge_{\alpha \in \text{ACT}} [\alpha]X$$

where $\text{ACT} \stackrel{\text{def}}{=} \{\text{ans}, \text{req}, \text{cls}\}$. It defines an invariant property requiring that at every reachable state, whenever the system produces an answer following a request, it cannot produce a subsequent answer, *i.e.*, [ans]ff. Using the semantics in Fig. 1, one can check that $s_{\mathbf{g}} \in [\![\varphi_0]\!]$, whereas $s_{\mathbf{b}} \notin [\![\varphi_0]\!]$ since it exhibits the violating trace $s_{\mathbf{b}} \xrightarrow{\text{req}} \cdot \xrightarrow{\text{ans}} \cdot \xrightarrow{\text{ans}} \ldots$, amongst others. $\Box$

3   Controlled System Synthesis and Suppression Enforcement

We present the simplified models for suppression enforcement and controlled system synthesis adapted from [5] and [24] respectively. Both models describe

$$\varphi, \psi \in \text{sHML}_{\text{inv}} ::= \text{tt} \mid \text{ff} \mid \varphi \wedge \psi \mid [\alpha]\varphi \mid \Box\varphi$$

Fig. 2. The syntax for sHML_{inv}.

the composite behaviour attained by the respective techniques. In suppression enforcement, the composite behaviour describes the *observable behaviour* obtained when the monitor and the SuS interact *at runtime*, while in controlled system synthesis, it describes the *structure* of the resulting controlled system obtained *statically prior to deployment.*

To enable our comparison between both approaches, we standardise the logics used in both works and restrict ourselves to sHML_{inv}, defined in Fig. 2. sHML_{inv} is a strict subset of sHML which results from the intersection of sHML, used for suppression enforcement in [5], and $\text{HML}_{\text{inv}}^{\text{reach}}$, used for controlled system synthesis in [24].

Although the work on CSS in [24] assumes that systems do not perform internal τ actions and that output labels may be associated to system states, the work on RE assumes the converse. We therefore equalise the system models by working with respect to LTSs that do not associate labels to states, and do not perform τ actions. We however assume that the resulting monitored and controlled systems may still perform τ actions.

Since we do not focus on state-based properties, the removal of state labels is not a major limitation as we are only forgoing additional state information from the SuS. Although the removal of τ actions requires the SuS to be fully observable, this does not impose significant drawbacks as the work on CSS can easily be extended to allow such actions.

Despite the fact that controlled system synthesis differentiates between system actions that can be removed (controllable) and those which cannot (uncontrollable), the work on enforcement does not. This is also not a major limitation since enforcement models can easily be adapted to make such a distinction. However, in our first attempt at a comparison, we opt to simplify the models as much as possible, and so to enable our comparison we assume that every system action is controllable and can be removed and suppressed by the respective techniques.

Finally, since we do not liberally introduce constructs that are not present in the original models of [5,24], the simplified models are just *restricted versions* of the original ones. Hence, the results proven with respect to these simplified models should either apply to the original ones or extend easily to the more general setting.

3.1   A Model for Suppression Enforcement

We use a simplified version of the operational model of enforcement presented in [5], which uses the transducers $m, n \in \text{TRN}$ defined in Fig. 3. Transducers define *transformation pairs*, $\{\beta, \mu\}$, consisting of: the *specifying action* β that determines whether or not the transformation should be applied to a system action α, and

Syntax

$$m, n \in \text{TRN} ::= \quad \{\alpha, \mu\}.m \quad (\text{where } \mu \in \{\alpha, \tau\}) \quad | \ \textstyle\sum_{i \in I} m_i \quad | \ \text{rec } x.m \quad | \ x$$

Dynamics

$$\text{ESEL} \frac{m_j \xrightarrow{\alpha \blacktriangleright \mu} n_j}{\sum_{i \in I} m_i \xrightarrow{\alpha \blacktriangleright \mu} n_j} \ j \in I \qquad \text{EREC} \frac{m\{\text{rec } x.m/x\} \xrightarrow{\alpha \blacktriangleright \mu} n}{\text{rec } x.m \xrightarrow{\alpha \blacktriangleright \mu} n}$$

$$\text{ETRN} \frac{}{\{\alpha, \mu\}.m \xrightarrow{\alpha \blacktriangleright \mu} m}$$

Instrumentation

$$\text{ITRN} \frac{s \xrightarrow{\alpha} s' \quad m \xrightarrow{\alpha \blacktriangleright \mu} n}{m[s] \xrightarrow{\mu} n[s']} \qquad \text{IDEF} \frac{s \xrightarrow{\alpha} s' \quad m \overset{\alpha}{\nrightarrow}}{m[s] \xrightarrow{\alpha} \text{id}[s']}$$

where $\text{id} \overset{\text{def}}{=} \text{rec } x. \sum_{\beta \in \text{ACT}} \{\beta\}.x$, $\text{sup} \overset{\text{def}}{=} \text{rec } x. \sum_{\beta \in \text{ACT}} \{\beta, \tau\}.x$ and $m \overset{\alpha}{\nrightarrow} \overset{\text{def}}{=} \nexists m', \mu \cdot m \xrightarrow{\alpha \blacktriangleright \mu} m'$.

Fig. 3. A model for transducers.

the *transformation action* μ that specifies whether the matched action α should be suppressed into a τ action, or be left intact. A transformation pair thus acts as a function that takes as input a system action α and transforms it into μ whenever α is equal to specifying action β. As a shorthand, we sometimes write $\{\beta\}$ in lieu of $\{\beta, \beta\}$ to signify that actions equal to β will remain unmodified.

The transition rules in Fig. 3 yield a LTS with labels of the form $\alpha \blacktriangleright \mu$. Intuitively, a transition $m \xrightarrow{\alpha \blacktriangleright \mu} n$ denotes the fact that the transducer in state m *transforms* the visible action α (produced by the system) into action μ and transitions into state n. In this sense, the transducer action $\alpha \blacktriangleright \alpha$ denotes the *identity* transformation, while $\alpha \blacktriangleright \tau$ encodes the *suppression* transformation of action α. The key transition rule is ETRN. It states that the transformation-prefix transducer $\{\alpha, \mu\}.m$ can transform action α into μ, as long as the specifying action α is the same as the action performed by the system. In this case, the transformed action is μ, and the transducer state that is reached is m.

The remaining rules ESEL and EREC respectively define the standard selection and recursion operations. A sum of transducers $\sum_{i \in I} m_i$ can reduce via ESEL to some n_j over some action $\alpha \blacktriangleright \mu$, whenever there exists a transducer m_j in the summation that reduces to n_j over the same action. Rule EREC enables a recursion transducer $\text{rec } x.m$ to reduce to some n when its unfolded instance $m\{\text{rec } x.m/x\}$ reduces to n as well. We encode the identity monitor, id, and the suppression monitor, sup, as $\text{rec } x. \sum_{\beta \in \text{ACT}} \{\beta\}.x$ and $\text{rec } x. \sum_{\beta \in \text{ACT}} \{\beta, \tau\}.x$ respectively, *i.e.*, as recursive monitors respectively defining an identity and suppression transformation for every possible action $\beta \in \text{ACT}$ that can be performed by the system.

Figure 3 also describes an *instrumentation* relation, which composes the behaviour of the SuS s with the transformations of a transducer monitor m

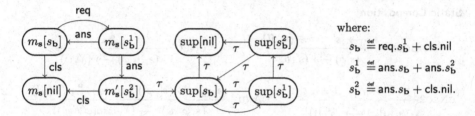

Fig. 4. The runtime execution graph of the monitored system.

that *agrees* with the (observable) actions ACT of s. The term $m[s]$ thus denotes the resulting *monitored system* whose behaviour is defined in terms of ACT $\cup \{\tau\}$ from the system's LTS. Concretely, rule ITRN states that when a system s transitions with an observable action α to s' and the transducer m can *transform* this action into μ and transition to n, the instrumented system $m[s]$ transitions with action μ to $n[s']$. Rule IDEF is analogous to standard monitor instrumentation rules for premature termination of the transducer [2,18,19,21], and accounts for underspecification of transformations. Thus, if a system s transitions with an observable action α to s', and the transducer m does not specify how to transform it $(m \xrightarrow{\alpha}\!\!\!\!\!/\ )$, the system is still allowed to transition while the transducer defaults to acting like the identity monitor, id, from that point onwards.

Example 2. Consider the suppression transducer $m_\mathbf{s}$ below:

$$m_\mathbf{s} \stackrel{\text{def}}{=} \text{rec}\, x.(\{\text{ans}\}.m'_\mathbf{s}) + \{\text{req}\}.x + \{\text{cls}\}.x$$
$$m'_\mathbf{s} \stackrel{\text{def}}{=} (\{\text{ans}, \tau\}.\text{sup} + \{\text{req}\}.x + \{\text{cls}\}.x)$$

where sup recursively suppresses every action $\beta \in$ ACT that can be performed by the system from that point onwards. When instrumented with system $s_\mathbf{b}$ from Example 1, the monitor prevents the monitored system $m_\mathbf{s}[s_\mathbf{b}]$ from answering twice in a row by suppressing the second answer and every subsequent visible action:

$$m_\mathbf{s}[s_\mathbf{b}] \xRightarrow{\ \text{req.ans}\ } \cdot \xrightarrow{\ \tau\ } \text{sup}[s_\mathbf{b}].$$

When equipped with this dynamic action suppression mechanism, the resulting monitored system $m_\mathbf{s}[s_\mathbf{b}]$ never violates formula φ_0 at runtime – this is illustrated by the runtime execution graph in Fig. 4.   □

We now formalise what we mean by a "static counterpart to suppression enforcement".

Definition 3 (Static Counterpart). *A static verification technique S is the static counterpart for suppression enforcement (in the context of safety properties) when, for every LTS $\langle$SYS, ACT, $\rightarrow\rangle$, formula $\varphi \in$ sHML$_{inv}$ and $s \in$ SYS, there exists a transducer m so that $m[s] \in [\![\varphi]\!]$ iff $S(s) \in [\![\varphi]\!]$ (where $S(s)$ is a statically reformulated version of s obtained from applying S).*   □

Static Composition

$$\text{cBool} \frac{s \xrightarrow{\alpha} s' \quad b \in \{\text{tt}, \text{ff}\}}{(s,b) \xmapsto{\alpha} (s',b)} \qquad \text{cNec1} \frac{s \xrightarrow{\alpha} s'}{(s,[\alpha]\varphi) \xmapsto{\alpha} (s',\varphi)}$$

$$\text{cNec2} \frac{s \xrightarrow{\beta} s' \quad \beta \neq \alpha}{(s,[\alpha]\varphi) \xmapsto{\beta} (s',\text{tt})} \qquad \text{cAnd} \frac{(s,\varphi) \xmapsto{\alpha} (s',\varphi') \quad (s,\psi) \xmapsto{\alpha} (s',\psi')}{(s,\varphi \wedge \psi) \xmapsto{\alpha} (s', min(\varphi' \wedge \psi'))}$$

$$\text{cMax} \frac{(s, \varphi\{max\,X.\varphi/X\}) \xmapsto{\alpha} (s',\psi)}{(s, max\,X.\varphi) \xmapsto{\alpha} (s', min(\psi))}$$

Synthesizability Test

$$\frac{\psi \in \{\text{tt}, X, [\alpha]\varphi\}}{(s,\varphi) \downarrow \psi} \qquad \frac{(s,\varphi) \downarrow \psi_1 \quad (s,\varphi) \downarrow \psi_2}{(s,\varphi) \downarrow (\psi_1 \wedge \psi_2)} \qquad \frac{(s,\varphi) \downarrow \psi}{(s,\varphi) \downarrow max\,X.\psi}$$

Invalid Transition Removal

$$\text{cTr} \frac{(s,\varphi) \xmapsto{\alpha} (s',\varphi') \quad (s',\varphi') \downarrow \varphi'}{(s,\varphi) \xrightarrow{\alpha} (s',\varphi')}$$

Fig. 5. The controlled system synthesis.

3.2 Synthesising Controlled Systems

Figure 5 presents a synthesis function that takes a system $\langle \text{Sys}, \text{Act}, \rightarrow \rangle$ and a formula φ and constructs a controlled version of the system that satisfies the formula. The new system is synthesised in two stages. In the first stage, a new transition relation $\mapsto \subseteq (\text{Sys} \times \text{sHML}) \times \text{Act} \times (\text{Sys} \times \text{sHML})$ is constructed over the state-formula product space, $(\text{Sys} \times \text{sHML})$. Intuitively, this transition relation associates a sHML formula to the initial system state and defines how this changes when the system transitions to other subsequent states. The composite behaviour of the formula and the system is statically computed using the first five rules in Fig. 5.

cBool always adds a transition when the formula is $b \in \{\text{tt}, \text{ff}\}$. Rules cNec1 and cNec2 add a transition from $[\alpha]\varphi$ to φ when s has a transition over α, and to tt if it reduces over $\beta \neq \alpha$. cAnd adds a transition for conjunct formulas, $\varphi \wedge \psi$, when both formulas can reduce independently to some φ' and ψ', with the formula of the end state of the new transition being $min(\varphi' \wedge \psi')$. Finally, cMax adds a fixpoint $max\,X.\varphi$ transition to $min(\psi)$, when its unfolding can reduce to ψ. In both cAnd and cMax, $min(\varphi)$ stands for a *minimal* logically equivalent formula of φ. This is an oversimplification of the minimisation techniques used in [24] to avoid synthesising an infinite LTS due to invariant formulas and conjunctions, see [24] for more details.

Example 3. Formulas $\varphi' \wedge \text{tt}$, $\varphi' \wedge \text{ff}$ and $\varphi \wedge \psi \wedge \psi$ are *logically equivalent* to (and can thus be minimized into) φ', ff and $\varphi \wedge \psi$ respectively. □

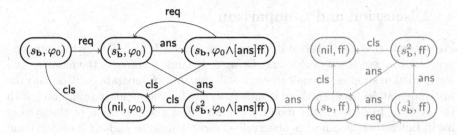

Fig. 6. The LTS obtained from controlling s_b via φ_0.

Instead of defining a rule for fixpoints, the authors of [24] define a synthesis rule directly for invariance stating that when $(s, \varphi) \overset{\alpha}{\longmapsto} (s', \varphi')$, then $(s, \Box\varphi) \overset{\alpha}{\longmapsto} (s', min(\Box\varphi \wedge \varphi'))$. We, however, opted to generalize this rule to fixpoints to simplify our comparison, while still limiting ourselves to $\text{sHML}_{\mathbf{inv}}$ formulas. This is possible since by encoding $\Box\varphi$ as $\max X.\varphi \wedge \bigwedge_{\beta \in \text{ACT}} [\beta]X$, we get that $(s, \max X.\varphi \wedge \bigwedge_{\beta \in \text{ACT}} [\beta]X) \overset{\alpha}{\longmapsto} (s', min((\max X.\varphi \wedge \bigwedge_{\beta \in \text{ACT}} [\beta]X) \wedge \varphi'))$ when $(s, \varphi) \overset{\alpha}{\longmapsto} (s', \varphi')$ where $min((\max X.\varphi \wedge \bigwedge_{\beta \in \text{ACT}} [\beta]X) \wedge \varphi')$ is the encoded version of $min(\Box\varphi \wedge \varphi')$.

The second stage of the synthesis involves using rule CTR to remove invalid transitions that lead to violating states; this yields the required transition function for the controlled system. This rule relies on the synthesizability test rules to tell whether a controlled state, (s, φ), is valid or not. Intuitively, the test rules fail whenever the current formula φ is semantically equivalent to ff, e.g., formulas $\max X.([\alpha]X \wedge \text{ff})$ and $\varphi \wedge \text{ff}$ both fail the synthesizability test rules as they are equivalent to ff. Concretely, the test is vacuously satisfied by truth, tt, logical variables, X, and guarded formulas, $[\alpha]\varphi$, as none of them are logically equivalent to ff. Conjunct formulas, $\psi_1 \wedge \psi_2$, pass the test when both ψ_1 and ψ_2 pass independently. A fixpoint, $\max X.\varphi'$, is synthesisable if φ' passes the test.

Transitions that lead to a state that fails the test are therefore removed, and transitions outgoing from failing states become redundant as they are unreachable. The resulting transition function is then used to construct the controlled LTS $\langle(\text{SYS} \times \text{sHML}_{\mathbf{inv}}), \text{ACT}, \rightarrow\rangle$.

Example 4. From φ_0 and s_b of Example 1 we can synthesise a controlled system in two stages. In the first stage we compose them together using the composition rules of Fig. 5. We start by generating the composite transition $(s_b, \varphi_0) \overset{\text{req}}{\longmapsto} (s_b^1, \varphi_0)$ via rules CMAX and CNEC since $s_b \overset{\text{req}}{\longrightarrow} s_b^1$, and keep on apply the respective rules to the rest of s_b's transitions until we obtain the LTS of Fig. 6. The (grey) ans transition leading to the test failing state, $(s_b, \text{ff})\,\not\downarrow$, is then removed in the second stage along with its outgoing (grey) transitions, therefore generating the required (black) controlled system. $\qquad\square$

4   Discussion and Comparison

We reiterate that controlled system synthesis is a static technique, while suppression enforcement is a dynamic one. Being a dynamic technique, the monitor and the system in suppression enforcement still remain two separate entities, and the instrumentation between them is merely a way for the monitor to interact with the system. In general, the monitor cannot affect the execution of the system itself, but rather modifies its observable trace of actions, such as its inputs and outputs. By contrast, when a controlled system is synthesised, an existing system is paired up with a formula and statically reconstructed into a *new* (valid) system that is incapable of executing the erroneous behaviour.

By removing invalid transitions entirely, controlled system synthesis is more ideal to guarantee the property compliance of the *internal* (less observable) behaviour of a system. For example, this can be useful to ensure that the system does not use a shared resource before locking it. By contrast, the invalid actions are still executed by the system in suppression enforcement, but their effect is rendered invisible to any external observer. This makes suppression enforcement more suitable to ensure that the *external* (observable) behaviour of the system complies with a desired property. For instance, one can ensure that the system does not perform an output that is innocuous to the system itself, but may be providing harmful information to the external environment.

One way of assessing the difference between these two techniques is to use observational equivalence as a yardstick, thus:

$$\forall \varphi \in \text{sHML}, s \in \text{Sys}, \exists m \in \text{Trn} \cdot m[s] \approx (s, \varphi). \tag{1}$$

We show by means of a counter example that (1) is in fact *false* and as a result prove Theorem 2.

Theorem 2 (Non Observational Equivalence). *There exist an* sHML_{inv} *formula* φ, *an LTS* $\langle \text{Sys}, \text{Act}, \rightarrow \rangle$ *and a system state* $s \in \text{Sys}$ *such that for every monitor* $m \in \text{Trn}$, $m[s] \not\approx (s, \varphi)$. $\qquad \square$

Proof Sketch. Recall the controlled LTS with initial state (s_b, φ_0) obtained in Example 4. To prove Theorem 2 we must show that *for every action suppression monitor m* (that can only apply suppression and identity transformations), one *cannot* find a weak bisimulation relation $\mathcal{R}$ so that $(m[s_b], (s_b, \varphi_0)) \in \mathcal{R}$. An elegant way of showing this claim, is by playing the *weak bisimulation games* [7] starting from the pair $(m[s_b], (s_b, \varphi_0))$, for every possible m. The game is played between two players, namely, the attacker and the defender. The attacker wins the game by finding a sequence of moves from the monitored state $m[s_b]$ (or the controlled state (s_b, φ_0)), which the defender cannot counter, *i.e.*, the move sequence cannot be performed by the controlled state (s_b, φ_0) (resp. monitored state $m[s_b]$). Note that the attacker is allowed to play a transition from either the current monitored state or the controlled state at each round of the game. A winning strategy for the attacker entails that the composite systems are *not* observationally equivalent.

We start playing the game from the initial pair $(m[s_\mathbf{b}], (s_\mathbf{b}, \varphi_0))$ for every monitor m. Pick any monitor that suppresses any action other than a second consecutive ans, such as $m_0 \overset{\text{def}}{=} \{\text{req}, \tau\}.m_0'$. In this case, it is easy to deduce that the defender always loses the game, that is, if the attacker attacks with $(s_\mathbf{b}, \varphi_0) \xrightarrow{\text{req}} (s_\mathbf{b}^1, \varphi_0)$ the defender is defenceless since $m_0[s_\mathbf{b}] \overset{\text{req}}{\not\Longrightarrow}$. This remains true regardless of the "depth" at which the suppression of the first req transition occurs.

On the one hand, using the same game characterisation, one can also deduce that by picking a monitor that *fails to suppress* the second consecutive ans action, such as $m_1 \overset{\text{def}}{=} \{\text{req}\}.\{\text{ans}\}.\{\text{ans}\}.m_1'$, also prevents the defender from winning. If the attacker plays with $m_1[s_\mathbf{b}] \xxrightarrow{\text{req.ans.ans}} m_1'[s_\mathbf{b}]$, the defender loses since it can only counter the first two transitions, *i.e.*, $(s_\mathbf{b}, \varphi_0) \xxrightarrow{\text{req.ans}} \overset{\text{ans}}{\not\Longrightarrow}$. Again, this holds regardless of the "depth" of the first such failed suppression.

On the other hand, any monitor that actually suppresses the second consecutive ans action, such as $m_\mathbf{s}$ from Example 2, still negates a win for the defender. In this case, the attacker can play $(s_\mathbf{b}, \varphi_0) \xxrightarrow{\text{req.ans}} (s_\mathbf{b}^2, \varphi_0 \wedge [\text{ans}]\text{ff})$ to which the defender may reply either with $m_\mathbf{s}[s_\mathbf{b}] \xxrightarrow{\text{req.ans}} m_\mathbf{s}[s_\mathbf{b}]$ or $m_\mathbf{s}[s_\mathbf{b}] \xxrightarrow{\text{req.ans}} m_\mathbf{s}'[s_\mathbf{b}^2]$. In the former option, the attacker can subsequently play req in the monitored system, to which the defender cannot reply via the controlled system, *i.e.*, $m_\mathbf{s}[s_\mathbf{b}] \xrightarrow{\text{req}} m_\mathbf{s}[s_\mathbf{b}^1]$ but $(s_\mathbf{b}^2, \varphi_0 \wedge [\text{ans}]\text{ff}) \overset{\text{req}}{\not\longrightarrow}$. In the latter case, the attacker can now play $m_\mathbf{s}'[s_\mathbf{b}^2] \xrightarrow{\tau} \text{sup}[s_\mathbf{b}]$, which can only be countered by an inaction on behalf of the defender, *i.e.*, the controlled system remains in state $(s_\mathbf{b}^2, \varphi_0 \wedge [\text{ans}]\text{ff})$. However, the attacker can subsequently play $(s_\mathbf{b}^2, \varphi_0 \wedge [\text{ans}]\text{ff}) \xrightarrow{\text{cls}} (\text{nil}, \varphi_0)$ which is indefensible since $\text{sup}[s_\mathbf{b}] \overset{\text{cls}}{\not\Longrightarrow}$. As in the previous cases, the above reasoning applies.

These cases therefore suffice to deduce that for every possible monitor the attacker always manages to win the game, and hence we conclude that Theorem 2 holds as required.   □

This result is important since it proves that powerful external observers, such as the ones presented by Abramsky in [1], can still distinguish between the resulting monitored and controlled systems.

5   Establishing a Static Counterpart to Enforcement

Despite not being observationally equivalent, Examples 2 and 4 provide the intuition that there still exists some level of correspondence between these two techniques. In fact, from the monitored execution graph of Fig. 4 and the controlled LTS in Fig. 6 one can notice that they both execute the *same set of traces*, and are therefore *trace equivalent*. Hence, since trace equivalent systems satisfy the same set of safety properties (Theorem 1), it suffices to conclude that the controlled LTS is statically achieving the same result obtained dynamically by the monitored one, and that it is therefore its static counterpart.

In what follows, we prove that this observation (*i.e.*, trace equivalence) also applies in the general case.

Theorem 3 (Trace Equivalence). *For every LTS* $\langle \text{SYS}, \text{ACT}, \rightarrow \rangle$, *formula* $\varphi \in \text{sHML}_{inv}$ *and* $s \in \text{SYS}$, *there exists a monitor* m *such that* $traces(m[s]) = traces((s, \varphi))$. □

To be able to prove this result, we first define a function that maps $\text{sHML}_{\mathbf{inv}}$ formulas to enforcement transducers. We reduce the complexity of this mapping by defining it over the normalised sHML formulas instead.

Definition 4 (sHML normal form). *The set of normalised* sHML *formulas is defined as:*

$$\varphi, \psi \in \text{sHML}_{nf} ::= \text{tt} \quad | \quad \text{ff} \quad | \quad \bigwedge_{i \in I} [\alpha_i]\varphi_i \quad | \quad X \quad | \quad \max X.\varphi .$$

In addition, a normalised sHML *formula* φ *must satisfy the following conditions:*

1. *In each subformula of* φ *of the form* $\bigwedge_{i \in I} [\alpha_i]\varphi_i$, *the* α_i's *are pairwise different, i.e.,* $\forall i, j \in I \cdot$ *if* $i \neq j$ *then* $\alpha_i \neq \alpha_j$.
2. *For every* $\max X.\varphi$ *we have* $X \in \boldsymbol{fv}(\varphi)$.
3. *Every logical variable is guarded by a modal necessity.* □

In previous work, [3,5] we proved that despite being a syntactic subset of sHML, $\text{sHML}_{\mathbf{nf}}$ is *semantically equivalent* to sHML. Hence, since $\text{sHML}_{\mathbf{inv}}$ is a (strict) subset of sHML, for every $\text{sHML}_{\mathbf{inv}}$ formula we can always find an equivalent $\text{sHML}_{\mathbf{nf}}$ formula. This means that by defining our mapping function in terms of $\text{sHML}_{\mathbf{nf}}$, we can still map every formula in $\text{sHML}_{\mathbf{inv}}$ to the respective monitor.

We proceed to define our mapping function over normalised sHML formulas.

Definition 5. *Recall the definitions of* id *and* sup *from Fig. 3. We define our mapping* $(\!| - |\!) : \text{sHML}_{nf} \mapsto \text{TRN}$ *inductively as:*

$$(\!| X |\!) \overset{\text{def}}{=} x \qquad (\!| \text{tt} |\!) \overset{\text{def}}{=} id \qquad (\!| \text{ff} |\!) \overset{\text{def}}{=} sup \qquad (\!| \max X.\varphi |\!) \overset{\text{def}}{=} rec\, x.(\!| \varphi |\!)$$

$$(\!| \bigwedge_{i \in I} [\{p_i, c_i\}]\varphi_i |\!) \overset{\text{def}}{=} \sum_{i \in I} m_i \quad \text{where } m_i \overset{\text{def}}{=} \begin{cases} \{\alpha_i, \alpha_i\}.(\!| \varphi_i |\!) & \text{if } \varphi_i \neq \text{ff} \\ \{\alpha_i, \tau\}.(\!| \text{ff} |\!) & \text{otherwise} \end{cases} \quad □$$

The function is compositional. It assumes a bijective mapping between fixpoint variables and monitor recursion variables and converts logical variables X accordingly, whereas maximal fixpoints, $\max X.\varphi$, are converted into the corresponding recursive monitor. The function also converts truth and falsehood formulas, tt and ff, into the identity monitor id and the suppression monitor sup respectively. Normalized conjunctions, $\bigwedge_{i \in I} [\alpha_i]\varphi_i$, are mapped into a *summation* of monitors, $\sum_{i \in I} m_i$, where every branch m_i can be either prefixed by an identity transformation when $\varphi_i \neq \text{ff}$, or by a suppression transformation otherwise. Notice that the requirement that, $\varphi_i \neq \text{ff}$, is in some sense analogous to the synthesisability test applied by the CSS rule cTR of Fig. 5 to retain the valid transitions only. In this mapping function, this requirement is essential to ensure that only the valid actions remain unsuppressed by the resulting monitor.

Example 5. Recall formula φ_0 from Example 1 which can be normalised as:

$$\varphi_0 \overset{\text{def}}{=} \max X.([\text{ans}]([\text{ans}]\text{ff} \wedge [\text{req}]X \wedge [\text{cls}]X)) \wedge [\text{req}]X \wedge [\text{cls}]X.$$

Using the mapping function defined in Definition 5, we generate monitor

$$(\!|\varphi_0|\!) = \text{rec}\, x.(\{\text{ans}\}.(\{\text{ans}, \tau\}.\text{sup} + \{\text{req}\}.x + \{\text{cls}\}.x)) + \{\text{req}\}.x + \{\text{cls}\}.x$$

which is identical to m_s from Example 2. $\qquad\square$

With this mapping function in hand, we are able to prove Theorem 3 as a corollary of Proposition 1.

Proposition 1. *For every LTS* $\langle\text{SYS}, \text{ACT}, \rightarrow\rangle$, *sHML$_{nf}$ formula* φ, $s \in$ SYS *and trace* t, *when* $(\!|\varphi|\!) = m$ *then* $t \in traces(m[s])$ *iff* $t \in traces((s, \varphi))$. $\qquad\square$

Proof Sketch. The if and only-if cases are proven separately and both proofs are conducted by induction on the length of trace t and by case analysis of φ. $\qquad\square$

Having concluded the proof of Theorem 3 and knowing Theorem 1, we can finally obtain our main result with respect to Definition 3.

Theorem 4. *Controlled system synthesis is the* static *counterpart of suppression enforcement in the context of safety properties.* $\qquad\square$

6 Related Work

Several works comparing formal verification techniques can be found in the literature. In [24] van Hulst *et al.* explore the relationship between their work on controlled system synthesis and the synthesis problem in Ramadge and Wonham's Supervisory Control Theory (SCT) [31]. The aim in SCT is to generate a *supervisor controller* from the SuS and its specification (*e.g.*, a formal property). If successfully generated, the synchronous product of the SuS and the controller is computed to obtain a supervised system. To enable the investigation, van Hulst *et al.* developed language-based notations akin to that used in [31], and proved that Ramadge and Wonham's work can be expressed using their theory.

Ehlers *et al.* in [14] establish a connection between SCT and reactive synthesis – a formal method that attempts to automatically derive a valid reactive system from a given specification. To form this connection, the authors first equalise both fields by using a simplified version of the standard supervisory control problem and focus on a class of reactive synthesis problems that adhere to the requirements imposed by SCT. They then show that the supervisory control synthesis problem can be reduced to a reactive synthesis problem.

Basile *et al.* in [10] explore the gap between SCT and coordination of services, which describe how control and data exchanges are coordinated in distributed systems. This was achieved via a new notion of controllability that allows one to reduce the classical SCT synthesis algorithms to produce orchestrations and choreographies describing the coordination of services as contract automata.

Falcone *et al.* made a brief, comparison between runtime enforcement and SCT in [16] in the context of K-step opacity, but established no formal results that relate these two techniques.

7   Conclusion

We have presented a novel comparison between suppression enforcement and controlled system synthesis — two verification techniques that automate system correction for erroneous systems. Using a counter-example we have proven that those techniques are different modulo observational equivalence, Theorem 2. An Abramsky-type external observer [1] can therefore tell the difference between a monitored and controlled system resulting from the same formula and SuS. However, we were still able to conclude that controlled system synthesis is the static counterpart to suppression enforcement in the context of safety, as defined by Definition 3. This required developing a function that maps logic formulas to suppression monitors, Definition 5, and proving inductively that for every system and formula, one can obtain a monitored and a controlled system that execute the same set of traces at runtime, Theorem 3. As trace equivalent systems satisfy the same safety properties, this result was enough to reach our conclusion, Theorem 4. To our knowledge this is the first formal comparison to be made between these two techniques.

Future Work. Having established a connection between suppression enforcement and control system synthesis with respect to safety properties, it is worth expanding this work at least along two directions and explore how:

(i) runtime enforcement and controlled system synthesis are related with respect to properties other than those representing safety, and how

(ii) suppression enforcement relates to other verification techniques such as supervisory control theory, reactive synthesis, *etc.*

Exploring (i) may entail looking into other work on enforcement and controlled system synthesis that explores a wider set of properties. It might be worth investigating how other enforcement transformations, such as action replacements and insertions, can be used to widen the set of enforceable properties, and how this relates to controlled system synthesis. The connection established by van Hulst *et al.* in [24] between control system synthesis and supervisory control, along with the other relationships reviewed in Sect. 6, may be a starting point for conducting our future investigations on (ii).

References

1. Abramsky, S.: Observation equivalence as a testing equivalence. Theoret. Comput. Sci. **53**, 225–241 (1987). https://doi.org/10.1016/0304-3975(87)90065-X
2. Aceto, L., Achilleos, A., Francalanza, A., Ingólfsdóttir, A.: A framework for parameterized monitorability. In: Baier, C., Dal Lago, U. (eds.) FoSSaCS 2018. LNCS, vol. 10803, pp. 203–220. Springer, Cham (2018). https://doi.org/10.1007/978-3-319-89366-2_11
3. Aceto, L., Achilleos, A., Francalanza, A., Ingólfsdóttir, A., Kjartansson, S.Ö.: Determinizing monitors for HML with recursion. arXiv preprint (2016)

4. Aceto, L., Achilleos, A., Francalanza, A., Ingólfsdóttir, A., Lehtinen, K.: Adventures in monitorability: from branching to linear time and back again. Proc. ACM Program. Lang. **3**(POPL), 52:1–52:29 (2019). https://doi.org/10.1145/3290365. http://doi.acm.org/10.1145/3290365

5. Aceto, L., Cassar, I., Francalanza, A., Ingólfsdóttir, A.: On runtime enforcement via suppressions. In: 29th International Conference on Concurrency Theory, CONCUR 2018, Beijing, China, 4–7 September 2018, pp. 34:1–34:17 (2018). https://doi.org/10.4230/LIPIcs.CONCUR.2018.34

6. Aceto, L., Ingólfsdóttir, A.: Testing Hennessy-Milner logic with recursion. In: Thomas, W. (ed.) FoSSaCS 1999. LNCS, vol. 1578, pp. 41–55. Springer, Heidelberg (1999). https://doi.org/10.1007/3-540-49019-1_4

7. Aceto, L., Ingólfsdóttir, A., Larsen, K.G., Srba, J.: Reactive Systems: Modelling, Specification and Verification. Cambridge University Press, New York (2007)

8. Alur, R., Černý, P.: Streaming transducers for algorithmic verification of single-pass list-processing programs. In: Proceedings of the 38th Annual ACM SIGPLAN-SIGACT Symposium on Principles of Programming Languages, pp. 599–610. ACM (2011)

9. Arnold, A., Walukiewicz, I.: Nondeterministic controllers of nondeterministic processes. In: Flum, J., Grädel, E., Wilke, T. (eds.) Logic and Automata. Texts in Logic and Games, vol. 2, pp. 29–52. Amsterdam University Press, Amsterdam (2008)

10. Basile, D., ter Beek, M.H., Pugliese, R.: Bridging the gap between supervisory control and coordination of services: synthesis of orchestrations and choreographies. In: Riis Nielson, H., Tuosto, E. (eds.) COORDINATION 2019. LNCS, vol. 11533, pp. 129–147. Springer, Cham (2019). https://doi.org/10.1007/978-3-030-22397-7_8

11. Cassar, I., Francalanza, A., Aceto, L., Ingólfsdóttir, A.: A survey of runtime monitoring instrumentation techniques. In: PrePost 2017, pp. 15–28 (2017)

12. Clarke, E.M., Grumberg, O., Peled, D.: Model Checking. MIT Press, Cambridge (1999)

13. Desai, A., Dreossi, T., Seshia, S.A.: Combining model checking and runtime verification for safe robotics. In: Lahiri, S., Reger, G. (eds.) RV 2017. LNCS, vol. 10548, pp. 172–189. Springer, Cham (2017). https://doi.org/10.1007/978-3-319-67531-2_11

14. Ehlers, R., Lafortune, S., Tripakis, S., Vardi, M.Y.: Bridging the gap between supervisory control and reactive synthesis: case of full observation and centralized control. In: WODES, pp. 222–227. International Federation of Automatic Control (2014)

15. Erlingsson, U., Schneider, F.B.: SASI enforcement of security policies: a retrospective. In: Proceedings of the 1999 Workshop on New Security Paradigms, NSPW 1999, pp. 87–95. ACM, New York (1999)

16. Falcone, Y., Marchand, H.: Runtime enforcement of k-step opacity. In: 52nd IEEE Conference on Decision and Control, pp. 7271–7278, December 2013. https://doi.org/10.1109/CDC.2013.6761043

17. Falcone, Y., Fernandez, J.C., Mounier, L.: What can you verify and enforce at runtime? Int. J. Softw. Tools Technol. Transfer **14**(3), 349 (2012)

18. Francalanza, A.: A theory of monitors. In: Jacobs, B., Löding, C. (eds.) FoSSaCS 2016. LNCS, vol. 9634, pp. 145–161. Springer, Heidelberg (2016). https://doi.org/10.1007/978-3-662-49630-5_9

19. Francalanza, A.: Consistently-detecting monitors. In: 28th International Conference on Concurrency Theory (CONCUR 2017). Leibniz International Proceedings in Informatics (LIPIcs), vol. 85, pp. 8:1–8:19. Schloss Dagstuhl-Leibniz-Zentrum fuer Informatik, Dagstuhl (2017)

20. Francalanza, A., et al.: A foundation for runtime monitoring. In: Lahiri, S., Reger, G. (eds.) RV 2017. LNCS, vol. 10548, pp. 8–29. Springer, Cham (2017). https://doi.org/10.1007/978-3-319-67531-2_2

21. Francalanza, A., Aceto, L., Ingólfsdóttir, A.: Monitorability for the Hennessy-Milner logic with recursion. Formal Methods Syst. Des. **51**(1), 87–116 (2017)

22. Havelund, K., Pressburger, T.: Model checking Java programs using Java PathFinder. Int. J. Softw. Tools Technol. Transfer **2**(4), 366–381 (2000). https://doi.org/10.1007/s100090050043

23. Havelund, K., Roşu, G.: An overview of the runtime verification tool Java PathExplorer. Formal Methods Syst. Des. **24**(2), 189–215 (2004)

24. van Hulst, A.C., Reniers, M.A., Fokkink, W.J.: Maximally permissive controlled system synthesis for non-determinism and modal logic. Discrete Event Dyn. Syst. **27**(1), 109–142 (2017)

25. Kejstová, K., Ročkai, P., Barnat, J.: From model checking to runtime verification and back. In: Lahiri, S., Reger, G. (eds.) RV 2017. LNCS, vol. 10548, pp. 225–240. Springer, Cham (2017). https://doi.org/10.1007/978-3-319-67531-2_14

26. Könighofer, B., et al.: Shield synthesis. Formal Methods Syst. Des. **51**(2), 332–361 (2017)

27. Leucker, M., Schallhart, C.: A brief account of runtime verification. J. Logic Algebraic Program. **78**(5), 293–303 (2009)

28. Ligatti, J., Bauer, L., Walker, D.: Edit automata: enforcement mechanisms for run-time security policies. Int. J. Inf. Secur. **4**(1), 2–16 (2005)

29. Milner, R., Parrow, J., Walker, D.: A calculus of mobile processes, I. Inf. Comput. **100**(1), 1–40 (1992)

30. Pnueli, A., Rosner, R.: On the synthesis of a reactive module. In: Proceedings of the 16th ACM SIGPLAN-SIGACT Symposium on Principles of Programming Languages, POPL 1989, pp. 179–190. ACM, New York (1989). https://doi.org/10.1145/75277.75293. http://doi.acm.org/10.1145/75277.75293

31. Ramadge, P.J., Wonham, W.M.: Supervisory control of a class of discrete event processes. SIAM J. Control Optim. **25**(1), 206–230 (1987)

32. Sakarovitch, J.: Elements of Automata Theory. Cambridge University Press, New York (2009)

33. Sangiorgi, D.: Introduction to Bisimulation and Coinduction. Cambridge University Press, New York (2011)

34. Schneider, F.B.: Enforceable security policies. ACM Trans. Inf. Syst. Secur. (TISSEC) **3**(1), 30–50 (2000)

Assumption-Based Runtime Verification with Partial Observability and Resets

Alessandro Cimatti, Chun Tian$^{(\boxtimes)}$ (iD), and Stefano Tonetta

Fondazione Bruno Kessler, Trento, Italy
{cimatti,ctian,tonettas}@fbk.eu

Abstract. We consider Runtime Verification (RV) based on Propositional Linear Temporal Logic (LTL) with both future and past temporal operators. We generalize the framework to monitor partially observable systems using models of the system under scrutiny (SUS) as assumptions for reasoning on the non-observable or future behaviors of the SUS. The observations are general predicates over the SUS, thus both static and dynamic sets of observables are supported. Furthermore, the monitors are *resettable*, i.e. able to evaluate any LTL property at arbitrary positions of the input trace (roughly speaking, $[\![u, i \models \varphi]\!]$ can be evaluated for any u and i with the underlying assumptions taken into account). We present a symbolic monitoring algorithm that can be efficiently implemented using BDD. It is proven correct and the monitor can be double-checked by model checking. As a by-product, we give the first automata-based monitoring algorithm for Past-Time LTL. Beside feasibility and effectiveness of our approach, we also demonstrate that, under certain assumptions the monitors of some properties are predictive.

1 Introduction

Runtime Verification (RV) [15, 26] as a lightweight verification technique, aims at checking whether a *run* of a system under scrutiny (SUS) satisfies or violates a given correctness specification (or *monitoring property*). Given any monitoring property, the corresponding runtime monitor takes as input an execution (i.e. finite prefix of a run, or finite word) and outputs a *verdict* for each input letter (or *state*).

The applicability of RV techniques on *black box systems* for which no system model is at hand, is usually considered as an advantage over other verification techniques like model checking. However, as systems are often partially observable, this forces one to specify the monitoring property in terms of the external interface of the SUS and diagnosis condition on its internals must be reflected in input/output sequence with an implicit knowledge about the SUS behavior. For example, the sequence to verify that an embedded system does not fail during the booting phase may involve observing that an activity LED blinks until it becomes steady within a certain amount of time; the booting failure is not

This work has received funding from European Union's *Horizon 2020* research and innovation programme under the Grant Agreement No. 700665 (Project *CITADEL*).

B. Finkbeiner and L. Mariani (Eds.): RV 2019, LNCS 11757, pp. 165–184, 2019.
https://doi.org/10.1007/978-3-030-32079-9_10

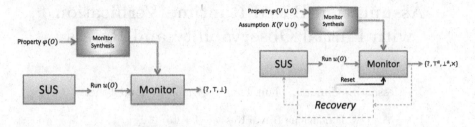

Fig. 1. Traditional RV (left) v.s. ABRV with partial observability & resets (right)

directly observable and the sequence assumes that the LEDs are not broken. In practice, one almost always knows something about the SUS. This information can be derived, for example, from models produced during the system design, or from the interaction with operators (person) of the system. Such information can be leveraged to monitor properties on unobservable parts of the SUS, assuming it behaves the same as specified by its model.

In this paper, we consider the RV problem for Propositional Linear Temporal Logic (PLTL or LTL) with both future and past temporal operators [28]. We extend a traditional RV approach where the monitor synthesis is based on a black-box specification of the system (Fig. 1, on the left) to the practical case where the property to monitor refers to some internal unobservable part of the SUS (Fig. 1, on the right). In order to cope with the partial observability of the SUS, we rely on certain assumption on its behavior, which is expressed in (symbolic) fair transition systems in our framework. Essentially the monitor output in our RV framework can be: the specification is satisfied ($\top^a$) or violated ($\bot^a$) *under* the assumption; the SUS *violates* its assumption ($\times$); or *unknown* (?) otherwise. The output of the monitor depends on the knowledge that can be derived from the partial observations of the system and the semantics of RV is extended to consider all infinite runs of the SUS having the same observed finite execution as prefixes. As for predictive semantics [25,36], by considering the assumption during the synthesis of runtime monitors, the resulting monitors may obtain more precise results: (1) conclusive verdicts could be given on shorter execution prefixes; (2) conclusive verdicts may be obtained from properties that are in general non-monitorable (without assumption).

We also generalize the RV framework to encompass *resettable monitors*. In addition to the observations from SUS, a resettable monitor also takes as input *reset* signals that can change the reference time for the evaluation of the specification without losing the observation history. Consider the case where the monitor is currently evaluating a property φ from the initial position (as done in the traditional case and denoted by $[\![u, 0 \models \varphi]\!]$). Upon a sequence u of observations, receiving as next input a reset, together with a new observation a, the monitor will evaluate φ from the last position. Taking one more observation b but without reset, the monitor will evaluate φ still in the previous position. In general, the monitor can evaluate φ at any position i (denoted by $[\![u, i \models \varphi]\!]$) as long as a reset is sent to the monitor with the observation at position i in the sequence u. We remark that in this framework if the properties are evaluated under assumptions or contain past operators, the observations before the reset may contribute to the evaluation of the property in the new position.

The motivation for introducing resettable monitors is twofold. First, most monitors based on LTL_3-related semantics are monotonic: once the monitor has reached conclusive true ($\top$) or false ($\bot$), the verdict will remain unchanged for all future inputs, rendering them useless from now on. However, when a condition being monitored occurs (e.g. a fault is detected), and necessary countermeasures (e.g. reconfiguration) have been taken, we want the monitoring process to provide fresh information. Given that the SUS (and maybe also other monitors) is still running, it would be desirable to retain the beliefs of the current system state. The monitor after reset will be evaluating the property at the current reference time, without losing the knowledge of the past. Hence, our reset is different from the simple monitor restart mechanisms found in most RV tools: our monitors keep in track the underlying assumptions and memorize all notable events ever happened in the past, whilst the monitor restart is too coarse in that it wipes out the history, and may thus lose fundamental information. Second, the concept of reset significantly enhances the generality of the formal framework. For example, by issuing the reset signal at every cycle, we capture the semantics of Past-Time LTL, i.e. we monitor $[\![u, |u| - 1 \models \varphi]\!]$ where φ is evaluated with reference to the time point of the most recent observation. As a by-product, this results in the first automata-based monitoring algorithm for Past-Time LTL.

As an example, consider a property $\varphi = \mathbf{G}\,\neg p$, which means that p never occurs, with an assumption K stating that "p occurs at most once." For every sequence u that contains p, the monitor should report a violation of the property (independently of the assumption). After a violation, if the monitor is reset, given the assumption K on the occurrence of p, the monitor should predict that the property is satisfied by any continuation. However, this requires that the reset does not forget that a violation already occurred in the past. Should the SUS produce a trace violating the assumption, where p occurs twice at i and at $j > i$, the assumption-based monitor will output "$\times$" at j.

We propose a new algorithm for assumption-based monitor synthesis with partial observability and resets. It naturally extends the LTL_3 RV approach [4]. Our work is based on a *symbolic* translation from LTL to ω-automata, used also by NUXMV model checker. Using symbolic algorithms, assumptions can be easily supported by (symbolically) composing the ω-automata with a system model representing the assumptions. The algorithm explores the space of beliefs, i.e. the sets of SUS states compatible with the observed signals (traces). The symbolic computation of forward images naturally supports partially observed inputs. Finally, the support of resettable monitors exploits some properties of the symbolic translation from LTL to ω-automata.

The new RV approach has been implemented on top of the NUXMV model checker [8]. We have evaluated our approach on a number of benchmarks showing its feasibility and applicability and the usefulness of assumptions. Beside the correctness proof, we have also used the NUXMV model checker to verify the correctness and the effectiveness of the synthesized monitors.

The rest of this paper is organized as follows. Preliminaries are presented in Sect. 2. In Sect. 3 our extended RV framework is presented. The symbolic monitoring algorithm and its correctness proof are given in Sect. 4. In Sect. 5 we describe implementation details and the experimental evaluation. Some related work is discussed in Sect. 6. Finally, in Sect. 7, we make conclusions and discuss future directions.

2   Preliminaries

Let Σ be a finite alphabet. A finite word u (or infinite word w) over Σ is a finite (or countably infinite) sequence of letters in Σ, i.e. $u \in \Sigma^*$ and $w \in \Sigma^\omega$. Empty words are denoted by ϵ. u_i denotes the zero-indexed ith letter in u ($i \in \mathbb{N}$ here and after), while u^i denotes the *sub-word* of u starting from u_i. $|u|$ is the length of u. Finally, $u \cdot v$ is the *concatenation* of a finite word u with another finite (or infinite) word v.

Linear Temporal Logic. Let AP be a set of Boolean variables, the set of Propositional Linear Temporal Logic (LTL) [28] formulae, LTL(AP), is inductively defined as

$$\varphi ::= \text{true} \mid p \mid \neg\varphi \mid \varphi \vee \varphi \mid \mathbf{X}\varphi \mid \varphi\mathbf{U}\varphi \mid \mathbf{Y}\varphi \mid \varphi\mathbf{S}\varphi$$

with $p \in AP$. Here $\mathbf{X}$ stands for *next*, $\mathbf{U}$ for *until*, $\mathbf{Y}$ for *previous*, and $\mathbf{S}$ for *since*. Other logical constants and operators like false, $\wedge$, $\rightarrow$ and $\leftrightarrow$ are used as syntactic sugars with the standard meaning. The following abbreviations for temporal operators are also used: $\mathbf{F}\varphi \doteq \text{true}\,\mathbf{U}\,\varphi$ (*eventually*), $\mathbf{G}\varphi \doteq \neg\mathbf{F}\neg\varphi$ (*globally*), $\mathbf{O}\varphi \doteq \text{true}\,\mathbf{S}\,\varphi$ (*once*), $\mathbf{H}\varphi \doteq \neg\mathbf{O}\neg\varphi$ (*historically*). Additionally, $\mathbf{X}^n p$ denotes a sequence of n nested unary operators: $\mathbf{XX}\cdots\mathbf{X}p$; similar for $\mathbf{Y}^n p$.

The semantics of LTL formulae over an infinite word $w \in (2^{AP})^\omega$ is given below:

$$w, i \models \text{true}$$
$$w, i \models p \quad\Leftrightarrow\quad p \in w_i$$
$$w, i \models \neg\varphi \quad\Leftrightarrow\quad w, i \not\models \varphi$$
$$w, i \models \varphi \vee \psi \Leftrightarrow\quad w, i \models \varphi \vee w, i \models \psi$$
$$w, i \models \mathbf{X}\varphi \quad\Leftrightarrow\quad w, i+1 \models \varphi$$
$$w, i \models \varphi\mathbf{U}\psi \Leftrightarrow\quad \exists k.\, i \leqslant k \wedge w, k \models \psi \wedge \forall j.\, i \leqslant j < k \Rightarrow w, j \models \varphi$$
$$w, i \models \mathbf{Y}\varphi \quad\Leftrightarrow\quad 0 < i \wedge w, i-1 \models \varphi$$
$$w, i \models \varphi\mathbf{S}\psi \Leftrightarrow\quad \exists k.\, k \leqslant i \wedge w, k \models \psi \wedge \forall j.\, k < j \leqslant i \Rightarrow w, j \models \varphi$$

We write $w \models \varphi$ for $w, 0 \models \varphi$ and $\mathcal{L}(\varphi) \doteq \{w \in (2^{AP})^\omega \mid w \models \varphi\}$ for the *language* (or the set of models) of φ. Two formulae ϕ and ψ are equivalent, $\phi \equiv \psi$, iff $\mathcal{L}(\phi) = \mathcal{L}(\psi)$.

Boolean Formulae. Let $\mathbb{B} = \{\top, \bot\}$ denote the type of Boolean values, a set of *Boolean formulae* $\Psi(V)$ over a set of propositional variables $V = \{v_1, \ldots, v_n\}$, is the set of all *well-formed formulae* (wff) [1] built from variables in V, propositional logical operators like $\neg$ and $\wedge$, and parenthesis. Henceforth, as usual in symbolic model checking, any Boolean formula $\psi(V) \in \Psi(V)$ is used to denote the set of truth assignments that make $\psi(V)$ true. More formally, following McMillan [30], a Boolean formula $\psi(V)$ as a set of truth assignments, is the *same* thing as a λ-function of type $\mathbb{B}^{|V|} \to \mathbb{B}$, which takes a vector of these variables and returns a Boolean value, i.e. $\lambda(v_1, \ldots, v_n). \psi(v_1, \ldots, v_n)$ or $\lambda V. \psi(V)$, assuming a fixed order of variables in V. Thus $\Psi(V)$ itself has the type $(\mathbb{B}^{|V|} \to \mathbb{B}) \to \mathbb{B}$. Whenever V is clear from the context, we omit the whole λ prefix. Therefore, set-theoretic operations such as intersection and union are interchangeable with logical connectives on sets of Boolean formulae.

Fair Kripke Structures. The system models, assumptions and ω-automata used in our RV framework are expressed in a symbolic presentation of Kripke structures called *Fair Kripke Structure* (FKS) [23] (or *Fair Transition System* [29]):

Definition 1. *Let V be a set of Boolean variables, and $V' \doteq \{v' \mid v \in V\}$ be the set of* next state *variables (thus $V \cap V' = \emptyset$). An* FKS $K = \langle V, \Theta, \rho, \mathcal{J} \rangle$ *is given by V, a set of initial states $\Theta(V) \in \Psi(V)$, a transition relation $\rho(V, V') \in \Psi(V \cup V')$, and a set of Boolean formulae $\mathcal{J} = \{J_1(V), \ldots, J_k(V)\} \subseteq \Psi(V)$ called* justice *requirements.*

Given any FKS $K \doteq \langle V, \Theta, \rho, \mathcal{J} \rangle$, a *state* $s(V)$ of K is an element in 2^V representing a full truth assignment over V, i.e., for every $v \in V$, $v \in s$ if and only if $s(v) = \top$. For example, if $V = \{p, q\}$, a state $\{p\}$ means $p = \top$ and $q = \bot$. Whenever V is clear from the context, we write s instead of $s(V)$. The transition relation $\rho(V, V')$ relates a state $s \in 2^V$ to its successor $s' \in 2^{V'}$. We say that s' is a *successor* of s (and that s is a predecessor of s') iff $s(V) \cup s'(V') \models \rho(V, V')$. For instance, if $\rho(V, V') = (p \leftrightarrow q')$, $s'(V') = \{q'\}$ is a successor of $s(V) = \{p\}$, since $s(V) \cup s'(V') = \{p, q'\}$ and $\{p, q'\} \models (p \leftrightarrow q')$. A path in K is an infinite sequence of states $s_0, s_1, \ldots$ where $s_0(V) \models \Theta$ and, for all $i \in \mathbb{N}$, $s_i(V) \cup s_{i+1}(V') \models \rho(V, V')$. The *forward image* of a set of states $\psi(V)$ on $\rho(V, V')$ is a Boolean formula $\mathrm{fwd}(\psi, \rho)(V) \doteq (\exists V. \rho(V, V') \wedge \psi(V))[V/V']$, where $[V/V']$ substitutes all (free) variables from V' to V.

A *fair path* of K is a path $s_0 s_1 \ldots \in \Sigma^\omega$ of K such that, for *all* i we have $s_i \cup s'_{i+1} \models \rho$, and, for all $J \in \mathcal{J}$, for *infinitely many* i, we have that $s_i \models J$. We denote by $\mathrm{FP}^\rho_{\mathcal{J}}(\psi)$ the set of fair paths starting from ψ (i.e., such that $s_0 \models \psi$). The language $\mathcal{L}(K)$ is the set of initial fair paths, i.e. $\mathrm{FP}^\rho_{\mathcal{J}}(\Theta)$ and $L(K)$ is the set of finite prefixes of paths in $\mathcal{L}(K)$. A state s is *fair* iff it occurs in a fair path. The set of all fair states, denoted by $\mathcal{F}_K$, can be computed by standard algorithms like Emerson-Lei [14]. Finally, let $K_1 = \langle V_1, \Theta_1, \rho_1, \mathcal{J}_1 \rangle$ and $K_2 = \langle V_2, \Theta_2, \rho_2, \mathcal{J}_2 \rangle$, the *synchronous product* of K_1 and K_2 is defined as $K_1 \otimes K_2 \doteq \langle V_1 \cup V_2, \Theta_1 \wedge \Theta_2, \rho_1 \wedge \rho_2, \mathcal{J}_1 \cup \mathcal{J}_2 \rangle$.

Translating LTL to ω-Automata. Our work relies on a linear-time symbolic translation from LTL to ω-automata. The algorithm traces its roots back to [7,10] where only future operators are supported, with additional support of past operators [17]. A set of propositional *elementary variables* of φ, denoted by $\mathrm{el}(\varphi)$, is used for converting any LTL formula into an equivalent propositional formula. It can be defined recursively as follows (where $p \in V$, ϕ and ψ are sub-formulae of φ):

$$
\begin{aligned}
\mathrm{el}(\mathrm{true}) &= \emptyset, & \mathrm{el}(\mathbf{X}\phi) &= \{\mathrm{X}_\phi\} \cup \mathrm{el}(\phi), \\
\mathrm{el}(p) &= \{p\}, & \mathrm{el}(\phi\mathbf{U}\psi) &= \{\mathrm{X}_{\phi\mathbf{U}\psi}\} \cup \mathrm{el}(\phi) \cup \mathrm{el}(\psi), \\
\mathrm{el}(\neg\phi) &= \mathrm{el}(\phi), & \mathrm{el}(\mathbf{Y}\phi) &= \{\mathrm{Y}_\phi\} \cup \mathrm{el}(\phi), \\
\mathrm{el}(\phi \vee \psi) &= \mathrm{el}(\phi) \cup \mathrm{el}(\psi), & \mathrm{el}(\phi\mathbf{S}\psi) &= \{\mathrm{Y}_{\phi\mathbf{S}\psi}\} \cup \mathrm{el}(\phi) \cup \mathrm{el}(\psi).
\end{aligned}
$$

For any LTL formula φ, $\mathrm{el}(\varphi) = \mathrm{el}(\neg\varphi)$, and φ can be rewritten into a Boolean formula $\chi(\varphi)$ using only variables in $\mathrm{el}(\varphi)$. Below is the full definition of $\chi(\cdot)$:

$$
\chi(\varphi) = \begin{cases}
\varphi & \text{for } \varphi \text{ an elementary variable in } \mathrm{el}(\cdot), \\
\neg\chi(\phi) & \text{for } \varphi = \neg\phi, \\
\chi(\phi) \vee \chi(\psi) & \text{for } \varphi = \phi \vee \psi, \\
\mathrm{X}_\phi \text{ (or } \mathrm{X}_{\phi\mathbf{U}\psi}) & \text{for } \varphi \text{ in forms of } \mathbf{X}\phi (\text{or } \mathbf{X}(\phi\mathbf{U}\psi), \text{ resp.}), \\
\mathrm{Y}_\phi \text{ (or } \mathrm{Y}_{\phi\mathbf{S}\psi}) & \text{for } \varphi \text{ in forms of } \mathbf{Y}\phi (\text{or } \mathbf{Y}(\phi\mathbf{S}\psi), \text{ resp.}) .
\end{cases}
\tag{1}
$$

To apply (1), all sub-formulae of φ leading by $\mathbf{U}$ and $\mathbf{S}$ must be wrapped within $\mathbf{X}$ and $\mathbf{Y}$, respectively. This can be done (if needed) by using the following *Expansion Laws*:

$$
\psi\mathbf{U}\phi \equiv \phi \vee (\psi \wedge \mathbf{X}(\psi\mathbf{U}\phi)), \qquad \psi\mathbf{S}\phi \equiv \phi \vee (\psi \wedge \mathbf{Y}(\psi\mathbf{S}\phi)).
\tag{2}
$$

For instance, $\chi(p\mathbf{U}q) = q \vee (p \wedge \mathrm{X}_{p\mathbf{U}q})$, and $\chi'(p\mathbf{U}q) = q' \vee (p' \wedge \mathrm{X}'_{p\mathbf{U}q})$.

The FKS translated from φ is given by $T_\varphi \doteq \langle V_\varphi, \Theta_\varphi, \rho_\varphi, \mathcal{J}_\varphi \rangle$, where $V_\varphi \doteq \mathrm{el}(\varphi)$.

The initial condition Θ_φ is given by $\Theta_\varphi \doteq \chi(\varphi) \wedge \bigwedge_{\mathrm{Y}_\psi \in \mathrm{el}(\varphi)} \neg\mathrm{Y}_\psi$. Here each $\mathrm{Y}_\psi \in \mathrm{el}(\varphi)$ has an initial false assignment in Θ_φ. This is essentially a consequence of LTL semantics for past operators, i.e. for any word w and formula ψ, $w, 0 \not\models \mathbf{Y}\psi$.

The transition relation ρ_φ (as a formula of variables in $\mathrm{el}(\varphi) \cup \mathrm{el}'(\varphi)$) is given by

$$
\rho_\varphi \doteq \bigwedge_{\mathrm{X}_\psi \in \mathrm{el}(\varphi)} \left(\mathrm{X}_\psi \leftrightarrow \chi'(\psi)\right) \wedge \bigwedge_{\mathrm{Y}_\psi \in \mathrm{el}(\varphi)} \left(\chi(\psi) \leftrightarrow \mathrm{Y}'_\psi\right).
\tag{3}
$$

Intuitively, the purpose of ρ_φ is to relate the values of elementary variables to the future/past values: for any $\psi \in \mathrm{el}(\varphi)$, the current value of ψ is *memorized* by the value of Y_ψ in next state; and the next value of ψ is *guessed* by the current value of X_ψ.

The justice set $\mathcal{J}_\varphi$ is given by $\mathcal{J}_\varphi \doteq \{\chi(\psi\mathbf{U}\phi) \to \chi(\phi) \mid \mathrm{X}_{\psi\mathbf{U}\phi} \in \mathrm{el}(\varphi)\}$. It guarantees that, whenever a sub-formula $\psi\mathbf{U}\phi$ is satisfied, eventually ϕ is satisfied. Thus an infinite sequence of ψ cannot be accepted by the FKS translated from $\psi \mathbf{U} \phi$.

Notice that T_φ and $T_{\neg\varphi}$ only differ at their initial conditions Θ_φ and $\Theta_{\neg\varphi}$.

3   The Generalized RV Framework

Now we formally present the generalized RV framework which extends the traditional RV with three new features: assumptions, partial observability and resets.

Let $\varphi \in \text{LTL}(AP)$ be a monitoring property[1], $K \doteq \langle V_K, \Theta_K, \rho_K, \mathcal{J}_K \rangle$ be an FKS representing the assumptions under which φ is monitored. Note that K can be a detailed model of the SUS or just a simple constraint over the variables in AP. In general, we do not have any specific assumption on the sets AP and V_K; although it is quite common that $AP \subseteq V_K$, V_K can be even empty if there is no assumption at all. Let $V \doteq V_K \cup AP$.

We say that the SUS is *partially observable* when the monitor can observe only a subset $O \subseteq V$ of variables (O is called the *observables*). Thus, the input trace of the monitor contains only variables from O. However, it is *not* required that all variables in O must be observable in each input state of the input trace. For instance, if $O = \{p, q\}$, it could be imagined that an observation reads the value of p holds but do not know anything about q, or vice versa. It is even possible that an observation does not know anything about p and q, except for knowing that the SUS has moved to its next state. Thus, in general, an observation is a set of assignments to O. If $O = V$ and the observation contains a single assignment to V, then we speak of *full observability*.

As recalled in Sect. 2, this can be represented by a Boolean formula over O. Thus, in our framework, the monitor takes as input a sequence of formulas over O. For example, if the input trace is $\mu = p \cdot q \cdot \top$, then μ represents the following sequence of assignments: $\{\{p\}, \{p, q\}\} \cdot \{\{q\}, \{p, q\}\} \cdot \{\emptyset, \{p\}, \{q\}, \{p, q\}\}$ (recall that, knowing nothing about p and q actually means all 4 possible value assignments are possible, just the monitor does not know which one actually happened in the SUS).

Now we present the *ABRV-LTL* semantics as an extension of Leucker's LTL₃:

Definition 2 *(ABRV-LTL).   Let $K \doteq \langle V_K, \Theta_K, \rho_K, \mathcal{J}_K \rangle$ be an FKS, $\varphi \in \text{LTL}(AP)$, $\mu \in \Psi(O)^*$ be a finite sequence of Boolean formulae over $O \subseteq V_K \cup AP$, and*

$$\mathcal{L}^K(\mu) \doteq \{ w \in \mathcal{L}(K) \mid \forall i < |\mu|.\, w_i(V_K \cup AP) \models \mu_i(O) \} \qquad (4)$$

be the set of runs in K which are compatible with μ. The ABRV-LTL semantics of φ over μ under the assumption K, denoted by $[\![\cdot]\!]_4^K \in \mathbb{B}_4 \doteq \{\top^a, \bot^a, ?, \times\}$, is defined as

$$[\![\mu, i \models \varphi]\!]_4^K \doteq \begin{cases} \times, & \text{if } \mathcal{L}^K(\mu) = \emptyset \\ \top^a, & \text{if } \mathcal{L}^K(\mu) \neq \emptyset \wedge \forall w \in \mathcal{L}^K(\mu).\, w, i \models \varphi \\ \bot^a, & \text{if } \mathcal{L}^K(\mu) \neq \emptyset \wedge \forall w \in \mathcal{L}^K(\mu).\, w, i \models \neg\varphi \\ ?, & \text{otherwise.} \end{cases} \qquad (5)$$

---

[1] Here $AP \subseteq V_\varphi$ (the set of variables in T_φ).

ABRV-LTL has four verdicts: *conclusive true* ($\top^a$), *conclusive false* ($\bot^a$), *inconclusive* (?) and *out-of-model* ($\times$). Due to partial observability, the finite trace μ is actually *a set* of finite traces over O, where each u_i of each $u \in \mu$ is a full assignment of truths over O. When $\mathcal{L}^K(\mu) = \emptyset$, K is unable to "follow" the behaviour shown from the SUS, hence the fourth verdict *out-of-model* ($\times$) comes.

The sequence of observations is paired with a sequence of Boolean reset signals. Intuitively, if the monitor receives a reset at cycle i, then it starts to evaluate the truth of φ at i (and does so until the next reset). Formally, the monitor receives inputs in $\Psi(O) \times \mathbb{B}$, the cross-product between formulas over the observables and the reset values. Thus $u = (\mu_0, \mathrm{res}_0), (\mu_1, \mathrm{res}_1), \ldots, (\mu_n, \mathrm{res}_n)$. We denote by $\mathrm{RES}(u)$ and $\mathrm{OBS}(u)$ the projection of u respectively on the reset and observation components, i.e. $\mathrm{RES}(u) = \mathrm{res}_0, \mathrm{res}_1, \ldots, \mathrm{res}_n$ and $\mathrm{OBS}(u) = \mu_0, \mu_1, \ldots, \mu_n$.

Definition 3 *(ABRV with Partial Observability and Resets). Let K, φ and O have the same meaning as in Definition 2, Let $u \in (\Psi(O) \times \mathbb{B})^*$ be a finite sequence of observations paired with resets. The problem of Assumption-based Runtime Verification (ABRV) w.r.t. K, φ and O is to construct a function $\mathcal{M}_\varphi^K : (\Psi(O) \times \mathbb{B})^* \to \mathbb{B}_4$ such that*

$$\mathcal{M}_\varphi^K(u) = [\![\mathrm{OBS}(u), \mathrm{MRR}(u) \models \varphi]\!]_4^K \tag{6}$$

where $\mathrm{MRR}(u)$ (the most recent reset) is the maximal i such that $\mathrm{RES}(u_i) = \top$.

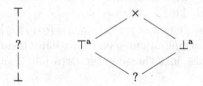

Fig. 2. LTL$_3$ lattice (left) v.s. ABRV-LTL lattice (right)

Here are some basic properties of the monitor defined in Definition 3. Let $(\mathbb{B}_4, \sqsubseteq)$ be a lattice with the partial order ? $\sqsubseteq \top^a/\bot^a \sqsubseteq \times$, shown in Fig. 2 (with a comparison to the LTL$_3$ lattice). It is not hard to see that, if there is no reset in the inputs, the monitor $\mathcal{M}_\varphi^K$ is always mono-increasing, i.e. $\mathcal{M}_\varphi^K(u) \sqsubseteq \mathcal{M}_\varphi^K(u \cdot (\psi, \bot))$. On the other hand, the monitor is *anti-monotonic* w.r.t. the assumption, i.e. if $\mathcal{L}(K_2) \subseteq \mathcal{L}(K_1)$, then $\mathcal{M}_\varphi^{K_1}(u) \sqsubseteq \mathcal{M}_\varphi^{K_2}(u)$. We omit the proofs of above properties due to page limits, instead the related experiments that use model checkers to prove them on the generated monitors are briefly reported in Sect. 5 with two samples of K_2.

If K_1 is taken as an empty FKS, i.e. $\mathcal{L}(K_1) = (2^O)^\omega$, we say that the assumption K_2 is *valuable* for φ if there exists $u \in (\Psi(O) \times \{\bot\})^*$ such that $\mathcal{M}_\varphi^{K_1}(u) = ?$

and $\mathcal{M}_\varphi^{K_2}(u) = \top^a$ or $\bot^a$. This can happen when the monitor $\mathcal{M}_\varphi^{K_2}$ is *diagnostic*, deducing some non-observable values from the assumption and observations, or when the monitor $\mathcal{M}_\varphi^{K_2}$ is *predictive*, deducing some future facts from the assumption and observations.

Monitoring Past-time LTL. If the monitor is reset on each input state, i.e. $\forall i.\,\mathrm{RES}(u_i) = \top$, then $\mathcal{M}_\varphi^K(u) = [\![\mathrm{OBS}(u), |u| - 1]\!]_4^K$. Furthermore, if φ has only past operators (**Y** and **S**), this monitor actually follows the (finite-trace) semantics ($\models_p$) of *Past-Time LTL* [22], where $[\![u \models_p \varphi]\!] \doteq [\![u, |u|-1 \models \varphi]\!]_4^K$ (for $|u| > 0$). The corresponding RV problem (under full observability, without assumptions) is usually handled by rewriting-based approaches or dynamic programming. Using our BDD-based algorithm now it is possible to generate an automaton monitoring Past-Time LTL.

4 The Symbolic Algorithm

Now we present Algorithm 1 for the RV problem given in Definition 3. This algorithm leverages Boolean formulae and can be effectively implemented in Binary Decision Diagrams (BDD) [6]. A monitor is built from an assumption $K \doteq \langle V_K, \Theta_K, \rho_K, \mathcal{J}_K \rangle$ and an LTL property $\varphi \in \mathrm{LTL}(AP)$. Then it can be used to monitor any finite trace $u \in (\Psi(O) \times \mathbb{B})^*$, where $O \subseteq V_K \cup AP$ is the set of observables.

In the monitor building phase (L2–5), the LTL to ω-automata translation algorithm (c.f. Sect. 2) is called on φ and $\neg\varphi$ for the constructions of FKS T_φ and $T_{\neg\varphi}$. The set of fair states of $K \otimes T_\varphi$ and of $K \otimes T_{\neg\varphi}$ are computed as $\mathcal{F}_\varphi^K$ and $\mathcal{F}_{\neg\varphi}^K$. Starting from L6, the purpose is to update two belief states r_φ and $r_{\neg\varphi}$ according to the input trace u. If we imagine $K \otimes T_\varphi$ and $K \otimes T_{\neg\varphi}$ as two NFAs, then r_φ and $r_{\neg\varphi}$ are the sets of current states in them. They are initialized with the initial conditions of $K \otimes T_\varphi$ and $K \otimes T_{\neg\varphi}$ (restricted to fair states). Indeed, their initial values are given by a chain of conjunctions (L6–7). They are then intersected with the first input state u_0 (L9–10). For the remaining inputs (if they exist), when there is no reset (L13–14), the purpose is to walk simultaneously in $K \otimes T_\varphi$ and $K \otimes T_{\neg\varphi}$ by computing the forward images of r_φ and $r_{\neg\varphi}$ with respect to the current input state and the set of fair states.

If any input state comes in with a reset signal, now the monitor needs to be reset (L16–18). Our most important discovery in this paper is that, a simple $r_\varphi \vee r_{\neg\varphi}$ at L16 just did the work. The resulting Boolean formula r actually contains the *history* of the current input trace and the current "position" in the assumption. (c.f. the correctness proof below for more details.) Then the forward image computed in 17–18 is for shifting the current values of all elementary variables by one step into the past, then the conjunction of $\chi(\varphi)$ (or $\chi(\neg\varphi)$, resp.) makes sure that from now on the "new" automata will accept φ (or $\neg\varphi$, resp.) from the beginning, just like in L9–10. We cannot use Θ_φ or $\Theta_{\neg\varphi}$ here, because they contain the initial all-false assignments of the past elementary variables, which may wrongly overwrite the history stored in r, as some of these variables

---

Algorithm 1: The symbolic (offline) monitor

```
 1  function symbolic_monitor(K ≐ ⟨V_K, Θ_K, ρ_K, 𝒥_K⟩, φ(AP), u ∈ (Ψ(O) × 𝔹)*)
 2  │  T_φ ≐ ⟨V_φ, Θ_φ, ρ_φ, 𝒥_φ⟩ ⟵ ltl_translation(φ);
 3  │  T_¬φ ≐ ⟨V_φ, Θ_¬φ, ρ_φ, 𝒥_φ⟩ ⟵ ltl_translation(¬φ);
 4  │  ℱ_φ^K ⟵ fair_states(K ⊗ T_φ);
 5  │  ℱ_¬φ^K ⟵ fair_states(K ⊗ T_¬φ);
 6  │  r_φ ⟵ Θ_K ∧ Θ_φ ∧ ℱ_φ^K;                              /* no observation */
 7  │  r_¬φ ⟵ Θ_K ∧ Θ_¬φ ∧ ℱ_¬φ^K;
 8  │  if |u| > 0 then                                      /* first observation */
 9  │  │  r_φ ⟵ r_φ ∧ OBS(u_0);
10  │  │  r_¬φ ⟵ r_¬φ ∧ OBS(u_0);
11  │  for 1 ≤ i < |u| do                                   /* more observations */
12  │  │  if RES(u_i) = ⊥ then                              /* no reset */
13  │  │  │  r_φ ⟵ fwd(r_φ, ρ_K ∧ ρ_φ)(V_K ∪ V_φ) ∧ OBS(u_i) ∧ ℱ_φ^K;
14  │  │  │  r_¬φ ⟵ fwd(r_¬φ, ρ_K ∧ ρ_φ)(V_K ∪ V_φ) ∧ OBS(u_i) ∧ ℱ_¬φ^K;
15  │  │  else                                              /* with reset */
16  │  │  │  r ⟵ r_φ ∨ r_¬φ;
17  │  │  │  r_φ ⟵ fwd(r, ρ_K ∧ ρ_φ)(V_K ∪ V_φ) ∧ χ(φ) ∧ OBS(u_i) ∧ ℱ_φ^K;
18  │  │  │  r_¬φ ⟵ fwd(r, ρ_K ∧ ρ_φ)(V_K ∪ V_φ) ∧ χ(¬φ) ∧ OBS(u_i) ∧ ℱ_¬φ^K;
19  │  if r_φ = r_¬φ = ⊥ then return ×;
20  │  else if r_φ = ⊥ then return ⊥^a;
21  │  else if r_¬φ = ⊥ then return ⊤^a;
22  │  else return ?;
```

---

may not be false any more. The whole reset process completes here, then the current input observation $\mathrm{OBS}(u_i)$ is finally considered and the new belief states must be restrict in fair states. Finally (L19–22) the monitor outputs a verdict in $\mathbb{B}_4$, depending on four possible cases on the emptiness of r_φ and $r_{\neg\varphi}$. This is in line with ABRV-LTL given in Definition 2.

Sample Run. Suppose we monitor $\varphi = p\,\mathbf{U}\,q$ (fully observable) assuming $p \neq q$. Here $O = \{p, q\}$, $V_\varphi = \{p, q, x \doteq \mathrm{X}_{p\mathbf{U}q}\}$, $\Theta_\varphi = q \vee (p \wedge x)$, $\Theta_{\neg\varphi} = \neg(q \vee (p \wedge x))$, $\rho_\varphi = x \leftrightarrow (q' \vee (p' \wedge x'))$, and $K = \langle O, \top, p' \neq q', \emptyset \rangle$. ($\mathcal{J}_\varphi$ and $\mathcal{J}_{\neg\varphi}$ can be ignored since all states are fair, i.e. $\mathcal{F}_\varphi^K = \mathcal{F}_{\neg\varphi}^K = \top$.) Let $u = \{p\}\{p\}\cdots\{q\}\{q\}\cdots$ (no reset). Initially (L6–7) $r_\varphi = \Theta_\varphi$, $r_{\neg\varphi} = \Theta_{\neg\varphi}$, taking the initial state $\{p\}$ they become (L9–10) $r_\varphi = \Theta_\varphi \wedge (p \wedge \neg q) \equiv p \wedge \neg q \wedge x$, and $r_{\neg\varphi} = \Theta_{\neg\varphi} \wedge (p \wedge \neg q) \equiv p \wedge \neg q \wedge \neg x$. Since both r_φ and $r_{\neg\varphi}$ are not empty, the monitor outputs ? (if ends here.) If the next state is still $\{p\}$, the values of r_φ and $r_{\neg\varphi}$ actually remain the same, because $\rho_\varphi \wedge (p' \wedge \neg q') \equiv x \leftrightarrow x'$ and L13–14 does not change anything. Thus the monitor still outputs ?, until it received $\{q\}$: in this case $\rho_\varphi \wedge (\neg p' \wedge q') \equiv x \leftrightarrow \top$, and $\mathrm{fwd}(r_{\neg\varphi}, \rho_\varphi)(V_\varphi) \wedge (\neg p' \wedge q')$ (L14) is unsatisfiable, i.e. $r_{\neg\varphi} = \bot$, while r_φ is still not empty, thus the output is $\top^a$. Taking more $\{q\}$ does not change the output, unless the assumption $p \neq q$ is broken (then $r_\varphi = r_{\neg\varphi} = \bot$, the output is × and remains there, unless the monitor were reset).

Online Monitoring. Algorithm 1 returns a single verdict after processing the entire input trace. This fits into Definition 3. However, runtime monitors are usually required to return verdicts for each input state and "*should* be designed to consider executions in an incremental fashion" [26]. Our algorithm can be easily modified for online monitoring, it outputs one verdict for each input state. It is indeed incremental since r_φ and $\bar{r}_{\neg\varphi}$ are updated on each input state, and the time complexity of processing one input state is only in terms of the size of K and φ, thus *trace-length independent* [12]. Space complexity is also important, as a monitor may eventually blow up after storing enough inputs. Our algorithm is *trace non-storing* [31] with bounded memory consumption.

Example. Let us consider again the example proposed in Sect. 1: the LTL property $\varphi = \mathbf{G}\,\neg p$ (p never occurs) under the assumption K stating that "p occurs at most once" (expressed in LTL: $\mathbf{G}(p \to \mathbf{XG}\,\neg p)$). Figure 3 shows the automaton that results from pre-computing the states that Algorithm 1 can reach, given φ and K. Each state reports the monitor output (N stands for $\perp^a$, Y for $\top^a$ and X for $\times$), while inputs are represented on the edges (R stands for reset). Starting from state 1, the monitors goes and remains in state 2 with the output ? as long as it reads $\neg p$ independently of the reset; it goes to state 3 with output $\perp$ as soon as it reads p (again independently of the reset); then, either it goes to state 4 with output $\perp$ while still reading $\neg p$ without reset; as soon as a reset is received it goes to state 5 with output $\top$ where it remains while reading $\neg p$; from states 3–5, whenever the monitor receives p (which would be the second occurrence violating the assumption), it goes to the sink state 0 with output $\times$.

Now we show the correctness of Algorithm 1:

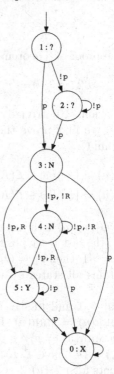

Fig. 3. The monitor of $\mathbf{G}\,\neg p$ under assumption $\mathbf{G}(p \to \neg\mathbf{XF}\,p)$

Theorem 1. *The function* symbolic_monitor *given in Algorithm 1 correctly implements the monitor function* $\mathcal{M}_\varphi^K(\cdot)$ *given in Definition 3.*

Proof (sketch). Fix a trace $u \in (2^O \times \mathbb{B})^*$, we define the following abbreviations:

$$u \lesssim w \Leftrightarrow \forall i.\ i < |u| \Rightarrow w_i(V_k \cup AP) \models \mathrm{OBS}(u_i)(O), \tag{7}$$

$$\mathcal{L}_\varphi^K(u) \doteq \{w \in \mathcal{L}(K) \mid (w, \mathrm{MRR}(u) \models \varphi) \wedge u \lesssim w\}, \tag{8}$$

$$L_\varphi^K(u) \doteq \{v \mid \exists w.\ v \cdot w \in \mathcal{L}_\varphi^K(u) \wedge |v| = |u|\}. \tag{9}$$

Intuitively, if $u \lesssim w$ holds, w is an (infinite) run of the FKS K *compatible* with the input trace u; $\mathcal{L}_\varphi^K(u)$ is the set of (infinite) u-*compatible* runs of K which satisfies φ w.r.t. the last reset position; And $L_\varphi^K(u)$ is the set of $|u|$-length prefixes from $\mathcal{L}_\varphi^K(u)$.

It is not hard to see that, Definition 3 can be rewritten in terms of $L_\varphi^K(u)$ and $L_{\neg\varphi}^K(u)$:

$$\mathcal{M}_\varphi^K(u) = [\![\mathrm{OBS}(u), \mathrm{MRR}(u) \models \varphi]\!]_4^K = \begin{cases} \times, & \text{if } L_\varphi^K(u) = \emptyset \wedge L_{\neg\varphi}^K(u) = \emptyset, \\ \top^a, & \text{if } L_\varphi^K(u) \neq \emptyset \wedge L_{\neg\varphi}^K(u) = \emptyset, \\ \bot^a, & \text{if } L_\varphi^K(u) = \emptyset \wedge L_{\neg\varphi}^K(u) \neq \emptyset, \\ ?, & \text{if } L_\varphi^K(u) \neq \emptyset \wedge L_{\neg\varphi}^K(u) \neq \emptyset. \end{cases}$$

Now the proof of Theorem 1 can be reduced to the following sub-goals:

$$L_\varphi^K(u) = \emptyset \Rightarrow r_\varphi(u) = \emptyset \quad \text{and} \quad L_{\neg\varphi}^K(u) = \emptyset \Rightarrow r_{\neg\varphi}(u) = \emptyset. \tag{10}$$

Equation (10) trivially holds when $u = \epsilon$, i.e. $|u| = 0$. Below we assume $|u| > 0$. We first prove the *invariant properties* of r_φ and $r_{\neg\varphi}$: (c.f. L12–18 of Algorithm 1)

$$r_\varphi(u) = \{s \mid \exists w \in \mathcal{L}(K \otimes T_\varphi). (w, \mathrm{MRR}(u) \models \varphi) \wedge u \lesssim w \wedge w_{|u|-1} = s\},$$
$$r_{\neg\varphi}(u) = \{s \mid \exists w \in \mathcal{L}(K \otimes T_{\neg\varphi}). (w, \mathrm{MRR}(u) \models \neg\varphi) \wedge u \lesssim w \wedge w_{|u|-1} = s\} \tag{11}$$

Intuitively, $r_\varphi(u)$ is the set of last states of u-compatible runs in $K \otimes T_\varphi$, satisfying φ w.r.t. the last reset position. Now we prove (11) by induction:

If $|u| = 1$, then $r_\varphi = \Theta_K \wedge \Theta_\varphi \wedge \mathcal{F}_{K,\varphi} \wedge \mathrm{OBS}(u_0)$. ($\mathrm{MRR}(u)$ is not used.) Thus, r_φ contains all states s such that $\exists w \in \mathcal{L}(K \otimes T_\varphi), (w, 0 \models \varphi), \cdot u_0 \lesssim w_0$ and $w_0 = s$.

If $|u| > 1$ and $\mathrm{RES}(u_n) = \bot$, let $|u| = n + 1$ and $u = v \cdot u_n$ with $|v| > 0$. Here $\mathrm{MRR}(u) = \mathrm{MRR}(v)$. By induction hypothesis, $r_\varphi(v) = \{s \mid \exists w \in \mathcal{L}(K \otimes T_\varphi). (w, \mathrm{MRR}(v) \models \varphi) \wedge v \lesssim w \wedge w_{n-1} = s\}$. Thus $r_\varphi(u) = \mathrm{fwd}(r_\varphi(v), \rho_K \wedge \rho_\varphi) \wedge \mathrm{OBS}(u_n) = \{s \mid \exists w \in \mathcal{L}(K \otimes T_\varphi). (w, \mathrm{MRR}(v) \models \varphi) \wedge v \cdot u_n \lesssim w \wedge w_n = s\}$. Same arguments for $r_{\neg\varphi}(u)$.

If $|u| > 1$ and $\mathrm{RES}(u_n) = \top$, let $|u| = n + 1$ and $u = v \cdot u_n$ with $|v| > 0$. Here $\mathrm{MRR}(u) = n$. By induction hypothesis, we have

$$r_\varphi(v) = \{s \mid \exists w \in \mathcal{L}(K \otimes T_\varphi). (w, \mathrm{MRR}(v) \models \varphi) \wedge v \lesssim w \wedge w_{n-1} = s\},$$
$$r_{\neg\varphi}(v) = \{s \mid \exists w \in \mathcal{L}(K \otimes T_{\neg\varphi}). (w, \mathrm{MRR}(v) \models \neg\varphi) \wedge v \lesssim w \wedge w_{n-1} = s\}.$$

Here, if we take the *union* of $r_\varphi(v)$ and $r_{\neg\varphi}(v)$, the two conjugated terms $(w, \mathrm{MRR}(v) \models \varphi)$ and $(w, \mathrm{MRR}(v) \models \neg\varphi)$ will be just neutralized, i.e., $r_\varphi(v) \vee r_{\neg\varphi}(v) = \{s \mid \exists w \in \mathcal{L}(K \otimes T_\varphi^0). v \lesssim w \wedge w_{n-1} = s\}$, where $T_\varphi^0 = \langle V_\varphi, \Theta_\varphi^0, \rho_\varphi, \mathcal{J}_\varphi \rangle$ and $\Theta_\varphi^0 = \bigwedge\limits_{Y_p \in \mathrm{el}(\varphi)} \neg Y_p$. It can be seen that $\forall w \in \mathcal{L}(K \otimes T_\varphi^0), n. (w, n \models \varphi) \Leftrightarrow (w^n \models \Theta_\varphi^0)$. Thus $r_\varphi(u) = \mathrm{fwd}(r_\varphi(v) \vee r_{\neg\varphi}(v), \rho_K \wedge \rho_\varphi) \wedge \mathrm{OBS}(u_n) \wedge \chi(\varphi) = \{s \mid \exists w \in$

$\mathcal{L}(K \otimes T_\varphi)$. $(w, n \models \varphi) \wedge (v \cdot u_n \lesssim w) \wedge w_n = s\}$. Same procedure for $r_{\neg\varphi}(u)$, thus (11) is proven.

To finally prove (10), we first unfold (8) into (9) and get $L_\varphi^K(u) = \{v \mid \exists w.\ v \cdot w \in \mathcal{L}(K) \wedge (v \cdot w, \text{MRR}(u) \models \varphi) \wedge u \lesssim v \wedge |v| = |u|\}$. If $L_\varphi^K(u)$ is empty, then by (11) $r_\varphi(u)$ must be also empty, simply because $\mathcal{L}(K \otimes T_\varphi) \subseteq \mathcal{L}(K)$. This proves the first part of (10), the second part follows in the same manner.   □

5   Experimental Evaluation

The RV approach presented in this paper has been implemented as an extension of NUXMV [8] in which the BDD library is based on CUDD 2.4.1.1. Besides the offline monitoring in NUXMV, it is also possible to synthesize the symbolic monitors into explicit-state monitors as independent code in various languages as online monitors without dependencies on NUXMV and BDD. The correctness of generated explicit-state monitor code has been extensively tested by comparing the outputs with those from the symbolic monitors, on a large set of LTL properties and random traces.

The comparison of the baseline implementation (no assumption, no reset) with other RV tools is not in the scope of this paper. However, a comparison with the RV-Monitor [27] has been reported in our companion tool paper [9], where our Java-based monitors are shown to be about 200x faster than RV-Monitor at generation-time and 2-5x faster at runtime, besides the capacity of generating monitors from long LTL formulae. As no other tool supports all our extended RV features, here we only focus on experimental evaluations on the usefulness and correctness of our ABRV approach.[2]

Tests on LTL Patterns. To show the feasibility and effectiveness of our RV approach, we have generated monitors from a wide coverage of practical specifications, i.e. Dwyer's LTL patterns [13][3]. To show the impact of assumptions, we generated two groups of monitors, with and without assumption. The chosen assumption says that *the transitions to s-states occur at most 2 times*, which can be expressed in LTL as $((\neg s)\,\mathbf{W}\,(s\,\mathbf{W}\,((\neg s)\,\mathbf{W}\,(s\,\mathbf{W}\,(\mathbf{G}\,\neg s)))))$, where $\mathbf{W}$ denotes *weak until*: $\varphi\,\mathbf{W}\,\psi \doteq (\mathbf{G}\,\varphi) \vee (\varphi\,\mathbf{U}\,\psi) = \varphi\,\mathbf{U}\,(\psi \vee \mathbf{G}\,\varphi)$. Under this assumption we found that, non-monitorable properties like $\mathbf{G}(p \rightarrow \mathbf{F}s)$ now become monitorable, i.e. the monitor may output conclusive verdicts on certain inputs. This is because, if the transitions to s-state have already occurred 2 times, there should be no s any more in the remaining inputs. Thus whenever p occurs, for whatever future inputs it is impossible to satisfy $\mathbf{F}s$, thus the property is violated conclusively. Eight monitors (Pattern 25, 27, 40, 42, 43, 44, 45, 50) are found to be monitorable under this fairness assumption.

---

[2] All test data, models and other artifacts for reproducing all experiments here are available at https://es.fbk.eu/people/ctian/papers/rv2019/rv2019-data.tar.gz.

[3] The latest version (55 in total) is available at http://patterns.projects.cs.ksu.edu/documentation/patterns/ltl.shtml. We call them Pattern $0, 1, \ldots, 54$ in the same order.

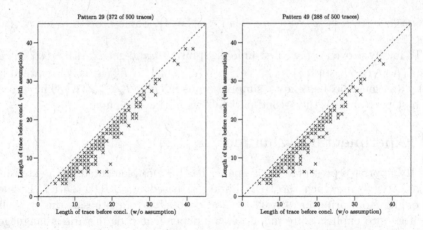

Fig. 4. The number of observations before a conclusive verdict with and w/o assumption

On the other hand, under this assumption some patterns result in predictive monitors, which output conclusive verdicts earlier than those without assumptions. For showing it, we generated 500 random traces (uniformly distributed), each with 50 states, under the assumption (thus the monitor outputs cannot be *out-of-model*). For each pair of monitors (with and without assumption), we record two numbers of states before reaching a conclusive verdict. Whenever the two numbers are the same, the related plot is omitted. In summary, fifteen monitors (Pattern 25, 27, 29, 37, 38, 39, 40, 41, 42, 43, 44, 45, 49, 50, 54) are predictive, and five of them (Pattern 29, 37, 41, 49, 54) have more than 50 traces showing the difference. Figure 4 shows, for example, the tests of Pattern 29 (*s responds to p after q until r*) and 49 (*s, t responds to p after q until r*). The time needed to run the tests on all traces is almost negligible (less than one second) for each pattern.

The *interesting* traces (which show predictive verdicts) can be also obtained by model checking on monitors generated into SMV models. Suppose we have two monitors M1 (with assumption) and M2 (w/o assumption), and AV := (M1._concl $\wedge$ ¬M2._concl) (the assumption is valuable iff M1 has reached conclusive verdicts ($\top^a$, $\bot^a$ or ×) while M2 has not), then the counterexample of model-checking ¬**F** AV (AV *cannot* eventually be true) will be a trace showing that the monitor M1 is predictive: $\emptyset, \{p, s\}, \emptyset, s, p, \emptyset, \ldots$. Furthermore, it is possible to find a trace such that the distance of conclusive outputs from the two monitors is arbitrary large. For this purpose, we can setup a bounded counter c, whose value only increases when AV is true and then verify if c can reach a given maximum value, say, 10. By checking the *invariance* specification $c < 10$, the counterexample will be the desired trace. Similarly, the monotonicity (**G** M._unknown $\vee$ (M._unknown **U** M._concl)), the correctness ((**F** M._true) $\rightarrow \varphi$ and (**F** M._false) $\rightarrow \neg\varphi$), and the correctness of resets ($\mathbf{X}^n$(M._reset $\wedge$ **X**(¬ M._reset **U** M._true)) $\rightarrow \mathbf{X}^n\varphi$) of any monitor M generated from φ can also be checked in NUXMV. Details are omitted due to page limits.

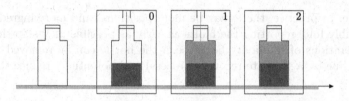

Fig. 5. The factory

Tests on a Factory Model. The assumption used in previous tests may look too artificial, so we present a real-world example taken from [16] and shown in Fig. 5. It models a (simplified) assembly line in a factory, in which some empty bottles need to pass three positions in the assembly line to have two ingredients filled. The red ingredient is filled at position 0, while the green ingredient is filled at position 1. In case of faults, either ingredient may not be correctly filled. The goal is to make sure that all bottles at position 2 have both ingredients filled successfully. There is a belt (the grey bottom line) moving all bottles to their next positions, and the filling operations can only be done when the belt is not moving. All variables in the model are Boolean: `bottle_present[]` (with index 0–2) denotes the existence of a bottle at a position. Similarly, `bottle_ingr1[]` denotes the existence of the red ingredient in the bottle at a position, and `bottle_ingr2[]` for the green ingredient. Besides, `move_belt` denotes if the belt is moving, and `new_bottle` denotes if there is a new bottle coming at position 0 before the belt starts to move. Finally, an unobservable variable `fault` denotes the fault: whenever it happens, the current filling operations (if any) fail and the corresponding ingredients are not filled into the bottle. (The related model files are part of the downloadable artifacts.)

The basic requirement is that all bottles at position 2 have both ingredients filled, if the belt is not moving. It can be expressed by safety property $\mathbf{G}\,((\texttt{bottle\_present[2]} \wedge \neg\texttt{move\_belt}) \rightarrow (\texttt{bottle\_ingr1[2]} \wedge \texttt{bottle\_ingr2[2]}))$ (*whenever the belt is not moving and there is a bottle at position 2, both ingredients are filled in that bottle*). We found that, the monitor of the same property, generated with the factory model as assumption, is predictive: it outputs $\perp^{a}$ *almost immediately* after the first fault happens, *before* the bottle arrived at position 2. To see such a possible trace, again we used model checking. By checking LTL specification $\neg\mathbf{F}$ AV where $AV := (\texttt{M1.\_concl} \wedge \neg\texttt{M2.\_concl})$ and M1 (M2) are monitors of the above safety property built with (without) assumption, respectively. The counterexample shows one such trace: the fault happens at state 4, and the filling of the red ingredient at position 0 failed at position 1; the monitor with assumption outputs $\perp^{a}$ at state 6, before the bottle is moved to position 1, while the monitor without assumption can only output $\perp^{a}$ at state 10, after the bottle is moved to position 2. This is because, any unfilled bottle at position 0 or 1 will remain unfilled at position 2 under the model, thus the monitor with assumption should have known the faults before any unfilled bottle arrived at position 2, even if the fault itself is not directly observable. In practice, there may be more positions (and more ingredients) in the assembly line, reporting the faults as early as possible may skip the rest of filling operations of the faulty bottle (e.g. the bottle can be removed from the assembly line by a separate recovery process) and potentially reduce the costs.

6   Related Work

The idea of leveraging partial knowledge of a system to improve monitorablity is not altogether new. Leucker [25] considers an LTL_3-based predictive semantics $LTL_{\mathcal{P}}$, where, given a finite trace u, an LTL formula φ is evaluated on every extension of u that are paths of a model $\hat{\mathcal{P}}$ of the SUS $\mathcal{P}$. Our proposal is a proper conservative extension of this work: in case of full observability, no reset, if the system always satisfies the assumption, i.e. $\mathcal{L}(\mathcal{P}) \subseteq \mathcal{L}(\hat{\mathcal{P}})$, our definition coincides with [25]. As $\mathcal{L}(\mathcal{P}) \subseteq \mathcal{L}(\hat{\mathcal{P}})$ is a strong assumption there, if it is violated, the monitor output will be undefined, while we explicitly take that possibility into account. On the other hand, partial observability is essential for extending traditional RV approaches such that assumptions are really needed to evaluate the property (not only for prediction). In fact, under full observability, if the model $\hat{\mathcal{P}}$ is expressed in LTL, the monitor of [25] coincides with the monitor for $\hat{\mathcal{P}} \to \phi$ given in [26]. Due to the partial observability, ABRV-LTL monitors cannot be expressed in traditional RV approach (quantifiers over traces would be necessary).

In another three-valued predictive LTL semantics [36], the assumption is based on predictive words. Given a sequence u, a predictive word v of subsequent inputs is computed with static analysis of the monitored program and the monitor output evaluates $[\![u \cdot v \models \varphi]\!]_3$. The assumption used in our framework can be also used to predict the future inputs, but can associate to each u an infinite number of words. Thus our assumption-based RV framework is more general than [36], even without partial observability and resets. On the other side, while our assumptions can be violated by the system execution, the predictive word of [36] is assured by static analysis.

The research of partial observability in Discrete-Event Systems is usually connected with diagnosability [32] and predicability [18,19]. The presence of system models plays a crucial role here, although technically speaking the support of partial observation is orthogonal with the use of system models (or assumptions) in the monitoring algorithm. Given a model of the system which includes faults (eventually leading the system to a failure) and which is partially-observable (observable only with a limited number of events or data variables), diagnosability studies the problem of checking if the faults can be detected within a finite amount of time. On the other hand, if we take an empty specification (true) and use the system model as assumptions, then our monitors will be checking if the system implementation is always consistent with its model—the monitor only outputs $\top^a$ and $\times$ in this case. This is in spirit of Model-based Runtime Verification [2,38], sometimes also combined with extra temporal specifications [34,35,37].

Other work with partial observability appears in decentralised monitoring of distributed systems [3,11], where an LTL formula describing the system's global behavior may be decomposed into a list (or tree) of sub-formulae according to the system components, whose local behaviours are fully observable.

To the best of our knowledge, the concept of resettable monitors was never published before. In general, if we do not consider assumptions or past operators, restarting monitors for LTL is not an issue. For example, in [33], the authors extend a runtime monitor for regular expressions with recovery. Comparing with our work, it is specific to the given pattern and considers neither past operators, nor the system model.

7   Conclusion

In this paper, we proposed an extended RV framework where assumptions, partial observability and resets are considered. We proposed a new four-valued LTL semantics called ABRV-LTL and have shown its necessity in RV monitors under assumptions. As the solution, we gave a simple symbolic LTL monitoring algorithm and demonstrated that, under certain assumptions the resulting monitors are predictive, while some non-monitorable properties becomes monitorable.

Future work includes: (1) analyzing monitorability, fixing the assumption and in the presence of resets; (2) characterizing monitors with partial observability and resets in terms of epistemic operators [21] and forgettable past [24]; (3) synthesizing the minimal assumption and/or the minimal number of observables to make a property monitorable or to detect every violation (this is related to [5,20]).

References

1. Ackermann, W.: Solvable Cases of the Decision Problem. North-Holland Publishing Company (1954). https://doi.org/10.2307/2964059
2. Azzopardi, S., Colombo, C., Pace, G.: A model-based approach to combining static and dynamic verification techniques. In: Margaria, T., Steffen, B. (eds.) ISoLA 2016, Part I. LNCS, vol. 9952, pp. 416–430. Springer, Cham (2016). https://doi.org/10.1007/978-3-319-47166-2_29
3. Bauer, A., Falcone, Y.: Decentralised LTL monitoring. Formal Methods Syst. Des. 48(1–2), 46–93 (2016). https://doi.org/10.1007/s10703-016-0253-8
4. Bauer, A., Leucker, M., Schallhart, C.: Runtime verification for LTL and TLTL. ACM Trans. Softw. Eng. Methodol. 20(4), 14–64 (2011). https://doi.org/10.1145/2000799.2000800
5. Bittner, B., Bozzano, M., Cimatti, A., Olive, X.: Symbolic synthesis of observability requirements for diagnosability. In: Proceedings of the Twenty-Sixth AAAI Conference on Artificial Intelligence, Toronto, Ontario, Canada, 22–26 July 2012. http://www.aaai.org/ocs/index.php/AAAI/AAAI12/paper/view/5056
6. Bryant, R.E.: Binary decision diagrams. In: Clarke, E., Henzinger, T., Veith, H., Bloem, R. (eds.) Handbook of Model Checking, pp. 191–217. Springer, Cham (2018). https://doi.org/10.1007/978-3-319-10575-8_7

7. Burch, J.R., Clarke, E.M., McMillan, K.L., Dill, D.L., Hwang, L.J.: Symbolic model checking: 10^{20} states and beyond. Inf. Comput. **98**(2), 142–170 (1992). https://doi.org/10.1016/0890-5401(92)90017-A

8. Cavada, R., et al.: The NUXMV symbolic model checker. In: Biere, A., Bloem, R. (eds.) CAV 2014. LNCS, vol. 8559, pp. 334–342. Springer, Cham (2014). https://doi.org/10.1007/978-3-319-08867-9_22

9. Cimatti, A., Tian, C., Tonetta, S.: NuRV: a nuXmv extension for runtime verification. In: Finkbeiner, B., Mariani, L. (eds.) RV 2019. LNCS, vol. 11757, pp. 382–392. Springer, Cham (2019)

10. Clarke, E.M., Grumberg, O., Hamaguchi, K.: Another look at LTL model checking. Formal Methods Syst. Des. **10**(1), 47–71 (1997). https://doi.org/10.1023/A:1008615614281

11. Colombo, C., Falcone, Y.: Organising LTL monitors over distributed systems with a global clock. Formal Methods Syst. Des. **49**(1), 109–158 (2016). https://doi.org/10.1007/s10703-016-0251-x

12. Du, X., Liu, Y., Tiu, A.: Trace-length independent runtime monitoring of quantitative policies in LTL. In: Bjørner, N., de Boer, F. (eds.) FM 2015. LNCS, vol. 9109, pp. 231–247. Springer, Cham (2015). https://doi.org/10.1007/978-3-319-19249-9_15

13. Dwyer, M.B., Avrunin, G.S., Corbett, J.C.: Patterns in property specifications for finite-state verification. In: Proceedings of the 21st International Conference on Software Engineering, pp. 411–420. ACM Press, New York (1999). https://doi.org/10.1145/302405.302672

14. Emerson, E.A., Lei, C.-L.: Temporal reasoning under generalized fairness constraints. In: Monien, B., Vidal-Naquet, G. (eds.) STACS 1986. LNCS, vol. 210, pp. 21–36. Springer, Heidelberg (1986). https://doi.org/10.1007/3-540-16078-7_62

15. Falcone, Y., Havelund, K., Reger, G.: A tutorial on runtime verification. Eng. Dependable Softw. Syst. **34**, 141–175 (2013). https://doi.org/10.3233/978-1-61499-207-3-141

16. Fauri, D., dos Santos, D.R., Costante, E., den Hartog, J., Etalle, S., Tonetta, S.: From system specification to anomaly detection (and back). In: Proceedings of the 2017 Workshop on Cyber-Physical Systems Security and PrivaCy, pp. 13–24. ACM Press, New York, November 2017. https://doi.org/10.1145/3140241.3140250

17. Fuxman, A.D.: Formal analysis of early requirements specifications. Ph.D. thesis, University of Toronto (2001). http://dit.unitn.it/~ft/papers/afthesis.ps.gz

18. Genc, S., Lafortune, S.: Predictability of event occurrences in partially-observed discrete-event systems. Automatica **45**(2), 301–311 (2009). https://doi.org/10.1016/j.automatica.2008.06.022

19. Genc, S., Lafortune, S.: Predictability in discrete-event systems under partial observation. IFAC Proc. Vol. **39**(13), 1461–1466 (2006). https://doi.org/10.3182/20060829-4-CN-2909.00243

20. Graf, S., Peled, D., Quinton, S.: Monitoring distributed systems using knowledge. In: Bruni, R., Dingel, J. (eds.) FMOODS/FORTE -2011. LNCS, vol. 6722, pp. 183–197. Springer, Heidelberg (2011). https://doi.org/10.1007/978-3-642-21461-5_12

21. Halpern, J.Y., Vardi, M.Y.: The complexity of reasoning about knowledge and time. I. Lower bounds. Journal of Computer and System Sciences **38**(1), 195–237 (1989). https://doi.org/10.1016/0022-0000(89)90039-1

22. Havelund, K., Roşu, G.: Synthesizing monitors for safety properties. In: Katoen, J.-P., Stevens, P. (eds.) TACAS 2002. LNCS, vol. 2280, pp. 342–356. Springer, Heidelberg (2002). https://doi.org/10.1007/3-540-46002-0_24

23. Kesten, Y., Pnueli, A., Raviv, L.: Algorithmic verification of linear temporal logic specifications. In: Larsen, K.G., Skyum, S., Winskel, G. (eds.) ICALP 1998. LNCS, vol. 1443, pp. 1–16. Springer, Heidelberg (1998). https://doi.org/10.1007/BFb0055036

24. Laroussinie, F., Markey, N., Schnoebelen, P.: Temporal logic with forgettable past. In: Proceedings of the 17th Annual IEEE Symposium on Logic in Computer Science (LICS 2002), pp. 383–392. IEEE Comput. Soc., July 2002. https://doi.org/10.1109/LICS.2002.1029846

25. Leucker, M.: Sliding between model checking and runtime verification. In: Qadeer, S., Tasiran, S. (eds.) RV 2012. LNCS, vol. 7687, pp. 82–87. Springer, Heidelberg (2013). https://doi.org/10.1007/978-3-642-35632-2_10

26. Leucker, M., Schallhart, C.: A brief account of runtime verification. J. Logic Algebraic Program. **78**(5), 293–303 (2009). https://doi.org/10.1016/j.jlap.2008.08.004

27. Luo, Q., et al.: RV-Monitor: efficient parametric runtime verification with simultaneous properties. In: Bonakdarpour, B., Smolka, S.A. (eds.) RV 2014. LNCS, vol. 8734, pp. 285–300. Springer, Cham (2014). https://doi.org/10.1007/978-3-319-11164-3_24

28. Manna, Z., Pnueli, A.: The Temporal Logic of Reactive and Concurrent Systems: Specification. Springer, New York (1992). https://doi.org/10.1007/978-1-4612-0931-7

29. Manna, Z., Pnueli, A.: Temporal Verification of Reactive Systems: Safety. Springer, New York (1995). https://doi.org/10.1007/978-1-4612-4222-2

30. McMillan, K.L.: Symbolic Model Checking. Springer, Boston (1993). https://doi.org/10.1007/978-1-4615-3190-6

31. Roşu, G., Havelund, K.: Rewriting-based techniques for runtime verification. Autom. Softw. Eng. **12**(2), 151–197 (2005). https://doi.org/10.1007/s10515-005-6205-y

32. Sampath, M., Sengupta, R., Lafortune, S., Sinnamohideen, K., Teneketzis, D.: Diagnosability of discrete-event systems. IEEE Trans. Autom. Control **40**(9), 1555–1575 (1995). https://doi.org/10.1109/9.412626

33. Selyunin, K., et al.: Runtime monitoring with recovery of the SENT communication protocol. In: Majumdar, R., Kunčak, V. (eds.) CAV 2017, Part I. LNCS, vol. 10426, pp. 336–355. Springer, Cham (2017). https://doi.org/10.1007/978-3-319-63387-9_17

34. Tan, L.: Model-based self-monitoring embedded programs with temporal logic specifications. Autom. Softw. Eng. 380–383 (2005). https://doi.org/10.1145/1101908.1101975

35. Tan, L., Kim, J., Sokolsky, O., Lee, I.: Model-based testing and monitoring for hybrid embedded systems. In: IEEE International Conference on Information Reuse and Integration, pp. 487–492. IEEE, November 2004. https://doi.org/10.1109/IRI.2004.1431508

36. Zhang, X., Leucker, M., Dong, W.: Runtime verification with predictive semantics. In: Goodloe, A.E., Person, S. (eds.) NFM 2012. LNCS, vol. 7226, pp. 418–432. Springer, Heidelberg (2012). https://doi.org/10.1007/978-3-642-28891-3_37

37. Zhao, Y., Oberthür, S., Kardos, M., Rammig, F.J.: Model-based runtime verification framework for self-optimizing systems. Electron. Notes Theor. Comput. Sci. **144**(4), 125–145 (2006). https://doi.org/10.1016/j.entcs.2006.02.008

38. Zhao, Y., Rammig, F.: Model-based runtime verification framework. Electron. Notes Theor. Comput. Sci. **253**(1), 179–193 (2009). https://doi.org/10.1016/j.entcs.2009.09.035

Decentralized Stream Runtime Verification

Luis Miguel Danielsson[1,2(✉)] and César Sánchez[1(✉)]

[1] IMDEA Software Institute, Madrid, Spain
{luismiguel.danielsson,cesar.sanchez}@imdea.org
[2] Universidad Politécnica de Madrid (UPM), Madrid, Spain

Abstract. We study the problem of decentralized monitoring of stream runtime verification specifications. Decentralized monitoring uses distributed monitors that communicate via a synchronous network, a communication setting common in many cyber-physical systems like automotive CPSs. Previous approaches to decentralized monitoring were restricted to logics like LTL logics that provide Boolean verdicts. We solve here the decentralized monitoring problem for the more general setting of stream runtime verification. Additionally, our solution handles network topologies while previous decentralized monitoring works assumed that every pair of nodes can communicate directly. We also introduce a novel property on specifications, called decentralized efficient monitorability, that guarantees that the online monitoring can be performed with bounded resources. Finally, we report the results of an empirical evaluation of an implementation and compare the expressive power and efficiency against state-of-the-art decentralized monitoring tools like Themis.

1 Introduction

We study the problem of decentralized runtime verification of stream runtime verification (SRV) specifications. Runtime verification (RV) is a dynamic technique for software quality assurance that consists of generating a monitor from a formal specification, that then inspects a single trace of execution of the system under analysis. One of the problems that RV must handle is to generate monitors from a specification. Early approaches for specification languages were based on temporal logics [6,11,18], regular expressions [25], timed regular expressions [2], rules [3], or rewriting [23]. Stream runtime verification, pioneered by Lola [10], defines monitors by declaring the dependencies between output streams of results and input streams of observations. SRV is a richer formalism that goes beyond Boolean verdicts, like in logical techniques, to allow specifying the collection of statistics and the generation richer (non-Boolean) verdicts. Examples include counting events, specifying robustness or generating models or quantitative verdicts. See [10,14,17] for examples illustrating the expressivity of SRV languages.

This work was funded in part by the Madrid Regional Government under project "S2018/TCS-4339 (BLOQUES-CM)", by EU H2020 project 731535 "Elastest" and by Spanish National Project "BOSCO (PGC2018-102210-B-100)".

B. Finkbeiner and L. Mariani (Eds.): RV 2019, LNCS 11757, pp. 185–201, 2019.
https://doi.org/10.1007/978-3-030-32079-9_11

Another important aspect of RV is the operational execution of monitors: how to collect information and how to monitor incrementally. In this paper we consider using a network of distributed monitors connected via a synchronous network, together with periodic sampling of inputs. This problem is known as *decentralized monitoring*. Our goal is to generate local monitors at each node that collaborate to monitor the specification, distributing the computational load while minimizing the network bandwidth and the latency of the computation of verdicts. Apart from more efficient evaluation, decentralized monitoring can provide fault-tolerance as the process can partially evaluate a specification with the part of the network that does not fail.

Our Solution. In this paper we provide a solution to the decentralized monitoring problem for Lola specifications for arbitrary network topologies and placement of the local monitors. We assume a connected network topology where nodes can only communicate directly with their neighbors. In general, messages between two nodes require several hops, and all nodes have initially deployed a local routing table that contains the next hop depending on the final destination. We follow the synchronous distributed model of computation, where computation (input readings from the system, message routing and local monitor computations) proceeds in rounds. We also assume a reliable system: nodes do not crash, and messages are not lost or duplicated. These assumptions are realistic, for example in automotive CPSs like solutions based on a synchronous BUS, like CAN networks [19] and Autosar [1]. In our solution, different parts of the specification (modeled as streams), including input readings, will be deployed in different nodes as a local monitor. Local monitors will communicate when necessary to resolve the streams assigned to them, trying to minimize the communication overhead.

A degenerated case of this setting is a centralized solution: nodes with mapped observations send their sensed values to a fixed central node that is responsible of computing the whole specification. The SRV language that we consider is Lola [10] including future dependencies. We will identify those specifications that can be monitored decentralized with finite memory, independently of the trace length.

Motivating Example. Our motivation is to build rich monitors for decentralized synchronous networks, used in automotive CPSs [20] for example using the Autosar standard over the CAN network. This example is inspired by the Electronic Stability Program (ESP) and models the under steering to the left scenario in an attempt to avoid an obstacle. The ESP must detect the sudden turn of the steering wheel and the deviation produced with the actual movement of the car (yaw). When this deviation is perceived and maintained over a

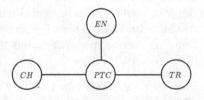

Fig. 1. Autosar simplified topology

period of time, the ESP must act on the brakes, the torque distribution and the engine in order to produce the desired movement without any lose of control over the vehicle. The topology is shown on the right. The monitor in node *CH* (chassis) detects the under-steering and whether the ESP must be activated. The monitor in *EN* (engine) checks that the throttle is ready to react to the evasive maneuver. Our intention is to define the following streams:

- ESP_on: represents whether there is under-steering or the wheel is slipping,
- req_thr: the requested throttle,
- good_thro: whether the throttle is correct

We achieve this by using input values, like yaw (the direction of the wheels), the desired steering, drive_wheel_slip (whether the drive wheels are slipping), and the throttle.

```
@Chassis{ input num yaw, steering, drive_wheel_slip
  define num dev = steering - yaw
  define bool under_steering_l = dev > 0 and dev > 0.2
  output bool ESP_on = under_steering_left or drive_wheel_slip
}
@Engine{ input num throttle
  output num req_thr = if ESP_on then req_thr[-1|0]-dev else 0
  output bool good_thro = req_thr[-1|0]/throttle <= 0.1
}
```

Related Work. The work in [4] shows how monitoring Metric Temporal Logic specifications of distributed systems (including failures and message reordering) where the nodes communicate in a tree fashion and the root emits the final verdict. Sen et al. [26] introduces PT-DTL, a variant of LTL logic for monitoring distributed systems. The work in [16] uses slices to support node crashes and message errors when monitoring distributed message passing systems with a global clock. Bauer et al. [5] introduce a first-order temporal logic and trace-length independent spawning automaton. Bauer et al. [7] shows a decentralized solution to monitor LTL$_3$ in synchronous systems using formula rewriting. This is improved in [12,13] using an Execution History Encoding (EHE). All these approaches consider only Boolean verdicts. SRV can generate verdicts from arbitrary data domains, but all previous SRV efforts, from Lola [10], Lola2.0 [14], Copilot [21,22] and extensions to timed event streams, like TeSSLa [8], RTLola [15] or Striver [17] assume a centralized monitoring setting.

Contributions and Structure. The main contribution of this paper is a solution, described in Sect. 3, to the decentralized stream runtime verification problem. A second contribution, included in Sect. 4, is the identification of a fragment of specifications, called decentralized efficiently monitorable, that ensure that monitoring can be performed with bounded memory (independently of the length of the input trace). A third contribution, detailed in Sect. 5, is a prototype implementation and an empirical evaluation. Section 2 contains the preliminaries and Sect. 6 concludes.

2   Preliminaries. Stream Runtime Verification

We recall now SRV briefly (see [10] and the tutorial [24]). The fundamental idea of SRV, pioneered by Lola [10] is to cleanly separate the temporal dependencies from the individual operations to be performed at each step, which leads to generalization of monitoring algorithms for logics to the computation of richer values. A Lola specification declares the relation between output streams and input streams, including both future and past temporal dependencies. The streams are typed using arbitrary multi-sorted first-order theories. A type has a collection of symbols used to construct expressions, together with an interpretation of these symbols to evaluate ground expressions.

Lola Syntax. Given a set Z of (typed) stream variables the set of *stream expressions* consists of (1) variables from Z, (2) offsets $v[k, d]$ where v is a stream variable of type D, k is a natural number and d a value from D, and (3) function applications $f(t_1, \ldots, t_n)$ using constructors f from the theories to previously defined terms. Stream variables represent streams (sequences of values). The intended meaning of expression $v[-1, false]$ is the value of stream v in the previous position of the trace (or *false* if there is no such previous position, that is, at the beginning). We assume that all theories have a constructor if · then · else · that given an expression of type Bool and two expressions of type D constructs a term of type D. We use $Term_D(Z)$ for the set of stream expressions of type D constructed from variables from Z (and drop Z if clear from the context). Given a term t, $sub(t)$ represents the set of sub-terms of t.

Definition 1 (Specification). *A Lola specification $\varphi(I, O)$ consists of a set $I = \{r_1, \ldots, r_m\}$ of input stream variables, a set $O = \{s_1, \ldots, s_n\}$ of output stream variables, and a set of defining equations, $s_i = e_i(r_1, \ldots, r_m, s_1, \ldots, s_n)$ one per output variable $s_i \in O$, from $Term_D(I \cup O)$ where D is the type of s_i.*

A specification describes the relation between input streams and output streams. We will use $r, r_i, \ldots$ to refer to input stream variables; $s, s_i, \ldots$ to refer to output stream variables; and u, v for an arbitrary input or output stream variable. Given $\varphi(I, O)$ we use $appears(u)$ for the set of output streams that use u, that is $\{s_i \mid u[-k, d] \in sub(e_i) \text{ or } u \in sub(e_i)\}$. Also, $ground(t)$ indicates whether expression t is a ground (contains no variables or offsets) and can be evaluated into a value.

Example 1. The property "*sum the previous values in input stream y, but if the reset stream is true, reset the count*", can be expressed as follows, where stream variable root uses the accumulator acc and the input reset to compute the desired sum:

```
input   bool reset , int i
define int acc  = i + root [-1|0]
output int root = if reset then 0 else acc
```

Lola Semantics. At runtime, input stream variables are associated with input streams (sequence of values of the appropriate type and of the same length M). The intended meaning of a Lola specification is to associate output streams to output stream variables (of the same length M) that satisfy the equations in the specification. Formally, this semantics are defined denotationally. Given input streams σ_I (one sequence per input stream variable) and given an output candidate σ_O (one sequence per output stream) the semantics describe when the pair (σ_I, σ_O) matches the specification, which we write $(\sigma_I, \sigma_O) \vDash \varphi$. We use σ_r for the stream in σ_I corresponding to input variable r and $\sigma_r(k)$ for the value at position k (with $0 \le k \le M$).

A *valuation* is a pair $\sigma : (\sigma_I, \sigma_O)$. Given a valuation the *evaluation* $[\![t]\!]_\sigma$ of a term t is a sequence of length M of values of the type of t defined as follows:

- If t is a stream variable u, then $[\![u]\!]_\sigma(j) = \sigma_u(j)$.
- If t is $f(t_1, \ldots, t_k)$ then $[\![f(t_1, \ldots, t_k)]\!]_\sigma(j) = f([\![t_1]\!]_\sigma(j), \ldots, [\![t_k]\!]_\sigma(j))$
- If t is $v[i, c]$ then $[\![v[i, c]]\!]_\sigma(j) = [\![v]\!]_\sigma(j + i)$ if $0 \le j + i < M$, and c otherwise.

Definition 2 (Evaluation Model). *A valuation (σ_I, σ_O) satisfies a Lola specification φ whenever for every output variable s_i, $[\![s_i]\!]_{(\sigma_I, \sigma_O)} = [\![e_i]\!]_{(\sigma_I, \sigma_O)}$. In this case we say that σ is an evaluation model of φ and write $(\sigma_I, \sigma_O) \vDash \varphi$.*

This semantics capture when a candidate valuation is an evaluation model, but the intention of a Lola specification is to compute the unique output streams given input streams.

A *dependency graph* D_φ of a specification $\varphi(I \cup O)$ is a weighted multi-graph (V, E) whose vertices are the stream variables $V = I \cup O$, and E contains a directed weighted edge $u \xrightarrow{w} v$ whenever $v[w, d]$ is a subterm in the defining equation of u. If a dependency graph D_φ contains no cycles with 0 weight then the specification is called well-formed, and it guarantees that for every σ_I there is a unique σ_O such that $(\sigma_I, \sigma_O) \vDash \varphi$. This is because the value of a stream at a given position cannot depend on itself.

Given a stream variable u and position $i \ge 0$ the *instant stream variable* (or simply instant variable) $u[i]$ is a fresh variable of the same type as u.

Definition 3 (Evaluation Graph). *Given $\varphi(I, O)$ and a trace length M the evaluation graph $G_{\varphi,M}$ has as vertices the set of instant variables $\{u[k]\}$ for $u \in I \cup O$ and $0 \le k < M$, and has edges $u[k] \to v[k']$ if the dependency graph contains an edge $u \xrightarrow{j} v$ and $k + j = k'$.*

For example, if the defining equations of u contains $v[-1, d]$ then $u[16]$ points to $v[15]$ in all evaluation graphs with $M \ge 16$. In well-formed specifications there are no cycles in any evaluation graph, which enables to reason by induction on evaluation graphs.

Lola Online Monitoring. The Lola online monitoring algorithm [10,24] maintains two storages:

- R: for instant variables that have been resolved (that is, pairs $(u[k], c)$ that denote that $u[k]$ is known to have value c);

– U: for instant variables $u[k]$ whose value is not determined yet (that is, whose instantiated equation still contains variables).

At instant k the equation e_i for s_i gets instantiated as follows: every variable u in e_i is converted into $u[k]$ and every offset $u[j,d]$ is turned into $u[k+j]$ (or into d if $k+j$ falls out of bounds). After instantiating all equations, the monitor substitutes instant variables by their value if these values are resolved (in R). If the resulting equation is not ground then it remains in U. Eventually, all values will be discovered and every term will be resolved and moved from U to R.

3   Decentralized Stream Runtime Verification

In this section we describe our solution to the decentralized SRV problem. Given a well-formed Lola specification, the decentralized online algorithm that we present here will incrementally compute a value for each output instant variable, reading values from the input stream variables at every clock instant. The starting point of the solution is a map that associates each variable in the specification to a network node. The node associated to an input variable corresponds to the location where readings of new values are performed, and the node associated to an output variable s is the node responsible to incrementally compute the stream for s. Each node will run a local monitor, that will collaborate with other monitors by exchanging messages to perform the global monitoring task.

The main correctness criteria is that the output produced by our network of cooperating monitors corresponds to the denotational semantics. However, the decentralized algorithm may compute some output values at different time instants than the centralized version, due to the different location of the inputs and the delays caused by the communication.

3.1   Problem Description

The description of the decentralized SRV monitoring problem consists of a specification, a network topology and a stream assignment.

Network. A network topology $\mathcal{T} : \langle N, \rightarrow \rangle$ is given by a set of nodes N connected by directed edges $\rightarrow \subseteq N \times N$ that represent communication links between the nodes. We assume that the graph is connected. A route between two nodes n and m is list of nodes $[n_0, \ldots, n_k]$ such that consecutive nodes are neighbors (i.e. $n_i \rightarrow n_{i+1}$), no node is repeated, and $n = n_0$ and $m = n_k$. We statically fix routes between every two nodes with the following properties: (1) if two nodes n, m are neighbors then they communicate directly (that is $[n, m]$ is the route from n to m); (2) if $[n_0, \ldots, n_i, \ldots n_k]$ is a route, then the route from n_i to n_k is the sub-list $[n_i \ldots n_k]$. These properties can be enforced easily in a connected graph, and they imply that routing tables can be encoded locally in every node by just encoding at every node the next hop for every destination.

We use $next_n(m)$ for the next hop in the routing table of n for messages with destination m, and $dist(n, m)$ for the number of hops between n and m. This is precisely the number of routing operations that are needed for a message from n to arrive to m. Consider the topology in Fig. 1. A message inserted at time 17 in CH with destination EN will arrive to PTC at time 18, which will be routed, arriving at EN at time 19.

We assume reliable unicast communication (no message loss or duplication) over a synchronous network, from which we build a synchronous distributed system where computation proceeds as a sequence of cycles. In this computational model, all nodes in the network execute in every cycle—in parallel and to completion— the following actions: (1) read input messages, (2) perform a terminating local computation, (3) generate output messages. We describe below our decentralized monitoring solution as a synchronous distributed system. In our solution we use two types of messages:

- **Requests** messages: $(\mathbf{req}, s[k], n_s, n_d)$ where $s[k]$ is an instant variable, n_s is the source node and n_d is the destination node of the message.
- **Response** messages: $(\mathbf{resp}, s[k], c, n_s, n_d)$ where $s[k]$ is an instant variable, c is a value, n_s is the source node and n_d is the destination node.

Let $msg = (\mathbf{resp}, s[k], c, n_s, n_d)$, then $msg.src = n_s$, $msg.dst = n_d$, $msg.type = \mathbf{resp}$, $msg.stream = s[k]$ and $msg.val = c$ (the analogous definitions apply for a request message except that $msg.val$ is not applicable). The intention of request messages is that n_s requests the value of $s[k]$ from n_d, which is the node in charge of stream s. Response messages are used to inform of the actual values read or computed.

Stream Assignment and Communication Strategies. Given a specification $\varphi(I, O)$ and a network topology $\mathcal{T} : \langle N, \rightarrow \rangle$ a *stream assignment* is a map $\mu : I \cup O \rightarrow N$ that assigns a network node to each stream variable. The node $\mu(r)$ for an input stream variable r is the location in the network where r is sensed in every clock tick. At runtime, at every instant k new input values for variables mapped to different nodes are read simultaneously. The node $\mu(s)$ for an output stream variable s is the location whose local monitor is responsible for resolving the values of s.

Additionally, each stream variable v can be assigned one of the following two *communication strategies* to denote whether an instant value $v[k]$ is automatically communicated to all potentially interested nodes, or whether its value is obtained on request only. Let v and u be two stream variables such that v appears in the equation of u and let $n_v = \mu(v)$ and $n_u = \mu(u)$.

- **Eager communication**: the node n_v informs n_u of every value $v[k] = c$ that it resolves by sending a message $(\mathbf{resp}, v[k], c, n_v, n_u)$.
- **Lazy communication**: node n_u requests n_v the value of $v[k]$ (in case n_u needs it to resolve $u[k']$ for some k') by sending a message $(\mathbf{req}, v[k], n_u, n_v)$. When n_u receives this message and resolves $v[k]$ to a value c, n_u will respond with $(\mathbf{resp}, v[k], c, n_v, n_u)$.

Each stream variable can be independently declared as eager or lazy. We use two predicates $eager(u)$ and $lazy(u)$ (which is defined as $\neg eager(u)$) to indicate the communication strategy of stream variable u. Note that the lazy strategy involves two messages and eager only one, but eager sends every instant variable resolved, while lazy will only sends those that are requested. In case the values are almost always needed, eager is preferable while if values are less frequently required lazy is preferred. We are finally ready to define the decentralized SRV problem.

Definition 4. *A decentralized SRV problem $\langle \varphi, \mathcal{T}, \mu, eager \rangle$ is characterized by a specification φ, a topology $\mathcal{T}$, a stream assignment μ and a communication strategy for every stream variable.*

3.2 Decentralized Stream Runtime Verification

Our solution consists of a collection of local monitors, one for each network node n. A local monitor $\langle Q_n, U_n, R_n, P_n, W_n \rangle$ for n consists of an input queue Q_n and four storages:

- **Resolved** storage R_n, where n stores resolved instant variables $(v[k], c)$.
- **Unresolved** storage U_n, where n stores unresolved equations $v[k] = e$ where e is not a value, but an expression that contains other instant variables.
- **Pending** requests P_n, where n records instant variables that have been requested from n by other monitors but that n has not resolved yet.
- **Waiting** for responses W_n, where n records instant variables that n has requested from other nodes but has received no response yet.

When n receives a response from remote nodes, the information is added to R_n, so future local requests for the same value can be resolved immediately. The storage W_n is used to prevent n from requesting the same value twice while waiting for the first request to be responded. An entry in W_n is removed when the value is received, since the value will be subsequently fetched directly from R_n and not requested through the network. The storage P_n is used to record that a value that n is responsible for has been requested, but n does not know the answer yet. When n computes the answer, then n sends the corresponding response message and removes the entry from P_n.

Informally, in each cycle, the local monitor for n processes the incoming messages from its input queue Q_n. Then n reads the values for input streams assigned to it and also instantiates for the current instant the output stream variables that n is responsible for. After that, the equations obtained are simplified using the knowledge acquired so far by n. Finally, new response and request messages are generated and inserted in the queues of the corresponding neighbors.

More concretely, every node n will execute the procedure MONITOR shown in Algorithm 1, which invokes STEP in every clock tick until the input terminates. The procedure FINALIZE is used to resolve the pending values at the end of the trace to their default. The procedure STEP executes the following steps:

1. **Process Messages**: Lines 11–20 deal with the processing of incoming messages. First, Lines 13–14 route messages with a different destination. Lines 16–17 annotate requests in P, which will be later resolved and responded. Lines 19–20 handle response arrivals, adding them to R and removing them from W.
2. **Read New Inputs and Outputs:** Line 21 reads new inputs for current time k, and line 22 instantiates the equation of every output stream that n is responsible for.
3. **Evaluate:** Line 23 evaluates the unresolved equations using EVALUATE.
4. **Send Responses:** Lines 24–27 send messages for all eager variables. Lines 28–31 deal with pending lazy variables. If a pending instant variable is now resolved, the response message is sent and the entry is removed from P_n.
5. **Send new Requests:** Lines 32–35 send new request messages for all lazy instant streams that are now needed, to the corresponding responsible nodes.
6. **Prune:** Line 37 prunes the set R from information that is no longer needed.

The pruning algorithm appears in Algorithm 2 and it is described in Sect. 4. We now show that our solution is correct by proving that the output computed is the same as in the denotational semantics, and that every output is eventually computed.

Theorem 1. *All of the following hold for every instant variable $u[k]$:*

(1) If $lazy(u)$ then all request messages for $u[k]$ are eventually responded.
(2) If $eager(u)$ then a response message for $u[k]$ is eventually sent.
(3) The value of $u[k]$ is eventually resolved.
(4) The value of $u[k]$ is c if and only if $(u[k], c) \in R$ at some instant.

The proof proceeds by induction in the evaluation graph, showing simultaneously in the induction step (1)–(4) as these depend on each other (in the previous inductive steps). Theorem 1 implies that every value of every defined stream at every point is eventually resolved by our network of cooperating monitors. Therefore, given input streams σ_I, the algorithm computes (by (4)) the unique output streams σ_i one for each s_i. The element $\sigma_i(k)$ is the value resolved for $s_i[k]$ by the local monitor for $\mu(s_i)$. The following theorem captures that Algorithm 1 computes the right values (according to the denotational semantics) and Theorem 1 that all values are eventually computed.

Theorem 2. *Let φ be a specification, $S = \langle \varphi, \mathcal{T}, \mu \rangle$ be a decentralized SRV problem, and σ_I an input. Then $(\sigma_I, out(\sigma_I)) \models \varphi$.*

3.3 Simplifiers

The evaluation of expressions in Algorithm 1 assumes that all instant variables in an expression e are known (i.e., e is ground), so the interpreted functions in the data theory can evaluate e. Sometimes, expressions can be partially evaluated (or even the value fully determined) knowing only some of the instant variables. A *simplifier* is a function $f : Term_D \rightarrow Term_D$ such that

- for every term t of type D, $Vars(f(t)) \subseteq Vars(t)$
- for every substitution ρ of $Vars(t)$, $[\![t \triangleleft \rho]\!]_{(\sigma_I,\sigma_O)} = [\![f(t) \triangleleft \rho]\!]_{(\sigma_I,\sigma_O)}$

For example, the following are sound simplifications

if true then $s[0]$ else $t[1]$ $\mapsto s[0]$	$0 + s[7] \mapsto s[7]$	*true* $\vee$ $s[0] \mapsto$ *true*
if false then $s[0]$ else $t[1]$ $\mapsto t[1]$	$1 \cdot t[23] \mapsto t[23]$	*false* $\vee$ $s[0] \mapsto s[0]$

Simplifiers can dramatically affect the performance in terms of the instant at which an instant variable is resolved and the number of messages exchanged.

It is easy to see that for every term t obtained by instantiating a defining equation and for every simplifier f, $[\![t]\!]_{\sigma_I,\sigma_O} = [\![f(t)]\!]_{(\sigma_I,\sigma_O)}$, because the values of the variables in t and in $f(t)$ are filled with the same values (from σ_I and σ_O). The following also holds for every φ and valuation (σ_I, σ_O).

Lemma 1. *Let e be an instant term and let $\rho = \{u[k] \mapsto c\}$ be the substitution such that $c = [\![u[k]]\!]_{(\sigma_I,\sigma_O)}$. Then, $[\![e]\!]_{(\sigma_I,\sigma_O)} = [\![e \triangleleft \rho]\!]_{(\sigma_I,\sigma_O)}$.*

Lemma 1 holds immediately because the substitution ρ is just the partial application of one of the values of the variables that may appear in e. Now, consider arbitrary simplifiers *simp* used in line 43 to simplify expressions. Let U_n be the unresolved storage for node n and let $u[k]$ be an instant variable with $\mu(u) = n$. By Algorithm 1 the sequence of terms $(u[k], t_0), (u[k], t_1), \ldots (u[k], t_k)$ that U_n will store are such that $t_{i+1} = simp(t_i)$ or $t_{i+1} = t_1 \triangleleft \rho$ where $\rho = \{v_i[k_i] \leftarrow c_i\}$ corresponds to the substitution of values of instant variables that are discovered at the given time step. By Lemma 1, it follows that $[\![t_i]\!]_{(\sigma_I,\sigma_O)} = [\![t_{i+1}]\!]_{(\sigma_I,\sigma_O)}$ which in particular when $t_k = c$ implies that the value computed is $[\![u[k]]\!]_{(\sigma_I,\sigma_O)} = c$. The following theorem follows.

Theorem 3. *The decentralized algorithm using simplifiers terminates and computes the unique output for every well-formed specification φ.*

In fact, it is easy to show that the algorithm using simplifiers obtains the value of every instant variable no later than the algorithm that uses no simplifier. This is because in the worst case every instant variable is resolved when all its depending variables are known, and all response messages are sent at the moment they are resolved.

4   Decentralized Efficient Monitorability

In this section we identify a fragment of specifications, called *decentralized efficiently monitorable*, for which the local monitors only need bounded memory to compute every output value. To guarantee that a given storage in a local monitor for node n is bounded, one must provide a bound on both: (1) when a value $(u[k], c)$ in R_n can be removed; and (2) when it is guaranteed that an unresolved value from U_n is resolved. Note that if $s[k]$ is resolved in bounded time then all occurrences of $s[k]$ in W_n and P_n are also removed in bounded time, because it only takes a bounded amount of time for response messages to arrive.

Pruning the Resolved Storage. We show now that the memory necessary in the resolve storage R_n can be bounded (for all specifications). If a stream s is $eager(s)$ then once $s[k]$ is resolved it is sent to the potentially interested remote nodes. However, the value of $s[k]$ has to remain in R_n (and in R_m for remote nodes that receive it) until it is no longer needed. For streams s that are $lazy(s)$, the value must remain in R_n until it is guaranteed that the value will not be requested any more. This information is captured by the notion of back reference.

Definition 5. *Let φ be a Lola specification with dependency graph D_φ. The back reference of a stream s is*

$$\Delta(s) \stackrel{def}{=} \begin{cases} \max(0, \{-k & | \ r \xrightarrow{k} s\}) & if \ eager(s) \\ \max(0, \{-k + dist(r,s) \mid r \xrightarrow{k} s\}) & if \ lazy(s) \end{cases}$$

Note that for lazy streams the request is guaranteed to be received after $dist(\mu(r), \mu(s))$ steps of the instantiation of the correspondent instance of r. Therefore, a node responsible for s will have received all requests for $u[k]$ at $k + \Delta(u)$. Similarly, a fetch for $u[k]$ in R_n locally at n is guaranteed to be done no later than $k + \Delta(u)$. Therefore, the following results holds.

Lemma 2. *A value $(u[k], c) \in R_n$ will not be fetched or requested after $k + \Delta(u)$.*

This implies that at every node n, all values of $u[k]$ can be removed at instant $k + \Delta(s)$, which allows to implement the algorithm for pruning shown in Algorithm 2. Therefore, the maximum size of R_n needed is bounded linearly by the maximum $\Delta(s)$ times the number of streams.

Time to Resolve. In centralized SRV monitoring [10,24] a specification is efficiently monitorable whenever all cycles in D_φ have negative weight. This guarantees that the online algorithm can be performed in a *trace length independent* way. However, this is not true for decentralized monitoring as illustrated in the following example.

Example 2. Consider the following specification deployed in monitors 1 and 2 with $dist(1,2) = dist(2,1) = 2$:

```
@1{output num a eval = b[-1|0]}
@2{output num b eval = a[-1|0]}
```

It is easy to see that $a[0]$ and $b[0]$ will be resolved at time 0, $a[1]$ and $b[1]$ at time 2, and $a[n]$ and $b[n]$ at time $2n$. Then, U_1 and U_2 will grow to contain a number of equations that depends on the length the trace.   □

We introduce the notion of *decentralized efficiently monitorable*, that guarantees an upper bound on the number of steps that it takes to resolve an equation in U_n. Note that Algorithm 1 removes an equation from U_n and moves it into R_n once it is resolved. In turn, this also gives a bound on the duration of the elements in P_n and W_n. It follows that for decentralized efficiently monitorable specifications, the monitoring process requires only a constant amount of memory (on the size of the specification) independently of the length of the trace.

Algorithm 1. Local monitoring algorithm at node n with $\langle Q_n, U_n, R_n, P_n, W_n \rangle$

```
 1: procedure MONITOR
 2:     U_n, R_n, P_n, W_n ← ∅
 3:     k ← 0
 4:     while not END do
 5:         STEP(k)
 6:         k ← k + 1
 7:     M ← k                                              ▷ Trace length M
 8:     FINALIZE(M)


 9: procedure STEP(k)
10:     R_old ← R_n
11:     for all msg ∈ Q do                                ▷ Process incoming messages
12:         Q_n ← Q_n \ msg
13:         if msg.dst ≠ n then
14:             route(msg)
15:         else
16:             if msg.type = req then
17:                 P_n ← P_n ∪ msg
18:             else
19:                 R_n ← R_n ∪ {(msg.stream, msg.val)}
20:                 W ← W \ {msg.stream}
21:     R_n ← R_n ∪ {r[k], new(r, k) | r ∈ inputs(n)}     ▷ Read inputs
22:     U_n ← U_n ∪ {s[k], instantiate(e_s, k) | s ∈ outputs(n)}   ▷ Instantiate outputs
23:     EVALUATE(U_n, R_n)
24:     for all (r[k'], c) ∈ R_n \ R_old do               ▷ New knowledge
25:         if eager(r) ∧ μ(r) = n then                   ▷ Eager new knowledge
26:             for all n_d ∈ μ(appears(r)) such that n ≠ n_d do
27:                 send(resp, r[k'], c, n, n_d)
28:     for all msg ∈ P_n do                              ▷ Pending lazy new knowledge
29:         if (msg.stream, c) ∈ R_n then
30:             send(resp, msg.stream, c, n, msg.src)
31:             P_n ← P_n \ {msg}
32:     for all (_, e) ∈ U do
33:         for all u[k'] ∈ sub(e) do
34:             if lazy(u) ∧ u[k'] ∉ W_n ∧ μ(u) ≠ n then  ▷ Send needed new requests
35:                 send(req, u[k'], n, μ(u))
36:                 W_n ← W_n ∪ {u[k']}
37:     PRUNE(R_n)


38: procedure EVALUATE(U_n, R_n)
39:     done ← false
40:     while not done do
41:         done ← true
42:         for all (s[k], e) ∈ U_n do
43:             e' ← SUBST(e, R_n)
44:             if ground(e') then
45:                 done ← false
46:                 U_n ← U_n \ {(s[k], e)}
47:                 R_n ← R_n ∪ {(s[k], e')}
48:             else
49:                 U_n ← U_n \ {(s[k], e)} ∪ {(s[k], e')}
```

Algorithm 2. Pruning R_n at node n at instant k

1: **procedure** PRUNE
2:     **for all** $(u[j], c) \in R_n$ **do**
3:         **if** $k \geq j + \Delta(u)$ **then**   ▷ If $u[j]$ will not be needed
4:             $R_n \leftarrow R_n \setminus \{(u[j], c)\}$ ▷ Remove

Definition 6 (Decentralized Efficiently monitoriable). *A specification φ is decentralized efficiently monitoriable whenever it is efficiently monitorable and no cycle in D_φ visits two streams r and s assigned to different nodes $\mu(r) \neq \mu(s)$.*

Note that since Lola is very expressive many decision problems for Lola specs (well-formedness, equivalence, etc.) are undecidable. However, well-definedness (which guarantee that the monitoring algorithm always computes a verdict), efficient monitorability and decentralized efficient monitorability are syntactic properties which are very easy to check.

We now define the notion of look-ahead of a stream s, that bounds for decentralized efficiently monitorable specifications the maximum between the moment at which $s[k]$ is inserted in U_n and $s[k]$ is resolved into a value. Note that a decentralized efficiently monitorable specification can be decomposed into a DAG of sets of stream variables such that each set is mapped to a single node (because cycles in the graph must belong to a single node). We use $S(s)$ for the set of streams that are grouped with s. In order to define the look-ahead distance $\nabla(s)$ we use an auxiliary definition: $\nabla_{rem}(s)$. This provides an upper-bound on the time to receive from a remote node the value of an instant variable $r[k']$ that $s[k]$ directly depends on.

– If r is eager, this value depends on $\nabla(r)$ to guarantee that $r[k']$ is known at $k' + \nabla(r)$ and the time $dist(r, s)$ to communicate this value.
– If r is lazy, the instant at which the network node of r sends the value of $r[k']$ is the later instant between $k' + \nabla(r)$ and the reception of the request, that is $k + dist(s, r)$. After receiving the request, the response takes $dist(r, s)$ to arrive to s.

Once ∇_{rem} has been determined for all edges in the dependency graph that leave a component $S(s)$, $\nabla(s)$ can be determined by the weight of the maximum simple path in $S(s)$ adding also the additional time to resolve the remote dependencies. Note that the definition of $\nabla(s)$ is identical to the look-ahead in a centralized specification with $S(s)$ as streams that considers directly accessible streams r at remote nodes as input streams. Formally:

Definition 7 (Look-ahead). *The remote look-ahead distance $\nabla_{rem}(s)$ of a stream s is $\nabla_{rem}(s) \stackrel{def}{=} \max(0, \{delay(r \xrightarrow{w} s) \mid \mu(r) \neq \mu(s)\})$, where*

$$delay(r \xrightarrow{w} s) \stackrel{def}{=} \begin{cases} dist(r, s) + w + \nabla(r) & \text{if eager } (r) \\ dist(r, s) + \max(w + \nabla(r), d(s, r)) & \text{if lazy } (r) \end{cases}$$

The look-ahead distance is $\nabla(s) \stackrel{def}{=} \max(0, \{w + \nabla_{rem}(r) \mid s \xrightarrow{w}^* r \text{ with } S(s) = S(r)\})$

The definition is well-defined because the graph is a DAG of components, each of which is mapped to single network node. Intuitively, the remote look-ahead $\nabla_{rem}(s)$ captures how long it takes to receive information from $\mu(r)$ that is relevant to compute $s[k]$. Note that if the specification is centralized, then there is a single component, $\nabla_{rem}(s)$ is 0 and the look-ahead distance coincides with the look-ahead for centralized Lola evaluation [24].

Lemma 3. *Every unresolved $s[k] = e$ in U_n is resolved at most at $k + \nabla(s)$.*

Lemmas 2 and 3 imply that decentralized efficiently monitorable specifications can be monitored with bounded resources. The bound depends only linearly on the size of the specification and the diameter of the network.

5   Empirical Evaluation

We have implemented our solution in a prototype tool dLola, written in the Go programming language (available at http://github.com/imdea-software/dLola). We describe now (1) an empirical comparison of dLola versus Themis [13]—a state-of-the-art tool for decentralized runtime verification of LTL specifications—and (2) the effect on dLola of the network placement on richer specifications (not supported by Themis).

Themis Comparison. Themis can only monitor Boolean specifications while dLola can monitor arbitrary values from richer domains. Also, Themis can only handle a clique topology while dLola supports arbitrary connected networks. In this comparison, we restrict to specifications and topologies that Themis can handle, and we translate directly LTL formulas to Lola specifications. We evaluate both tools against 213, 196 synthesized input tests in a network with 5 nodes. The results from Themis where obtained from the database provided openly at https://gitlab.inria.fr/monitoring/themis. Our tool reached a final verdict on all cases, which coincided with Themis on all experiments for which Themis had a verdict in the database (85% of our input cases). Figure 2 report metrics collected using these experiments. We compared our centralized setting (with decentralized observation) with the Themis' Orchestration algorithm and our decentralized setting with Themis' Choreography algorithm. Figure 2(a) shows the number of messages exchanged to compute the final verdict. In the best case a lazy strategy requires less messages than an eager strategy because many remote values are not required. In the worst case the eager strategy consumes less messages than the lazy, because the request messages are not sent.

In comparison with Themis, dLola requires less messages on average and in the worst case, but more messages in the minimum case. Figure 2(b) shows the size of the message payload used for the computation of verdicts. Again, dLola uses smaller payloads except in the minimum case. Figure 2(c) contains the maximum delay, which shows that dLola incurs in a higher maximum delay for the centralized cases, but significantly lower when decentralized.

	min			avg			max		
	dLola		Themis	dLola		Themis	dLola		Themis
	Lazy	Eager		Lazy	Eager		Lazy	Eager	
decentr	6.00	12.00	0.00	564.19	332.50	6751.12	4201.00	2101.00	66000.00
centr	1.00	9.00	0.00	98.33	140.88	7085.40	1001.00	801.00	48400.00

(a) Number of messages exchanged

decentr	139.50	279.00	0.00	13186.87	7792.24	60743.17	97862.00	49074.50	594000.00
centr	24.50	204.50	0.00	2208.38	3171.91	83833.05	82759.45	22462.00	576950.00

(b) Payload size (in bits)

decentr	2.00	1.00	0.00	23.72	20.49	84.46	115.00	110.00	4070.00
centr	0.00	0.00	0.00	17.61	16.59	6.52	101.00	100.00	110.00

(c) Time delay (in cycles)

Fig. 2. Comparison dLola vs Themis

	Ring			Ringshort			Line			Clique			Star		
	best	even	worst	best	even	worst	best	even	worst	best	even	worst	best	even	worst
4	301	1301	2901	301	1301	1301	301	1501	2401	301	901	1101	301	1401	2101
5	301	1301	3903	301	1301	2103	301	1501	3401	301	901	1101	301	1501	2101
7	301	1301	5701	301	1301	3001	301	1801	5401	301	901	1101	301	2401	3901
9	301	1301	5901	301	1301	4301	301	1301	7401	301	901	1101	301	2301	3901
10	301	1301	6501	301	1301	4501	301	1301	8401	301	901	1101	301	2701	5701

Fig. 3. Number of messages exchanged by topology and placement (for $4, \ldots, 10$ nodes)

Topologies. Intuitively speaking, the performance depends on the placement of streams, as more locality reduces the latency and the number of messages required. We selected five representative topologies (ring, ringshort, linear, clique, star) and for each topology selected three different placements: (1) maximizing manually the locality, (2) assigning output streams evenly, and (3) minimizing manually the locality. For all experiments we use the following specification, where we make a chain of four output streams depend on an input and on the previous stream. Figure 3 illustrates how the placement of subformulas affect the overall efficiency of the monitors, which confirms that placement is crucial for efficiency and suggests that in most cases, values can be resolved with a number of messages independently of the topology and size of the network by careful placement. This is relevant since the topology may be fixed by the system design, while the placement is part of the monitoring solution.

6   Conclusions and Future Work

We have studied the problem of decentralized stream runtime verification, that starts from a specification, a topology and a placement of the input streams. Our solution consists of a placement of output streams and an online local monitoring algorithm that runs on every node. We have captured specifications that guarantee that the monitoring can be performed with constant memory independently of the length of the trace. We report on an empirical evaluation of our prototype tool dLola. Our empirical evaluation shows that placement is crucial for performance and suggest that in most cases careful placement can lead to constant costs and delays. As future work we plan to extend our solution to timed asynchronous distributed systems [9], to monitor under failures and uncertainties and to support reading at different nodes (alternatively or simultaneously).

References

1. Autosar. https://www.autosar.org/
2. Asarin, E., Caspi, P., Maler, O.: Timed regular expressions. J. ACM **49**(2), 172–206 (2002)
3. Barringer, H., Goldberg, A., Havelund, K., Sen, K.: Rule-based runtime verification. In: Steffen, B., Levi, G. (eds.) VMCAI 2004. LNCS, vol. 2937, pp. 44–57. Springer, Heidelberg (2004). https://doi.org/10.1007/978-3-540-24622-0_5
4. Basin, D., Klaedtke, F., Zalinescu, E.: Failure-aware runtime verification of distributed systems. In: Proceedings of the 35th IARCS Annual Conference on Foundations of Software Technology and Theoretical Computer Science (FSTTCS 2015). LIPIcs. vol. 45, pp. 590–603. Schloss Dagstuhl-Leibniz-Zentrum fuer Informatik (2015)
5. Bauer, A., Küster, J.-C., Vegliach, G.: From propositional to first-order monitoring. In: Legay, A., Bensalem, S. (eds.) RV 2013. LNCS, vol. 8174, pp. 59–75. Springer, Heidelberg (2013). https://doi.org/10.1007/978-3-642-40787-1_4
6. Bauer, A., Leucker, M., Schallhart, C.: Runtime verification for LTL and TLTL. ACM Trans. Softw. Eng. Methodol. **20**(4), 14 (2011)
7. Bauer, A., Falcone, Y.: Decentralised LTL monitoring. In: Giannakopoulou, D., Méry, D. (eds.) FM 2012. LNCS, vol. 7436, pp. 85–100. Springer, Heidelberg (2012). https://doi.org/10.1007/978-3-642-32759-9_10
8. Convent, L., Hungerecker, S., Leucker, M., Scheffel, T., Schmitz, M., Thoma, D.: TeSSLa: temporal stream-based specification language. In: Massoni, T., Mousavi, M.R. (eds.) SBMF 2018. LNCS, vol. 11254, pp. 144–162. Springer, Cham (2018). https://doi.org/10.1007/978-3-030-03044-5_10
9. Cristian, F., Fetzer, C.: The timed asynchronous distributed system model. IEEE Trans. Parallel Distrib. Syst. **10**(6), 642–657 (1999)
10. D'Angelo, B., et al.: LOLA: runtime monitoring of synchronous systems. In: Proceedings of the 12th International Symposium of Temporal Representation and Reasoning (TIME 2005), pp. 166–174. IEEE CS Press (2005)
11. Eisner, C., Fisman, D., Havlicek, J., Lustig, Y., McIsaac, A., Van Campenhout, D.: Reasoning with temporal logic on truncated paths. In: Hunt, W.A., Somenzi, F. (eds.) CAV 2003. LNCS, vol. 2725, pp. 27–39. Springer, Heidelberg (2003). https://doi.org/10.1007/978-3-540-45069-6_3
12. El-Hokayem, A., Falcone, Y.: Monitoring decentralized specifications. In: Proceedings of the 26th ACM SIGSOFT International Symposium on Software Testing and Analysis (ISSTA 2017), pp. 125–135. ACM (2017)

13. El-Hokayem, A., Falcone, Y.: THEMIS: a tool for decentralized monitoring algorithms. In: Proceedings of the 26th ACM SIGSOFT International Symposium on Software Testing and Analysis (ISSTA 2017), pp. 125–135. ACM, July 2017

14. Faymonville, P., Finkbeiner, B., Schirmer, S., Torfah, H.: A stream-based specification language for network monitoring. In: Falcone, Y., Sánchez, C. (eds.) RV 2016. LNCS, vol. 10012, pp. 152–168. Springer, Cham (2016). https://doi.org/10.1007/978-3-319-46982-9_10

15. Faymonville, P., et al.: StreamLAB: stream-based monitoring of cyber-physical systems. In: Dillig, I., Tasiran, S. (eds.) CAV 2019. LNCS, vol. 11561, pp. 421–431. Springer, Cham (2019). https://doi.org/10.1007/978-3-030-25540-4_24

16. Francalanza, A., Pérez, J.A., Sánchez, C.: Runtime verification for decentralised and distributed systems. In: Bartocci, E., Falcone, Y. (eds.) Lectures on Runtime Verification. LNCS, vol. 10457, pp. 176–210. Springer, Cham (2018). https://doi.org/10.1007/978-3-319-75632-5_6

17. Gorostiaga, F., Sánchez, C.: Striver: stream runtime verification for real-time event-streams. In: Colombo, C., Leucker, M. (eds.) RV 2018. LNCS, vol. 11237, pp. 282–298. Springer, Cham (2018). https://doi.org/10.1007/978-3-030-03769-7_16

18. Havelund, K., Roşu, G.: Synthesizing monitors for safety properties. In: Katoen, J.-P., Stevens, P. (eds.) TACAS 2002. LNCS, vol. 2280, pp. 342–356. Springer, Heidelberg (2002). https://doi.org/10.1007/3-540-46002-0_24

19. ISO Central Secretary: Road vehicles interchange of digital information controller area network (CAN) for high speed communication. Standard ISO 11898, International Standards Organisation (1993)

20. Liebemann, E.K., Meder, K., Schuh, J., Nenninger, G.: Safety and performance enhancement: the Bosch electronic stability control (ESP). In: SAE, pp. 421–428 (2004)

21. Pike, L., Goodloe, A., Morisset, R., Niller, S.: Copilot: a hard real-time runtime monitor. In: Barringer, H., Falcone, Y., Finkbeiner, B., Havelund, K., Lee, I., Pace, G., Roşu, G., Sokolsky, O., Tillmann, N. (eds.) RV 2010. LNCS, vol. 6418, pp. 345–359. Springer, Heidelberg (2010). https://doi.org/10.1007/978-3-642-16612-9_26

22. Pike, L., Wegmann, N., Niller, S., Goodloe, A.: Copilot: monitoring embedded systems. Innovations Syst. Softw. Eng. 9(4), 235–255 (2013)

23. Roşu, G., Havelund, K.: Rewriting-based techniques for runtime verification. Autom. Softw. Eng. 12(2), 151–197 (2005)

24. Sánchez, C.: Online and offline stream runtime verification of synchronous systems. In: Colombo, C., Leucker, M. (eds.) RV 2018. LNCS, vol. 11237, pp. 138–163. Springer, Cham (2018). https://doi.org/10.1007/978-3-030-03769-7_9

25. Sen, K., Roşu, G.: Generating optimal monitors for extended regular expressions. In: Sokolsky, O., Viswanathan, M. (eds.) Electronic Notes in Theoretical Computer Science, vol. 89. Elsevier (2003)

26. Sen, K., Vardhan, A., Agha, G., Rosu, G.: Efficient decentralized monitoring of safety in distributed systems. In: Proceedings of the 26th International Conference on Software Engineering (ICSE 2004), pp. 418–427. IEEE CS Press (2004)

Explaining Violations of Properties in Control-Flow Temporal Logic

Joshua Heneage Dawes[1,2(✉)] and Giles Reger[1]

[1] University of Manchester, Manchester, UK
joshua.dawes@cern.ch
[2] CERN, Geneva, Switzerland

Abstract. Runtime Verification is the process of deciding whether a run of a program satisfies a given property. This work considers the more challenging problem of *explaining* why a run does or does not satisfy the property. We look at this problem in the context of CFTL, a low-level temporal logic. Our main contribution is a method for reconstructing representative execution paths, separating them into *good* and *bad* paths, and producing *partial parse trees* explaining their differences. This requires us to extend CFTL and our second contribution is a partial semantics used to identify the first violating observation in a trace. This is extended with a notion of *severity* of violation, allowing us to handle real-time properties sensitive to small timing variations. These techniques are implemented as an extension to the publicly available VYPR2 tool. Our work is motivated by results obtained applying VYPR2 to a web service on the CMS Experiment at CERN and initial tests produce useful explanations for realistic use cases.

1 Introduction

The Runtime Verification (RV) problem [5] is typically phrased as *given a run of a system (e.g. a trace) τ and a property φ, does τ satisfy φ?* Over the last 20 years many techniques and tools [6,15,16,18,20,24] have been introduced to answer this question and most of these will answer *yes*, *no*, or some form of *maybe* but few attempt to explain *why* they return the given result. This work considers this challenge within the context of online monitoring of Control-Flow Temporal Logic [10,11] (CFTL) properties but we argue that the approach generalises to the broader RV problem. As such, the technical details of the approach will use CFTL but we will comment on the general application of the idea throughout the paper. An advantage of using CFTL as a vehicle for this idea is that its semantics are already closely aligned with the control-flow of the monitored program, which will be useful when using this to explain violations.

CFTL is a low-level temporal logic with real-time constraints. Specifications in CFTL are written directly over program constructs (e.g. variable assignments and function calls) occuring within the scope of a single function. For example,

$$\forall t \in \mathsf{calls}(\mathtt{save}) : \mathsf{duration}(t) \in [0, 10] \land \mathsf{dest}(t)(\mathtt{result}) = 1$$

B. Finkbeiner and L. Mariani (Eds.): RV 2019, LNCS 11757, pp. 202–220, 2019.
https://doi.org/10.1007/978-3-030-32079-9_12

specifies that every local call to save should take no more than 10 s and the value of result afterwards should be 1. If a set of traces violate this property then it could either be due to the save call taking too long or the result being incorrect, we would like to know which. Furthermore, if it were the former we would like to be able to quantify by *how much* we violate this time constraint. Lastly, but most importantly, there may be many calls to save in our function; we would like to know which one(s) are the source of the violations and which parts of the code contribute to the bad behaviour.

The general idea behind our approach is to take sets of violating and successful paths and abstract these to identify the parts of the function that influence the verdict. This requires two main steps. Firstly, we reconstruct paths through the monitored function from an observation trace. A key property of the monitoring approach for CFTL is that it admits an automatic and (in some sense) minimal instrumentation strategy. To reconstruct paths we modify this strategy to record sufficient information for full reconstruction. Secondly, once paths have been reconstructed, we generate *explanations* as generalised path objects (represented as context-free grammars) through a (symbolic) control flow graph of the monitored function. These explanations are further enhanced by a measure of the *severity* of time constraint violations. This work (and our previous work developing CFTL) is motivated by our experience working with engineers to apply runtime verification at the CMS Experiment at CERN.

We begin by introducing CFTL (Sect. 2) and an extension to partial traces (Sect. 3). We then describe a method for *reconstructing* paths (through the monitored function) from observation traces (Sect. 4), followed by our approach for producing *explanations* from sets of paths (Sect. 5). We then describe the implementation and an experiment demonstrating its use (Sect. 6). We conclude with related work and final remarks.

2   Control-Flow Temporal Logic (CFTL)

In this section we introduce the main concepts behind CFTL but refer the reader to previous work [9–11] for further details and formal definitions. CFTL is a linear-time temporal logic whose formulas reason over two central types of objects: *states*, instantaneous *checkpoints* in a program's runtime; and *transitions*, the computation that must happen to move between states.

2.1   CFTL Formulas

CFTL specifications take prenex form e.g. a list of quantifiers followed by a boolean combination of *atoms*, which are expressions (possibly containing temporal operators) over states and transitions. Given a CFTL formula φ, we use Vars_φ to refer to the set of quantified variables in φ, $A(\varphi)$ to refer to the set of atoms in φ and, for $\alpha \in A(\varphi)$, we use $\mathsf{var}(\alpha)$ for the variable on which α is based. At the top-level, atoms are assertions over the value of variables in a state or duration of a transition. States and transitions within atoms either come from the outer quantification or from temporal operators that find the next state or transition satisfying a given constraint.

As another example of a CFTL formula consider

$$\forall q \in \mathsf{changes}(\mathtt{var}) : q(\mathtt{var}) = \mathtt{True} \implies \mathsf{duration}(\mathsf{next}(q, \mathsf{calls}(\mathtt{func}))) \in [0, 1].$$

which captures the property "for every change to $\mathtt{var}$, if the new value is $\mathtt{True}$, then the next call to the function $\mathtt{func}$ should take no more than $1\,\mathrm{s}$".

2.2   What CFTL Formulas Mean

The semantics of CFTL formulas are defined over *dynamic runs*, which are sequences of observations with each observation relating directly to a point in the monitored function taken from the function's *symbolic control-flow graph*. It is important to note that a CFTL formula is defined in terms of elements in the control-flow graph and this is needed to understand the meaning of the formula. This close relation to the control-flow graph is what makes instrumentation points easy to define and helps later in explanation.

Symbolic Control-Flow Graphs. Given a program P (we assume a basic language with assignments, conditionals, and loops, see [10][1]), its Symbolic Control-Flow Graph $\mathsf{SCFG}(P)$ captures (1) the change in state generated by variable assignments and function calls in programs and (2) reachability in control-flow.

We associate with each node in the abstract syntax tree of P a unique *program point* and let Sym be a set of symbols representing variables and functions in P. Then, a *symbolic state* σ is a pair $\langle p, m \rangle$ where p is a program point and m is a map (partial function with finite domain) from symbols to the set of statuses {changed, unchanged, called, undefined}. We abuse notation and denote by $\sigma(x)$ the value to which m maps x. SCFGs are then directed graphs with symbolic states as vertices.

Definition 1. *A symbolic control-flow graph (SCFG) is a directed graph $\langle V, E, v_s \rangle$ with a finite set of symbolic states V, a finite set of edges $E \subseteq V \times V$, and an initial symbolic state $v_s \in V$.*

A symbolic state σ is *final* if it has no successors e.g. there is no edge $\langle \sigma, \sigma' \rangle$ in E. A *path* π through $\mathsf{SCFG}(P) = \langle V, E, v_s \rangle$ is a finite sequence of symbolic states $\sigma_1, \ldots, \sigma_k$ such that for every pair of adjacent symbolic states σ_i, σ_{i+1} there is an edge $\langle \sigma_i, \sigma_{i+1} \rangle$ in E. A path is *complete* if $\sigma_1 = v_s$ and σ_k is final. Our previous work [10] gave a construction to generate $\mathsf{SCFG}(P)$ for a given program P.

---

[1] Practically, in our implementation we target a subset of Python.

Dynamic Runs. A *dynamic run* is an abstraction of a run of a program P and is associated with a path through $\mathsf{SCFG}(P)$. Let Val be the finite set of possible values to which the elements of Sym can be mapped at runtime. Then a *concrete state* is a triple $\langle t, \sigma, \tau \rangle$ for timestamp $t \in \mathbb{R}^{\geq}$, symbolic state σ and a map $\tau : \mathsf{Sym} \rightharpoonup \mathsf{Val}$ from program symbols to values. A dynamic run $\mathcal{D}$ is a finite sequence of such concrete states.

Definition 2. *A dynamic run over $SCFG(P) = \langle V, E, v_s \rangle$ is a finite sequence $\mathcal{D} = \langle t_1, \sigma_1, \tau_1 \rangle, \ldots, \langle t_n, \sigma_n, \tau_n \rangle$ such that timestamps t_i are strictly increasing, $\sigma_1 = v_s, \sigma_n$ is final, and there is a path in $SCFG(P)$ between every pair of symbolic states σ_i and σ_{i+1} i.e. $\sigma_1, \ldots, \sigma_n$ can be extended to a complete path.*

A *transition* is a pair of concrete states. A transition $\langle \langle t, \sigma, \tau \rangle, \langle t', \sigma', \tau' \rangle \rangle$ is *atomic* if $\langle \sigma, \sigma' \rangle$ is an edge in $\mathsf{SCFG}(P)$. A dynamic run $\mathcal{D}$ is *most-general* if every transition is atomic. Later we will restrict the condition on σ_n to get *partial dynamic runs*, therefore we sometimes refer to these as *total*. Given some concrete state $q = \langle t, \sigma, \tau \rangle$, the *symbolic support* $\mathsf{support}(q)$ of q is symbolic state σ. Similarly for a transition $tr = \langle \langle t, \sigma, \tau \rangle, \langle t', \sigma', \tau' \rangle \rangle$, the symbolic support $\mathsf{support}(tr)$ is the edge $\langle \sigma, \sigma' \rangle$.

Evaluation of CFTL Formulas. The semantics of a CFTL formula φ with respect to a dynamic run $\mathcal{D}$ is defined by iterating over the quantifiers of φ (by the well-formedness criteria [10] there must be at least one) to generate sets of *points of interest*, and then evaluating the inner part of the formula at each of these points. This evaluation relies on an eval function that gives the next state or transition satisfying a state or transition constraint. More formally, given a dynamic run $\mathcal{D}$, a point of interest θ, and an expression Exp, $\mathsf{eval}(\mathcal{D}, \theta, \mathsf{Exp})$ gives the unique concrete state or transition to which Exp refers based on $\mathcal{D}$ and θ. In the total semantics (for total dynamic runs) this is guaranteed to exist. A full definition is omitted here but can be found in previous work [10].

2.3   Instrumentation and Observations

Given $\mathsf{SCFG}(P) = \langle V, E, v_s \rangle$, instrumentation is the process of choosing a subset $\mathsf{Inst} \subset V$ of *instrumentation points* such that φ can be evaluated given concrete states and transitions whose symbolic supports are the elements of Inst. One could of course take $\mathsf{Inst} = V$, but the intention of instrumentation is to throw away concrete states from a most-general dynamic run which are not needed to monitor φ, thus reducing work for a monitoring algorithm.

To compute Inst, we first inspect the quantification sequence of φ to determine which symbolic states could generate *points of interest*. We call such symbolic states *candidate points of interest*. For example, a formula with quantification sequence $\forall q \in \mathsf{calls}(f)$ would lead us to identify all pairs of symbolic states that may correspond to calls to the function f in a dynamic run. Once these points of interest are obtained, we then inspect the quantifier-free part of φ to determine the actual instrumentation points.

We then use Inst to filter $\mathcal{D}$ to give a second dynamic run $\mathcal{D}'$ whose concrete states are only those with symbolic supports in Inst. This filtered dynamic run has the property that $\mathcal{D}, [] \models \varphi$ if and only if $\mathcal{D}', [] \models \varphi$ (see [10]). Given a computed set Inst and a (not necessarily most-general) dynamic run $\mathcal{D}$, we call a concrete state or transition an *observation* if its symbolic support is in Inst. We call any concrete state/transition that is not an observation *redundant with respect to* φ.

2.4   What Matters for Explanation?

If we wanted to replace CFTL with another specification language we would need to ensure that there is a direct correspondence between the assertions/predicates in that language and points in the SCFG. Properly defined, this should be compatible with the above notion of redundancy. To take advantage of the concept of *verdict severity* the language should contain real-time constraints.

3   Identifying Failing Observations

Later we will explain violations using paths through the associated SCFG to the observation causing the failure. To do this we assume that the property is a safety property (CFTL only captures safety properties), e.g. all violations are witnessed by finite prefixes, and the semantics for incomplete runs is *impartial* [17] e.g. the verdict cannot change from true to false or vice versa with more information. In the following we outline a partial semantics for CFTL that holds the impartiality property. We also give a quantitative extension of this semantics called *verdict severity*, which will be helpful later when determining the extent to which a violation has occurred.

3.1   Partial Semantics for CFTL

Our aim is to identify the observation in a most-general dynamic run $\mathcal{D}$ after which a CFTL formula φ can no longer be satisfied. We call such an observation a *falsifying observation*. If $\mathcal{D}$ violates φ there is exactly one such observation. Unfortunately, CFTL semantics is defined over total dynamic runs corresponding to *complete* paths through SCFGs, hence we have no way to talk about such an observation. We now describe a partial semantics over dynamic runs that do not finish at final symbolic states in SCFGs.

We define a *partial dynamic run* as a dynamic run where the last symbolic state is not final in the SCFG. This ensures that the semantics is well defined: the total semantics (with truth domain {true, false}) should be used for total dynamic runs.

The first change required is to update the evaluation function (which returns the unique concrete state or transition corresponding to an expression) so that it is partial and returns null when the expression cannot be evaluated. For example, for the property

$$\forall q \in \text{changes}(\text{var}) : q(\text{var}) = \text{True} \implies \text{duration}(\text{next}(q, \text{calls}(\text{func}))) \in [0,1].$$

when evaluating $\text{next}(q, \text{calls}(\text{func}))$ we would get null if there is no next transition satisfying the condition. Note that this extended evaluation function coincides with the original function for total dynamic runs.

Once the evaluation function has been updated it is then necessary to update the way that points of interest are defined so that they can also be partial. For example, if the quantification were $\forall q \in \text{changes}(\text{var}) : \forall t \in \text{future}(q, \text{calls}(f))$ we would include a partial quantification for all satisfying states q even if no satisfying transitions t exist.

Finally, we get a partial semantics with a truth domain {false, notSure, trueSoFar}. Expressions are evaluated as false if their value is known and they are false, otherwise (if their value is known and it is true) we get trueSoFar. If the expression cannot be fully evaluated then the result is notSure. For the above example, if $\text{next}(q, \text{calls}(\text{func}))$ evaluates to null then the atom $\text{duration}(\text{next}(q, \text{calls}(\text{func}))) \in [0,1]$ would evaluate to notSure. The truth domain has the ordering false < notSure < trueSoFar with ¬false ≡ trueSoFar, and ¬notSure ≡ notSure. We take ⊓ to be the greatest lower bound with respect to this order, and ⊔ to be the least upper bound. This can be used to interpret the boolean operators in the language as expected e.g. using ⊔ for ∨.

As soon as a dynamic run is extended to be total, its satisfaction of some CFTL formula φ is subject to the normal semantics with the truth domain {true, false}. To ensure well-definedness on which semantics to use, we consider dynamic runs before filtering by instrumentation (this could remove the last concrete state corresponding to a final symbolic state in the SCFG).

The resulting partial semantics holds the *verdict impartiality* property [17]: true can never be declared for a dynamic run identifying with a path that is not complete because extensions to a complete path can introduce new points of interest that cause violations. In addition, the partial semantics will be able to give a false verdict since CFTL formulas are universally quantified, hence a single falsifying observation means false for every possible extension of the dynamic run (they are safety properties).

With a partial semantics defined for partial dynamic runs, we can now isolate the observation in a total dynamic run that prevented satisfaction of a property φ. We do this by taking a total dynamic run and extracting a partial dynamic run whose final state causes the partial semantics to switch to the false verdict.

Given a total dynamic run $\mathcal{D}$ let $\mathcal{D}_p(q)$ be the partial dynamic run that is the prefix of $\mathcal{D}$ ending with concrete state q. For a CFTL formula φ such that $\mathcal{D}, [] \not\models \varphi$, the *falsifying observation* is $q \in \mathcal{D}$ such that:

1. $[\mathcal{D}_p(q), []\models \varphi] = \text{false}$.
2. Given the previous state q' in $\mathcal{D}$ (if it exists), $[\mathcal{D}_p(q'), []\models \varphi] = \text{trueSoFar}$ or $[\mathcal{D}_p(q'), []\models \varphi] = \text{notSure}$.

It suffices to consider the previous state due to the impartiality of the partial semantics.

3.2 Verdict Severity

Later we will divide a set of runs into *good* and *bad*. This can be trivially done based on whether the runs satisfy the given property or not. However, for timing properties things are not so clear-cut; perhaps small deviations are acceptable, or more likely, the more problematic violations are grouped with less problematic ones. To handle this situation we introduce a quantitative extension to our semantics that uses a notion of *severity* of violation such that a negative severity means violation and a positive one means success, with the magnitude indicating the level to which this verdict is reached. In essence, this gives a metric of *by how much* some function call was or was not a falsifying observation. As mentioned later, this can also be used to decide whether a path is only a borderline satisfaction/violation i.e. whether it could be included in the paths that generated the opposite verdict.

Given an observation c it is always possible to identify the atom α that is evaluated for c (indeed, our monitoring algorithm makes this explicit). We define the verdict severity of c with respect to this atom α.

Definition 3. *Given an observation c evaluated at atom α, the verdict severity Sev(α, c) is 1 if the atom is satisfied and -1 otherwise, with the exception of the case where $\alpha = (\mathsf{duration}(t) \in I) \in A_\varphi$ for some finite, bounded $I \subset \mathbb{R}_{>0}$, in which case*

$$\mathsf{Sev}(\alpha, c) = \inf\{|\mathsf{duration}(c) - n| : n \in I\} \cdot \mathcal{X}(\alpha, c)$$

such that $\mathcal{X}(\alpha, c) = 1$ if $\mathsf{duration}(c) \in I, -1$ otherwise.

The term $\mathcal{X}(\alpha, c)$ allows us to differentiate between satisfaction and violation of the constraint, and the infimum captures by how much.

As an example, consider again the property

$$\forall q \in \mathsf{changes}(\mathtt{var}) : q(\mathtt{var}) = \mathtt{True} \implies \mathsf{duration}(\mathsf{next}(q, \mathsf{calls}(\mathtt{func}))) \in [0, 1].$$

which can only be violated by breaking the duration constraint. If the duration of the failing transition were 2 then the severity would be -1, whereas if it were 1.3, then the severity would be -0.3.

4   Path Reconstruction

As discussed previously, the first step in generating explanations is to reconstruct the path through the monitored program that leads to the observation we want to explain (often the falsifying observation, which we showed how to identify for CFTL in the previous section). Note that later we may also want to reconstruct paths for satisfying runs, so this section talks about reconstructing paths for an observation in general.

Given an observation and a symbolic control-flow graph $\mathsf{SCFG}(P)$, we consider the task of deciding precisely which path was taken through $\mathsf{SCFG}(P)$ to reach the observation. When the dynamic run given is most-general, this is straightforward, but if it has been filtered by instrumentation, it is not necessarily possible.

Let $\mathsf{SCFG}(P) = \langle V, E, v_s \rangle$ be the symbolic control-flow graph of P and q be an observation in a most-general dynamic run $\mathcal{D}$ over $\mathsf{SCFG}(P)$. We consider the dynamic run $\mathcal{D}'$ obtained by removing concrete states that are redundant with respect to a formula φ, and what can be done to determine the path taken through $\mathsf{SCFG}(P)$ by $\mathcal{D}'$. Given that $\mathcal{D}'$ contains only the concrete states required to check φ, it is clear that, for consecutive concrete states $\langle t, \sigma, \tau \rangle, \langle t', \sigma', \tau' \rangle$, there may be multiple paths between σ and σ'. This means there may not be enough information in $\mathcal{D}'$ to decide the exact path taken. We therefore introduce the notion of a *branch-aware dynamic run*, which is a dynamic run whose concrete states allow the exact path taken to be reconstructed.

Definition 4. *A dynamic run $\mathcal{D}_b$ is a* branch-aware dynamic run *if between any two consecutive concrete states $\langle t, \sigma, \tau \rangle$ and $\langle t', \sigma', \tau' \rangle$, there is a single path from σ to σ'.*

Let us denote the set of concrete states added to some $\mathcal{D}$ to make it branch-aware by $\mathsf{branching}(\mathcal{D}_b)$. If there is no branching in P, possibly $\mathsf{branching}(\mathcal{D}_b) = \emptyset$. The concrete states in $\mathsf{branching}(\mathcal{D}_b)$ are considered redundant with respect to φ since they are added after instrumentation allowed removal of states.

The most obvious example of a branch-aware dynamic run is a most-general dynamic run, since all transitions correspond to single edges. However, given that making a dynamic run branch-aware makes additional instrumentation necessary, a most-general dynamic run is not economical.

A dynamic run $\mathcal{D}_b$ is *minimally branch-aware* if it is branch-aware and there is no concrete state which is redundant with respect to φ and whose removal would not stop $\mathcal{D}_b$ being branch-aware. This definition captures the intuition that a minimally branch-aware dynamic run should have additional concrete states placed in strategic places.

4.1   Instrumentation for Branch-Aware Dynamic Runs

To make $\mathsf{branching}(\mathcal{D}_b)$ minimal we determine the minimal set of symbolic states $\mathsf{SCFG}(P)$ which will be the symbolic supports of the elements of $\mathsf{branching}(\mathcal{D}_b)$. We now present a strategy for determining such a set of symbolic states.

There are multiple structures that result in multiple possible directions for a path to take . For conditionals the branch taken can be determined if the first vertex on that branch is known, hence we instrument the first vertex on each branch. Further, it is necessary to instrument the first vertex after the branches have converged, distinguishing observations from inside and after the body. For

---

Algorithm 1. Path reconstruction algorithm given a minimally branch-aware dynamic run $\mathcal{D}_b$ and a symbolic control-flow graph $\mathsf{SCFG}(P) = \langle V, E, v_s \rangle$.

1: $\pi \leftarrow \langle \rangle$ ▷ Initialise an empty path.
2: branchingIndex $\leftarrow 0$ ▷ Initialise the index of the element of branching($\mathcal{D}_b$) to be used next.
3: curr $\leftarrow v_s$
4: **while** branchingIndex $< |$branching($\mathcal{D}_b$)$|$ **do**
5:    **if** $\exists \langle$curr$, \sigma \rangle \in$ outgoing(curr) $: \sigma =$ support(L(branchingIndex)) **then**
6:       curr $\leftarrow$ the σ from $\langle$curr$, \sigma \rangle$
7:       branchingIndex $+= 1$
8:    **else**
9:       curr $\leftarrow$ the σ such that there is $\langle$curr$, \sigma \rangle \in E$
10:    $\pi += \langle$curr$, \sigma \rangle$

---

loops we instrument the first vertex of the loop body (to capture the number of iterations) and the post-loop vertex. For try-catch blocks we insert instruments at the beginning of each block but, so far, we have no efficient way to capture the jump from an arbitrary statement inside the try block to the catch block. However, it would be possible to use an error trace to determine the statement at which the exception was thrown, and use this in path reconstruction.

Applying this method for instrumentation to the entire SCFG gives a minimally branch-aware dynamic run, e.g. one whose path we can reconstruct, using a small and conservative set of new instrumentation points.

4.2   Computing Reconstructed Paths

In order to finally determine the path taken to reach some observation we step through the (minimally) branch-aware dynamic run collecting the relevant symbolic states. Algorithm 1 takes a minimally branch-aware dynamic run $\mathcal{D}_b$ with n concrete states and a symbolic control-flow graph $\mathsf{SCFG}(P)$, and reconstructs the path taken by $\mathcal{D}_b$ as a sequence of edges. It makes use of:

– A labelling $L(i)$ on branching($\mathcal{D}_b$) giving the ith concrete state with respect to timestamps and $L(0)$ being the first concrete state.
– A function outgoing(σ) which gives $\{\langle \sigma, \sigma' \rangle \in E\}$.

The intuition is that we follow edges in the symbolic control-flow graph until we arrive at a symbolic state at which branching occurs. At this point, we use branching($\mathcal{D}_p$) to decide on which direction to take.

4.3   What Matters for Explanation?

If we wanted to replace CFTL with another specification language we would need to solve the path reconstruction problem separately. The main challenge would be to ensure that enough information is captured in the recorded dynamic run for path reconstruction. This is made easier in CFTL as the semantics is defined in terms of the SCFG.

5   Explaining Verdicts with Paths

We now consider the following problem: given a set of dynamic runs (for a CFTL formula φ over a single symbolic control-flow graph $\mathsf{SCFG}(P)$) containing a violating dynamic run $\mathcal{D}^v$ how can we explain what makes this run a *bad* run?

Our first step is identify the other dynamic runs in our original set that follow the same edge in $\mathsf{SCFG}(P)$. Let $c^\perp$ be the falsifying observation for $\mathcal{D}^v$ and consider $\mathsf{support}(c^\perp)$, the edge in $\mathsf{SCFG}(P)$ corresponding to $c^\perp$. To save space, we consider only the case where $c^\perp$ is the only transition with this symbolic support (ie, it is not inside a loop). Let $\mathcal{F} = \mathcal{D}_1, \ldots, \mathcal{D}_n$ be the set of dynamic runs containing an observation c_i such that $\mathsf{support}(c_i) = \mathsf{support}(c^\perp)$. To explain the violating run $\mathcal{D}^v$ (which must appear in $\mathcal{F}$), we will take the reconstructed paths up to each observation c_i and compare them. Note that for satisfying runs we will only examine the behaviour up until the corresponding observation.

We use the notion of verdict severity (or if there are no timing constraints, just the satisfaction relation) to separate these paths. Let $C_\top$ be the set of pairs $\langle c_i, \mathsf{Sev}(\alpha, c_i) \rangle$ such that $\mathsf{Sev}(\alpha, c_i) \geq 0$ for each c_i. We define $C_\perp$ similarly, but with $\mathsf{Sev}(\alpha, c_i) < 0$. Using these sets, we will reconstruct paths up to each observation and associate each path with the verdict severity to which it leads. The differences between these two sets will then be used to construct the explanation.

5.1   Reconstructed Paths as Parse Trees

We now consider what all the paths in $C_\top$ and $C_\perp$ have in common. If there are common characteristics, we may conclude that such characteristics could affect the verdict. This requires us to represent reconstructed paths (computed by Algorithm 1) in a concise way that makes it easy to isolate divergent behaviours. Our solution is to derive a context-free grammar from the SCFG and use this to parse the paths and then compare the parse trees. This representation will allow comparison of path characteristics such as branches taken and number of iterations completed by loops. Our approach is similar to the standard approach to deriving context free grammars from finite state automata, with the major difference being that we recognise that there are commonly found structures in symbolic control-flow graphs, such as conditionals and loops. Such structures are used to generate grammars that yield parse trees which make it easy to compare path characteristics.

Figure 1 gives a detailed schema for deriving these grammars. For each *component* of a SCFG we give the corresponding generated grammar. The grammar of an entire SCFG can be constructed by recursively applying this schema. An application of this is illustrated in Fig. 2, which shows a SCFG on the left with a grammar derived on the right. Non-terminal symbols (symbolic states) are written in bold. The grammar on the right works by mapping symbolic states in the SCFG to sequences of edges and other symbolic states. Symbolic states are always non-terminal, so any path generated by such a grammar is a sequence of edges. The difference between our approach to deriving a grammar vs the traditional approach is reflected in the right hand side of rule $\boldsymbol{\sigma_1}$. Using this fact

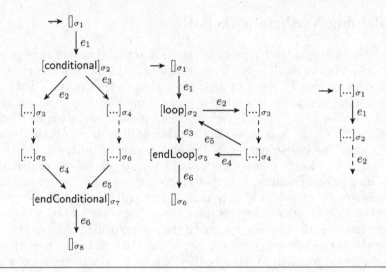

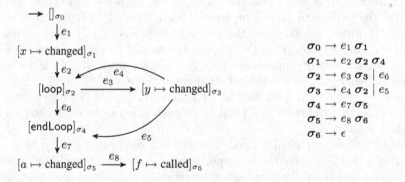

Fig. 1. A subset of the full schema for deriving a context free grammar from a SCFG.

Fig. 2. A symbolic control-flow graph and its context free grammar.

that all complete paths through the SCFG must pass through the edge e_7 to exit the loop, we encode loops in grammars by using one rule for the loop body, and another for the post-loop control-flow.

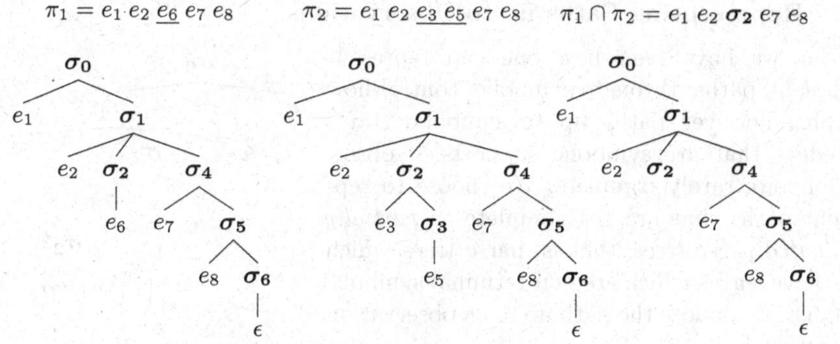

$$\pi_1 = e_1 \, e_2 \, \underline{e_6} \, e_7 \, e_8 \qquad\qquad \pi_2 = e_1 \, e_2 \, \underline{e_3} \, \underline{e_5} \, e_7 \, e_8 \qquad \pi_1 \cap \pi_2 = e_1 \, e_2 \, \boldsymbol{\sigma_2} \, e_7 \, e_8$$

Fig. 3. The parse trees of two paths, and their intersection.

Once we have constructed these parse trees we want to find commanalities between them. Figure 3 shows how we can take parse trees from multiple paths and form the *intersection*. We define the intersection of two parse trees $T(\pi_1)$ and $T(\pi_2)$, written $T(\pi_1) \cap T(\pi_2)$, by the parse tree which contains a subtree if and only if that subtree is found in both $T(\pi_1)$ and $T(\pi_2)$ at the same path. Intersection is given by the recursive definition in Fig. 4. In this definition, a subtree is a pair $\langle r, \{h_1, \ldots, h_n\} \rangle$ for root r and child vertices $h_1, \ldots, h_n$, and the empty tree is denoted by null. The base case of recursion is for leaves l and l'.

We abuse notation and write $\pi_1 \cap \pi_2$ for the path obtained by reading the leaves from left to right from the intersection of the parse trees $T(\pi_1)$ and $T(\pi_2)$. If such a path contains symbolic states, we call it a *parametric path* and call a symbolic state contained by such a path a *path parameter*. In particular, the vertex to which this symbolic state corresponds in the intersection parse tree is given different subtrees by at least two parse trees in the intersection. The values given to those parameters by each path in the intersection can be determined by following the path to the path parameter's vertex through each parse tree.

$$\text{intersect}(l, l') = \begin{cases} \text{null} & \text{if } l \neq l' \\ l & \text{otherwise} \end{cases}$$

$$\text{intersect}(\langle r, \{h_1, \ldots, h_n\} \rangle, \\ \langle r', \{h'_1, \ldots, h'_m\} \rangle) = \begin{cases} \langle r, \{\ldots \text{intersect}(h_i, h'_i) \ldots \} \rangle & \text{if } r = r' \wedge n = m \\ r & \text{if } r = r' \wedge n \neq m \\ \text{null} & \text{if } r \neq r' \end{cases}$$

Fig. 4. A recursive definition of parse tree intersection.

5.2   Representing Paths up to Observations

So far we have seen how one can represent *complete* paths through symbolic control-flow graphs, however paths up to symbolic states or edges that are symbolic supports of observations are rarely complete. We choose to represent paths that are not complete as *partially evaluated parse trees*, that is, parse trees which still have leaves which are non-terminal symbols. Further, we denote the path up to an observation q by $\pi(q)$.

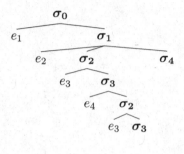

Fig. 5. A partial parse tree.

As an example, consider the path $e_1 \, e_2 \, e_3 \, e_4 \, e_3$ through the symbolic control-flow graph in Fig. 2. This path is not complete, since it does not end with the edge e_8, hence its parse tree with respect to the context free grammar must contain non-terminal symbols. Figure 5 shows its partial parse tree.

5.3   Producing Explanations

We show how we can use intersections of the paths up to observations c_i of pairs $\langle c_i, \mathsf{Sev}(\alpha, c_i) \rangle$ in our *good*, $C_\top$, and *bad*, $C_\bot$, sets to determine whether certain parts of code may be responsible for violations or not. This intersection is our *explanation*. In the case that the path taken is not likely to be responsible, we give an alternative method that is a sensible approach for our work at the CMS Experiment at CERN.

For each $\langle c_i, \mathsf{Sev}(\alpha, c_i) \rangle \in C_\top$, we compute $\pi(c_i)$, the path taken by $\mathcal{D}_i$ to reach $\mathsf{support}(c_i)$. We then form the intersection of the parse trees $\bigcap_{c_i \in C_\top} T(\pi(c_i))$. Any path parameter in the resulting intersection tells us that this part of the path is unlikely to contribute to the verdict reached by the observations c_i which are not falsifying. We draw a similar conclusion when we compute the parse trees for $c_i \in C_\bot$; any parts of the paths that disagree across dynamic runs in which an observation was always falsifying are unlikely to affect the verdict.

Verdict severity is useful if there are multiple paths $\pi(c_i)$ which disagree with all others on a specific path parameter, but which have verdict severity $\mathsf{Sev}(\alpha, c_i)$ close to 0, ie, borderline. In these cases, we could move the associated runs to the other set and redo the analysis e.g. reclassify a run that should not contribute to a particular class.

In the case of disagreement of values of path parameters for the same verdict, we capture input parameters of the relevant function calls. The space of maps from input parameters to their values will then give us an indication of whether state, rather than control flow, contributed to a verdict. For example, all violations may occur when an input variable is negative. If neither factor shows to affect the verdict, in the cases we have dealt with so far at the CMS Experiment at CERN, it is reasonable to conclude that external calls (e.g. network operations) are a contributing factor.

6   Implementation in VYPR2

We have implemented our explanation technique as an extension of the VYPR2 framework [11] (http://cern.ch/vypr). The code used to perform the analysis in this section is found at http://github.com/pyvypr/. The necessary modifications to VYPR2 included (1) additional instrumentation, to make the dynamic run derived by VYPR2 *branch-aware*; (2) changes to the relational verdict schema to allow detailed querying of the data now being obtained by VYPR2 during monitoring; and (3) path reconstruction and comparison tools to allow construction of explanations.

We now demonstrate how our prototype implementation can be used on a representative program to conclude that one branch is more likely to cause violation than another when an observation generated after the branches converge is checked. Work is currently underway at the CMS Experiment at CERN to build an analysis library, since everything in the remainder of this section required custom scripts.

A representative program and PyCFTL specification are given in Fig. 6. Since the current implementation of VYPR2 works with Python-based web services that are based on the Flask [1] framework (this being a commonly used framework at the CMS Experiment), the code in Fig. 6 is typical of the code seen in a Flask-based web service. In this case, the result of the function `test` is returned when the URL `test/n/`, where `n` is a natural number, is accessed.

6.1   Performing an Analysis

Path Reconstruction. This step generates sequences of edges in the SCFG of the function being monitored using Algorithm 1. The minimal amount of information is stored in the verdict database to perform such reconstruction by storing

```
1   def f(l):
2       for item in l:
3           time.sleep(0.1)
4
5   @app.route(
6       '/test/<int:n>/',
7       methods=["GET", "POST"]
8   )
9   def test(n):
10      a = 10
11      if n > 10:
12          l = []
13          for i in range(n):
14              l.append(i**2)
15          print(''test'')
16      else:
17          l = []
18      f(l)
19      return "..."
```

```
1   "app.routes" : {
2       "test" : [
3           Forall(
4               s = changes('a')
5           ).\
6           Check(
7               lambda s : (
8                   If(
9                       s('a').equals(10)
10                  ).then(
11                      s.next_call('f').\
12                          duration()._in([0, 1])
13                  )
14              )
15          )
16      ]
17  }
```

Fig. 6. The program (left) and PyCFTL specification (right) we use to demonstrate our path comparison approach.

observations and *mapping* them to the previous branching condition that was satisfied to reach them. This way, the complexity of the specification has no effect on the efficiency of path reconstruction. The results of this step are not visible to the user.

Path Comparison. Our initial implementation of path comparison processes all recorded dynamic runs, and then focuses on observations generated by the call to f at line 18 in Fig. 6. These observations are grouped into two sets; those generating the false verdict, and those generating trueSoFar. Figure 7 (top) shows the intersection of all parse trees derived from observations that generated trueSoFar, and Fig. 7 (middle) those that generated false. We call these parse trees *representatives*.

Finally, in the implementation used for these experiments, Fig. 7 (bottom) is the result of our analysis. It shows the intersection of the representative parse trees from trueSoFar and false verdicts with the single *path parameter* highlighted in bold. It is clear from the path parameter that variation in paths is found at an if-statement, and the branch taken here may affect the verdict, since the representatives show that good and bad paths follow single paths.

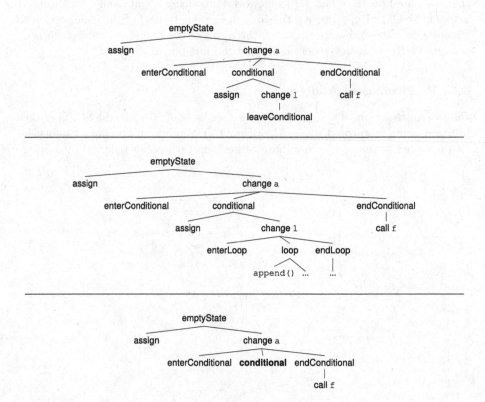

Fig. 7. The intersection (bottom) of the good (top) and bad (middle) path representatives, with the single path parameter highlighted in bold.

Our notion of verdict severity would come in useful if there were observations on the borderline of a verdict that were stopping us from obtaining a single path parameter value for all paths giving a single verdict. We could redo our analysis, counting the anomalous observation(s) as contributing to different verdicts.

6.2   Performance

The overhead induced by additional instrumentation for path reconstruction has been shown to be minimal. When the program in Fig. 6 traverses the branch starting at line 17, the overhead is large (approximately 43%), but we observe, exactly as in [10], that this is due to Python's Global Interpreter Lock preventing truly asynchronous monitoring. When the branch starting at line 12 is traversed, the overhead becomes negligible because `time.sleep` is called, which is thread-local.

Our implementation of offline path comparison (including path reconstruction, context free grammar construction, parse tree derivation and intersection) has shown to scale approximately quadratically with the number of paths. Reconstruction and comparison of 400 paths (200 good, 200 bad) took approximately 3.6 s, while 1000 paths (500 good, 500 bad) took approximately 16.6 s. These measurements were taken by turning off many of the writes to disk used to store SCFGs and parse trees, since these are performed by the `graphviz` [2] library. We observe that it is possible to use previously computed parts of an intersection since intersection is commutative and that deriving the parse trees of multiple paths with respect to a context free grammar is parallelisable, with a possibly small increase in memory usage.

7   Related Work

An alternative approach to explaining violations measures the *distance* between a violating trace and the language of the specification [3,19,22]. Other work considers error traces and what changes could be made to prune violating extensions [8]. The idea is that, if a fix can be found that prunes all possible erroneous extensions, the code to be fixed could be regarded as a fault. This work lies inside the general field of Fault Localisation [26], where much work has been done, including Spectra-based [25] and Model-based [21] approaches. Our work differs from the existing work in that we consider *faults* to be potentially problematic control flow with respect to CFTL formulas.

Reconstructing paths is also not a new idea [4], where some approaches have compared paths [23]. Our work differs in its context free grammar-based comparison, and the subsequent use to construct explanations of violations of CFTL specifications.

Much work has been done on explanation in the Model Checking community. For example, finding the closest satisfying traces to the set of counterexamples and describing the differences [14] or localising the parts of an input signal violating the property [7,13]. There has also been work quantifying the degree of severity of a violation/satisfaction [12]. Although the setting is different (in RV we deal with concrete runs), there are similarities with our approach, which will be explored in the future.

8   Conclusion

We introduced a new partial semantics for CFTL that allows isolation of the observation that causes a CFTL formula to evaluate to false. Following that, we extended the notion of dynamic runs to define *branch-aware dynamic runs* which allow reconstruction of the execution path of a program as a path through its symbolic control-flow graph. Finally, we gave our approach for comparing paths using context free grammars. Implementation of this approach in VyPR2 allows construction of explanations based on comparison of the paths taken with respect to verdicts generated.

Our next step is already underway: we are developing analysis tools for VyPR2, with services used at the CMS Experiment at CERN serving as use cases.

References

1. Flask for Python. http://flask.pocoo.org
2. Graphviz for Python. https://graphviz.readthedocs.io/en/stable/
3. Babenko, A., Mariani, L., Pastore, F.: Ava: automated interpretation of dynamically detected anomalies. In: Proceedings of the Eighteenth International Symposium on Software Testing and Analysis, ISSTA 2009, pp. 237–248. ACM, New York, NY, USA (2009). https://doi.org/10.1145/1572272.1572300
4. Ball, T., Larus, J.R.: Efficient path profiling. In: Proceedings of the 29th Annual ACM/IEEE International Symposium on Microarchitecture MICRO, vol. 29, pp. 46–57. IEEE Computer Society, Washington, DC, USA (1996). http://dl.acm.org/citation.cfm?id=243846.243857
5. Bartocci, E., Falcone, Y., Francalanza, A., Leucker, M., Reger, G.: An introduction to runtime verification. In: Lectures on Runtime Verification - Introductory and Advanced Topics. LNCS, vol. 10457, pp. 1–23 (2018)
6. Basin, D., Krstić, S., Traytel, D.: Almost event-rate independent monitoring of metric dynamic logic. In: Lahiri, S., Reger, G. (eds.) RV 2017. LNCS, vol. 10548, pp. 85–102. Springer, Cham (2017). https://doi.org/10.1007/978-3-319-67531-2_6
7. Beer, I., Ben-David, S., Chockler, H., Orni, A., Trefler, R.: Explaining counterexamples using causality. Form. Methods Syst. Des. **40**(1), 20–40 (2012). https://doi.org/10.1007/s10703-011-0132-2
8. Christakis, M., Heizmann, M., Mansur, M.N., Schilling, C., Wüstholz, V.: Semantic fault localization and suspiciousness ranking. In: Vojnar, T., Zhang, L. (eds.) Tools and Algorithms for the Construction and Analysis of Systems, pp. 226–243. Springer International Publishing, Cham (2019)

9. Dawes, J.H., Reger, G.: Specification of State and Time Constraints for Runtime Verification of Functions (2018). arXiv:1806.02621

10. Dawes, J.H., Reger, G.: Specification of temporal properties of functions for runtime verification. In: Proceedings of the 34th ACM/SIGAPP Symposium on Applied Computing, pp. 2206–2214. SAC 2019. ACM, New York, NY, USA (2019). https://doi.org/10.1145/3297280.3297497

11. Dawes, J.H., Reger, G., Franzoni, G., Pfeiffer, A., Govi, G.: VyPR2: a framework for runtime verification of python web services. In: Vojnar, T., Zhang, L. (eds.) Tools and Algorithms for the Construction and Analysis of Systems, pp. 98–114. Springer International Publishing, Cham (2019)

12. Donzé, A., Maler, O.: Robust satisfaction of temporal logic over real-valued signals. In: Chatterjee, K., Henzinger, T.A. (eds.) Formal Modeling and Analysis of Timed Systems, pp. 92–106. Springer, Heidelberg (2010)

13. Ferrère, T., Maler, O., Ničković, D.: Trace diagnostics using temporal implicants. In: Finkbeiner, B., Pu, G., Zhang, L. (eds.) Automated Technology for Verification and Analysis, pp. 241–258. Springer International Publishing, Cham (2015)

14. Groce, A., Chaki, S., Kroening, D., Strichman, O.: Error explanation with distance metrics. Int. J. Softw. Tools Technol. Transfer 8(3), 229–247 (2006). https://doi.org/10.1007/s10009-005-0202-0

15. Havelund, K., Reger, G.: Specification of parametric monitors - quantified event automata versus rule systems. In: Formal Modeling and Verification of Cyber-Physical Systems (2015)

16. Kim, M., Viswanathan, M., Kannan, S., Lee, I., Sokolsky, O.: Java-MaC: a run-time assurance approach for java programs. Form. Methods Syst. Des. 24(2), 129–155 (2004). https://doi.org/10.1023/B:FORM.0000017719.43755.7c

17. Leucker, M., Schallhart, C.: A brief account of runtime verification. J. Logic Algebr. Program. 78(5), 293–303 (2009). https://doi.org/10.1016/j.jlap.2008.08.004. http://www.sciencedirect.com/science/article/pii/S1567832608000775. The 1st Workshop on Formal Languages and Analysis of Contract-Oriented Software (FLACOS 2007)

18. Meredith, P.O., Jin, D., Griffith, D., Chen, F., Rosu, G.: An overview of the MOP runtime verification framework. STTT 14(3), 249–289 (2012). https://doi.org/10.1007/s10009-011-0198-6

19. Reger, G.: Suggesting edits to explain failing traces. In: Bartocci, E., Majumdar, R. (eds.) RV 2015. LNCS, vol. 9333, pp. 287–293. Springer, Cham (2015). https://doi.org/10.1007/978-3-319-23820-3_20

20. Reger, G., Cruz, H.C., Rydeheard, D.: MARQ: monitoring at runtime with QEA. In: Baier, C., Tinelli, C. (eds.) TACAS 2015. LNCS, vol. 9035, pp. 596–610. Springer, Heidelberg (2015). https://doi.org/10.1007/978-3-662-46681-0_55

21. Reiter, R.: A theory of diagnosis from first principles. Artif. Intell. 32(1), 57–95 (1987). https://doi.org/10.1016/0004-3702(87)90062-2,. http://www.sciencedirect.com/science/article/pii/0004370287900622

22. Renieris, M., Reiss, S.P.: Fault localization with nearest neighbor queries. In: Proceedings of the 18th IEEE International Conference on Automated Software Engineering, ASE 2003, pp. 30–39. IEEE Press, Piscataway, NJ, USA (2003). https://doi.org/10.1109/ASE.2003.1240292

23. Reps, T., Ball, T., Das, M., Larus, J.: The use of program profiling for software maintenance with applications to the year 2000 problem. In: Jazayeri, M., Schauer, H. (eds.) Software Engineering – ESEC/FSE 1997, pp. 432–449. Springer, Berlin Heidelberg, Berlin, Heidelberg (1997)
24. Signoles, J.: E-ACSL: Executable ANSI/ISO C Specification Language, version 1.5-4, March 2014. frama-c.com/download/e-acsl/e-acsl.pdf
25. de Souza, H.A., Chaim, M.L., Kon, F.: Spectrum-based software fault localization: A survey of techniques, advances, and challenges. CoRR abs/1607.04347 (2016). http://arxiv.org/abs/1607.04347
26. Wong, W.E., Gao, R., Li, Y., Abreu, R., Wotawa, F.: A survey on software fault localization. IEEE Trans. Softw. Eng. **42**(8), 707–740 (2016). https://doi.org/10.1109/TSE.2016.2521368

FastCFI: Real-Time Control Flow Integrity Using FPGA Without Code Instrumentation

Lang Feng[1]([⊠]), Jeff Huang[2], Jiang Hu[1,2], and Abhijith Reddy[1]

[1] Department of Electrical and Computer Engineering, Texas A&M University,
College Station, TX 77843, USA
{flwave,jianghu,abreddy}@tamu.edu
[2] Department of Computer Science and Engineering,
Texas A&M University, College Station, TX 77843, USA
jeffhuang@tamu.edu

Abstract. Control Flow Integrity (CFI) is an effective defense technique against a variety of memory-based cyber attacks. CFI is usually enforced through software methods, which entail considerable performance overhead. Hardware-based CFI techniques can largely avoid performance overhead, but typically rely on code instrumentation, which forms a non-trivial hurdle to the application of CFI. We develop FastCFI, an FPGA based CFI system that can perform fine-grained and stateful checking without code instrumentation. We also propose an automated Verilog generation technique that facilitates fast deployment of FastCFI. Experiments on popular benchmarks confirm that FastCFI can detect fine-grained CFI violations over unmodified binaries. The measurement results show an average of 0.36% performance overhead on SPEC 2006 benchmarks.

1 Introduction

Control Flow Integrity (CFI) [1] is to regulate instruction flow transitions, such as branch, toward target addresses conforming to the original design intention. Such regulation can prevent software execution from being redirected to erroneous address or malicious code. It is widely recognized as an effective approach to defend against a variety of security attacks including return oriented programming (ROP) [34] and jump oriented programming (JOP) [3].

Software-based CFI usually competes for the same processor resource as the software application being protected [1,9,30,41], and therefore it tends to incur large performance overhead unless its resolution is very coarse-grained. Alternatively, CFI can be realized through hardware-based enforcement, which is performed largely external to software execution and thus involves much lower overhead. Indeed, hardware-based CFI has attracted significant research attention recently [13,15,26,40].

Apart from relatively low overhead, there are some other issues of hardware CFI which are worth a close look.

This work is partially supported by NSF (CNS-1618824).

1. **Code instrumentation.** Previous hardware CFI methods often rely on code instrumentation [5, 10, 22, 23, 25, 26, 37]. Additional code is added to the application software being protected for more executing information. This causes performance overhead, may introduce extra security vulnerability, and is not always practically feasible [18].

2. **Granularity.** Fine-grained CFI can detect detailed violations that would be missed by coarse-grained CFI. For example, the only legal instruction flow transitions are from code segment A to B, denoted by $A \to B$, and $C \to D$. A coarse-grained CFI may only check if a transition target is legitimate without examining the transition source. As such, an illegal transition $A \to D$ would pass such coarse-grained CFI check as D is a legitimate target, while fine-grained CFI can detect this violation.

3. **Stateful CFI.** Whether or not a transition is legal may depend on its history. For example, a transition $C \to D$ is legal only when its previous transition is $A \to C$, while transition $B \to C$ is also legal. Therefore, transition $B \to C \to D$ is illegal. Most previous hardware CFI works [17, 32, 40] are stateless, and in this case only check $C \to D$ without examining its history.

The first issue affects practical applications. The next two issues are for security in term of CFI coverage. To the best of our knowledge, there is no previous work that well addresses all of these issues along with low overhead.

In this paper, we present FastCFI, which is an FPGA-based CFI system. FPGA implementation is a customized hardware solution that is much more power-efficient than software-based solution on general purpose microprocessors. In embedded applications, such as

Table 1. Comparison among different methods.

Method	Fine-grained	Stateful	No instrumentation	<1% overhead	No false alarm
FastCFI	✓	✓	✓	✓	✓
Lee [26]	×	✓	×	×	✓
CONVERSE [17]	✓	×	✓	✓	×
Griffin [15]	✓	✓	✓	×	✓
FlowGuard [27]	×	✓	✓	×	✓
CFIMon [40]	×	×	✓	×	×
MoCFI [9]	✓	✓	×	×	×
Zhang [41]	×	✓	×	×	✓
kBouncer [30]	×	✓	✓	✓	✓
Ding [13]	✓	✓	✓	×	✓
Abadi [1]	✓	✓	×	×	✓

autonomous vehicles, such power-efficiency is particularly desirable. At the same time, the reconfigurability of FPGAs provides an important flexibility that is not available in dedicated ASIC solutions. Largely due to these appealing advantages, Microsoft adopts FPGA for its datacenters [31]. FastCFI also inherits the computing efficiency and flexibility of FPGA. The computing efficiency arises from the fact that FPGA computing can considerably circumvent system overhead and intrinsically support parallel processing.

FastCFI is the first fine-grained and stateful CFI system with negligible overhead and without using code instrumentation. Moreover, FastCFI does not produce any false alarm and has low detection latency.

A comparison between FastCFI and some major works is provided in Table 1.

The source code of FastCFI is available at [35]. The main contributions of our paper are:

- A CFI system without code instrumentation or processor architecture/instruction set modification.
- A detailed design of a hardware-based fine-grained and stateful CFI system with low latency.
- A concrete system implementation based on FPGA, instead of simulation.
- A new circuit design technique that can automatically generate Verilog HDL for the application dependent component and therefore facilitates fast deployment of FastCFI systems.
- An extensive evaluation on both popular security and performance benchmarks (never done before in FPGA-based work to the best of our knowledge).

We anticipate several application scenarios of FastCFI. FastCFI can be applied to various electronic systems, especially those security-critical ones such as banks, public security systems, and military defense systems. These systems often have high real-time and security requirements, and can afford additional hardware resources, such as FPGAs which are relatively expensive as of today. FastCFI can also be applied in software supply chain to secure users of potentially vulnerable third-party software, the binaries of which can be analyzed, but do not allow code instrumentation. FastCFI has low latency (Sect. 5.4) and low overhead (Sect. 5.3), indicating its high real-time capability. On one hand, the programs running on the processors will not be disturbed. On the other hand, once there is an attack, FastCFI can identify it immediately. FastCFI also has high precision (Sect. 5.2) without any false alarm. These properties ensure the system's security. Furthermore, FastCFI does not depend on code instrumentation and thus, makes the implementation be practical.

The rest of this paper is organized as follows. Section 2 introduces the background on CFI and control flow graph; Sect. 3 discusses previous work; Sect. 4 presents our proposed system design; Sect. 5 reports the experimental results and Sect. 6 concludes the paper.

2   CFI and Control Flow Graph

The specification of CFI is a control flow graph (CFG) of the target program, in which each node corresponds to one segment or block of instructions and each directed edge indicates a legal transition between instruction segments. In the example of Fig. 1(a), the instructions are divided into seven segments, each of which corresponds to a node in Fig. 1(b). The solid and

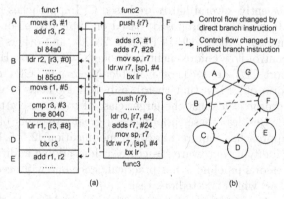

Fig. 1. Example of control flow graph.

dashed edges in Fig. 1(b) indicate transitions by direct and indirect branch instructions, respectively. For example, the edge from node A to F implies that the branch instruction bl 84a0 in A is taken and the software execution switches from A to F.

Once a CFG is constructed for a software, CFI of this software execution is enforced by verifying if an execution trace conforms to the CFG. For instance, transition $A \to B$ is illegal as there is no edge from A to B in the CFG. CFI for function returns can be stateful. For example, there are edges from F to both B and E. However, if F is invoked by function call from A, the last instruction in F should only return to the instruction right after A, which is in B. Therefore, function return $F \to B$ is legal while transition $F \to E$ is illegal.

3   Previous Work

3.1   Software-Based CFI

Early work on CFI was mostly realized by software implementation. The seminal work by Abadi et al. [1] proposes two code instrumentation approaches, which have average overhead of 16% and 21%, respectively, on the SPEC 2000 benchmark. Later work targeted CFI at specific application scenarios. For example, the method of Davi et al. [9] is designed for smartphones, and the work by Zhang and Sekar [41] addresses how to handle COTS binary codes. Several works [4, 11, 30] attempt to reduce performance overhead or avoid code instrumentation by sacrificing granularity or security coverage. For example, kBouncer [30] has very low overhead and code instrumentation is avoided in [4]. However, both methods handle ROP attacks only.

FastCFI is hardware-based CFI, which avoids some disadvantages in software-base CFI, such as high performance overhead [1,9], coarse-grained CFI policy [4,11,30], and requiring code instrumentation [1,9,41].

3.2   Hardware-Based CFI

Recently, several hardware-based CFI approaches [2,5,8,10,12–17,22–29,32,37, 40] have been proposed, based on Intel Processor Trace [13,15,16,27], performance counters [40], FPGA [8,25,26], and others [17]. Intel also proposed the control-flow enforcement technology (CET) [20]. However, processors that support CET are still not available. Meanwhile, CET only implements the weakest form of CFI in that there's only a single class of valid targets and is too weak to protect against the larger class of code reuse attacks.

Besides these approaches, great amount of the hardware-based CFI approaches require hardware modification [2,5,8,10,12,14,22–24,28,29,32,37]. Modifying hardware structure such as adding additional modules inside the processor's pipeline is not practical, since one will need to repeat the whole design flow, which is a tedious task.

Compared to previous hardware-based CFI, FastCFI has novelties in multiple directions. Firstly, FastCFI does not depend on code instrumentation. Previous hardware-based approaches leverage code instrumentation for getting more information [5,10,22,23,25,26,37]. However, this results in large overhead, and code instrumentation itself is also not secure and sometimes even impossible. Secondly, FastCFI has a low overhead compared to some previous works [12,13,15,25,26]. High overhead is unacceptable in some real-time applications. Also, not all the hardware-based CFI are fine-grained and stateful [8,17,25,26,40]. They may miss some attacks. In operating system, false positive may delay all the processes, but some techniques used in previous works lead to this [17,40]. Through results obtained in FastCFI we show that such cases are avoided in our CFI solution. Hardware-based CFI is harder to be implemented than software-based CFI due to the cost, difficulties in manufacturing, resources, etc. A few previous works prefer using simulator for implementation [8,10,14,22,23], but this will not guarantee the functionality because there are differences between simulation and real world conditions. We use FPGA to implement the hardware design. By taking advantage of existing devices in the processor, we avoid changing the structure of the processor and are able to build a real system for CFI verification.

4   The Proposed System Design

4.1   System Platform

FastCFI is developed on a platform depicted in Fig. 2. It is composed of an ARM Cortex-A9 processor and an FPGA. The CFI of a software execution on the ARM core is verified by the FPGA. Program Trace Macrocell (PTM) generates compressed control-flow traces according to instructions processed by the ARM core. The CoreSight Debug module in the ARM core can obtain traces from PTM and send the traces to FPGA through the Trace Port Interface Unit (TPIU), which acts as a bridge between the trace data and a data stream. The key ideas of FastCFI can be applied to other platforms such as x86 architecture.

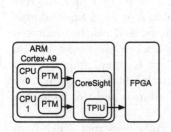

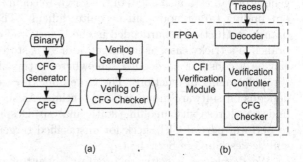

(a)   (b)

Fig. 2. System platform for the proposed CFI.

Fig. 3. System design overview: (a) offline CFG checker generator; (b) online CFI verifier.

4.2 System Design Overview

The system design of FastCFI consists of an offline CFG checker generator and an online CFI verifier, as depicted in Fig. 3. The CFG checker generator is a software that takes application software binary as input and generates CFG checker design in Verilog. During online software execution, a trace captured through ARM CoreSight is first decoded in order to understand its semantics. The decoded trace data is then fed to the CFI verification module, which is composed of a verification controller and a CFG checker. Both the decoder and the verification module are implemented on FPGA.

4.3 Offline CFG Checker Generator

To give the hardware verification circuits the correct execution information which can be represented by CFG, target software binary has to be analyzed, and CFG should be extracted. Since we implement the CFG as a hardware circuit called CFG checker in the verification module for higher speed, the output of the CFG checker generator is the CFG checker's Verilog HDL file.

Given software binary, the generator first converts it to assembly code. It extracts CFG from the assembly code and generates the Verilog design of CFG checker circuit. Then, the CFG checker is mapped on FPGA. The generator is able to help the fast implementation of CFI verification given a system to be protected, and only the target vulnerable binary is required.

We denote a sequence of assembly instructions as $I_1, I_2, ...I_{m1}, B_1, I_{m1+1}, I_{m1+2}, ..., I_{m2}, B_2, ...B_n...$; where $B_1, B_2, ...B_n$ are branch instructions (e.g., jmp, call, ret, etc.) and the others are non-branch instructions. Then, the instruction sequence is partitioned into multiple segments $\{I_1, I_2, ...I_{m1}, B_1\}$, $\{I_{m1+1}, I_{m1+2}, ..., I_{m2}, B_2\}$,..., each of which has a single branch instruction at its end. Each instruction segment forms a node in the CFG. In the sequel, we use CFG node and instruction segment interchangeably when the context is clear.

By examining the source node and target node of each branch instruction, the generator can establish edges of the CFG. Recognizing the source node is trivial, but finding target node can be quite difficult. The target address of a direct branch instruction is hardcoded in the binary and can be easily found. Indirect branch is a tricky case, as its target address is stored in a register. Such address can be a constant hardcoded somewhere in the binary, and can be recovered through tracing instructions. The more difficult case is where the target address depends on software input data at runtime. As such, it is almost impossible to find the address with an offline static analysis. Despite this difficulty, we find how to perform partial CFI check for unspecified target address and this technique will be described in Sect. 4.5.

We developed a software program to automatically construct CFG from binary code. The generator further creates Verilog description for the CFG checker circuit. Meanwhile, our framework is general and can accommodate other tools such as IDA [19].

4.4   Trace Decoder

The decoder takes software execution trace from TPIU as input, interprets its semantic and extracts information that is relevant to CFI. A trace consists of many packets, each of which is usually a few bytes. Two types of packets are of particular relevance to CFI, *Atom* and *Branch address* [6], which is simply called *Branch* subsequently. An *Atom* tells if a direct branch is taken or not, and indicates the case that an indirect branch is not taken. If an indirect branch is taken, its target address is contained in *Branch*. Some other types of packets, such as *I-sync* [6], can periodically indicate the current instruction address.

The decoder extracts the following required information:

- Context ID that identifies the current program.
- The current program state.
- The current packet type: *Atom*, *Branch*, or *I-sync*, etc.
- The current instruction address, which is obtained from *Branch*, or *I-sync*. Note that this information is not always available and the scenarios of its availability are complex. The starting address of a program is available at *I-sync*, which continues to provide current address periodically.
- T/N from *Atom*, where T indicates that a branch is taken and N means an indirect branch is not taken.
- Program exception and PTM buffer overflow information.

The TPIU channel in the ARM core has 32-bit bitwidth, which means 4 bytes of packets can be sent to FPGA in every clock cycle. When implementing, we design a 3-phase pipeline decoder to increase the throughput and match the speed of the TPIU.

4.5   CFI Verification Module

The CFI verification module is to examine if flow transitions in a software execution trace are consistent with transitions specified in CFG, which is embedded in the CFG checker. In order to do so, we need to obtain the source node and target node of a branch instruction from the execution trace. The source node of a branch instruction, which is equivalent to the current instruction address of the branch,

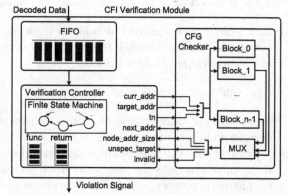

Fig. 4. Architecture of CFI verification module.

is often unavailable in trace packets. In [26], it is acquired through code instrumentation. Without code instrumentation, identifying the source/current node is much more difficult. We solve this difficulty by using the periodically available instruction address information and tracking the other addresses by following the CFG.

Consider the example in Fig. 1. Suppose we know the address of the first instruction of node A. The last instruction of A, bl 84a0, is a branch to node F, whose execution results in an *Atom* with T indicating that the branch is taken. Note that every direct branch has only one deterministic target when it is taken. When Write⊕Execute [39] feature is applied in an operating system, an attacker is not able to change the code and the target of each direct branch. Therefore, by observing T from trace decoder and examining the CFG in the CFG checker, we know that the software execution now moves to node F even if the current instruction address is not available at trace packets. Since the transition from A to F changes the current function from func1 to func2, bl 84a0 is inferred as a function call. Therefore, func2 should return to the next instruction of bl 84a0 of func1, which is the first instruction of B. The last instruction of node F is function return, which is an indirect branch. Its execution leads to a *Branch* in decoded trace packet. By receiving this *Branch*, we can be aware of the occurrence of a transition from F. The target address is contained in *Branch* and we can examine if it is consistent with the target node B in the CFG.

The architecture of the CFI verification module is shown in Fig. 4. Its key components, CFG checker and verification controller, are described as follows.

CFG Checker. The CFG checker is an FPGA circuit that contains CFG information and outputs specific CFG details for given execution trace information. It has n blocks, as shown in Fig. 4, each of which corresponds to a node in CFG. Assigning each CFG node in one block makes the CFG node search run in parallel, and this will greatly increase the performance of FastCFI.

In detail, there are three main inputs to the checker circuit, all of which are from the decoded trace packets or earlier computations.

- *curr_addr*: current instruction address from trace or earlier calculation.
- *target_addr*: indirect branch target address decoded from *Branch*.
- *tn*: T/N information decoded from *Atom*.

The four main outputs are:

- *next_addr*: the next program counter address after executing the branch of current node according to CFG.
- *node_addr_size*: the start address and size of current node, and function size if the current node is the first node of a function, where the size is equivalent to difference between end and start addresses of a node/function.
- *invalid*: a binary signal whose assertion indicates that the *target_addr* does not conform to the *next_addr*.
- *unspec_target*: a binary signal whose assertion indicates that an indirect branch target depends on application input and is not specified in CFG.

Each block first checks if an input *curr_addr* is within the node corresponding to this block. If so, the block is activated and always generates its *node_addr_size* output. The other outputs vary depending on three different types of blocks. Since each node in CFG contains only one branch instruction at its end, the categorization of blocks is based on their branch instructions.

1. **Direct branch.** An activated block with direct branch generates *next_addr* according to input *tn*. If *tn* is *T*, indicating that the branch is taken, the *next_addr* can be found in CFG and is hardcoded in the FPGA. Otherwise, the *next_addr* is the address of the next instruction.
2. **Indirect branch with constant target.** If *tn* is *T*, the *target_addr* is compared with the possible *next_addr* from CFG. If they are the same, the *next_addr* is sent to output. Otherwise, signal *invalid* asserts.
3. **Indirect branch with unspecified target.** In this case, *next_addr* is not specified in CFG as the target address depends on software application input and cannot be identified in the offline analysis. Then, *next_addr* is output as *target_addr* and at the same time signal *unspec_target* asserts.

Note that at most one block can be activated in the checker circuit. When the CFG checker is implemented in Verilog HDL, we use *if* statement for each block, where the condition is that the current address is within the range of instructions' addresses of the corresponding CFG node. Inside *if*, the *tn* and *target_addr* are examined by the three rules above. Since the only difference among the same type blocks is the parameter but not the structure, we can write three Verilog description templates for all the three types and use software to automatically instantiate one of them for each block, which is the way that the CFG checker generator in Sect. 4.3 works.

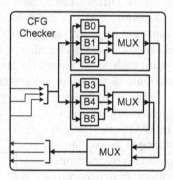

Fig. 5. An example of grouping blocks in CFG checker.

The checker outputs cover the following scenarios.

C1 **No output:** Current address is not in any CFG nodes.
C2 **There is output:** Current address is in one CFG node, whose start address is found. The start address of the next node is also found.
C3 **Output contains function size:** The current node is at the beginning of a function. The address range of this function is found.
C4 **No *invalid* or *unspec_target* assertion:** The actual control flow is valid after executing the branch instruction in the current node. The next address after the current node is found so that the actual software execution position is located. Meanwhile, the current node has a direct branch or has an indirect branch with constant target, which the actual execution target address.
C5 **invalid asserts but no *unspec_target* assertion:** The current node has an indirect branch with constant target, which is different from the target address of the actual software execution.

C6 *unspec_target* **asserts but no** *invalid* **assertion:** The current node has an indirect branch with unspecified target in CFG and the verification module is to perform other checks for CFI which will be discussed later in this section.

For the Verilog compilation tool, optimizing a large number of blocks is more difficult than optimizing fewer blocks. Therefore, in our implementation, we develop a hierarchical approach that groups blocks into small Verilog modules. Each small module takes the checker input to all of its internal blocks, and selects an output among all of its internal blocks. For example, in Fig. 5, the CFG checker has 6 blocks, $B0$ to $B5$, which are grouped into two small modules. In this way, the compiling optimization is directed to perform in a hierarchical manner to reach different resource use and compiling time tradeoffs.

Verification Controller. The verification controller takes the decoded trace packets as input, feeds input to the CFG checker, and analyzes the checker results to locate current instruction address, if not available from the trace packets, and performs CFI verification. It is mainly a finite state machine with state transition diagram provided in Fig. 6. It also has a function stack, which stores information about the current function, and a return stack that stores function return addresses. These two stacks are the critical parts for realizing the stateful attribute of the proposed system.

The controller operations start from the WAIT state, which attempts to capture executing instruction address from decoded trace packets. This address provides a reference for the verification module to track the software execution location, and can be obtained from *Branch* or *I-sync*.

Once an executing instruction address is acquired, the controller enters the SCOPE_CHECK state, where the instruction address is sent to the CFG checker as *curr_addr* to tell

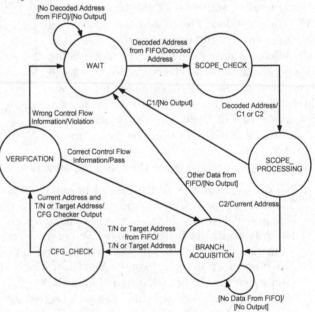

Fig. 6. State transition diagram of the controller.

if it is in the scope of CFG. After the scope checking is finished, SCOPE_PROCESSING state is entered where the controller analyzes the checking result and decides what to do next. If the result is C1, the instruction address is not in the CFG and the next state is WAIT. If the result is C2, the controller records the context ID, which identifies the software execution to be verified, and then moves to state BRANCH_ACQUISITION.

At BRANCH_ACQUISITION, the controller attempts to capture decoded *Atom* or *Branch*, and feeds *tn* or *target_addr* to the CFG checker. If the received trace packet is *I-sync* with current instruction address, the controller switches to the WAIT so as to update the reference instruction address. If branch information, *Atom* or *Branch*, is received, it enters the CFG_CHECK state, where the CFG checker processes the *Atom* or *Branch* information, along with *curr_addr*.

When the CFG checking is finished, the controller switches to VERIFICATION. This state is to analyze the checking results and keep track of instruction execution location. If condition C3 occurs, the function address range is pushed in to the function stack. The function stack top always stores the address range of the current function. C3 also implies that the previous node made a function call, and notifies the controller to push the return address onto the return stack.

If the target address of a branch instruction is specified in the CFG, either C4 or C5 will hold when the corresponding block is activated. Condition C4 indicates that CFI verification is passed without seeing any violations. Then, the controller updates the current address with the next address and the state goes back to BRANCH_ACQUISITION. Condition C5 shows CFI violation, then the controller outputs a violation signal and goes back to the WAIT state.

Otherwise, if the target address of an indirect branch is not specified, condition C6 will hold, which is a very difficult case for CFI verification as the CFG alone does not immediately tell if the actual target address is legal or not. Despite the difficulty, our controller continues to evaluate three sub-cases and detect as many CFI violations as possible. The first case is function return. The controller compares the actual target address from a trace packet with the return address at the top of the return stack. If they are same, the current indirect branch is confirmed to be a function return, which is legal. Note that this check is stateful as it relies on historical information stored in the return stack. The second one is Branch within current function. The controller checks if the actual target address is within the range of function address at the top of the function stack. If the check result is yes, no violation signal is triggered. The third one is Branch as a new function call. If the actual target address is not in current function, the only legal scenario is that a new function call is made. To verify if a new function call is indeed made, the controller updates the current address with the next address and waits for the next BRANCH_ACQUISITION and CFG_CHECK result. If the next result indicates C3 and the current address is the same as the new function entry address, a new function call is confirmed. Evidently, this is also a stateful check. Any other scenario beyond the above three is illegal and then a CFI violation signal is triggered.

The verification is not only stateful, but also fine-grained as its resolution is on each individual edge in the CFG. We also re-emphasize that our work is general and flexible enough to be applied with other code static analysis tools.

5   Experiments and Results

5.1   Experiment Setup

All our experiments were run and measured on an Altera DE1-SoC board, containing a Cyclone V FPGA working at 50 MHz and an ARM Cortex-A9 dual core processor working at 1 GHz on which we loaded a Linux kernel. In addition, we use Quartus Prime 17.1 [21] for Verilog compilation and FPGA layout synthesis, and Signal Tap Logic Analyzer for FPGA signal monitoring. The Verilog compilation is done on a desktop with an Intel 3.8 GHz CPU and 16 GB RAM.

5.2   Security

We use RIPE [33,38] to evaluate the effectiveness of FastCFI. RIPE is a popular benchmark that has been used frequently in previous works [13,15] for evaluating control flow defenses. However, RIPE is designed for Intel processors, and does not directly run on our ARM platform. There are numerous processor architecture specific assembly and shell codes in RIPE, which we had to modify for the ARM processor.

Table 2. Security performance for different attack methods.

No.	Overflow Technique	Attack Code	Target Code Pointer	Location	Identify?	No.	Overflow Technique	Attack Code	Target Code Pointer	Location	Identify?
1	direct	createfile	ret	stack	√	24	indirect	createfile	funcptrheap	bss	√
2	direct	createfile	funcptrstackvar	stack	√	25	indirect	createfile	funcptrbss	bss	√
3	direct	createfile	structfuncptrstack	stack	√	26	indirect	createfile	funcptrdata	bss	√
4	direct	createfile	funcptrheap	heap	√	27	indirect	createfile	ret	data	√
5	direct	createfile	structfuncptrheap	heap	√	28	indirect	createfile	funcptrstackvar	data	√
6	direct	createfile	structfuncptrbss	bss	√	29	indirect	createfile	funcptrstackparam	data	√
7	direct	createfile	funcptrdata	data	√	30	indirect	createfile	funcptrheap	data	√
8	direct	createfile	structfuncptrdata	data	√	31	indirect	createfile	funcptrbss	data	√
9	indirect	createfile	ret	stack	√	32	indirect	createfile	funcptrdata	data	√
10	indirect	createfile	funcptrstackvar	stack	√	33	direct	returnintolibc	ret	stack	√
11	indirect	createfile	funcptrstackparam	stack	√	34	direct	returnintolibc	funcptrstackvar	stack	√
12	indirect	createfile	funcptrheap	stack	√	35	direct	returnintolibc	structfuncptrstack	stack	√
13	indirect	createfile	funcptrbss	stack	√	36	direct	returnintolibc	funcptrheap	heap	√
14	indirect	createfile	funcptrdata	stack	√	37	direct	returnintolibc	structfuncptrheap	heap	√
15	indirect	createfile	ret	heap	√	38	direct	returnintolibc	structfuncptrbss	bss	√
16	indirect	createfile	funcptrstackvar	heap	√	39	direct	returnintolibc	funcptrdata	data	√
17	indirect	createfile	funcptrstackparam	heap	√	40	direct	returnintolibc	structfuncptrdata	data	√
18	indirect	createfile	funcptrheap	heap	√	41	direct	rop	ret	stack	√
19	indirect	createfile	funcptrbss	heap	√	42	-	-	-	-	No False Alarm
20	indirect	createfile	funcptrdata	heap	√						
21	indirect	createfile	ret	bss	√	SP1	-	-	-	-	√
22	indirect	createfile	funcptrstackvar	bss	√	SP2	-	-	-	-	√
23	indirect	createfile	funcptrstackparam	bss	√						

Due to the engineering difficulties, it is hard to port all RIPE functions to ARM. In total, we recovered 41 attacks (which can run successfully on ARM), including both return oriented programming (ROP) and jump oriented programming (JOP) attacks, as shown in Table 2 (Row #1-41). To assess the precision (i.e., no false positive), we also added a new function (Row #42) in RIPE and let it run without attack.

The results in Table 2 show that all these attacks can be identified by FastCFI. In addition, FastCFI does not report any false positive (for the newly introduced function with no attack).

Fine-Grained, Stateful Attacks. We also designed two special attacks not included in RIPE, as shown in the last two rows of Table 2.

SP1 is a stateful attack that cannot be detected by stateless CFI techniques. As shown in Fig. 7(a), in SP1, there is a function *vuln* which may be called by function *func1* or *func2*. So in the CFG, the node with function return of *vuln* has edges to nodes in both *func1* and *func2*. However, only one of them is valid each time *vuln* is called. If *func1* calls *vuln*, then *vuln* can only return to *func1*. In our test, we use buffer overflow to change the return address of *vuln* to *func2*, even if it is called by *func1*. Our experiment shows that FastCFI can easily identify this attack. However, stateless CFI such as [17,40] and the coarse-grained approach in [15], would not be able to identify this attack.

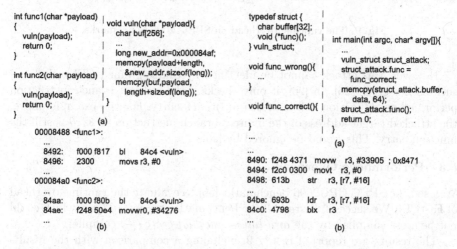

Fig. 7. Code illustrating the stateful SP1 attack.

Fig. 8. Code illustrating the fine-grained SP2 attack.

SP2 is a fine-grained attack. In SP2, the attack changes a function call, making it call another unintended function in the program's binary. The C code is shown in Fig. 8(a). In *main*, there is a structure *struct_attack*, which contains a buffer and a function pointer. Usually, the function pointer in the memory is right after the buffer. The user data, which can be controlled by the attacker, is copied to the buffer through *memcpy*. An attacker can input the data with a larger size than the buffer, and put the address of the function *func_wrong* right after the 32-byte's data. In this way, when the *struct_attack.func()* is called, function *func_wrong* will be executed rather than the correct function *func_correct*.

For our fine-grained CFI, FastCFI can easily identify this attack. Figure 8(b) shows part of the assembly in *main*. The instruction at *84c0* is the function call *struct_attack.func()*. The program would jump to the address stored in *r3*. By backtracking the value in r3, we can find that it should be *0x8471*, where there is the entry of *func_correct*. This is a typical example of indirect branch with constant target address that we discussed before. We create the CFG with a node containing the instruction at *84c0*, and the only outgoing edge of this node is to the node containing the entry of *func_correct*. If the buffer overflow is performed by an attacker, then the control flow will not go through the correct edge in CFG. This will be detected by FastCFI.

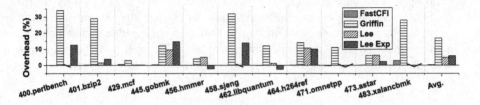

Fig. 9. The runtime overhead on SPEC 2006 benchmarks.

However, this attack cannot be identified by coarse-grained CFI techniques such as Lee et al. [26]. In [26], it only checks if the indirect branch instruction performed as a function call is at the function's entry. For the example above, the attacked target address of the indirect branch instruction at *84c0* is still the function entry. This would be ignored by [26].

5.3   Performance Overhead

We used the SPEC CPU2006 benchmarks [36] to evaluate the runtime overhead of FastCFI. We successfully ran all the benchmarks, except *403.gcc*, which could not be cross compiled by the *arm-linux-gnueabihf-gcc(g++)* compiler.

The results are reported in Fig. 9, including a comparison with the results from two recent works: *Griffin* [15] and *Lee* [26]. Both results of *Lee* and *Griffin* are copied from the original papers [15, 26]. For *Lee* [26], some benchmarks are marked with "\", because they were not evaluated in *Lee*'s work. Besides, we also did the code instrumentation and repeated the overhead experiments in [26], the results are shown as *Lee Exp*. The benchmarks not evaluated in *Lee Exp* (marked with "/") are also not evaluated by *Lee*'s original work [26]. Moreover, *400.perlbench* and *458.sjeng* are not evaluated by *Lee* but evaluated by our repeated experiment *Lee Exp*. There are some benchmarks, such as *471.omnetpp*, which have overhead less than 0. This is likely due to cache effects or the noise of the measurement, since the actual overhead is negligible.

Overall, FastCFI has the lowest performance overhead, only 0.36% on average. The reason is that we do not add or modify anything on the software side, and there is no code instrumentation or running of other programs. The only overhead is caused by enabling the PTM device.

5.4 Latency

We also evaluated the latency introduced by FPGA to detect CFI violations, since it relies on TPIU to communicate the trace between the ARM core and FPGA. The latency is the clock cycles needed by FPGA to identify the attacks after receiving the trace packet containing the CFI violation information. The results are shown in Fig. 10. Overall, FastCFI has a latency within dozens of clock cycles only. We note that some other hardware-based techniques such as [7] incur a latency of tens of thousands of clock cycles, due to a more complex architectural design.

The latency varies between different attacks. This depends on the quantity of data in the FIFO when the wrong control flow information comes. The data in the FIFO must be processed sequentially by the CFI verification module. The more data, the longer latency. In general, this can be affected by many factors, such as the target program itself, the input, or the other programs running on the same processor.

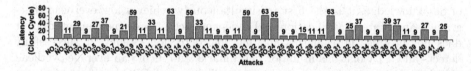

Fig. 10. The latency for FPGA to identify attacks.

5.5 Circuit Resource Use and Compilation Time

Resource use is important for hardware design. Due to the resource limitation of our FPGA, for some benchmarks the system may not fully verify the whole CFG, but a sub-CFG, and ignores the instruction flow transitions happened outside the sub-CFG. In our experiments, we always create the complete CFG first, and then select as many CFG nodes as our FPGA can contain for the sub-CFG. In practice, the sub-CFG can be specified by the user or developer, who may choose the most security sensitive parts of the code to protect against CFI attacks.

The resource use results are reported in Table 3. The ALM means adaptive logic module in Altera FPGA, which is the basic element of FPGA and similar to LUT (Lookup Tables). For these experiments, we group 100 blocks in one small Verilog module as discussed in Sect. 4.5. Overall, our current FPGA

Table 3. Resource use on SPEC 2006 benchmarks.

Benchmark	Sub-CFG Nodes	Total CFG Nodes	# of ALMs	Compile Time	False Alarm?
400.perlbench	4563	65083	32070	18 m 55 s	None
401.bzip2	2247	2247	22840	15 m 32 s	None
429.mcf	471	471	16171	13 m 48 s	None
445.gobmk	4585	37019	31604	19 m 11 s	None
456.hmmer	4602	12286	31449	19 m 10 s	None
458.sjeng	4591	6458	18738	15 m 08 s	None
462.libquantum	1300	1300	18738	15 m 08 s	None
464.h264ref	4513	15195	32070	19 m 15 s	None
471.omnetpp	4763	31811	30250	18 m 07 s	None
473.astar	1345	1345	18995	15 m 07 s	None
483.xalancbmk	4807	173204	31576	18 m 39 s	None

can support 4500−4600 CFG nodes. Note that even though with only the sub-CFGs, FastCFI does not report any false alarms on the studied benchmarks. As also reported in Table 3, the Verilog compilation time, including FPGA layout synthesis, in our experiments is less than 20 min for each benchmark.

6   Conclusion

We have presented an FPGA-based CFI system named FastCFI. To the best of our knowledge, it is the first to simultaneously achieves low overhead, fine-grained and stateful verification and independence of code instrumentation. It does not produce false alarms and has low detection latency. It successfully detects all CFI violations in major benchmarks and incurs an average overhead of 0.36%. While it offers the computing efficiency of FPGAs, its deployment is nearly as convenient as software due to our automated Verilog generation technique. These advantages make FastCFI be feasible to be applied to the systems having high real-time and security requirements.

References

1. Abadi, M., Budiu, M., Erlingsson, U., Ligatti, J.: Control-flow Integrity. In: ACM Conference on Computer and Communications Security, pp. 340–353 (2005)
2. Arora, D., Ravi, S., Raghunathan, A., Jha, N.K.: Hardware-assisted run-time monitoring for secure program execution on embedded processors. IEEE Trans. Very Large Scale Integr. Syst. **14**(12), 1295–1308 (2006)
3. Bletsch, T., Jiang, X., Freeh, V.W., Liang, Z.: Jump-oriented programming: a new class of code-reuse attack. In: ACM Symposium on Information, Computer and Communications Security, pp. 30–40 (2011)
4. Cheng, Y., Zhou, Z., Miao, Y., Ding, X., Deng, H.R.: ROPecker: a generic and practical approach for defending against ROP attacks. In: Symposium on Network and Distributed System Security (2014)
5. Christoulakis, N., Christou, G., Athanasopoulos, E., Ioannidis, S.: HCFI: Hardware-enforced Control-Flow Integrity. In: ACM Conference on Data and Application Security and Privacy, pp. 38–49 (2016)

6. CoreSight^{TM} Program Flow Trace^{TM}. http://infocenter.arm.com/help/topic/com. arm.doc.ihi0035b/IHI0035B_cs_pft_v1_1_architecture_spec.pdf

7. Das, S., Liu, Y., Zhang, W., Mahinthan, C.: Semantics-based online malware detection: towards efficient real-time protection against malware. IEEE Trans. Inf. Forensics Secur. **11**(2), 289–302 (2016)

8. Das, S., Zhang, W., Liu, Y.: A fine-grained control flow integrity approach against runtime memory attacks for embedded systems. IEEE Trans. Very Large Scale Integr. Syst. **24**(11), 3193–3207 (2016)

9. Davi, L., et al.: MoCFI: a framework to mitigate control-flow attacks on smartphones. In: Symposium on Network and Distributed System Security (2012)

10. Davi, L., et al.: HAFIX: Hardware-assisted Flow Integrity Extension. In: Annual Design Automation Conference, pp. 74:1–74: 6 (2015)

11. Davi, L., Sadeghi, A.-R., Lehmann, D., Monrose, F.: Stitching the gadgets: on the ineffectiveness of coarse-grained control-flow integrity protection. In: USENIX Conference on Security, pp. 401–416 (2014)

12. de Clercq, R., Gtzfried, J., Bler, D., Maene, P., Verbauwhede, I.: SOFIA: Software and Control Flow Integrity Architecture. Comput. Secur. **68**(C), 16–35 (2017)

13. Ding, R., Qian, C., Song, C., Harris, B., Kim, T., Lee, W.: Efficient protection of path-sensitive control security. In: USENIX Conference on Security, pp. 131–148 (2017)

14. Francillon, A., Perito, D., Castelluccia, C.: Defending embedded systems against control flow attacks. In: ACM Workshop on Secure Execution of Untrusted Code, pp. 19–26 (2009)

15. Ge, X., Cui, W., Jaeger, T.: GRIFFIN: guarding control flows using Intel Processor trace. In: International Conference on Architectural Support for Programming Languages and Operating Systems, pp. 585–598 (2017)

16. Gu, Y., Zhao, Q., Zhang, Y., Lin, Z.: PT-CFI: transparent backward-edge control flow violation detection using Intel Processor Trace. In: ACM Conference on Data and Application Security and Privacy, pp. 173–184 (2017)

17. Guo, Z., Bhakta, R., Harris, I.G.: Control-flow checking for intrusion detection via a real-time debug interface. In: International Conference on Smart Computing Workshops, pp. 87–92 (2014)

18. Huang, J., Rajagopalan, A.K.: Precise and maximal race detection from incomplete traces. In: ACM SIGPLAN International Conference on Object-Oriented Programming, Systems, Languages, and Applications, pp. 462–476 (2016)

19. IDA. https://www.hex-rays.com/products/ida/index.shtml

20. Intel CET. https://software.intel.com/sites/default/files/managed/4d/2a/controlflow-enforcement-technology-preview.pdf

21. Intel Quartus Prime. https://fpgasoftware.intel.com/17.1/?edition=lite

22. Kayaalp, M., Ozsoy, M., Abu-Ghazaleh, N., Ponomarev, D.: Branch regulation: low-overhead protection from code reuse attacks. In: Annual International Symposium on Computer Architecture, pp. 94–105 (2012)

23. Kayaalp, M., Ozsoy, M., Abu-Ghazaleh, N., Ponomarev, D.: Efficiently securing systems from code reuse attacks. IEEE Trans. Comput. **63**(5), 1144–1156 (2014)

24. Kayaalp, M., Schmitt, T., Nomani, J., Ponomarev, D., Abu-Ghazaleh, N.: SCRAP: architecture for signature-based protection from code reuse attacks. In: IEEE International Symposium on High Performance Computer Architecture, pp. 258–269 (2013)

25. Lee, Y., Lee, J., Heo, I., Hwang, D., Paek, Y.: Integration of ROP/JOP Monitoring IPs in an ARM-based SoC. In: Conference on Design, Automation & Test in Europe, pp. 331–336 (2016)

26. Lee, Y., Lee, J., Heo, I., Hwang, D., Paek, Y.: Using CoreSight PTM to Integrate CRA Monitoring IPs in an ARM-Based SoC. ACM Trans. Des. Autom. Electron. Syst. **22**(3), 52:1–52:25 (2017)
27. Liu, Y., Shi, P., Wang, X., Chen, H., Zang, B., Guan, H.: Transparent and efficient CFI enforcement with Intel processor trace. In: IEEE International Symposium on High Performance Computer Architecture, pp. 529–540 (2017)
28. Mao, S., Wolf, T.: Hardware support for secure processing in embedded systems. In: Annual Design Automation Conference, pp. 483–488 (2007)
29. Ozdoganoglu, H., Vijaykumar, T.N., Brodley, C.E., Kuperman, B.A., Jalote, A.: SmashGuard: a hardware solution to prevent security attacks on the function return address. IEEE Trans. Comput. **55**(10), 1271–1285 (2006)
30. Pappas, V., Polychronakis, M., Keromytis, A.D.: Transparent ROP exploit mitigation using indirect branch tracing. In: USENIX Conference on Security, pp. 447–462 (2013)
31. Putnam, A., et al.: A reconfigurable fabric for accelerating large-scale datacenter services. IEEE Micro **35**(3), 10–22 (2015)
32. Rahmatian, M., Kooti, H., Harris, I.G., Bozorgzadeh, E.: Hardware-assisted detection of malicious software in embedded systems. IEEE Embedd. Syst. Lett. **4**(4), 94–97 (2012)
33. RIPE. https://github.com/johnwilander/RIPE
34. Shacham, H.: The geometry of innocent flesh on the bone: Return-into-libc without function calls (on the x86). In: ACM Conference on Computer and Communications Security, pp. 552–561 (2007)
35. Source Code of FastCFI. https://github.com/flwave/FastCFI
36. SPEC CPU 2006 Benchmark. https://www.spec.org/cpu2006/
37. Sullivan, D., Arias, O., Davi, L., Larsen, P., Sadeghi, A.-R., Jin, Y.: Strategy without tactics: policy-agnostic hardware-enhanced control-flow integrity. In: Annual Design Automation Conference, pp. 1–6 (2016)
38. Wilander, J., Nikiforakis, N., Younan, Y., Kamkar, M., Joosen, W.: RIPE: Runtime Intrusion Prevention Evaluator. In: Annual Computer Security Applications Conference, pp. 41–50 (2011)
39. Write XOR Execute. https://en.wikipedia.org/wiki/W%5EX
40. Xia, Y., Liu, Y., Chen, H., Zang, B.: CFIMon: detecting violation of control flow integrity using performance counters. In: IEEE/IFIP International Conference on Dependable Systems and Networks, pp. 1–12 (2012)
41. Zhang, M., Sekar, R.: Control flow integrity for COTS binaries. In: USENIX Conference on Security, pp. 337–352 (2013)

An Extension of LTL with Rules and Its Application to Runtime Verification

Klaus Havelund[1(✉)] and Doron Peled[2(✉)]

[1] Jet Propulsion Laboratory, California Institute of Technology, Pasadena, USA
klaus.havelund@jpl.nasa.gov, doron.peled@gmail.com
[2] Department of Computer Science, Bar Ilan University, Ramat Gan, Israel

Abstract. Runtime Verification (RV) consists of analyzing execution traces using formal techniques, e.g., monitoring executions against Linear Temporal Logic (LTL) properties. Propositional LTL is, however, limited in expressiveness, as first shown by Wolper [32]. Several extensions to propositional LTL, which promote the expressive power to that of regular expressions, have therefore been proposed; however, none of which was, by and large, adopted for RV. In addition, for many practical cases, there is a need in RV to monitor properties that carry data. This problem has been addressed by numerous authors, and in previous work we addressed this by providing an algorithm that uses BDDs to represent relations over data elements. We show expressiveness deficiencies of first-order LTL and suggest an extension of (propositional as well as first-order) LTL with rules to address these limitations. We describe how the DEJAVU tool is correspondingly extended and provide some experimental results.

1 Introduction

Runtime verification (RV) [3,20] refers to the use of rigorous (formal) techniques for *processing* execution traces emitted by a system being observed. The purpose is typically to evaluate the behavior of the observed system. We focus here on *specification-based* runtime verification, where an execution trace is checked against a property expressed in a formal logic, in our case variants of Linear Temporal Logic (LTL).

LTL is a common specification formalism for reactive and concurrent systems. It is often used in model checking and runtime verification. Another formalism that is used for the same purpose is finite automata, often over infinite words. This includes Büchi, Rabin, Street, Muller and Parity automata [31], all having the same expressive power. In fact, model checking of an LTL specification is usually performed by first translating the specification into a Büchi automaton. The automata formalisms are more expressive than LTL, with a classical example by Wolper [32], showing that it

---

K. Havelund—The research performed by this author was carried out at Jet Propulsion Laboratory, California Institute of Technology, under a contract with the National Aeronautics and Space Administration.

D. Peled—The research performed by this author was partially funded by Israeli Science Foundation grant 1464/18: "Efficient Runtime Verification for Systems with Lots of Data and its Applications".

B. Finkbeiner and L. Mariani (Eds.): RV 2019, LNCS 11757, pp. 239–255, 2019.
https://doi.org/10.1007/978-3-030-32079-9_14

is not possible to express in LTL that every even state in the sequence satisfies some proposition *p*. This has motivated extending LTL in various ways to achieve the same expressive power as Büchi automata: Wolper's ETL [32,33] uses right-linear grammars, Sistla's QLTL extends LTL with dynamic (i.e., state-dependent, second-order) *quantification over propositions* [30] and the PSL standard [23] extends LTL with regular expressions. However, these and other extensions have not been extensively used for RV.

We therefore first present an alternative extension of propositional LTL with *rules*, named RLTL. These rules define and use auxiliary propositions, not appearing in the execution itself. These propositions obtain their values in a state as a function of the prefix of the execution up to and including that state, expressed as a past time temporal formula. This extension fits easily and naturally to existing RV algorithms that use incremental summaries of prefixes, e.g., the classical algorithm [21] for past time LTL (denoted here PLTL), maintaining also its linear time complexity (in the length of the trace and the size of the formula). In fact, our extension of the logic is inspired by that RV algorithm. The logic RLTL is shown to be equivalent to QLTL and its restriction to past properties is equivalent to Büchi automata and regular expressions.

Another expressiveness dimension is runtime verification of events that carry data, for which a first-order LTL supporting *quantification over data* is appropriate, here referred to as FLTL. We demonstrate the weakness of FLTL in expressing Wolper's example, relativized to the first-order case, and in expressing the transitive closure of temporal relations over events. We therefore introduce two alternative ways of extending the expressive power of FLTL, corresponding, respectively, to the propositional logics QLTL and RLTL. The first adds quantification over relations of data, obtaining a logic referred to as QFLTL. The second extension adds rules for the first-order case, and is referred to as RFLTL. Both of these extended logics can express the above examples. We show that for the first-order case, in contrast to the propositional case, the extension of the logic with quantification is more expressive than the extension with rules.

Runtime verification is commonly restricted to the *past time* versions of LTL, i.e., to *safety* properties [1], where a violation can be detected and demonstrated after a finite prefix of the execution. We refer to the logic PLTL for the propositional case and to PFLTL for the first-order case; these logics also enjoy elegant RV algorithms, based on the ability to compute summaries of the observed prefixes [18,21], as opposed to future temporal logics [25]. The RV algorithm, presented here for RPFLTL (the safety part of RFLTL) naturally extends the RV algorithm for PFLTL in [18] in the same way that the algorithm we present for RPLTL (the safety part of RLTL) extends the RV algorithm in [21] for PLTL.

We further present a corresponding extension of the DEJAVU tool [17–19], that realizes the extension of first-order past time LTL with rules (RPFLTL). The DEJAVU tool allows runtime verification of past time first-order temporal logic over infinite domains (e.g., the integers, strings, etc.). It achieves efficiency by using a unique BDD representation of the data part; BDDs correspond to relations over a Boolean enumeration of the input data (with a hash table representing the correspondence between the data and the enumerations). This is a very different use of BDDs from the classical model checking representation of sets of Boolean states[1]. A garbage collection algorithm tailored for that representation also assists in obtaining efficiency.

Our main contribution is the LTL logics extended with rules (extensions prefixed with 'R'), and in particular the logic RPFLTL and its implementation. The structure of the paper reflects our step-wise approach by first exploring the problem in the propositional case to form a basic understanding, and then by addressing the more interesting first-order case.

Numerous monitoring related expressive logics and systems have been developed over the past decades. In the database community, relations have been added to temporal databases for aggregation [22], calculating functions (sums etc.). Aggregations were also used in the runtime verification tool MONPOLY [4]. Numerous other systems have been produced for monitoring execution traces with data against formal specifications. These include e.g. MOP [27], QEA [29], and LARVA [12], which provide automaton-based data parameterized logics; LOLA [2], which is based on stream processing; BEEPBEEP [15] which is temporal logic-based; and the rule-based LOGFIRE [16]. These systems address the expressiveness issues discussed in this paper in different ways. Our approach differs from earlier such work by taking a starting point in LTL and extending it with rules, implemented using BDDs.

Conventions. As already outlined above, we present several versions of LTL. We name the different versions by prefixing LTL with the following letters. 'P' : restricted to *Past*-time temporal operators; 'F' : allowing *First*-order (static) quantification over data assigned to variables; 'Q' : adding second-order (dynamic) *Quantification* over propositions/predicates; and finally 'R' : adding *Rules*, our main contribution.

2   Propositional LTL

The classical definition of linear temporal logic [26] has the following syntax:

$$\varphi ::= true \mid p \mid (\varphi \wedge \varphi) \mid \neg \varphi \mid \bigcirc \varphi \mid (\varphi \, \mathcal{U} \, \varphi) \mid \ominus \varphi \mid (\varphi \, \mathcal{S} \, \psi)$$

where p is a proposition from a finite set of propositions P, and $\bigcirc$, $\mathcal{U}$, $\ominus$, $\mathcal{S}$ stand for *next-time, until, previous-time* and *since*, respectively. The models for LTL formulas are infinite sequence of states, of the form $\sigma = s_1 s_2 s_3 \ldots$, where $s_i \subseteq P$ for each $i \geq 1$. These are the propositions that *hold* in that state. LTL's semantics is defined as follows:

- $(\sigma, i) \models true$.
- $(\sigma, i) \models p$ if $p \in s_i$.
- $(\sigma, i) \models \neg \varphi$ if $(\sigma, i) \not\models \varphi$.
- $(\sigma, i) \models (\varphi \wedge \psi)$ if $(\sigma, i) \models \varphi$ and $(\sigma, i) \models \psi$.
- $(\sigma, i) \models \bigcirc \varphi$ if $(\sigma, i+1) \models \varphi$.
- $(\sigma, i) \models (\varphi \, \mathcal{U} \, \psi)$ if for some $j, j \geq i$, $(\sigma, j) \models \psi$, and for each $k, i \leq k < j, (\sigma, k) \models \varphi$.
- $(\sigma, i) \models \ominus \varphi$ if $i > 1$ and $(\sigma, i-1) \models \varphi$.

---

[1] E.g., in [6], BDDs are used to represent sets of program locations, and the data elements are represented symbolically as a formula.

- $(\sigma, i) \models (\varphi \, S \, \psi)$ if there exists j, $1 \leq j \leq i$, such that $(\sigma, j) \models \psi$ and for each k, $j < k \leq i$, $(\sigma, k) \models \varphi$.

Then $\sigma \models \varphi$ when $(\sigma, 1) \models \varphi$. We can use the following abbreviations: $false = \neg true$, $(\varphi \vee \psi) = \neg(\neg\varphi \wedge \neg\psi)$, $(\varphi \rightarrow \psi) = (\neg\varphi \vee \psi)$, $\Diamond\varphi = (true \, \mathcal{U} \, \varphi)$, $\Box\varphi = \neg\Diamond\neg\varphi$, $\mathbf{P}\,\varphi = (true \, S \, \varphi)$ ($\mathbf{P}$ stands for *Previously*) and $\mathbf{H}\,\varphi = \neg\mathbf{P}\,\neg\varphi$ ($\mathbf{H}$ stands for *History*).

The expressive power of different versions of propositional LTL is often compared to regular expressions over the alphabet $\sigma = 2^P$ and to *monadic* first and second-order logic. Accordingly, we have the following characterizations: LTL is equivalent to monadic first-order logic, star-free regular expressions[2] and counter-free Büchi automata. For an overview of logic and automata see [31]. Restricting the temporal operators to the *future* operators $\mathcal{U}$ and $\bigcirc$ (and the ones derived from them $\Box$ and $\Diamond$) maintains the same expressive power. An important subset of LTL, called here PLTL, allows only past temporal operators: S, $\ominus$ and the operators derived from them, $\mathbf{H}$ and $\mathbf{P}$. The past time logic is sometimes interpreted over finite sequences, where $\sigma \models \varphi$ when $(\sigma, |\sigma|) \models \varphi$. It is also a common practice to use a PLTL formula, prefixed with a single $\Box$ (always) operator; in this case, *each of the prefixes* has to satisfy φ. This later form expresses *safety* LTL properties [1]. When PLTL is interpreted over finite sequences, its expressive power is the same as star-free regular expressions, first-order monadic logic over finite sequences and counting-free automata. Wolper [32] demonstrated that the expressive power of LTL is lacking using the property that all the states with even[3] indexes in a sequence satisfy some proposition p.

Extending LTL with Dynamic Quantification. Adding quantification over propositions, suggested by Sistla in [30], allows writing a formula of the form $\exists q \varphi$, where $\exists q$ represents *existential* quantification over a proposition q that can appear in φ. To define the semantics, let $X \subseteq P$ and denote $\sigma|_X = s_1 \setminus X \, s_2 \setminus X \ldots$. (Note that $\sigma|_X$ denotes projecting *out* the propositions in X.) The semantics is defined as follows:

- $(\sigma, i) \models \exists q \varphi$ if there exists σ' such that $\sigma'|_{\{q\}} = \sigma$ and $(\sigma', i) \models \varphi$.

Universal quantification is also allowed, where $\forall q \varphi = \neg \exists q \neg \varphi$. This kind of quantification is considered to be *dynamic*, since the quantified propositions can have different truth values depending on the states. It is also called *second-order* quantification, since the quantification establishes the *set* of states in which a proposition has the value *true*. Extending LTL with such quantification, the logic QLTL has the same expressive power as regular expressions, full Büchi automata, or monadic second-order logic with unary predicates over the naturals (see again [31]). In fact, it is sufficient to restrict the quantification to existential quantifiers that prefix the formula to obtain the full expressiveness of QLTL [31]. Restricting QLTL to the past modalities, one obtains the logic QPLTL. QPLTL has the same expressive power as regular expressions and finite automata. Wolper's property can be rewritten in QPLTL as:

$$\exists q \, \mathbf{H}((q \leftrightarrow \ominus \neg q) \wedge (q \rightarrow p)) \tag{1}$$

---

[2] Regular expressions without the star operator (or ω).

[3] This is different than stating that p alternates between *true* and *false* on consecutive states.

Since $\ominus\varphi$ is interpreted as *false* in the first state of any sequence, regardless of φ, then q is *false* in the first state. Then q alternates between even and odd states.

Extending LTL with Rules. We introduce another extension of LTL, which we call RLTL. As will be showed later, this extension is very natural for runtime verification. We partition the propositions P into *auxiliary propositions* $A = \{a_1, \ldots, a_n\}$ and *basic propositions* B. An RLTL property η has the following form:

$$\psi \text{ where } a_j := \varphi_j : j \in \{1,\ldots,n\} \tag{2}$$

where each a_j is a distinct auxiliary proposition from A, ψ is an LTL property and each φ_i is a PLTL property where propositions from A can only occur within the scope of a $\ominus$ operator. We refer to ψ as the *statement* of η and to $a_j := \varphi_j$ as a *rule* (in text, rules will be separated by commas). The semantics can be defined as follows.

$$\sigma \models \eta \text{ if there exists } \sigma', \text{ where } \sigma'|_A = \sigma \text{ s.t. } \sigma' \models (\psi \wedge \square \bigwedge_{1 \leq j \leq n}(a_j \leftrightarrow \varphi_j))$$

RLTL extends the set of propositions with new propositions, whose values at a state are functions of (i.e., uniquely defined by) the prefix of the model up to that state. This differs from the use of auxiliary propositions in QLTL, where the values assigned to the auxiliary propositions do not have to extend the states of the model in a unique way throughout the interpretation of the property over a model. The constraint that auxiliary propositions appearing in the formulas φ_i must occur within the scope of a $\ominus$ operator is required to prevent conflicting rules, as in $a_1 := \neg a_2$ and $a_2 := a_1$. Wolper's example can be written in RLTL as follows:

$$\square(q \to p) \text{ where } q := \ominus \neg q \tag{3}$$

where $A = \{q\}$ and $B = \{p\}$. The auxiliary proposition q is used to augment the input sequence such that each *odd* state will satisfy $\neg q$ and each *even* state will satisfy q.

Lemma 1 (Well foundedness of auxiliary propositions). *The values of the auxiliary propositions of an RLTL formula η are uniquely defined in a state of an execution by the prefix of the execution up to and including that state.*

Proof. Let η be a formula over auxiliary propositions A and basic propositions B, with rules $a_j := \varphi_j : j \in \{1,\ldots,n\}$. Let σ be a model with states over B. Then there is a unique model σ' such that $\sigma'|_A = \sigma$ and $\sigma' \models \square \bigwedge_{1 \leq j \leq n}(a_j \leftrightarrow \varphi_j)$: inductively, the value of each auxiliary proposition a_j at the ith state of σ' is defined, via a rule $a_j := \varphi_j$, where φ_j is a PLTL formula; hence it depends on the values of the propositions B in the ith state of σ, and on the values of $A \cup B$ in the previous states of σ'. $\square$

Theorem 1. *The expressive power of RLTL is the same as QLTL.*

Sketch of Proof. Each RLTL formula η, as defined in (2), is expressible using the following equivalent QLTL formula:

$$\exists a_1 \ldots \exists a_n (\psi \wedge \square \bigwedge_{1 \leq j \leq n} (a_j \leftrightarrow \varphi_j))$$

For the other direction, one can first translate the QLTL property into a second-order monadic logic formula, then to a deterministic Muller automata and then construct an RLTL formula that holds for the accepting executions of this automaton. The rules of this formula encode the automata states, and the statement describes the acceptance condition of the Muller automaton.   □

We define RPLTL by disallowing the future time temporal operators in RLTL. Every top level formula is interpreted as implicitly being prefixed with a □ operator, hence is checked in every state. This results in a formalism that is equivalent to a Büchi automata, where all the states except one are accepting and where the non-accepting state is a sink. We can use a related, but simpler construction than in Theorem 1 to prove the following:

Lemma 2. *The expressive power of RPLTL is the same as QPLTL.*

Lemma 3. *RPLTL can, with no loss of expressive power, be restricted to the form:*

$$\Box p \text{ where } a_j = \varphi_j : j \in \{1,\ldots,n\}$$

with p being one of the auxiliary propositions a_j and φ_j contains only a single occurrence of the $\ominus$ temporal operator (and the Boolean operators).

In this form, the value of the Boolean variables a_j encodes the states of an automaton, and the rules encode the transitions.

3   RV for Propositional Past Time LTL and Its Extension

Runtime verification of temporal specifications often concentrates on the past portion of the logic. Past time specifications have the important property that one can distinguish when they are violated after observing a finite prefix of an execution. For an extended discussion of this issue of *monitorability*, see e.g., [5,13]. The RV algorithm for PLTL, presented in [21], is based on the observation that the semantics of the past time formulas $\ominus\varphi$ and $(\varphi S \psi)$ in the current state i is defined in terms of the semantics of its subformula(s) in the previous state $i-1$. To demonstrate this, we rewrite the semantic definition of the S operator to a form that is more applicable for runtime verification.

– $(\sigma,i) \models (\varphi S \psi)$ if $(\sigma,i) \models \psi$ or: $i > 1$ and $(\sigma,i) \models \varphi$ and $(\sigma,i-1) \models (\varphi S \psi)$.

The semantic definition is recursive in both the length of the prefix and the structure of the property. Thus, subformulas are evaluated based on smaller subformulas, and the evaluation of subformulas in the previous state. The algorithm shown below uses two vectors of values indexed by subformulas: pre, which summarizes the truth values of the subformulas for the execution prefix that ends just *before* the current state, and now, for the execution prefix that ends with the current state. The order of calculating now for subformulas is bottom up, according to the syntax tree.

1. Initially, for each subformula φ of η, $\text{now}(\varphi) := \textit{false}$.
2. Observe a new event (as a set of propositions) s as input.
3. Let pre := now.

4. Make the following updates for each subformula. If φ is a subformula of ψ then $\text{now}(\varphi)$ is updated before $\text{now}(\psi)$.
   - $\text{now}(true) := true$.
   - $\text{now}(\varphi \wedge \psi) := \text{now}(\varphi)$ *and* $\text{now}(\psi)$.
   - $\text{now}(\neg\varphi) := not\ \text{now}(\varphi)$.
   - $\text{now}(\varphi S \psi) := \text{now}(\psi)$ *or* $(\text{now}(\varphi)$ *and* $\text{pre}((\varphi S \psi)))$.
   - $\text{now}(\ominus \varphi) := \text{pre}(\varphi)$.
5. If $\text{now}(\eta) = false$ then report a violation, otherwise goto step 2.

Runtime Verification for RPLTL. For RPLTL, we need to add to the above algorithm calculations of $\text{now}(a_j)$ and $\text{now}(\varphi_j)$ for each rule of the form $a_j := \varphi_j$ (the corresponding pre entries will be updated as in line 3 in the above algorithm). Because the auxiliary propositions can appear recursively in RPLTL rules, the order of calculation is subtle. To see this, consider, for example, Formula (3). It contains the definition $q := \ominus\neg q$. We cannot calculate this bottom up, as we did for PLTL, since $\text{now}(q)$ is not computed yet, and we need to calculate $\text{now}(\ominus\neg q)$ in order to compute $\text{now}(q)$. However, notice that the calculation is not dependent on the value of q to calculate $\ominus\neg q$; in Step 4 above, we have that $\text{now}(\ominus \varphi) := \text{pre}(\varphi)$ so $\text{now}(\ominus\neg q) := \text{pre}(\neg q)$.

Mixed Evaluation Order. Under mixed evaluation order, one calculates now as part of Step 4 of the above algorithm in the following order.

a. Calculate $\text{now}(\delta)$ for each subformula δ that appears in φ_j of a rule $a_j := \varphi_j$, but *not* within the scope of a $\ominus$ operator (observe that $\text{now}(\ominus\gamma)$ is set to $\text{pre}(\gamma)$).
b. Set $\text{now}(a_j)$ to $\text{now}(\varphi_j)$ for each j.
c. Calculate $\text{now}(\delta)$ for each subformula δ that appears in φ_j of a rule $a_j := \varphi_j$ *within* the scope of a $\ominus$ operator.
d. Calculate $\text{now}(\delta)$ for each subformula δ that appears in the statement ψ, using the calculated $\text{now}(a_j)$.

4   First-Order LTL

Assume a finite set of infinite domains[4] $D_1, D_2, \ldots$, e.g., integers or strings. Let V be a finite set of *variables*, with typical instances x, y, z. An *assignment* over a set of variables V maps each variable $x \in V$ to a value from its associated domain $domain(x)$, where multiple variables (or all of them) can be related to the same domain. For example $[x \rightarrow 5, y \rightarrow$ "abc"$]$ assigns the values 5 to x and the value "abc" to y.

We define models for FLTL based on *temporal* relations [9], that is, relations with last parameter that is a natural number, representing a time instance in the execution. So a tuple of a relation R can be ("a", 5, "cbb", 3), where 3 is the value of the time parameter. The last parameter i represents a discrete progress of time rather than modeling *physical real time*. It is used to allow the relations to have different tuples in different instances of i, corresponding to states in the propositional temporal logics.

For a relation R, $R[i]$ is the relation obtained from R by restricting it to the value i in the last parameter, and removing that last i from the tuples. For simplicity, we will

---

[4] Finite domains are handled with some minor changes, see [18].

describe henceforth the logic with relations R that have exactly two parameters, the second of which is the time instance. Hence $R[i]$ is a relation with just one parameter over a domain that will be denoted as $dom(R)$. The definition of the logic that allows relations with more parameters is quite straightforward. Our implementation, and the examples described later, fully support relations with zero or more parameters.

Syntax. The formulas of the core FLTL logic are defined by the following grammar, where p denotes a relation, a denotes a constant and x denotes a variable.

$$\varphi ::= true \mid p(a) \mid p(x) \mid (\varphi \wedge \varphi) \mid \neg\varphi \mid \bigcirc\varphi \mid (\varphi \; \mathcal{U} \; \varphi) \mid \ominus \varphi \mid (\varphi \; \mathcal{S} \; \varphi) \mid \exists x \; \varphi$$

Additional operators are defined as in the propositional logic. We define $\forall x \; \varphi = \neg\exists x \neg\varphi$. Restricting the modal operators to the past operators ($\mathcal{S}$, $\ominus$ and the ones derived from them) forms the logic PFLTL.

Semantics. A model is a set of temporal relations $\mathcal{R} = \{R_1 \ldots, R_m\}$. Since the standard definition of temporal logic is over a sequence ("the execution"), let $\mathcal{R}[i] = \{R_1[i] \ldots, R_m[i]\}$. $\mathcal{R}[i]$ represents a *state*. A model $\mathcal{R}$ can thus be seen as a sequence of states $\mathcal{R}[1]\mathcal{R}[2]\ldots$. Let m be a bijection from relation names (syntax) to the relations $\mathcal{R}$ (semantics).

Let $free(\varphi)$ be the set of free (i.e., unquantified) variables of a subformula φ. We denote by $\gamma|_{free(\varphi)}$ the restriction (projection) of an assignment γ to the free variables appearing in φ. Let ε be the empty assignment (with no variables). In any of the following cases, $(\gamma, \mathcal{R}, i) \models \varphi$ is defined where γ is an assignment over $free(\varphi)$, and $i \geq 1$.

- $(\varepsilon, \mathcal{R}, i) \models true$.
- $(\varepsilon, \mathcal{R}, i) \models p(a)$ if $m(p)(a, i)$, where a denotes a constant from $dom(m(p))$.
- $([x \mapsto a], \mathcal{R}, i) \models p(x)$ if $m(p)(a, i)$, where $domain(x) = dom(m(p))$.
- $(\gamma, \mathcal{R}, i) \models (\varphi \wedge \psi)$ if $(\gamma|_{free(\varphi)}, \mathcal{R}, i) \models \varphi$ and $(\gamma|_{free(\psi)}, \mathcal{R}, i) \models \psi$.
- $(\gamma, \mathcal{R}, i) \models \neg\varphi$ if not $(\gamma, \mathcal{R}, i) \models \varphi$.
- $(\gamma, \mathcal{R}, i) \models \bigcirc\varphi$ if $(\gamma, \mathcal{R}, i+1) \models \varphi$.
- $(\gamma, \mathcal{R}, i) \models (\varphi \; \mathcal{U} \; \psi)$ if for some j, $j \geq i$, $(\gamma|_{free(\psi)}, \mathcal{R}, j) \models \psi$ and for each k, $i \leq k < j$, $(\gamma|_{free(\varphi)}, \mathcal{R}, k) \models \varphi$.
- $(\gamma, \mathcal{R}, i) \models \ominus\varphi$ if $i > 1$ and $(\gamma, \mathcal{R}, i-1) \models \varphi$.
- $(\gamma, \mathcal{R}, i) \models (\varphi \; \mathcal{S} \; \psi)$ if for some j, $1 \leq j \leq i$, $(\gamma|_{free(\psi)}, \mathcal{R}, j) \models \psi$ and for each k, $j < k \leq i$, $(\gamma|_{free(\varphi)}, \mathcal{R}, k) \models \varphi$.
- $(\gamma, \mathcal{R}, i) \models \exists x \; \varphi$ if there exists $a \in domain(x)$ such that[5] $(\gamma[x \mapsto a], \sigma, i) \models \varphi$.

For an FLTL (PFLTL) formula with no free variables, denote $\mathcal{R} \models \varphi$ when $(\varepsilon, \mathcal{R}, 1) \models \varphi$. We will henceforce, less formally, use the same symbols both for the relations (semantics) and their representation in the logic (syntax). Note that the letters p, q, r, which were used for representing propositions in the propositional versions of the logic in previous sections, will represent relations in the first-order versions. The quantification over values of variables, denoted with $\exists$ and $\forall$, here is *static* in the sense that they are independent of the state in the execution. We demonstrate that the lack of expressiveness carries over from LTL (PLTL) to FLTL (PFLTL).

---

[5] $\gamma[x \mapsto a]$ is the overriding of γ with the binding $[x \mapsto a]$.

Example 1. Let p and q be temporal relations. The specification that we want to monitor is that for each value a, $p(a)$ appears in all the states where $q(a)$ has appeared an even number of times so far (for the odd occurrences, $p(a)$ can also appear, but does not have to appear). To show that this is not expressible in FLTL (and PFLTL), consider models (executions) where only one data element a appears. Assume for the contradiction that there is an FLTL formula ψ that expresses this property. We recursively replace in ψ, each subformula of the form $\exists\varphi$ by a disjunction over copies of φ, in which the quantified occurrences of $p(x)$ and $q(x)$ are replaced by p_a and q_a, respectively or to *false*; the *false* represents the Boolean value of $p(x)$ and $q(x)$ for any $x \neq a$, since only $p(a)$ and $q(a)$ may appear in the input. For example, $\exists x(q(x)Sp(x))$ becomes $(q_a S p_a) \vee (false S false)$ (which can be simplified to $(q_a S p_a)$). Similarly, subformulas of the form $\forall\varphi$ are replaced by conjunctions. This results in an LTL formula that holds in a model, where each $p(a)$ is replaced by p_a and each $q(a)$ is replaced by q_a, iff ψ holds for the original model. But Wolper's example [32] contradicts the assumption that such a formula exists. Using parametric automata as a specification formalism, as in [14,20,27,29], can express this property, where for each value a there is a separate automaton that counts the number of times that $q(a)$ has occurred.

Example 2. Consider the property that asserts that when $report(y,x,d)$ appears in a state, denoting that process y sends some data d to a process x, there was a chain of process spawns: $spawn(x,x_1), spawn(x_1,x_2) \ldots spawn(x_l,y)$. i.e., y is a descendent process of x. The required property involves the transitive closure of the relation $spawn$. FLTL can be translated (in a way similar to the standard translation of *LTL* into monadic first-order logic formula [31]) to a first-order formula, with explicit occurrences of time variables over the naturals and the linear order relation $<$ (or $\leq$) between them. For example, $\Box\forall x(p(x) \rightarrow \Diamond q(x))$ will be translated into $\forall x\forall t(p(x,t) \rightarrow \exists t'(t \leq t' \wedge q(x,t')))$. However, the transitive closure of $spawn$ cannot be expressed in first-order setting. This can be shown based on the compactness theory of first-order logic [11].

Extending FLTL with Dynamic Quantification. Relations play in FLTL a similar role to propositions in LTL. Hence, in correspondence with the relation between LTL and QLTL, we extend FLTL (PFLTL) with dynamic quantification over relations, obtaining QFLTL (and the past-restricted version QPFLTL). The syntax includes $\exists p\varphi$, where p denotes a relation. We also allow $\forall p\, \varphi = \neg\exists p\neg\varphi$. The semantics is as follows.

- $(\gamma,\mathcal{R},i) \models \exists q\varphi$ if there exists $\mathcal{R}'$ such that $\mathcal{R}' \setminus \{q\} = \mathcal{R}$ and $(\gamma,\mathcal{R}',i) \models \varphi$.

Consequently, quantification over relations effectively extends the model $\mathcal{R}$ into a model $\mathcal{R}'$ within the scope of the quantifier. Note that quantification here is dynamic (as in QLTL and QPLTL) since the relations are temporal and can have different sets of tuples in different states.

Extending FLTL with Rules. We now extend FLTL into RFLTL in a way that is motivated by the propositional extension from LTL (PLTL) to RLTL (RPLTL). We allow the following formula:

$$\psi \text{ where } r_j(x_j) := \varphi_j(x_j) : j \in \{1,\ldots,n\} \quad \text{such that,} \tag{4}$$

1. ψ, the *statement*, is an FLTL formula with no free variables,
2. φ_j are PFLTL formulas with a single[6] free variable x_j,
3. r_j is an auxiliary temporal relation with two parameters: the first parameter is of the same type as x_j and the second one is, as usual, a natural number that is omitted in the temporal formulas. An auxiliary relation r_j can appear within ψ. They can also appear in φ_k of a *rule* $r_k := \varphi_k$, but only within the scope of a previous-time operator $\ominus$.

We define the semantics for the RFLTL (RPFLTL) specification (4) by using the following equivalent QFLTL (QPFLTL, respectively) formula[7]:

$$\exists r_1 \dots \exists r_n (\psi \wedge \Box \bigwedge_{j \in \{1,\dots,n\}} (r_j(x_j) \leftrightarrow \varphi_i(x_j))) \tag{5}$$

The logic RPFLTL is obtained by restricting the temporal modalities of RFLTL to the past ones: S and $\ominus$, and those derived from them.

Lemma 4 (Well foundedness of auxiliary relations). *The auxiliary temporal relations of an RFLTL formula at state i are uniquely defined by the prefix of the execution up to and including that state.*

Proof. By a simple induction, similar to Lemma 1. □

The following formula expresses the property described in Example 1, which was shown to be not expressible using FLTL.

$$\Box \forall x (r(x) \rightarrow p(x)) \text{ where } r(x) = (q(x) \leftrightarrow \ominus \neg r(x)) \tag{6}$$

The property that corresponds to Example 2 appears as the property spawning in Fig. 1 in the implementation Sect. 6.

Theorem 2. *The expressive power of RPFLTL is strictly weaker than that of QPFLTL.*

Sketch of Proof. The proof of this theorem includes encoding of a property that observes sets of data elements, where elements a, appears separately, i.e., one per state, as $v(a)$, in between states where r appears. The domain of data elements is unbounded. The set of a-values observed in between two consecutive r's is called a *data set*. The property asserts that there are no two consecutive data sets that are equivalent. This property can be expressed in QPFLTL.

We use a combinatorial argument to show by contradiction that one cannot express this property using any RPFLTL formula φ. The reason is that every prefix of a model for an RPFLTL property is extended uniquely with auxiliary relations, according to Lemma 4. Each prefix can be summarized by a finite number of relations: the ones in the model, the auxiliary relations and the assignments satisfying the subformulas. The size of each such relation is bounded by $O(m^N)$ where m is the number of values

---

[6] Again, the definition can be extended to any number of parameters.
[7] Formal semantics can also be given by constructing a set of temporal relations extended with the auxiliary ones inductively over growing prefixes.

appearing in the prefix, and N is the number of parameters of the relations. However, the number of different data sets over m values is 2^m. This means that with large enough number of different values, each RPFLTL formula φ over the models of this property can have two prefixes with the same summary, where one of them has a data set that the other one does not. The semantics of RPFLTL implies that extending two prefixes with the same summary in the same way would have the same truth value. Consequently, we can extend the two prefixes where some data set appears in one of them but not in the other into a complete model, and φ will not be able to distinguish between these models. □

From Theorem 2 and Eq. (5) we immediately obtain:

Corollary 1. *Restricting the quantification of QPFLTL to existential quantification, strictly weakens its expressive power*[8].

5   RV for Past Time First-Order LTL and Its Extension

Runtime verification of FLTL is performed on an input that consists of *events* in the form of tuples of relations. (A typical use of runtime verification restricts the events for each state to a single event.) In our notation, the input consists of a sequence $\mathcal{R}[1]\,\mathcal{R}[2]\ldots$, which we earlier identified with states, where each $\mathcal{R}[i]$ consists of the relations in $\mathcal{R}$ with the last parameter is restricted to i. The RV algorithm will make use of sets of assignments over a set of variables, satisfying a subformula at some state (and stored in pre and now), also represented as relations (instead of propositions, as used for LTL in Sect. 3).

Set Semantics. The RV algorithm for (R)PLTL, presented in Sect. 3 calculates $\text{now}(\varphi)$, for φ a subformula of the monitored property, to be the Boolean truth value of φ over the prefix inspected by the RV algorithm so far. For (R)PFLTL, $\text{now}(\varphi)$ denotes the set of assignments satisfying φ (in the form of relations over the free variables in the subformula), rather than a Boolean value. We provide an alternative *set semantics* for the logic RPFLTL, without changing its interpretation, in a way that is more directly related to the calculation of values in now by the RV algorithm that will be presented below. Under the set semantics (introduced in [18] for PFLTL, and extended here for RPFLTL), $I[\varphi,\sigma,i]$ denotes a set of assignments such that $\gamma \in I[\varphi,\sigma,i]$ iff $(\gamma,\sigma,i) \models \varphi$. We present here only two simple cases of the set semantics.

- $I[(\varphi \wedge \psi),\sigma,i] = I[\varphi,\mathcal{R},i] \cap I[\psi,\sigma,i]$.
- $I[(\varphi\,S\,\psi),\mathcal{R},i] = I[\psi,\mathcal{R},i] \cup (I[\varphi,\mathcal{R},i] \cap I[(\varphi S\psi),\mathcal{R},i-1])$.

Runtime Verification Algorithm for PFLTL. We start by describing an algorithm for monitoring PFLTL properties, presented in [18] and implemented in the tool DEJAVU. We enumerate data values appearing in monitored events, as soon as we first see them. We represent relations over the Boolean encoding of these enumeration, rather than over

---

[8] It is interesting to note that for QPLTL, restriction to existential quantification does not change the expressive power.

the data values themselves. A hash function is used to connect the data values to their enumerations to maintain consistency between these two representations. The relations are represented as BDDs [7]. For example, if the runtime-verifier sees the input events *open*("a"), *open*("b"), *open*("c"), it will encode the argument values as 000, 001 and 010 (say, we use 3 bits b_0, b_1 and b_2 to represent each enumeration, with b_2 being the most significant bit). A Boolean representation of the *set* of values {"a", "b"} would be equivalent to a Boolean function $(\neg b_1 \wedge \neg b_2)$ that returns 1 for 000 and 001.

Since we want to be able to deal with infinite domains (where only a finite number of elements may appear in a given observed prefix) and maintain the ability to perform complementation, unused enumerations represent the values that have not been seen yet. In fact, it is sufficient to have just one enumeration representing these values per each variable of the LTL formula. We guarantee that at least one such enumeration exists by preserving for that purpose the enumeration 11...11. We present here only the basic algorithm. For versions that allow extending the number of bits used for enumerations and garbage collection of enumerations, consult [17].

Given some ground predicate $p(a)$, observed in the monitored execution, matching with $p(x)$ in the monitored property, let **lookup**(x, a) be the enumeration of a (a lookup in the hash table). If this is a's first occurrence, then it will be assigned a new enumeration. Otherwise, **lookup** returns the enumeration that a received before. We can use a counter, for each variable x, counting the number of different values appearing so far for x. When a new value appears, this counter is incremented and converted to a Boolean representation. The function **build**(x, A) returns a BDD that represents the set of assignments where x is mapped to (the enumeration of) v for $v \in A$. This BDD is independent of the values assigned to any variable other than x, i.e., they can have any value. For example, assume that we use the three Boolean variables (bits) x_0, x_1 and x_2 for representing enumerations over x (with x_0 being the least significant bit), and assume that $A = \{a, b\}$, **lookup**$(x, a) = 000$, and **lookup**$(x, b) = 001$. Then **build**(x, A) is a BDD representation of the Boolean function $(\neg x_1 \wedge \neg x_2)$.

Intersection and union of sets of assignments are translated simply into conjunction and disjunction of their BDD representation, respectively; complementation becomes BDD negation. We will denote the Boolean BDD operators as **and**, **or** and **not**. To implement the existential (universal, respectively) operators, we use the BDD existential (universal, respectively) operators over the Boolean variables that represent (the enumerations of) the values of x. Thus, if B_φ is the BDD representing the assignments satisfying φ in the current state of the monitor, then **exists**$(\langle x_0, \ldots, x_{k-1} \rangle, B_\varphi)$ is the BDD that represents the assignments satisfying $\exists x \, \varphi$ in the current state. Finally, BDD$(\bot)$ and BDD$(\top)$ are the BDDs that return always 0 or 1, respectively. The algorithm for monitoring a formula η is as follows.

1. Initially, for each subformula φ of η, now$(\varphi) := $ BDD$(\bot)$.
2. Observe a new state (as a set of ground predicates) s_i as input.
3. Let pre $:=$ now.
4. Make the following updates for each subformula. If φ is a subformula of ψ then now(φ) is updated before now(ψ).
   - now$(true) := $ BDD$(\top)$.
   - now$(p_k(a)) := $ if $R_k[i](a)$ then BDD$(\top)$ else BDD$(\bot)$.

- $\text{now}(p_k(x)) := \textbf{build}(x, \{a \mid R_k[i](a)\})$.
- $\text{now}((\varphi \wedge \psi)) := \textbf{and}(\text{now}(\varphi), \text{now}(\psi))$.
- $\text{now}(\neg \varphi) := \textbf{not}(\text{now}(\varphi))$.
- $\text{now}((\varphi \, \mathcal{S} \, \psi)) := \textbf{or}(\text{now}(\psi), \textbf{and}(\text{now}(\varphi), \text{pre}((\varphi \, \mathcal{S} \, \psi))))$.
- $\text{now}(\ominus \varphi) := \text{pre}(\varphi)$.
- $\text{now}(\exists x \, \varphi) := \textbf{exists}(\langle x_0, \ldots, x_{k-1} \rangle, \text{now}(\varphi))$.
5. If $\text{now}(\eta) = false$ then report a violation, otherwise goto step 2.

RV Algorithm for RPFLTL. We extend now the algorithm to capture RPFLTL. The auxiliary relations r_j extend the model, and we need to keep BDDs representing $\text{now}(r_j)$ and $\text{pre}(r_j)$ for each relation r_j. We also need to calculate the subformulas φ_i that appear in a specification, as part of the runtime verification, as per the above PFLTL algorithm. One subtle point is that the auxiliary relations r_j may be defined in a rule with respect to a variable x_j as in $r_j(x_j) := \varphi_j(x_j)$ (this can be generalized to any number of variables), but r_j can be used as a subformula with other parameters in other rules or in the statement e.g., as $r_j(y)$. This can be resolved by a BDD renaming function $\textbf{rename}(r_j(x_j), y)$. We then add the following updates to step 4 of the above algorithm.

For each rule $r_j(x_j) := \varphi_j(x_j)$:
  calculate $\text{now}(\varphi_j)$;
  $\text{now}(r_j) := \text{now}(\varphi_j)$;
  $\text{now}(r_j(y)) := \textbf{rename}(r_j(x_j), y)$;
  $\text{now}(r_j(a)) :=$ if $\text{now}(r_j)(a)$ then $\text{BDD}(\top)$ else $\text{BDD}(\bot)$

As in the propositional case, the evaluation order cannot be simply top down or bottom up, since relations can appear both on the left and the right of a definition such as $r(x) := p(x) \vee \ominus r(x)$; we need to use the *mixed evaluation order*, described in Sect. 3.

Complexity. BDDs were first introduced to model checking [8] since they can often (but not always) allow a very compact representation of states. In our context, each BDD in pre or now represents a relation with k parameters, which summarizes the value of a subformula of the checked PFLTL or RPFLTL property with k free variables over the prefix observed so far. Hence, it can grow up to a size that is polynomial in the number of values appearing in the prefix, and exponential in k (with k being typically very small). However, the marriage of BDDs and Boolean enumeration is in particular efficient, since collections of adjacent Boolean enumerations tend to compact well.

6 Implementation

DEJAVU is implemented in SCALA. DEJAVU takes as input a specification file containing one or more properties, and synthesizes the monitor as a self-contained SCALA program. This program takes as input the trace file and analyzes it. The tool uses the JavaBDD library for BDD manipulations [24].

Example Properties. Figure 1 shows four properties in the input ASCII format of the tool, the first three of which are related to the examples in Sect. 4, which are not expressible in (P)FLTL. That is, these properties are not expressible in the original first-order

prop telemetry1 : **Forall** x . closed(x) → !telem(x) **where**
  closed(x) := toggle(x) ↔ @!closed(x)

prop telemetry2 : **Forall** x . closed(x) → !telem(x) **where**
  closed(x) := (!@**true** & !toggle(x)) | (@closed(x) & !toggle(x)) |
          (@open(x) & toggle(x)),
  open(x) := (@open(x) & !toggle(x)) | (@closed(x) & toggle(x))

prop spawning : **Forall** x . **Forall** y . **Forall** d . report(y,x,d) → spawned(x,y) **where**
  spawned(x,y) := @spawned(x,y) | spawn(x,y) |
          Exists z . (@spawned(x,z) & spawn(z,y))

prop commands : **Forall** c . dispatch(c) → ! already_dispatched(c) **where**
  already_dispatched(c) := @ [dispatch(c) , complete(c)),
  dispatch(c) := **Exists** t . CMD_DISPATCH(c,t),
  complete(c) := **Exists** t . CMD_COMPLETE(c,t)

Fig. 1. Properties stated in DEJAVU's logic

logic of DEJAVU presented in [18]. The last property illustrates the use of rules to perform conceptual abstraction. The ASCII version of the logic uses @ for ⊖, | for ∨, & for ∧, and ! for ¬. The first property telemetry1 is a variant of formula 6, illustrating the use of a rule to express a first-order version of Wolper's example [32], that all the states with even indexes of a sequence satisfy a property. In this case we consider a radio on board a spacecraft, which communicates over different channels (quantified over in the formula) that can be turned on and off with a toggle(x); they are initially off. Telemetry can only be sent to ground over a channel x with the telem(x) event when radio channel x is toggled on.

The second property, telemetry2, expresses the same property as telemetry1, but in this case using two rules, reflecting how we would model this using a state machine with two states for each channel x: closed(x) and open(x). The rule closed(x) is defined as a disjunction between three alternatives. The first states that this predicate is true if we are in the initial state (the only state where @**true** is false), and there is no toggle(x) event. The next alternative states that closed(x) was true in the previous state and there is no toggle(x) event. The third alternative states that in the previous state we were in the open(x) state and we observe a toggle(x) event. Similarly for the open(x) rule.

The third property, spawning, expresses a property about threads being spawned in an operating system. We want to ensure that when a thread y reports some data d back to another thread x, then thread y has been spawned by thread x either directly, or transitively via a sequence of spawn events. The events are spawn(x,y) (thread x spawns thread y) and report(y,x,d) (thread y reports data d back to thread x). For this we need to compute a transitive closure of spawning relationships, here expressed with the rule spawned(x,y).

The fourth property, commands, concerns a realistic log from the Mars rover Curiosity [28]. The log consists of events (here renamed) CMD_DISPATCH(c,t) and CMD_COMPLETE(c,t), representing the dispatch and subsequent completion of a command c at time t. The property to be verified is that a command, once dispatched, is not dispatched again before completed. Rules are used to break down the formula to conceptually simpler pieces.

Evaluation. In [18, 19] we evaluated DEJAVU without the rule extension against the MONPOLY tool [4], which supports a logic close to DEJAVU's. In [17] we evaluated DEJAVU's garbage collection capability. In this section we evaluate the rule extension for the properties in Figure 1 on a collection of traces. Table 1 shows the analysis time (excluding time to compile the generated monitor) and maximal memory usage in MB for different traces (format is 'trace length : time/memory'). The processing time is generally very reasonable for very large traces. However, the spawning property requires considerably larger processing time and memory compared to the other properties since more data (the transitive closure) has to be computed and stored. The evaluation was performed on a Mac laptop, with the Mac OS X 10.10.5 operating system, on a 2.8 GHz Intel Core i7 with 16 GB of memory.

Table 1. Evaluation - trace lengths, analysis time in seconds, and maximal memory use

Property	Trace 1	Trace 2	Trace 3
telemetry1	1,200,001 : 2.6 s/194 MB	5,200,001 : 5.9 s/210 MB	10,200,001 : 10.7 s/239 MB
telemetry2	1,200,001 : 3.8 s/225 MB	5,200,001 : 8.7 s/218 MB	10,200,001 : 16.6 s/214 MB
spawning	9,899 : 29.5 s/737 MB	19,999 : 117.3 s/1,153 MB	39,799 : 512.5 s/3,513 MB
commands	49,999 : 1.5 s/169 MB	N/A	N/A

7   Conclusions

Propositional linear temporal logic (LTL) and automata are two common specification formalisms for software and hardware systems. While temporal logic has a more declarative flavor, automata are more operational, describing how the specified system progresses. There has been several proposed extensions to LTL that extend its expressive power to that of related automata formalisms. We proposed here a simple extension for propositional LTL that adds auxiliary propositions that summarize the prefix of the execution, based on rules written as past formulas. Conceptually, this extension puts the specification in between propositional LTL and automata, as the additional variables can be seen as representing the state of an automaton that is synchronized with the temporal property. It is shown to have the same expressive power as Büchi automata, and is in particular appealing for runtime verification of past (i.e., safety) temporal properties, which already are based on summarizing the value of subformulas over observed prefixes. We demonstrated that first-order linear temporal logic (FLTL), which can be used to assert properties about systems with data, also has expressiveness deficiencies, and similarly extended it with rules that define *relations* that summarize prefixes of the execution. We proved that for the first-order case, unlike the propositional case, this extension is not identical to the addition of dynamic (i.e., state dependent) quantification. We presented a monitoring algorithm for propositional past time temporal logic with rules, extending a classical algorithm, and similarly presented an algorithm for first-order past temporal logic with rules. Finally we described the implementation of this extension in the DEJAVU tool and provided experimental results. The code and many more examples appear at [10]. Future work includes performing additional experiments, and making further comparisons to other formalisms. We intend to study further extensions, exploring the space between logic and programming.

References

1. Alpern, B., Schneider, F.B.: Recognizing safety and liveness. Distrib. Comput. **2**(3), 117–126 (1987)
2. D'Angelo, B., et al.: LOLA: runtime monitoring of synchronous systems. In: TIME 2005, pp. 166– 174 (2005)
3. Bartocci, E., Falcone, Y., Francalanza, A., Reger, G.: Introduction to runtime verification. In: Bartocci, E., Falcone, Y. (eds.) Lectures on Runtime Verification. LNCS, vol. 10457, pp. 1–33. Springer, Cham (2018). https://doi.org/10.1007/978-3-319-75632-5_1
4. Basin, D.A., Klaedtke, F., Marinovic, S., Zalinescu, E.n.: Monitoring of temporal first-order properties with aggregations. Formal Methods Syst. Des. **46**(3), 262–285 (2015)
5. Bauer, A., Leucker, M., Schallhart, C.: The good, the bad, and the ugly, but how ugly is ugly? In: Sokolsky, O., Taşıran, S. (eds.) RV 2007. LNCS, vol. 4839, pp. 126–138. Springer, Heidelberg (2007). https://doi.org/10.1007/978-3-540-77395-5_11
6. Bohn, J., Damm, W., Grumberg, O., Hungar, H., Laster, K.: First-order-CTL model checking. In: Arvind, V., Ramanujam, S. (eds.) FSTTCS 1998. LNCS, vol. 1530, pp. 283–294. Springer, Heidelberg (1998). https://doi.org/10.1007/978-3-540-49382-2_27
7. Bryant, R.E.: Symbolic Boolean manipulation with ordered binary-decision diagrams. ACM Comput. Surv. **24**(3), 293–318 (1992)
8. Burch, J.R., Clarke, E.M., McMillan, K.L., Dill, D.L., Hwang, L.J.: Symbolic model checking: 10^{20} states and beyond. Inf. Comput. **98**(2), 142–170 (1992)
9. Chomicki, J.: Efficient checking of temporal integrity constraints using bounded history encoding. ACM Trans. Database Syst. **20**(2), 149–186 (1995)
10. DejaVu. https://github.com/havelund/dejavu
11. Ebbinghaus, H.-D., Flum, J., Thomas, W.: Mathematical Logic. Undergraduate Texts in Mathematics. Springer, New York (1984). https://doi.org/10.1007/978-1-4757-2355-7
12. Colombo, C., Pace, G.J., Schneider, G.: LARVA - safer monitoring of real-time Java programs. In: 7th IEEE International Conference on Software Engineering and Formal Methods (SEFM 2009), Hanoi, Vietnam, 23–27 November 2009, pp. 33–37. IEEE Computer Society (2009)
13. Falcone, Y., Fernandez, J.-C., Mounier, L.: What can you verify and enforce at runtime? STTT **14**(3), 349–382 (2012)
14. Frenkel, H., Grumberg, O., Sheinvald, S.: An automata-theoretic approach to modeling systems and specifications over infinite data. In: Barrett, C., Davies, M., Kahsai, T. (eds.) NFM 2017. LNCS, vol. 10227, pp. 1–18. Springer, Cham (2017). https://doi.org/10.1007/978-3-319-57288-8_1
15. Hallé, S., Villemaire, R.: Runtime enforcement of web service message contracts with data. IEEE Trans. Serv. Comput. **5**(2), 192–206 (2012)
16. Havelund, K.: Rule-based runtime verification revisited. STTT **17**(2), 143–170 (2015)

17. Havelund, K., Peled, D.: Efficient runtime verification of first-order temporal properties. In: Gallardo, M.M., Merino, P. (eds.) SPIN 2018. LNCS, vol. 10869, pp. 26–47. Springer, Cham (2018). https://doi.org/10.1007/978-3-319-94111-0_2
18. Havelund, K., Peled, D.A., Ulus, D.: First-order temporal logic monitoring with BDDs. In: FMCAD 2017, pp. 116–123 (2017)
19. Havelund, K., Peled, D.A., Ulus, D.: First-order temporal logic monitoring with BDDs. Formal Methods Syst. Des. 1–21 (2019)
20. Havelund, K., Reger, G., Thoma, D., Zălinescu, E.: Monitoring events that carry data. In: Bartocci, E., Falcone, Y. (eds.) Lectures on Runtime Verification. LNCS, vol. 10457, pp. 61–102. Springer, Cham (2018). https://doi.org/10.1007/978-3-319-75632-5_3
21. Havelund, K., Roşu, G.: Synthesizing monitors for safety properties. In: Katoen, J.-P., Stevens, P. (eds.) TACAS 2002. LNCS, vol. 2280, pp. 342–356. Springer, Heidelberg (2002). https://doi.org/10.1007/3-540-46002-0_24
22. Hella, L., Libkin, L., Nurmonen, J., Wong, L.: Logics with aggregate operators. J. ACM **48**(4), 880–907 (2001)
23. IEEE Standard for Property Specification Language (PSL), Annex B. IEEE Std 1850TM-2010 (2010)
24. JavaBDD. http://javabdd.sourceforge.net
25. Kupferman, O., Vardi, M.Y.: Model checking of safety properties. Formal Methods Syst. Des. **19**(3), 291–314 (2001)
26. Manna, Z., Pnueli, A.: The Temporal Logic of Reactive and Concurrent Systems. Specification. Springer, New York (1992). https://doi.org/10.1007/978-1-4612-0931-7
27. Meredith, P.O., Jin, D., Griffith, D., Chen, F., Rosu, G.: An overview of the MOP runtime verification framework. STTT **14**, 249–289 (2011)
28. Mars Science Laboratory (MSL) mission website. http://mars.jpl.nasa.gov/msl
29. Reger, G., Cruz, H.C., Rydeheard, D.: MARQ: monitoring at runtime with QEA. In: Baier, C., Tinelli, C. (eds.) TACAS 2015. LNCS, vol. 9035, pp. 596–610. Springer, Heidelberg (2015). https://doi.org/10.1007/978-3-662-46681-0_55
30. Sistla, A.P.: Theoretical issues in the design and analysis of distributed systems, Ph.D. Thesis, Harvard University (1983)
31. Thomas, W.: Automata on Infinite Objects, Handbook of Theoretical Computer Science, Volume B: Formal Models and Semantics, pp. 133–192 (1990)
32. Wolper, P.: Temporal logic can be more expressive. Inf. Control **56**(1/2), 72–99 (1983)
33. Wolper, P., Vardi, M.Y., Sistla, A.P.: Reasoning about infinite computation paths (Extended Abstract). In: FOCS 1983, pp. 185–194 (1983)

Monitorability over Unreliable Channels

Sean Kauffman[1(✉)], Klaus Havelund[2], and Sebastian Fischmeister[1]

[1] University of Waterloo, Waterloo, Canada
skauffma@uwaterloo.ca
[2] Jet Propulsion Laboratory, California Institute of Technology, Pasadena, USA

Abstract. In Runtime Verification (RV), monitoring a system means checking an execution trace of a program for satisfactions and violations of properties. The question of which properties can be effectively monitored over ideal channels has mostly been answered by prior work. However, program monitoring is often deployed for remote systems where communications may be unreliable. In this work, we address the question of what properties are monitorable over an unreliable communication channel. We describe the different types of mutations that may be introduced to an execution trace and examine their effects on program monitoring. We propose a fixed-parameter tractable algorithm for determining the immunity of a finite automaton to a trace mutation and show how it can be used to classify ω-regular properties as monitorable over channels with that mutation.

1 Introduction

In Runtime Verification (RV) the correctness of a program execution is determined by another program, called a monitor. In many cases, monitors run remotely from the systems they monitor, either due to resource constraints or for dependability. For example, ground stations monitor a spacecraft, while an automotive computer may monitor emissions control equipment. In both cases, the program being monitored must transmit data to a remote monitor.

Communication between the program and monitor may not always be reliable, however, leading to incorrect or incomplete results. For example, data from the Mars Science Laboratory (MSL) rover is received out-of-order, and some low priority messages may arrive days after being sent. Even dedicated debugging channels like ARM Embedded Trace Macrocell (ETM) have finite bandwidth and may lose data during an event burst [1]. Some works in the field of RV have begun to address the challenges of imperfect communication, but the problem has been largely ignored in the study of monitorability.

In this work, we propose a definition for a property to be considered monitorable over an unreliable communication channel. To reach our definition, we

The research performed by the second author was carried out at Jet Propulsion Laboratory, California Institute of Technology, under a contract with the National Aeronautics and Space Administration.

© Springer Nature Switzerland AG 2019
B. Finkbeiner and L. Mariani (Eds.): RV 2019, LNCS 11757, pp. 256–272, 2019.
https://doi.org/10.1007/978-3-030-32079-9_15

must determine what constitutes a monitorable property and whether monitorability is affected by a mutation of the property's input. We first examine the concept of uncertainty in monitoring and four common notions of monitorability in Sects. 3 and 4. We then define possible trace mutations due to unreliable channels and describe what makes a property immune to a trace mutation in Sects. 5 and 6. The combination of immunity to a trace mutation and monitorability (under an existing definition) is what defines the monitorability of a property under that mutation. To reach a decision procedure for the immunity of an ω-regular property, we map the definition of immunity to a property of derived monitor automata in Sect. 7. We finally present a decision procedure for the immunity of an automaton to a mutation and prove it correct in Sect. 8.

2 Notation

We use $\mathbb{N}$ to denote the set of all natural numbers and ∞ to denote infinity. We write $\perp$ to denote *false* and $\top$ to denote *true*. A finite sequence σ of n values, is written $\sigma = \langle v_1, \cdots, v_n \rangle$ where both v_i and $\sigma(i)$ mean the i'th item in the sequence. A value x is in a sequence σ, denoted by $x \in \sigma$, iff $\exists\, i \in \mathbb{N}$ such that $\sigma(i) = x$. The length of a sequence σ is written $|\sigma| \in \mathbb{N} \cup \{\infty\}$. The suffix of a sequence σ beginning at the i'th item in the sequence is written σ^i. The concatenation of two sequences σ, τ is written $\sigma \cdot \tau$ where σ is finite and τ is either finite or infinite.

We denote the cross product of A and B as $A \times B$ and the set of total functions from A to B as $A \to B$. Given a set S, S^* denotes the set of finite sequences over S where each sequence element is in S, S^ω denotes the set of infinite sequences of such elements, and $S^\infty = S^* \cup S^\omega$. Given a set S, we write 2^S to mean the set of all subsets of S. The cardinality of a set S is written $|S|$. A map is a partial function $M : K \nrightarrow V$ where K is a finite domain of keys mapped to the set V of values. We write $M(k) \leftarrow v$ to denote M updated with k mapped to v. AP is a finite, non-empty set of *atomic propositions*. An *alphabet* is denoted $\Sigma = 2^{\mathrm{AP}}$, and an element of the alphabet is a symbol $s \in \Sigma$. A *trace*, *word*, or *string* is a sequence of symbols.

In this work, we use *Finite Automata (FAs)* to represent both regular and ω-regular languages. We use Non-deterministic Büchi Automata (NBAs) to represent ω-regular languages, which accept infinite strings, and Non-deterministic Finite Automata (NFAs) to represent regular languages, which accept finite strings. Both an NBA and an NFA are written $\mathcal{A} = (Q, \Sigma, q_0, \delta, F)$, where Q is the set of states, Σ is the alphabet, $q_0 \in Q$ is the initial state, $\delta : Q \times \Sigma \to 2^Q$ is the transition function, and $F \subseteq Q$ is the set of accepting states. The two types of FAs differ in their accepting conditions. An NFA is a Deterministic Finite Automaton (DFA) iff $\forall q \in Q$, $\forall \alpha \in \Sigma$, $|\delta(q, \alpha)| = 1$.

A *path* (or *run*) through an FA $\mathcal{A}$ from a state $q \in Q$ over a word $\sigma \in \Sigma^\infty$ is a sequence of states $\pi = \langle q_1, q_2, \cdots \rangle$ such that $q_1 = q$ and $q_{i+1} \in \delta(q_i, \sigma_i)$. We write $\mathcal{A}(q, \sigma)$ to denote the set of all runs on $\mathcal{A}$ starting at state q with the word σ. The set of all *reachable states* in an FA $\mathcal{A}$ from a starting state q_0 is denoted

$Reach(\mathcal{A}, q_0) = \{q \in \pi : \pi \in \mathcal{A}(q_0, \sigma), \ \sigma \in \Sigma^\infty\}$. Given a DFA $(Q, \Sigma, q_0, \delta, F)$, a state $q \in Q$, and a finite string $\sigma \in \Sigma^* : |\sigma| = n$, $\delta^* : Q \times \Sigma^* \to Q$ denotes the terminal (nth) state of the run over σ beginning in q.

A finite run on an NFA $\pi = \langle q_1, q_2, \cdots, q_n \rangle$ is considered *accepting* if $q_n \in F$. For an infinite run on an NBA ρ, we use $Inf(\rho) \subseteq Q$ to denote the set of states that are visited infinitely often, and the run is considered *accepting* when $Inf(\rho) \cap F \neq \varnothing$. $\mathcal{L}(\mathcal{A})$ denotes the language accepted by an FA $\mathcal{A}$. The complement or negation of an FA $\mathcal{A} = (Q, \Sigma, q_0, \delta, F)$ is written $\overline{\mathcal{A}}$ where $\mathcal{L}(\overline{\mathcal{A}}) = \Sigma^* \setminus \mathcal{L}(\mathcal{A})$ for NFAs and $\mathcal{L}(\overline{\mathcal{A}}) = \Sigma^\omega \setminus \mathcal{L}(\mathcal{A})$ for NBAs.

We use Linear Temporal Logic (LTL) throughout the paper to illustrate examples of properties because it is a common formalism in the RV area. The syntax of these formulae is defined by the following inductive grammar where p is an atomic proposition, U is the *Until* operator, and X is the *Next* operator.

$$\varphi ::= p \mid \neg\varphi \mid \varphi \vee \varphi \mid X\varphi \mid \varphi\,U\varphi$$

The symbols $\neg$ and $\vee$ are defined as expected and the following inductive semantics are used for X and U, where $\sigma \in \Sigma^\omega$.

- $\sigma \models X\varphi$ iff $\sigma^2 \models \varphi$
- $\sigma \models \varphi\,U\phi$ iff $\exists k \geq 1 : \sigma^k \models \phi \wedge \forall j : 1 \leq j < k, \ \sigma^j \models \varphi$

We also define the standard notation: $true = p \vee \neg p$ for any proposition p, $false = \neg true$, $\varphi \wedge \phi = \neg(\neg\varphi \vee \neg\phi)$, $\varphi \to \phi = \neg\varphi \vee \phi$, $F\varphi = true\,U\varphi$ (eventually φ), $G\varphi = \neg F\neg\varphi$ (globally φ), and $\overline{X}\varphi = X\varphi \vee \neg X true$ (weak-next φ, true at the end of a finite trace).

3   Uncertainty

Program properties are typically specified as languages of infinite length strings, for example by writing LTL formulae. However, in RV, a finite prefix of an execution trace must be checked. We say a finite string *determines* inclusion in (or exclusion from) a language of infinite words only if all infinite extensions of the prefix are in (or out of) the language. If some infinite extensions are in the language and some are out, then the finite prefix does not determine inclusion and the result is uncertainty. The problem appears with an LTL property such as Fa, which is satisfied if an a appears in the string. However, if no a has yet been observed, and the program is still executing, it is unknown if the specification will be satisfied in the future.

To express notions of uncertainty in monitoring, extensions to the Boolean truth domain $\mathbb{B}_2 = \{\top, \bot\}$ have been proposed. $\mathbb{B}_3$ adds a third verdict of $?$ to the traditional Boolean notion of *true* or *false* to represent the idea that the specification is neither satisfied nor violated by the current finite prefix [5]. $\mathbb{B}_4$ replaces $?$ with *presumably true* ($\top_p$) and *presumably false* ($\bot_p$) to provide more information on what has already been seen [6].

The verdicts $\top_p$ and $\perp_p$ differentiate between prefixes that would satisfy or violate the property interpreted with finite trace semantics. The intuition is that $\perp_p$ indicates that something is required to happen in the future, while $\top_p$ means there is no such outstanding event. For example, if the formula $a \rightarrow Fb$ is interpreted as four-value LTL (LTL$_4$) (also called Runtime Verification LTL (RV-LTL) [6], which uses $\mathbb{B}_4$), the verdict on a trace $\langle b \rangle$ is $\top_p$ because a has not occurred, and therefore no b is required, while the verdict on $\langle a \rangle$ is $\perp_p$ because there is an a but as yet no b. If the same property is interpreted as three-value LTL (LTL$_3$) (which uses $\mathbb{B}_3$) the verdicts on both traces would be $?$.

The above intuitions are formalized in Definition 1, which is based on notation from [13]. Here, φ is a language that includes both finite and infinite traces.

Definition 1 (Evaluation Functions). *Given a property $\varphi \subseteq \Sigma^\infty$ (here understood as the language it accepts) for each of the truth domains $\mathbb{B} \in \{\mathbb{B}_3, \mathbb{B}_4\}$, we define evaluation functions of the form $[\![\cdot]\!]_{\mathbb{B}}(\cdot) : 2^{\Sigma^\infty} \times \Sigma^* \rightarrow \mathbb{B}$ as the following. For $\mathbb{B}_3 = \{\perp, ?, \top\}$,*

$$[\![\varphi]\!]_{\mathbb{B}_3}(\sigma) = \begin{cases} \perp & \text{if } \sigma \cdot \mu \notin \varphi \; \forall \mu \in \Sigma^\omega \\ \top & \text{if } \sigma \cdot \mu \in \varphi \; \forall \mu \in \Sigma^\omega \\ ? & \text{otherwise} \end{cases}$$

For $\mathbb{B}_4 = \{\perp, \perp_p, \top_p, \top\}$,

$$[\![\varphi]\!]_{\mathbb{B}_4}(\sigma) = \begin{cases} [\![\varphi]\!]_{\mathbb{B}_3}(\sigma) & \text{if } [\![\varphi]\!]_{\mathbb{B}_3}(\sigma) \neq \; ? \\ \perp_p & \text{if } [\![\varphi]\!]_{\mathbb{B}_3}(\sigma) = \; ? \text{ and } \sigma \notin \varphi \\ \top_p & \text{if } [\![\varphi]\!]_{\mathbb{B}_3}(\sigma) = \; ? \text{ and } \sigma \in \varphi \end{cases}$$

Introducing the idea of uncertainty in monitoring causes the possibility that some properties might never reach a definite, *true* or *false* verdict. A monitor that will only ever return a $?$ result does not have much utility. The *monitorability* of a property captures on this notion of the reachability of definite verdicts.

4 Monitorability

In this section, we examine the four most common definitions of monitorability. To define monitorability for properties over unreliable channels, we must first define monitorability for properties over ideal channels. Rather than choose one definition, we introduce four established definitions and allow the reader to select that of their preference.

4.1 Classical σ-Monitorability

Pnueli and Zaks introduced the first formal definition of monitorability in their work on Property Specification Language (PSL) model checking in 2006 [24]. They define what languages are monitorable given a trace prefix σ.

Definition 2 (Classical σ-Monitorability). *Given an alphabet Σ, and a finite sequence $\sigma \in \Sigma^*$ a language $\varphi \subseteq \Sigma^\infty$ is σ-monitorable iff* $\exists \eta \in \Sigma^* : \sigma \cdot \eta \cdot s \models \varphi \, \forall s \in \Sigma^\infty \, \vee \, \sigma \cdot \eta \cdot s \not\models \varphi \, \forall s \in \Sigma^\infty.$

That is, there exists another finite sequence η such that $\sigma \cdot \eta$ determines inclusion in or exclusion from φ.

For example, GFp is non-monitorable for any finite prefix, because the trace needed to determine the verdict must be infinite. If a reactive system is expected to run forever, then it is useless to continue monitoring after observing σ such that φ is not monitorable.

4.2   Classical Monitorability

Bauer, Leuker, and Schallhart restated this definition of monitorability and proved that safety and guarantee (co-safety) properties represent a proper subset of the class of monitorable properties [7]. It was already known that the class of monitorable properties was not limited to safety and guarantee properties from the work of d'Amorim and Roşu on monitoring ω-regular languages [10], however that work did not formally define monitorability.

The definition of monitorability given by Bauer et al. is identical to Definition 2 except that it considers all possible trace prefixes instead of a specific prefix [12,13] and it excludes languages with finite words. The restriction to infinite words is due to their interest in defining monitorable LTL$_3$ properties, which only considers infinite traces.

They use Kupferman and Vardi's definitions of *good* and *bad* prefixes of an infinite trace [17] to define what they call an *ugly* prefix. That is, given an alphabet Σ and a language of infinite strings $\varphi \subseteq \Sigma^\omega$,

- a finite word $b \in \Sigma^*$ is a *bad prefix* for φ iff $\forall s \in \Sigma^\omega$, $b \cdot s \notin \varphi$, and
- a finite word $g \in \Sigma^*$ is a *good prefix* for φ iff $\forall s \in \Sigma^\omega$, $g \cdot s \in \varphi$.

Bauer et al. use good and bad prefixes to define *ugly* prefixes and then use ugly prefixes to define Classical Monitorability.

Definition 3 (Ugly Prefix). *Given an alphabet Σ and a language of infinite strings $\varphi \subseteq \Sigma^\omega$, a finite word $u \in \Sigma^*$ is an* ugly prefix *for φ iff $\nexists s \in \Sigma^* : u \cdot s$ is either a good or bad prefix.*

Definition 4 (Classical Monitorability). *Given a language of infinite strings $\varphi \subseteq \Sigma^\omega$, φ is* classically monitorable *iff $\nexists u \in \Sigma^* : u$ is an ugly prefix for φ.*

4.3   Weak Monitorability

Recently, both Chen et al. and Peled and Havelund proposed a weaker definition of monitorability that includes more properties than either the Classical or Alternative definitions [9,22]. They observed that there are properties that are classically non-monitorable, but that are still useful to monitor. For example, the property $a \wedge GFa$ is non-monitorable under Definition 4 because any trace that begins with a must then satisfy or violate GFa, which is not possible. However, $a \wedge GFa$ is violated by traces that do not begin with a, so it may have some utility to monitor.

Definition 5 (Weak Monitorability). *Given a property* $\varphi \subseteq \Sigma^{\infty}$, φ *is weakly monitorable iff* $\exists p \in \Sigma^{*} : p$ *is not an ugly prefix for* φ.

4.4   Alternative Monitorability

Falcone et al. observed that the class of monitorable properties should depend on the truth domain of the monitored formula. However, they noticed that changing from $\mathbb{B}_3$ to $\mathbb{B}_4$ does not influence the set of monitorable properties under classical monitorability [12,13]. To resolve this perceived shortcoming, the authors of [12,13] introduce an *alternative* definition of monitorability. They introduce the notion of an *r-property* (runtime property) which separates the property's language of finite and infinite traces into disjoint sets. We do not require this distinction and treat the language of a property as a single set containing both finite and infinite traces. Falcone et al. then define an alternative notion of monitorability for a property using a variant of Definition 1.

Definition 6 (Alternative Monitorability). *Given a truth domain* $\mathbb{B}$ *and an evaluation function for* $\mathbb{B}$ $[\![\cdot]\!]_{\mathbb{B}}(\cdot) : 2^{\Sigma^{\infty}} \times \Sigma^{*} \to \mathbb{B}$, *a property* $\varphi \subseteq \Sigma^{\infty}$ *is alternatively monitorable iff* $\forall \sigma_g \in \varphi \cap \Sigma^{*}$, $\forall \sigma_b \notin \varphi \cap \Sigma^{*}$ $[\![\varphi]\!]_{\mathbb{B}}(\sigma_g) \neq [\![\varphi]\!]_{\mathbb{B}}(\sigma_b)$

Definition 6 says that, given a truth domain, a language with both finite and infinite words is monitorable if evaluating the finite strings in the language always yield different verdicts from evaluating the finite strings out of the language.

5   Unreliable Channels

For a property to be monitorable over an unreliable channel it must be monitorable over ideal channels, and it must reach the correct verdict despite the unreliable channel. To illustrate this idea, we introduce an example.

5.1   An Example with Unreliable Channels

Consider the LTL property Fa over the alphabet $\Sigma = \{a, b\}$. That is, all traces that contain at least one a satisfy φ. We assume that the trace is monitored remotely, and, for this example, we will adopt a $\mathbb{B}_3$ truth domain. With LTL$_3$ semantics, the verdict on finite prefixes without an a, is $?$, while the verdict when an a is included is $\top$. Figure 1a shows the NBA for such a property.

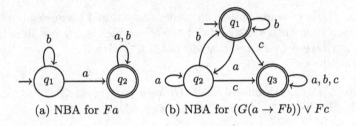

(a) NBA for Fa (b) NBA for $(G(a \to Fb)) \vee Fc$

Fig. 1. Example properties

Monitorability Under Reordering. Suppose that the channel over which the trace is transmitted may reorder events. That is, events are guaranteed to be delivered, but not necessarily in the same order in which they were sent.

We argue that Fa should be considered monitorable over a channel that reorders the trace. First, the property is monitorable over an ideal channel (see Sect. 4). Second, given any trace prefix, reordering the prefix would not change the verdict of a monitor. Any a in the trace will cause a transition to state q_2, regardless of its position.

Monitorability Under Loss. Now suppose that, instead of reordering, the channel over which the trace is transmitted may lose events. That is, the order of events is guaranteed to be maintained, but some events may be missing from the trace observed by the monitor.

We argue that Fa should not be considered monitorable over a channel that loses events, even though the property is deemed to be monitorable over an ideal channel. It is possible for the verdict from the monitor to be different from what it would be given the original trace. For example, assume a trace $\langle a, b \rangle$. For this trace, the verdict from an LTL_3 monitor would be $\top$. However, if the a is lost, the verdict would be $?$.

5.2 Trace Mutations

To model unreliable channels, we introduce *trace mutations*. A mutation represents the possible modifications to traces from communication over unreliable channels. These mutations are defined as relations between unmodified original traces and their mutated counterparts. Trace mutations include only finite traces because only finite prefixes may be mutated in practice.

There are four trace mutations $\mathcal{M}^k \subseteq \Sigma^* \times \Sigma^*$ where $\mathcal{M}$ denotes any of the relations in Definitions 7, 8, 9, and 10 or a union of any number of them, and k denotes the number of inductive steps.

Definition 7 (Loss Mutation)

$$Loss = \{(\sigma, \sigma') : \sigma = \sigma' \vee \exists \alpha, \beta \in \Sigma^*, \exists x \in \Sigma : \sigma = \alpha \cdot \langle x \rangle \cdot \beta \wedge \sigma' = \alpha \cdot \beta\}$$

Definition 8 (Corruption Mutation)

$$Corruption = \{(\sigma, \sigma') : \exists \alpha, \beta \in \Sigma^*, \exists x, y \in \Sigma : \sigma = \alpha \cdot \langle x \rangle \cdot \beta \wedge \sigma' = \alpha \cdot \langle y \rangle \cdot \beta\}$$

Definition 9 (Stutter Mutation)

$$Stutter = \{(\sigma, \sigma') : \sigma = \sigma' \vee \exists \alpha, \beta \in \Sigma^*, \exists x \in \Sigma : \sigma = \alpha \cdot \langle x \rangle \cdot \beta \wedge \sigma' = \alpha \cdot \langle x, x \rangle \cdot \beta\}$$

Definition 10 (Out-of-Order Mutation)

$$OutOfOrder = \{(\sigma, \sigma') : \exists \alpha, \beta \in \Sigma^*, \exists x, y \in \Sigma : \sigma = \alpha \cdot \langle x, y \rangle \cdot \beta \wedge \sigma' = \alpha \cdot \langle y, x \rangle \cdot \beta\}$$

Definition 11 (Inductive k-Mutations). *Given any mutation or union of mutations $\mathcal{M}^k$, we define $\mathcal{M}^{k+1}$ inductively as the following.*

$$\mathcal{M}^1 \in \{\bigcup m : m \in 2^{\{Loss, Corruption, Stutter, OutOfOrder\}}, m \neq \varnothing\}$$

$$\mathcal{M}^{k+1} = \{(\sigma_1, \sigma_3) : \exists (\sigma_1, \sigma_2) \in \mathcal{M}^k, \exists (\sigma_2, \sigma_3) \in \mathcal{M}^1\} \cup \mathcal{M}^k$$

These mutations are based on Lozes and Villard's interference model [21]. Other works on the verification of unreliable channels, such as [8], have chosen to include *insertion* errors instead of *Corruption* and *OutOfOrder*. We prefer to define *Corruption* and *OutOfOrder* because the mutations more closely reflect our real-world experiences. For example, packets sent using the User Datagram Protocol (UDP) may be corrupted or arrive out-of-order, but packets must be sent before these mutations occur.

We say a mutation M is *prefix-assured* when $\forall(\sigma, \sigma') \in M$ such that $|\sigma| > 1$, $\exists(\sigma_p, \sigma'_p) \in M$, where σ_p is a prefix of σ and σ'_p is a prefix of σ'. All mutations $\mathcal{M}^1$ are prefix-assured. Combining mutations is possible under Definition 11, and it is possible to form any combination of strings by doing so. This capability is important to ensure the mutation model is complete.

Theorem 1 (Completeness of Mutations). *Given any set of non-empty traces $S \subseteq \Sigma^* \setminus \{\varepsilon\}$, $(Loss \cup Corruption \cup Stutter)^\infty = S \times \Sigma^*$.*

Proof: First, Definition 8 allows an arbitrary symbol in a string to be changed to any other symbol. Thus, $\forall \sigma' \in \Sigma^*$, $\exists \sigma : (\sigma, \sigma') \in Corruption^n$, $|\sigma| = |\sigma'|$ where $n \geq |\sigma|$. A string can also be lengthened or shortened arbitrarily, so long as it is non-empty. Definition 9 allows lengthening, because $Stutter(\sigma, \sigma') \implies |\sigma| < |\sigma'|$, while Definition 7 allows shortening, because $Loss(\sigma, \sigma') \implies |\sigma| > |\sigma'|$.   □

These mutations are general and it may be useful for practitioners to define their own, more constrained mutations based on domain knowledge. For example, even Definition 10 is unnecessary for the completeness of the mutation model, but the combination of Definitions 7, 8, and 9 cannot completely specify the *OutOfOrder* relation. That is, $OutOfOrder^n \subset Corruption^{2n} \; \forall n \in \mathbb{N}$.

6   Immunity to Trace Mutations

The two requirements for a property to be monitorable over an unreliable channel are that the property is monitorable over an ideal channel and that the property is *immune* to the effects of the unreliable channel. A monitor must be able to reach a meaningful, actionable verdict for a trace prefix, and the verdict must also be *correct*. If a monitored property is immune to a mutation then we can trust the monitor's verdict whether or not the observed trace is mutated.

Definition 12 characterizes properties where the given trace mutation will have no effect on the evaluation verdict. For example, the LTL property Fa from Fig. 1a is immune to $OutOfOrder^\infty$ with truth domain $\mathbb{B}_3$ or $\mathbb{B}_4$ because reordering the input trace cannot change the verdict.

Definition 12 (Full Immunity to Unreliable Channels). *Given a trace alphabet Σ, a property $\varphi \subseteq \Sigma^\infty$, a trace mutation $\mathcal{M}^k \subseteq \Sigma^* \times \Sigma^*$, a truth domain $\mathbb{B}$, and an evaluation function $[\![\cdot]\!]_\mathbb{B}(\cdot) : 2^{\Sigma^\infty} \times \Sigma^* \to \mathbb{B}$, φ is immune to $\mathcal{M}^k$ iff $\forall(\sigma, \sigma') \in \mathcal{M}^k$, $[\![\varphi]\!]_\mathbb{B}(\sigma) = [\![\varphi]\!]_\mathbb{B}(\sigma')$.*

Definition 12 specifies a k-Mutation from Definition 11, but a property that is immune to a mutation for some k is immune to that mutation for *any* k. This significant result forms the basis for checking for mutation immunity in Sect. 8. The intuition is that, since we assume any combination of symbols in the alphabet is a possible ideal trace, and a mutation could occur at any time, one mutation is enough to violate immunity for any vulnerable property.

Theorem 2 (Single Mutation Immunity Equivalence). *Given a trace alphabet Σ, a property $\varphi \subseteq \Sigma^\infty$, a trace mutation $\mathcal{M} \subseteq \Sigma^* \times \Sigma^*$, and a number of applications of that mutation k, φ is immune to $\mathcal{M}^k$ iff φ is immune to $\mathcal{M}^1$.*

Proof: Since k-Mutations are defined inductively, Theorem 2 is equivalent to the statement that φ is immune to $\mathcal{M}^{k+1}$ iff φ is immune to $\mathcal{M}^k$. Now assume by way of contradiction a property $\varphi_{\text{bad}} \subseteq \Sigma^\infty$ such that φ_{bad} is immune to some k-Mutation M^k but not to M^{k+1}. That is, given a truth domain $\mathbb{B}$, $\exists(\sigma_1, \sigma_3) \in M^{k+1} : [\![\varphi_{\text{bad}}]\!]_\mathbb{B}(\sigma_1) \neq [\![\varphi_{\text{bad}}]\!]_\mathbb{B}(\sigma_3)$. From Definition 11, either $(\sigma_1, \sigma_3) \in M^k$, or $\exists(\sigma_1, \sigma_2) \in \mathcal{M}^k, \exists(\sigma_2, \sigma_3) \in \mathcal{M}^1 : [\![\varphi_{\text{bad}}]\!]_\mathbb{B}(\sigma_1) \neq [\![\varphi_{\text{bad}}]\!]_\mathbb{B}(\sigma_3)$. It cannot be true that $(\sigma_1, \sigma_3) \in M^k$ since φ_{bad} is immune to M^k so there must exist pairs $(\sigma_1, \sigma_2) \in \mathcal{M}^k$ and $(\sigma_2, \sigma_3) \in \mathcal{M}^1$. Since φ_{bad} is immune to $\mathcal{M}^k$, $[\![\varphi_{\text{bad}}]\!]_\mathbb{B}(\sigma_1) = [\![\varphi_{\text{bad}}]\!]_\mathbb{B}(\sigma_2)$ so it must be true that $[\![\varphi_{\text{bad}}]\!]_\mathbb{B}(\sigma_2) \neq [\![\varphi_{\text{bad}}]\!]_\mathbb{B}(\sigma_3)$. However, it is clear from Definition 11 that $M^k \subseteq M^{k+1}$, so $M^1 \subseteq M^k$ for any k, which is a contradiction.

For the reverse case, assume a property $\varphi_{\text{sad}} \subseteq \Sigma^\infty$ such that φ_{sad} is not immune to some k-Mutation M^k but immune to M^{k+1}. However, as we saw before, $M^k \subseteq M^{k+1}$ so φ_{sad} must not be immune to M^{k+1}, a contradiction.   □

Immunity under Definition 12 is too strong to be a requirement for monitorability over an unreliable channel, however. Take, for example, the property $(G(a \to Fb)) \vee Fc$, as shown in Fig. 1b. By Definition 12 with truth domain

$\mathbb{B}_4$ this property is vulnerable (not immune) to $OutOfOrder^1$ because reordering symbols may change the verdict from $\top_p$ to $\bot_p$ and vice versa. However, this property is monitorable under all definitions in Sect. 4, so we would like to weaken the definition of immunity only to consider the parts of a property that affect its monitorability.

To weaken the definition of immunity we consider only the determinization of the property to be crucial. Definition 13 characterizes properties for which satisfaction and violation are unaffected by a mutation. We call this *true-false immunity*, and it is equivalent to immunity with truth domain $\mathbb{B}_3$. The intuition is that $\mathbb{B}_3$ treats all verdicts outside $\{\top, \bot\}$ as the symbol *?* so immunity with this truth domain does not concern non-*true-false* verdicts.

Definition 13 (True-False Immunity to Unreliable Channels). *Given a trace alphabet Σ, a property $\varphi \subseteq \Sigma^\infty$, a trace mutation $\mathcal{M}^k \subseteq \Sigma^* \times \Sigma^*$, and the evaluation function $[\![\cdot]\!]_{\mathbb{B}_3}(\cdot) : 2^{\Sigma^\infty} \times \Sigma^* \to \mathbb{B}_3$, φ is true-false immune to $\mathcal{M}^k$ iff $\forall(\sigma, \sigma') \in \mathcal{M}^k$, $[\![\varphi]\!]_{\mathbb{B}_3}(\sigma) = [\![\varphi]\!]_{\mathbb{B}_3}(\sigma')$.*

The true-false immunity of a property to a mutation is necessary but not sufficient to show that the property is monitorable over an unreliable channel. For example, $G(a \to Fb)$ is true-false immune to all mutations because the verdict will be *?* for any prefix, but the property is not monitorable. We can now define monitorability over unreliable channels in the general case.

Definition 14 (Monitorability over Unreliable Channels). *Given a trace alphabet Σ, a property $\varphi \subseteq \Sigma^\infty$, a trace mutation $\mathcal{M}^k \subseteq \Sigma^* \times \Sigma^*$, and a definition of monitorability $\mathcal{V}$, φ is monitorable over $\mathcal{M}^k$ iff φ is considered monitorable by $\mathcal{V}$, and φ is true-false immune to $\mathcal{M}^k$.*

By Rice's Theorem, monitorability over unreliable channels is undecidable in the general case, but we now provide a decision procedure for properties expressible by an NBA. As decision procedures for the monitorability of ω-regular languages exist, we focus on determining the true-false immunity of a property to a given mutation.

7   Deciding Immunity for ω-Regular Properties

To determine the immunity of an ω-regular property to a trace mutation, we must construct automata that capture the notion of uncertainty from $\mathbb{B}_3$. Bauer et al. defined a simple process to build a $\mathbb{B}_3$ monitor using two DFAs in their work on LTL$_3$ [5].

The procedure begins by complementing the language. A language of infinite words φ is represented as an NBA $\mathcal{A}_\varphi = (Q, \Sigma, q_0, \delta, F_\varphi)$, for example, LTL can be converted to an NBA by tableau construction [25]. The NBA is then complemented to form $\overline{\mathcal{A}_\varphi} = (\overline{Q}, \Sigma, \overline{q_0}, \overline{\delta}, \overline{F_\varphi})$. *Remark:* The upper bound for NBA complementation is $2^{O(n \log n)}$, so it is cheaper to complement an LTL property and construct its NBA if starting from temporal logic [18].

To form the monitor, create two NFAs based on the NBAs and then convert them to DFAs. The two NFAs are defined as $\mathcal{A} = (Q, \Sigma, q_0, \delta, F)$ and $\overline{\mathcal{A}} = (\overline{Q}, \Sigma, \overline{q_0}, \overline{\delta}, \overline{F})$ The new accepting states are the states from which an NBA accepting state is reachable. That is, we make $F = \{q \in Q : \mathcal{R}each(\mathcal{A}_\varphi, q) \cap F_\varphi \neq \varnothing\}$, and $\overline{F} = \{q \in \overline{Q} : \mathcal{R}each(\overline{\mathcal{A}_\varphi}, q) \cap \overline{F_\varphi} \neq \varnothing\}$. The two NFAs are then converted to DFAs via powerset construction. The verdict for a finite trace σ is then given as the following:

Definition 15 ($\mathbb{B}_3$ Monitor Verdict). *Given an alphabet Σ and a language $\varphi \subseteq \Sigma^\omega$, derive $\mathbb{B}_3$ monitor DFAs $\mathcal{A} = (Q, \Sigma, q_0, \delta, F)$ and $\overline{\mathcal{A}} = (\overline{Q}, \Sigma, \overline{q_0}, \overline{\delta}, \overline{F})$. The $\mathbb{B}_3$ verdict for a string $\sigma \in \Sigma^*$ is the following.*

$$[\![\varphi]\!]_{\mathbb{B}_3}(\sigma) = \begin{cases} \bot & \text{if } \sigma \notin \mathcal{L}(\mathcal{A}) \\ \top & \text{if } \sigma \notin \mathcal{L}(\overline{\mathcal{A}}) \\ ? & \text{otherwise} \end{cases}$$

We can now restate Definition 13 using monitor automata. This new definition will allow us to construct a decision procedure for a property's immunity to a mutation.

Theorem 3 (True-False Immunity to Unreliable Channels for ω-Regular Properties). *Given an alphabet Σ and an ω-regular language $\varphi \subseteq \Sigma^\omega$, derive $\mathbb{B}_3$ monitor DFAs $\mathcal{A} = (Q, \Sigma, q_0, \delta, F)$ and $\overline{\mathcal{A}} = (\overline{Q}, \Sigma, \overline{q_0}, \overline{\delta}, \overline{F})$. φ is true-false immune to a trace mutation $\mathcal{M}^k \subseteq \Sigma^* \times \Sigma^*$ iff $\forall (\sigma, \sigma') \in \mathcal{M}^k, (\sigma \notin \mathcal{L}(\mathcal{A}) \Leftrightarrow \sigma' \notin \mathcal{L}(\mathcal{A})) \wedge (\sigma \notin \mathcal{L}(\overline{\mathcal{A}}) \Leftrightarrow \sigma' \notin \mathcal{L}(\overline{\mathcal{A}}))$.*

Proof: By Definition 13 it is only necessary to show that $[\![\varphi]\!]_{\mathbb{B}_3}(\sigma) = [\![\varphi]\!]_{\mathbb{B}_3}(\sigma')$ is equivalent to $(\sigma \notin \mathcal{L}(\mathcal{A}) \Leftrightarrow \sigma' \notin \mathcal{L}(\mathcal{A})) \wedge (\sigma \notin \mathcal{L}(\overline{\mathcal{A}}) \Leftrightarrow \sigma' \notin \mathcal{L}(\overline{\mathcal{A}}))$. There are three cases: $\bot$, $\top$, and $?$. For $\bot$ and $\top$ it is obvious from Definition 15 that the verdicts are derived from exclusion from the languages of $\mathcal{A}$ and $\overline{\mathcal{A}}$. As there are only three possible verdicts, this also shows the $?$ case.   □

We say that an automaton is immune to a trace mutation in a similar way to how a property is immune. To show that a property is true-false immune to a mutation, we only need to show that its $\mathbb{B}_3$ monitor automata are also immune to the property. Note that, since the implication is both directions, we can use either language inclusion or exclusion in the definition.

Definition 16 (Finite Automaton Immunity). *Given a finite automaton $\mathcal{A} = (Q, \Sigma, q_0, \delta, F)$ and a trace mutation $\mathcal{M}^k \subseteq \Sigma^* \times \Sigma^*$, $\mathcal{A}$ is immune to $\mathcal{M}^k$ iff $\forall (\sigma, \sigma') \in \mathcal{M}^k, \sigma \in \mathcal{L}(\mathcal{A}) \Leftrightarrow \sigma' \in \mathcal{L}(\mathcal{A})$.*

With this definition we can provide a decision procedure for the monitorability of an ω-regular property over an unreliable channel. The procedure will check the immunity of the $\mathbb{B}_3$ monitor automata to the mutations from the channel, as well as the property's monitorability. If the DFAs are both immune to the mutations and the property is monitorable, then the property is monitorable over the unreliable channel.

8   Decision Procedure for Finite Automaton Immunity

We propose Algorithm 1 for deciding whether a DFA is immune to a trace mutation. The algorithm is loosely based on Hopcroft and Karp's near-linear algorithm for determining the equivalence of finite automata [15].

Algorithm 1. Determine if a DFA is immune to a given trace mutation.

1: **procedure** IMMUNE($\mathcal{A} = (\Sigma, Q, q_0, \delta, F), M$)
2:     **for** $q \in Q$ **do** $E(q) \leftarrow \{q\}$ ▷ E is a map $E : Q \twoheadrightarrow 2^Q$
3:     $R \leftarrow \mathcal{R}each(\mathcal{A}, q_0)$ ▷ R is the reachable states
4:     $T \leftarrow \{\ \}$ ▷ T is a set of pairs, used like a worklist
5:     **for** $(\sigma, \sigma') \in M$ **where** $|\sigma| = minLength(M)$ **do**   ▷ M is a mutation relation
6:         **for** $q \in R$ **do**
7:             $q_1 \leftarrow \delta^*(q, \sigma); q_2 \leftarrow \delta^*(q, \sigma')$ ▷ Follow mutated strings
8:             $E(q_1) \leftarrow E(q_2) \leftarrow \{q_1, q_2\}$ ▷ Update E for both states
9:             $T \leftarrow T \cup \{(q_1, q_2)\}$ ▷ Add the pair to T
10:     **while** T is not empty **do**
11:         **let** $(q_1, q_2) \in T$ ▷ Get a pair from the worklist
12:         $T \leftarrow T \setminus \{(q_1, q_2)\}$ ▷ Remove the pair from T
13:         **for** $\alpha \in \Sigma$ **do**
14:             $n_1 \leftarrow \delta(q_1, \alpha); n_2 \leftarrow \delta(q_2, \alpha)$ ▷ Follow transitions to the next states
15:             $C \leftarrow \{E(n_1), E(n_2)\}$ ▷ C is a set of two sets
16:             **if** $|C| > 1$ **then**   ▷ If those sets weren't equal
17:                 $E(n_1) \leftarrow E(n_2) \leftarrow \bigcup C$ ▷ Merge sets in E
18:                 $T \leftarrow T \cup \{(n_1, n_2)\}$ ▷ The new pair is added to T
19:     **if** Any set in E contains both final and non-final states **then return False**
20:     **else return True**

The parameters to Algorithm 1 are the DFA to check ($\mathcal{A}$) and the mutation (M) which is a relation given by $\mathcal{M}^1$ in Definition 11. The intuition behind Algorithm 1 is to follow transitions for pairs of unmutated and corresponding mutated strings in M and verify that they lead to the same acceptance verdicts. More specifically, Algorithm 1 finds sets of states which must be equivalent for the DFA to be immune to a given mutation. The final verdict of IMMUNE is found by checking that no equivalence class contains both final and non-final states. If an equivalence class contains both, then there are some strings for which the verdict will change due to the given mutation.

If all mutations required only a string of length one, the step at Line 7 could follow transitions for pairs of single symbols. However, mutations like *OutOfOrder* require strings of at least two symbols, so we must follow transitions for short strings. We express this idea of a minimum length for a mutation in the $minLength : 2^{\Sigma^* \times \Sigma^*} \to \mathbb{N}$ function. For mutations in Sect. 5, $minLength(Loss) = minLength(Corruption) = minLength(Stutter) = 1$ and $minLength(OutOfOrder) = 2$. Note that $minLength$ for unions must increase to permit the application of both mutations on a string. For example, $minLength(Loss \cup Corruption) = 2$. This length guarantees that each string has at least one mutation, which is sufficient to show immunity by Theorem 2.

The algorithm works as follows. We assume a mutation can occur at any time, so we begin by following transitions for pairs of mutated and unmutated strings from every reachable state (stored in the set R). On Lines 5–9, for each pair (σ, σ') in M and for each reachable state, we compute the states q_1 and q_2 reached from σ (respectively σ'). The map E contains equivalence classes, which we update for q_1 and q_2 to hold the set containing both states. The pair of states is also added to the worklist T, which contains equivalent states from which string suffixes must be explored.

The loop on Lines 10–18 then explores those suffixes. It takes a pair of states (q_1, q_2) from the worklist and follows transitions from those states to reach n_1 and n_2. If n_1 and n_2 are already marked as equivalent to other states in E or aren't marked as equivalent to each other, those states are added to the worklist, and their equivalence classes in E are merged. If at the end, there is an equivalence class with final and non-final states, then $\mathcal{A}$ is not immune to M.

Theorem 4 (Immunity Procedure Correctness). *Algorithm 1 is sound and complete for any DFA and prefix-assured mutation. That is, given a DFA $\mathcal{A} = (\Sigma, Q, q_0, \delta, F)$, and a mutation, M, $\textsc{Immune}(\mathcal{A}, M) \Leftrightarrow \mathcal{A}$ is immune to M.*

Proof: By Definition 16, this is equivalent to showing that $\textsc{Immune}(\mathcal{A}, M) \Leftrightarrow (\forall (\sigma, \sigma') \in M, \ \sigma \in \mathcal{L}(\mathcal{A}) \Leftrightarrow \sigma' \in \mathcal{L}(\mathcal{A}))$.

We will prove the $\Rightarrow$ direction (soundness) by contradiction. Suppose at the completion of the algorithm that all sets in E contain only final or non-final states, but that $\mathcal{A}$ is not immune to M. There is at least one pair $(\sigma_b, \sigma'_b) \in M$ where one leads to a final state, and one does not. If Algorithm 1 had checked this pair then these states would be in an equivalence class in E. Since the loop on Line 7 follows transitions for pairs in M of length $minLength(M)$, the reason (σ_b, σ'_b) was not checked must be because $|\sigma_b| \neq minLength(M)$. The length of σ_b must be greater than $minLength(M)$ since strings shorter than $minLength(M)$ cannot be mutated by M. Since M is prefix-assured, there must be a pair $(\sigma, \sigma') : |\sigma| = minLength(M)$ that are prefixes of (σ_b, σ'_b). The loop on Line 10 will check $(\sigma \cdot s, \sigma' \cdot s)$, $\forall s \in \Sigma^*$. Therefore it must be the case that $\sigma_b = \sigma \cdot t$, $\sigma'_b = \sigma' \cdot u : t, u \in \Sigma^*$, $t \neq u$. However, if $t \neq u$ then $(\sigma_b, \sigma'_b) \in M^k : k > 1$, so $\mathcal{A}$ is immune to M^1 but not M^k, but from Theorem 2 this is a contradiction.

We prove the $\Leftarrow$ direction (completeness) by induction. We will show that if $\mathcal{A}$ is immune to M then no set in E, and no pair in T will contain both final and non-final states. The base case at initialization is obviously true since every set in E contains only one state and T is empty. The induction hypothesis is that at a given step i of the algorithm if $\mathcal{A}$ is immune to M then every set in E and every pair in T contains only final or non-final states.

At step $i + 1$, in the loop on Line 7, E and T are updated to contain states reached by following σ and σ'. Clearly, if $\mathcal{A}$ is immune to M then these states must be both final or non-final since we followed transitions from reachable states for a pair in M. In the loop on Line 10, n_1 and n_2 are reached by following the same symbol in the alphabet from a pair of states in T. If $\mathcal{A}$ is immune to M, the strings leading to that pair of states must both be in, or both be out of the language. So, extending both strings by the same symbol in the alphabet creates two strings that must both be in or out of the language. These states reached by following these strings are added to T on Line 18.

On Lines 15 and 17, the two sets in E corresponding to n_1 and n_2 are merged. Since both sets must contain only final or non-final states, and one-or-both of n_1 and n_2 are contained in them, the union of the sets must also contain only final or non-final states.   □

Theorem 5 (Immunity Procedure Complexity). *Algorithm 1 is Fixed-Parameter Tractable. That is, given a DFA $\mathcal{A} = (\Sigma, Q, q_0, \delta, F)$, and a mutation, M, its maximum running time is $|Q|^{O(1)} f(k)$, where f is some function that depends only on some parameter k.*

Proof: The run-time complexity of Algorithm 1 is $O(n)O(m^l f(M))$ where $n = |Q|$, $m = |\Sigma|$, $l = minLength(M)$, and f is a function on M. First, Lines 4, 7, 8, 9, 11, 12, 14, 15, 16, 17, and 18 execute in constant time, while each of Lines 2, 3, and 19 run in time bounded by n.

The initialization loop at Line 5 runs once for each pair in the mutation where the length of σ is bounded by $minLength(M)$. This count is m^l times a factor $f(M)$ determined by the mutation. For example, $f(Loss) = l$ because each σ is mutated to remove each symbol in the string. Critically, this factor $f(M)$ must be finite, which it is for the mutations $\mathcal{M}^1$. The loop at Line 6 runs in time bounded by n, so the body of the loop is reached at most $m^l f(M)n$ times.

The loop at Line 10 may run at most $m^l f(M) + n$ times. The loop continues while the worklist T is non-empty. Initially, T has $m^l f(M)$ elements. Each time Line 12 runs, an element is removed from the worklist. For an element to be added to T, it must contain states corresponding to sets in E which are not identical. When this occurs, those two corresponding sets are merged, so the number of unique sets in E is reduced by at least one. Therefore, the maximum number of times Line 18 can be reached and an element added to T is n.   □

Note that, in practice, $minLength(M)$ is usually small (often only one), so Algorithm 1 achieves near linear performance in the size of the FA. The size of the alphabet has an effect but it is still quadratic.

9   Discussion

The mutations from Definitions 7 to 10 are useful abstractions of common problems in communication. However, in many cases, they are stronger than is needed as practitioners may have knowledge of the channel that constrains the mutations. For example, in MSL, messages contain sequence numbers which can be used to narrow the range of missing symbols. An advantage of our method is that custom mutations can be easily defined and then tested using Algorithm 1.

Custom mutations should avoid behavior that requires long strings to mutate, however, as this causes exponential slowdown.

Well designed mutations like those in Sect. 5 can be checked quickly. However, the method relies on $\mathbb{B}_3$ monitor construction to obtain DFAs, and the procedure to create them from an NBA is in 2EXPSPACE. We argue that this is an acceptable cost of using the procedure since a monitor must be derived to check the property in any case. Future work should explore ideas from the study of monitorability [11,22] to find a theoretical bound on deciding immunity.

Another avenue for improving on our work is to characterize classes of properties that are immune to different mutations. The classes of monitorable properties under different definitions in Sect. 4 are mostly understood [13,22]. Finding a similar classification for the immunity of properties to mutations would be useful. It is already understood that all LTL properties without the next (X) operator are immune to *Stutter* [19,23].

10   Related Work

Unreliable channels have been acknowledged in formal methods research for some time. One area where the unreliable communication channels are commonly modeled is where Communicating Finite State Machines (CFSMs) are used to verify network protocols. Abdulla and Jonsson provided algorithms for deciding the termination problem for protocols on lossy first-in first-out (FIFO) buffers, as well as algorithms for some safety and eventuality properties [2]. Cécé et al. also considered channels with insertion errors and duplication errors [8].

Work has been done to show which properties are verifiable on a trace with mutations and to express degrees of confidence when they are not. Stoller et al. used Hidden Markov Models (HMMs) to compute the probability of a property being satisfied on a lossy trace [26]. Their definition of lossy included a "gap" marker indicating where symbols were missing. They used HMMs to predict the missing states where gaps occurred and aided their estimations with a learned probability distribution of state transitions. Joshi et al. introduced an algorithm to determine if a specification could be monitored soundly in the presence of a trace with transient loss, meaning that eventually it contained successfully transmitted events [16]. They defined monotonicity to identify properties for which the verdicts could be relied upon once a decision was made.

Garg et al. introduced a first-order logic with restricted quantifiers for auditing incomplete policy logs [14]. The authors used restricted quantifiers to allow monitoring policies that would, in principle, require iterating over an infinite domain. Basin et al. also specified a first-order logic for auditing incomplete policy logs [4]. Basin et al. also proposed a semantics and monitoring algorithm for Metric Temporal Logic (MTL) with freeze quantifiers that was sound and complete for unordered traces [3]. Their semantics were based on a three-value logic, and the monitoring algorithm was evaluated over ordered and unordered traces. All three of these languages used a three value semantics ($t, f, \perp$) to model a lossy trace, where $\perp$ represented missing information.

Li et al. examined out-of-order data arrival in Complex Event Processing (CEP) systems and found that SASE [27] queries processed using the Active Instance Stack (AIS) data structure would fail in several ways [20]. They proposed modifications to AIS to support out-of-order data and found acceptable experimental overhead to their technique.

11   Conclusion

The ability to check properties expressible by NBAs for monitorability over unreliable channels allows RV to be considered for applications where RV would have previously been ignored. To arrive at this capability, we first needed to define monitorability over unreliable channels using both existing notions of monitorability and a new concept of mutation immunity. We proved that immunity to a single application of a mutation is sufficient to show immunity to any number of applications of that mutation, and we defined true-false immunity using $\mathbb{B}_3$ semantics. We believe unreliable communication is an important topic for RV and other fields that rely on remote systems, and we hope that this work leads to further examination of unreliable channels in the RV community.

Acknowledgements. The authors would like to thank Rajeev Joshi for his contributions to the work.

References

1. Embedded trace macrocell architecture specification, May 2019. http://infocenter.arm.com/help/index.jsp?topic=/com.arm.doc.ihi0014q/
2. Abdulla, P.A., Jonsson, B.: Verifying programs with unreliable channels. Inf. Comput. **127**(2), 91–101 (1996)
3. Basin, D., Klaedtke, F., Zălinescu, E.: Runtime verification of temporal properties over out-of-order data streams. In: Majumdar, R., Kunčak, V. (eds.) CAV 2017. LNCS, vol. 10426, pp. 356–376. Springer, Cham (2017). https://doi.org/10.1007/978-3-319-63387-9_18
4. Basin, D., Klaedtke, F., Marinovic, S., Zălinescu, E.: Monitoring compliance policies over incomplete and disagreeing logs. In: Qadeer, S., Tasiran, S. (eds.) RV 2012. LNCS, vol. 7687, pp. 151–167. Springer, Heidelberg (2013). https://doi.org/10.1007/978-3-642-35632-2_17
5. Bauer, A., Leucker, M., Schallhart, C.: Monitoring of real-time properties. In: Arun-Kumar, S., Garg, N. (eds.) FSTTCS 2006. LNCS, vol. 4337, pp. 260–272. Springer, Heidelberg (2006). https://doi.org/10.1007/11944836_25
6. Bauer, A., Leucker, M., Schallhart, C.: Comparing LTL semantics for runtime verification. J. Logic Comput. **20**(3), 651–674 (2010)
7. Bauer, A., Leucker, M., Schallhart, C.: Runtime verification for LTL and TLTL. ACM Trans. Softw. Eng. Methodol. (TOSEM) **20**(4), 14:1–14:64 (2011)
8. Cécé, G., Finkel, A., Iyer, S.P.: Unreliable channels are easier to verify than perfect channels. Inf. Comput. **124**(1), 20–31 (1996)
9. Chen, Z., Wu, Y., Wei, O., Sheng, B.: Deciding weak monitorability for runtime verification. In: Proceedings of the 40th International Conference on Software Engineering: Companion Proceedings, ICSE 2018, pp. 163–164. ACM, New York (2018)

10. d'Amorim, M., Roşu, G.: Efficient monitoring of ω-languages. In: Etessami, K., Rajamani, S.K. (eds.) CAV 2005. LNCS, vol. 3576, pp. 364–378. Springer, Heidelberg (2005). https://doi.org/10.1007/11513988_36

11. Diekert, V., Muscholl, A., Walukiewicz, I.: A note on monitors and Büchi automata. In: Leucker, M., Rueda, C., Valencia, F.D. (eds.) ICTAC 2015. LNCS, vol. 9399, pp. 39–57. Springer, Cham (2015). https://doi.org/10.1007/978-3-319-25150-9_3

12. Falcone, Y., Fernandez, J.-C., Mounier, L.: Runtime verification of safety-progress properties. In: Bensalem, S., Peled, D.A. (eds.) RV 2009. LNCS, vol. 5779, pp. 40–59. Springer, Heidelberg (2009). https://doi.org/10.1007/978-3-642-04694-0_4

13. Falcone, Y., Fernandez, J.C., Mounier, L.: What can you verify and enforce at runtime? Int. J. Softw. Tools Technol. Transf. 14(3), 349–382 (2012)

14. Garg, D., Jia, L., Datta, A.: Policy auditing over incomplete logs: theory, implementation and applications. In: Proceedings of the 18th ACM Conference on Computer and Communications Security, CCS 2011, pp. 151–162. ACM, New York (2011)

15. Hopcroft, J.E., Karp, R.M.: A linear algorithm for testing equivalence of finite automata. Technical report, Cornell University (1971)

16. Joshi, Y., Tchamgoue, G.M., Fischmeister, S.: Runtime verification of LTL on lossy traces. In: Proceedings of the Symposium on Applied Computing, SAC 2017, pp. 1379–1386. ACM, New York (2017)

17. Kupferman, O., Vardi, M.Y.: Model checking of safety properties. Formal Methods Syst. Des. 19(3), 291–314 (2001)

18. Kupferman, O., Vardi, M.Y.: Weak alternating automata are not that weak. ACM Trans. Comput. Logic 2(3), 408–429 (2001)

19. Lamport, L.: What good is temporal logic? In: IFIP Congress, vol. 83, pp. 657–668 (1983)

20. Li, M., Liu, M., Ding, L., Rundensteiner, E.A., Mani, M.: Event stream processing with out-of-order data arrival. In: 27th International Conference on Distributed Computing Systems Workshops, ICDCSW 2007, p. 67, June 2007

21. Lozes, É., Villard, J.: Reliable contracts for unreliable half-duplex communications. In: Carbone, M., Petit, J.-M. (eds.) WS-FM 2011. LNCS, vol. 7176, pp. 2–16. Springer, Heidelberg (2012). https://doi.org/10.1007/978-3-642-29834-9_2

22. Peled, D., Havelund, K.: Refining the safety–liveness classification of temporal properties according to monitorability. In: Margaria, T., Graf, S., Larsen, K.G. (eds.) Models, Mindsets, Meta: The What, the How, and the Why Not?. LNCS, vol. 11200, pp. 218–234. Springer, Cham (2019). https://doi.org/10.1007/978-3-030-22348-9_14

23. Peled, D., Wilke, T.: Stutter-invariant temporal properties are expressible without the next-time operator. Inf. Process. Lett. 63(5), 243–246 (1997)

24. Pnueli, A., Zaks, A.: PSL model checking and run-time verification via testers. In: Misra, J., Nipkow, T., Sekerinski, E. (eds.) FM 2006. LNCS, vol. 4085, pp. 573–586. Springer, Heidelberg (2006). https://doi.org/10.1007/11813040_38

25. Sistla, A.P., Clarke, E.M.: The complexity of propositional linear temporal logics. J. ACM 32(3), 733–749 (1985)

26. Stoller, S.D., Bartocci, E., Seyster, J., Grosu, R., Havelund, K., Smolka, S.A., Zadok, E.: Runtime verification with state estimation. Runtime Verification 11, 193–207 (2011)

27. Wu, E., Diao, Y., Rizvi, S.: High-performance complex event processing over streams. In: Proceedings of the 2006 ACM SIGMOD International Conference on Management of Data, SIGMOD 2006, pp. 407–418. ACM, New York (2006)

Runtime Verification for Timed Event Streams with Partial Information

Martin Leucker[1]([⊠]), César Sánchez[2]([⊠]), Torben Scheffel[1]([⊠]),
Malte Schmitz[1]([⊠]), and Daniel Thoma[1]([⊠])

[1] University of Lübeck, Lübeck, Germany
{leucker,scheffel,schmitz,thoma}@isp.uni-luebeck.de
[2] IMDEA Software Institute, Madrid, Spain
cesar.sanchez@imdea.org

Abstract. Runtime Verification (RV) studies how to analyze execution traces of a system under observation. Stream Runtime Verification (SRV) applies stream transformations to obtain information from observed traces. Incomplete traces with information missing in gaps pose a common challenge when applying RV and SRV techniques to real-world systems as RV approaches typically require the complete trace without missing parts. This paper presents a solution to perform SRV on incomplete traces based on abstraction. We use TeSSLa as specification language for non-synchronized timed event streams and define abstract event streams representing the set of all possible traces that could have occurred during gaps in the input trace. We show how to translate a TeSSLa specification to its abstract counterpart that can propagate gaps through the transformation of the input streams and thus generate sound outputs even if the input streams contain gaps and events with imprecise values. The solution has been implemented as a set of macros for the original TeSSLa and an empirical evaluation shows the feasibility of the approach.

1 Introduction

Runtime verification (RV) is a dynamic formal method for software system reliability. RV studies how to analyze and evaluate traces against formal specifications and how to obtain program traces from the system under observation, e.g., through software instrumentation or utilization of processors' embedded trace units. Since RV only inspects one execution trace of the system, it is often regarded to be a readily applicable but incomplete approach, that combines formal verification with testing and debugging.

Most early RV languages were based on logics common in static verification, like LTL [21], past LTL adapted for finite paths [4,11,18], regular expressions [22] or timed regular expressions [2]. For these logics, the monitoring problem consists on computing a Boolean verdict indicating whether the trace fulfills the

This work was funded in part by the Madrid Regional Government under project *S2018/TCS-4339 (BLOQUES-CM)*, by EU H2020 projects 731535 *Elastest* and 732016 *COEMS*, by Spanish National Project *BOSCO (PGC2018-102210-B-100)* and by the BMBF project *ARAMiS II* with funding ID 01 IS 16025.

B. Finkbeiner and L. Mariani (Eds.): RV 2019, LNCS 11757, pp. 273–291, 2019.
https://doi.org/10.1007/978-3-030-32079-9_16

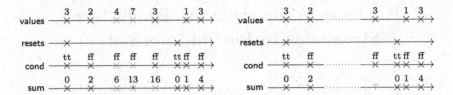

Fig. 1. Example trace for a typical SRV specification (left) with two input streams values (with numeric values) and resets (with no internal value). The intention of the specification is to accumulate in the output stream sum all values since the last reset. The intermediate stream cond is derived from the input streams indicating if reset has currently the most recent event, and thus the sum should be reset to 0. If the input streams contain gaps (dotted regions on the right) some information can no longer be computed, but after a reset event the computation recovers from the data loss during the gap. ⊤ denotes events with unknown data.

specification. In contrast to static analysis, however, considering only a single concrete trace enables the application of more complex analyses: Stream Runtime Verification (SRV) [6,7,10] uses stream transformations to derive additional streams as verdicts from the input streams. Using SRV one can still check if the input stream is conformant with a specification, but additionally verify streams in terms of their events' data: streams in SRV can store data from richer domains than Booleans, including numerical values or user defined data-types, so SRV languages can extract quantitative values and express quantitative properties like "*compute the average retransmission time*" or "*compute the longest duration of a function*". SRV cleanly separates the temporal dependencies that the stream transformation algorithms follow from the concrete operations to be performed on the data, which are specific to each data-type. As an example for SRV consider the trace diagram on the left of Fig. 1. We consider non-synchronized event streams, i.e., sequences of events with increasing timestamps and values from a data domain. Using non-synchronized event streams one can represent events arriving on different streams with different frequencies in a compact way with little computation overhead because there is no need to process additional synchronization events in the stream-transformation process. In this paper we use the TeSSLa specification language [7], an SRV language for non-synchronized, timed event streams. TeSSLa has been defined to be general enough to allow for a natural translation from other common SRV formalisms, e.g., Lola [10] and Striver [16]. Therefore, our results carry over to these languages as well.

Since RV is performed on traces obtained from the system under test in the deployed environment, it is a common practical problem for RV techniques that the traces do not cover the entire run of the system. However, most of the previous RV approaches require the trace to be available without any interruptions in order to obtain a verdict, because this knowledge is assumed in the semantics of the specification logics. Especially in the case of interrupted traces with some data losses applying previous RV techniques can be very challenging. Unfortunately those traces occur very often in practical testing and debugging scenarios, e.g., due to interrupted experiments, buffer overflows, network errors or any other temporary problem with the trace retrieval.

In this paper we present a solution to the problem of evaluating traces with imprecise values and even interrupted traces. Our only assumption is that we have exact knowledge of the imprecision of the trace in the following sense: (1) for events with imprecise values we know the range of values and (2) for data losses we know when we stop getting information and when the trace becomes reliable again. We call such a sequence of uncertainty a *gap* in the trace. Our solution automatically propagates gaps and imprecisions, and allows to obtain sound verdicts even in the case of missing information in the input trace.

Figure 1 on the right displays a case where the input stream values has a long gap in the middle. It is not possible to determine the events in the output stream sum during that gap, because we do not even know if and how many events might have happened during that gap. Thus, the intermediate stream cond and the output stream sum simply copy that gap representing any possible combination of events that might occur. The first event after the gap is the one with the value 3 on values. Because no reset happened after the end of the gap, we would add 3 to the latest event's value on sum, but the gap is the latest on sum. Thus, we only know that this input event on values causes an event on sum independently of what might have happened during the gap, but the value of that event completely depends on possible events occurring during the gap. After the next event on reset the values of the following events on sum are independent of any previous events. The monitor can fully recover from the missing information during the gap and can again produce events with precise values.

In order to realize this propagation of gaps through all the steps of the stream-transformation we need to represent all potentially infinitely many concrete traces (time is dense and values are for arbitrary domains) that might have happened during gaps and imprecise events. An intuitive approach would be a symbolic representation in terms of constraint formulas to describe the set of all possible streams. These formulas would then be updated while evaluating the input trace. While such a symbolic execution might work for shorter traces, the representation can grow quickly with each input event. Consequently the computational cost could grow prohibitively with the trace length for many input traces. Instead, in this paper we introduce a framework based on abstraction [8,9]. We use abstraction in two ways:

(1) Streams are lifted from concrete domains of data to abstract domains to model possible sets of values. For example, in our solution a stream can store intervals as abstract numerical values.
(2) We define the notion of abstract traces, which extend timed streams with the capabilities of representing gaps. Intuitively, an abstract trace over-approximates the sets of concrete traces that can be obtained by filling the gaps with all possible concrete events.

Our approach allows for both gaps in the input streams as well as events carrying imprecise values. Such imprecise values can be modelled by abstract domains, e.g., intervals of real numbers. Since we rely on abstraction, we can avoid false negatives and false positives in the usual sense: concrete verdicts are guaranteed to hold and imprecise verdicts are clearly distinguished from concrete verdicts. The achievable precision depends on the specification and the input trace.

After reproducing the semantics of the basic TeSSLa operators in Sect. 2, we introduce abstract semantics of the existing basic operators of TeSSLa in Sect. 3. Using these abstract TeSSLa operators, we can take a TeSSLa specification on streams and replace every TeSSLa operator with its abstract counterpart and derive an abstraction of the specification on abstract event streams. We show that the abstract specification is a sound abstraction of the concrete specification, i.e., every concrete verdict generated by the original specification on a set S of possible input traces is represented by the abstract verdict applied to an abstraction of S. We further show that the abstract TeSSLa operators are a perfect abstraction of their concrete counterparts, i.e., that applying the concrete operator on all individual elements of S doesn't get you more accurate results. Finally, we show that an abstract TeSSLa specification can be implemented using the existing TeSSLa basic operators by representing an abstract event stream as multiple concrete event streams carrying information about the events and the gaps. Since the perfect accuracy of the individual abstract TeSSLa operators does not guarantee perfect accuracy of their compositions, we discuss the accuracy of composed abstract TeSSLa specifications in Sect. 4. Next we present in Sect. 5 an advanced use-case where we apply abstract TeSSLa to streams over a complex data domain of unbounded queues, which are used to compute the average of all events that happened in the sliding window of the last five time units. Section 6 evaluates the overhead and the accuracy of the presented abstractions on representative example specifications and corresponding input traces with gaps. An extended preprint version of this paper is available as [19].

Related Work. SRV was pioneered by LOLA [10,13,14]. TeSSLa [7] generalises to asynchronous streams the original idea of LOLA of recursive equations over stream transformations. Its design is influenced by formalisms like stream programming languages [5,15,17] and functional reactive programming [12]. Other approaches to handle data and time constraints include Quantitative Regular Expressions QRE [1] and Signal Temporal Logic [20].

While ubiquitous in practice, the problem of gaps in an observation trace has not been studied extensively. To the best of our knowledge, abstraction techniques have not been applied to the evaluation of stream-based specifications. However, approaches to handle the absence of events or ordering information have been presented for MTL [3] and past-time LTL [24]. State estimation based on Markov models has been applied to replace absent information by a probabilistic estimation [23]. The concept of abstract interpretation used throughout this paper has been introduced in [8].

2   The TeSSLa Specification Language

A *time domain* is a totally ordered semi-ring $(\mathbb{T}, 0, 1, +, \cdot, \leq)$ that is positive, i.e., $\forall_{t \in \mathbb{T}} \, 0 \leq t$. We extend the order on time domains to the set $\mathbb{T}_\infty = \mathbb{T} \cup \{\infty\}$ with $\forall_{t \in \mathbb{T}} \, t < \infty$. Given a time domain $\mathbb{T}$, an *event stream* over a data domain $\mathbb{D}$ is a finite or infinite sequence $s = t_0 d_0 t_1 \cdots \in \mathcal{S}_\mathbb{D} = (\mathbb{T} \cdot \mathbb{D})^\omega \cup (\mathbb{T} \cdot \mathbb{D})^* \cdot (\mathbb{T}_\infty \cup \mathbb{T} \cdot \mathbb{D}_\perp)$ where $\mathbb{D}_\perp := \mathbb{D} \cup \{\perp\}$ and $t_i < t_{i+1}$ for all i with $0 < i + 1 < |s|$ ($|s|$ is ∞ for infinite sequences). An infinite event stream is an infinite sequence of timestamps and data values representing the stream's events. A finite event stream is a finite sequence of timestamped events up to a certain timestamp that indicates the progress of the stream. A stream can end with:

- a timestamp without a data value that denotes progress up to but not including that timestamp,
- a timestamp followed by $\perp$ (or a data value) which denotes progress up to and including that timestamp (and an event at that timestamp),
- ∞, which indicates that no additional events will ever arrive on this stream.

We refer to these cases as *exclusive, inclusive* and *infinite progress*, resp.

Streams $s \in \mathcal{S}_\mathbb{D}$ can be seen as functions $s : \mathbb{T} \to \mathbb{D} \cup \{\perp, ?\}$ such that $s(t)$ is a value d if s has an event with value d at time t or $\perp$ if there is no event at time t. For timestamps after the progress of the stream $s(t)$ is $?$. Formally, $s(t) = d$ if s contains td, $s(t) = \perp$ if s does not contain t, but contains a $t' > t$ or s ends in $t\perp$, and $s(t) = ?$ otherwise. We use $ticks(s)$ for the set $\{t \in \mathbb{T} \mid s(t) \in \mathbb{D}\}$ of timestamps where s has events. A stream s is a *prefix* of stream r if $\forall_{t \in \mathbb{T}} s(t) \in \{r(t), ?\}$. We use the unit type $\mathbb{U} = \{\square\}$ for streams carrying only the single value $\square$. A TeSSLa specification consists of a collection of stream variables and possibly recursive equations over these variables using the operators **nil**, **unit**, **time**, **lift**, **last** and **delay**. The semantics of recursive equations is given as the least fixed-point of the equations seen as a function of the stream variables and fixed input streams. See [7] for more details.

- ▶ **nil** $= \infty \in \mathcal{S}_\emptyset$ is the stream without any events and infinite progress.
- ▶ **unit** $= 0 \, \square \, \infty \in \mathcal{S}_\mathbb{U}$ is the stream with a single unit event at timestamp zero and infinite progress.
- ▶ **time** $: \mathcal{S}_\mathbb{D} \to \mathcal{S}_\mathbb{T}$, **time**$(s) := z$ maps the event's values to their timestamps: $z(t) = t$ if $t \in ticks(s)$ and $z(t) = s(t)$ otherwise.
- ▶ **lift** $: (\mathbb{D}_{1\perp} \times \ldots \times \mathbb{D}_{n\perp} \to \mathbb{D}_\perp) \to (\mathcal{S}_{\mathbb{D}_1} \times \ldots \times \mathcal{S}_{\mathbb{D}_n} \to \mathcal{S}_\mathbb{D})$, **lift**$(f)(s_1, \ldots, s_n) := z$ lifts a function f on values to a function on streams by applying f to the stream's values for every timestamp. The function f must not generate new events, i.e., must fulfill $f(\perp, \ldots, \perp) = \perp$.

$$z(t) = \begin{cases} f(s_1(t), \ldots, s_n(t)) & \text{if } s_1(t) \neq ?, \ldots, s_n(t) \neq ? \\ ? & \text{otherwise} \end{cases}$$

- ▶ **last** $: \mathcal{S}_\mathbb{D} \times \mathcal{S}_{\mathbb{D}'} \to \mathcal{S}_\mathbb{D}$, **last**$(v, r) := z$ takes a stream v of values and a stream r of triggers. It outputs an event with the previous value on v for every event on r.

$$z(t) = \begin{cases} d & t \in \text{ticks}(r) \text{ and } \exists_{t' < t} \text{isLast}(t, t', v, d) \\ \bot & r(t) = \bot \text{ and } \text{defined}(z, t), \text{ or } \forall_{t' < t} v(t') = \bot \\ ? & \text{otherwise} \end{cases}$$

$\text{isLast}(t, t', v, d) \overset{\text{def}}{=} v(t') = d \wedge \forall_{t'' | t' < t'' < t} v(t'') = \bot$ holds if $t'd$ is the last event on v until t, and $\text{defined}(z, t) \overset{\text{def}}{=} \forall_{t' < t} z(t') \neq ?$ holds if z is defined until t (exclusive).

Using the basic operators we can now derive the following utility functions:

▷ $\text{const}(c)(a) := \textbf{lift}(f_c)(a)$ with $f_c(d) := c$. This function maps the values of all events of the input stream a to a constant value c. Using const we can lift constants into streams representing a constant signal with this value, e.g., $\text{true} := \text{const}(\text{true})(\textbf{unit})$ or $\text{zero} := \text{const}(0)(\textbf{unit})$.

▷ $\text{merge}(x, y) := \textbf{lift}(f)(x, y)$ with $f(a \neq \bot, b) = a$ and $f(\bot, b) = b$, which combines events from two streams, prioritizing the first stream.

Event streams in TeSSLa can also be interpreted as a *continuous signals*. Using **last** one can query the last known value of an event stream s and interpret the events on s as points where a piece-wise constant signal changes its value. By combining the **last** and **lift** operators, we can realize:

▷ *signal lift* for total functions $f : \mathbb{D} \times \mathbb{D}' \to \mathbb{D}''$ as $\text{slift}(f)(x, y) := \textbf{lift}(g_f)(x', y')$ with $x' := \text{merge}(x, \textbf{last}(x, y))$ and $y' := \text{merge}(y, \textbf{last}(y, x))$, as well as $g_f(a \neq \bot, b \neq \bot) := f(a, b)$, $g_f(\bot, b) := \bot$, and $g_f(a, \bot) := \bot$.

Example 1. We can now specify the stream transformations shown on the left in Fig. 1 in TeSSLa. Let $\text{resets} \in \mathcal{S}_\mathbb{U}$ and $\text{values} \in \mathcal{S}_\mathbb{Z}$ be two external input event streams. We then derive $\text{cond} \in \mathcal{S}_\mathbb{B}$ and $\text{lst}, \text{sum} \in \mathcal{S}_\mathbb{Z}$ as follows:

$$\text{cond} = \text{slift}(\leq)(\textbf{time}(\text{resets}), \textbf{time}(\text{values})) \qquad f : \mathbb{B} \times \mathbb{Z} \times \mathbb{Z} \to \mathbb{Z} \text{ with}$$
$$\text{lst} = \text{merge}(\textbf{last}(\text{sum}, \text{values}), \text{zero})$$
$$\text{sum} = \text{slift}(f)(\text{cond}, \text{lst}, \text{values}) \qquad f(c, l, v) = \begin{cases} 0 & \text{if } c = \text{true} \\ l + v & \text{otherwise} \end{cases}$$

Using the operators described above one can only derive streams with timestamps that are already present in the input streams. To derive streams with events at computed timestamps one can use the **delay** operator, which is described in [7].

3   Abstract TeSSLa

Preliminaries. Given two partial orders $(A, \preceq)$ and $(B, \preceq)$, a *Galois Connection* is a pair of monotone functions $\alpha : A \to B$ and $\gamma : B \to A$ such that, for all $a \in A$ and $b \in B$, $\alpha(a) \preceq b$ if and only if $a \preceq \gamma(b)$. Let $(A, \preceq)$ be a partial order, $f : A \to A$ a monotone function and $\gamma : B \to A$ a function. The function $f^{\#} : B \to B$ is an *abstraction* of f whenever, for all $b \in B$, $f(\gamma(b)) \preceq \gamma(f^{\#}(b))$. If (α, γ) is a Galois Connection between A and B, the function $f^{\#} : B \to B$ such that $f^{\#}(b) := \alpha(f(\gamma(b))$ is a *perfect abstraction* of f.

In this section we define the abstract counterparts of the TeSSLa operators, listed in Sect. 2. A *data abstraction* of a data domain $\mathbb{D}$ is an abstract domain $\mathbb{D}^{\#}$ with an element $\top \in \mathbb{D}^{\#}$ and an associated concretisation function $\gamma : \mathbb{D}^{\#} \to 2^{\mathbb{D}}$ with $\gamma(\top) = \mathbb{D}$. The abstract value $\top$ represents any possible value from the data domain and can be used to model an event with known timestamp but unknown value. A *gap* is a segment of an abstract event stream that represents all combinations of events that could possibly occur in that segment (both in terms of timestamps and values). Hence an abstract event stream consists of an event stream over a data abstraction and an associated set of known timestamps:

Definition 1 (Abstract Event Stream). *Given a time domain* $\mathbb{T}$, *an abstract event stream over a data domain* $\mathbb{D}$ *is a pair* (s, Δ) *with* $s \in \mathcal{S}_{\mathbb{D}}^{\#}$ *and* $\Delta \subseteq \mathbb{T}$ *such that* Δ *can be represented as union of intervals whose (inclusive or exclusive) boundaries are indicated by events in an event stream. Further, we require* $s(t) \neq \bot \Rightarrow t \in \Delta$. *The set of all abstract event streams over* $\mathbb{D}$ *is denoted as* $\mathcal{P}_{\mathbb{D}}$. *The concretisation function* $\gamma : \mathcal{P}_{\mathbb{D}} \to 2^{\mathcal{S}_{\mathbb{D}}}$ *is defined as*

$$\gamma((s, \Delta)) = \{s' \mid \forall_{t \in ticks(s)} s(t) \in \gamma(s'(t)) \land \forall_{t \in \Delta \setminus ticks(s)} s(t) = s'(t)\}$$

If the data abstraction is defined in terms of a Galois Connection a refinement ordering and abstraction function can be obtained. The refinement ordering $(\mathcal{P}_{\mathbb{D}}, \preceq)$ is defined as $(s_1, \Delta_1) \preceq (s_2, \Delta_2)$ iff $\Delta_1 \supseteq \Delta_2$ and $\forall_{t \in ticks(s_2)} s_1(t) \preceq s_2(t) \land \forall_{t \in \Delta_2 \setminus ticks(s_2)} s_1(t) = s_2(t)$. The abstraction function $\alpha : 2^{\mathcal{S}_{\mathbb{D}}} \to \mathcal{P}_{\mathbb{D}}$ is defined as $\alpha(S) = \sup\{(s, \mathbb{T}) \mid s \in S\}$. Note, if the data abstraction is defined in terms of a Galois Connection, (α, γ) is a Galois Connection between $2^{\mathcal{S}_{\mathbb{D}}}$ and $\mathcal{P}_{\mathbb{D}}$.

An abstract event stream $s = (s', \Delta) \in \mathcal{P}_{\mathbb{D}}$ can also be seen as a function $s : \mathbb{T} \to \mathbb{D}^{\#} \cup \{?, \bot, \smile\}$ with $s(t) = s'(t)$ if $t \in \Delta$ and $s(t) = \smile$ otherwise. A particular point t of an abstract event stream s can be either (a) directly at an event $(s(t) \in \mathbb{D})$, (b) in a gap $(s(t) = \smile)$, (c) in a gapless segment without an event at t $(s(t) = \bot)$, or (d) after the known end of the stream $(s(t) = ?)$.

We denote $\mathbb{D}_{\bot}^{\#} \overset{\text{def}}{=} \mathbb{D}^{\#} \cup \{\bot, \smile\}$. If $\mathbb{D}^{\#}$ is a data abstraction of a data domain $\mathbb{D}$ with an associated concretisation function γ, then $\mathbb{D}_{\bot}^{\#}$ is a data abstraction of $\mathbb{D}_{\bot}$ with an associated concretisation function $\gamma_{\bot} : \mathbb{D}_{\bot}^{\#} \to 2^{\mathbb{D} \cup \{\bot\}}$ with

$$\gamma_{\bot}(d) = \begin{cases} \bot & \text{if } d = \bot \\ \mathbb{D} \cup \{\bot\} & \text{if } d = \smile \\ \gamma(d) & \text{if } d \in \mathbb{D}^{\#} \end{cases}$$

The above diagram shows a possible data abstraction $\mathbb{B}^{\#}$ of $\mathbb{B}$ and the corresponding data abstraction $\mathbb{B}_{\bot}^{\#}$. Using the functional representation of an abstract event stream we can now define the abstract counterparts of the TeSSLa operators:

▶ $\mathbf{nil}^{\#} = (\infty, \mathbb{T}) \in \mathcal{P}_{\emptyset}$ is the empty abstract stream without any gaps.

▶ $\mathbf{unit}^{\#} = (0 \,\square\, \infty, \mathbb{T}) \in \mathcal{P}_{\mathbb{U}}$ is the abstract stream without any gaps and a single event at timestamp 0.

▶ $\mathbf{time}^{\#} : \mathcal{P}_{\mathbb{D}} \to \mathcal{P}_{\mathbb{T}}, \mathbf{time}^{\#}(s) := z$ is equivalent to its concrete counterpart; only the data domain is extended: $z(t) = t$ if $t \in ticks(s)$ and $z(t) = s(t)$ otherwise.

▶ $\mathbf{lift}^{\#} : (\mathbb{D}_{1\perp}^{\#} \times \cdots \times \mathbb{D}_{n\perp}^{\#} \to \mathbb{D}_{\perp}^{\#}) \to (\mathcal{P}_{\mathbb{D}_1} \times \cdots \times \mathcal{P}_{\mathbb{D}_n} \to \mathcal{P}_{\mathbb{D}})$, $\mathbf{lift}^{\#}(f^{\#})(s_1, \ldots, s_n) := z$ can be defined similarly to its concrete counterpart, because the abstract function $f^{\#}$ takes care of the gaps:

$$z(t) = \begin{cases} f^{\#}(s_1(t), \ldots, s_n(t)) & \text{if } s_1 \neq ?, \ldots, s_n \neq ? \\ ? & \text{otherwise} \end{cases}$$

The operator $\mathbf{lift}^{\#}$ is restricted to those functions $f^{\#}$ that are an abstraction of functions f that can be used in $\mathbf{lift}$, that is, $f(\perp, \ldots, \perp) = \perp$. Using the abstract lift we can derive the abstract counterparts of const and merge:

▷ $\mathsf{const}^{\#}(c)(a) := \mathbf{lift}^{\#}(f_c)(a)$ with $f_c(d) := c$ if $d \neq \smile$ and $f_c(\smile) := \smile$ otherwise maps all events' values to a constant while preserving the gaps. Using $\mathsf{const}^{\#}$ we can define constant signals without any gaps, e.g., $\mathsf{true}^{\#} := \mathsf{const}^{\#}(\mathsf{true})(\mathbf{unit}^{\#})$ or $\mathsf{zero}^{\#} := \mathsf{const}^{\#}(0)(\mathbf{unit}^{\#})$.

▷ $\mathsf{merge}^{\#}(x, y) := \mathbf{lift}^{\#}(f)(x, y)$ with $f(a \notin \{\smile, \perp\}, b) = a$, $f(\perp, b) = b$, $f(\smile, b \in \{\smile, \perp\}) = \smile$, and $f(\smile, b \notin \{\smile, \perp\}) = \top$.

The diagram on the right shows an example trace merging the events of the streams x and y. The symbol $\circ$ indicates a point-wise gap. Note how an event on the first stream takes precedence over a gap on the second stream, but not the other way round, similarly to how events from the first stream are prioritized if both streams have an event at the same timestamp.

▶ $\mathsf{last}^{\#} : \mathcal{P}_{\mathbb{D}_1} \times \mathcal{P}_{\mathbb{D}_2} \to \mathcal{P}_{\mathbb{D}_1}, \mathsf{last}^{\#}(v, r) := z$ has three major extensions over its concrete counterpart:

(1) $\top$ is added as an output in case an event on r occurs and there were events on the stream v of values but all followed by a gap.

(2) $\smile$ is outputted for all gaps on the stream r of trigger events if there have been events on the stream v of values.

(3) $\smile$ can also be output if an event occurs on r and no event occurred on v before except for a gap.

The parts similar to the concrete operator are typeset in gray:

$$z(t) = \begin{cases} d & t \in ticks(r) \wedge \exists_{t' <_t t} isLast(t, t', v, d) \wedge \forall_{t'' | t' <_t t'' <_t t} v(t'') \neq \smile \\ \top & t \in ticks(r) \wedge \exists_{t' <_t t} isLast(t, t', v, \smile) \wedge \exists_{t'' | t' <_t t'' <_t t} v(t'') = \smile & (1) \\ \perp & r(t) = \perp \wedge defined(z, t) \vee \forall_{t' <_t t} v(t') = \perp \\ \smile & defined(z, t) \wedge r(t) = \smile \wedge \exists_{t' <_t t} v(t') \neq \perp & (2) \\ \smile & defined(z, t) \wedge t \in ticks(r) \wedge \forall_{t' <_t t} t' \notin ticks(v) \wedge \exists_{t' <_t t} v(t') = \smile & (3) \\ ? & \text{otherwise} \end{cases}$$

The trace diagram on the right shows an example trace covering most edge cases of the abstract last. The output stream z is a point-wise gap if triggered after initial gaps (3); z is $\top$ if triggered after non-initial gaps (1); z is an event if triggered after a gapless sequence (d); and z inherits all gaps from the stream of trigger events (2).

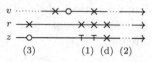

We can now combine the $\mathbf{last}^{\#}$ and the $\mathbf{lift}^{\#}$ operators to realize:

▷ abstract signal lift for total functions $f : \mathbb{D} \times \mathbb{D}' \rightarrow \mathbb{D}''$ as $\mathbf{slift}^{\#}(f)(x,y) := \mathbf{lift}^{\#}(g_f)(x',y')$ with $x' := \mathbf{merge}^{\#}(x, \mathbf{last}^{\#}(x,y))$ and $y' := \mathbf{merge}^{\#}(y, \mathbf{last}^{\#}(y,x))$, as well as $g_f(a \notin \{\smile, \bot\}, b \notin \{\smile, \bot\}) = f(a,b)$, $g_f(\bot, b) = g_f(a, \bot) = \bot$, $g_f(\smile, \smile) = \smile$, and $g_f(\smile, b \notin \{\smile, \bot\}) = g_f(a \notin \{\smile, \bot\}, \smile) = \smile$.

Example 2. By replacing every TeSSLa operator in Example 1 with their abstract counterparts and applying it to the abstract input streams values $\in \mathcal{P}_{\mathbb{Z}}$ and resets $\in \mathcal{P}_{\mathbb{U}}$, we derive the abstract stream cond $\in \mathcal{P}_{\mathbb{B}}$ and the recursively derived abstract stream sum $\in \mathcal{P}_{\mathbb{Z}}$: After the large gap on values, the sum stream eventually recovers completely. The first reset after the point-wise gap does not lead to full recovery, because at that point the last event on values cannot be accessed, because of the prior gap. The next reset falls into the gap, so again cond cannot be evaluated. In a similar fashion one can define an abstract $\mathbf{delay}^{\#}$ operator as counterpart of the concrete $\mathbf{delay}$. See [19] for details.

Following from the definitions of the abstract TeSSLa operators we get:

Theorem 1. *Every abstract TeSSLa operator is an abstraction of its concrete counterpart.*

Theorem 1 implies that abstract TeSSLa operators are sound in the following way. Let o be a concrete TeSSLa operator with the abstract counterpart $o^{\#}$ and let $s \in \mathcal{P}_{\mathbb{D}}$ be an abstract event stream with a concretization function γ. Then, $o(\gamma(s)) \preceq \gamma(o^{\#}(s))$. Since abstract interpretation is compositional we can directly follow from the above theorem:

Corollary 1. *If a concrete TeSSLa specification φ is transformed into a specification ψ by replacing every concrete operator in φ with its abstract counterpart, then ψ is an abstraction of φ.*

Theorem 1 guarantees that applying abstract TeSSLa operators to the abstract event stream is still sound regarding the underlying set of possible concrete event streams. However, we have established no result so far about the accuracy of the abstract TeSSLa operators. The abstraction returning only the completely unknown stream ($\Delta = \emptyset$) is sound but useless. The following theorem states, that our abstract TeSSLa operators are optimal in terms of accuracy.

Using a perfect abstraction guarantees the abstract TeSSLa operators preserve as much information as can possibly be encoded in the resulting abstract event streams.

Theorem 2. *Every abstract TeSSLa operator is a perfect abstraction of its concrete counterpart.*

Given a concrete TeSSLa operator o and its abstract counterpart $o^{\#}$, and any abstract event stream $s \in \mathcal{P}_{\mathbb{D}}$ with the Galois Connection (α, γ) between $2^{S_{\mathbb{D}}}$ and $\mathcal{P}_{\mathbb{D}}$ one can show that $o^{\#}(s) = \alpha(o(\gamma(s)))$. Applying the abstract operator on the abstract event stream is as good as applying the concrete operator on every possible event stream represented by the abstract event stream. Thus $o^{\#}$ is a perfect abstraction of o. (The detailed proof can be found in [19].) Note that we assume that $f^{\#}$ is a perfect abstraction of f to conclude that $\mathbf{lift}^{\#}(f^{\#})$ is a perfect abstraction of $\mathbf{lift}(f)$.

In Corollary 1 we have shown that a specification ψ (generated by replacing the concrete TeSSLa operator in φ with their abstract counterparts) is an abstraction of φ. Note that ψ is in general not a perfect abstraction of φ. We study some special cases of perfect abstractions of compositional specifications in Sect. 4.

The next result states that the abstract operators can be defined in terms of concrete TeSSLa operators. Realizing the abstract operators in TeSSLa does not require an enhancement in the expressivity of TeSSLa.

Theorem 3. *The semantics of the abstract TeSSLa operators can be encoded in TeSSLa using only the concrete operators.*

Proof. One can observe that the abstract TeSSLa operators are monotone and future independent (the output stream up to t only depends on the input streams up to t.) As shown in [7], TeSSLa can express every such function. □

3.1 Fixpoint Calculations Ensuring Well-Formedness

A concrete TeSSLa specification consists of stream variables and possibly recursive equations applying concrete TeSSLa operators to the stream variables. Theorem 1 and Corollary 1 guarantee that a concrete TeSSLa specification can be transformed into an abstract TeSSLa specification, which is able to handle gaps in the input streams. Additionally, Theorem 3 states that the abstract TeSSLa operators can be implemented using concrete TeSSLa operators. Combining these two results, one can transform a given concrete specification φ into a corresponding specification ψ, which realizes the abstract TeSSLa semantics of the operators in φ, but only uses concrete TeSSLa operators.

However, using the realization of the abstract TeSSLa operators in TeSSLa adds additional cyclic dependencies in ψ between the stream variables. A TeSSLa specification is well-formed if every cycle of its dependency graph contains at least one edge guarded by a last (or a delay) operator, which is required to guarantee the existence of a unique fixed-point and hence computability (see [7]).

Consider the trace diagram on the right showing $\mathbf{last}^{\#}(v, r)$. If v is used in a recursive manner, i.e., v is defined in terms of $\mathbf{last}^{\#}(v, r)$, then the first event on v could start a gap on $\mathbf{last}^{\#}(v, r)$ that could start a gap on v at the same timestamp. As a result v has an unguarded cyclic dependency and hence the specification is not well-formed. To overcome this issue one can split up the value and gap calculation sequentially, reintroducing guards in the cyclic dependency:

Definition 2 (Unrolled Abstract Last). *We define two variants of the abstract last,* $\mathbf{last}^{\#}_{\perp}$ *and* $\mathbf{last}^{\#}_{\smile}$ *as follows. Let* $z = \mathbf{last}^{\#}(v, r)$*, then* $\mathbf{last}^{\#}_{\perp}(v, r) := z_{\perp}$ *and* $\mathbf{last}^{\#}_{\smile}(v, r, d) := z_{\smile}$*.*

$$z_{\perp}(t) = \begin{cases} z(t) & \text{if } z(t) \neq \smile \\ \perp & \text{otherwise} \end{cases} \qquad z_{\smile}(t) = \begin{cases} d(t) & \text{if } t \in \mathit{ticks}(d) \\ \smile & \text{if } t \notin \mathit{ticks}(d) \wedge z(t) = \smile \\ \perp & \text{otherwise} \end{cases}$$

Function $\mathbf{last}^{\#}_{\perp}$ executes a normal calculation of the events, in the same way an abstract last would do, but neglecting gaps and outputting $\perp$ as long as there is no event. Function $\mathbf{last}^{\#}_{\smile}$ takes a third input stream and outputs its events directly, but calculates gaps correctly as $\mathbf{last}^{\#}$ would do.

Since the trigger input of a $\mathbf{last}$ operator cannot be recursive in a well-formed specification, a recursive equation using one last has the form $x = \mathbf{last}^{\#}(v, r)$ and $v = f(x, \mathbf{c})$, where $\mathbf{c}$ is a vector of streams not involved in the recursion and f does not introduce further last (or delay) operators. Now, this equation system can be rewritten in the following equivalent form:

$$x' = \mathbf{last}^{\#}_{\perp}(v, r) \qquad v' = f(x', \mathbf{c}) \qquad x = \mathbf{last}^{\#}_{\smile}(v', r, x') \qquad v = f(x, \mathbf{c})$$

This pattern can be repeated if multiple recursive abstract lasts are used and can also be applied in a similar fashion to mutually recursive equations and the delay operator.

4   Perfection of Compositional Specifications

A concrete TeSSLa specification φ can be transformed into an abstract TeSSLa specification ψ by replacing the concrete operators with their abstract counterparts. For two functions f and g with corresponding abstractions $f^{\#}$ and $g^{\#}$ the function composition $f^{\#} \circ g^{\#}$ is an abstraction of $f \circ g$. Unfortunately, even if $f^{\#}$ and $g^{\#}$ are perfect abstractions, $f^{\#} \circ g^{\#}$ is not necessarily a perfect abstraction. Hence, ψ needs not be a perfect abstraction of φ. In this section we discuss the perfection of two common compositional TeSSLa operators: (1) the $\mathbf{slift}^{\#}$ defined in Sect. 3 is a composition of $\mathbf{last}^{\#}$ in $\mathbf{lift}^{\#}$, which realizes signal semantics; (2) $\mathbf{last}^{\#}(\mathbf{time}^{\#}(v), r)$, which is a common pattern used when comparing timestamps.

The slift$^\#$ is defined as the **lift**$^\#$ applied to the synchronized versions x' and y' of the input streams x and y. The input stream x is synchronized with y by keeping the original events of x and reproducing the last known value of x for every timestamp with an event on y, but not on x.

Theorem 4. *If $f^\#$ is a perfect abstraction of f then $\mathsf{slift}(f^\#)^\#$ is a perfect abstraction of $\mathsf{slift}(f)$.*

Proof. Since slift$^\#$ is defined on abstract event streams we need to consider gaps. The stream x' does not have any gap or event until the first gap or event on x. After the first gap or event on x the synchronized stream x' contains a gap or event at every timestamp where x or y contain a gap or event. Because slift$^\#$ is symmetric in terms of the event pattern the same holds for y'. By definition, slift$^\#(f^\#)(x,y) = z$ contains an event or gap iff x' and y' contain an event or gap, because f is a total function. The output stream z contains an event iff x' and y' contain events. The events values are ensured to be as precise as possible, because $f^\#$ is a perfect abstraction of f.   □

TeSSLa allows arbitrary computations on the timestamps of events using the **time** operator. The specification $z = $ **time**(v) derives a stream z from v by replacing all event's values in v with the event's timestamps. The stream variable z can now be used in any computation expressible in TeSSLa. Hence,

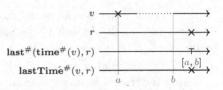

TeSSLa does not distinguish between timestamps and other values, and consequently abstract TeSSLa specifications cannot make use of the monotonicity of time. As an example consider the trace diagram on the right. The stream **last**$^\#(\mathbf{time}^\#(v), r)$ is derived from v by composing **time**$^\#$ and **last**$^\#$. Since **time**$^\#$ changes the events values with their timestamps, the **last**$^\#$ does not know any longer that we are interested in the last timestamp of v and can only produce an event with the value $\top$ representing all possible values. To overcome this issue we define **lastTime**$(v, r) := \mathbf{last}(\mathbf{time}(v), r)$ and provide a direct abstraction, which allows a special treatment of timestamps.

Definition 3 (Time Aware Abstract Last). *Let $y = \mathbf{last}^\#(\mathbf{time}^\#(v), r)$, we define* **lastTime**$^\# : \mathcal{P}_\mathbb{D} \times \mathcal{P}_{\mathbb{D}'} \to \mathcal{P}_{2^\top}$, **lastTime**$^\#(v, r) := z$ *as* $z(t) = [a, b]$ *if* $y(t) = \top$ *with* $a = \inf\{t' < t \mid \forall_{t' < t'' < t} v(t'') \neq {\smile}\}$ *and* $b = \max\{t' < t \mid t' \in ticks(v)\}$ *and* $z(t) = y(t)$ *otherwise.*

Now the following result holds (the proof can be found in [19]).

Theorem 5. **lastTime**$^\#$ *is a perfect abstraction of* **lastTime**.

A similar problem occurs if slift$^\#$ is used to compare event's timestamps. In Example 2 the stream cond derived by comparing the timestamps of values and resets has two events with the unknown data value $\top$ because of prior gaps on values. Since the slift$^\#$ is defined in terms of **lift**$^\#$ and **last**$^\#$ we can define the function $\mathsf{sliftTime}^{\#}(f^{\#})(x,y)$ as an abstraction for the special case $\mathsf{sliftTime}(f)(x,y) = \mathsf{slift}(f)(\mathbf{time}(x),\mathbf{time}(y))$ by using $\mathsf{lastTime}^{\#}$ instead of $\mathsf{last}^{\#}$ and ensuring that $f^{\#}$ uses interval arithmetics to abstract f. Note that $\mathsf{sliftTime}^{\#}(f^{\#})$ is a perfect abstraction of $\mathsf{sliftTime}(f)$.

Example 3. To illustrate the perfect abstraction $\mathsf{sliftTime}^{\#}$ we update the definition of cond in Example 2 as follows: cond $= \mathsf{sliftTime}(\leq)(\mathsf{resets},\mathsf{values})$. The events drawn in red now have concrete values instead of $\top$ as in Example 2.

values	3	2 4		5			3 6 1
resets							
cond	tt ff ff		tt ff		tt		ff tt ff
sum	0 2 6		0 5		0		0 1

5   Abstractions for Sliding Windows

In this section we demonstrate how to apply the techniques presented in this paper to specifications with richer data domains. In particular, we show now a TeSSLa specification that uses a queue to compute the average load of a processor in the last five time units. The moving window is realized using a queue storing all events that happened in the time window. The stream $\mathsf{load} \in \mathcal{S}_{\mathbb{R}}$ contains an event every time the input load changes:

$$\mathsf{stripped} = \mathsf{slift}(\mathit{remOlder}_5)(\mathbf{time}(\mathsf{load}), \mathbf{merge}(\mathbf{last}(\mathsf{queue},\mathsf{load}),\langle\rangle)))$$
$$\mathsf{queue} = \mathbf{lift}(\mathit{enq})(\mathbf{time}(\mathsf{load}), \mathsf{load}, \mathsf{stripped})$$
$$\mathsf{avg} = \mathbf{lift}(\mathit{int})(\mathsf{queue}, \mathbf{time}(\mathsf{load}))$$
$$\mathit{int}(q,u) = \mathit{fold}(f,q,0,u) \qquad f(a,b,v,acc) = acc + v \cdot (b-a)/5$$

The queue operation *enq* adds elements to the queue, while *remOlder*$_5$ removes elements with a timestamp older than five time units. The function *int* accumulates all values in the queue weighted by the length of the corresponding signal piece. The queue operation *fold* is used to fold the function f over all elements from the queue with the initial accumulator 0 until the timestamp u. Hence f is called for every element in the queue with the timestamps a and b, the element's value v and the accumulator. Consequently, the specification adds elements to the queue, removes the expired elements and accumulates the remaining values. Using our approach we replace every operator with its abstract counterpart and represent abstract queues appropriately such that also queues with partly unknown entries can be modeled. By doing this we obtain a specification that is able to handle gaps in the input stream, as illustrated in Fig. 2.

We can extend the example such that the queue only holds a predefined maximum number of events (to guarantee a finite state implementation). When removing events we represent these as unknown entries in the abstract queues. The abstract *fold*$^{\#}$ is capable of computing the interval of possible average loads for queues with unknown elements anyhow.

Note that the average load is only updated for every event on the input stream. Using a delay operator, we can set a timeout whenever an element leaves

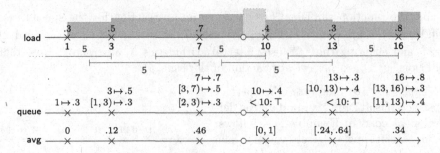

Fig. 2. Example trace of the abstract queue specification.

the sliding window in the abstract setting. The element is removed from the queue at that timeout and the new value of the queue is updated with the remaining elements. Formal definitions of the queue functions as well as the complete specifications are available online[1].

6   Implementation and Empirical Evaluation

As discussed in Sect. 3.1 the abstract TeSSLa operators can be implemented using only the existing concrete TeSSLa operators. We implemented the abstract TeSSLa operators as macros specified in the TeSSLa language itself such that the existing TeSSLa engine presented in [7] can handle abstract TeSSLa specifications. An abstract event stream $(s, \Delta) \in \mathcal{P}_\mathbb{D}$ can be represented as two TeSSLa streams $s \in \mathcal{S}_{\mathbb{D}\#}$ and $s_d \in \mathcal{S}_X$, where X contains the following six possible changes of Δ: inclusive start, exclusive start, inclusive end, exclusive end, point-wise gap and point-wise event in a gap. Using this encoding it is sufficient to look up the latest $s_d(t')$ with $t' \leq t$ to decide whether $t \in \Delta$. While this encoding already allows a decent implementation of abstract TeSSLa we go one step further and assume a finite time domain with a limited precision, e.g., 64 bit integers or floats. Under this assumption there is always a known smallest relative timestamp ε. Hence, we can use the encoding $s_d \in \mathcal{S}_\mathbb{B}$ where an event $s_d(t) = \text{true}$ encodes a start inclusive and $s_d(t) = \text{false}$ an end exclusive. This encoding captures the most common cases and simplifies the implementation of union and intersection on Δ enormously since they can now be realized as slift($\vee$) and slift($\wedge$), resp. The other possible switches at timestamp t can be represented as follows: $s_d(t + \varepsilon) = \text{true}$ encodes an exclusive start, $s_d(t + \varepsilon) = \text{false}$ encodes an inclusive end, $s_d(t) = \text{true}$ and $s_d(t + \varepsilon) = \text{false}$ encodes a point-wise event in a gap, and $s_d(t) = \text{false}$ and $s_d(t + \varepsilon) = \text{true}$ encodes a point-wise gap. Using this encoding the abstract TeSSLa operators do not need to handle these additional cases explicitly.

Furthermore, assuming the smallest relative timestamp ε, we can avoid the need to perform the unrolling defined in Definition 2 by delaying the second part of the computation to the next possible timestamp $t + \varepsilon$.

---

[1] http://tessla-a.isp.uni-luebeck.de/.

As a final efficiency improvement we simplified **last**$^\#$ before the first event on the stream of values, which are not relevant in practice. The abstract operator and hence abstract specifications are of course still a sound abstraction of their concrete counterparts, but due to over-abstractions no longer a perfect one during this initial event-less phase of the stream of values.

The implementation in form of a macro library for the existing TeSSLa engine is available together with all the examples and scripts used in the following empirical evaluation and can be experimented with in a web IDE (see Footnote 1).

In the following empirical evaluation we measure the accuracy of the abstractions presented in this paper. An abstract event stream represents input data with some sequences of data loss, where we do not know if any events might have been occurred or what their values have been. Applying an abstract TeSSLa specification to such an input stream takes these gaps into account and provides output streams that in turn contain sequences of gaps and sequences containing concrete events. To evaluate the accuracy of this procedure we compare the output of an abstract TeSSLa specification with the best possible output.

Let $r \in \mathcal{P}_\mathbb{D}$ be an abstract event stream. We obtain the set R of all possible input streams containing all possible variants that might have happened during gaps in r by applying the concretization function γ on the abstract input stream. Now we can apply the concrete TeSSLa specification φ to all streams in R and get the set S of concrete 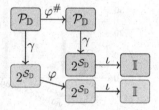 output streams. On the other hand we apply the abstract TeSSLa specification $\varphi^\#$ directly to r and get the abstract output stream s. Now S is the set of all possible output streams and $\gamma(s)$ is the set of output streams defined by the abstract TeSSLa specification. The diagram on the right depicts this comparison process.

To compare $\gamma(s)$ and S in a quantitative way we define the *ignorance measure* $\iota : 2^{S_\mathbb{D}} \to \mathbb{I} = [0,1]$ scoring the ambiguity of such a set of streams, i.e., how similar the different streams in the set are. Events in non-synchronized streams might not have corresponding events at the same timestamp on the other streams. Hence we refer to the signal seman- 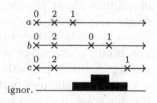 tics of event streams where the events represent the changes of a piece-wise constant signal. As depicted on the right with three event streams over the finite data domain $\{0, 1, 2\}$, we score timestamps based on how many event streams have the same value with respect to the signal semantics at that timestamp. These scores are then integrated and normalized throughout the length of the streams. See [19] for the technical details. Using this ignorance measure we can now compute the optimal ignorance $i := \iota(S) \in \mathbb{I}$ and the ignorance $k := \iota(\gamma(s)) \in \mathbb{I}$ of the streams produced by the abstract TeSSLa specification.

For the evaluation we took several example specifications and corresponding input traces representing different use-cases of TeSSLa and compared the optimal ignorance with the ignorance of abstract TeSSLa. Note that computing the optimal ignorance requires to derive all possible variants of events that might have happened during gaps, which are in general infinitely many and in the special case of only point-wise gaps still exponentially many. Hence this can only be done on rather short traces with only a few point-wise gaps. As a measure for the overhead imposed by using the abstraction compared to the concrete TeSSLa specification we use the computation depth, i.e., the depth of the dependency graph of the computation nodes of the specifications. While runtimes are highly depending on implementation details of the used TeSSLa engines, the computation depth is a good indicator for the computational overhead in terms of how many concrete TeSSLa operators are needed to realize the abstract TeSSLa specification. Figure 3 shows the empirical results.

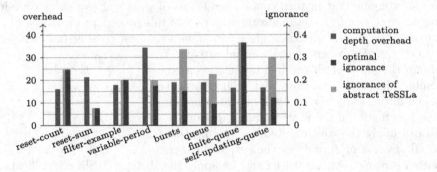

Fig. 3. Empirical results.

The first three examples represent the class of common, simple TeSSLa specifications without complex interdependencies and no generation of additional events with **delay**: Reset-count counts between reset events; reset-sum sums up events between reset events; and filter-example filters events occurring in a certain timing-pattern. For these common specifications the overhead is small and the abstraction is perfectly accurate. The burst example checks if events appear according to a complex pattern. In the abstraction we loose accuracy because the starting point of a burst is not accessible by **last**$^\#$ after a gap. A similar problem occurs in the queue example where we use a complex data domain to develop a queue along an event stream. If **last**$^\#$ produces $\top$ after a gap all information about the queue before the gap is lost. For variable-period the abstraction is not perfectly accurate, because the **delay** is used to generate events periodically depending on an external input. This gets even worse for the self-updating queue where complex computations are performed depending on events generated by a **delay**. Surprisingly, the finite-queue is again perfectly accurate, because the size of the queue is limited in a way that eliminates the inaccuracy of the abstraction in this particular example.

7   Conclusion

By replacing the basic operators of TeSSLa with abstract counterparts, we obtained a framework where properties and analyses can be specified with respect to complete traces and automatically evaluated for partially known traces. We have shown that these abstract operators can be encoded in TeSSLa, allowing existing evaluation engines to be reused. This is particularly useful as TeSSLa comprises a very small core language suitable for implementation in soft- as well as hardware. Using the example of sliding windows, we demonstrated how complex data structures like queues can be abstracted. Using finite abstractions, our approach even facilitates using complex data structures when only limited memory is available. Evaluating the abstract specification typically only increases the computational cost by a constant factor. In particular, if a concrete specification can be monitored in linear time (in the size of the trace) its abstract counterpart can be as well. Finally, we illustrated the practical feasibility of our approach by an empirical evaluation using the freely available TeSSLa engine.

References

1. Alur, R., Fisman, D., Raghothaman, M.: Regular programming for quantitative properties of data streams. In: Thiemann, P. (ed.) ESOP 2016. LNCS, vol. 9632, pp. 15–40. Springer, Heidelberg (2016). https://doi.org/10.1007/978-3-662-49498-1_2
2. Asarin, E., Caspi, P., Maler, O.: Timed regular expressions. J. ACM **49**(2), 172–206 (2002)
3. Basin, D.A., Klaedtke, F., Zalinescu, E.: Failure-aware runtime verification of distributed systems. In: FSTTCS. LIPIcs, vol. 45, pp. 590–603. Schloss Dagstuhl - Leibniz-Zentrum fuer Informatik (2015)
4. Bauer, A., Leucker, M., Schallhart, C.: Runtime verification for LTL and TLTL. ACM T. Softw. Eng. Meth. **20**(4), 14 (2011)
5. Berry, G.: The foundations of Esterel. In: Plotkin, G., Stirling, C., Tofte, M. (eds.) Proof, Language, and Interaction: Essays in Honour of Robin Milner, pp. 425–454. MIT Press, Cambridge (2000)
6. Bozzelli, L., Sánchez, C.: Foundations of Boolean stream runtime verification. In: Bonakdarpour, B., Smolka, S.A. (eds.) RV 2014. LNCS, vol. 8734, pp. 64–79. Springer, Cham (2014). https://doi.org/10.1007/978-3-319-11164-3_6
7. Convent, L., Hungerecker, S., Leucker, M., Scheffel, T., Schmitz, M., Thoma, D.: TeSSLa: temporal stream-based specification language. In: Massoni, T., Mousavi, M.R. (eds.) SBMF 2018. LNCS, vol. 11254, pp. 144–162. Springer, Cham (2018). https://doi.org/10.1007/978-3-030-03044-5_10
8. Cousot, P., Cousot, R.: Abstract interpretation: a unified lattice model for static analysis of programs by construction or approximation of fixpoints. In: POPL, pp. 238–252. ACM Press (1977)
9. Cousot, P., Cousot, R.: Abstract interpretation frameworks. J. Log. Comput. **2**(4), 511–547 (1992)
10. D'Angelo, B., et al.: LOLA: runtime monitoring of synchronous systems. In: TIME, pp. 166–174. IEEE (2005)

11. Eisner, C., Fisman, D., Havlicek, J., Lustig, Y., McIsaac, A., Van Campenhout, D.: Reasoning with temporal logic on truncated paths. In: Hunt, W.A., Somenzi, F. (eds.) CAV 2003. LNCS, vol. 2725, pp. 27–39. Springer, Heidelberg (2003). https://doi.org/10.1007/978-3-540-45069-6_3

12. Eliot, C., Hudak, P.: Functional reactive animation. In: Proceedings of ICFP '07, pp. 163–173. ACM (1997)

13. Faymonville, P., Finkbeiner, B., Schirmer, S., Torfah, H.: A stream-based specification language for network monitoring. In: Falcone, Y., Sánchez, C. (eds.) RV 2016. LNCS, vol. 10012, pp. 152–168. Springer, Cham (2016). https://doi.org/10.1007/978-3-319-46982-9_10

14. Faymonville, P., et al.: StreamLAB: stream-based monitoring of cyber-physical systems. In: Dillig, I., Tasiran, S. (eds.) CAV 2019. LNCS, vol. 11561, pp. 421–431. Springer, Cham (2019). https://doi.org/10.1007/978-3-030-25540-4_24

15. Gautier, T., Le Guernic, P., Besnard, L.: SIGNAL: a declarative language for synchronous programming of real-time systems. In: Kahn, G. (ed.) FPCA 1987. LNCS, vol. 274, pp. 257–277. Springer, Heidelberg (1987). https://doi.org/10.1007/3-540-18317-5_15

16. Gorostiaga, F., Sánchez, C.: Striver: stream runtime verification for real-time event-streams. In: Colombo, C., Leucker, M. (eds.) RV 2018. LNCS, vol. 11237, pp. 282–298. Springer, Cham (2018). https://doi.org/10.1007/978-3-030-03769-7_16

17. Halbwachs, N., Caspi, P., Pilaud, D., Plaice, J.: LUSTRE: a declarative language for programming synchronous systems. In: Proceedings of POPL 1987, pp. 178–188. ACM Press (1987)

18. Havelund, K., Roşu, G.: Synthesizing monitors for safety properties. In: Katoen, J.-P., Stevens, P. (eds.) TACAS 2002. LNCS, vol. 2280, pp. 342–356. Springer, Heidelberg (2002). https://doi.org/10.1007/3-540-46002-0_24

19. Leucker, M., Sanchez, C., Scheffel, T., Schmitz, M., Thoma, D.: Runtime verification for timed event streams with partial information. arXiv:1907.07761 (2019). https://arxiv.org/abs/1907.07761

20. Maler, O., Nickovic, D.: Monitoring temporal properties of continuous signals. In: Lakhnech, Y., Yovine, S. (eds.) FORMATS/FTRTFT -2004. LNCS, vol. 3253, pp. 152–166. Springer, Heidelberg (2004). https://doi.org/10.1007/978-3-540-30206-3_12

21. Manna, Z., Pnueli, A.: Temporal Verification of Reactive Systems: Safety. Springer, New York (1995). https://doi.org/10.1007/978-1-4612-4222-2

22. Sen, K., Roşu, G.: Generating optimal monitors for extended regular expressions. ENTCS 89(2), 226–245 (2003)

23. Stoller, S.D., et al.: Runtime verification with state estimation. In: Khurshid, S., Sen, K. (eds.) RV 2011. LNCS, vol. 7186, pp. 193–207. Springer, Heidelberg (2012). https://doi.org/10.1007/978-3-642-29860-8_15

24. Wang, S., Ayoub, A., Sokolsky, O., Lee, I.: Runtime verification of traces under recording uncertainty. In: Khurshid, S., Sen, K. (eds.) RV 2011. LNCS, vol. 7186, pp. 442–456. Springer, Heidelberg (2012). https://doi.org/10.1007/978-3-642-29860-8_35

Shape Expressions for Specifying and Extracting Signal Features

Dejan Ničković[1]([✉]), Xin Qin[2], Thomas Ferrère[3], Cristinel Mateis[1], and Jyotirmoy Deshmukh[2]

[1] AIT Austrian Institute of Technology, Vienna, Austria
dejan.nickovic@ait.ac.at
[2] University of Southern California, Los Angeles, USA
[3] IST Austria, Klosterneuburg, Austria

Abstract. Cyber-physical systems (CPS) and the Internet-of-Things (IoT) result in a tremendous amount of generated, measured and recorded time-series data. Extracting temporal segments that encode patterns with useful information out of these huge amounts of data is an extremely difficult problem. We propose *shape expressions* as a declarative formalism for specifying, querying and extracting sophisticated temporal patterns from possibly noisy data. Shape expressions are regular expressions with arbitrary (linear, exponential, sinusoidal, etc.) shapes with parameters as atomic predicates and additional constraints on these parameters. We equip shape expressions with a novel *noisy* semantics that combines regular expression matching semantics with statistical regression. We characterize essential properties of the formalism and propose an efficient approximate shape expression matching procedure. We demonstrate the wide applicability of this technique on two case studies.

1 Introduction

Cyber-physical systems (CPS) and Internet-of-Things (IoT) applications are everywhere around us - smart buildings that adapt heating control to the user's habit, intelligent transportation systems that optimize traffic based on the continuous monitoring of the road conditions, wearable health monitoring devices, and medical devices that fine-tune a given therapy depending on sensing a patient's health. These applications are inherently data-driven – the decisions of the system rely on the measurement and analysis of the dynamic behavior of the environment. Low-cost sensing solutions combined with the availability of powerful edge and cloud devices to store and process data has led to a tremendous increase in the generation, measurement and recording of time-series data. Processing these huge streams of available data in an efficient manner to extract useful information is challenging. It is often the case that only specific segments of the time series contain interesting and relevant patterns. For instance, an electricity provider may be interested in observing spikes or oscillations in the voltage signals. A medical device manufacturer may want to detect anomalous cardiac

© Springer Nature Switzerland AG 2019
B. Finkbeiner and L. Mariani (Eds.): RV 2019, LNCS 11757, pp. 292–309, 2019.
https://doi.org/10.1007/978-3-030-32079-9_17

behavior. A wearable device maker would like to associate specific patterns in the measurements from accelerometer and gyroscope sensors to a concrete user activity, such as running or walking.

Such patterns can be often characterized with geometric shapes observed in the time-series data; e.g., a spike can be specified as an "upward triangle", i.e. a sequence of two contiguous line segments with slopes that have opposite signs. There are also instances where the time-series data is multi-dimensional (say $(x(t), y(t))$), and the user may be interested in knowing if a "pulse" shape in $x(t)$ is followed by an "exponential decay" shape in $y(t)$.

We propose *shape expressions*, a novel declarative language for specifying sophisticated temporal patterns over (possibly multi-dimensional) time series. A shape expression is in essence a regular expression where atomic predicates are arbitrary (linear, exponential, sinusoidal, etc.) shapes with (slope, offset, frequency, etc.) parameters, and with additional parameter constraints. We associate to shape expressions a *noisy language* that allows observed data to approximately match the expression. The noisy expression semantics combines classical regular expression semantics with statistical regression, which is used to match atomic shapes and infer parameter valuations that minimize the noise between the ideal shape and the observation. We allow either using *mean squared error* (MSE) or the *coefficient of determination* (CoD), statistical measures of how close the observed data are to the fitted regression (atomic) shape, as our noise metric. We define *shape automata* as an executable formalism for matching shape expressions and propose a heuristic for querying time series with shape expressions efficiently. We apply this algorithm to two case studies from different CPS and IoT domains to demonstrate its applicability.

Illustrating Example. We use the example depicted in Fig. 1 to illustrate the concepts presented in this paper. This figure shows a raw noisy signal that contains two pulses. The two pulses differ both in duration, depth and offset, but have the same qualitative shape that characterizes them as pulses. Figure 1b shows a specification of an ideal pulse. We characterize a pulse as a sequence of 5 segments: (1) constant segment at some b; (2) linearly decreasing segment with slope $a_2 < 0$; (3) constant segment at some b_3; (4) linearly increasing segment with slope $a_4 > 0$; and (5) constant segment at b. We observe that the

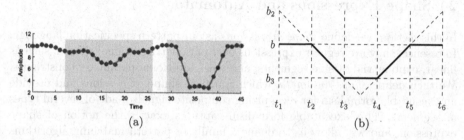

(a)   (b)

Fig. 1. (a) Two pulses shapes (b) Idealized Pulse shape (Color figure online)

above specification uses parametric shapes, where the parameters are possibly constrained (e.g. $a_2 < 0$) or shared between shapes (e.g. b), and describes a perfect shape without accounting for noise.

Related Work. Regular expressions and temporal logics are the most common general purpose specification languages for expressing temporal patterns in the formal methods community. However, specifying temporal patterns in data is a problem that has been pervasively studied. For instance, specification and recognition of a pulse in pulse-based communications is an IEEE standard [1] in its own right. Extracting unspecified motifs in time series has been studied in data-mining [21], and feature extraction using patterns has been studied in machine learning [12,20]. More recently, time series shapelets were introduced in [29] as a data mining primitive. A shapelet is a time series segment representing a certain shape identified from data. Our work is partially motivated by the concept of shapelets. In contrast to shapelets that are extracted from unlabelled data, shape expressions provide a more supervised feature extraction mechanism, in which domain-specific knowledge is used to express shapes of interest.

In the context of CPS, timed regular expressions (TRE) [6,7], quantitative regular expressions (QRE) [2–4,19], Signal Temporal Logic (STL) [18] and various stream languages [10,11,15–17] have been used as popular formalisms for specifying properties of CPS behaviors. QREs is a powerful formalism that combines quantitative computations over data with regular expression-based matching. An offline algorithm for matching TREs was proposed in [22,23]. This thread of work was extended to online pattern matching in [24]. Automata-based matching for TREs has been developed in [25–27]. In contrast to our approach, pattern matching with QREs and TREs is sensitive to noise in data. The problem of uncertainty has been studied through parameterized TRE specifications, either by having parameters in time bounds [5] or in spatial atomic predicates [8]. These approaches are orthogonal to ours – instead of having parameters on standard TRE operators, we focus on a rich class of parameterized atomic shapes. Finally, a sophisticated algorithm to incrementally detect exponential decay patterns in CO_2 measurements was proposed in [28] in the context of smart building applications. We adapt and extend this basic idea to a general purpose specification language that allows combining such atomic shapes with regular operators.

2   Shape Expressions and Automata

In this section, we define *shape expressions* as our pattern specification language. In essence, they are regular expressions over parametrized signal shapes, such as linear, exponential or sine segments, and with additional parameter constraints. We then define *shape automata*, which translate shape expressions and provide an executable formalism for recognizing composite signals made of several types of segments. This executable formalism captures exactly the notion of shape expression, and will allow us to define a family of pattern matching algorithms as we will see in Sect. 3. We first give a few basic definitions necessary to our framework, such as notions of *signals*, *parameters*, and *shapes*.

2.1   Definitions

Let $P = \{p_1, \ldots, p_n\}$ be a set of *parameters*. A parameter valuation v maps parameters $p \in P$ to values $v(p) \in \mathbb{R} \cup \{\bot\}$, where $\bot$ represents the *undefined* value. We use the shortcut $v(P)$ to denote $\{v(p_1), \ldots, v(p_n)\}$. A *constraint* γ over P is a Boolean combination of inequalities over P. We write $v \models \gamma$ when the constraint γ is satisfied by the valuation v. Given $p \in P$ and $p \circ k$ for $\circ \in \{=, <, \leq, >, \geq\}$ and some $k \in \mathbb{R}$, we have that $v(p) = \bot$ implies that $v \not\models p \circ k$. We denote by $\Gamma(P)$ the set of all constraints over P.

Let X be a set of signal variables. A *signal* w over X is a function $w : X \times [0, d) \to \mathbb{R}$, where $[0, d)$ is the time domain of w, which we assume to be discrete, hence a subset of $\mathbb{Z}$. We denote by $|w| = d$ the length of w.

Given two signals $w_1 : X \times [0, d_1) \to \mathbb{R}$ and $w_2 : X \times [0, d_2) \to \mathbb{R}$, we denote by $w \equiv w_1 \cdot w_2$ their concatenation $w : X \times [0, d_1 + d_2) \to \mathbb{R}$, where for all $x \in X$, $w(x, t) = w_1(x, t)$ if $t \in [0, d_1)$ and $w(x, t) = w_2(x, t - d_1)$ if $t \in [d_1, d_1 + d_2)$. Let $w : X \times [0, d) \to \mathbb{R}$ be a signal, and d_1 and d_2 be two constants such that $0 \leq d_1 < d_2 \leq d$. We denote by $w^{[d_1, d_2)} : X \times [0, d_2 - d_1) \to \mathbb{R}$ the restriction of w to the time domain $[d_1, d_2)$, such that for all $x \in X$ and $t \in [0, d_2 - d_1)$, $w^{[d_1, d_2)}(x, t) = w(x, t + d_1)$. We allow signals of null duration $d = 0$, which results in the unique signal with the empty time domain[1].

Consider two sequences $\mathbf{y} = y_1, \ldots, y_n$ and $\mathbf{f} = f_1, \ldots, f_n$ of values, where $\mathbf{y}$ represents a sequence of observations and $\mathbf{f}$ the corresponding sequence of predictions given by a model which approximates the distribution of $\mathbf{y}$. The *mean squared error* $\mathrm{MSE}(\mathbf{y}, \mathbf{f})$ of $\mathbf{f}$ relative to $\mathbf{y}$ is a statistical measure of how well the predictions of a (regression) model approximates the observations, and is defined as follows.

$$\mathrm{MSE}(\mathbf{y}, \mathbf{f}) = \frac{1}{n} \Sigma_{i=1}^{n} (y_i - f_i)^2$$

Another statistical measure in a regression analysis of how well the predictions of a (regression) model approximates the observations is the *coefficient of determination* R^2, defined in terms of the *mean* $\bar{y}$ of the sequence $\mathbf{y}$, its total sum of squares SS_{tot} and the residual sum of squares SS_{res} as follows:

$$R^2(\mathbf{y}, \mathbf{f}) = 1 - \frac{SS_{res}(\mathbf{y}, \mathbf{f})}{SS_{tot}(\mathbf{y})} \qquad \bar{y} = \frac{1}{n} \Sigma_{i=1}^{n} y_i$$
$$SS_{tot}(\mathbf{y}) = \Sigma_{i=1}^{n} (y_i - \bar{y})^2 \quad SS_{res}(\mathbf{y}, \mathbf{f}) = \Sigma_{i=1}^{n} (y_i - f_i)^2$$

The coefficient of determination R^2 typically ranges from 0 to 1. An R^2 of 1 indicates that the predictions are a perfect match of the observations. On the contrary, an R^2 of 0 indicates that the model explains none of the variability of the response data around its mean. Negative values of R^2 can occur if the predictions fit the observations worse than a horizontal hyperplane.

---

[1] The signal with the empty time domain is equivalent to the empty word in the classical language theory.

2.2 Shape Expressions

We now define the syntax and semantics of *shape expressions* defined over the set X of signals and the set P of parameter variables. A *shape* $\sigma_x(P')$ is an expression that maps parameter variables $P' \subseteq P$ and the signal variable $x \in X$ to a parameterized family of idealized signals. To every shape σ_x, we associate a special *duration* variable $l_{\sigma,x}$ that is included in the set P of parameter variables.[2] Consider the basic shapes below.

$$\text{lin}_x(a, b, \underline{l}) \equiv \{w \mid \exists v.|w| = v(\underline{l}) \wedge w(x, t) = t \cdot v(a) + v(b)\} \tag{1}$$

$$\text{exp}_x(a, b, c, \underline{l}) \equiv \{w \mid \exists v.|w| = v(\underline{l}) \wedge w(x, t) = v(a) + v(b)e^{t \cdot v(c)}\} \tag{2}$$

$$\text{sin}_x(a, b, c, d, \underline{l}) \equiv \{w \mid \exists v.|w| = v(\underline{l}) \wedge w(x, t) = v(a) + v(b)\sin(v(c)t + v(d))\} \tag{3}$$

In (1), we describe a line segment parameterized by its slope a, and intercept b. In (2), we describe an exponential shape with parameters a, b, c, and $\underline{l}$, while (3) describes a parameterized family of sinusoidal shapes with the specified parameters[3]. Given a valuation v and a shape $\sigma_x(P')$, we denote by $w(x) = \sigma_x(v(P'))$ the signal w that instantiates the shape σ_x to concrete parameter values defined by v. We assume a finite set Σ of shapes, without imposing further restrictions. Shape expressions (SE) are regular expressions, where shapes with unknown parameters play the role of atomic primitives, and which have an additional restriction operator for enforcing parameter constraints.

Definition 1 (SE syntax). *The shape expressions are given by the grammar*

$$\varphi ::= \epsilon \mid \sigma_x(P') \mid \varphi_1 \cup \varphi_2 \mid \varphi_1 \cdot \varphi_2 \mid \varphi^* \mid \varphi : \gamma$$

where $\sigma \in \Sigma$, $x \in X$, $P' \subseteq P$, and $\gamma \in \Gamma(P)$.

The symbol ϵ denotes the *empty word*, the operators $\varphi_1 \cup \varphi_2$, $\varphi_1 \cdot \varphi_2$ and φ^* denote the classical regular expression *union*, *concatenation* and *Kleene star* respectively, while $\varphi : \gamma$ says that φ is *constrained* by γ. We write φ^i as an abbreviation of $\varphi \cdots \varphi$ (i times). We denote by $\Sigma_X(P)$ the set of expressions of the form $\sigma_x(P')$ for $\sigma \in \Sigma$, $x \in X$ and $P' \subseteq P$. The set of shape expressions over P and X is denoted $\Phi(P, X)$.

Example 1. Consider the visual pulse specification from Fig. 1b. We describe an ideal pulse as a shape expression φ_{pulse} as follows[4]:

$$\varphi \equiv \text{lin}_x(0, b) \cdot \text{lin}_x(a_2, b_2) : a_2 < 0 \cdot \text{lin}_x(0, b_3) \cdot \text{lin}_x(a_4, b_4) : a_4 > 0 \cdot \text{lin}_x(0, b)$$

---

[2] We use $\underline{l}$ instead of $l_{\sigma,x}$ whenever its association to σ_x is clear from the context, and omit $l_{\sigma,x}$ altogether when not interested in the duration of the shape.

[3] We omit the duration variable $\underline{l}$ whenever we are not interested in the duration of a shape - for instance we then use the notation $\sin(a, b, c, d)$.

[4] We abuse the notation and replace a parameter variable by a constant, for instance $\text{lin}_x(0, b)$, as a shortcut for $\text{lin}_x(a_1, b)$: $a_1 = 0$.

The semantics of shape expressions is given as a relation between signals and parameter valuations, which we call a *language*. We associate with every shape expression a *noisy language* $\mathcal{L}_\nu$ for some noise tolerance threshold $\nu \geq 0$, capturing the ν-approximate meaning of the expression. The *exact language* $\mathcal{L}$ capturing the precise meaning of the expression is obtained by setting ν to zero.

To define the noisy language of an expression, we associate a goodness of fit measure of a signal to an ideal shape, describing how far is the observed signal from the ideal shape. We derive this measure by combining mean squared error (MSE) computed on atomic shapes. The overall measure gives the quality of a match to a shape expression.

We formally define the noisy language as follows.

Definition 2 (SE noisy language). *Let $\nu \in \mathbb{R}_{\geq 0}$ be a noise tolerance threshold. The noisy language $\mathcal{L}_\nu$ of a shape expression is defined as follows:*

$$\mathcal{L}_\nu(\epsilon) = \{(w,v) \mid |w| = 0\}$$
$$\mathcal{L}_\nu(\sigma_x(P')) = \{(w,v) \mid |w| = v(\underline{l}) \text{ and } \mu(w(x), \sigma_x(v(P'))) \leq \nu\}$$
$$\mathcal{L}_\nu(\varphi_1 \cdot \varphi_2) = \{(w_1 \cdot w_2, v) \mid (w_1, v) \in \mathcal{L}_\nu(\varphi_1) \text{ and } (w_2, v) \in \mathcal{L}_\nu(\varphi_2)\}$$
$$\mathcal{L}_\nu(\varphi_1 \cup \varphi_2) = \mathcal{L}_\nu(\varphi_1) \cup \mathcal{L}_\nu(\varphi_2)$$
$$\mathcal{L}_\nu(\varphi^*) = \bigcup_{i=0}^{\infty} \mathcal{L}_\nu(\varphi^i)$$
$$\mathcal{L}_\nu(\varphi : \gamma) = \{(w,v) \mid (w,v) \in \mathcal{L}_\nu(\varphi) \text{ and } v \models \gamma\}$$

where $\mu(\boldsymbol{y}, \boldsymbol{f})$ is substituted by either $\mathrm{MSE}(\boldsymbol{y}, \boldsymbol{f})$ or $1 - \mathrm{CoD}(\boldsymbol{y}, \boldsymbol{f})$.

The noisy SE language is defined as the set of all signal/parameter valuation pairs, such that the distance of the signal from the ideal shape signal defined by the shape expression and instantiated by the parameter valuation is smaller or equal than the noise threshold.

Example 2. Consider the shape expression φ_{pulse} specifying a pulse, the signal w depicted in Fig. 1a, and the signal $w' = w^I$ the restriction of w to the interval $I = [7, 26)$. Let us consider $v = (v(a_2), v(a_4), v(b), v(b_2), v(b_3), v(b_4)) = (-0.67, 0.67, 9, 17, 7, -5)$ the valuation of parameter variables in φ_{pulse} that instantiates the ideal shape (red line) of the first pulse depicted in Fig. 1a. Let $w_1 = w^{[7,12)}$, $w_2 = w^{[12,15)}$, $w_3 = w^{[15,18)}$, $w_4 = w^{[18,21)}$ and $w_5 = w^{[21,26)}$, with:

$$\begin{aligned}
\mathrm{MSE}(w_1(x), \mathrm{lin}_x(0, v(b))) &= 0.04 & \mathrm{MSE}(w_4(x), \mathrm{lin}_x(v(a_4), v(b_4))) &= 0.35 \\
\mathrm{MSE}(w_2(x), \mathrm{lin}_x(v(a_2), v(b_2))) &= 0.49 & \mathrm{MSE}(w_5(x), \mathrm{lin}_x(0, v(b))) &= 0.10 \\
\mathrm{MSE}(w_3(x), \mathrm{lin}_x(0, v(b_3))) &= 0.13
\end{aligned}$$

It follows that $(w', v) \in \mathcal{L}_{0.5}(\varphi_{pulse})$ but $(w', v) \notin \mathcal{L}_{0.1}(\varphi_{pulse})$.

2.3   Shape Automata

We now define *shape automata*, which will act as recognizers for shape expressions. They are akin to finite state automata in which edges are labeled by shape expressions with unknown parameters, and parameter constraints. We will then show that they are inter-translatable to shape expressions.

Definition 3 (Shape automata). *A shape automaton is a tuple $\langle P, X, Q, \Delta, S, F \rangle$, where (1) P is the set of parameters, (2) X is the set of real-valued signal variables, (3) Q is the set of control locations, (4) $\Delta \subseteq Q \times \Sigma_X(P) \times \Gamma(P) \times Q$ is the set of edges, (5) $S \subseteq Q$ is the set of starting locations, and (6) $F \subseteq Q$ is the set of final locations.*

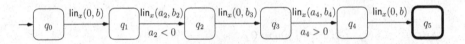

Fig. 2. Shape automaton $\mathcal{A}_{pulse}$

Example 3. The shape automaton $\mathcal{A}_{pulse}$, shown in Fig. 2 recognizes pulse shapes specified by the shape expression φ_{pulse}.

A state in a shape automaton is a pair (q, v) where q is a location and v is a parameter valuation. The runs of shape automata are akin to those in weighted automata and defined as follows. For a signal w we define transitions $\xrightarrow[c]{w}$ between two states as follows. We have $(q, v) \xrightarrow[c]{w} (q', v')$ if there exists $(q, \sigma_x(P'), \gamma, q') \in \Delta$ such that $P' \subseteq P$, $c = \mu(w(x), \sigma_x(v'(P')))$, $v' \models \gamma$, $v'(p) = v(p)$ for all $p \in P \backslash P'$ and $v'(p) = v(p)$ also for all $p \in P \cap P'$ such that $v(p) \neq \perp$. The semantics of a shape automaton are given as follows.

Definition 4 (Shape automaton run). *A run of a shape automaton over some signal w is a sequence of transitions*

$$(q_0, v_0) \xrightarrow[c_1]{w_1} (q_1, v_1) \xrightarrow[c_2]{w_2} \ldots \xrightarrow[c_n]{w_n} (q_n, v_n)$$

such that $q_0 \in S$, $v_0 = (\perp, \ldots, \perp)$ and $q_n \in F$, where $w_1 \cdot w_2 \ldots w_n$ is a decomposition of w. Such a run ρ induces $\mathrm{cost}(\rho) = \max_{i=1}^n c_i$ and the parameter valuation $\mathsf{val}(\rho) = v_n$.

The set of runs of a shape automaton $\mathcal{A}$ over some signal w is denoted $\mathcal{R}(\mathcal{A}, w)$. A shape automaton $\mathcal{A}$ associates any given signal w to a similarity measure that is the minimum among the similarity measures of all runs.

Definition 5 (SA language and noisy language). *The noisy language of a shape automaton for a given noise tolerance threshold $\nu \in \mathbb{R}_+$ is $\mathcal{L}_\nu(\mathcal{A}) = \{(w, v) \mid \exists \rho \in \mathcal{R}(\mathcal{A}, w) \text{ s.t. } \mathsf{val}(\rho) = v \text{ and } \mathrm{cost}(\rho) \leq \nu\}$. The exact language of a shape automaton is $\mathcal{L}(\mathcal{A}) = \mathcal{L}_0(\mathcal{A})$.*

Example 4. Consider the signal $w' = w_1 w_2 w_3 w_4 w_5$ from Example 2 and let:

$$v_1 = (\bot, \bot, 9, \bot, \bot, \bot) \qquad c_1 = 0.04 \quad v_4 = (-0.67, 0.67, 9, 17, 7, -5) \; c_4 = 0.35$$
$$v_2 = (-0.67, \bot, 9, 17, \bot, \bot) \; c_2 = 0.49 \quad v_5 = (-0.67, 0.67, 9, 17, 7, -5) \; c_5 = 0.10$$
$$v_3 = (-0.67, \bot, 9, \bot, 7, \bot) \quad c_3 = 0.13$$

We then have, assuming $v_0 = (\bot, \bot, \bot, \bot, \bot, \bot)$, that

$$\rho = (q_0, v_0) \xrightarrow[c_1]{w_1} (q_1, v_1) \xrightarrow[c_2]{w_2} \cdots \xrightarrow[c_5]{w_5} (q_5, v_5)$$

is a run of $\mathcal{A}_{pulse}$ over w' with $\mathrm{cost}(\rho) = 0.49$ and $w' \in \mathcal{L}_{0.5}(\mathcal{A}_{pulse})$.

We now formally show the equivalence between shape expressions and shape automata. The first direction of the theorem allows to construct automata recognizers for arbitrary expressions. The second direction of the theorem shows that shape expressions are expressively complete relative to the class of automata under consideration.

Theorem 1 (SE $\Leftrightarrow$ SA). *For any shape expression φ there exists a shape automaton $\mathcal{A}_\varphi$ such that $\mathcal{L}_\nu(\mathcal{A}_\varphi) = \mathcal{L}_\nu(\varphi)$ for all $\nu \geq 0$. For any shape automaton $\mathcal{A}$ there exists a shape expression $\varphi_{\mathcal{A}}$ such that $\mathcal{L}_\nu(\varphi_{\mathcal{A}}) = \mathcal{L}_\nu(\mathcal{A})$ for all $\nu \geq 0$.*

3 Pattern Matching

In Sect. 2.3, we introduced shape automata to recognize signals that are close to a specified shape. However, a shape expression is not intended to represent a whole signal, but only a segment thereof. In this section, we extend shape automata to enable them identifying all signal segments that match specific shapes. We first define the notion of noisy match sets.

Definition 6 (Noisy match set). *For any signal w defined over a time domain $\mathbb{T} = [0, d)$, shape expression φ and noise tolerance threshold ν, we define the match set $\mathcal{M}(\varphi, w)$ and the noisy match set $\mathcal{M}_\nu(\varphi, w)$ as follows:*

$$\mathcal{M}_\nu(\varphi, w) = \{(t, t') \in \mathbb{T}^2 \mid t \leq t' \text{ and } w^{[t, t')} \in \mathcal{L}_\nu(\varphi)\}$$

Given a shape automaton $\mathcal{A}$, its associated *shape pattern matching automaton* $\hat{\mathcal{A}}$ is another shape automaton that extends $\mathcal{A}$ with dedicated initial and final locations, which allow $\hat{\mathcal{A}}$ to silently consume a prefix and a suffix of a signal. The construction follows [9] and is given in the definition below.

Definition 7 (Shape pattern matching automaton). *Let* $\mathcal{A} = \langle P, X, Q, \Delta,$ $S, F \rangle$ *be a shape automaton. Then the corresponding shape pattern matching automaton is* $\hat{\mathcal{A}} = \langle P, X, \hat{Q}, \hat{\Delta}, \hat{S}, \hat{F} \rangle$, *where*

- $\hat{Q} = Q \cup \{\hat{s}, \hat{f}\}$, $\hat{S} = \{\hat{s}\}$, $\hat{F} = \{\hat{f}\}$,
- $\hat{\Delta} = \Delta \cup \{(\hat{s}, \textsf{any}, \textsf{true}, q) \mid q \in S\} \cup \{(q, \textsf{any}, \textsf{true}, \hat{f}) \mid q \in F\}$, *where* **any** *is a special shape such that* $\mu(w, \textsf{any}) = 0$ *for all* w.

Intuitively, given a signal w, a shape expression φ and its associated shape pattern matching automaton $\hat{\mathcal{A}}_\varphi$, an accepting run ρ over w decomposed into $w_0 \cdot w_1 \cdots w_{n+1}$ in $\hat{\mathcal{A}}_\varphi$

$$(\hat{s}, v_0) \xrightarrow[0]{w_0} (q_0, v_0) \xrightarrow[c_1]{w_1} \cdots \xrightarrow[c_n]{w_n} (q_n, v_n) \xrightarrow[0]{w_{n+1}} (\hat{f}, v_n)$$

represents one potential match (defined by segment (t, t') in w where $t = |w_0|$ and $t' = |w| - |w_{n+1}|$) with one specific parameter instantiation (v_n) and its associated similarity measure $\text{cost}(\rho) = \max_{i=1}^{n} c_i$. We denote by $\lambda(\rho) = (t, t')$ the *label* of run ρ over w in $\hat{\mathcal{A}}$. We first note that for a given decomposition of w, there is an infinite number of runs over w in $\hat{\mathcal{A}}_\varphi$ that follow that decomposition due to the parameters being valued as real numbers. We also note that for a given signal w, there is a finite (but large) number of its decompositions.

Example 5. Figure 3 shows three runs ρ_1, ρ_2 and ρ_3 over w in $\hat{\mathcal{A}}_{pulse}$ and the corresponding ideal shapes defined by the valuations computed during the runs. We can see that each run identifies one segment of w that could be a potential match of the shape expression φ_{pulse} with specific parameter values and cost. In particular, we can observe that runs ρ_1 and ρ_2 decompose w in the same manner but with different parameter valuations, resulting in $\text{cost}(\rho_1) < \text{cost}(\rho_2)$.

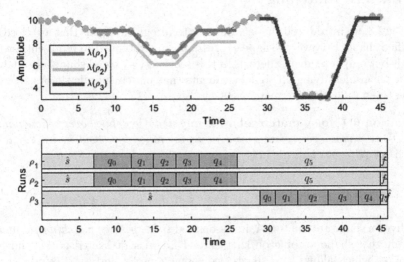

Fig. 3. Pulse train - three runs ρ_1, ρ_2 and ρ_3 over w in $\hat{\mathcal{A}}_{pulse}$.

From the above observations, we obtain that the labeling of the set of runs associated to a shape pattern matching automaton $\hat{\mathcal{A}}$ and a signal w gives us exactly the match set of $\mathcal{L}(\mathcal{A})$ relative to w.

Theorem 2. *Let φ be a shape expression, $\hat{\mathcal{A}}_\varphi$ the corresponding shape pattern matching automaton, w a signal and ν a noise tolerance threshold. We have that $\mathcal{M}_\nu(\varphi, w) = \{(t, t') \mid \exists \rho \in \mathcal{R}(\hat{\mathcal{A}}_\varphi, w) \text{ s.t. } \lambda(\rho) = (t, t') \text{ and } \mathrm{cost}(\rho) \leq \nu\}$.*

We observe that while this in principle solves the SE pattern-matching problem, the complexity in terms of signal length is not practical. Let us define the dot-depth of some expression φ the maximal number of concatenations featured on any branch of its syntax tree.

Theorem 3. *The size of the set of runs of a shape matching automaton $\hat{\mathcal{A}}_\varphi$ is $\Omega(n^{k+2})$, where n is the size of the trace, and k is the dot-depth of φ.*

The dot-depth of any expression is nonnegative, hence this lower bound is at least quadratic in the length of the signal. This means that any exhaustive algorithm will not scale in many practical applications, where typical signal can be over 10^6 samples long.

We propose two ways to handle complexity: (1) bound the length of matches, or (2) develop heuristics to efficiently match shape expressions. Bounding the length of matches is reflected in the following definition.

Definition 8 (Bounded shape expressions). *A shape expression is said to be bounded (by k) when for all words w we have that $w \in \mathcal{L}(\varphi)$ implies $|w| \leq k$.*

Theorem 4 (Linear-time upper bound). *For an expression φ bounded by k the size of the set of accepting runs of the shape matching automaton can be represented by a dag of size $O(nk2^{m \cdot k^m})$, where n is the length of the trace and m is the length of the expression.*

4   Policy Scheduler for Shape Matching Automata

In this section, we propose a heuristic in the form of a policy scheduler that efficiently approximates the complete match set by computing a representative subset of non-overlapping matches.

Let w be a signal defined over X and $\sigma_x(P')$ a shape with $x \in X$. We denote by reg the *statistical regression* with constraints which returns the pair of the parameter values $v(P')$ which minimizes MSE under the constraint γ and the associated $\mu(w, \sigma_x(v(P')))$, defined as follows:

$$\mathrm{reg}(w, \sigma_x, \gamma) = (\mathrm{argmin}_v\{\mathrm{MSE}(w, \sigma_x(v(P'))) \mid v \models \gamma\}, \mu(w, \sigma_x(v(P')))).$$

We now show that μ (MSE and CoD) can be computed in an online fashion. Given the two sequences $\mathbf{y} = y_1, \ldots, y_n$ and $\mathbf{f} = f_1, \ldots, f_n$ of observations and predictions, we define a recursive definition of MSE and CoD as follows.

Algorithm 1. Shape expression match expression_match

Input: Set of locations S, current end match time t
Output: New end match time t'

1   $t' \leftarrow -\infty$
2   **if** $S \cap F \neq \emptyset$ **then** $t' \leftarrow t$
3   **else if** $t < |w|$ **then**
4   **foreach** $\delta = (q, \sigma_x, \gamma, q') \in out_{\Delta}(S)$ **do**
5         $\tau \leftarrow$ atomic_match(δ, t)
6   **if** $\tau > -\infty$ **then** $\tau' \leftarrow$ expression_match$(\{q'\}, \tau)$
7         $t' \leftarrow \max\{t', \tau'\}$

8   **return** t'

$$
\begin{aligned}
\mathrm{MSE}(\mathbf{y}, \mathbf{f}, n+1) &= \tfrac{n}{n+1}\,\mathrm{MSE}(\mathbf{y}, \mathbf{f}, n) + \tfrac{1}{n+1}(y_{n+1} - f_{n+1})^2 \\
\bar{y}(n+1) &= \tfrac{n}{n+1}\bar{y}(n) + \tfrac{1}{n+1}y_{n+1} \\
SS_{tot}(\mathbf{y}, n+1) &= SS_{tot}(\mathbf{y}, n) + (y_{n+1} - \bar{y}(n))(y_{n+1} - \bar{y}(n+1)) \\
SS_{res}(\mathbf{y}, \mathbf{f}, n+1) &= SS_{res}(\mathbf{y}, \mathbf{f}, n) + (y_{n+1} - f_{n+1})^2 \\
R^2(\mathbf{y}, \mathbf{f}, n+1) &= 1 - \tfrac{SS_{res}(\mathbf{y},\mathbf{f},n+1)}{SS_{tot}(\mathbf{y},n+1)}
\end{aligned}
$$

We require a minimum length $\lambda > 1$ for atomic shape matches[5]. We define the auxiliary method out_{Δ} as follows:

$$
out_{\Delta}(S) = \{\delta \mid \exists\, \delta = (q, \sigma_x, \gamma, q') \in \Delta \text{ for some } q \in S\}
$$

The method policy_scheduler searches for non-overlapping SE matches in w from time 0, using method expression_match. The call of expression_match at time t returns another time t'. If $t' > t$, the segment $[t, t']$ successfully matches the expression. The segment $[t, t']$ is added to the set of matches and the procedure expression_match is invoked again at time $t' + 1$. If $t' \leq t$, it means that the expression could not be matched from time t. The procedure expression_match is invoked again at time $t + 1$.

The shape matching procedure expression_match (see Algorithm 1) attempts in a recursive fashion to reach a final location from a set of locations S and time index t. The procedure returns another time index t', where $t' \geq t$ if a final location can be reached in $t' - t$ steps from a location in S, or $t' = -\infty$ (the initial value of t', see line 1) otherwise. If one of the locations is a final location, we have that $t' = t$ (lines 2). If none of the locations in S is final, and we have not yet reached the end of w (lines 3–7), the procedure does the following. For every transition with a source location in S, labeled by σ_x and γ (lines 4–7), atomic_match computes the end time τ of the longest match of σ_x that satisfies γ and starts at t (line 5). If there is no such match, τ equals to $-\infty$, otherwise

---

[5] We also assume that the SMA $\hat{A}$, the signal w, the noise tolerance threshold ν and the minimum match length λ are given as global parameters to the main procedure policy_scheduler and are implicitly propagated to all the other methods.

Algorithm 2. Atomic shape match atomic_match.

Input: Transition $\delta = (q, \sigma_x, \gamma, q')$, start match time index t
Output: End match time t'

1 $t' \leftarrow -\infty$
2 **if** $t + \lambda \leq |w|$ **then**
3       $\tau \leftarrow \lambda$; $w' \leftarrow w^{[t,t+\tau]}$; $(v, c) \leftarrow \text{reg}(w', \sigma_x(P'), \gamma)$
4   **while** $c \leq \nu$ **do**
5           $t' \leftarrow t + \tau$
6   **if** $t' < |w|$ **then**
7               $\tau \leftarrow \tau + 1$; $w' \leftarrow w' \cdot w(t')$
8               $c \leftarrow \mu(w', \sigma_x(v(P')))$
9   **if** $c > \nu$ **then** $(v, c) \leftarrow \text{reg}(w', \sigma_x(P'), \gamma)$
10   **else break**

11 **return** t'

$\tau \geq t + \lambda$[6]. For all the transitions that result in a match ending at time τ, we recursively call expression_match with the target location q' and time τ as inputs, and τ' as output (line 6). The procedure keeps the longest from the successful expression matches (line 7). This effectively allows the procedure to concurrently follow multiple paths and select the one that provides the longest match.

The atomic shape matching procedure atomic_match, shown in Algorithm 2, efficiently computes the longest match of an atomic shape starting from a given time index. It takes as inputs a transition $\delta = (q, \sigma_x, \gamma, q')$ and the time index t, and returns the end time t' of the longest σ_x ν-noisy match $[t, t']$ that satisfies γ. The algorithm starts by fitting the shape σ_x to the segment $w' = w^{[t,t+\tau]}$ under the constraint γ, using the regression method reg, and thus estimating the parameters v (lines 3). The procedure reg also returns the corresponding μ-value c of the performed regression. If the associated μ-value c is greater than the allowed noise tolerance ν, the procedure returns $t' = -\infty$, meaning that the segment is not a good candidate for matching the shape. Otherwise, the algorithm iteratively extends the size τ of the segment as long as the μ-value between the extended prefix and $\sigma_x(v(P'))$ instantiated with the fixed parameter valuation v remains lower than or equal to ν (lines 4–10). We note that each extension of the signal prefix updates μ but not the parameter valuation. There are two possible reasons for μ becoming greater than ν: (i) either the estimated parameter valuation v needs to be updated, or (ii) the current prefix does not fit the shape under the constraint ν anymore with any valuation v. In the first case, the procedure re-estimates the new parameter valuation and re-computes μ (line 9). If the re-computed μ is smaller than or equal to ν and we didn't reach the end of the signal, we repeat the match extension procedure. Otherwise, we terminate the procedure and return the time index t' where the current match (if any, otherwise t' equals to $-\infty$) ended.

---

[6] Recall that we require atomic matches of minimum length λ.

5   Implementation and Evaluation

We implemented the Algorithm 2 into a prototype tool using the Python programming language. We employed pattern matching of shape expressions to two applications – detection of patterns in electro-cardiograms (ECG) and oscillatory behaviors in an aircraft elevator control system. All experiments were run on MacBook Pro with the Intel Core i7 2.6 GHz processor and 16 GB RAM.

5.1   Detection of Anomalous Patterns in ECG

In this case study, we consider ECG signals from the PhysioBank database [14], which contains 549 records from 290 subjects (209 male and 81 female, aged from 17 to 87). Each record includes 15 simultaneously measured signals, digitized at 1,000 samples per second, with 16-bit resolution over a range of ±16.384 mV. The diagnostic classes for the subjects participating in the recordings include cardiovascular diseases such as myocardial infarction, cardiomyopathy, dysrythmia and myocardial hypertrophy.

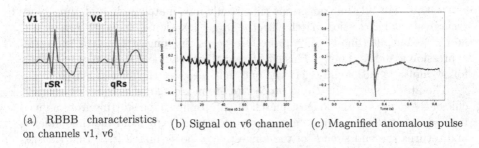

(a) RBBB characteristics on channels v1, v6   (b) Signal on v6 channel   (c) Magnified anomalous pulse

Fig. 4. Recognizing pulses in ECG signals

Specification of an Anomalous Heart Pulse. We consider the *right bundle branch block* (RBBB) heart condition, in which the right ventricle is not directly activated by impulses traveling through the right bundle branch. Figure 4a depicts a visual characterization of the RBBB heart condition as it can be observed on channels v1 and v6[7]. In this work, we concentrate on specifying the shape of the pulse depicted in v6 using shape expressions. The specification φ of the anomalous v6 pulse consists of a sequence of 7 atomic shapes:

$$\varphi = \exp(a_1, b_1, c_1) \; : \; b_1 > 0 \cdot \exp(a_2, b_2, c_2) \; : \; b_2 < 0 \cdot$$
$$\lin(a_3, b_3) \; : \; a_3 > 0 \cdot \lin(a_4, b_4) \; : \; a_4 < 0 \cdot \lin(a_5, b_5) \; : \; a_5 > 0 \cdot$$
$$\exp(a_6, b_6, c_6) \; : \; b_6 > 0 \cdot \exp(a_7, b_7, c_7) \; : \; b_7 < 0$$

Evaluation. We evaluated our SE matching procedure with respect to the recordings of a 70 year old patient that suffers from RBBB condition. The v6

---

[7] The figure is under copyright by A. Rad.

Table 1. Experimental results

<table>
<tr><td colspan="4">(a) Sensitivity to the noise threshold</td><td colspan="3">(b) Runtime and memory requirements</td></tr>
<tr><td>ν</td><td>$|H|$</td><td>$|\mathcal{M}_\nu(\varphi)|$</td><td>$|\mathcal{M}_\nu(\varphi')|$</td><td>Num.
Samples</td><td>Runtime
(s)</td><td>Mem.
(MB)</td></tr>
<tr><td>0.70</td><td>4</td><td>9</td><td>4</td><td></td><td></td><td></td></tr>
<tr><td>0.24</td><td>4</td><td>7</td><td>4</td><td>1,000</td><td>0.46</td><td>33.13</td></tr>
<tr><td>0.20</td><td>4</td><td>5</td><td>4</td><td>2,500</td><td>1.43</td><td>48.82</td></tr>
<tr><td>0.10</td><td>4</td><td>4</td><td>4</td><td>5,000</td><td>3.39</td><td>70.80</td></tr>
<tr><td>0.02</td><td>4</td><td>4</td><td>4</td><td>7,500</td><td>6.39</td><td>72.83</td></tr>
<tr><td>0.01</td><td>4</td><td>0</td><td>0</td><td>10,000</td><td>10.12</td><td>89.18</td></tr>
</table>

channel recording of the patient, shown in Fig. 4b, has 10,000 samples. In this experiment, we use CoD as our noise metric[8]. With noise threshold $\nu = 0.02$, we were able to identify all the segments that match φ in 28.98 s. The matches are depicted as colored vertical bands in Fig. 4b. Figure 4c zooms in on a single match and shows the ideal shape that was inferred to match the pattern.

We now experimentally study how sensitive is the quality of the procedure outcome with respect to the noise threshold and the constraints on the parameters, and how well the procedure scales with the size of the input.

Sensitivity to the Noise Threshold and the Constraints on the Parameters. Domain knowledge in a particular application field can be used to derive more precise specifications. In the case of anomalous v6 pulses for patients with RBBB condition, such knowledge can be for instance used to refine its specification φ by further constraining the slope a_3 to be greater than 0.5, resulting in specification φ'. We demonstrate the impact of the noise threshold to the quality of pattern matching in the cases of under-specified (φ) and over-specified (φ') shape expressions. Table 1a shows the results of the experiments, where column $|H|$ denotes the number of segments matched by the inspection of the signal by a human with domain knowledge and columns $|\mathcal{M}_\nu(\varphi)|$ and $|\mathcal{M}_\nu(\varphi')|$ denotes the number of the segments matching the expressions φ and φ' by our procedure, respectively.

We first observe that domain knowledge improves the quality of both the specification the robustness of the monitor. Second, our approach can result in missing patterns or detecting false patterns. This result is expected – very low ν enables to only match shapes that are very close to the ideal one, while very high ν results in matching shapes that are far away from the specification. Hence, our procedure may require tuning parameters.

Scalability. We now evaluate the scalability of our procedure with respect to the size of the signal, taking into account the computation time and the memory requirements. Table 1b summarizes the results. The computation time in this

---

[8] We recall that $\nu = 0$ denotes zero noise tolerance and $\nu = 1$ allows arbitrary level of noise.

experiment exhibits an almost linear behavior, while the memory consumption appears to grow in a sub-linear fashion with respect to the size of the input.

5.2   Detection of Ringing in an Aircraft Elevator Control System

In many electronics applications, step response is used to study how the system responds to sudden changes in inputs. *Ringing* is an oscillation in the output signal, which is encountered in response to a step in input. It is considered to be an undesirable behavior, which nevertheless cannot be fully avoided. It is hence important to investigate properties of the oscillations (amplitude, frequency, etc.) to determine the quality of the output response.

We use SEs to detect and study ringing behavior in an aircraft elevator control system [13]. It is a Simulink model of a redundant actuator control system with one elevator on the left and one on the right side. In essence, the pilot gives a command with the intended position of the aircraft, which must be followed by the left and right elevators. When the pilot gives a step command, this results in the ringing response by the control system, as shown in Fig. 5(a).

Specification of a Ringing Behavior. We are interested in detecting both the rising and falling edge and the subsequent ringing behavior. We chose to specify such behavior as a line, followed by a sinc wave $(sinc(a, b, c, d, t) = a + b\frac{sin(ct+d)}{ct+d})$.

$$\varphi = \lin_x(a_1, b_1) : a_1 > 0.5 \cdot \mathrm{sinc}_x(a_2, b_2, c_2, d_2).$$

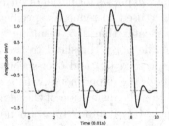
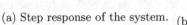
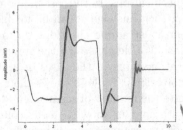

(a) Step response of the system.   (b) Segments matching ringing patterns.

Fig. 5. Aircraft elevator control system step response

Inferring Parameters of Ringing Patterns. Figure 5(b) shows the segments in the output response of the aircraft elevator control system that match the ringing pattern. We stimulate the system with input steps of different amplitudes and show how this change in inputs

Table 2. Parameters inferred from segments matching φ.

Amp	a_1	b_1	a_2	b_2	c_2	d_2
1	1.36	−8.98	−0.40	3.03	−2.05	17.73
2	2.83	−18.55	−1.51	2.83	−3.31	25.80
3	4.75	−30.75	−2.78	−8.76	−5.21	13.09

affects the step response and the resulting ringing oscillations. For each response signal, we report the inferred parameters in Table 2. We can observe that the rising edge of the step response becomes steeper with input steps of higher amplitude. We can also see that both the amplitude and the frequency of the sinc monotonically decrease with the input amplitude.

6   Conclusion

In this paper, we proposed *shape expressions* as a language for specification of rich and complex temporal patterns. We studied essential properties of shape expressions and developed an efficient heuristic pattern matching procedure for this specification language. We believe that this work explores the expressiveness boundaries of declarative specification languages.

We will pursue this work in several directions. We will apply our technique to examples from more application domains. We will study more sophisticated matching methods that will minimize the need of tuning parameter constraints. We will compare more closely our approach to the work on classical regular expression matching on one hand, and purely machine learning feature extraction methods on the other hand. We will finally investigate the application of shape expressions in testing CPS with the particular focus on generating test cases from such a specification language.

Acknowledgments. This research was supported in part by the Austrian Science Fund (FWF) under grants 27 S11402-N23 (RiSE/SHiNE) and Z211-N23 (Wittgenstein Award), and by the Productive 4.0 project (ECSEL 737459).

References

1. IEEE standard on pulse Measurement and analysis by objective techniques. IEEE Std. 181–1977 (1977)
2. Abbas, H., Rodionova, A., Bartocci, E., Smolka, S.A., Grosu, R.: Quantitative regular expressions for arrhythmia detection algorithms. In: Feret, J., Koeppl, H. (eds.) CMSB 2017. LNCS, vol. 10545, pp. 23–39. Springer, Cham (2017). https://doi.org/10.1007/978-3-319-67471-1_2
3. Alur, R., Fisman, D., Raghothaman, M.: Regular programming for quantitative properties of data streams. In: Thiemann, P. (ed.) ESOP 2016. LNCS, vol. 9632, pp. 15–40. Springer, Heidelberg (2016). https://doi.org/10.1007/978-3-662-49498-1_2
4. Alur, R., Mamouras, K., Stanford, C.: Modular quantitative monitoring. In: Proceedings of the ACM on Programming Languages, vol. 3(POPL), p. 50 (2019)
5. André, É., Hasuo, I., Masaki, W.: Offline timed pattern matching under uncertainty. In: 23rd International Conference on Engineering of Complex Computer Systems, ICECCS 2018, Melbourne, Australia, 12–14 December 2018, pp. 10–20 (2018)
6. Asarin, E., Caspi, P., Maler, O.: A Kleene theorem for timed automata. In: Logic in Computer Science (LICS), pp. 160–171 (1997)
7. Asarin, E., Caspi, P., Maler, O.: Timed regular expressions. J. ACM **49**(2), 172–206 (2002)

8. Bakhirkin, A., Ferrère, T., Maler, O., Ulus, D.: On the quantitative semantics of regular expressions over real-valued signals. In: Abate, A., Geeraerts, G. (eds.) FORMATS 2017. LNCS, vol. 10419, pp. 189–206. Springer, Cham (2017). https://doi.org/10.1007/978-3-319-65765-3_11

9. Bakhirkin, A., Ferrère, T., Nickovic, D., Maler, O., Asarin, E.: Online timed pattern matching using automata. In: Jansen, D.N., Prabhakar, P. (eds.) FORMATS 2018. LNCS, vol. 11022, pp. 215–232. Springer, Cham (2018). https://doi.org/10.1007/978-3-030-00151-3_13

10. D'Angelo, B., et al.: LOLA: runtime monitoring of synchronous systems. In: 12th International Symposium on Temporal Representation and Reasoning (TIME 2005), 23–25 June 2005, Burlington, Vermont, USA, pp. 166–174 (2005)

11. Faymonville, P., Finkbeiner, B., Schirmer, S., Torfah, H.: A stream-based specification language for network monitoring. In: Falcone, Y., Sánchez, C. (eds.) RV 2016. LNCS, vol. 10012, pp. 152–168. Springer, Cham (2016). https://doi.org/10.1007/978-3-319-46982-9_10

12. Geurts, P.: Pattern extraction for time series classification. In: De Raedt, L., Siebes, A. (eds.) PKDD 2001. LNCS (LNAI), vol. 2168, pp. 115–127. Springer, Heidelberg (2001). https://doi.org/10.1007/3-540-44794-6_10

13. Ghidella, J., Mosterman, P.: Requirements-based testing in aircraft control design. In: AIAA Modeling and Simulation Technologies Conference and Exhibit, p. 5886 (2005)

14. Goldberger, A.L., et al.: Physiobank, physiotoolkit, and physionet: components of a new research resource for complex physiologic signals. Circulation 101(23), e215–e220 (2000)

15. Gorostiaga, F., Sánchez, C.: Striver: stream runtime verification for real-time event-streams. In: Colombo, C., Leucker, M. (eds.) RV 2018. LNCS, vol. 11237, pp. 282–298. Springer, Cham (2018). https://doi.org/10.1007/978-3-030-03769-7_16

16. Hallé, S., Khoury, R.: Event stream processing with beepbeep 3. In: RV-CuBES 2017. An International Workshop on Competitions, Usability, Benchmarks, Evaluation, and Standardisation for Runtime Verification Tools, 15 September 2017, Seattle, WA, USA, pp. 81–88 (2017)

17. Leucker, M., Sánchez, C., Scheffel, T., Schmitz, M., Schramm, A.: TeSSLa: runtime verification of non-synchronized real-time streams. In: Proceedings of the 33rd Annual ACM Symposium on Applied Computing, SAC 2018, Pau, France, 09–13 April 2018, pp. 1925–1933 (2018)

18. Maler, O., Nickovic, D.: Monitoring temporal properties of continuous signals. In: Lakhnech, Y., Yovine, S. (eds.) FORMATS/FTRTFT -2004. LNCS, vol. 3253, pp. 152–166. Springer, Heidelberg (2004). https://doi.org/10.1007/978-3-540-30206-3_12

19. Mamouras, K., Raghothaman, M., Alur, R., Ives, Z.G., Khanna, S.: StreamQRE: modular specification and efficient evaluation of quantitative queries over streaming data. In: ACM SIGPLAN Notices, vol. 52, pp. 693–708. ACM (2017)

20. Olszewski, R.T.: Generalized feature extraction for structural pattern recognition in time-series data. Technical report, Carnegie-Mellon Univ. School of Computer Science (2001)

21. Rakthanmanon, T., et al.: Searching and mining trillions of time series subsequences under dynamic time warping. In: Proceedings of the 18th ACM SIGKDD International Conference on Knowledge Discovery and Data Mining, pp. 262–270. ACM (2012)

22. Ulus, D.: MONTRE: a tool for monitoring timed regular expressions. In: Majumdar, R., Kunčak, V. (eds.) CAV 2017. LNCS, vol. 10426, pp. 329–335. Springer, Cham (2017). https://doi.org/10.1007/978-3-319-63387-9_16
23. Ulus, D., Ferrère, T., Asarin, E., Maler, O.: Timed pattern matching. In: Legay, A., Bozga, M. (eds.) FORMATS 2014. LNCS, vol. 8711, pp. 222–236. Springer, Cham (2014). https://doi.org/10.1007/978-3-319-10512-3_16
24. Ulus, D., Ferrère, T., Asarin, E., Maler, O.: Online timed pattern matching using derivatives. In: Chechik, M., Raskin, J.-F. (eds.) TACAS 2016. LNCS, vol. 9636, pp. 736–751. Springer, Heidelberg (2016). https://doi.org/10.1007/978-3-662-49674-9_47
25. Waga, M., Hasuo, I.: Moore-machine filtering for timed and untimed pattern matching. IEEE Trans. CAD Integr. Circ. Syst. **37**(11), 2649–2660 (2018)
26. Waga, M., Hasuo, I., Suenaga, K.: Efficient online timed pattern matching by automata-based skipping. In: Abate, A., Geeraerts, G. (eds.) FORMATS 2017. LNCS, vol. 10419, pp. 224–243. Springer, Cham (2017). https://doi.org/10.1007/978-3-319-65765-3_13
27. Waga, M., Hasuo, I., Suenaga, K.: MONAA: a tool for timed pattern matching with automata-based acceleration. In: 3rd Workshop on Monitoring and Testing of Cyber-Physical Systems, MT@CPSWeek 2018, Porto, Portugal, 10 April, pp. 14–15 (2018)
28. Wenig, F., Klanatsky, P., Heschl, C., Mateis, C., Dejan, N.: Exponential pattern recognition for deriving air change rates from CO_2 data. In: 26th IEEE International Symposium on Industrial Electronics, ISIE 2017, Edinburgh, United Kingdom, 19–21 June 2017, pp. 1507–1512 (2017)
29. Ye, L., Keogh, E.J.: Time series shapelets: a new primitive for data mining. In: Proceedings of the 15th ACM SIGKDD International Conference on Knowledge Discovery and Data Mining, Paris, France, 28 June–1 July 2009, pp. 947–956 (2009)

A Formally Verified Monitor for Metric First-Order Temporal Logic

Joshua Schneider[✉], David Basin, Srđan Krstić[✉], and Dmitriy Traytel[✉]

Institute of Information Security, Department of Computer Science, ETH Zürich, Zurich, Switzerland
{joshua.schneider,srdan.krstic,traytel}@inf.ethz.ch

Abstract. Runtime verification tools must correctly establish a specification's validity or detect violations. This task is difficult, especially when the specification is given in an expressive declarative language that demands a non-trivial monitoring algorithm. We use a proof assistant to not only solve this task, but also to gain confidence in our solution. We formally verify the correctness of a monitor for metric first-order temporal logic specifications using the Isabelle/HOL proof assistant. From our formalization, we extract an executable algorithm with correctness guarantees and use differential testing to find discrepancies in the outputs of two unverified monitors for first-order specification languages.

Keywords: First-order monitoring · Temporal logic · Proof assistant

1 Introduction

Runtime verification (RV) tools are used today in safety, mission, and security-critical applications, where mistakes are too costly to be tolerated. These tools rely on complex monitoring algorithms for expressive specification languages. The correctness of these algorithms and their implementations is important and rarely obvious.

The RV community has considered different ways of improving monitors' trustworthiness by model checking monitoring algorithms [15,21,22] and using proof assistants to formally verify monitor instances for fixed specifications [6,30] or entire monitors for linear temporal logic (LTL) on finite words [24] and differential dynamic logic (d$\mathcal{L}$) [7,18]. We add to these lines of work and use the Isabelle/HOL proof assistant (Sect. 2) to develop and prove correct a monitor that supports a large fragment of metric first-order temporal logic with past and future operators (MFOTL) (Sect. 3).

Basin et al. [2] describe an efficient monitoring algorithm for MFOTL, which is implemented in the state-of-the-art monitoring tool MonPoly [3]. Our implementation deviates from the algorithm's informal description [2] in several fine points, in particular regarding the concrete representation of the monitor's state. Our formally verified algorithm closely follows MonPoly's implementation, while incorporating several simplifications regarding the evaluation order of subformulas and using simpler, less optimized data structures.

Like MonPoly, we consider a fragment of MFOTL that is monitorable using finite relations, which we represent as tables (Sect. 4). (Another version of MonPoly also supports full MFOTL using automata to represent regular relations, but is orders of magnitude less efficient.) Our monitoring algorithm processes a parametric event stream

B. Finkbeiner and L. Mariani (Eds.): RV 2019, LNCS 11757, pp. 310–328, 2019.
https://doi.org/10.1007/978-3-030-32079-9_18

online, incrementally updates its state, and outputs verdicts specifying for every position in the event stream whether a violation has occurred and which parameters caused it (Sect. 5). We have proved the algorithm correct by establishing a complex invariant on its state and verifying that the outputted violations faithfully reflect MFOTL's semantics (Sect. 6).

Using Isabelle's code generator [9], we extract an executable OCaml implementation from our formalization. The resulting certified algorithm is integrated into MonPoly by replacing its core algorithm, while reusing its (unverified) formula and log parsers. The certified algorithm is slower than MonPoly's original algorithm. Yet it is efficient enough to process roughly 4 000 events per second on a formula with non-trivial past and future operators, whereas the original algorithm can process 23 000 events per second.

To demonstrate the verified monitor's usefulness, we perform a case study in differential testing: We compare our algorithm's output to MonPoly's on randomly generated inputs (Sect. 7). We also compare with DejaVu [11–13], a monitor for past-only first-order temporal logic. We find some discrepancies in the outputs of both tools, exhibiting corner cases where the unverified tools deviate from MFOTL's standard semantics.

In summary, we contribute a highly trustworthy monitor implementation by verifying its correctness in Isabelle/HOL. The monitor features an expressive parametric specification language with past and future metric temporal operators. Our case study confirms the usefulness of having a trusted testing oracle. We describe the formalized algorithm using concrete Isabelle syntax, demonstrating that programming in Isabelle is not different from programming in any other functional programming language. Moreover, the described algorithm can be seen as a more faithful and precise description of the MFOTL monitor than the original paper by Basin et al. [2]. With only 3 000 lines of Isabelle definitions and proofs, the verification effort was modest. The formalization is publicly available [29].

Related Work. Monitoring parametric traces and first-order specifications is bread-and-butter business in runtime verification [2,3,10–13,23,25,26]. We refer to Havelund et al. [14] for a recent overview. Here, we discuss verification efforts targeting monitors.

Pike et al. [15,21,22] use SMT-based model-checking to increase the trustworthiness of monitors within the Copilot framework. Blech et al. [6] extract executable monitors for regular expressions from a formalization in the Coq proof assistant. However, the monitors must be proved correct manually for every property because their construction is not verified. Völlinger [30] develops a framework for certifying the output of distributed algorithms in Coq. The certification procedures that are part of this framework can be seen as concrete monitors for specific properties. Their correctness, too, must be proved manually for every distributed algorithm considered. Rizaldi et al. [24] verify a dynamic programming monitor for LTL on finite traces in Isabelle/HOL as part of their work on monitoring traffic rules. The finite trace semantics significantly simplifies their algorithm. ModelPlex is a framework for synthesizing correct-by-construction monitors for cyber-physical systems [18]. Bohrer et al. [7] further extend this work to an entire verified pipeline that culminates in the usage of a verified compiler. Both works use differential dynamic logic, which targets cyber-physical systems, but cannot easily express metric temporal properties.

More distantly related verification efforts in proof assistants include regular expression matchers [1,20], a model checker for LTL [8], a library of timed automata [31] including a model checker [32], and relational database management systems [4,5,16].

In a separate line of work [27], we have extended our formalization with a framework for adaptive parallel monitoring. There parallel instances of the verified monitor must exchange parts of their states. Having the formalization of the monitor in the first place was crucial to gain trust in the correctness of this nontrivial extension.

2 Isabelle/HOL

Proof assistants are tools that mechanically check human-written proofs. They provide the highest level of trustworthiness by being built around a small, well-understood inference kernel. All proofs must pass through the kernel, which rules out invalid arguments.

Isabelle/HOL [19] is a proof assistant based on classical higher-order logic (HOL) with Hilbert choice, the axiom of infinity, and rank-1 polymorphism. HOL's syntax resembles that of functional programming languages, but with quantifiers. Isabelle features a code generator [9], which exports executable specifications to Haskell, OCaml, and Scala.

HOL's basic types include type variables $'a, 'b, \ldots$, Booleans *bool*, natural numbers *nat*, sets $'a\,set$, pairs $'a \times 'b$, and functions $'a \Rightarrow 'b$. Functions are usually curried, and $\Rightarrow$ is right-associative. Type constructors such as $'a\,set$ are written postfix, e.g., *nat set* denotes the type of sets of natural numbers. The command **type_synonym** $t = u$ introduces an abbreviation t for an existing type u. The command **typedef** $t = S$ defines a genuinely new type from a nonempty set S over an existing type. Recursive datatypes are defined by the **datatype** command, similar to Haskell's `data`. For example, **datatype** $'a\,list = []$ | Cons $'a\,('a\,list)$ defines finite lists. The Cons constructor is usually written infix as #.

Terms are built from variables $x, y, \ldots$, constants, function applications $f\,x$, and abstractions $\lambda x. z$. Function application is left-associative. We use additional notation, e.g., conditionals <u>if</u> b <u>then</u> z_1 <u>else</u> z_2, case distinctions for datatypes <u>case</u> d <u>of</u> $x\#xs \Rightarrow z \mid \ldots$, and infix operators. The expression $z :: t$ denotes that the term z has type t. The command **definition** $c :: t$ **where** $c = z$ defines a new constant c from the term $z :: t$, which may not contain c. Recursive functions are defined by pattern-matching using **fun**. For example,

> **fun** map :: $('a \Rightarrow 'b) \Rightarrow 'a\,list \Rightarrow 'b\,list$ **where**
> map $f\,[] = []$ | map $f\,(x\#xs) = f\,x\#$map $f\,xs$

defines the standard list map function. Inductive predicates can be introduced differently:

> **inductive** list_all2 :: $('a \Rightarrow 'b \Rightarrow bool) \Rightarrow 'a\,list \Rightarrow 'b\,list \Rightarrow bool$ **where**
> list_all2 $P\,[]\,[]$ | $P\,x\,y \wedge$ list_all2 $P\,xs\,ys \longrightarrow$ list_all2 $P\,(x\#xs)\,(y\#ys)$

The **inductive** command defines list_all2 as the least (inductive) predicate closed under the two given rules (implications). In other words, list_all2 $P\,xs\,ys$ is true iff the lists xs and ys have the same lengths, and their elements satisfy the binary predicate P pairwise.

type_synonym *name* = *string*   **type_synonym** *domain* = *string*
type_synonym *db* = (*name* × *domain list*) *set*   **type_synonym** *ts* = *nat*

typedef *trace* = {*s* :: (*db* × *ts*) *stream*. wf_trace *s*}

datatype *trm* = V *nat* | C *domain*   **typedef** $\mathcal{I}$ = {(*a* :: *nat*, *b* :: *enat*). *a* ≤ *b*}

datatype *frm* = Pred *name* (*trm list*) | Eq *trm trm* | Neg *frm* | Or *frm frm* | Exists *frm*
| Since *frm* $\mathcal{I}$ *frm* | Until *frm* $\mathcal{I}$ *frm*

fun eval_trm :: *domain list* ⇒ *trm* ⇒ *domain* **where** eval_trm *v* (V *x*) = *v*!*x* | eval_trm *v* (C *x*) = *x*

fun sat :: *trace* ⇒ *domain list* ⇒ *nat* ⇒ *frm* ⇒ *bool* **where**
   sat σ *v i* (Pred *r ts*) = ((*r*, map (eval_trm *v*) *ts*) ∈ Γ σ *i*)
   | sat σ *v i* (Eq t_1 t_2) = (eval_trm *v* t_1 = eval_trm *v* t_2) | sat σ *v i* (Neg ψ) = (¬sat σ *v i* ψ)
   | sat σ *v i* (Exists ψ) = (∃z. sat σ (z#v) *i* ψ) | sat σ *v i* (Or α β) = (sat σ *v i* α ∨ sat σ *v i* β)
   | sat σ *v i* (Since α *I* β) = (∃j ≤ *i*. τ σ *i*−τ σ *j* ∈$_\mathcal{I}$ *I* ∧ sat σ *v j* β ∧ (∀k ∈ {*j* <.. *i*}. sat σ *v k* α))
   | sat σ *v i* (Until α *I* β) = (∃j ≥ *i*. τ σ *j*−τ σ *i* ∈$_\mathcal{I}$ *I* ∧ sat σ *v j* β ∧ (∀k ∈ {*i* ..< *j*}. sat σ *v k* α))

Fig. 1. Syntax and semantics of MFOTL

We use many constructs from Isabelle's library: e.g., projections fst and snd on pairs and the minimum operator min. The type *enat* extends *nat* with infinity ∞. The set {*x*. *P x*} contains all *x* satisfying *P*. Other set operations are *A* × *B* (Cartesian product), *A* − *B* (set difference), ⋃*x* ∈ *A*. *F x* (indexed union, i.e., {*y*. ∃x ∈ *A*. *y* ∈ *F x*}), Inf *A* (infimum), and *f* '*A* (image of *A* under *f*, i.e., ⋃*x* ∈ *A*. {*f x*}). The sets {*a* ..< *b*} and {*a* <.. *b*} contain all natural numbers *n* with *a* ≤ *n* < *b* and *a* < *n* ≤ *b*, respectively. The list [*a* ..< *b*] contains all of {*a* ..< *b*} in ascending order. The datatype '*a option* has two constructors ⊥ and ⟨*x* :: '*a*⟩. The term map_option *f* maps ⊥ to ⊥ and ⟨*x*⟩ to ⟨*f x*⟩. Options can be converted to sets via ⌈⊥⌉ = {} and ⌈⟨*x*⟩⌉ = {*x*}. The function these :: '*a option set* ⇒ '*a set* maps *A* to ⋃*x* ∈ *A*. ⌈*x*⌉. The term foldr *f xs z* combines the elements of the list *xs* with the binary function *f*, using *z* as the initial value, e.g., foldr (−) [1,2] 3 = 1 − (2 − 3). The set of all elements in the list *xs* is set *xs*, the length of *xs* is length *xs*, the *i*-th element of *xs* is *xs*!*i* (zero-based, requires *i* < length *xs*), and list concatenation is *xs*@*ys*. Strings *string* are character lists. Streams '*a stream* are infinite sequences of values of type '*a*.

3   Metric First-Order Temporal Logic

We interpret MFOTL over infinite streams of time-stamped events. Figure 1 shows the types of event streams and formulas along with the relation sat defining the semantics. Events consist of a name and a list of parameters from some domain (*name* × *domain list*). The *name* and *domain* types are arbitrary; we choose strings for convenience. We group concurrent events into databases (*db*). Time-stamps are discrete and modeled as natural numbers (*ts*). An event stream (*trace*) is an infinite stream of time-stamped databases. We write Γσ*i* for the *i*-th database in event stream σ and τσ*i* for the corresponding time-stamp, where *i* is a zero-based index. The predicate wf_trace in *trace*'s definition ensures that the time-stamp sequence is monotonic (∀i. τ σ *i* ≤ τ σ (*i* + 1)) and unbounded (∀t. ∃i. *t* < τ σ *i*). A (stream) prefix π is a finite list of time-stamped databases. It satisfies wf_prefix iff the prefix π has monotonic time-stamps. We write prefix_of π σ if the event stream σ extends the prefix π, i.e., the sequence of σ's first length π elements equals π.

The datatypes for terms (*trm*) and formulas (*frm*) are mostly standard. We use De Bruijn indices to represent free and bound variables, e.g., $\exists y.\ A(x,y)$ is encoded as Exists (Pred A [V 1, V 0]). In examples, we will show both the standard notation and the concrete encoding. The term fvφ denotes the set of φ's free variables. The degree nfv φ is the least number n such that for than any $x \in$ fvφ we have $x < n$. The predicate is_Const tests whether its argument is C d for some d. The type $\mathcal{I}$ models nonempty intervals over the natural numbers. The term interval a b represents the interval from a to b (both inclusive), and point c = interval c c. We write left I and right I for the endpoints of $I : \mathcal{I}$, and $n \in_{\mathcal{I}} I$ for the membership of n in I. We use abbreviations for some derived operators: And α β = Neg (Or (Neg α) (Neg β)), AndNot α β = Neg (Or (Neg α) β), TT = Eq (C d) (C d), where d is an arbitrary domain value, and Eventually I ψ = Until TT I ψ. We omit the operators *previous* and *next* from our presentation. These operators are implemented in the formalization [29].

We have sat σ v i φ iff the formula φ is satisfied by the valuation v at index i, given the event stream σ. Valuations are modeled as lists of domain values, the first element being the assignment to the variable with index 0, the second to the variable 1, and so forth.

4   Finite Tables

Our monitor computes and outputs all satisfying valuations of a formula at all indices. To do so efficiently, it operates on finite sets of valuations, which can be viewed as finite tables, and manipulates them using standard relational operations like natural join.

A way to represent finite sets of valuations for a given formula φ is to use sets of n-ary tuples (i.e., lists of length n), where n is the number of free variables in φ. The representation must map free variables to positions in the tuple and the natural join operation changes the arity of tuples. We chose a slightly different representation to simplify the implementation of union and join: Our tuples xs are lists of *optional* domain values, which assign values only to those variables i whose corresponding entries $xs!i$ are not $\perp$. This allows us to use tuples of a fixed length n, regardless of the formula's free variables, while ensuring that for any subformula all its free variables given by a set V are assigned, as specified by the well-formedness predicate wf_tuple (Fig. 2). We use the statement wf_tuple$n$ (fvφ) v with nfv$\varphi \leq n$ to express that v is a well-formed tuple for φ. We obtain the corresponding valuation $\bar{v}$ = map the v, where the function the maps $\langle x \rangle$ to x and $\perp$ to some unspecified domain element. The actual value assigned to $\perp$ is irrelevant for the valuation's satisfaction since it is only assigned to variables that are not free in φ.

A well-formed table A, written wf_table n V Q A, is a set of well-formed tuples. The parameter Q is a predicate on tuples that further restricts our attention to those tuples satisfying Q. Typically, Q will be instantiated by sat expressing that a table A consists of precisely the well-formed tuples that satisfy a given formula φ on stream σ at index i, i.e., wf_table$n$ (fvφ) ($\lambda v.$ sat $\sigma \bar{v} i \varphi$) A, where nfv$\varphi \leq n$. The abbreviation table$n$ V A = wf_table$n$ V ($\lambda v. v \in A$) A expresses that A only contains well-formed tuples.

type_synonym *tuple = domain option list*   **type_synonym** *table = tuple set*

definition wf_tuple :: *nat* $\Rightarrow$ *nat set* $\Rightarrow$ *tuple* $\Rightarrow$ *bool* **where**
    wf_tuple $n\ V\ v = (\text{length } v = n \wedge (\forall i < n.\ v\,!\,i = \bot \longleftrightarrow i \notin V))$

definition wf_table :: *nat* $\Rightarrow$ *nat set* $\Rightarrow$ *(tuple* $\Rightarrow$ *bool)* $\Rightarrow$ *table* $\Rightarrow$ *bool* **where**
    wf_table $n\ V\ Q\ A = (\forall v.\ v \in A \longleftrightarrow (Q\ v \wedge \text{wf\_tuple } n\ V\ v))$

fun join1 :: *tuple* $\times$ *tuple* $\Rightarrow$ *tuple option* **where**
    join1 $([], []) = \langle[]\rangle$
| join1 $(\bot \# xs, \bot \# ys) = \text{map\_option } (\lambda zs.\ \bot \# zs)\ (\text{join1 } (xs, ys))$
| join1 $(\langle x\rangle \# xs, \bot \# ys) = \text{map\_option } (\lambda zs.\ \langle x\rangle \# zs)\ (\text{join1 } (xs, ys))$
| join1 $(\bot \# xs, \langle y\rangle \# ys) = \text{map\_option } (\lambda zs.\ \langle y\rangle \# zs)\ (\text{join1 } (xs, ys))$
| join1 $(\langle x\rangle \# xs, \langle y\rangle \# ys) = (\underline{\text{if }} x = y \underline{\text{ then }} \text{map\_option } (\lambda zs.\ \langle x\rangle \# zs)\ (\text{join1 } (xs, ys)) \underline{\text{ else }} \bot)$
| join1 $(\_, \_) = \bot$

definition join :: *bool* $\Rightarrow$ *table* $\Rightarrow$ *table* $\Rightarrow$ *table* **where**
    join $p\ A\ B = (\underline{\text{if }} p \underline{\text{ then }} \text{these } (\text{join1 } `\ (A \times B)) \underline{\text{ else }} A - \text{these } (\text{join1 } `\ (A \times B)))$

Fig. 2. Finite tables

Using this representation, the union of tables A and B both satisfying table $n\ V$ is just the set union $A \cup B$, satisfying table $n\ V\ (A \cup B)$. The natural join operation is more involved. We first show how to join two individual tuples. We define this function join1 recursively (Fig. 2) assuming that the two input tuples have the same length (but not necessarily the same variables being set to $\bot$). The function join1 returns an optional tuple, where $\bot$ indicates either that the inputs do not have the same length (last equation) or that they are not joinable, i.e., have conflicting assigned domain values (the $\underline{\text{else}}$ branch in the $\underline{\text{if}}$-expression). The key property of join1 is its correspondence to logical conjunction:

$$\text{wf\_tuple } n\ V\ v \wedge \text{wf\_tuple } n\ W\ w \longrightarrow$$
$$\text{join1 } (v, w) = \langle z \rangle \longleftrightarrow (\text{wf\_tuple } n\ (V \cup W)\ z \wedge v = z \downarrow V \wedge w = z \downarrow W),$$

where $v \downarrow V$ maps all domain elements assigned to variables outside of the set V to $\bot$; formally, $v \downarrow V = \text{map } (\lambda i.\ \underline{\text{if }} i \in V \underline{\text{ then }} v\,!\,i \underline{\text{ else }} \bot)\ [0\ ..< \text{length } v]$.

The function join (Fig. 2) lifts join1 to tables, where the Boolean p indicates whether a join ($p = \text{True}$) or an anti-join ($p = \text{False}$) is computed. Naturally, join's key property is similar to join1's, but now expressed on tables. For the anti-join, the negated part's variables (W) must be contained in those of the non-negated part (V) to ensure finiteness.

$$\text{table } n\ V\ A \wedge \text{table } n\ W\ B \wedge (\neg p \longrightarrow W \subseteq V) \longrightarrow$$
$$z \in \text{join } p\ A\ B \longleftrightarrow (\text{wf\_tuple } n\ (V \cup W)\ z \wedge z \downarrow V \in A \wedge (p \longleftrightarrow z \downarrow W \in B))$$

Above, join computes $A \times B$ before applying join1. We prove and use for code generation the more space-efficient definition join True $A\ B = \bigcup v \in A.\ \bigcup w \in B.\ \lceil \text{join1 } (v, w) \rceil$.

5 Monitor

A monitor takes an MFOTL formula φ and an event stream σ as inputs. It computes *satisfactions*: pairs (i, v) of indices i and valuations v that satisfy the formula, i.e.,

type_synonym *buf = table list × table list*   **type_synonym** *saux = (ts × table) list*
type_synonym *uaux = (ts × table × table) list*

datatype *state* = Eq$_S$ *table* | Pred$_S$ *name (trm list)*
  | And$_S$ *state bool state buf* | Or$_S$ *state state buf* | Exists$_S$ *state*
  | Since$_S$ *bool state* $\mathcal{I}$ *state buf (ts list) saux* | Until$_S$ *bool state* $\mathcal{I}$ *state buf (ts list) uaux*

datatype *mstate* = MState *nat nat state*

definition init :: *frm* $\Rightarrow$ *mstate* **where** ...
fun step :: *db × ts* $\Rightarrow$ *mstate* $\Rightarrow$ *(nat × tuple) set × mstate* **where** ...
fun steps :: *(db × ts) list* $\Rightarrow$ *mstate* $\Rightarrow$ *(nat × tuple) set* **where**
  steps [] _ = {} | steps (*tdb*#π) s = (let (A,s') = step *tdb* s in A∪steps π s')

Fig. 3. The monitor's state and its high-level interface

sat σ $\bar{v}$ i φ. One is often interested in finding the *violations* of a formula φ, which are the pairs (i,v) such that $\neg$sat σ $\bar{v}$ i φ. Violations can be obtained by monitoring the negated formula.

A monitor cannot directly process an infinite event stream. Instead, in the *offline* setting, the monitor computes satisfactions for a single stream prefix. In the *online* setting, the monitor processes an unbounded stream incrementally and produces intermediate outputs. Our monitor always receives a whole time-stamped database at once, since MFOTL formulas cannot distinguish the order and arrival time of events within a database.

Figure 3 shows our monitor's state type (*mstate*) and its online and offline interface. The online interface is a transition system given by two functions: init, which computes the initial state, and step, which updates the state with a new input (a time-stamped database) and outputs satisfactions. The offline interface is the function monitor φ π = steps π (init φ), where steps iterates step on a prefix and collects all satisfactions in a set.

Example 1. Consider the formula $A(x) \longrightarrow \Diamond_{[1,2]}(\exists y. B(x,y))$, i.e., all A events must be followed by a matching B event after one or two time units. To obtain violations, we monitor the negation $A(x) \wedge \neg \Diamond_{[1,2]}(\exists y. B(x,y))$, which we encode as

φ_{ex} = AndNot (Pred A [V 0]) (Eventually (interval 1 2) (Exists (Pred B [V 1,V 0]))).

Given the prefix $\pi_{ex} = [(\{(A,[d]),(A,[e])\},1),(\{(B,[d,f])\},2),(\{(B,[e,f])\},5)]$, which consists of three databases with indices 0, 1, 2 and time-stamps 1, 2, and 5, with four events in total, there is one satisfaction: monitor φ_{ex} π_{ex} = $\{(0,[\langle e \rangle])\}$. The satisfaction originates from the event $(A,[e])$, which is part of the database with index 0 in π_{ex}. The satisfaction's valuation is $[\langle e \rangle]$ because the parameter of $(A,[e])$ is bound to φ_{ex}'s first (and only) free variable. The satisfaction is output after processing the third database:

$$\text{step } (\{(A,[d]),(A,[e])\},1) \text{ (init } \varphi_{ex}) = (\{\},s_1)$$
$$\text{step } (\{(B,[d,f])\},2) \quad\quad s_1 \quad\quad = (\{\},s_2)$$
$$\text{step } (\{(B,[e,f])\},5) \quad\quad s_2 \quad\quad = (\{(0,[\langle e \rangle])\},s_3),$$

where s_1, s_2, and s_3 are the monitor's states after processing each input.

fun mf :: *frm* ⇒ *bool* **where**
    mf (Eq t_1 t_2) = (is_Const t_1 ∨ is_Const t_2)
    | mf (Pred *e trms*) = True
    | mf (Neg (Or (Neg α) β)) = (mf α ∧ (mf β ∧ fv β ⊆ fv α ∨ mf ?$_\mathrm{Neg}$ β)
    | mf (Or α β) = (fv α = fv β ∧ mf α ∧ mf β)
    | mf (Exists ψ) = mf ψ
    | mf (Since α I β) = (fv α ⊆ fv β ∧ (mf α ∨ mf ?$_\mathrm{Neg}$ α) ∧ mf β)
    | mf (Until α I β) = (fv α ⊆ fv β ∧ (mf α ∨ mf ?$_\mathrm{Neg}$ α) ∧ mf β ∧ right $I \neq \infty$)
    | mf _ = False

Fig. 4. Monitorable formulas (f ?$_\mathrm{Neg}$ φ abbreviates <u>case</u> φ <u>of</u> Neg φ' ⇒ f φ' | _ ⇒ False)

Overview of the Algorithm. We require satisfactions to be output in the order they occur. Namely, (i_1, v_1) cannot be output after (i_2, v_2) if $i_1 < i_2$. Therefore, the monitor's state is characterized by its *progress*, which we represent by a stream index i. The progress is the smallest index for which new satisfactions cannot be computed without receiving more databases. It is initially zero and always at most the number of databases received. It is generally not possible to compute all satisfactions for an index j after processing the j-th input when monitoring a formula with future operators. For example, if the j-th input contains the event $(A, [d])$, we do not know whether $(j, [\langle d \rangle])$ satisfies φ_{ex} from Example 1 until we either observe a matching B event or a time-stamp that is at least three units ahead.

For every input database, step advances i by recursively evaluating the monitored formula. The evaluation of a subformula ψ at index i yields a table containing all valuations v with sat $\sigma \bar{v} i \psi$. For any binary operator in the formula, it may be possible to evaluate its subformulas up to different indices, e.g., if one subformula contains a future operator and the other does not. Our monitor evaluates subformulas as far as possible. Therefore, every subformula ψ has its own progress i_ψ describing how far it has been evaluated. (We omit the subscript when it is clear from the context.) Since several indices might be resolved at once by a new input, the evaluation result is a list xs :: *table list*. Its elements correspond to indices $[i ..< i + \mathrm{length}\ xs]$ according to their position in the list.

Recall that tables are finite sets. Evaluation of a subformula must therefore not result in infinitely many satisfying valuations. This is not guaranteed for all MFOTL formulas. For example, the formula $\neg A(x)$ (i.e., Neg (Pred A [V 0])) has infinitely many satisfying valuations at each index, regardless of the event stream. We, therefore, adopt the restriction to a syntactic fragment of MFOTL that is used in the table-based variant of MonPoly [2]. A formula is *monitorable* if and only if its satisfies the recursive predicate mf (Fig. 4). Note that the negation of φ must be monitorable if we search for violations of φ, which is generally different from the monitorability of φ itself. Basin et al. [2] describe a heuristic that attempts to rewrite formulas into equivalent, monitorable ones.

An equality Eq t_1 t_2 is only monitorable if at least one of the terms is a constant (otherwise, an infinite number of valuations satisfy $x = x$, i.e., Eq (V 0) (V 0)). In general, monitorable formulas may contain negations only in specific places. The pattern Neg (Or (Neg α) (Neg β)) corresponds to a conjunction And α β, which is always

fun init0 :: $nat \Rightarrow frm \Rightarrow state$ **where** ...

fun eval :: $nat \Rightarrow ts \Rightarrow db \Rightarrow state \Rightarrow table\ list \times state$ **where** ...

definition init :: $frm \Rightarrow mstate$ **where** init $\varphi = (\underline{let}\ n = \text{nfv}\ \varphi\ \underline{in}\ \text{MState}\ n\ 0\ (\text{init0}\ n\ \varphi))$

. **fun** step :: $db \times ts \Rightarrow mstate \Rightarrow (nat \times tuple)\ set \times mstate$ **where**
    step (db,t) (MState $n\ i\ s) = (\underline{let}\ (xs, s') = \text{eval}\ n\ t\ db\ s$
    $\underline{in}\ (\bigcup(k,V) \in \text{set}\ (\text{enumerate}\ i\ xs).\ \bigcup v \in V.\ \{(k,v)\}, \text{MState}\ n\ (i + \text{length}\ xs)\ s'))$

Fig. 5. Initialization and step functions of the monitor

monitorable if α and β are monitorable. For AndNot $\alpha\ \beta$, we additionally require that all variables free in β are free in α. This rules out formulas like $A(x) \wedge \neg B(y)$ (i.e., AndNot (Pred A [V 0]) (Pred B [V 1])), which has infinitely many satisfactions if the stream contains at least one A event. The subformulas α and β of Or $\alpha\ \beta$ must have exactly the same free variables for similar reasons. The temporal operators Since and Until allow a negated left subformula $\alpha = \text{Neg}\ \alpha'$ even if α itself is not monitorable. However, there is always a restriction on the free variables. For example, Since $\alpha\ I\ \beta$ is already satisfied at index i if β is satisfied at i. Any free variable in α that is not free in β could thus be assigned any value, and the resulting table would be infinite. Moreover, the future reach of Until $\alpha\ I\ \beta$ must be bounded to ensure that the monitor can make progress.

The monitor's state MState $n\ i\ s$ consists of the formula's degree $n = \text{nfv}\ \varphi$ (to avoid recomputation), the progress i, and a formula state s. The formula state datatype *state* (Fig. 3) extends the abstract syntax tree of formulas with the state that is associated with the formula's operators. It restricts the syntax to a superset of the monitorable formulas, such that the evaluation can be implemented directly as a recursive function on *state*.

The monitor's entry points are defined in Fig. 5. The function init uses init0 to convert the formula recursively into a formula state. We omit init0's definition, which follows mf's definition. Some of *state*'s constructors carry a Boolean flag p that indicates whether one of the subformulas is positive ($p = \text{True}$) or negated ($p = \text{False}$). In those cases where a negated subformula is not monitorable, we remove the negation before the recursive conversion and set p to False. For example, $\alpha \wedge \neg\beta$ (i.e., AndNot $\alpha\ \beta$) is converted to Ands (init0 $n\ \alpha$) False (init0 $n\ \beta$) ([], []). All lists in the *state* are initially empty.

The step function step is a wrapper for eval that evaluates a formula state given the formula's degree and the new time-stamp and database. It returns a list of tables for all indices that could be evaluated, and the updated *state*. We cover all cases of eval's definition in the following subsections. The standard function enumerate $i\ xs$ maps the elements V of xs to pairs (k, V), where the numbers k increase sequentially starting at i.

Atomic Formulas. The constructor Eqs of *state* represents constant tables corresponding to (monitorable) equalities. The associated *state* is always the same table, which is returned upon evaluation. For a predicate's state Preds $e\ trms$, we first select all events in the database db with the name e. The auxiliary function match, defined in Fig. 6, is applied to each selected event. This function attempts to compute the unique valuation for the variables in *trms* that makes the terms match the event's parameters. It returns

fun match :: *trm list* $\Rightarrow$ *domain list* $\Rightarrow$ *(nat* $\Rightarrow$ *domain option) option* **where**
   match [] [] = $\langle \lambda x.\ \bot \rangle$
  | match (C x # $trms$) (y # ys) = (<u>if</u> $x = y$ <u>then</u> match $trms\ ys$ <u>else</u> $\bot$)
  | match (V x # $trms$) (y # ys) = (<u>case</u> match $trms\ ys$ <u>of</u> $\bot \Rightarrow \bot$
    | $\langle f \rangle \Rightarrow$ (<u>case</u> $f\ x$ <u>of</u> $\bot \Rightarrow \langle f(x \mapsto y) \rangle$ | $\langle z \rangle \Rightarrow$ <u>if</u> $y = z$ <u>then</u> $\langle f \rangle$ <u>else</u> $\bot$))
  | match _ _ = $\bot$

Fig. 6. The match function

fun buf_add :: *table list* $\Rightarrow$ *table list* $\Rightarrow$ *buf* $\Rightarrow$ *buf* **where**
  buf_add $xs'\ ys'\ (xs, ys) = (xs\ @\ xs', ys\ @\ ys')$
fun buf_take :: *(table* $\Rightarrow$ *table* $\Rightarrow$ *'b)* $\Rightarrow$ *buf* $\Rightarrow$ *'b list* $\times$ *buf*
  buf_take $f\ (x$ # xs, y # $ys) = $ (<u>let</u> $(zs, b) = $ buf_take $f\ (xs, ys)$ <u>in</u> $(f\ x\ y$ # $zs, b))$
  | buf_take $f\ (xs, ys) = ([], (xs, ys))$

Fig. 7. Buffer operations

$\langle f \rangle$ if such a valuation f exists, and $\bot$ otherwise. To simplify match's definition, f is encoded as a partial function *nat* $\Rightarrow$ *domain option*. We convert it into a tuple using map $f\ [0\ ..< n]$.

  eval $n\ t\ db$ (Eq$_S\ r$) = $([r], $ Eq$_S\ r$)
  | eval $n\ t\ db$ (Pred$_S\ e\ trms$) = $([(\lambda f.\ $map $f\ [0\ ..< n]) \text{ 'these}$
    (match $trms\ \text{'}(\bigcup(e', x) \in db.$ <u>if</u> $e = e'$ <u>then</u> $\{x\}$ <u>else</u> $\{\}))], $ Pred$_S\ e\ trms$)

Non-Temporal Operators. It may be possible to evaluate the two subformulas α and β of a binary operator up to different indices $i_\alpha \neq i_\beta$. Then, the operator itself can only be evaluated up to the minimum of i_α and i_β. The remaining tables obtained from the subformula that is further ahead must be stored until more results are available from the other subformula. We store the tables in a *buffer* of type *buf*, which consists of one list for each subformula. The lists act as queues: new results are appended, and whenever both lists are nonempty, the subformula can be evaluated by removing pairs of tables from the front. The function buf_add $xs'\ ys'\ b$ (Fig. 7) adds the result lists xs' and ys' from the two subformulas to the buffer b. The function buf_take $f\ b$ removes pairs of tables from the front of the buffer and applies the operator-specific function f to them, collecting a list of results.

For And$_S$ and Or$_S$, we evaluate both subformulas and obtain two result lists xs and ys, as well as the updated subformula states s_1' and s_2'. The results are added to the buffer b. Then, buf_take combines the results that are available for both subformulas into the results of the operator, using an (anti-)join for conjunctions and a union for disjunctions.

  | eval $n\ t\ db$ (And$_S\ s_1\ p\ s_2\ b$) = (<u>let</u> $(xs, s_1') = $ eval $n\ t\ db\ s_1$; $(ys, s_2') = $ eval $n\ t\ db\ s_2$
    $(zs, b) = $ buf_take (join p) (buf_add $xs\ ys\ b$) <u>in</u> $(zs, $ And$_S\ s_1'\ p\ s_2'\ b)$
  | eval $n\ t\ db$ (Or$_S\ s_1\ s_2\ b$) = (<u>let</u> $(xs, s_1') = $ eval $n\ t\ db\ s_1$; $(ys, s_2') = $ eval $n\ t\ db\ s_2$;
    $(zs, b) = $ buf_take ($\cup$) (buf_add $xs\ ys\ b$) <u>in</u> $(zs, $ Or$_S\ s_1'\ s_2'\ b)$

definition update_since :: $\mathcal{I} \Rightarrow bool \Rightarrow table \Rightarrow table \Rightarrow ts \Rightarrow saux \Rightarrow table \times saux$ **where**
  update_since $I\ p\ r_1\ r_2\ nt\ aux = (\underline{let}\ aux = (\underline{case}\ [(t, join\ r\ p\ r_1).\ (t, r) \leftarrow aux,\ nt - t \leq right\ I]\ \underline{of}$
    $[] \Rightarrow [(nt, r_2)]$
    $\mid x \# aux' \Rightarrow (\underline{if}\ fst\ x = nt\ \underline{then}\ (fst\ x, snd\ x \cup r_2)\ \# aux'\ \underline{else}\ (nt, r_2)\ \# x \# aux'))$
    $\underline{in}\ (foldr\ (\cup)\ [r.\ (t, r) \leftarrow aux,\ left\ I \leq nt - t]\ \{\}, aux)$

fun update_until :: $\mathcal{I} \Rightarrow bool \Rightarrow table \Rightarrow table \Rightarrow ts \Rightarrow uaux \Rightarrow uaux$ **where**
  update_until $I\ p\ r_1\ r_2\ nt\ aux = (map\ (\lambda x.\ \underline{case}\ x\ \underline{of}\ (t, a_1, a_2) \Rightarrow$
    $(t, \underline{if}\ p\ \underline{then}\ join\ a_1\ True\ r_1\ \underline{else}\ a_1 \cup r_1, \underline{if}\ nt - t \in_{\mathcal{I}} I\ \underline{then}\ a_2 \cup join\ r_2\ p\ a_1\ \underline{else}\ a_2))\ aux)\ @$
    $[(nt, r_1, \underline{if}\ left\ I = 0\ \underline{then}\ r_2\ \underline{else}\ \{\})]$

fun eval_until :: $\mathcal{I} \Rightarrow ts \Rightarrow uaux \Rightarrow table\ list \times uaux$
  eval_until $I\ nnt\ [] = ([], [])$
  $\mid$ eval_until $I\ nnt\ ((t, a_1, a_2) \# aux) = (\underline{if}\ t + right\ I < nnt$
    $\underline{then}\ (\underline{let}\ (xs, aux) = $ eval_until $I\ nnt\ aux\ \underline{in}\ (a_2 \# xs, aux))\ \underline{else}\ ([], (t, a_1, a_2) \# aux))$

fun tbuf_take :: $(table \Rightarrow table \Rightarrow ts \Rightarrow {}'b \Rightarrow {}'b) \Rightarrow {}'b \Rightarrow buf \Rightarrow ts\ list \Rightarrow {}'b \times buf \times ts\ list$ **where**
  tbuf_take $f\ z\ (x \# xs, y \# ys)\ (t \# ts) = $ tbuf_take $f\ (f\ x\ y\ t\ z)\ (xs, ys)\ ts$
  $\mid$ tbuf_take $f\ z\ (xs, ys)\ ts = (z, (xs, ys), ts)$

Fig. 8. Auxiliary operations for evaluating $Since_S$ and $Until_S$

We increment the degree in the recursive computation of an existential quantifier $Exists_S$ to account for the variables' De Bruijn encoding. Each computed tuple v (which is a list) is then replaced by its tail tl v to remove the assignment to the bound variable.

  $\mid$ eval $n\ t\ db\ (Exists_S\ s) = (\underline{let}\ (xs, s') = $ eval $(n + 1)\ t\ db\ s$
    $\underline{in}\ (map\ (\lambda r.\ tl\ {}^{`}r)\ xs, Exists_S\ s')$

Since and Until. The monitoring algorithm implements $Since\ \alpha\ I\ \beta$ by decomposing the interval I. Note that $Since\ \alpha\ I\ \beta$ is equivalent to a disjunction of $Since\ \alpha\ (point\ c)\ \beta$, where c ranges over I. We can additionally bound c from above by the time-stamp $\tau\ \sigma\ (i-1)$, where i is the operator's progress. This ensures that the disjunction always consists of finitely many terms (even if right $I = \infty$). We store the satisfactions for $Since\ \alpha\ (point\ c)\ \beta$ in a list in the monitor's state, together with time-stamps $\tau\ \sigma\ (i-1) - c$. The list, called the *auxiliary state*, is sorted on the time-stamps c. It also contains satisfactions for $c < left\ I$ (if left $I > 0$) because these may move into the interval I as time progresses.

  For every new input database, the function update_since (Fig. 8) updates the list to maintain the correspondence with $Since\ \alpha\ (point\ c)\ \beta$. It also computes the satisfactions by taking the union over all tables in the list that satisfy $c \in_{\mathcal{I}} I$. The arguments of update_since are the interval I of the $Since$ operator, a flag p indicating whether the left subformula is positive (not negated), the subformulas' results r_1 and r_2 at index i, the time-stamp $nt = \tau\ \sigma\ i$, and the old auxiliary state aux. We assume that the left subformula is evaluated without the negation. If the new time-stamp $\tau\ \sigma\ i$ differs from the previous time-stamp $\tau\ \sigma\ (i-1)$, i.e., $\Delta = \tau\ \sigma\ i - \tau\ \sigma\ (i-1) \neq 0$, the tables in the old auxiliary state now represent $Since\ \alpha\ (point\ (c + \Delta))\ \beta$, but without taking the satisfactions of α and β at i into account. First, update_since removes all tables for which $c + \Delta$ exceeds the right bound of the interval. It then joins each remaining table with the result r_1 for α, and adds the satisfactions r_2 for β either to the first table (if $c + \Delta = 0$) or as a new list element to the list.

Decomposing a formula $\psi = \text{Until } \alpha \, I \, \beta$ into point intervals is not as useful because there is no obvious way to compute the satisfactions of Until α (point c) β at index $i + 1$ from those at index i, which would allow us to reuse previous computations. Another difference to Since is that we cannot immediately output the satisfactions once we have the subformulas' results. A new input may still change the satisfactions for previous indices.

Let i^* be the minimum of i_α and i_β. The auxiliary state for Until, which has type $uaux$, stores for all k in $\{i_\psi \,..< i^*\}$ the time-stamp $\tau \, \sigma \, k$ and two tables a_1 and a_2, sorted by k. The meaning of the tables depends on the flag p, which indicates whether the left subformula α is positive. If $p = \text{True}$, the table a_1 contains the valuations satisfying α at all indices in $\{k \,..< i^*\}$. If $p = \text{False}$, it contains the valuations satisfying Neg α at some index in $\{k \,..< i^*\}$. The table a_2 contains the valuation satisfying β at some index k' in $\{k \,..< i^*\}$ with $\tau \, \sigma \, k' - \tau \, \sigma \, k \in_{\mathcal{I}} I$, and satisfying α for all indices in $\{k \,..< k'\}$. Note that this is not the same as the satisfactions for Until $\alpha \, I \, \beta$ at k because the interval may be incomplete between k and i^*. The function update_until (Fig. 8) maintains this invariant for every advance of i^*. Its arguments have the same meaning as for update_since. However, it does not compute the results, which is instead done by eval_until. Its argument nnt denotes the time-stamp $\tau \, \sigma \, (i^* + 1)$, or $\tau \, \sigma \, j$ if j is the most recent input database and $i^* = j$. The function retrieves those tables a_2 for which the interval is complete, i.e., nnt is more than right I units ahead of the associated time-stamp t.

The implementation of eval for Since$_S$ and Until$_S$ follows the other binary operators, but with an additional update step for the auxiliary state.

```
| eval n t db (Sinceₛ p s₁ I s₂ b ts aux) = (let (xs, s₁′) = eval n t db s₁;
    (ys, s₂′) = eval n t db s₂; ((zs, aux), b, ts) = tbuf_take (λr₁ r₂ t (zs, aux).
        let (z, aux) = update_since I p r₁ r₂ t aux in (zs @ [z], aux))
        ([], aux) (buf_add xs ys b) (ts @ [t])
    in (zs, Sinceₛ p s₁′ I s₂′ b ts aux)
| eval n t db (Untilₛ p s₁ I s₂ b ts aux) = (let (xs, s₁′) = eval n t db s₁;
    (ys, s₂′) = eval n t db s₂; ((zs, aux), b, ts) =
        tbuf_take (update_until I p) aux (buf_add xs ys b) (ts @ [t]);
    (zs, aux) = eval_until I (case ts of [] ⇒ t | t′#_ ⇒ t′) aux
    in (zs, Untilₛ p s₁′ I s₂′ b ts aux)
```

Here, tbuf_take (Fig. 8) is used instead of buf_take as we must consider the time-stamps $ts @ [t]$ corresponding to the subformulas' (future) results. Unlike buf_take, this function does not apply f individually, but it folds all results from left to right.

6 Correctness

We define a formal invariant for the monitor's state, which connects its structure with MFOTL's semantics and the stream prefix observed so far. We then prove that init establishes and that step preserves the invariant. Moreover, we show that the satisfactions output by steps are sound and eventually complete for monitorable formulas.

fun prog :: *trace* ⇒ *frm* ⇒ *nat* ⇒ *nat* **where**

  prog σ (Pred e ts) $j = j$ | prog σ (Eq t_1 t_2) $j = j$

  | prog σ (Neg ψ) $j =$ prog σ ψ j | prog σ (Or α β) $j =$ min (prog σ α j) (prog σ β j)

  | prog σ (Exists ψ) $j =$ prog σ ψ j | prog σ (Since α I β) $j =$ min (prog σ α j) (prog σ β j)

  | prog σ (Until α I β) $j =$

    Inf $\{i.\ \forall k.\ k < j \wedge k \le$ min (prog σ α j) (prog σ β j) $\longrightarrow \tau\ \sigma\ i +$ right $I \ge \tau\ \sigma\ k\}$

definition prog2 σ α β $j =$ min (prog σ α j) (prog σ β j)

Fig. 9. Progress of the monitor

definition wf_mstate :: *frm* ⇒ ($db \times ts$) *list* ⇒ *mstate* ⇒ *bool* **where**

  wf_mstate φ π (MState n i s) $\longleftrightarrow$ wf_prefix $\pi \wedge n =$ nfv $\varphi \wedge (\forall \sigma.$ prefix_of π σ $\longrightarrow$

    $i =$ prog σ φ (length π) $\wedge$ wf_state σ (length π) n s φ)

inductive wf_state :: *trace* ⇒ *nat* ⇒ *nat* ⇒ *state* ⇒ *frm* ⇒ *bool* **where**

  ...

  | wf_state σ j n s_1 $\alpha \wedge$ wf_state σ j n s_2 $\beta \wedge$

    $(p \longrightarrow \alpha' = \alpha) \wedge (\neg p \longrightarrow \alpha' =$ Neg $\alpha) \wedge$ mf $\alpha = p \wedge$ fv $\alpha \subseteq$ fv $\beta \wedge$

    wf_buf σ j n α β $b \wedge$ wf_ts σ j α β $ts \wedge$ wf_uaux σ j n p α I β $aux \longrightarrow$

    wf_state σ j n (Until$_S$ p s_1 I s_2 b ts aux) (Until α' I β)

Fig. 10. Main invariant predicates (excerpt)

The invariant relates the tables stored in a formula state to the semantics of the corresponding subformulas. In Sect. 5, we introduced the notion of progress i_ψ, which states how far the subformula ψ has been evaluated. The function prog in Fig. 9 defines i_ψ concretely. Its arguments are the trace σ, an arbitrary MFOTL formula ψ, and the index j of the next time-stamped database to be received by the monitor. (Initially, j is zero, and every application of step increases it by one.) Predicates and equalities can always be evaluated up to j. For Until α I β, we take the least index i at which we cannot evaluate the operator yet. Recall that these are the indices for which we do not have complete information up to and including the time $\tau\ \sigma\ i +$ right I. The index k in the definition ranges over all indices for which the time-stamp (condition $k < j$) and the results from both subformulas (condition min (prog σ α j) (prog σ β j)) are available. All other operators are only constrained by the progress of their subformula(s). We note some basic properties of prog.

Lemma 1. (a) *Monotonicity:* $j \le j'$ implies prog σ φ $j \le$ prog σ φ j'. (b) *Upper bound:* prog σ φ $j \le j$. (c) *Completeness:* mf φ implies $\exists j.\ i \le$ prog σ φ j, for all i.

The predicate wf_mstate φ π mst (Fig. 10) is the invariant for a monitor state mst after monitoring φ on the stream prefix π. We require that π is a well-formed prefix and that the cached degree n agrees with the formula. All auxiliary invariants that are used to define wf_mstate are expressed in terms of infinite streams instead of prefixes. This includes wf_state σ j n s φ, which holds iff s :: *state* corresponds to the monitorable formula φ :: *frm* after monitoring the first j databases of σ. Therefore, we consider all event streams σ that extend the prefix π, i.e., prefix_of π σ.

definition wf_buf :: *trace* $\Rightarrow$ *nat* $\Rightarrow$ *nat* $\Rightarrow$ *frm* $\Rightarrow$ *frm* $\Rightarrow$ *buf* $\Rightarrow$ *bool* **where**
  wf_buf σ j n α β b $\longleftrightarrow$ (case b of (xs, ys) $\Rightarrow$
    list_all2 (λk. wf_table n (fv α) (λv. sat σ $\bar{v}$ k α)) [prog2 σ α β j ..< prog σ α j] xs $\wedge$
    list_all2 (λk. wf_table n (fv β) (λv. sat σ $\bar{v}$ k β)) [prog2 σ α β j ..< prog σ β j] ys)

definition wf_ts :: *trace* $\Rightarrow$ *nat* $\Rightarrow$ *frm* $\Rightarrow$ *frm* $\Rightarrow$ *ts list* $\Rightarrow$ *bool* **where**
  wf_nts σ j α β ts $\longleftrightarrow$ list_all2 (λk t. $t = \tau$ σ k) [prog2 σ α β j ..< j] ts

definition wf_uaux :: *trace* $\Rightarrow$ *nat* $\Rightarrow$ *nat* $\Rightarrow$ *bool* $\Rightarrow$ *frm* $\Rightarrow$ $\mathcal{I}$ $\Rightarrow$ *frm* $\Rightarrow$ *uaux* $\Rightarrow$ *bool* **where**
  wf_uaux σ j n p α I β aux $\longleftrightarrow$ prog σ (Until α I β) j + length aux = prog2 σ α β j $\wedge$
    list_all2 (λx k. case x of (t, r_1, r_2) $\Rightarrow$ $t = \tau$ σ k $\wedge$
      wf_table n (fv α) (λv. if p then ($\forall k' \in \{k ..<$ prog2 σ α β $j\}$. sat σ $\bar{v}$ k' α)
        else ($\exists k' \in \{k ..<$ prog2 σ α β $j\}$. sat σ $\bar{v}$ k' α)) $\wedge$
      wf_table n (fv β) (λv. $\exists k'$. $k \leq k'$ $\wedge k' <$ prog2 σ α β $j \wedge \tau$ σ $k' - \tau$ σ $k \in_{\mathcal{I}}$ I $\wedge$
        sat σ $\bar{v}$ k' $\beta \wedge (\forall k'' \in \{k ..< k'\}$. if p then sat σ $\bar{v}$ k'' α else $\neg$sat σ $\bar{v}$ k'' α)))
    aux [prog σ (Until α I β) j ..< prog2 σ α β j])

Fig. 11. Invariants of the state's components

We only show the case for Until$_S$ in wf_state here. This case states the conditions under which Until$_S$ p s_1 I s_2 b ts aux is a well-formed state corresponding to Until α' I β. Depending on the flag p, α' is either a negated subformula $\alpha' = $ Neg α for some α, or its outermost operator is not a negation and $\alpha' = \alpha$. The invariant inherits the condition fv $\alpha \subseteq$ fv β from the mf predicate (Sect. 5). The two subformula states m_1 and m_2 must be recursively well-formed and correspond to α and β, respectively.

The predicate wf_buf (Fig. 11) encodes the invariant for buffers of type *buf*. These store all results of the formulas α and β from index prog2 σ α β j to indices prog σ α j and prog σ β j, respectively. The results must be tables assigning values to the free variables of the corresponding formula. The invariant wf_ts ensures that the additional time-stamp list *ts*, which is used by binary temporal operators, contains all time-stamps from the start of the result buffer to the most recent input, which has index j.

The invariant for the auxiliary states *aux* of type *uaux* for the $\psi = $ Until α' I β operator is shown in Fig. 11. The elements of *aux* are in a one-to-one correspondence with the indices in $[i_\psi ..< i^*]$, where $i_\psi = $ prog σ ψ j and $i^* = $ prog2 σ α' β $j = $ prog2 σ α β j (the possible negation in α' does not affect the progress). Each element for such an index k with time-stamp t is a triple (t, r_1, r_2). The content of the tables r_1 and r_2 is described in Sect. 5.

We state the correctness of the satisfactions output by step (and hence monitor) in terms of a function verdicts, which characterizes the monitor's output semantically. For a formula φ and stream prefix π, it returns exactly the pairs (k, v) where the monitor has made progress beyond k, and for which sat σ $\bar{v}$ i φ is true for all traces σ that extend π.

definition verdicts :: *frm* $\Rightarrow$ (*db* $\times$ *ts*) *list* $\Rightarrow$ (*nat* $\times$ *tuple*) *set* **where**
  verdicts φ $\pi = \{(k, v)$. wf_tuple (nfv φ) (fv φ) $v \wedge (\forall \sigma$. prefix_of π σ $\longrightarrow$
    $k <$ prog σ φ (length π) $\wedge$ sat σ $\bar{v}$ k $\varphi)\}$

Using the completeness of prog, we show that verdicts behaves according to the informal description of a monitor, which we gave in the beginning of Sect. 5.

Lemma 2. *For all monitorable formulas φ, verdicts φ is sound and eventually complete, i.e., for all prefixes π extending the stream σ, indices k, and tuples v,*

(a) $(k, v) \in$ verdicts $\varphi\, \pi \longrightarrow$ sat $\sigma\, \bar{v}\, k\, \varphi$, *and*
(b) $k <$ length $\pi \wedge$ wf_tuple (nfv φ) (fv φ) $v \wedge (\forall \sigma'.\ \text{prefix\_of } \pi\, \sigma' \longrightarrow$ sat $\sigma'\, \bar{v}\, k\, \varphi) \longrightarrow$
$\quad\ (\exists \pi'.\ \text{prefix\_of } \pi'\, \sigma \wedge (k, v) \in$ verdicts $\varphi\, \pi')$.

We can now state the main correctness result for the more general online interface consisting of init and step. The correctness of monitor follows easily. Let last_ts π denote the last time-stamp of π, and 0 if π is empty.

Theorem 1. *(a)* init *establishes the invariant:* mf φ *implies* wf_mstate φ [] (init φ).
$\quad$*(b)* step *preserves the invariant and its output can be described in terms of* verdicts: *Let* step (db, t) mst $= (A, mst')$. *If* wf_mstate $\varphi\, \pi$ mst *and* last_ts $\pi \leq t$, *then we have* $A =$ verdicts $\varphi\ (\pi @ [(db, t)]) -$ verdicts $\varphi\, \pi$ *and* wf_mstate $\varphi\ (\pi @ [(db, t)])$ mst'.

Corollary 1. *If* mf φ *and* wf_prefix π, monitor $\varphi\, \pi =$ verdicts $\varphi\, \pi$.

7   Case Study in Differential Testing

To demonstrate the benefit of our verified monitor we perform differential testing [17] to compare our monitor to two existing unverified state-of the-art monitors, MonPoly [3] and DejaVu [13], which support first-order temporal logic specifications.

We used Isabelle/HOL's code generator [9] to export a certified implementation of our monitoring algorithm (called *VeriMon*) for the monitorable fragment of MFOTL. The generated file consists of about 2 800 lines of OCaml code and includes code generated from an Isabelle library of red-black trees, which are used to efficiently implement sets. To be used as a standalone monitor, the verified monitor must be augmented with a formula and log parser. We reused MonPoly's parsing components, as they were implemented in OCaml and extensively used and tested. About 130 lines of straightforward, unverified OCaml code integrates these unverified components with the verified algorithm, translating between the analogous types for formulas and traces.

We focus on randomized differential testing. We generate random stream prefixes and formulas, invoke the monitors, and validate the results using VeriMon. For this purpose, we have developed a random MFOTL formula generator that takes as parameters the formula size (in terms of number of operators) and the number of free variables that occur in the formula, and outputs a random formula and a signature describing the name, arity, and parameter types for each predicate used in the formula. The generator creates a random formula of size n by randomly selecting an operator op and then recursively creating its subformula of size $n - 1$ (if op is unary) or its two subformulas of size m and $n - m - 1$ (if op is binary) for some random non-negative $m < n$. The generator creates predicate or equality formulas for size $n = 0$. Since each monitor can be tested on the logical fragment it mutually supports with VeriMon, our formula generator only generates monitorable MFOTL formulas for testing MonPoly and monitorable, past-only, non-metric formulas for testing DejaVu. Monitorable formulas are generated by sampling only the operators that correspond to the cases in the definition of the recursive predicate mf (Fig. 4). Whenever an operator op is sampled, free variables for its subformulas are sampled to satisfy mf's conditions for op. DejaVu requires the generator to sample only past temporal operators, use only interval 0 ∞ in temporal formulas, and since it does not support free variables, all generated formulas are closed. DejaVu can only monitor traces with databases containing a single event, which results in formulas like $P \wedge Q$ (i.e., And (Pred P []) (Pred Q [])) evaluating to false. The generator avoids this by ensuring that binary Boolean formulas have at least one temporal subformula referring to the past.

The generated signature file is used by a random stream prefix generator to sample random event names defined in the file. For each event, the generator uniformly samples its parameter values from the domain $D = \{0, 1, \ldots, 10^9 - 1\}$. With a given probability r, the last q unique values that were previously sampled are sampled again to ensure that events have common parameter values. This makes the subsequent monitoring less trivial.

DejaVu's output differs from MonPoly's and VeriMon's. DejaVu does not output variable valuations that violate the formula, but only the prefix indices where the formula is violated. We use these indices as the basis for comparing its output with VeriMon.

We ran our testing suite for formula sizes ranging from 2 to 5, having up to 6 free variables. For each combination of these parameters, we generated 1 000 random formulas and for each formula 4 random prefixes with lengths of 20, 40, 60, and 100 databases.

Our results reveal two classes of inconsistencies in MonPoly's output and three in DejaVu's output. The inconsistencies in MonPoly's output correspond to two implementation errors. The first error manifests in MonPoly's handling of finite trace semantics. Specifically, after reading the entire stream prefix MonPoly outputs an additional violation for a non-existing index (beyond the last index present in the prefix). MonPoly's second implementation error was exhibited by its failure to correctly monitor a formula of the form $\alpha \wedge \neg(\beta \, S \, \alpha)$ (i.e., AndNot α (Since β (interval 0 ∞) α)) where nfv $\beta > 0$, fv $\beta \subset$ fv α, and the order of occurrences of free variables in the two instances of α is different. These conditions trigger a heavily optimized part of MonPoly's code, confirming our intuition that complex performance optimizations can lead to implementation errors.

The problems exhibited by DejaVu's implementation are arguably less severe and all related to monitoring formulas with equalities. The most benign issue is that formulas containing only arithmetic relations (and no predicates) fail to parse. Next, we discovered that DejaVu does not produce any violation on a prefix satisfying a propositional formula α, when monitoring a formula of the form $\neg \exists x. \alpha \wedge x = 24$ (i.e., Neg (Exists (And α (Eq (V 0) (C 24))))). DejaVu's authors documented that the formula semantics changes if a variable occurs in arithmetic relations [11, §5]. Specifically, the variable's quantifier becomes bounded: it quantifies only over the active domain defined as values seen in the prefix so far. The change has an (unintuitive) effect on the subformulas where the variable does not occur as shown in the example above. Finally, DejaVu does not output any violation for the formula $\neg \exists x. x = 24 \wedge \neg P(x)$ (i.e., Neg (Exists (AndNot (Eq (V 0) (C 24))(Pred P [V 0])))) when monitored on a prefix without the event $(P, [24])$. This formula's violations coincide under both standard and active domain quantifier semantics. However, DejaVu's definition of the active domain does not include the constants occurring in the formula, which causes the discrepancy.

In addition to using random formulas, we included the tool's benchmarks in our testing. All the experiments are available in an easy to reproduce Docker image [28].

8 Conclusion

We demonstrated an approach to increase the trustworthiness of runtime verification by formally verifying a monitor for MFOTL in the Isabelle/HOL proof assistant. Our formalization of the non-trivial monitoring algorithm is essentially a high-level implementation as one would write it in a functional programming language. To prove its correctness, we had to characterize the algorithm's output, which precisely documents its behavior. Being able to execute a verified monitor with acceptable performance enables the systematic testing of more performant implementations. Our results from differential testing, which uncovered two genuine errors in MonPoly, show that this is beneficial.

One possible use case of our verified monitor is as a referee in tool competitions, where it can provide the ground truth. We also believe that it is a good starting point for extensions of the monitoring algorithm, whose correctness may not be obvious, as in our unpublished draft on adaptive monitoring [27]. Other future extensions may include the use of more optimized and verified data structures, which would make the generated code even more efficient. Finally, we hope that our compact formalization encourages machine-checked proofs for other algorithms and tools.

Acknowledgment. Joshua Schneider is supported by the US Air Force grant "Monitoring at Any Cost" (FA9550-17-1-0306). Srđan Krstić is supported by the Swiss National Science Foundation grant "Big Data Monitoring" (167162). Martin Raszyk pointed us to DejaVu's non-standard semantics for formulas with equality. Anonymous reviewers gave numerous helpful suggestions on how to improve the presentation.

References

1. Ausaf, F., Dyckhoff, R., Urban, C.: POSIX lexing with derivatives of regular expressions (proof pearl). In: Blanchette, J.C., Merz, S. (eds.) ITP 2016. LNCS, vol. 9807, pp. 69–86. Springer, Cham (2016). https://doi.org/10.1007/978-3-319-43144-4_5
2. Basin, D., Klaedtke, F., Müller, S., Zălinescu, E.: Monitoring metric first-order temporal properties. J. ACM **62**(2), 15:1–15:45 (2015)
3. Basin, D., Klaedtke, F., Zălinescu, E.: The MonPoly monitoring tool. In: RV-CuBES 2017. Kalpa Publications in Computing, vol. 3, pp. 19–28. EasyChair (2017)
4. Benzaken, V., Contejean, E.: A Coq mechanised formal semantics for realistic SQL queries: formally reconciling SQL and bag relational algebra. In: Mahboubi, A., Myreen, M.O. (eds.) CPP 2019, pp. 249–261. ACM, New York (2019)
5. Benzaken, V., Contejean, É., Keller, C., Martins, E.: A Coq formalisation of SQL's execution engines. In: Avigad, J., Mahboubi, A. (eds.) ITP 2018. LNCS, vol. 10895, pp. 88–107. Springer, Cham (2018). https://doi.org/10.1007/978-3-319-94821-8_6

6. Blech, J.O., Falcone, Y., Becker, K.: Towards certified runtime verification. In: Aoki, T., Taguchi, K. (eds.) ICFEM 2012. LNCS, vol. 7635, pp. 494–509. Springer, Heidelberg (2012). https://doi.org/10.1007/978-3-642-34281-3_34

7. Bohrer, B., Tan, Y.K., Mitsch, S., Myreen, M.O., Platzer, A.: VeriPhy: verified controller executables from verified cyber-physical system models. In: Foster, J.S., Grossman, D. (eds.) PLDI 2018, pp. 617–630. ACM, New York (2018)

8. Esparza, J., Lammich, P., Neumann, R., Nipkow, T., Schimpf, A., Smaus, J.-G.: A fully verified executable LTL model checker. In: Sharygina, N., Veith, H. (eds.) CAV 2013. LNCS, vol. 8044, pp. 463–478. Springer, Heidelberg (2013). https://doi.org/10.1007/978-3-642-39799-8_31

9. Haftmann, F.: Code generation from specifications in higher-order logic. Ph.D. thesis, Technical University Munich (2009)

10. Havelund, K.: Rule-based runtime verification revisited. STTT **17**(2), 143–170 (2015)

11. Havelund, K., Peled, D.: Efficient runtime verification of first-order temporal properties. In: Gallardo, M.M., Merino, P. (eds.) SPIN 2018. LNCS, vol. 10869, pp. 26–47. Springer, Cham (2018). https://doi.org/10.1007/978-3-319-94111-0_2

12. Havelund, K., Peled, D., Ulus, D.: First order temporal logic monitoring with BDDs. In: FMCAD 2017, pp. 116–123. IEEE (2017)

13. Havelund, K., Peled, D., Ulus, D.: DejaVu: a monitoring tool for first-order temporal logic. In: MT@CPSWeek 2018, pp. 12–13 (2018)

14. Havelund, K., Reger, G., Thoma, D., Zălinescu, E.: Monitoring events that carry data. In: Bartocci, E., Falcone, Y. (eds.) Lectures on Runtime Verification. LNCS, vol. 10457, pp. 61–102. Springer, Cham (2018). https://doi.org/10.1007/978-3-319-75632-5_3

15. Laurent, J., Goodloe, A., Pike, L.: Assuring the guardians. In: Bartocci, E., Majumdar, R. (eds.) RV 2015. LNCS, vol. 9333, pp. 87–101. Springer, Cham (2015). https://doi.org/10.1007/978-3-319-23820-3_6

16. Malecha, J.G., Morrisett, G., Shinnar, A., Wisnesky, R.: Toward a verified relational database management system. In: Hermenegildo, M.V., Palsberg, J. (eds.) POPL 2010, pp. 237–248. ACM, New York (2010)

17. McKeeman, W.M.: Differential testing for software. Digit. Tech. J. **10**(1), 100–107 (1998)

18. Mitsch, S., Platzer, A.: ModelPlex: verified runtime validation of verified cyber-physical system models. Formal Methods Syst. Des. **49**(1–2), 33–74 (2016)

19. Nipkow, T., Wenzel, M., Paulson, L.C. (eds.): Isabelle/HOL - A Proof Assistant for Higher-Order Logic. LNCS, vol. 2283. Springer, Heidelberg (2002). https://doi.org/10.1007/3-540-45949-9

20. Nipkow, T., Traytel, D.: Unified decision procedures for regular expression equivalence. In: Klein, G., Gamboa, R. (eds.) ITP 2014. LNCS, vol. 8558, pp. 450–466. Springer, Cham (2014). https://doi.org/10.1007/978-3-319-08970-6_29

21. Pike, L., Niller, S., Wegmann, N.: Runtime verification for ultra-critical systems. In: Khurshid, S., Sen, K. (eds.) RV 2011. LNCS, vol. 7186, pp. 310–324. Springer, Heidelberg (2012). https://doi.org/10.1007/978-3-642-29860-8_23

22. Pike, L., Wegmann, N., Niller, S., Goodloe, A.: Experience report: a do-it-yourself high-assurance compiler. In: Thiemann, P., Findler, R.B. (eds.) ICFP 2012, pp. 335–340. ACM, New York (2012)

23. Reger, G., Rydeheard, D.: From first-order temporal logic to parametric trace slicing. In: Bartocci, E., Majumdar, R. (eds.) RV 2015. LNCS, vol. 9333, pp. 216–232. Springer, Cham (2015). https://doi.org/10.1007/978-3-319-23820-3_14

24. Rizaldi, A., et al.: Formalising and monitoring traffic rules for autonomous vehicles in Isabelle/HOL. In: Polikarpova, N., Schneider, S. (eds.) IFM 2017. LNCS, vol. 10510, pp. 50–66. Springer, Cham (2017). https://doi.org/10.1007/978-3-319-66845-1_4

25. Roşu, G., Chen, F.: Semantics and algorithms for parametric monitoring. Log. Methods Comput. Sci. **8**(1:9), 1–47 (2012)
26. Sánchez, C.: Online and offline stream runtime verification of synchronous systems. In: Colombo, C., Leucker, M. (eds.) RV 2018. LNCS, vol. 11237, pp. 138–163. Springer, Cham (2018). https://doi.org/10.1007/978-3-030-03769-7_9
27. Schneider, J., Basin, D., Brix, F., Krstić, S., Traytel, D.: Adaptive online first-order monitoring. In: Chen, Y.F., Cheng, C.H., Esparza, J. (eds.) ATVA 2019. Springer (2019, to appear). http://people.inf.ethz.ch/trayteld/papers/atva19-adaptive/aom.pdf
28. Schneider, J., Basin, D., Krstić, S., Traytel, D.: Case study associated with this paper (2019). https://hub.docker.com/r/infsec/verified-monpoly-exps. Docker image (tag 1.3.0)
29. Schneider, J., Traytel, D.: Formalization of a monitoring algorithm for metric first-order temporal logic. Archive of Formal Proofs (2019). http://isa-afp.org/entries/MFOTL_Monitor.html
30. Völlinger, K.: Verifying the output of a distributed algorithm using certification. In: Lahiri, S., Reger, G. (eds.) RV 2017. LNCS, vol. 10548, pp. 424–430. Springer, Cham (2017). https://doi.org/10.1007/978-3-319-67531-2_29
31. Wimmer, S.: Formalized timed automata. In: Blanchette, J.C., Merz, S. (eds.) ITP 2016. LNCS, vol. 9807, pp. 425–440. Springer, Cham (2016). https://doi.org/10.1007/978-3-319-43144-4_26
32. Wimmer, S., Lammich, P.: Verified model checking of timed automata. In: Beyer, D., Huisman, M. (eds.) TACAS 2018. LNCS, vol. 10805, pp. 61–78. Springer, Cham (2018). https://doi.org/10.1007/978-3-319-89960-2_4

Efficient Detection and Quantification of Timing Leaks with Neural Networks

Saeid Tizpaz-Niari[✉], Pavol Černý, Sriram Sankaranarayanan,
and Ashutosh Trivedi

University of Colorado Boulder, Boulder, USA
{saeid.tizpazniari,pavol.cerny,srirams,ashutosh.trivedi}@colorado.edu

Abstract. Detection and quantification of information leaks through timing side channels are important to guarantee confidentiality. Although static analysis remains the prevalent approach for detecting timing side channels, it is computationally challenging for real-world applications. In addition, the detection techniques are usually restricted to "yes" or "no" answers. In practice, real-world applications may need to leak information about the secret. Therefore, quantification techniques are necessary to evaluate the resulting threats of information leaks. Since both problems are very difficult or impossible for static analysis techniques, we propose a dynamic analysis method. Our novel approach is to split the problem into two tasks. First, we learn a timing model of the program as a neural network. Second, we analyze the neural network to quantify information leaks. As demonstrated in our experiments, both of these tasks are feasible in practice—making the approach a significant improvement over the state-of-the-art side channel detectors and quantifiers. Our key technical contributions are (a) a neural network architecture that enables side channel discovery and (b) an MILP-based algorithm to estimate the side-channel strength. On a set of micro-benchmarks and real-world applications, we show that neural network models learn timing behaviors of programs with thousands of methods. We also show that neural networks with thousands of neurons can be efficiently analyzed to detect and quantify information leaks through timing side channels.

1 Introduction

Programs often handle sensitive data such as credit card numbers or medical histories. Developers are careful that eavesdroppers cannot easily access the secrets (for instance, by using encryption algorithms). However, a side channel might arise even if the transferred data is encrypted. For example, in timing side channels [12], an eavesdropper who observes the response time of a server might be able to infer the secret input, or at least significantly reduce the remaining entropy of possible secret values. Studies show that side-channel attacks are practical [14,27,30].

Detecting timing side channels are difficult problems for static analysis, especially in real-world Java applications. From the theoretical point of view, side-channel presence cannot be inferred from one execution trace, but rather, an

© Springer Nature Switzerland AG 2019
B. Finkbeiner and L. Mariani (Eds.): RV 2019, LNCS 11757, pp. 329–348, 2019.
https://doi.org/10.1007/978-3-030-32079-9_19

analysis of equivalence classes of traces is needed [43]. From a practical perspective, the problem is hard because timing is not explicitly visible in the code. A side channel is a property of the code and the platform on which the program is executed. In addition, most existing static techniques rely on taint analysis that is computationally difficult for applications with dynamic features [33].

A large body of work addresses the problem of detecting timing side channels [5,13,41]. However, detection approaches are often restricted to either "yes" or "no" answers. In practice, real-world applications may need to leak information about the secret [44]. Then, it is important to know "how much" information is being leaked to evaluate the resulting threats. Quantification techniques with entropy-based measures are the primary tools to calculate the amount of leaks.

We propose a data-driven dynamic analysis for detecting and quantifying timing leaks. Our approach is to split the problem into two tasks: first, to learn a timing model of the program as the neural network (NN) and second, to analyze the NN, which is a simpler object than the original program. The key insight that we exploit is that *timing models of the program are easier to learn than the full functionality of the program*. The advantages of this approach are two-fold. First, although general verification problems are difficult in theory and practice, learning the timing models is efficiently feasible, as shown in our experiments. We conjecture that this is because timing behaviors reflect the computational complexity of a program, which is usually a simpler function of the input rather than the program. Second, neural networks, especially with ReLU units, are easier models to analyze than programs.

Our key technical ideas are enabling a side channel analysis using a specialized neural network architecture and a mixed integer linear programming (MILP) algorithm to estimate an entropy-based measure of side-channel strengths. First, our NN consists of three parts: (a) encoding the secret inputs, (b) encoding the public inputs, and (c) combining the outputs of the first two parts to produce the program timing model. This architecture has the advantage that we can easily change the "strength" (the number of neurons k) of the connection from the secret inputs. This enables us to determine whether there is a side channel. If timing can not be accurately predicted based on just public inputs ($k = 0$), then there is a timing side channel. Second, for $k > 0$, the trained NN can be analyzed to estimate the strength of side-channel leaks. Each valuation of the k binarized output of secret part corresponds to one observationally distinguishable class of secret values. We use an MILP encoding to estimate the size of classes and calculate the amount of information leaks with entropy-based objectives such as *Shannon* entropy.

Our empirical evaluation shows both that timing models of programs can be represented as neural networks and that these NNs can be analyzed to discover side channels and their strengths. We implemented our techniques using Tensorflow [2] and Gurobi [25] for learning timing models as NN objects and analyzing the NNs with MILP algorithms, respectively. We ran experiments on a Linux machine with 24 cores of 2.5 GHz. We could learn timing model of programs (relevant to the observed traces) with few thousands methods in less than 10 min with the accuracy of 0.985. Our analysis can handle NN models with thousands of neurons and retrieve the number of solutions for each class of observation. The number of solutions enables us to quantify the amount of information leaks. In summary, our key contributions are:

- An approach for side channel analysis based on learning execution times of a program as a NN.
- A tunable specialized NN architecture for timing side-channel analysis.
- An MILP-based algorithm for estimating entropy-based measures of information leaks over the NN.
- An empirical evaluation that shows our approach is scalable and quantifies leaks for real-world Java applications.

2   Overview

We illustrate on examples the key ingredients of our approach: learning timing models of programs using neural networks and a NN architecture that enables us to detect and quantify timing leaks.

Learning Timing Models of Programs. Learning the functionality of the sorting algorithms from programs is difficult, while learning their timing model is much easier. We picked the domain of sorting algorithms as these algorithms have well-known different timing behaviors. We implement six different sorting algorithms namely bubble sort, selection sort, insertion sort, bucketing sort, merging sort, and quick sort in one sorting application. We generate random arrays of different sizes from 100 to 20,000 elements and run the application for each input array with different sorting algorithms. This implies that we consider the average-case computational complexities of different algorithms. Each data point consists of the input array, the indicator of sorting algorithm, and the execution time of sorting application. In addition, the data points are independent from each other, and the neural network learns end-to-end execution times of the entire application, not individual sorting algorithms. Figure 1(a) shows the learned execution times for the sorting application. The neural network model has 6 layers with 825 neurons. The accuracy of learning based on coefficient of determination (R^2) over test data is 0.999, and the learning takes 308.7 s (the learning rate is 0.01). As we discussed earlier, the NN model predicts (approximates) execution times for the whole sorting application. Further analysis is required to decompose the NN model for individual sorting algorithms that is not relevant in our setting since we are only interested in learning end-to-end execution times of applications. Using the neural network model to estimate execution times has two important advantages over the state-of-the-art techniques [23,50]. First, the neural network can approximate an arbitrary timing model as a function of input features, while the previous techniques can only approximate linear or polynomial functions. Second, the neural network does not require feature engineering, whereas the previous techniques require users to specify important input features such as work-load (size) features.

(a)

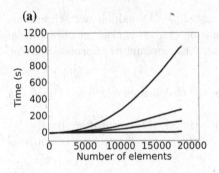

(b)

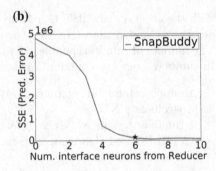

Fig. 1. (a) Timing models of the sorting application as learned by NNs. (b) Prediction error vs. the number of neurons (k) in the interface layer of SnapBuddy.

Neural Network Architecture for Side Channel Discovery. With the observations that the neural networks can learn programs' execution times precisely, we consider a special architecture to analyze timing side channels of programs. We propose the neural network architecture shown in Fig. 2. The NN architecture consists of three parts: (1) A reducer function that learns a map from n secret features (inputs) to k binarized interface neurons (we call them interface neurons as they connect the secret inputs to the rest of the network); (2) A neural network function that connects the public features to the overall model; (3) A joint function that uses the output of the reducer and public-features functions to predict the execution times. The architecture makes it easy to change the number of neurons (k) in the connection from the reducer, which enables us to estimate the side-channel strength. In this architecture, there are timing side channels if the value for k is greater than or equal to 1. The NN learning is to find the weights in different layers with the optimal number of neurons in the interface layer (k) such that the NN approximates execution times accurately.

Estimating the Side Channel Strength. The side-channel strength is estimated by finding the minimal value of k in the learning of accurate NN models. We use Sum of Squared Error (SSE) measure to compute prediction errors. Figure 1(b) shows the SSE versus the number of interface neurons (k) for the SnapBuddy application (described in Sect. 6.2). As shown in the plot, the prediction error decreases as the number of neurons increase from 0 to 6. But, after 6, the prediction error stays almost the same. We thus choose 6 as the optimal number of interface neurons. Since each neuron is a binary unit, there are 2^6 distinct outputs from the reducer function. Each distinct output forms a class of observation over the secret inputs. However, some classes of observations might be empty and are not feasible from any secret value. Furthermore, for feasible classes, the entropy measures require the number of elements in each class. We encode the reducer function as a mixed integer linear programming (MILP) problem. Then, we calculate the number of feasible solutions for each class. For SnapBuddy, it takes 16.6 s to analyze the reducer function and find the number of solutions for non-empty classes. Using Shannon entropy, the analysis shows 3.0 bits of information about secret inputs are leaking in SnapBuddy.

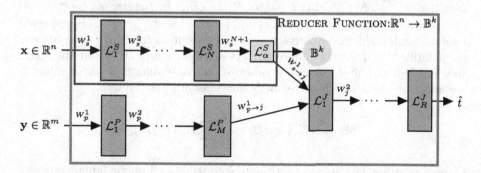

Fig. 2. Neural network architecture for side-channel discovery and quantification. The NN takes secret features ($\mathbf{x}$) and public features ($\mathbf{y}$), and it learns weights W with the minimal number of neurons in the interface layer ($\mathcal{L}_\alpha^S$) to precisely predict execution times. The reducer function maps n-dimensional $\mathbf{x}$ to k binary outputs. The MILP analysis of reducer function is used for the quantification.

3   Problem Statement

We develop a framework for detecting and quantifying information leaks due to the execution time of programs. Our framework is suitable for *known-message* and *chosen-message* threat [32] settings where the variations in the execution times depend on both public and secret inputs.

The *timing model* $[\![\mathcal{P}]\!]$ of a program $\mathcal{P}$ is a tuple $(X, Y, \mathcal{S}, \delta)$ where $X = \{x_1, \dots, x_n\}$ is the set of *secret* input variables, $Y = \{y_1, y_2, \dots, y_m\}$ is the set of *public* input variables, and $\mathcal{S} \subseteq \mathbb{R}^n$ is a finite set of *secret* inputs, and $\delta : \mathbb{R}^n \times \mathbb{R}^m \to \mathbb{R}_{\geq 0}$ is the execution-time of the program as a function of secret and public inputs. A *timing function* of the program $\mathcal{P}$ for a secret input $s \in \mathcal{S}$ is the function $\delta(s)$ defined as $\mathbf{y} \in \mathbb{R}^m \mapsto \delta(s, \mathbf{y})$. Let $\mathcal{F}$ be the set of all timing functions in $\mathcal{P}$.

Given a timing model $[\![\mathcal{P}]\!]$ and a tolerance $\varepsilon > 0$, a k-bit ε-approximate secret reducer is a pair

$$(\alpha, \beta) \in [\mathbb{R}^n \to \mathbb{B}^k] \times [\mathbb{B}^k \to \mathbb{R}^n]$$

such that $\|\delta(\mathbf{x}) - \delta(\beta(\alpha(\mathbf{x})))\| \leq \varepsilon$ for every $\mathbf{x} \in \mathcal{S}$ where $\| \cdot \|$ is some fixed norm over the space of timing function. In this paper, we work with ∞-norm. We write $R_{(\varepsilon, k)}$ for the set of all k-bit ε-approximate reducers for $[\![\mathcal{P}]\!]$. We say that $(\alpha, \beta) \in R_{(\varepsilon, k)}$ is an optimal ε-approximate reducer if for all $k' < k$ the set $R_{(\varepsilon, k')}$ is empty. Given a tolerance $\varepsilon > 0$, we say that there are information leaks in execution times, if there is no 0-bit ε-approximate optimal secret reducer.

A reducer (α, β) characterizes an equivalence relation $\equiv_\alpha$ over the set of secrets $\mathcal{S}$, defined as the following: $s \equiv_\alpha s'$ if $\alpha(s) = \alpha(s')$. Let $\mathcal{S}_{[\alpha]} = \langle \mathcal{S}_1, \mathcal{S}_2, \ldots, \mathcal{S}_K \rangle$ be the quotient space of $\mathcal{S}$ characterized by the reducers (α, β); note that $2^{k-1} < K \le 2^k$. Let $\mathcal{B} = \langle B_1, B_2, \ldots, B_K \rangle$ be the size of observational equivalence class in $\mathcal{S}_\alpha$, i.e. $B_i = |\mathcal{S}_i|$ and let $B = |\mathcal{S}| = \sum_{i=1}^{K} B_i$. The expected information leaks due to observations on the execution times of a program can be quantified by using the difference between the uncertainty about the secret values before and after the timing observations. Assuming that secret values $\mathcal{S}$ are uniformly distributed, we quantify information leaks [31] as

$$\mathsf{SE}(\mathcal{S}|\alpha) \stackrel{\text{def}}{=} \log_2(B) - \frac{1}{B} \sum_{i=1}^{K} B_i \log_2(B_i). \qquad (1)$$

Given a program with inputs partitioned into secret and public inputs, our goal is to quantify the information leaks through timing side channels. However, such programs often have complex functionality with black-box components. Moreover, the shape of timing functions may be non-linear and unknown. We propose a neural-network architecture to approximate the timing model as well as to quantify information leakage due to the timing side channels in the program. We then analyze this network to precisely quantify the information leaks based on the Eq. (1).

4   Neural Network Architecture to Detect and Quantify Information Leaks

A rectified linear unit (ReLU) is a function $\sigma : \mathbb{R} \to \mathbb{R}$ defined as $x \mapsto \max\{x, 0\}$. We can generalize this function from scalars to vectors as $\sigma : \mathbb{R}^n \to \mathbb{R}^n$ in a straightforward fashion by applying ReLU component-wise. In this paper, we primarily work with feedforward neural network (NN) with ReLU activation units. A $\mathbb{R}^{w_0} \to \mathbb{R}^{w_{N+1}}$ feedforward neural network $\mathcal{N}$ is characterized by its number of hidden layers (or depth) N, the input and output dimensions $w_0, w_{N+1} \in \mathbb{N}$, and width of its hidden layers $w_1, w_2, \ldots, w_N$. Each hidden layer i implements an affine mapping $T_i : \mathbb{R}^{w_{i-1}} \to \mathbb{R}^{w_i}$ corresponding to the weights in each layer. The function $f_\mathcal{N} : \mathbb{R}^{w_0} \to \mathbb{R}^{w_{N+1}}$ implemented by neural network $\mathcal{N}$ is:

$$f_\mathcal{N} = T_{k+1} \circ \sigma \circ T_k \circ \sigma \circ \cdots T_2 \circ \sigma \circ T_1.$$

It is well known that NNs with ReLU units implement a piecewise-linear function [8] and due to this property, it can readily be encoded [21] as a mixed integer linear programming (MILP).

Given a target (black-box) function $f : \mathbb{R}^{w_0} \to \mathbb{R}^{w_{N+1}}$ to be approximated and a neural network architecture $(w_0, w_1, \ldots, w_{N+1}) \in \mathbb{R}^{N+2}$, the process of training the network is to search for weights of various layers so as to closely approximate the function f based on noisy approximate examples from the function f. The celebrated universal approximation theorems about neural networks state that *deep feedforward neural networks* [16, 26]—equipped with simple activation units such as rectified linear unit (ReLU)—can approximate arbitrary continuous functions on a compact domain to an arbitrary precision. Assuming that the timing functions of a program have bounded discontinuities, it can be approximated with a continuous function to an arbitrary precision. It then follows that one can approximate the execution-time function to an arbitrary precision using feedforward neural networks.

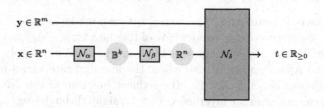

Fig. 3. Neural Network $\mathcal{N}_\delta$ approximating the execution-time function δ along with a reducer $(\mathcal{N}_\alpha, \mathcal{N}_\beta)$.

Figure 3 shows different components of our neural network model. We train a neural network $\mathcal{N}_\delta : \mathbb{R}^{n+m} \to \mathbb{R}$ (where the input variables are partitioned into secret and public and the output variable is the execution time) to approximate the execution times of a given program to a given precision $\varepsilon > 0$. In order to quantify the number of secret bits leaked in the timing functions, we train a pair of k-bit reducer neural networks $\mathcal{N}_\alpha : \mathbb{R}^n \to \mathbb{B}^k$ and $\mathcal{N}_\beta : \mathbb{B}^k \to \mathbb{R}^n$ with the output of $\mathcal{N}_\beta$ connected to the neural network $\mathcal{N}_\delta$. In this training, we only learn the weights of $\mathcal{N}_\alpha$ and $\mathcal{N}_\beta$ while keeping the weights of $\mathcal{N}_\delta$ unchanged. We call the composition of these networks $\mathcal{N}_k = \mathcal{N}_\alpha \circ \mathcal{N}_\beta \circ \mathcal{N}_\delta$. It is easy to see that the network pair $(\mathcal{N}_\alpha, \mathcal{N}_\beta)$ implements a k-bit secret reducer $(f_{\mathcal{N}_\alpha}, f_{\mathcal{N}_\beta})$. Let k be the smallest number such that the fitness of $\mathcal{N}_k$ is comparable to the fitness of $\mathcal{N}_\delta$. We find the smallest $k \in \mathbb{N}$ such that $\mathcal{N}_k$ approximate the execution time as closely as $\mathcal{N}$. The value k characterizes the number of observational classes over the secret inputs in the program and corresponding network $\mathcal{N}_\alpha$ characterizes the secret elements in each class of observation.

We use an MILP encoding, similar to [18, 21, 40] but in backward analysis fashions, to count the number of secret elements in each observational class as characterized by the network $\mathcal{N}_\alpha$. These counts can then be used to provide a quantitative measure of information leaks in the program due to the execution times. Since the function β is not directly useful in quantification process, we use a simpler network model, in our experiments, to compute the reducer function α as shown in Fig. 2.

5   Experiments

5.1   Implementations

Environment Setup. All timing measurements from programs are conducted on an NUC5i5RYH machine. We run each experiment multiple times and use the mean of running time for the rest of analysis. We use a super-computing machine for the training and analysis of the neural network. The machine has a Linux Red Hat 7 OS with 24 cores of 2.5 GHz CPU each with 4.8 GB RAM.

Neural Network Learning. The neural network model is implemented using TensorFlow [2]. We randomly choose 10% of the data for testing, and the rest for the training. We use ReLU units as activation functions and apply mini-batch SGD with the Adam optimizer [29] where the learning rate varies from 0.01 to 0.001 for different benchmarks. For the reducer function of our NN model, we binarize the output of every layer using the "straight-through" technique [15] to estimate the activation function in the backward propagation of errors known as backpropagation [35].

Quantification of Information Leaks. After training, we analyze the reducer function using mixed integer linear programming (MILP) [21,40]. We encode the MILP model in Gurobi [25] and use the *PoolSolutions* option to retrieve feasible solutions (up to 2 Billions). For each class of observation (each distinct output of interface layer), the Gurobi calculates possible solutions from the secret inputs such that the output value of interface layer is feasible from those inputs. We use the number of solutions for each class and apply Shannon entropy to quantify the amount of information leaks.

5.2   Micro-benchmarks

First, we show our approach for finding the (optimal) number of interface neurons (k) from the reducer function. Then, we show the scalability and usefulness of our approach. *scalability:* We use the size of neural network, computation time for learning, and the computation time for analyzing. *usefulness:* We consider the number of classes of observations, the fitness of predictions, and entropy measures. We also compare the entropy values to ground truth.

Programs. We use two sets of micro-benchmark programs for our studies. The first one, taken from [50], uses the names R_n where n is the number of secret bits in the program. The benchmarks were constructed to exhibit complex relationships between secret bits that influence the running time. Each relationship is a boolean formula over the secret input where the true evaluation triggers a (linear) loop statement over the public inputs.

For Branch_Loop (B_L) applications [51], the program does different computations with different complexities depending on the values of the secret input. There are four loop complexities: $O(\log(N))$, $O(N)$, $O(N.\log(N))$, and $O(N^2)$

where N is the public input. Each micro-benchmark B_L_i has all four loop complexities, and there are i types of each complexity with different constant factors such as $O(\log(N))$ and $O(2. \log(N))$ for B_L_2.

Optimal Number of Reducer Outputs. Since the number of observational classes of the secret inputs depends on the number of interface neurons (k) from the reducer function, we choose the optimal value for k. We consider the sum of squared error (SSE) versus the number of interface neurons (k). We choose a value k such that the SSE error decreases from 0 to k ($k \geq 0$) and stays almost same for larger values of k. Figure 4(a) and (b) show the plot of the SSE error vs number of interface neurons for R_n and B_L_n, respectively. For example, in B_L_5, the optimal number of interface neurons is 7.

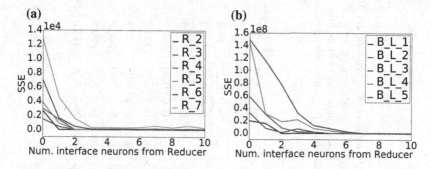

Fig. 4. (a) The SSE versus the number of interface neurons for R_n. (b) The SSE versus the number of interface neurons for B_L_n.

Scalability Results. Table 1 shows that our approach is scalable for learning *timing models* of programs. For example, we could learn the time model of B_L_5 program with the NN model of 7 internal layers and 717 neurons in 25 min. In addition, the growth in computation times of learning is proportional to the growth in the size of networks. The results show that our approach is scalable for *analyzing* the reducer function of NN. For this analysis, we only consider the secret parts of NN (shown with L_S in Table 1). The computation time for the analysis depends on the size of secret inputs and the size of reducer function. In B_L_5 program with 7 interface neurons of the reducer, we calculate feasible solutions over secret inputs for each 2^7 possible classes. It takes about 8 min to analyze the reducer function of B_L_5 program. The growth in the computation times of network analysis is also proportional to the growth in the size of secret inputs and the size of reducer. For example, the computation time for the analysis of B_L_4 example is increased by almost 12 times in comparison to B_L_3, but the size of input, the interface, and the internal neurons have increased by two times (from 2^{11} to 2^{12}), two times (from 2^6 to 2^7), and 6 times (2.5×2.5), respectively.

Table 1. #R: number of data records, #S: number of secret bits, #P: number of public bits, L_S: the size of secret part (reducer function) of NN, L_P: the size of public part of NN, L_J: the size of joint part of NN, α: learning rate, R^2: coefficient of determination, T_L: the computation time (s) for learning NNs, T_A: the computation time (s) for analyzing reducer functions, #k: number of interface neurons in the reducer function, #K: number of (feasible) classes of observations, SE_I: initial Shannon entropy (before any observations), SE_O: remaining Shannon entropy after timing observations.

App(s)	#R	#S	#P	L_S	L_P	L_J	α	R^2	T_L	T_A	#k	#K	SE_I	SE_O
R_2	400	2	7	[5 × 1]	[5]	[10]	1e-2	0.99	91.7	0.1	1	2	2.0	1.19
R_3	800	3	7	[10 × 2]	[10]	[20]	1e-2	0.99	91.7	0.1	2	3	3.0	1.44
R_4	1,600	4	7	[10 × 2]	[10]	[20]	1e-2	0.99	90.3	0.1	2	4	4.0	2.32
R_5	3,200	5	7	[10 × 10 × 2]	[10]	[20]	1e-2	0.99	127.3	0.2	2	3	5.0	3.4
R_6	6,400	6	7	[10 × 10 × 3]	[10 × 10]	[20]	1e-2	0.99	168.4	0.5	3	5	6.0	4.0
R_7	12,800	7	7	[20 × 20 × 3]	[10 × 10]	[20]	1e-2	0.99	185.4	1.8	3	5	7.0	5.0
B_L_1	756	9	7	[20 × 20 × 4]	[10]	[20 × 20]	1e-2	0.99	124.3	0.3	4	5	8.97	6.43
B_L_2	1,512	10	7	[40 × 5]	[10]	[40 × 40]	1e-2	0.99	129.4	2.5	5	10	9.97	6.40
B_L_3	3,024	11	7	[20 × 20 × 6]	[10]	[100 × 100]	5e-3	0.99	346.0	18.6	6	16	10.64	6.39
B_L_4	6,048	12	7	[50 × 50 × 7]	[10]	[200 × 200]	5e-3	0.99	889.8	216.7	7	39	11.93	6.0
B_L_5	12,096	13	7	[50 × 50 × 7]	[10]	[200 × 400]	2e-3	0.99	1,411.0	496.6	7	50	12.29	6.1

Usefulness Results. We use the statistical metric, coefficient of determination (R^2) [39], as the fitness indicator of our predictions. In all benchmarks, R^2 is 0.99. The analysis of the reducer function provides us: (1) whether a class of observation (a specific value of the reducer output) is reachable from at least one secret value; (2) how many secret elements exist in each class of observation. In B_L_5, there are 128 possible values for the 7 interface neurons. The analysis of network shows that only 50 values out of 128 are valid and reachable from secret inputs. To count the number of solutions for each class, we bound the number of possible solutions to be at most 100. We use Shanon entropy to measure the amount of information leaks in bits. For example, in R_7, the initial Shannon entropy is $SE_I = 7(bits)$. We obtain 5 feasible classes: $\{68, 16, 27, 1, 16\}$. Therefore, after the timing observations, the conditional Shannon entropy is $SE_O = 5.2\,(bits)$. The amount of information leaks is $SH_L = 1.8\,(bits)$. We note that the initial Shannon entropy may depend on the number of feasible classes of observations and the bounds on the possible solutions (see B_L_5 as an example). The ground truth of conditional Shannon entropy is the following: R_2 = 1.19, R_3 = 1.44, R_4 = 2.42, R_5 = 3.42, R_6 = 4.0, R_7 = 5.0, and B_L_1, B_L_2, B_L_3, B_L_4, B_L_5 are all equal to 6.64.

6 Case Studies

Table 2 summarizes 5 real-world Java applications used as case studies in this paper. Table 2 has similar structure to Table 1 in Sect. 5.2 and also lists the number of methods in the applications. Figure 5 shows the SSE (error) vs the number of interface neurons of the reducer function for case-study applications. The main research questions are "Does our approach of using neural networks for side-channel analysis of real-world applications (1) scale well, (2) learn timing models accurately, and (3) give useful information about the strength of leaks?"

6.1 GabFeed

Gabfeed [6] is a Java web application with 573 methods implementing a chat server [13]. The application and its users can mutually authenticate each other using public-key infrastructure. The server takes users' public key and its own private key and calculate a common key.

Inputs. We consider the secret and public keys with 1,024 bits. We generate 65,908 keys (combination of secret and public keys) that are uniformly taken from the space of secret and public inputs.

Neural Network Learning. We learn the timing model of GabFeed for generating common keys with $R^2 = 0.952$ where we set the learning rate to 0.01. The NN model consists of 1,024 binary secret and 1,024 binary public inputs. The network has more than 600 neurons. The optimal number of neurons for interface layer is 6. It takes 40 min to learn the timing model of GabFeed application.

Security Analysis. Since the output of the reducer is 6 bits, there are at most 64 classes of observations. Our analysis shows that there are only 26 feasible classes. With the assumption that each class can have at most 10,000 solutions, the initial Shannon entropy is 18.0 bits. By observing the 26 classes through timing side channels, the remaining Shannon entropy becomes 13.29 bits. Therefore, the amount of leaks is 4.71 bits. The security analysis of NN takes 300 min.

Research Questions. To answer our research questions: *Scalability:* The neural network model has 606 neurons. It takes 40 min to learn the time model of GabFeed applications. It takes 300 min to analyze the reducer function and obtain the number of elements in each class. *Usefulness:* We learn the time model of GabFeed as the function of public and secret inputs with $R^2 = 0.952$. Our analysis shows that there are 26 classes of observations over the secret inputs, and 4.71 bits of information about the secret key is leaking.

6.2   SnapBuddy

SnapBuddy is a mock social network application where each user has their own profiles with a photograph [49]. The profile page is publicly accessible.

Inputs. The secret is the identity of a user (among 477 available users in the network) who is currently interacting with the server. The public is the size of each profile (from 13 KB to 350 KB). Note that the size of profiles are observable from generated network traffics.

Neural Network Learning. We consider the response time of the SnapBuddy application to download public profiles of 477 users in the system [6]. We learn the response time using a neural network with 176 neurons and 6 neurons in the interface layer. The accuracy of neural network model in predicting response times based on the coefficient of determination is 0.985 where we set the learning rate to be 0.01. The learning takes less than 10 min.

Security Analysis. Our analysis finds only 8 classes of observations reachable out of 64. Since the number of users (secrets) in the current database is fixed to 477, we assume there can be at most 60 users in each class. The initial Shannon entropy is 8.91 bits. The remaining Shannon entropy after observing the execution times and obtaining the classes of observations with their characteristics is 5.91 bits. The amount of information leaks is 3.0 bits. The analysis of reducer function takes less than 17 s.

Research Questions. To answer our research questions: *Scalability:* It takes less than 10 min to learn the time model of SnapBuddy. It takes only 16.6 s to calculate feasible solutions for all of feasible classes of observations. *Usefulness:* We learn the time model of SnapBuddy as a function of public and secret inputs with $R^2 = 0.985$. Our analysis shows that there are 8 classes of observations over the secret inputs, and 3.0 bits of information about users' identities are leaking.

Table 2. Case Studies. Legends similar to Table 1 in Sect. 5.2 except that #M shows the number of methods in the application and SE_L is the difference between SE_O and SE_I and shows the amount of information leaked in bits.

App(s)	#M	#R	#S	#P	L_S	L_P	L_J	α	R^2	T_L	T_A	#k	#K	SE_L
GabF.	573	65,908	1,024	1,024	[50 × 50 × 6]	[100]	[200 × 200]	1e-2	0.95	2,410	18,010	6	26	4.7
Snap.	3,071	6,678	30	4	[30 × 30 × 6]	[10]	[100]	1e-2	0.98	579	17	6	8	3.0
Phon.	101	3,043	82	11	[50 × 50 × 10]	[5]	[100]	8e-3	0.99	566	10,151	10	60	5.9
Ther.	53	10,000	11	4	[100 × 100 × 9]	[100]	[200 × 200]	1e-3	0.8	4,236	5,148	9	9	7.0
PassM.	6	211,238	14	30	[50 × 50 × 3]	[50]	[100]	1e-2	0.98	202	16	3	4	1.6

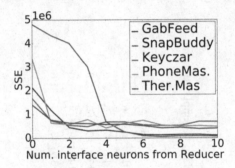

Fig. 5. The SSE versus the number of interface neurons k for case-study application.

6.3 PhoneMaster

Phonemaster [6] is a record keeping service for tracking phone calls and bills. The identity of a user who submits a request is secret, while the generated traffic from the interaction is public.

Inputs. There are at most 150 users. For each user, we send a random command from the set of possible commands.

Neural Network Learning. We use a neural network with 215 neurons. We find out that the optimal number of neurons in the interface layer is 10. We learn the time model of phoneMaster in less than 10 min with $R^2 = 0.993$.

Security Analysis. We analyze the reducer function of NN and find out that 60 classes of observations are feasible. We assume that there can be at most 3 users in each class. The initial Shannon entropy is 7.49 bits. The remaining Shannon entropy after observing the execution times is 1.58. The amount of information leakage is 5.91 bits. This shows that almost everything about the identity of users is leaking. The computation time of analysis is about 169 min.

6.4 Thermomaster

Thermomaster [6] is a temperature control and prediction system. The program takes the goal temperature (secret inputs) and the current temperature (public inputs) to simulate the controller for matching with the goal temperature.

Inputs. The goal temperature is between −10,000 and +10,000 and the current temperature is between −250 and +250. We generate 10,000 inputs uniformly from the space of goal and current temperatures.

Neural Network Learning. We use a NN model with 709 neurons. The optimal number of neurons for the interface layer is 9. We learn the timing models of thermomaster in 70 min with $R^2 = 0.80$.

Security Analysis. We analyze the reducer function of NN and find out that only 9 classes of observations are feasible. The initial Shannon entropy is 11.0

bits. The remaining Shannon entropy after observations is 4.0. Therefore, 7.0 bits of information about the goal temperature are leaking through timing side channels. The computation time of analysis is less than 86 min.

6.5   Password Matching (Keyczar)

We consider a vulnerability in a password matching algorithm similar to the side-channel vulnerability in Keyczar library [34]. This vulnerability allows one to recover the secret password through sequences of oracles where the attacker learns one letter of the secret password in each step.

Inputs. The secret input is target password stored in a server, and the public input is a guess oracle. We use libFuzzer [47] to generate 21,123 guesses for randomly selected passwords. We assume a password is at most 6 (lower-case) letters.

Neural Network Learning. We use a neural network with 253 neurons. The optimal number of neurons for the interface layer is 3. We learn the time model of the password matching algorithm in 202.3 s with $R^2 = 0.976$.

Security Analysis. There can be at most 8 classes of observations. Our analysis shows only 4 classes of observations are feasible. The initial Shannon entropy is 14 bits. The 4 classes (obtained from timing observation) have the following number of elements: $\{48, 6760, 4309, 5269\}$. So, the remaining entropy (after observing the classes through the time model) is 12.4 bits. It takes about 16 s to analyze the secret parts of NN and quantify the information leaks.

7   Related Work

Modeling Program Execution Times. Various techniques have been applied to model and predict computational complexity of software systems [7,23,50]. Both [23] and [50] consider cost measures such as execution time and predict the cost as a function of input features such as the number of bytes in an input file. The works [23,50] are restricted to certain classes of functions such as linear functions, while the neural network techniques can model arbitrary functions. Additionally, both techniques require feature engineering: the user needs to specify some features such as size or work-load features. However, neural network models do not require this and can automatically discover important features.

Neural Networks for Security Analysis. Neural network models have been used for software security analysis. For example, the approach in [46] uses the deep neural network for anomaly detection in software defined networking (SDN). The framework [36] uses a deep neural network model for detecting vulnerabilities such as buffer and resource management errors. We use neural network models to detect and quantify information leaks through timing side channels.

Dynamic Analysis for Side-Channel Detections. Dynamic analysis has been used for side-channel detections [38,41,42]. Diffuzz [41] is a fuzzing techniques for finding side channels. The approach extends AFL [1] and KELINCI [28] fuzzers to detect side channels. The goal of Diffuzz is to maximize the following objective: $\delta = |c(p, s_1) - c(p, s_2)|$, that is, to find two distinct secret values s_1, s_2 and a public value p that give the maximum cost (c) difference. The work [41] uses the noninterference notion of side channel leaks. Therefore, they do not quantify the amounts of information leaks. The cost function in [41] is the number of byte-code executed, whereas we consider the actual execution time in a fixed environment. Note that our approach can be used with the abstract cost model such as the byte-code executed in a straight-forward fashion. Diffuzz [41] can be combined with our technique to generate inputs and quantify leaks.

Static Analysis for Side-Channel Detections. Noninterference was first introduced by Goguen and Meseguer [22] and has been widely used to enforce confidentiality properties in various systems [4,43,48]. Various works [5,13] use static analysis for side-channel detections based on noninterference notion. The work [13] defines ε bounded noninterference that requires the resource usage behavior of the program executed from the same public inputs differ at most ε. Chen et al. [13] use Hoare Logic [11] equipped with taint analysis [37] to detect side channels. These static techniques including [13] rely on the taint analysis that is computationally difficult for real-world Java applications. The work [33] reported that 78% of 461 open-source Java projects use dynamic features such as reflections that are problematic for static analysis. In contrast, we use dynamic analysis that handles the reflections and scales well for the real-world applications. In addition, Chen et al. [13] answer either 'yes' or 'no' to the existence of side channels, which is restricted for many real-world applications that may need to disclose a small amounts of information about the secret. However, our approach quantifies the leaks using entropy measures.

Quantification of Information Leaks. Quantitative information flow [10,31,44] has been used for measuring the strength of side channels. The work [10] presents an approach based on finding the equivalence relation over secret inputs. The authors cast the problem of finding the equivalence relation as a reachability problem and use model counting to quantify information leaks. Their approach works only for a small program, limited to a few lines of code, while our approach can work for large applications. In addition, they consider the leaks through direct observations such as program outputs or public input values. In contrast, we consider the leaks through timing side channels, which are non-functional aspects of programs. Sidebuster [56] combines static and dynamic analyses for detection and quantification of information leaks. Sidebuster [56] also relies on taint analysis to identify the source of vulnerability. Once the source identified, Sidebuster uses dynamic analysis and measures the amounts of information leaks. The information leaks in Sidebuster [56] is because of generated network packets, while our information leaks are through timing side channels.

Hardening Against Side Channels. Hardening against side channels can be broadly divided to mitigation and elimination approaches. The mitigation approaches [9,32,52] aim to minimize the amounts of information leaks, while considering the performance of systems. The goal of elimination approaches [3, 19,55] is to completely transform out information leaks without considering the performance burdens. Our techniques can be combined with the hardening methods to mitigate or eliminate information leaks.

Other Types of Side Channels. Sensitive information can be leaked through other side channels such as power consumptions [20,53], network traffics [14], and cache behaviors [17,24,45,54]. We believe our approach could be useful for these types of side channels, however, we left further analysis for future work.

8 Conclusion and Discussion

We presented a data-driven dynamic analysis for detection and quantifying information leaks due to execution times of programs. The analysis performed over a specialized NN architecture in two steps: first, we utilized neural network objects to learn timing models of programs and second, we analyzed the parts of NNs related to secret inputs to detect and quantify information leaks. Our experiences showed that NNs learn timing models of real-world applications precisely. In addition, they enabled us to quantify information leaks, thanks to the simplicity of NN models in comparison to program models.

Throughout this work, we assume that the analyzer would be able to construct interesting inputs either with fuzzing tools, previously reported bugs, or domain knowledges. Nevertheless, we demonstrate practical solutions to generate inputs in each example with emphasis on the recent development in fuzzing for side-channel analysis [41].

Furthermore, our dynamic analysis approach can not prove the absent of side channels. Our NN model learns and generalizes the timing models for the observed program behaviors and is limited to observed paths in the program. We emphasize that the proof is also difficult for static analysis. Although static analysis can prove the absent of bugs or vulnerabilities in principle, the presence of dynamic features such as reflections in Java applications is problematic and can cause false negative in static analysis (see Limitations Section in [13]).

For *future work*, there are few interesting directions. One idea is to develop a SAT-based algorithm, similar to DPLL, on top of MILP algorithms to calculate the number of solutions more efficiently. Another idea is to define threat models based on the attackers capabilities to utilize neural networks for guessing secrets.

Acknowledgements. The first author thanks Shiva Darian for proofreading and providing useful suggestions. This research was supported by DARPA under agreement FA8750-15-2-0096.

References

1. American fuzzy lop (2016). http://lcamtuf.coredump.cx/afl/

2. Abadi, M., et al.: TensorFlow: a system for large-scale machine learning. In: OSDI 2016, pp. 265–283 (2016)
3. Agat, J.: Transforming out timing leaks. In: Proceedings of the 27th ACM SIGPLAN-SIGACT Symposium on Principles of Programming Languages, pp. 40–53. ACM (2000)
4. Almeida, J.B., Barbosa, M., Barthe, G., Dupressoir, F., Emmi, M.: Verifying constant-time implementations. In: USENIX Security Symposium, pp. 53–70 (2016)
5. Antonopoulos, T., Gazzillo, P., Hicks, M., Koskinen, E., Terauchi, T., Wei, S.: Decomposition instead of self-composition for proving the absence of timing channels. In: ACM SIGPLAN Notices, vol. 52, pp. 362–375. ACM (2017)
6. Apogee-Research: Space/time analysis for cybersecurity (STAC) repository. https://github.com/Apogee-Research/STAC
7. Arar, Ö.F., Ayan, K.: Software defect prediction using cost-sensitive neural network. Appl. Soft Comput. **33**, 263–277 (2015)
8. Arora, R., Basu, A., Mianjy, P., Mukherjee, A.: Understanding deep neural networks with rectified linear units. arXiv e-prints (2016)
9. Askarov, A., Zhang, D., Myers, A.C.: Predictive black-box mitigation of timing channels. In: Proceedings of the 17th ACM Conference on Computer and Communications Security, pp. 297–307. ACM (2010)
10. Backes, M., Köpf, B., Rybalchenko, A.: Automatic discovery and quantification of information leaks. In: S&P 2009 (2009)
11. Barthe, G., D'Argenio, P.R., Rezk, T.: Secure information flow by self-composition. In: Proceedings of the 17th IEEE Computer Security Foundations Workshop, pp. 100–114. IEEE (2004)
12. Brumley, D., Boneh, D.: Remote timing attacks are practical. Comput. Netw. **48**(5), 701–716 (2005)
13. Chen, J., Feng, Y., Dillig, I.: Precise detection of side-channel vulnerabilities using quantitative cartesian hoare logic. In: CCS (2017)
14. Chen, S., Wang, R., Wang, X., Zhang, K.: Side-channel leaks in web applications: a reality today, a challenge tomorrow. In: S&P 2010 (2010)
15. Courbariaux, M., Hubara, I., Soudry, D., El-Yaniv, R., Bengio, Y.: Binarized neural networks: training deep neural networks with weights and activations constrained to +1 or −1. arXiv preprint arXiv:1602.02830 (2016)
16. Cybenko, G.: Approximation by superpositions of a sigmoidal function. Math. Control Signals Systems **2**, 303–314 (1989)
17. Doychev, G., Köpf, B., Mauborgne, L., Reineke, J.: CacheAudit: a tool for the static analysis of cache side channels. ACM Trans. Inf. Syst. Secur. (TISSEC) **18**(1), 4 (2015)
18. Dutta, S., Jha, S., Sankaranarayanan, S., Tiwari, A.: Output range analysis for deep feedforward neural networks. In: Dutle, A., Muñoz, C., Narkawicz, A. (eds.) NFM 2018. LNCS, vol. 10811, pp. 121–138. Springer, Cham (2018). https://doi.org/10.1007/978-3-319-77935-5_9
19. Eldib, H., Wang, C.: Synthesis of masking countermeasures against side channel attacks. In: Biere, A., Bloem, R. (eds.) CAV 2014. LNCS, vol. 8559, pp. 114–130. Springer, Cham (2014). https://doi.org/10.1007/978-3-319-08867-9_8
20. Eldib, H., Wang, C., Schaumont, P.: Formal verification of software countermeasures against side-channel attacks. ACM Trans. Softw. Eng. Methodol. (TOSEM) **24**(2), 11 (2014)
21. Fischetti, M., Jo, J.: Deep neural networks and mixed integer linear optimization. Constraints **23**(3), 296–309 (2018)

22. Goguen, J.A., Meseguer, J.: Security policies and security models. In: IEEE Symposium on Security and Privacy, p. 11. IEEE (1982)
23. Goldsmith, S.F., Aiken, A.S., Wilkerson, D.S.: Measuring empirical computational complexity. In: FSE 2007, pp. 395–404. ACM (2007)
24. Guo, S., Wu, M., Wang, C.: Adversarial symbolic execution for detecting concurrency-related cache timing leaks. In: Proceedings of the 2018 26th ACM Joint Meeting on European Software Engineering Conference and Symposium on the Foundations of Software Engineering, pp. 377–388. ACM (2018)
25. Gurobi Optimization, Inc.: Gurobi optimizer reference manual (2018). http://www.gurobi.com
26. Hornik, K., Stinchcombe, M.B., White, H.: Multilayer feedforward networks are universal approximators. Neural Networks **2**, 359–366 (1989)
27. Hund, R., Willems, C., Holz, T.: Practical timing side channel attacks against kernel space ASLR. In: IEEE Symposium on Security and Privacy, pp. 191–205. IEEE (2013)
28. Kersten, R., Luckow, K., Păsăreanu, C.S.: POSTER: AFL-based fuzzing for Java with Kelinci. In: Proceedings of the 2017 ACM SIGSAC Conference on Computer and Communications Security, pp. 2511–2513. ACM (2017)
29. Kingma, D.P., Ba, J.: Adam: a method for stochastic optimization. arXiv preprint arXiv:1412.6980 (2014)
30. Kocher, P.C.: Timing attacks on implementations of Diffie-Hellman, RSA, DSS, and other systems. In: Koblitz, N. (ed.) CRYPTO 1996. LNCS, vol. 1109, pp. 104–113. Springer, Heidelberg (1996). https://doi.org/10.1007/3-540-68697-5_9
31. Köpf, B., Basin, D.: An information-theoretic model for adaptive side-channel attacks. In: CCS 2007, pp. 286–296 (2007)
32. Köpf, B., Dürmuth, M.: A provably secure and efficient countermeasure against timing attacks. In: CSF 2009 (2009)
33. Landman, D., Serebrenik, A., Vinju, J.J.: Challenges for static analysis of java reflection-literature review and empirical study. In: IEEE/ACM 39th International Conference on Software Engineering (ICSE), pp. 507–518. IEEE (2017)
34. Lawson, N.: Timing attack in Google Keyczar library (2009). https://rdist.root.org/2009/05/28/timing-attack-in-google-keyczar-library/
35. LeCun, Y., Bengio, Y., Hinton, G.: Deep learning. Nature **521**(7553), 436 (2015)
36. Li, Z., et al.: VulDeePecker: a deep learning-based system for vulnerability detection. arXiv:1801.01681 (2018)
37. Livshits, V.B., Lam, M.S.: Finding security vulnerabilities in Java applications with static analysis. In: USENIX Security Symposium, vol. 14, p. 18 (2005)
38. Milushev, D., Beck, W., Clarke, D.: Noninterference via symbolic execution. In: Giese, H., Rosu, G. (eds.) FMOODS/FORTE -2012. LNCS, vol. 7273, pp. 152–168. Springer, Heidelberg (2012). https://doi.org/10.1007/978-3-642-30793-5_10
39. Nagelkerke, N.J., et al.: A note on a general definition of the coefficient of determination. Biometrika **78**(3), 691–692 (1991)
40. Narodytska, N., Kasiviswanathan, S., Ryzhyk, L., Sagiv, M., Walsh, T.: Verifying properties of binarized deep neural networks. In: AAAI 2018 (2018)
41. Nilizadeh, S., Noller, Y., Pasareanu, C.S.: DIFFUZZ: differential fuzzing for side-channel analysis. In: ICSE (2019). http://arxiv.org/abs/1811.07005
42. Rosner, N., Burak Kadron, I., Bang, L., Bultan, T.: Profit: detecting and quantifying side channels in networked applications. In: NDSS (2019)
43. Sabelfeld, A., Myers, A.C.: Language-based information-flow security. IEEE J. Sel. Areas Commun. **21**, 5–19 (2003)

44. Smith, G.: On the foundations of quantitative information flow. In: de Alfaro, L. (ed.) FoSSaCS 2009. LNCS, vol. 5504, pp. 288–302. Springer, Heidelberg (2009). https://doi.org/10.1007/978-3-642-00596-1_21

45. Sung, C., Paulsen, B., Wang, C.: CANAL: a cache timing analysis framework via LLVM transformation. In: ASE 2018, pp. 904–907 (2018)

46. Tang, T.A., Mhamdi, L., McLernon, D., Zaidi, S.A.R., Ghogho, M.: Deep learning approach for network intrusion detection in software defined networking. In: WINCOM 2016 (2016)

47. libFuzzer Team Guided: LibFuzzer: coverage-based fuzz testing (2016). http://llvm.org/docs/LibFuzzer.html

48. Terauchi, T., Aiken, A.: Secure information flow as a safety problem. In: Hankin, C., Siveroni, I. (eds.) SAS 2005. LNCS, vol. 3672, pp. 352–367. Springer, Heidelberg (2005). https://doi.org/10.1007/11547662_24

49. Tizpaz-Niari, S., Černý, P., Chang, B.-Y.E., Sankaranarayanan, S., Trivedi, A.: Discriminating traces with time. In: Legay, A., Margaria, T. (eds.) TACAS 2017. LNCS, vol. 10206, pp. 21–37. Springer, Heidelberg (2017). https://doi.org/10.1007/978-3-662-54580-5_2

50. Tizpaz-Niari, S., Černý, P., Chang, B.E., Trivedi, A.: Differential performance debugging with discriminant regression trees. In: AAAI 2018, pp. 2468–2475 (2018)

51. Tizpaz-Niari, S., Černý, P., Trivedi, A.: Data-driven debugging for functional side channels. arXiv:1808.10502 (2018)

52. Tizpaz-Niari, S., Černý, P., Trivedi, A.: Quantitative mitigation of timing side channels. In: Dillig, I., Tasiran, S. (eds.) CAV 2019. LNCS, vol. 11561, pp. 140–160. Springer, Cham (2019). https://doi.org/10.1007/978-3-030-25540-4_8

53. Wang, J., Sung, C., Wang, C.: Mitigating power side channels during compilation. arXiv preprint arXiv:1902.09099 (2019)

54. Wang, S., Wang, P., Liu, X., Zhang, D., Wu, D.: Cached: Identifying cache-based timing channels in production software. In: 26th USENIX Security Symposium, pp. 235–252 (2017)

55. Wu, M., Guo, S., Schaumont, P., Wang, C.: Eliminating timing side-channel leaks using program repair. In: Proceedings of the 27th ACM SIGSOFT International Symposium on Software Testing and Analysis, pp. 15–26. ACM (2018)

56. Zhang, K., Li, Z., Wang, R., Wang, X., Chen, S.: Sidebuster: automated detection and quantification of side-channel leaks in web application development. In: Proceedings of the 17th ACM Conference on Computer and Communications Security, pp. 595–606. ACM (2010)

Predictive Runtime Monitoring for Linear Stochastic Systems and Applications to Geofence Enforcement for UAVs

Hansol Yoon[1], Yi Chou[1], Xin Chen[2], Eric Frew[1],
and Sriram Sankaranarayanan[1(✉)]

[1] University of Colorado, Boulder, USA
{hansol.yoon,yi.chou,eric.frew,srirams}@colorado.edu
[2] University of Dayton, Dayton, USA
xchen4@udayton.edu

Abstract. We propose a predictive runtime monitoring approach for linear systems with stochastic disturbances. The goal of the monitor is to decide if there exists a possible sequence of control inputs over a given time horizon to ensure that a safety property is maintained with a sufficiently high probability. We derive an efficient algorithm for performing the predictive monitoring in real time, specifically for linear time invariant (LTI) systems driven by stochastic disturbances. The algorithm implicitly defines a control envelope set such that if the current control input to the system lies in this set, there exists a future strategy over a time horizon consisting of the next N steps to guarantee the safety property of interest. As a result, the proposed monitor is oblivious of the actual controller, and therefore, applicable even in the presence of complex control systems including highly adaptive controllers. Furthermore, we apply our proposed approach to monitor whether a UAV will respect a "geofence" defined by a geographical region over which the vehicle may operate. To achieve this, we construct a data-driven linear model of the UAVs dynamics, while carefully modeling the uncertainties due to wind, GPS errors and modeling errors as time-varying disturbances. Using realistic data obtained from flight tests, we demonstrate the advantages and drawbacks of the predictive monitoring approach.

1 Introduction

We present efficient algorithms for the problem of monitoring viability in linear stochastic systems, and apply our approach to monitoring *geofencing* for UAVs. As UAVs become increasingly prevalent, the issue of such UAVs straying into critical infrastructure such as airports [3], residential buildings, military installations and other areas has gained critical importance. Geofences are virtual areas defined by a air traffic management authority inside which a UAV is permitted to operate [24]. However, breaches of these geofences, intentional or otherwise, need to be monitored. Furthermore, monitors need to provide advance warning to an operator that a breach is impending: such warnings can provide the

B. Finkbeiner and L. Mariani (Eds.): RV 2019, LNCS 11757, pp. 349–367, 2019.
https://doi.org/10.1007/978-3-030-32079-9_20

traffic manager valuable time to undertake possible defensive measures, or even help with post-incident investigations. Formally, a *geofence* is defined by a set $F \subseteq \mathbb{R}^3$, specifying legal (x, y, z) positions of the UAV.

Definition 1 (Geofence Monitoring Problem). *Given the current state of the aircraft (assume current time is $t = 0$), will its position $(x(t), y(t), z(t))$ remain inside a geofence F over a time interval $[0, T]$ in the future.*

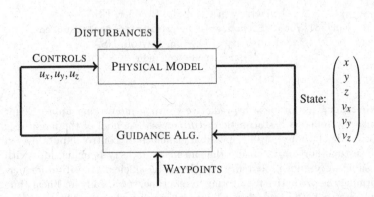

Fig. 1. Schematic diagram of the closed loop system showing the plant and the controller.

As such, geofences are safety properties and monitoring them over a finite time horizon requires over-approximating the set of possible reachable states $\mathcal{R}_T$ over the time interval $[0, T]$ of interest, enabling us to check the condition $\mathcal{R}_T \subseteq F$. Naturally, for runtime monitoring, the reachable state estimate must be computed and checked against the specifications during the deployment. However, reachability analysis is a difficult computation that is complicated by multiple factors. As shown in Fig. 1, the UAV system is a closed-loop consisting of the physical dynamics of the aircraft and the on-board navigation/guidance controller.

1. The physical dynamics are uncertain and influenced by unknown, stochastic disturbances such as the wind.
2. The navigation and guidance component are often nonlinear, involving proprietary autopilot systems and influenced by *waypoints* or other mission specifications provided by the operator.

Nonlinear reachability analysis for hybrid systems is an active area of research [2,7,9,12]. However, a rapid real-time stochastic reachability analysis of the closed loop in Fig. 1 to check geofence violations is beyond the capability of even the most sophisticated tools, at the time of writing. In this paper, we *sidestep* these issues to derive an efficient solution suitable for online monitoring:

1. We use data-driven linear forecast models for the UAVs that includes the effect of wind uncertainty and unmodeled dynamics.
2. Instead of monitoring whether the closed loop will satisfy the safety property, we ask a different question of *viability* rather than *safety*.

Definition 2 (θ-viable). *A state $x(0)$ of the plant is θ-viable at a future time T, iff there exists a control strategy over $[0, T]$ such that the probability of safety at time T is at least θ—i.e., $\mathbb{P}(x(T) \in F) \geq \theta$.*

In practice, θ is set to a number close to 1, indicating the desired level of confidence in the system state. Viability monitoring differs from the standard safety monitor in the following manner: rather than ask whether the particular control law can act to prevent a future failure, we ask the question whether there exists *some control strategies* that can prevent failure. In particular, this strategy may differ from the one used by the actual controller. It is possible that a system state is viable but the specific control law employed can lead to failure. On the other hand, if a system is deemed *not viable* for a future time, it is essentially at the mercy of the environment: no controller can guarantee safety for such a system with probability exceeding θ. The advantages of the viability monitoring approach used in this paper include:

(a) It is purely a property of the plant model and does not involve the controller. This allows us to handle systems that are controlled by complex control strategies that may be proprietary, or in general, hard to reason about in real-time. This may include neural networks and learning-based controllers that are now quite popular in autonomous systems.
(b) Finally, we show a sufficient condition that yields a sound monitor for viability for linear stochastic systems. This monitor can be implemented efficiently with an efficient online runtime monitoring strategy.

However, viability monitoring suffers from key disadvantages from the point of view of runtime monitoring for safety:

(a) A viability monitor can miss impending safety violation (false negatives). The closed loop system may, in fact, violate the safety property despite there being a strategy to avoid that violation.
(b) The approach can potentially yield *false alarms*, wherein a failure of viability does not necessarily lead to a property failure. It is entirely possible that the environment does not exhibit the worst case behavior leading to a failure of viability, but at the same time allowing the system to remain safe. Nevertheless, such situations are important to note and fix, lest they lead to an actual violation in a different instance.

The gap between safety monitoring and the notion of viability monitoring presented in this paper can be narrowed by constraining the definition of viability, in order to account for properties of the controller. The key here is to restrict the control strategies used in Definition 2 to a smaller set of strategies that include those employed by the controller. For instance, the range of control inputs used by the actual controller implementation can be used to restrict the strategies considered in Definition 2. More general abstractions of the controller, if available, can also be employed in this manner. In doing so, the drawbacks mentioned above can be partly addressed.

The rest of the paper is organized as follows: Sect. 2 describes the data-driven modeling approach, Sect. 3 presents the basic algorithm for monitoring viability efficiently, Sect. 4 presents how this algorithm is adapted and makes more efficient specifically for geofencing. Finally, an evaluation based on actual UAV test flight data under windy conditions is presented in Sect. 5. The evaluation shows that the approach is generally successful in monitoring violations of safety properties sufficiently ahead of time. Very few violations ($< 1\%$) are missed by our monitors, while at the same time the false positive rate is very small ($< 0.3\%$). Proofs have been omitted in order to conform to the page limits. All proofs are provided in an extended version of this paper that will be available upon request.

1.1 Related Work

The use of real-time monitors to predict and act against imminent property violations forms the basis for runtime assurance using L1-Simplex architectures that switch between a lower performance but formally validated control when an impending failure is predicted [23]. However, the key issue lies in the process of predicting impending failures with high confidence. Often, predicting failures involves computing control invariant sets, or solving reachability problems in real time [8,14]. Previous work by some of the authors use a game theoretic approach to monitor impending property violations for linear systems [10]. This paper directly extends our previous work to probabilistic models. Additionally, we showcase a realistic application to monitoring geofence violations. Recently, the idea of *shielding* has been proposed for runtime assurance of autonomous systems with human operators and learning-enabled systems. Formally, a shield is a component that interfaces between a human operator or a complex controller and the plant that can modify the control inputs in real time to avoid an erroneous state, or recover from one as quickly as possible [15]. The idea has been applied to safe reinforcement learning wherein the shield restricts the actions of the learner during the training phase and prevents a specification violation during deployment phase [1]. Although the present work focuses on efficient monitoring, our approach described here lends itself easily to the synthesis of a shield component. However, a key difference is that our work focuses on predicting the satisfaction of safety properties over a future state using a data-driven model. Such a prediction is complementary to the process of shield synthesis that focuses on corrective actions to avoid failures, or recover from them.

Recently, data-driven predictions of impending property violations have received much attention. Phan et al. demonstrate the use of neural network classifiers combined with offline statistical model checkers to predict if the current state is likely to violate a property during a future time horizon [20]. Neural networks are black boxes whose predictions must be trusted. Nevertheless, the recent surge of interest in verifying neural networks bodes well for the use of these models in monitoring applications.

Lygeros and Prandini (along with coworkers) have investigated stochastic reachability analysis approaches for detecting and avoiding collisions between aircrafts [16,22]. Their approach bears many similarities with ours: the use of stochastic models to predict future positions with uncertainties and the use of reachability analysis to estimate probability of collision. However, there are many key differences: first, we use discrete time data-driven models inferred in real time as we obtain recent historical data. We also monitor viability in order to avoid reasoning about the on-board controllers.

Stevens et al. investigate the problem of monitoring geofences: on one hand their work can monitor nonconvex geofence regions [25]. However, their monitoring is not predictive: to enable prediction they simply narrow the safety region so that a violation of the conservative region indicates a potential impending violation of the original specification. In this work, we tackle the problem of predicting future loss in viability, more systematically, while accounting for wind disturbances.

The work of Moosbrugger et al. presents another key application of data-driven models for the runtime monitoring of UAVs [19]. Their approach uses a combination of a Bayes network to model how various observable events may result in hardware/software failures or security threats during the operation of a UAV. Our approach also uses data-driven models, but to predict future positions and velocities. Also, we monitor viability properties involving future positions of the aircraft. We hope to investigate how ideas from Moosbrugger et al. (ibid) can be incorporated into our framework to fuse observable events on-board UAVs to better predict future positions. Besides predicting collisions, or monitoring onboard health, data-driven models can be applicable to other aspects of flight such as remaining fuel/power. Chati and Balakrishnan present a data-driven Gaussian process model of aircraft fuel consumption, an important prediction target during flight [6].

Vinod et al. consider the problem of finding control inputs to guarantee future safety property of a linear stochastic system using ideas such as dynamic programming, chance constrained optimization and Fourier transform approaches [26,27]. Our work in contrast attempts to get rid of the stochastic disturbances by finding a robust set to contain the disturbances. This has the advantage of computational speed suitable for real-time monitoring. However, we can only provide a sound rather than a precise solution for the monitoring problem. Quantifying the gap between the two approaches will be performed in our future work.

2   Data-Driven Model

In this section, we review our approach to formulating data-driven models that augment an existing physical model of aircraft dynamics. We first start with the overall structure of the model and explain how various parts of the model are infered as well as the process of modeling the uncertainty.

We start with a simple physical model of an aircraft with current position (x, y, z), velocities (v_x, v_y, v_z) along a static reference frame fixed to the earth and accelerations (u_x, u_y, u_z) that are treated as control inputs. Let δ be a fixed step size. Our experiments use $\delta = 0.4\,\text{s}$ based on the data refresh rate from our UAV platforms.

$$\begin{bmatrix} x(t + \delta) = x(t) + \delta v_x(t) + \frac{1}{2}\delta^2 u_x + e_x(t + \delta) \\ y(t + \delta) = y(t) + \delta v_y(t) + \frac{1}{2}\delta^2 u_y + e_y(t + \delta) \\ z(t + \delta) = z(t) + \delta v_z(t) + \frac{1}{2}\delta^2 u_z + e_z(t + \delta) \\ v_x(t + \delta) = v_x(t) + \delta u_x(t) + e_{vx}(t + \delta) \\ v_y(t + \delta) = v_y(t) + \delta u_y(t) + e_{vy}(t + \delta) \\ v_z(t + \delta) = v_z(t) + \delta u_z(t) + e_{vz}(t + \delta) \end{bmatrix} \tag{1}$$

We have introduced terms $e_x, e_y, e_z, e_{vx}, e_{vy}, e_{vz}$ model discrepancies between the observed data at time $t + \delta$ and that predicted by a simple Newtonian particle model of the UAV. We will call Eq. (1) as our core model that incorporates the physical knowledge as well as unexplained discrepancies that may arise due to model mismatch as well as the disturbances. The key is to model these discrepancies as a function of the *recent* historical data. We wish to model each error as a function of the past:

$$e_x(t + \delta) = a_0 e_x(t) + \cdots + a_{p-1} e_x(t - (p - 1)\delta) + w(t + \delta). \tag{2}$$

Here $a_0, \ldots, a_{p-1}$ are called the *autoregressive* coefficients, p is the history length and w is a random variable drawn from a known probability distribution, and independent of the current state variables. Such a model is called an *autoregressive* (AR) model. Likewise, we formulate AR models for $e_y, e_z, e_{vx}, \ldots, e_{vz}$. It is important to fix the form of this model and the length of the historical data needed.

2.1   Autoregressive Models

In this paper, we will model discrepancies e using a simple yet effective modeling paradigm called *auto-regressive* models with *exogenous inputs* (ARX) models [5,18]. ARX models are a simple approach to formulating linear models in time-series forecasting. They are widely used in numerous applications especially where simplicity and careful modeling of uncertainties are important. Furthermore, we prefer to explore the capabilities of such a simple approach to motivate whether more complex nonlinear models can be useful. Consider again the form of the discrepancy model in Eq. (2). To infer the coefficients $a_0, \ldots, a_{p-1}$, we first use our data to compute $e_x(t), e_y(t), \ldots, e_{vz}(t)$ for each time $t = \delta, \ldots, N\delta$ by substituting the known data in the core model (1).

Inferring Models (Regression): For discrepancy variables e_x, e_y, e_z, e_{vx}, e_{vy}, and e_{vz}, we set up models for fixed history lengths p as in Eq. (2). The disturbance term $w(t + \delta)$ is removed from the model and estimated later. For each time $t = 0, \delta, \ldots, (N-1)\delta$, we obtain a single equation involving the unknowns $c : (a_0, \ldots, a_{p-1})$. As a result of plugging in the data, we obtain a system of equations of the form: $Ac \approx b$, wherein A, b are formulated from the data. However, there will be more equations than there are unknowns. Thus, our goal is not to find a "perfect" solution to the equations, since one will not exist in all but the rarest of cases. We use linear regression to minimize the residual error $\min(\||Ac-b\||_2^2)$. Often, we wish to minimize the residual error subject to sparsity constraints on the coefficient. One approach to do is called *ridge regression* [13], wherein we minimize $\min(\||Ac-b\||_2^2 + \alpha\||c\||_2^2)$, wherein α is a constant. The objective function represents a tradeoff between achieving low residual errors versus keeping the sizes of the coefficients small. This is adjusted using the parameter α. The regression problem is solved using well-studied approaches from linear algebra such as Cholesky decomposition or conjugate gradient approaches. The resulting solution yields the coefficients c of the ARX model.

Once we finish solving the regression, we estimate the distribution of the residuals $w(t)$, by modeling the distribution of the residual error vector $Ac - b$. This can be achieved in one of two ways: (a) carrying the residual vector $Ac - b$ and randomly sampling a value from it when needed to obtain a sample; (b) modeling the error as a distribution such as a Gaussian distribution by computing its mean and standard deviation. Statistical tests such as the chi-squared tests can help us estimate how close the residual distribution is to being a Gaussian. We adopt the latter approach since for all our datasets seen in this paper, we obtain excellent fits to the Gaussian distribution. The distribution mean is obtained as the empirical mean of the residuals $Ac - b$ and the standard deviation is obtained as the empirical standard deviation. The final form of the ARX model is therefore given by Eq. (2) with w modeled as a sample from a Gaussian distribution with a given mean and standard deviation.

Example 1. The equation below partially illustrates a model for x, y, z with e_x, e_y and e_z. Note that $\delta = 0.4$.

$$x(t + \delta) = x(t) + \delta v_x(t) + \tfrac{1}{2}\delta^2 u_x + e_x(t)$$
$$y(t + \delta) = y(t) + \delta v_y(t) + \tfrac{1}{2}\delta^2 u_y + e_y(t)$$
$$z(t + \delta) = z(t) + \delta v_z(t) + \tfrac{1}{2}\delta^2 u_z + e_z(t)$$
$$e_x(t + \delta) = 0.57 e_x(t) + 0.39 e_x(t - \delta) + w_1 \ (\sigma_1 : \ 0.13)$$
$$e_y(t + \delta) = 0.49 e_y(t) + 0.27 e_y(t - \delta) + w_2 \ (\sigma_2 : \ 0.14)$$
$$e_z(t + \delta) = 1.35 e_z(t) - 0.39 e_z(t - \delta) + w_3 \ (\sigma_3 : \ 0.053)$$

The terms w_1, w_2, w_3 are Gaussian random variables with 0 mean and variances σ_1, σ_2 and σ_3, respectively, as shown.

Model Updating: We briefly comment on model updating. UAV environments involve changes to aircraft dynamics due to wear and tear, payload variations and fuel loss as well as changes in wind conditions. As a result, it is important to update the model using the "latest" available data. In our experiments, the process of constructing the model from nearly 2000 data points takes less than 0.1 s. As a result, it is possible to keep updating the model in real time. Another alternative is to update the distributions of $w(t)$ over time using the residuals computed based on real data. For the rest of the paper, we consider the model to remain fixed for all times. Schemes for updating the model in real time are beyond the scope of the current work. We hope to investigate them as part of future work.

3   Viability Monitoring

We will now present viability monitoring for linear stochastic systems.

Definition 3 (Plant Model). *A plant model $\mathscr{P}$ is given by a tuple $\langle \delta, A, B, C, \mathscr{U}, \mathscr{D} \rangle$ with a time step $\delta > 0$, state vector $x(t) \in \mathbb{R}^n$, a control input vector $u(t) \in \mathbb{R}^m$ and a disturbance input vector $w(t) \in \mathbb{R}^k$. At each step, the state of the plant model is updated according to the matrices $A \in \mathbb{R}^{n \times n}$, $B \in \mathbb{R}^{n \times m}$ and $C \in \mathbb{R}^{n \times k}$.*

$$x(t + \delta) = Ax(t) + Bu(t) + Cw(t),$$

wherein $u(t) \in \mathscr{U}$ and $w(t) \sim \mathscr{D}$, i.e., $w(t)$ is distributed according to $\mathscr{D}$.

We will make the following assumptions on the structure of the plant model.

(1) The set $\mathscr{U}$ is a box wherein each component u_i belongs to an interval $[a_{u_i}, b_{u_i}]$. Later, this assumption will enable us to simplify the overall monitoring algorithm.

(2) The distribution $\mathscr{D}$ is normal wherein each component $w_i(t)$ for $1 \leq i \leq k$ is distributed according to a gaussian random variable with mean 0 and standard deviation σ_i. Furthermore, random variable $w_i(t), w_j(t)$ are pairwise independent for $i \neq j$. Also, random variables $w(t), w(t')$ are independent for $t' \neq t$.

We note that the data-driven model discussed in Eqs. (1) and (2) in Sect. 2 fit the structure of our plant model. The state x consists of the following:

$$\underbrace{x(t), y(t), z(t)}_{\text{Position}}, \underbrace{v_x(t), v_y(t), v_z(t)}_{\text{Velocities}}, \underbrace{e_x(t), \ldots, e_x(t - (p-1)\delta)}_{\text{ARX model state}}, \cdots, \underbrace{e_{v_z}(t), \ldots, e_{v_z}(t - (p-1)\delta)}_{\text{ARX model state}}.$$

Let F be a set of safe states x defined by constraints of the form $Px \leq q$ for a $l \times n$ matrix P and $l \times 1$ vector q. For a fixed parameter $\theta \in (0, 1)$, we define θ viability formally in terms of the plant model.

Definition 4 (θ-viable). *A state x is said to be θ-viable with respect to a plant model $\mathscr{P}$ and time $T = N\delta$ if an only if*

$$(\exists u(0), \ldots, u((N-1)\delta) \in \mathscr{U}^N) \ \mathbb{P}_{w(0) \sim \mathscr{D}, \ldots, w((N-1)\delta) \sim \mathscr{D}} (x(N\delta) \in F) \geq \theta. \qquad (3)$$

3.1 Sufficient Condition for θ-Viability

We will now present the derivation for a sufficient condition for θ viability given an initial state $x(0)$. For simplicity, we will assume that there is no uncertainty with respect to the initial state itself. However, such uncertainties can be easily modeled in our framework. Let $u(t)$ denote the control inputs at time $t \in \{0, \ldots, (N-1)\delta\}$, such that $u(t) \in \mathcal{U}$. Let $v_j : \begin{pmatrix} u(0) \\ \vdots \\ u((j-1)\delta) \end{pmatrix}$ for $j \geq 1$, be the vector that collects the control inputs over time points $t \in \{0, \delta, \ldots, (j-1)\delta\}$.

Let $\mathcal{V}_j$ be the set of admissible values of v_j. Finally, let $z_j : \begin{pmatrix} w(0) \\ \vdots \\ w((j-1)\delta) \end{pmatrix}$ collect the disturbance inputs over the time points $\{0, \delta, \ldots, (j-1)\delta\}$. We can calculate $x(N\delta)$ as follows:

$$x(N\delta) = A_N x(0) + B_N v_N + C_N z_N. \tag{4}$$

The matrix A_N is defined by the recurrence: $A_j = A A_{j-1}$, $j \geq 2$, with base case $A_1 = A$. B_N is defined by the recurrence $B_j = [A B_{j-1}\ B]$ for $j \geq 2$, with base case $B_1 = B$. Likewise, $C_j = [A C_{j-1}\ C]$ for $j \geq 2$, with base case $C_1 = C$.

Lemma 1. *Given A_N, B_N, C_N and the vectors v_j, z_j, as described above, for any initial state x_0 at time $t = 0$, $x(N\delta) = A_N x_0 + B_N v_N + C_N z_N$.*

Note: All proofs are provided in the extended version made available upon request.

Robust Disturbance Sets: Equation (3) involves checking an existentially quantified formula involving an integration over z_N. Such assertions are called *chance constraints*, and can be quite expensive to verify [26]. We perform a reduction of the chance constraints through a simple trick of replacing the integration with a *forall* quantifier by using a *robust disturbance set*.

Definition 5 (θ-robust set). *Let $z \sim \mathcal{D}$. A set Z_θ is said to be θ-robust for distribution $\mathcal{D}$ if $\mathbb{P}(z \in Z_\theta) \geq \theta$.*

In general, there are many possible choices of θ-robust sets, given the distribution of each disturbance input vector $w(t)$. For instance, if $w(t)$ is a normally distributed random variable $\mathcal{N}(0, \sigma^2 I_{n \times n})$ with mean 0 and co-variance matrix $\Sigma : \sigma^2 I_{n \times n}$, then the following hyper-spherical region is θ-robust:

$$Z_{\theta, \Sigma} = \{w \mid w^T \Sigma^{-1} w \leq \chi_n^2 (1 - \theta)\}, \tag{5}$$

wherein $\chi_n^2 (1 - \theta)$ represents the upper $(1 - \theta)$ quantile of the standard chi-squared distribution with n-degrees of freedom, whose value can be looked up from a table. Therefore, to derive a sufficient condition for checking θ-viability, we first select a θ-robust set Z_θ such that $\mathbb{P}(z_N \in Z_\theta) \geq \theta$. Next, we check the assertion:

$$(\exists v_N \in \mathscr{V}_N)\ (\forall z_N \in Z_\theta)\ x(N\delta) \in F \tag{6}$$

Lemma 2. *The condition in Eq. (6) implies the viability definition in Eq. (3).*

Therefore, once Z_θ is chosen, the computation reduces to checking (6). However, this involves a single quantifier alternation and thus, computational expensive. However, the structure of the plant model can be exploited as follows:

First, we note that the set of possible states $x(N\delta)$ in Eq. (4) is the sum of three individual components that can each be chosen independently of the others: (a) constant vector $A_N x(0)$ (no real choice here), (b) a vector of the form $B_N v_N$ indicating the contribution from the control strategy, and (c) a disturbance vector chosen from the set:

$$\hat{Z}:\ \{C_N z_N \mid z_N \in Z_\theta\} \tag{7}$$

Thus, the key observation is that the reachable set at time $N\delta$ is a *Minkowski sum* of three sets, as described above. We will now define the operation of *Minkowski difference* of two sets and directly use it to remove the quantifier alternation in Eq. (6).

Definition 6 (Minkowski Difference). *Let $A, B \subseteq \mathbb{R}^n$ be two subsets. The Minkowski difference $A \ominus B$ is defined as the set: $A \ominus B:\ \{a \mid (\forall\ b \in B)\ a + b \in A\}$.*

Therefore, returning to Eq. (6), we use the definition of $\hat{Z}$ from Eq. (7), and the notion of Minkowski difference to obtain an equivalent condition:

$$(\exists\ v_N \in \mathscr{V}_N) A_N x_0 + B_N v_N \in (F \ominus \hat{Z}) \tag{8}$$

Lemma 3. *The condition in Eq. (8) is equivalent to that in Eq. (6).*

Computing Minkowski Difference: It is essential to compute the Minkowski difference between a polyhedron F given by constraints $Px \leq q$ and a set $\hat{Z}$. We use the following properties to compute this difference efficiently for polyhedral sets.

Lemma 4. *Consider a family of sets A_j for $j = 1, \ldots, l$. $(\bigcap_{j=1}^{l} A_j) \ominus B = \bigcap_{j=1}^{l}(A_j \ominus B)$.*

Lemma 5. *Let A_j be a set denoted by a half-space $\{x \mid a_j \cdot x \geq b_j\}$ and B be a compact set. Let Δ_j be the result of the optimization problem $\min\ a_j \cdot x$ s.t. $x \in B$. The set $A_j \ominus B$ is the half-space $\hat{A}_j$ given by $\{x \mid a_j \cdot x \geq b_j - \Delta_j\}$.*

The lemma above provides us the ingredients for computing $F \ominus \hat{Z}$ for a polyhedron F given by the intersection of $l > 0$ half-spaces, and a set $\hat{Z}$. This involves solving optimization problems of the form $(\min\ a \cdot z$ s.t. $z \in \hat{Z})$. If $\hat{Z}$ is a convex set, then computing Δ can be performed efficiently using convex optimization solvers [4].

Lemma 6. *The Minkowski difference of a polyhedron* $F : Px \leq q$ *and a compact set* $\hat{Z}$ *is given by a polyhedron* $G : F \ominus \hat{Z}$ *of the form* $G : Px \leq q - \Delta$, *wherein* $\Delta_j : \min P_j x$ *s.t.* $x \in \hat{Z}$.

3.2 Overall Monitoring Algorithm

We will now present the overall monitoring algorithm as a combination of (a) upfront offline calculations, and (b) the real-time online monitor.

Offline Calculations: The offline calculations are performed given the plant model $\mathscr{P} : \langle A, B, C, \mathscr{U}, \mathscr{D} \rangle$ (Definition 3), and the safety property F as a convex polyhedron $Px \leq q$.

1. Compute matrices A_N, B_N and C_N using $\Theta(N)$ matrix multiplication operations.
2. Compute a θ-robust set Z_θ. Since the disturbance inputs are distributed normally, we use Eq. (5) to choose one Z_θ.
3. Compute the polyhedron for $F \ominus \hat{Z}$, wherein $\hat{Z} : \{C_N z \mid z \in Z_\theta\}$ using Lemma 6. Since Z_θ is a convex quadratic, this is technically a *quadratically constrained quadratic program* (QCQP).

Online Calculations: The results of the offline calculations include matrices (A_N, B_N) and the set $G : F \ominus \hat{Z}$. The online monitor receives the current state estimate x_0 and the current controller input u_0. Since $v_N = (u(0), u(\delta), \cdots, u((N-1)\delta))^T$. We will set $u(0) = u_0$ and let $u(\delta), \ldots, u((N-1)\delta)$ be unknown decision variables. The monitor checks the following constraint (Eq. (8)):

$$(\exists\ u(\delta) \in \mathscr{U}, \cdots, u((N-1)\delta) \in \mathscr{U})\ A_N x_0 + B_N \begin{pmatrix} u_0 \\ u(\delta) \\ \vdots \\ u((N-1)\delta) \end{pmatrix} \in G \quad (9)$$

Note that we can use a linear programming (LP) solver to check the condition above. If it is feasible, we conclude that the system is viable. Otherwise, we flag a potential violation of viability. Solving a LP can be performed efficiently in polynomial time [11] and real-time solvers have been pioneered for applications to model-predictive control [17]. However, as we will examine in the subsequent section, it is possible to efficiently monitor a single half-space of the geofence, while completely avoiding the LP solver.

4 Monitoring for Geofence Violations

In this section, we use the implementation of the monitoring approach from Sect. 3 for checking geofences for UAVs. A *geofence* is defined by a (disjoint union of) polyhedral regions over $\mathbb{R}^3$ that defines the possible (x, y, z) coordinates of an aircraft over time. Let F denote the polyhedral region. We will use a data-driven plant model $\mathscr{P}$ that is inferred from the telemetry data including positions and velocities over time, as described in Sect. 2. The data is updated with a small time period δ (0.4 s). We will choose a time horizon $N\delta$ (typically in the range 5–20 s). The monitoring approach uses the following improvements on top of the base algorithm from Sect. 3:

1. *Monitoring Single Half-spaces:* We show that the approach in Sect. 3 can be simplified considerably if we can monitor one half-space at a time. This is natural for geofencing applications, wherein the safety property represents a large geographical region.
2. *Receding horizon monitoring:* We deploy N monitors $\mathscr{M}_1, \ldots, \mathscr{M}_N$ in parallel wherein $\mathscr{M}_j$ monitors the viability for time $j\delta$ into the future.

Monitoring Single Half-Spaces: We will now derive an efficient monitor when the safety property F is defined by a single half-space: $F : \{x \mid c \cdot x \geq d\}$. We will also assume that $\mathscr{U}$, the bounds on the control inputs is a box with each control input $u_i \in [a_i, b_i]$. The restriction to a single half-space can be justified for geofence regions that are large enough so that if they are violated, the violation will occur by crossing a single hyperplane of the polyhedron rather than crossing the intersection of multiple regions simultaneously. We will now derive the monitoring conditions, following the same approach as in Sect. 3. However, we will do so for the special case when F is a single half-space.

Given $x(N\delta) = A_N x_0 + B_N v_N + C_N z_N$, we have $c \cdot x(N\delta) = (c^T A_N)x_0 + (c^T B_N)v_N + (c^T C_N)z_N$. Therefore, $c \cdot x(N\delta) \geq d$ if and only if there exists $v_N \in \mathscr{V}_N$ such that the following condition holds with probability at least θ:

$$(c^T A_N)x_0 + (c^T B_N)v_N + (c^T C_N)z_N \geq d \tag{10}$$

Note that the disturbance term $(c^T C_N)z_N$ is a scalar normal random variable with 0 mean and whose standard deviation can be computed as a weighted sum of the individual standard deviations of the component random variables. Therefore, let $[-M, M]$ represent an interval such that $\mathbb{P}((c^T C_N)z_N \in [-M, M]) \geq \theta$. In other words, we choose a θ-robust set, that is an interval. Therefore, a sufficient condition for Eq. (10) is as follows:

$$(\exists \, v_N \in \mathscr{V}_N) \, (c^T B_N)v_N \geq d + M - (c^T A_N)x_0 \tag{11}$$

v_N collects all the control inputs $u(0), \ldots, u((N-1)\delta)$. Thus, Eq. (11) is "expanded" as

$$(\exists u(\delta) \in \mathscr{U}, \ldots, u((N-1)\delta) \in \mathscr{U}) \sum_{j=0}^{N-1} \sum_{i=1}^{m} \hat{c}_{i,j} u_i(j\delta) \geq \hat{d}, \tag{12}$$

wherein $\hat{c}_{i,j}$ represents the component of $c^T B_N$ corresponding to the control input $u_i(j\delta)$ (the ith component of the control input at time $t = j\delta$) and $\hat{d} = d + M - (c^T A_N)x_0$. Note that the value of $u_i(0)$ is known, and for $j \geq 1$, $u_i(j\delta) \in [a_i, b_i]$. We define $\hat{u}_{i,j}$ as follows:

$$\hat{u}_{i,j} = \begin{cases} b_i & \text{if } \hat{c}_{i,j} \geq 0 \\ a_i & \text{if } \hat{c}_{i,j} < 0 \end{cases}$$

Lemma 7. *The condition* (12) *is satisfiable iff*

$$\sum_{j=1}^{N-1} \sum_{i=1}^{m} \hat{c}_{i,j} \hat{u}_{i,j} \geq \hat{d} - \sum_{i=1}^{m} \hat{c}_{i,0} u_i(0). \tag{13}$$

In other words, monitoring a single half-space can avoid using LP solvers, and instead, rely on efficient matrix vector multiplication operations.

Finding largest θ value for viability: Rather than fixing a value of θ and checking θ-viability, a simple modification to Eq. (11) allows us to find the largest value of θ for which viability can be guaranteed. To do so, we find a value of M which corresponds to the minimum possible disturbance that can continue to maintain viability. This is convenient since it allows us to compute a *risk measure* rather than a yes/no answer.

5   Evaluation

We now present a preliminary evaluation of the ideas presented, thus far, based on viability monitoring applied to telemetry data collected from a test flight of the Talon UAV running a Pixhawk autopilot [21,28]. The test flight was carried out over the Pawnee national grassland in the USA during summer 2017 and the data recorded included GPS positions, velocities and accelerations in x, y, z directions. Note that accelerations are treated as the control inputs to our model. The Talon UAV flight data includes about 4500 s of flight data with data collected at $\delta = 0.4$ s intervals. We dropped the first 800 s that consisted of take off followed by *loitering*. The subsequent 800 s of data were used as the training set for inferring a data-driven model. The estimated average wind speed was about 3 m/s. However, detailed wind data was not collected for these experiments.

Data-Driven Model:
We used regres-
sion to infer AR
models for cap-
turing the devia-
tions, as explained
in Sect. 2. The value
of the *lookback* (p)
was chosen to be
$p = 4$, so that
the overall stan-
dard deviation of
the residuals was
minimized. The com-
bined model has
30 state variables
that include the

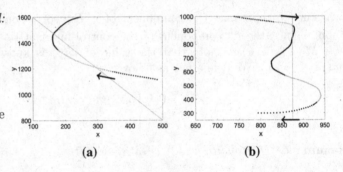

(a)   **(b)**

Fig. 2. Sample trajectory segments over time intervals (a) $[1600, 1680]$ s and (b) $[4000, 4080]$ s from start of flight test. Two geofence boundaries are shown as red lines. The monitor uses a time horizon $N = 15$ (6 s). Arrows denote the direction of the UAV's flight. Data points are shaded red if a violation results and blue/black depending on the magnitude of the viability probability $\theta(t)$. (Color figure online)

positions (x, y, z), velocities (v_x, v_y, v_z), and the AR model states for $e_x, e_y, e_z, e_{v_x}, e_{v_y}$, and e_{v_z}. The disturbances were taken to be normal random variable with mean and standard deviations estimated from the residual errors obtained after fitting the AR model. The mean values were very close to 0, lying in the range $[-0.05, 0.05]$ in all cases, and thus taken to be exactly zero. All calculations were performed in Matlab(tm) running on a macbook pro laptop with 3.1 GHz Intel Core i7 and 16 GB RAM. The time taken to perform regression was less than 0.05 s. The matrices A, B, C for the plant model are sparse and thus we use sparse matrix manipulations available in Matlab(tm).

To what extent can a viability monitor be used to flag safety violations? As mentioned earlier, viability and safety are rather different. On one hand, the UAV can violate the geofence without causing a failure of viability. This is because, there may always be a N step strategy to keep the violation from happening, whereas the actual controller is unable to implement this strategy. On the other, a loss of viability does not mean that safety will be violated. After all, the environment may not have manifested its worst case behavior. Model mismatch between the linear stochastic data-driven model and the underlying nonlinear model can potentially make the issue of missed violations and false alarms much worse. We will now perform an empirical evaluation of the viability monitor, focusing on its ability to predict an impending violation as well as the false alarm rate.

Figure 2 shows two example scenarios for a fixed geofence property shown, each corresponding to roughly 80 s of flying time taken from our data. We defined geofence boundaries and use our monitors with $N = 15$ to check for viability. Note that in both, the viability monitor is able to provide advance warning of an impending

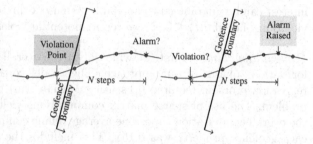

Fig. 3. (Left): For each violation point, is there an alarm raised N steps in the past for various values of N? **(Right):** For each alarm raised by the monitor, is there a violation of the geofence N steps into the future?

violation (shown using red circles). However, the viability monitor differs from a safety monitor: this is clearly seen at points that are shaded blue/black even though the UAV remains in violation of the geofence. This is because the monitor infers the existence of a strategy for the UAV to get back into the geofence within the time horizon.

Empirical Evaluation on Randomly Generated Geofence Specifications: The empirical evaluation is carried out over segments of the data past the initial 800 s of data used for training. We defined various randomly generated half-spaces $c_1 x + c_2 y + c_3 z \geq d$ as the geofences to be monitored. For each such geofence, we ran 30 monitors wherein the ith monitor has its time horizon of $N = i$. First, we define *violation points* for the geofence, wherein time t is said to be a violation point iff the position at time t violates the geofence whereas the position at the previous time step $t - \delta$ satisfies the geofence specification (see Fig. 3). We analyze our data in order to answer three questions **Q1–3**, with **Q1, Q2** focusing on missed alarms whereas **Q3** focusing on alarms that do not materialize in a violation.

1. **Q1:** How far ahead of a violation point do we obtain the earliest alarm corresponding to that point?
2. **Q2:** What fraction of the violation points are alarmed by monitor with lookahead time $N = i$ for various values of $i \in [1, 30]$?
3. **Q3:** If a monitor with lookahed of i, raises an alarm at time t, does the UAV position at $t + i\delta$ violate the geofence?

We studied 250 randomly generated geofence specifications and instantiated 30 monitors for each specification with time horizons ranging from 1–30. The offline calculations yield matrices $c^T A_N$, $c^T B_N$ and $c^T C_N$, wherein c represents the normal vector to the hyperplane describing the geofence. The online monitor uses the calculations presented in Sect. 4 using lower bounds and upper bounds on the accelerations. These were taken to be ± 2 m/s^2 for our calculations based on the acceleration inputs observed in the actual data. For each state $x(t)$ and control $u(t)$, we calculate $\theta(t)$ the largest value of θ for which the property of interest can be guaranteed to be viable. We use a threshold of 0.95 for reporting violations: i.e., if $\theta(t) \leq 0.95$, we report potential violations.

Computation Times: First, we will analyze the overall computation times taken for various phases of our approach. The model construction solving a linear regression problem required 0.1 s using Matlab (tm) to solve the least squares problem. The use of sparse matrix computations yielded significant savings in the overall computation time. The average offline computation time required for each geofence property was 0.15 s. This includes the offline computation time for all the 30 monitors that were instantiated corresponding to each geofence. Likewise, the average online computation time at each time instant was 0.09 s for all 30 monitors. Recalling that the monitors looked ahead between 1–30 steps with 0.4 s/step, these times are much smaller than the overall time horizon.

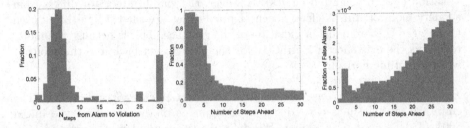

Fig. 4. (Left): Histogram showing the number of steps between a known violation event and the *earliest* alarm corresponding to the event using monitors with time horizon ranging from 1–30. 0 steps is used to indicate that all monitors deployed did not alarm for a given violation. **(Middle):** The fraction of violation points successfully predicted by a monitor looking ahead i steps for $i \in [1, 30]$. **(Right):** Fraction of false alarms for monitor looking ahead $N = i$ steps into the future for $i \in [1, 30]$. Notice that the y-axis numbers are scaled by 10^{-3}.

Analysis of Missed Violation Points: Figure 4 **(left)** plots the number of steps between a violation point and the *earliest* alarm corresponding to that violation. We use 0 steps to indicate that a violation point was missed by all monitors. We note that 99% of the violation points are detected at least 1 step (0.4 s ahead). In fact, nearly 98.5% of the violation points are detected 0.8 s ahead, while 65% of the violation points are detected more than 2 s ahead of time. At the other end, about 15% of the violation points are detected 12 s ahead of time. Interestingly, we note a strong correlation between violations that are predicted 15–29 steps in advance and those predicted 30 steps in advance. In other words, most violations that are predicted 15 steps in advance are also predicted 30 steps in advance.

Figure 4 **(middle)** focuses on individual monitors monitoring 1–30 steps ahead in the future and the fraction of violation points successfully predicted by each monitor. As expected, the monitors looking ahead less than 5 steps ($\leq 2s$) are successful more than 90% of the time in predicting violation points, whereas monitors 30 steps ahead predict less than 20% of the violation points. Overall, the analysis shows that using a bank of monitors in parallel wherein each monitor has a different lookahead time horizon can reduce the cumulative missed alarm rate to less than 1%. However, this also means that impending violations may be caught as early as 12 s in some cases, and as late as 0.4 s in advance in some cases with most alarms occuring between 2–4 s ahead of a violation.

Analysis for False Positives: Another key issue is that of false positives. To analyze for false positives, we focus on each alarm raised by the monitor that looks ahead $N = i$ steps into the future at time t and ask whether the UAV violates the geofence at time $t + i\delta$. Figure 4 **(right)** shows what fraction of the alarms do not result in corresponding violations i steps into the future. We note that the false positive rate is quite tiny: I.e., most alarms do result in violations.

6   Conclusions

To conclude, we present the notion of θ-viability and derive sufficient conditions for monitoring whether or not a linear system driven by stochastic disturbances is θ viable at its current state. We apply this to geofence monitoring of UAVs. Our experimental evaluation shows that the viability monitor can provide useful advance warnings 5–10 s before a violation. Our future work will investigate strategies for model validation and updating, which is not studied in this paper. We also plan to consider multi-modal approaches wherein different modes such as loitering, turning and waypoint following are modeled differently.

Acknowledgements. We are grateful to Drs. Jyotirmoy Deshmukh and Derek Kingston for valuable discussions. This work was funded in part by the US National Science Foundation (NSF) under award number 1815983, the US Airforce Research Laboratory and the NSF-IUCRC Center for Unmanned Aerial Systems (C-UAS). All ideas and opinions expressed here are those of the authors and do not necessarily represent those of NSF, AFRL or C-UAS.

References

1. Alshiekh, M., Bloem, R., Ehlers, R., Könighofer, B., Niekum, S., Topcu, U.: Safe reinforcement learning via shielding. In: Thirty-Second AAAI Conference on Artificial Intelligence (2018)
2. Althoff, M.: An introduction to CORA 2015. In: Proc. of the Workshop on Applied Verification for Continuous and Hybrid Systems, pp. 120–151 (2015)
3. BBC News: Heathrow airport: Drone sighting halts departures, bBC News 8 January 2019: Cf. https://www.bbc.com/news/uk-46803713
4. Boyd, S., Vandenberghe, S.: Convex Optimization. Cambridge University Press, Cambridge (2004)
5. Brockwell, P.J., Davis, R.A.: Time Series: Theory and Methods. Springer Series in Statistics, 2nd edn. Springer, New York (2009)
6. Chati, Y.S., Balakrishnan, H.: A gaussian process regression approach to model aircraft engine fuel flow rate. In: Proceedings of the 8th International Conference on Cyber-Physical Systems, ICCPS 2017, pp. 131–140 (2017)

7. Chen, X., Ábrahám, E., Sankaranarayanan, S.: Flow*: an analyzer for non-linear hybrid systems. In: Sharygina, N., Veith, H. (eds.) CAV 2013. LNCS, vol. 8044, pp. 258–263. Springer, Heidelberg (2013). https://doi.org/10.1007/978-3-642-39799-8_18

8. Chen, X., Sankaranarayanan, S.: Decomposed reachability analysis for nonlinear systems. In: 2016 IEEE Real-Time Systems Symposium (RTSS), pp. 13–24. IEEE Press, November 2016

9. Chen, X., Ábrahám, E., Sankaranarayanan, S.: Taylor model flowpipe construction for nonlinear hybrid systems. In: Proceedings RTSS 2012, pp. 183–192. IEEE (2012)

10. Chen, X., Sankaranarayanan, S.: Model-predictive real-time monitoring of linear systems. In: IEEE Real-Time Systems Symposium (RTSS), pp. 297–306. IEEE Press (2017)

11. Chvátal, V.: Linear Programming. Freeman (1983)

12. Duggirala, P.S., Potok, M., Mitra, S., Viswanathan, M.: C2E2: a tool for verifying annotated hybrid systems. In: Proceedings of the 18th International Conference on Hybrid Systems: Computation and Control, HSCC 2015, Seattle, WA, USA, 14–16 April 2015, pp. 307–308 (2015)

13. Hoerl, A.E., Kennard, R.W.: Ridge regression: biased estimation for nonorthogonal problems. Technometrics **12**(1), 55–67 (1970)

14. Johnson, T.T., Bak, S., Caccamo, M., Sha, L.: Real-time reachability for verified simplex design. ACM Trans. Embedd. Comput. Syst. **15**(2), 29 (2016)

15. Könighofer, B., et al.: Shield synthesis. Formal Methods Syst. Des. **51**(2), 332–361 (2017)

16. Lygeros, J., Prandini, M.: Aircraft and weather models for probabilistic collision avoidance in air traffic control. In: Proceedings of the 41st IEEE Conference on Decision and Control, 2002, vol, 3, pp. 2427–2432, December 2002

17. Mattingley, J., Wang, Y., Boyd, S.: Receding horizon control: automatic generation of high-speed solvers. IEEE Control Syst. Mag. **31**(3), 52–65 (2011)

18. McLeod, A.I., Li, W.K.: Diagnostic checking arma time series models using squared-residual autocorrelations. J. Time Series Anal. **4**(4), 1467–9892 (1983)

19. Moosbrugger, P., Rozier, K.Y., Schumann, J.: R2u2: monitoring and diagnosis of security threats for unmanned aerial systems. Formal Methods Syst. Des. **1**, 31–61 (2017)

20. Phan, D., Paoletti, N., Zhang, T., Grosu, R., Smolka, S.A., Stoller, S.D.: Neural state classification for hybrid systems. In: Lahiri, S.K., Wang, C. (eds.) ATVA 2018. LNCS, vol. 11138, pp. 422–440. Springer, Cham (2018). https://doi.org/10.1007/978-3-030-01090-4_25

21. Pixhawk: Independent open-hardware autopilot (2018), cf. pixhawk.org. Accessed October 2018

22. Prandini, M., Lygeros, J., Nilim, A., Sastry, S.: Randomized algorithms for probabilistic aircraft conflict detection. In: Proceedings of the IEEE Conference on Decision and Control, vol. 3, pp. 2444–2449, February 1999

23. Sha, L.: Using simplicity to control complexity. IEEE Softw. **18**(4), 20–28 (2001)

24. Stevens, M.N., Atkins, E.M.: Multi-mode guidance for an independent multicopter geofencing system. In: 16th AIAA Aviation Technology, Integration, and Operations Conference, p. 3150. AIAA (2016)

25. Stevens, M.N., Rastgoftar, H., Atkins, E.M.: Specification and evaluation of geofence boundary violation detection algorithms. In: International Conference on Unmanned Aircraft Systems (ICUAS), pp. 1588–1596. IEEE (2017)

26. Vinod, A.: Scalable Stochastic Reachability: Theory, Computation, and Control. Ph.D. thesis, University of New Mexico (2018)
27. Vinod, A.P., Gleason, J.D., Oishi, M.M.K.: SReachTools: A MATLAB Stochastic Reachability Toolbox, 16–18 April 2019. https://sreachtools.github.io
28. Watza, S.Z.: Assessment of an online RF propagation hybrid architecture for communication-aware small unmanned aircraft systems (2018)

Reactive Control Meets Runtime Verification: A Case Study of Navigation

Dogan Ulus[✉] and Calin Belta

Boston University, Boston, MA, USA
doganulus@gmail.com

Abstract. This paper presents an application of specification based runtime verification techniques to control mobile robots in a reactive manner. In our case study, we develop a layered control architecture where runtime monitors constructed from formal specifications are embedded into the navigation stack. We use temporal logic and regular expressions to describe safety requirements and mission specifications, respectively. An immediate benefit of our approach is that it leverages simple requirements and objectives of traditional control applications to more complex specifications in a non-intrusive and compositional way. Finally, we demonstrate a simulation of robots controlled by the proposed architecture and we discuss further extensions of our approach.

1 Introduction

Mobile robots are designed to work either in static and fully predictable environments such as automated warehouses or in open, partially unknown, and constantly changing environments. Classical deliberative control often works well for the former case while being inadequate or very inefficient for the latter. Alternatively, in reactive control approaches, robots continuously observe the environment at every level and thus are able to react and adapt to previously unknown circumstances. A common point between reactive control and runtime verification is that they both trade the completeness guarantees of deliberate control and model checking for online computation, practicality, and scalability. Following this synergy and growing interest in robotics using formal specifications, we think runtime verification techniques can raise the level of abstraction and assurance of reactive controllers in robotic applications.

In this paper, we explore the combination of reactive control and runtime verification techniques to construct controllers for mobile robots that satisfy given safety requirements and high-level mission specifications. To this end, we use a multi-layered architecture that can be seen in many reactive controllers and enhance each layer with runtime monitors[1] to search for desired behaviors on-the-fly. We depict our navigation architecture that contains several components from reactive control and runtime verification domains in Fig. 1. At the

---

[1] https://github.com/doganulus/python-monitors.

© Springer Nature Switzerland AG 2019
B. Finkbeiner and L. Mariani (Eds.): RV 2019, LNCS 11757, pp. 368–374, 2019.
https://doi.org/10.1007/978-3-030-32079-9_21

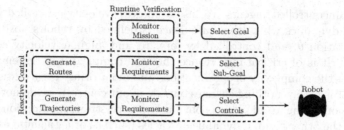

Fig. 1. The navigation stack used in the case study

bottom layer of the architecture, we employ limited trajectory search to devise the short-time motion of the robot. Runtime monitors are embedded to find trajectories that satisfy low-level safety properties such as collision avoidance and one-way regulations. The middle layer addresses the shortcomings of short-horizon trajectories by searching for a route over a connectivity graph of the environment. Mid-level safety properties for the graph traversal (e.g. avoiding specific areas) are similarly checked using runtime monitors in this layer. Once undesired trajectories and routes are filtered out, we use a number of features and heuristics to select the best one among the remaining. Repeating these procedures in real-time produces a safe motion for the robot to reach a specific (goal) location relative to trajectory/route generation specifics. Finally, the top layer is designated for high-level mission control that enforces the correct order of locations to be visited and we similarly employ runtime monitors constructed from mission specifications for the mission control.

2   Environment, Robots, and Specifications

For our case study, we will work on a relatively complex 2D environment designed to give a representative view of real challenges without introducing too much detail. Depicted on the left of Fig. 2, our environment represents an office space with rooms (R1–R6), narrow passages (such as doors D1–D6), named locations (A–D), and some regulations at certain regions (one-way regions) including other

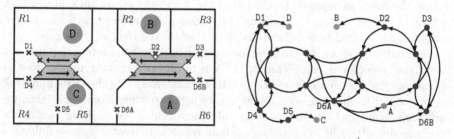

Fig. 2. Environment maps: Geometric on the left and topological on the right

(possibly uncontrolled) agents. We use a unicycle velocity-controlled model for the robot dynamics where the state space is defined by robot's position (x, y) and orientation θ, and controlled by forward and angular velocity commands $u = (v, \omega)$. It is of critical importance that the complexity of the environment determines the complexity of specifications and monitoring. For a static environment (that is to say, nothing changes outside of our control), we do not need any runtime monitoring at all. This is obviously a very strong assumption for many cases. On the other hand, if dynamic obstacles (such as other agents) exist in the environment, we have to at least add a basic monitoring mechanism that checks simple propositions—will the robot collide with anything soon or did the robot reach its goal? Moreover, if we have more complex regulations and tasks to complete in the environment, runtime monitors automatically constructed from rich specification languages seem a preferable option. Therefore, our robots in this study are assigned to perform complex navigation missions, specified by regular expressions, while avoiding static and dynamic obstacles as well as satisfying desired properties and regulations, specified by temporal logic formulas.

3   Search for Safe Motion

We here demonstrate an application of runtime monitors in searching for the desired safe behavior enhancing existing trajectory and route search algorithms. The general procedure can be summarized in three steps: (1) Generating a number of alternative behaviors (trajectories or routes), (2) discarding unsafe/undesired behaviors using runtime monitors, and (3) selecting the best remaining (thus safe) behaviors according to a predefined set of heuristics. Importantly, the extent of these search processes is limited due to available computational resources as well as that long-term complete plans may become invalid very quickly in dynamic and uncertain environments. In the following, we give more details about search procedures and actual properties used in the case study.

Trajectory Search. Dynamic Window Approach (DWA) [3] is a well-known collision avoidance and local motion planning algorithm that uses search procedures to find control actions (velocity commands) while considering robot's dynamics. The search space of DWA is limited by maximum acceleration available to the robot as depicted on the left of Fig. 3 and the algorithm samples a set of control actions. Then it calculates the future trajectories of each alternative action over a limited time horizon as illustrated on the right of the figure.

Originally being a collision avoidance algorithm, the only safety requirement over these trajectories considered in DWA is never getting dangerously close to obstacles, which is usually hard-coded into the algorithm. On the other hand, we are interested in checking such requirements using runtime monitors so that we can extend the approach for any temporal logic formula. We start our case study by expressing the collision avoidance requirement in temporal logic as follows.

$$\texttt{never(dangerously\_close(obstacles))} \hspace{2cm} \text{(CA)}$$

where `dangerously_close` is a predicate that computes whether any intersection occurs between obstacles and robot's footprint.

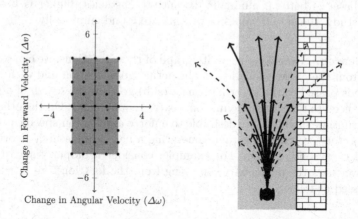

Fig. 3. (Left) A finite set of admissible velocity commands for the next time step relative to the current velocity. The search space, depicted in gray, is constrained by maximum allowed accelerations of the robot. (Right) Future trajectories of the robot simulated for each admissible velocity command. Dashed trajectories contain a violation in specification so commands that lead to these trajectories are discarded.

In this case study, besides collision avoidance, we also want our robot to obey one-way regulations of the environment, which state that robots have to move in a single direction inside certain regions. The direction of one-way regions is either west or east in our environment. We call these regions westways and eastways accordingly and predicates `inside_westway` and `inside_eastway` check whether the robot is in these regions. Moreover, we define some auxiliary formulas to detect whether the robot just entered a one-way region such that

```
entered_eastway : inside_eastway and not previously inside_eastway
entered_westway : inside_westway and not previously inside_westway
```

The desired direction in a one-way region is checked by predicates `going_east` and `going_west` and we write our safety properties for each type of one-way regions as follows:

$$\texttt{inside\_eastway implies (going\_east since entered\_eastway)} \qquad \text{(OW-E)}$$
$$\texttt{inside\_westway implies (going\_west since entered\_westway)} \qquad \text{(OW-W)}$$

Finally, we construct our runtime monitor to check the conjunction of (CA), (OW-E), and (OW-W) requirements over generated trajectories. Control actions that produce violating trajectories are discarded before the selection phase. This ensures the safety of selected control action if there exists one in alternatives otherwise we apply a full brake. The last piece of trajectory search is to select the best one among safe trajectories according to a weighted sum of some predefined heuristics, namely final speed of the trajectory (higher is better), final-distance-to-goal (lower is better), minimum-distance-to-obstacles (higher is better). In the case study, the actual values of weights are found empirically.

Route Search. Given a connectivity graph of these locations, we can search for a route from the current location to the actual goal location and each node on the route is passed to the lower layer as a (sub) goal. In the search of a suitable route, we need to take into account some extra requirements. On the other hand, external runtime monitors are desirable to enforce application-specific properties as in trajectory search rather than generating a new graph search algorithm for each and every one of them. For example, consider a property such that the robot never uses the door D6A when going from the location D to A, which can be expressed as follows.

$$\text{(visit(A) \&\& once visit(D)) -> (!visit(D6A) since visit(D))} \quad \text{(ND)}$$

We then construct a runtime monitor from the property (ND) to check routes generated over the graph. In particular, we use an off-the-shelf implementation of the shortest path algorithm [8] that generates simple paths starting from the shortest one. Sequentially checking these paths using runtime monitors constructed from temporal logic formulas [4,6] ensures that the we select the shortest route that satisfies specified properties and then we can update the route of the robot accordingly.

4   Navigate by Regular Expressions

In this section, we use regular expressions to specify complex navigation missions and guide the mission execution via runtime monitors constructed from the specification. Navigation missions describe the desired behavior of the robot over a set of observations and regular operations of sequential composition (;), alternative choice (|), and repetition (*) are used to express the ordering between these observations. For example, a robot is said to reach a region A when it was outside for a while and then entered the region A. We can specify such a behavior using regular expressions as follows:

$$\text{reach(A) = (outside(A))*; inside(A)}$$

where atomic propositions inside(A) and outside(A) check whether the robot is in the region A or not. Similarly more complex missions are obtained by composing simple missions as below.

$$\text{mission1 : (reach(C); reach(B)|reach(D); reach(A))*} \quad \text{(M1)}$$

which specifies a (robot) behavior to repeatedly visit the regions A, and C while visiting B or D in-between. From this expression, we construct a runtime monitor [7] that associates a Boolean state variable for each proposition and updates them according to previous states and robot's position at each time step. The next sub-goal of the robot is determined according to the state vector of the monitor.

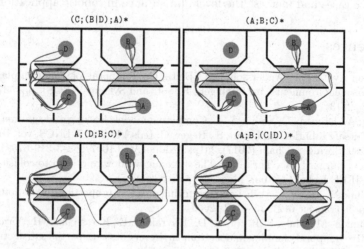

Fig. 4. Trajectories of robots G1–G4 assigned with missions M1–M4, respectively. (Color figure online)

Finally we present our simulation results of four robots G1–G4 operated in the same environment and controlled by the proposed architecture. We assign the first robot G1 with the mission M1 and the rest G2–G4 with missions M2–M4 below, respectively.

$$\text{mission2} : \; (\text{reach}(A); \; \text{reach}(B); \; \text{reach}(C))* \qquad (M2)$$

$$\text{mission3} : \; (\text{reach}(A); \; (\text{reach}(D); \; \text{reach}(B); \; \text{reach}(C))* \qquad (M3)$$

$$\text{mission4} : \; (\text{reach}(A); \; \text{reach}(B); \; (\text{reach}(C)|\text{reach}(D))* \qquad (M4)$$

In Fig. 4, we separately show the simulated trajectories of the robot for a certain duration that covers several loops as specified in the mission. The initial position of the robot is marked by a yellow star. Robots get close to each other quite frequently and evading maneuvers cause small variations among loops seen in the figure. Overall we see that the robots successfully avoid each other and static obstacles and obey regulations of the environment while performing their formally-specified missions over achieving reasonable trajectories.

5   Conclusion

We presented an example and novel use of provably correct runtime monitors to control a mobile robot subject to complex safety requirements and mission specifications in a dynamic environment. We embedded runtime monitors into a layered reactive control architecture together with other simple and scalable components to achieve a navigation solution that does not require strong assumptions. Our approach amounts to a more active use of runtime monitors beyond checking assumptions of an offline motion planner at runtime [1,2,5]. We believe the simplicity and breadth of runtime monitors would make them ideal to cover many use cases and increase the level of assurance in robotic applications.

References

1. Medina Ayala, A.I., Andersson, S.B., Belta, C.: Temporal logic motion planning in unknown environments. In: Intelligent Robots and Systems (IROS), pp. 5279–5284. IEEE (2013)
2. Desai, A., Dreossi, T., Seshia, S.A.: Combining model checking and runtime verification for safe robotics. In: Lahiri, S., Reger, G. (eds.) RV 2017. LNCS, vol. 10548, pp. 172–189. Springer, Cham (2017). https://doi.org/10.1007/978-3-319-67531-2_11
3. Fox, D., Burgard, W., Thrun, S.: The dynamic window approach to collision avoidance. IEEE Robot. Autom. Mag. **4**(1), 23–33 (1997)
4. Havelund, K., Rosu, G.: Efficient monitoring of safety properties. Int. J. Softw. Tools Technol. Transfer **6**(2), 158–173 (2004)
5. Lahijanian, M., Maly, M.R., Fried, D., Kavraki, L.E., Kress-Gazit, H., Vardi, M.Y.: Iterative temporal planning in uncertain environments with partial satisfaction guarantees. IEEE Trans. Rob. **32**(3), 583–599 (2016)
6. Ulus, D.: Online monitoring of metric temporal logic using sequential networks. arXiv preprint arXiv:1901.00175 (2019)
7. Ulus, D.: Sequential circuits from regular expressions revisited. arXiv preprint arXiv:1801.08979 (2018)
8. Yen, J.Y.: Finding the k shortest loopless paths in a network. Manage. Sci. **17**(11), 712–716 (1971)

Overhead-Aware Deployment of Runtime Monitors

Teng Zhang[1(✉)], Greg Eakman[2], Insup Lee[1], and Oleg Sokolsky[1]

[1] University of Pennsylvania, Philadelphia, PA 19104, USA
{tengz,lee,sokolsky}@cis.upenn.edu
[2] BAE Systems, Burlington, MA 01803, USA
gregory.eakman@baesystems.com

Abstract. One important issue needed to be handled when applying runtime verification is the time overhead introduced by online monitors. According to how monitors are deployed with the system to be monitored, the overhead may come from the execution of monitoring logic or asynchronous communication. In this paper, we present a method for deciding how to deploy runtime monitors with awareness of minimizing the overhead. We first propose a parametric model to estimate the overhead given the prior knowledge on the distribution of incoming events and the time cost of sending a message and executing monitoring logic. Then, we will discuss how to statically decide the boundary of synchronous and asynchronous monitors such that the lowest overhead can be obtained.

Keywords: Runtime verification · Monitor deployment · Overhead

1 Introduction

Runtime verification (RV) has been widely used to check properties of software systems. The time overhead brought by online monitors may influence the performance of the system to be monitored (denoted as the target system). Multiple factors can influence the overhead such as event sampling rate [6] or monitoring algorithm [8]. Deployment of monitors may also have impact on the overhead [5]. According to how to interact with the target system, monitors can be deployed synchronously or asynchronously with the target system. If multiple monitors are involved, they can be deployed in a hybrid way. A generally accepted assumption is that synchronous monitoring can detect the violation timely while asynchronous monitoring can incur less overhead [4]. In the real world, however, finding the deployment to achieve the least overhead is undecidable. Nevertheless, if the termination of monitors to handle each event is guaranteed and prior knowledge about the distribution of incoming events is available, it is possible to estimate the time overhead statically.

This paper presents an initial study on deciding deployment of monitors to reduce the overhead. More specifically, we propose a model to estimate the time

© Springer Nature Switzerland AG 2019
B. Finkbeiner and L. Mariani (Eds.): RV 2019, LNCS 11757, pp. 375–381, 2019.
https://doi.org/10.1007/978-3-030-32079-9_22

overhead of SMEDL [12] monitors, parameterized by the distribution of incoming events, the execution time of sending a message and making a transition. Then, by analyzing the structure of monitors given the knowledge about the incoming event stream, we will present a way to decide the boundary of synchronous and asynchronous monitors to obtain the lowest overhead.

Related Work. There are multiple approaches to reduce monitoring overhead. Considerable number of studies focus on event sampling [1,3,6,7,9]. In [8], efficient monitoring algorithms are proposed to reduce the overhead. By contrast, we are concerned with the overhead of event propagation. The RV framework in [5] supports tuning of deployments but does not offer a quantitative method. In [4], a hybrid instrumentation technique to dynamically switch between synchronous and asynchronous monitoring. The goal is to reduce the overhead by minimizing the synchronous instrumentation while ensuring timely detections. In their approach, synchronous monitoring is built upon the asynchronous communication and always has higher overhead. By contrast, we decide the deployment statically based on quantitative overhead model.

2   Preliminaries

This section briefly introduces the syntax and semantics of SMEDL. A SMEDL specification contains a set of monitor specifications and an architecture description that captures patterns of communication between them. During execution, each monitor can be instantiated statically during system startup. Specified in the architecture description, monitors can be deployed synchronously or asynchronously with the target system.

Single Monitor. A SMEDL monitor is a collection of EFSMs (Extended Finite State Machines) in which the transitions are performed by reacting to events sent from the environment, other monitors or raised within the monitor. EFSMs interact with each other using shared state variables or by triggering execution of other EFSMs through raised events. Each transition is triggered by an event and attached to a guard condition and a list of actions to be executed after the transition. Actions of transitions include raising events and updating state variables. Primitive data types, arithmetic and logical operations are supported in SMEDL. The reader can refer to [13] for detailed description and formal semantics.

Monitor Network. The target system and monitors interact with each other using events. Communication pattern of events among monitors is specified in the architecture description. For instance, Fig. 1(a) illustrates event connection between the target system and three monitors M_1, M_2 and M_3. During runtime, multiple instances are created with different identities as shown in Fig. 1(b). The architecture description specifies how events raised by a monitor instance are sent to specific instances of another monitor. For instance, when e_4 is sent from M_1 to M_2 as e_5, the first identity of $M_1(\text{x})$ must be equal to the identity of $M_2(\text{z})$. In Fig. 1(b), we can observe that instance $M_1(1,1)$ and $M_1(1,2)$

connect to $M_2(1)$ while $M_1(2,1)$ connects to $M_2(2)$, which is complying with the static specification. SMEDL supports specifying deployment form of monitors. As shown in Fig. 1(a), M_1 is deployed synchronously with the target system while M_2 and M_3 are asynchronous monitors. Event connection specification is independent of deployment form but the communication is decided by how they are deployed. The synchronous monitors interact with the target system by direct API calls while asynchronous communication can be implemented using communication middleware such as RabbitMQ [10].

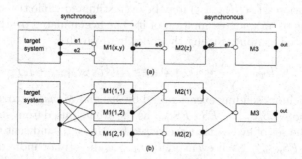

Fig. 1. An example of connections between monitors and the target system

3 Estimation and Comparison of Monitoring Overhead

Notation. The types of events generated by the target system sys is a set $ES = \{e_1, e_2, ..., e_k\}$. The event stream raised by sys and its corresponding length are respectively denoted as S and n. $Mons$ is the set of monitors in the monitor network. $Mons_{sync}$ and $Mons_{async}$ are respectively the subsets of monitors which are deployed synchronously and asynchronously with sys. Asynchronous monitors can receive events from synchronous monitors or the target system, but not vice versa. The accumulated overhead of the system is denoted as $OH(n)$, which is the sum of the overhead brought by the synchronous ($OH_{sync}(n)$) and the asynchronous part ($OH_{async}(n)$).

Assumptions. The time for sending an event asynchronously and making a transition, respectively denoted as t_m and t_s, can be accurately measured or estimated. Note that t_s includes time to make transition and executing actions in the transition. Actions are arithmetic/logical operations, raising and sending events to other synchronous monitors. For simplicity of analysis, we assume that transitions take approximately the same time to execute actions. It is straightforward to relax it by estimating execution time for each transition and aggregating them. The prior knowledge about the distribution of incoming events in S is also assumed to be available and simplified as the normalized frequency of appearance in S for all events in ES, denoted as $f_{e_1}, ... f_{e_2}, ..., f_{e_k}$ where $\Sigma_{e \in ES} f_e = 1$. This assumption is realistic in systems sending different types of events in a regular rate and enough data can be collected to estimate the distribution.

Overhead Model. Overhead for synchronous monitors come from execution of transitions. The set of external events to be consumed by $Mons_{sync}$ is denoted as $ES_{sync} = \{e_{s_1}, e_{s_2}, ..., e_{s_i}\}$, which is a subset of ES. Each event e in ES_{sync} may directly or indirectly trigger transitions in $Mons_{sync}$. The corresponding overhead is $t_s * tr_{(e, Mons_{sync})} * f_e$. The denotation $tr_{(e, MS)}$ represents the number of transitions triggered by e in the monitor set MS, which can be estimated by static analysis. However, the transitions triggered by an event depend on the dynamic state of the monitors and parameter values carried by the event so we do not know which transitions will be executed statically. If we choose the largest possible transition set, $OH_{sync}(n)$ may be overestimated while the smallest transition set leads to an underestimation of it. The accumulated overhead brought by S can then be computed using the following formulae:

$$OH_{sync}(n) = n * t_s * \Sigma_{e \in ES_{sync}}(tr_{(e, Mons_{sync})} * f_e)$$

$OH_{async}(n)$ includes sending events raised by sys and $Mons_{sync}$ to asynchronous monitors. Denote $ES_{async} = ES - ES_{sync}$ as the events raised from sys and sent to $Mons_{async}$. The set of events that are raised by $Mons_{sync}$ and sent to $Mons_{async}$ is denoted as ES_{raised}. Each event in ES_{raised} is directly or indirectly triggered by one or multiple events in ES_{sync}. We use $g_{(e', e)}$ to denote the number of instances of e generated by each instance of e'. $OH_{async}(n)$ can be computed using the following formula:

$$OH_{async}(n) = n * t_m * (\Sigma_{e \in ES_{async}} f_e + \Sigma_{e \in ES_{raised} \wedge e' \in ES_{sync}} f_{e'} * g_{(e', e)})$$

Note that to estimate the value of g and tr, we assume that all event instances of the same type are dispatched to the same monitor instances regardless of their parameter values. Furthermore, n will be ignored in the rest of the paper as both formula are the linear function of n.

Determine the Deployment. The SMEDL monitor network can be modeled as a direct acyclic graph (DAG) where nodes are the target system and monitors and edges are event connections. All instances of the same monitor are treated as one node in DAG. M is a direct upstream monitor to M' when M sends events to M' and M' is the direct downstream monitor of M. In this paper, we consider a simpler case in which the monitor network is a chain of monitors, which means each monitor in $Mons$ only has one direct upstream and downstream monitor and only one monitor directly receives events from the target system. Algorithm 1 computes $Mons_{sync}$, the set of monitors to be deployed synchronously. While traversing the monitor chain ($MonsChain$) and the current monitor is mon, the overall overhead OH_{cur} including mon as the synchronous monitor is computed (Line 4 to Line 9). If it is smaller than the least overhead seen so far (denoted as OH_{min}), mon and all pending monitors in $Temp_{sync}$ are added to $Mons_{sync}$ (Line 11 to Line 14). Otherwise, add mon to $Temp_{sync}$. Note that the set of input events of mon is the set of output events of its direct upstream monitor. As a result, f_e can be computed for every e in the set of output events since values of all f'_e are already available.

Algorithm 1. Determination of synchronous monitors

```
1: Mons_sync ← ∅, Temp_sync ← ∅, OH_min ← t_m, OH_async ← t_m, OH_cur ← t_m
2: while MonsChain ≠ ∅ do
3:     mon ← dequeue(MonsChain)
4:     Ev ← inputEvents(mon)
5:     tempOH_sync ← t_s * Σ_{e'∈Ev}(tr_{(e',{mon})} * f_{e'})
6:     for e ∈ outputEvents(mon) do
7:         f_e ← Σ_{e'∈Ev} f'_e * g_{(e',e)}
8:     tempOH_async ← t_m * Σ_{e∈outputEvents(mon)} f_e
9:     OH_cur ← OH_cur + tempOH_async + tempOH_sync - OH_async
10:    OH_async ← tempOH_async
11:    if OH_min > OH_cur then
12:        Mons_sync ← Mons_sync ∪ {mon} ∪ Temp_sync
13:        Temp_sync ← ∅
14:        OH_min ← OH_cur
15:    else
16:        Temp_sync ← Temp_sync ∪ {mon}
    return Mons_sync
```

To summarize, the method includes the following steps: (1) measure t_m and t_s on the actual platform for executing the target system and monitors; (2) estimate frequencies f_{e_i} of events raised by the system (3) for each monitor $m \in Mons$ with the set EI_m and EO_m of input and output events, compute $g_{(e',e)}$ and $tr_{(e',\{m\})}$ where $e' \in EI_m$ and $e \in EO_m$; (4) compute $Mons_{sync}$ using Algorithm 1.

4   Case Study

We present two examples to illustrate the use of method presented above. Both examples use a tracking application which receives sensor data of tracks. The experiments were conducted on a virtual machine of Ubuntu 18.04 64-bit run on a laptop with 2.5 GHz Intel i7 processor and 16 GB RAM. The first case study is a single monitor *checkFormat* which takes the input messages collected from the sensor. For each input event, one transition is taken to check whether the format complies with certain protocol. Only fully asynchronous and synchronous deployments need to be considered. The synchronous deployment has less overhead if $t_m/t_s > \Sigma_{e \in ES}(tr_{(e,\{checkFormat\})} * f_e)$. In this example, the right-hand side is equal to 1 and t_m/t_s is around 16. The testing results validate the estimate: the overhead of synchronous monitor is less than 5% while the overhead of the asynchronous monitor is about 20%.

The second example is the track quality monitors [11]. The monitors check output track quality of the tracking application by computing average duration over a sliding window time interval. There are two types of events generated from the target system, *track* which forms the track and *detection* which is used to generate *heartbeat* event as the boundary of the sliding window. The structure of

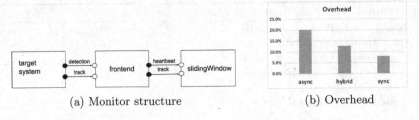

(a) Monitor structure   (b) Overhead

Fig. 2. Track quality monitor and the overhead for 10000 detection events

the monitor is illustrated in Fig. 2(a). We assume that both *frontend* and *sliding-Window* have one instance. This monitor has three possible deployments: fully synchronous, fully asynchronous, and hybrid, where only *frontend* is deployed synchronously.

Suppose the size of sliding window is 1000 ms and the time gap between each *detection* event is about 10 ms, then $g_{(detection,heartbeat)}$ is $1/100$. The input event stream has the identical number of *track* and *detection* events so $f_{detection}$ and f_{track} are equal to $1/2$. The overhead of fully asynchronous monitoring is t_m. According to Algorithm 1, we first compute the overhead when *frontend* is synchronously deployed. Each *detection* and *track* event trigger one transition in the *frontend* monitor so $tr_{(detection,\{frontend\})}$ and $tr_{(track,\{frontend\})}$ are equal to 1. Moreover, *frontend* immediately resends the *track* event. Consequently, the overhead is $t_s * (1/2 + 1/2) + t_m * (1/2 + 1/2 * 1/100) = t_s + 0.505 * t_m$. We can deduce that if $t_m/t_s > 200/99$, *frontend* should be deployed synchronously. Recall that t_m is 15 times greater than t_s. Figure 2(b) illustrates that the overhead of hybrid deployment is less than asynchronous deployment, which is consistent with the model.

5   Future Work

In this paper, we proposed a model to estimate the overhead of monitors statically given the prior knowledge of frequency among different type of events and the static structure of the monitor specification. We give an intuitive method to decide the deployment of chains of monitors. Although the model is specific to SMEDL monitors, it can also be used in other automata-based RV techniques. Moreover, the idea of trade-off between synchronous and asynchronous monitoring is not unique to specific formalisms and one future work would be the generalization of the model and algorithm to other formalisms for monitoring logics. For example, the model for rule-based monitors such as Eagle [2] can be expressed in terms of the number of rule firings rather than transitions.

Avenues of on-going work include: (1) more experiments on multiple applications to yield conclusive results for validation of the model; (2) monitor analysis to estimate the number of transitions triggered by each input event; and (3) for dynamic instantiation of monitors, we will extend the model to account for instantiation overhead. Finally, we will invest in a more accurate overhead measurement infrastructure. Currently, for computationally intensive systems, overhead calculation is often noisy, making it hard to validate predictions of our model when differences between deployments are small, as in the case with hybrid vs. synchronous deployment in the second example above.

References

1. Arnold, M., Vechev, M., Yahav, E.: QVM: an efficient runtime for detecting defects in deployed systems. ACM SIGPLAN Not. **43**(10), 143–162 (2008)
2. Barringer, H., Goldberg, A., Havelund, K., Sen, K.: Program monitoring with LTL in EAGLE. In: 18th International Parallel and Distributed Processing Symposium (IPDPS), April 2004. https://doi.org/10.1109/IPDPS.2004.1303336
3. Bonakdarpour, B., Navabpour, S., Fischmeister, S.: Sampling-based runtime verification. In: Butler, M., Schulte, W. (eds.) FM 2011. LNCS, vol. 6664, pp. 88–102. Springer, Heidelberg (2011). https://doi.org/10.1007/978-3-642-21437-0_9
4. Cassar, I., Francalanza, A.: On synchronous and asynchronous monitor instrumentation for actor-based systems. arXiv preprint: arXiv:1502.03514 (2015)
5. Colombo, C., Francalanza, A., Mizzi, R., Pace, G.J.: polyLARVA: runtime verification with configurable resource-aware monitoring boundaries. In: Eleftherakis, G., Hinchey, M., Holcombe, M. (eds.) SEFM 2012. LNCS, vol. 7504, pp. 218–232. Springer, Heidelberg (2012). https://doi.org/10.1007/978-3-642-33826-7_15
6. Fei, L., Midkiff, S.P.: Artemis: practical runtime monitoring of applications for execution anomalies. ACM SIGPLAN Not. **41**, 84–95 (2006)
7. Huang, X., et al.: Software monitoring with controllable overhead. Int. J. Softw. Tools Technol. Transf. **14**(3), 327–347 (2012)
8. Meredith, P.O., Jin, D., Griffith, D., Chen, F., Roşu, G.: An overview of the MOP runtime verification framework. Int. J. Softw. Tools Technol. Transf. **14**(3), 249–289 (2012)
9. Stoller, S.D., et al.: Runtime verification with state estimation. In: Khurshid, S., Sen, K. (eds.) RV 2011. LNCS, vol. 7186, pp. 193–207. Springer, Heidelberg (2012). https://doi.org/10.1007/978-3-642-29860-8_15
10. Videla, A., Williams, J.J.: RabbitMQ in Action: Distributed Messaging for Everyone. Manning (2012)
11. Zhang, T., Eakman, G., Lee, I., Sokolsky, O.: Flexible monitor deployment for runtime verification of large scale software. In: Margaria, T., Steffen, B. (eds.) ISoLA 2018, Part IV. LNCS, vol. 11247, pp. 42–50. Springer, Cham (2018). https://doi.org/10.1007/978-3-030-03427-6_6
12. Zhang, T., Gebhard, P., Sokolsky, O.: SMEDL: combining synchronous and asynchronous monitoring. In: Falcone, Y., Sánchez, C. (eds.) RV 2016. LNCS, vol. 10012, pp. 482–490. Springer, Cham (2016). https://doi.org/10.1007/978-3-319-46982-9_32
13. Zhang, T., et al.: Correct-by-construction implementation of runtime monitors using stepwise refinement. In: Feng, X., Müller-Olm, M., Yang, Z. (eds.) SETTA 2018. LNCS, vol. 10998, pp. 31–49. Springer, Cham (2018). https://doi.org/10.1007/978-3-319-99933-3_3

NuRV: A NuXmv Extension for Runtime Verification

Alessandro Cimatti, Chun Tian[⊠][iD], and Stefano Tonetta

Fondazione Bruno Kessler, Trento, Italy
{cimatti,ctian,tonettas}@fbk.eu

Abstract. We present NuRV, an extension of the NuXmv model checker for assumption-based LTL runtime verification with partial observability and resets. The tool provides some new commands for online/offline monitoring and code generations into standalone monitor code. Using the online/offline monitor, LTL properties can be verified incrementally on finite traces from the system under scrutiny. The code generation currently supports C, C++, Common Lisp and Java, and is extensible. Furthermore, from the same internal monitor automaton, the monitor can be generated into SMV modules, whose characteristics can be verified by Model Checking using NuXmv. We show the architecture, functionalities and some use scenarios of NuRV, and we compare the performance of generated monitor code (in Java) with those generated by a similar tool, RV-Monitor. We show that, using a benchmark from Dwyer's LTL patterns, besides the capacity of generating monitors for long LTL formulae, our Java-based monitors are about 200x faster than RV-Monitor at generation-time and 2–5x faster at runtime.

1 Introduction

Symbolic Model Checking [16] is a powerful formal verification technique for proving temporal properties of transition systems (a.k.a. models) represented by logical formulae. In the case of Linear Temporal Logic (LTL) [15], the properties can be translated into symbolically represented ω-automata, which is then conjoined with the model and proved by search-based techniques that exhaustively analyze the infinite traces of the system [7]. Runtime Verification (RV) [10,13] on the other hand, is a lightweight verification technique for checking if a given property is satisfied (or violated) on a finite trace of the system under scrutiny (SUS). In general, LTL-based RV problems can be resolved by automata-based [1], rewriting-based [17], or rule-based [11] approaches.

In this paper, we present a new tool called NuRV, an extension of the NuXmv [4] model checker for LTL-based RV. To the best of our knowledge, this is the first time that a model checker is directly modified (or extended) into a runtime monitor (or monitor generator). It is natural to do so, as NuXmv has

This work has received funding from European Union's *Horizon 2020* research and innovation programme under the Grant Agreement No. 700665 (Project *CITADEL*).

B. Finkbeiner and L. Mariani (Eds.): RV 2019, LNCS 11757, pp. 382–392, 2019.
https://doi.org/10.1007/978-3-030-32079-9_23

already provided the needed infrastructure, such as a symbolic translation from LTL to ω-automata, an algorithm for computing the "fair states" (those leading to infinite paths), together with an interface to BDD library [3] based on CUDD 2.4.1 [18].

For the monitoring algorithm implemented in NuRV (c.f. [6] for more details), our start point is the automata-based approach [1] based on LTL_3, implemented *symbolically*. Suppose the monitoring property is φ, we first run the LTL translations twice, on φ and $\neg\varphi$, to get two symbolic automata T_φ and $T_{\neg\varphi}$, resp. Then an input trace u is synchronously *simulated* on T_φ and $T_{\neg\varphi}$, by repeatedly computing forward images w.r.t. all fair states[1]. For each input state of u, we get two sets of *belief states*, r_φ and $r_{\neg\varphi}$. Based on their emptinesses, the monitor returns one of the following verdicts:

- *conclusive true* ($\top$), if $r_\varphi \neq \emptyset$ and $r_{\neg\varphi} = \emptyset$. φ is *verified* for all future inputs;
- *conclusive false* ($\bot$), if $r_\varphi = \emptyset$ and $r_{\neg\varphi} \neq \emptyset$. φ is *violated* for all future inputs;
- *inconclusive* (?), if $r_\varphi \neq \emptyset$ and $r_{\neg\varphi} \neq \emptyset$. In this case, the knowledge of the monitor is limited by the finiteness of u.

Besides the property φ, the monitoring algorithm takes in input a model K of the SUS. This is used to declare the variables in which the properties are expressed, but more importantly to define some constraints on their temporal evolution, which represent assumptions on the behavior of the SUS. By considering only (infinite) traces of K, the above algorithm may give more *precise* outputs (turning ? into $\top/\bot$). This is obtained by using $K \otimes T_\varphi$ (the *synchronous product* of K and T_φ) and $K \otimes T_{\neg\varphi}$ instead of T_φ and $T_{\neg\varphi}$, respectively. This coincides with [12], where the resulting monitor is called to be *predictive*.

The model is used by NuRV in different novel ways. First of all, there is the possibility that $u \notin L(K)$, because the model may be wrong, or it only captures a partial knowledge of the SUS, or due to unexpected faults. In this case we have $r_\varphi = r_{\neg\varphi} = \emptyset$ in above algorithm, and we naturally let the monitor returns a fourth verdict called *out-of-model* ($\times$). This is why we call K an *assumption*, and the two verdicts $\top/\bot$ are only conclusive under assumptions, thus renamed to $\top^a/\bot^a$. This extended RV approach may be called *assumption-based*. In particular, if one only cares whether the SUS always follows its model, we can use a dummy LTL property true in above procedure, so that $K \otimes T_{\neg\varphi}$ is always empty, and the monitor will output either $\top^a$ or $\times$, indicating whether $u \in L(K)$. This application coincides with *model-based RV* [19].

Second, the above monitoring algorithm directly supports *partially observable* traces, i.e. variables appeared in the monitoring property are not (always) known in each state of the input trace. This is because the symbolic forward-image computations do not require full observability—less restrictive inputs result to

---

[1] Emerson-Lei algorithm [9] is used here. This corresponds to the NBA-to-NFA conversions based on SCC (strongly connected components) detections in [1], while the forward-image computations determinize NFAs into DFAs *on the fly*. Thus, NuRV provides a full implementation of [1].

coarser belief states. Partial observability becomes more useful under assumptions, as an assumption may express a relation between observable and unobservable variables of the SUS.

Third, NuRV supports *resettable* monitors, i.e. it can evaluate an LTL property at arbitrary positions of the input trace. This idea was inspired by the observation that, in r_φ and $r_{\neg\varphi}$, all variables (some are generated by the LTL translations) related to the present and the past have the same values, while all variables related to the future have opposite values. There is no easy way to distinguish these two groups of variables. However, by taking $r_\varphi \cup r_{\neg\varphi}$ we smartly get a new belief state which represents the history of the system after a run given by the input trace seen so far. If we restart the monitor algorithm at state i using this history as the new initial condition of K (also with a reduced version of initial conditions of T_φ and $T_{\neg\varphi}$), the new monitor is essentially evaluating $[\![u, i \models \varphi]\!]$ for $|u| > i$, with the underlying assumptions taken into account. This is again an orthogonal feature, but having an assumption makes resetting of the monitor more interesting as the assumption evolves to take into consideration the history of the system.

Furthermore, NuRV can synthesize the symbolic monitors into explicit-state monitor automata and then generate them into standalone monitor code in various programming languages (currently we support C, C++, Java, and Common Lisp). Besides, it is possible to dump the monitor automata into SMV modules, which can be further analyzed in NUXMV for their correctness and other properties.

The rest of this paper is organized as follows: In Sect. 2 we describe its architecture and functionalities. Some use case scenarios (as running examples) are given in Sect. 3. Section 4 shows some experimental evaluation results. Finally, we conclude the paper in Sect. 5 with some directions for future work.

2   Architecture and Functionalities

NuRV implements the Assumption-based Runtime Verification (ABRV) with partial observability and resets described in [6]. Monitoring properties are expressed in Propositional Linear Temporal Logic (LTL) [15] with both future and past temporal operators. For each input state, the monitor outputs one of four verdicts in $\mathbb{B}_4 \doteq \{\top^a, \bot^a, ?, \times\}$. As a program, NuRV takes an assumption (as SMV model), some LTL properties and input traces, and output the verification results or some standalone monitor code, according to a batch of commands. The reader may refer to [6] for the formal definition of the LTL semantics and the related RV problems.

2.1   Architecture of NuRV

The internal structure of NuRV is shown in Fig. 1. The monitor construction starts from the modular description of a model K (used as assumptions in ABRV) and a set of LTL properties $\varphi_1, \ldots, \varphi_n$. The model is used also to declare

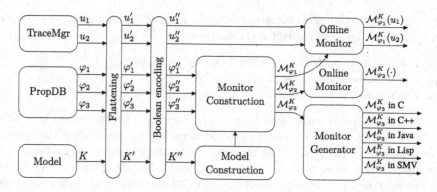

Fig. 1. The internal structure of NuRV

the variables (and their types) in which the LTL properties are expressed, thus the *alphabet* of the input words of the monitors. NuRV has inherited NUXMV's support of hierarchical models and rich variable types (such as bound integers and arrays), all input data (models, properties and traces) are flattened and boolean encoded before going to further steps. The *Model Construction* component generates (from the model) a BDD-based representation of the Finite State Machine (FSM), which is then used in the monitor construction step, together with the monitoring property, to produce another BDD-based FSM representing the symbolic monitor. The resulting monitor can be used in two ways: (1) as an online/offline monitor running inside NUXMV, accepting finite traces incrementally, outputting verification results for each input states. (2) as the input of the *Monitor Generator* component, resulting into standalone monitor code. From the end-users' point of view, NuRV extends NUXMV with the following new commands:

1. `build_monitor`: build the symbolic monitor for a given LTL property;
2. `verify_property`: verify a currently loaded trace in the symbolic monitor;
3. `heartbeat`: verify one input state in the symbolic monitor (online monitoring);
4. `generate_monitor`: generate standalone monitors in a target language.

The commands `build_monitor` and `verify_property` together implemented the offline monitoring algorithm described in [6]. The command `generate_monitor` further generates explicit-state monitors in various languages from the symbolic monitor built by the command `build_monitor`. These commands must work with other NUXMV commands [2] to be useful.

2.2   Structure of Explicit-State Monitors

The *Monitor Generator* components internally generate monitor code in two steps: (1) generating explicit-state monitor automata from the symbolic monitor;

(2) converting monitor automata into code in specific languages. NuRV can generate three levels of explicit-state monitors:

L1 The monitor synthesis stops at all conclusive states;
L2 The monitor synthesis explores all states;
L3 The monitor synthesis explores all states and reset states.

A sample explicit-state monitor for LTL property $p \, \mathbf{U} \, q$ generated by NuRV is shown in Fig. 2. The monitor is generated under the assumption that either p or q is true in the input. The monitor starts at location 1, and returns ? if the input is $p \wedge \neg q$ until it received $\neg p \wedge q$ which has the output $\top^a$ (Y). The **L1** monitor has no further transition at locations associated with conclusive verdicts ($\top^a$ or $\perp^a$), since it can be easily proved that ABRV-LTL monitors are monotonic if the assumption is always respected by the input trace. The **L2** monitor contains all locations and transitions, thus it may return × even after the monitor reached conclusive verdicts. The **L3** monitor additionally contains information for the resets: in case the monitor is reset, the current location will first *jump* to the location indicated in the bracket [], of current location, then goes to next location according to the input state. However, in the above monitor all reset locations are just the initial location (1), this is mostly because the assumption is an invariant property and the LTL property does not have any past operators.

Standalone monitor code are literally translated from these monitor automata (FSMs). The correctness of monitors in C, for instance, comes *indirectly* from the correctness of the symbolic algorithm and mode checking on SMV-based monitors.

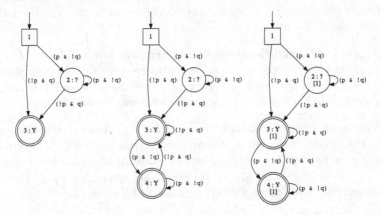

Fig. 2. Explicit-state monitors of $p \, \mathbf{U} \, q$ (assuming $p \neq q$) (L1–L3)

2.3   API of Generated Code

NuRV currently supports monitor code generation into five languages: C, C++, Java, Common Lisp and SMV. The structure of monitor code is simple yet efficient: it simply mimics the simulations of deterministic FSMs.

The monitor code generated (in C, for example) has the following signature:

```
int /* [out] (0 = unknown, 1 = true, 2 = false, 3 = out-of-model) */
  monitor
    (long /* state [in] */,
     int  /* reset [in] (0 = none, 1 = hard, 2 = soft) */,
     int* /* current_loc: [in/out] */);
```

The function name (*monitor* here) is given by the user. It takes three parameters: (1) `state`: an encoded long integer representing the current input state of the trace, (2) `reset`, an integer representing the possible reset signal, and (3) `current_loc`: a pointer of integer holding the internal state of the monitor. It is caller's responsibility to allocate an integer and provide the pointer to the monitor (otherwise the function returns -1 indicating *invalid locations*), and this is actually the only thing to identify a monitor instance. The sole purpose of the function is to update `*current_loc` (the value behind the pointer) according to `state` and `reset` and to return a monitoring output. NuRV supports two different encodings for `state`:

1. *Static* partial observability: `state` denotes a full assignment of the observables, encoded in binary bits: 0 for *false* ($\perp$), 1 for *true* ($\top$);
2. *Dynamic* partial observability: `state` denotes a ternary number, whose each ternary bit represents 3 possible values of an observable variable: 0 for *unknown* (?), 1 for *true* ($\top$) and 2 for *false* ($\perp$).

Note that the symbolic monitoring algorithm can take in general input states expressed in Boolean formulae (e.g., if the observables are p and q, our monitor may take an input state "p xor q", either p or q is true but not both), but this is not supported by the generated code.

BDD operations are implemented by the BDD manager. Their performance strongly depends on the variable ordering used in the BDD construction. This can be controlled by setting an `input_order_file` in NUXMV. The input of generated monitor code requires an encoding of BDDs into long integers according to this file. This encoding is done from the least to the most significant bit. For instance, if the observables are p and q with the same order, an binary encoding for the state $\{p = \top, q = \perp\}$ would be $(01)_2 = 1$, and a ternary encoding for the same state would be $(21)_3 = 7$. The design purpose is to make sure that the comparison of two encoded states can be as fast as possible. The signatures of monitors in other languages are quite similar, except that the parameter `current_loc` can be put inside C++/Java classes as an member variable, and each monitor is an instance of the generated monitor class.

3   Use Case Scenario

Now we briefly demonstrate the process of generating a monitor for LTL properties $\varphi_0 = p\,\mathbf{U}\,q$ and $\varphi_1 = \mathbf{Y}p \vee q$, assuming $p \neq q$. A batch of commands shown in Fig. 3 does the work (also c.f. Fig. 4 for the contents of two helper files).

The command go builds the model from the input file disjoint.smv which defines two Boolean variables p and q, together with the invariant $p \neq q$.

The generated monitors M0.c and M1.c (together with their C headers) are under the full observability of p and q. The variable

```
set input_file "disjoint.smv"
set input_order_file "default.ord"
go
add_property -l -p "p U q"
add_property -l -p "Y p | q"
build_monitor -n 0
build_monitor -n 1
generate_monitor -n 0 -l 3 -L "c" -o "M0"
generate_monitor -n 1 -l 3 -L "c" -o "M1"
quit
```

Fig. 3. The batch commands

ordering is given by the file default.ord, in which each line denotes one variable in the model.

The simplest way to use the generated monitor, M0 for instance, is to declare an integer and call the monitor function like this: (e.g. when monitoring a C program linked with the generated monitor code, p and q may denote two assertions in the program)

```
int monitor_loc, out;
out = M0 (0b01 /* p & !q */, 1 /* hard */, &monitor_loc);
out = M0 (0b10 /* !p & q */, 0 /* none */, &monitor_loc);
```

There is no need to initialize the integer monitor_loc as the first M0 call with a value 1 will also do the monitor initialization. (Actually it just set monitor_loc to 1, we may call it a *hard reset*.) The first function call returns 0 indicating ABRV-LTL value ? (unknown); the second call returns 1 indicating $\top^a$ (conclusive true).

```
MODULE main
VAR    p : boolean; q : boolean;
INVAR p != q
```

_____

```
p
q
```

Fig. 4. disjoint.smv and default.ord

For offline monitoring, there is no need to call generate_monitor in above batch command. Suppose a trace $u = pppqqq$ has been loaded (by read_trace), the command verify_property verifies the trace against the symbolic monitor of φ_0, shown in Fig. 5 (here "−n 0" denotes the first monitor, and 1 denotes the first loaded trace).

```
MODULE main
VAR    p : boolean; q : boolean;
INVAR p != q
```

_____

```
p
q
```

Fig. 5. Offline monitoring in NuRV

It is also possible to verify just one input state by heartbeat (online monitoring). It has a similar interface with verify_property, just the trace ID is replaced by a single state expressed by a logical formula (as a string), e.g. "p & !q".

4 Experimental Evaluation

We have done some comparison tests[2] between NuRV and the latest release of RV-Monitor [14]. To show the feasibility and effectiveness of RV tools, we tried to generate LTL monitors from a wide coverage of practical specifications, i.e. Dwyer's LTL patterns[3] [8]. The purpose is to generate the same monitors from NuRV and RV-Monitor (rvm) and compare their performances and other characteristics. All these patterns are expressed in six Boolean variables (p, q, r, s, t and z). RV-Monitor is event-based, i.e. the alphabet is the set of these variables instead of their power set. This means our monitors can be built under the assumption that all six variables are disjoint.

Table 1. Eight long formulae from Dwyer's patterns

ID	Pattern	LTL
13	Trans to p occur at most twice (between q and r)	$\mathbf{G}\,((q \wedge \mathbf{F}\,r) \rightarrow ((\neg p \wedge \neg r)\,\mathbf{U}\,(r \vee ((p \wedge \neg r)\,\mathbf{U}\,(r \vee ((\neg p \wedge \neg r)\,\mathbf{U}\,(r \vee ((p \wedge \neg r)\,\mathbf{U}\,(r \vee (\neg p\,\mathbf{U}\,r))))))))))$
14	Trans to p occur at most twice (after q until r)	$\mathbf{G}\,(q \rightarrow ((\neg p \wedge \neg r)\,\mathbf{U}\,(r \vee ((p \wedge \neg r)\,\mathbf{U}\,(r \vee ((\neg p \wedge \neg r)\,\mathbf{U}\,(r \vee ((p \wedge \neg r)\,\mathbf{U}\,(r \vee (\neg p\,\mathbf{W}\,r) \vee \mathbf{G}\,p))))))))))$
39	p precedes s, t (after q until r)	$\mathbf{G}\,(q \rightarrow (\neg(s \wedge (\neg r) \wedge \mathbf{X}\,(\neg r\,\mathbf{U}\,(t \wedge \neg r)))\,\mathbf{U}\,(r \vee p) \vee \mathbf{G}\,(\neg(s \wedge \mathbf{X}\,\mathbf{F}\,t))))$
43	p responds to s, t (between q and r)	$\mathbf{G}\,((q \wedge \mathbf{F}\,r) \rightarrow (s \wedge \mathbf{X}\,(\neg r\,\mathbf{U}\,t) \rightarrow \mathbf{X}\,(\neg r\,\mathbf{U}\,(t \wedge \mathbf{F}\,p)))\,\mathbf{U}\,r)$
44	p responds to s, t (after q until r)	$\mathbf{G}\,(q \rightarrow (s \wedge \mathbf{X}\,(\neg r\,\mathbf{U}\,t) \rightarrow \mathbf{X}\,(\neg r\,\mathbf{U}\,(t \wedge \mathbf{F}\,p)))\,\mathbf{U}\,(r \vee \mathbf{G}\,(s \wedge \mathbf{X}\,(\neg r\,\mathbf{U}\,t) \rightarrow \mathbf{X}\,(\neg r\,\mathbf{U}\,(t \wedge \mathbf{F}\,p)))))$
49	s, t responds to p (after q until r)	$\mathbf{G}\,(q \rightarrow (p \rightarrow (\neg r\,\mathbf{U}\,(s \wedge \neg r \wedge \mathbf{X}\,(\neg r\,\mathbf{U}\,t))))\,\mathbf{U}\,(r \vee \mathbf{G}\,(p \rightarrow (s \wedge \mathbf{X}\,\mathbf{F}\,t))))$
53	s, t without z responds to p (between q and r)	$\mathbf{G}\,((q \wedge \mathbf{F}\,r) \rightarrow (p \rightarrow (\neg r\,\mathbf{U}\,(s \wedge \neg r \wedge \neg z \wedge \mathbf{X}\,((\neg r \wedge \neg z)\,\mathbf{U}\,t))))\,\mathbf{U}\,r)$
54	s, t without z responds to p (after q until r)	$\mathbf{G}\,(q \rightarrow (p \rightarrow (\neg r\,\mathbf{U}\,(s \wedge \neg r \wedge \neg z \wedge \mathbf{X}\,((\neg r \wedge \neg z)\,\mathbf{U}\,t))))\,\mathbf{U}\,(r \vee \mathbf{G}\,(p \rightarrow (s \wedge \neg z \wedge \mathbf{X}\,(\neg z\,\mathbf{U}\,t)))))$

Unfortunately, RV-Monitor (rvm) fails in generating monitors from eight long formulae (Pattern 13, 14, 39, 43, 44, 49, 53 and 54), shown in Table 1. Also it

---

[2] All test data and materials for reproducing these experiments are available at https://es.fbk.eu/people/ctian/papers/rv2019/rv2019-data.tar.gz.

[3] The latest version (55 in total) is available at http://patterns.projects.cs.ksu.edu/documentation/patterns/ltl.shtml. We call them Pattern $0, 1, \ldots, 54$ in the same order.

does not generate[4] monitors from all ten safety properties (Pattern 5, 7, 22, 25, 27, 40, 41, 42, 45 and 50). Eventually we got only 37 monitors out of 55 LTL patterns, and we confirmed that, whenever rvm monitors report violations, our monitors behave the same. Our 55 monitors were quickly generated in 0.467 s (MacBook Pro with Intel Core i7 2.6 GHz, 4 cores) using a single core, while the 37 rvm monitors were generated in 78.619 s on the same machine using multiple cores.

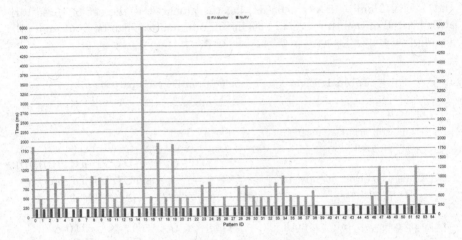

Fig. 6. Performance of generated Java monitors on 10^7 states.

We observed that rvm monitors does not report further violations once the first violation happens, and goes into terminal states. To get visible performance metrics we chose to reset all monitors once a violation is reported. Also, to prevent extra performance loss in rvm monitors by creating multiple monitor instances [5], we have used a single trace (stored in a vector) with 10^7 random states. For each of the 37 LTL patterns, we recorded the time (in ms) spent by both monitors (running in the same Java process), the result is shown in Fig. 6. Our monitors (in Java) have shown a constant-like time complexity (approx. 250 ms), i.e. the time needed for processing one input trace is almost the same for all patterns. This reflects the spirit of automata-based approaches. Rvm monitors vary from 500 ms to more than 6 s, depending on the number of resets.

5   Conclusions and Future Work

We presented NuRV, a NUXMV extension for Runtime Verification. It supports assumption-based RV for propositional LTL with both future and past operators, with the supports of partial observability and resets. It has functionalities

---

[4] The error message is "violation is not a supported state in this logic, ltl.".

for offline and online monitoring, and code generation of the monitors in various programming languages. The experimental evaluation on standard LTL patterns shows that NuRV is quite efficient in both generation and running time. In the future, we plan to participate in the RV competition to broaden the tool comparison and to extend the monitor specification language beyond the propositional case.

Acknowledgment. We thank the anonymous reviewers for their helpful comments.

References

1. Bauer, A., Leucker, M., Schallhart, C.: Runtime verification for LTL and TLTL. ACM Trans. Softw. Eng. Methodol. **20**(4), 14–64 (2011). https://doi.org/10.1145/2000799.2000800
2. Bozzano, M., et al.: nuXmv 1.1.1 User Manual (2016). https://es.fbk.eu/tools/nuxmv/downloads/nuxmv-user-manual.pdf
3. Bryant, R.E.: Binary decision diagrams. In: Clarke, E.M., Henzinger, T.A., Veith, H., Bloem, R. (eds.) Handbook of Model Checking, pp. 191–217. Springer, Cham (2018). https://doi.org/10.1007/978-3-319-10575-8_7
4. Cavada, R., et al.: The NUXMV symbolic model checker. In: Biere, A., Bloem, R. (eds.) CAV 2014. LNCS, vol. 8559, pp. 334–342. Springer, Cham (2014). https://doi.org/10.1007/978-3-319-08867-9_22
5. Chen, F., Roşu, G.: Parametric trace slicing and monitoring. In: Kowalewski, S., Philippou, A. (eds.) TACAS 2009. LNCS, vol. 5505, pp. 246–261. Springer, Heidelberg (2009). https://doi.org/10.1007/978-3-642-00768-2_23
6. Cimatti, A., Tian, C., Tonetta, S.: Assumption-based runtime verification with partial observability and resets. In: Finkbeiner, B., Mariani, L. (eds.) RV 2019. LNCS, vol. 11757, 165–184. Springer, Cham (2019). https://doi.org/10.1007/978-3-030-32079-9_10
7. Clarke, E.M., Grumberg, O., Hamaguchi, K.: Another look at LTL model checking. Formal Methods Syst. Des. **10**(1), 47–71 (1997). https://doi.org/10.1023/A:1008615614281
8. Dwyer, M.B., Avrunin, G.S., Corbett, J.C.: Patterns in property specifications for finite-state verification. In: Proceedings of the 21st International Conference on Software Engineering, pp. 411–420. ACM Press, New York (1999). https://doi.org/10.1145/302405.302672
9. Allen Emerson, E., Lei, C.-L.: Temporal reasoning under generalized fairness constraints. In: Monien, B., Vidal-Naquet, G. (eds.) STACS 1986. LNCS, vol. 210, pp. 21–36. Springer, Heidelberg (1986). https://doi.org/10.1007/3-540-16078-7_62
10. Falcone, Y., Havelund, K., Reger, G.: A tutorial on runtime verification. Eng. Dependable Softw. Syst. **34**, 141–175 (2013). https://doi.org/10.3233/978-1-61499-207-3-141
11. Havelund, K.: Rule-based runtime verification revisited. Int. J. Softw. Tools Technol. Transfer **17**(2), 143–170 (2014). https://doi.org/10.1007/s10009-014-0309-2
12. Leucker, M.: Sliding between model checking and runtime verification. In: Qadeer, S., Tasiran, S. (eds.) RV 2012. LNCS, vol. 7687, pp. 82–87. Springer, Heidelberg (2013). https://doi.org/10.1007/978-3-642-35632-2_10
13. Leucker, M., Schallhart, C.: A brief account of runtime verification. J. Logic Algebraic Program. **78**(5), 293–303 (2009). https://doi.org/10.1016/j.jlap.2008.08.004

14. Luo, Q., et al.: RV-Monitor: efficient parametric runtime verification with simultaneous properties. In: Bonakdarpour, B., Smolka, S.A. (eds.) RV 2014. LNCS, vol. 8734, pp. 285–300. Springer, Cham (2014). https://doi.org/10.1007/978-3-319-11164-3_24

15. Manna, Z., Pnueli, A.: The Temporal Logic of Reactive and Concurrent Systems: Specification. Springer-Verlag, New York (1992). https://doi.org/10.1007/978-1-4612-0931-7

16. McMillan, K.L.: Symbolic Model Checking. Springer, Heidelberg (1993). https://doi.org/10.1007/978-1-4615-3190-6

17. Roşu, G., Havelund, K.: Rewriting-based techniques for runtime verification. Autom. Softw. Eng. **12**(2), 151–197 (2005). https://doi.org/10.1007/s10515-005-6205-y

18. Somenzi, F.: CUDD: CU Decision Diagram Package, Release 2.4.1. University of Colorado at Boulder (2005)

19. Zhao, Y., Rammig, F.: Model-based runtime verification framework. Electron. Notes Theoret. Comput. Sci. **253**(1), 179–193 (2009). https://doi.org/10.1016/j.entcs.2009.09.035

AllenRV: An Extensible Monitor for Multiple Complex Specifications with High Reactivity

Nic Volanschi[(✉)] and Bernard Serpette

Inria Bordeaux - Sud-Ouest, Talence, France
{eugene.volanschi,bernard.serpette}@inria.fr

Abstract. AllenRV is a tool for monitoring temporal specifications, designed for ensuring good scalability in terms of size and number of formulae, and high reactivity. Its features reflect this design goal. For ensuring scalability in the number of formulae, it can simultaneously monitor a set of formulae written in past and future, next-free LTL, with some metric extensions; their efficient simultaneous monitoring is supported by a let construct allowing to share computations between formulae. For ensuring scalability in the size of formulae, it allows defining new abstractions as user-defined operators, which take discrete time boolean signals as arguments, but also constant parameters such as delays. For ensuring high reactivity, its monitoring algorithm does not require clock tick events, unlike many other tools. This is achieved by recomputing output signals both upon input signals changes and upon internally generated timeout events relative to such changes. As a consequence, monitoring remains efficient on arbitrarily fine-grained time domains.

AllenRV is implemented by extending the existing Allen language and compiler, initially targeting ubiquitous applications using binary sensors, with temporal logic operators and a comprehensive library of user-defined operators on top of them. The most complex of these operators, including a complete adaptation of Allen-logic relations as selection operators, are proven correct with respect to their defined semantics.

Thus, AllenRV offers an open platform for cooperatively developing increasingly complex libraries of high level, general or domain-specific, temporal operators and abstractions, without compromising correctness.

Keywords: Online monitoring · Allen logic · Linear time logic

1 Introduction

AllenRV is a monitoring tool for detecting temporal conditions about boolean signals over discrete time. Such boolean signals may directly originate from binary sensors, or be abstracted from non-binary sensors based on value thresholds. These signals typically correspond to the monitoring of cyber-physical systems such as smart homes, smart buildings, or other sensor deployments for

B. Finkbeiner and L. Mariani (Eds.): RV 2019, LNCS 11757, pp. 393–401, 2019.
https://doi.org/10.1007/978-3-030-32079-9_24

IoT applications. It is assumed that input signals are piecewise constant, and are represented as timestamped values that are emitted upon significant value switches (for boolean sensors, this means any value switches). Timestamps are typically labeled in seconds or milliseconds. Based on the input signals and a set of specifications, AllenRV incrementally computes an output boolean signal for each specification. The output signal reports the satisfaction or violation of each monitored condition at each time point.

The AllenRV monitoring algorithm [12] and its language for expressing temporal specifications [11] are designed to satisfy several key requirements for monitoring applications in this domain:

- It supports the efficient monitoring of multiple specifications over a shared sensor infrastructure, by providing a 'let' construct for sharing common computations between different formulae. This avoids repeatedly computing the same sub-formulae many times. Monitoring multiple related specifications is a key need in applications that simultaneously monitor different aspects at different levels, such as low-level concerns (e.g. detecting basic interactions) and application-level concerns (e.g. detecting human activities), where higher-level aspects commonly reuse formulae of lower-level aspects.
- It supports the efficient development of complex specifications by providing the possibility to define new user-defined operators on boolean signals, extending the comprehensive set of predefined operators. This allows to define programming abstractions that can be instantiated for different set of signals and which can also be parameterized with constant values such as delays or dates. The need for developing complex specifications is key when addressing real use cases, where programming abstractions are typically layered on top of each other. As a complement for the 'let' construct, addressing the reuse of common computations, a 'def' construct allows to reuse programming abstractions by instantiating them in different contexts.
- It supports highly reactive applications that rely on the quick detection of conditions being satisfied or violated, by computing changes in the output signals even when they occur between two input events. In contrast, many of the available RV monitoring tools (e.g., [1,2,6]) only recompute output signals upon change events, and rely on the introduction of regular clock events for ensuring their reactivity; however, increasing the rate of regular clock events typically hampers efficient monitoring, and therefore is subject to a reactivity *vs.* efficiency tradeoff. AllenRV does not impose such a dilemma, thanks to the self-generation of timeout events relative to value changes, which trigger additional output signals recomputing, without waiting the next input event. The high reactivity requirement is key in many interactive or security-related applications.

While each individual feature is not necessarily novel, this combination of features ensures unprecedented scalability in terms of number and size of the monitored formulae and towards fine-grained reactivity.

For the specification of conditions on boolean signals, AllenRV uses a Next-free subset of past/future LTL, with some metric extensions. This propositional temporal logic, equivalent to a subset of MTL [9], has proven to be sufficient in practice for expressing various real services of ambient assisted living (AAL) in smart homes (SH), as pointed out in Sect. 3.

AllenRV is implemented by extending an existing tool for expressing context detection logic in ubiquitous applications called Allen [11]. The original tool offered domain-specific operators on boolean signals, extensible with user-defined operators. Domain-specific operators included adaptations of the Allen-logic relations (during, overlaps, etc.) working on boolean signals, hence the name of the tool. AllenRV adds standard LTL operators Since and Until to the set of native operators, and adds a comprehensive library of system-defined operators, (1) re-implementing all the native operators, and (2) adding classical temporal operators such as bounded Historically/Once past operators. The correctness of the most complex operators, namely from the Allen logic, is ensured by formal proofs [10]. The AllenRV implementation is open-source software distributed under the GPL licence.[1]

2 Tool Description

2.1 Foundations

AllenRV monitors temporal formulae over discrete time boolean signals, which are functions $s : \mathbb{N} \to \mathbb{B}$. In practice, signals typically originate from binary sensors, and are given as a non-empty, possible infinite sequence of timestamped value changes $s(t_i)_{i \geq 0}$ where $t_0 = 0$, and $\forall i > 0, t_i > t_{i-1} \wedge s(t_i) = \neg s(t_{i-1})$ (repeated values reported by the sensor are dropped). The *current value* of the signal on the interval $[t_i, t_{i+1})$ is $s(t_i)$. Non-binary sensors can also be used as inputs by converting them to boolean signals using a command option that associates a sensor name to a threshold value.

A discrete time boolean signal can also be viewed as a set of *states*, that is, the discrete time intervals where its current value is 1: $\{[t_i, t_{i+1}) \subseteq \mathbb{N} \mid s(t_i)\}$. If the sequence of timestamped values from a sensor is finite $s(t_i)_{0 \leq i \leq n}$, the last interval is $[s(t_n), \infty)$. Note that, as the timestamps t_i of a signal are strictly increasing, its states are non-empty, disjoint and non-adjacent.

A *log* is a sequence of timestamped value changes for a finite set of signals $s \in \mathcal{S}$. The definition of signals over the infinite domain of natural numbers allows to use the standard LTL definitions of temporal operators on infinite traces. By putting $\Sigma = 2^{\mathcal{S}}$, each log may be interpreted as an infinite trace in Σ^{ω}, namely the infinite sequence $(a_t)_{t \in \mathbb{N}}$ where $a_t = \{s \in \mathcal{S} \mid s(t)\}$ is the set of signals whose current value at time t is 1. In particular, a finite log analyzed in offline mode is seen as its infinite constant continuation, that is, the last sensor values reported in the log are prolonged indefinitely.

---

[1] https://github.com/NicVolanschi/Allen.

2.2 Specifications

All operators in AllenRV take a fixed number of signals as input and produce a signal as output. Besides the boolean operators, having the expected pointwise semantics, there are 4 native operators in AllenRV, defined in Fig. 1. Since and Until are the standard past/future LTL operators. Operator delay[T] is delaying a signal by a given period $T \in \mathbb{N}^*$, filling the beginning interval $[0, T)$ with 0.[2] Thus, delay[1] is equivalent to a classical Previous operator with a strong sense, i.e. false at $t=0$. Moreover, delay[T] is equivalent to the Once operator $O_{[T,T]}$ in the MTL logic, when interpreted synchronously over the discrete domain of natural numbers, seen as timestamps [8]. Finally, the $>!!$ operator selects from a signal the states longer than a given duration T, but dropping their initial period of length T. This operator is similar to the Historically operator $H_{\leq T}$ in MTL, but has a strong sense, meaning that $true >!! T$ is 0 on $[0, T)$,[3] while $H_{\leq T} true$ is 1 on $[0, T)$. Nevertheless, the MTL operator $H_{\leq T}$ can be expressed in terms of the Allen operator $>!!$, as will be shown in Sect. 2.3. In this sense, we may say that the logic implemented by AllenRV is a subset of MTL, containing unbounded past/future operators, the Previous operator but not the Next operator, and a subset of bounded past operators, including $H_{[T,T]}$ and $H_{\leq T}$ (or, equivalently, $O_{[T,T]}$ and $O_{\leq T}$).

$$since(p, q)(t) \leftrightarrow \exists t' \leq t . q(t') \wedge \forall t'' \in (t', t] . p(t'')$$
$$until(p, q)(t) \leftrightarrow \exists t' \geq t . q(t') \wedge \forall t'' \in [t, t') . p(t'')$$
$$delay[T](p) = \{[t + T, t' + T) \mid [t, t') \in p\}$$
$$p >!! T = \{[t + T, t') \mid [t, t') \in p \wedge t' - t > T\}$$

Fig. 1. The native operators in AllenRV.

Among these 4 operators, only delay[T] existed in the original Allen tool. The other three are extensions belonging to AllenRV.

The complete syntax of the specification language is given in Fig. 2. A specification may start with a list of **def** constructs, introducing user-defined operators, and a list of global **let** constructs, introducing named expressions common to all the monitored formulae. After this optional prologue, comes the non-empty list of named monitored formulae, also called 'contexts'. The formulae may use boolean operators, duration operators such as $>!!$ and its variations, and named operators, either defined in the system library or user-defined. Atomic formulae may be named expressions introduced via **let** or signals from the log referred by their name as a string. Constant delays and durations are by default in milliseconds, but can be also given in other units such as seconds or minutes. Expressions may also contain local **let** constructs, introducing named sub-expressions local to one formula.

---

[2] From its definition, the first state of delay[T] cannot start sooner that time 0+T.

[3] From its definition, the first state of $p >!! T$ cannot start sooner that time 0+T.

```
Prog -> Lib LetRules
Lib -> Def*
Def -> "def" id ("[" id+(",") "]")? ("(" id*(",") ")")?
       "=" Context
LetRules -> "let" id "=" Expr "in" LetRules | Rules
Rules -> id ":" Context (";" Rules)?
Context -> "let" id "=" Expr "in" Context | Expr
Expr -> Prod "|" Expr | Prod
Prod -> Comp "&" Prod | Comp
Comp -> Expr1 (">=!"|"<="|">="|">!"|">!!"|"<"|">") Int | Expr1
Expr1 -> true | false | "~" Expr1 | "(" Expr ")" | str
       | id ("[" Int+(",") "]")? ("(" Expr*(",") ")")?
Int -> id | int ("hr" | "min" | "sec")?
```

Fig. 2. The syntax of the specification language for AllenRV.

User-defined operators are expanded as macros, by instantiating their definition with the given constant parameters and signal arguments. In contrast, the computation of each `let` expressions is shared by all the containing formulae. The global `let` construct is an extension belonging to AllenRV. Although it adds no expressiveness to the language, this extension allows to greatly improve performance when multiple formulae rely on common sub-formulae.

2.3   The AllenRV Library

Based on the 4 native operators and leveraging the `def` construct, AllenRV offers a comprehensive library of more than 50 system-defined temporal operators, defined in the AllenRV specification language (complete listing in the Appendix). Some of these operators came from needs experienced in practical applications in the SH and AAL domains, but should be useful in other domains, too. Other operators are well-known shorthands in temporal logics. Most, but not all of these operators existed in the original Allen tool, but they were implemented as native operators independently of each other, in ad-hoc ways.

Classic operators include the weak variants Z (weak Since) and W (weak Until), the unbounded past and future logic quantifiers O (Once), H (Historically), F (Finally), G (Globally), defined as expected using Since and Until, and also the bounded versions of past MTL operators $H_{\leq T}$ and $O_{\leq T}$, defined in Fig. 3 using the native operators. Other classical operators are the unary operators recognizing the raising edges of a signal (up), its falling edges (dn), or both (sw).

Operators derived from practice include:

- different duration operators $(<=, >)$, which are variants of the $>!!$ native operator. They all select states from a signal, or sub-intervals thereof, by comparing them to a given duration T.
- selection binary operators derived from the 13 relations in the Allen logic. The Allen-logic relations define all the possible positions of two time interval with respect to each other: : during, contains, starts, started, ends, ended, overlaps, overlapped, meets, met, eq, before, after. For each interval relation IRJ, we

```
def occ(p,q) = since(q, p&q)   # p has already occurred in this state of q
def step[T] = delay[T](true)   # step function, 0 on [0,T) and 1 afterwards
def orig = ~step[1]            # true only at the origin of time, when t=0
def init(s) = occ(orig(), s)   # selects the state of s starting at t=0
def H_le[T](s) = s >!! T | init(s)   # Historically_<=T in MTL
def O_le[T](s) = ~H_le[T](~s)        # Once_<=T in MTL
```

Fig. 3. Defining the bounded past operators $O_{\leq T}$ and $H_{\leq T}$ in AllenRV.

implemented a binary operator $r(p, q)$ on signals which selects all the states of p which are in relation R with *some* state of q. To improve the practical usefulness, the before and after have been interpreted as immediately before and immediately after, respectively.

- variants of the O (Once) and F (Finally) operators bounded by a signal, instead of a relative delay. This gives binary operators occ(p,q), meaning "p has occurred at least once in the current state of q", and possible(p,q), meaning "p is still possible in the current state of q".
- different forms of a binary flat(p,q) operator, which glue together the different states of p which occur during a same state of q. This operator is frequently used to reconstitute a whole period within a slot out of fragments of it: for instance, reconstituting a presence in a room out of sporadic movements while no other movements are sensed elsewhere.
- other operators such as a binary operator far[T](p,q) selecting states of p that are far away (i.e. more than T away) from any state in q.

2.4   Online Monitoring

The online monitoring algorithm of Allen, first described in [12], is based on detecting informative prefixes. The compiler constructs a graph for the set of monitored formulae, in which let-bound sub-expressions are shared by all the containing expressions, be it in the same or in different monitored formulae. The monitor pushes from bottom up the value changes for each formula from the corresponding signals; other events in the log are dropped. Evaluating certain kinds of operators may generate timer events that are merged in the event input stream. This way, output signals may change either triggered by input value changes or by delays relative to such changes.

For example, the $p >!! T$ operator schedules a timer event at time $t + T$ when signal p raises to 1 at time t, and cancels the scheduled event when signal p falls to 0. If the timer event is encountered, this means that p has been continuously 1 on the interval $[t, t + T)$, so the output signal is switched to 1.

Future time operators are handled by computing three-valued output signals $\{0,1,?\}$, like in LTL3 monitoring [3]. However, our monitoring, like any algorithm based on informative prefixes, does not guarantee that a definite signal (0 or 1) is computed the earliest possible for a monitored formula, but rather when sufficient evidence was gathered to evaluate it from bottom to top. However, it is important to note that, when computing an operator over the three-valued domain, our algorithm does not always block on unknown values. Indeed, some operators may return defined values (0 or 1) even when some of the inputs are unknown (equal to '?'). For instance, the value computed for a node since(p,q) is always 1 when the current value of q is 1, independently of the current value of p, and in particular even if p is currently unknown.

Another salient feature of our algorithm, already mentioned in the Introduction, is that the current output of any operator is recomputed both when the current value of its input changes (in the three-valued domain) *and* possibly on timer events, such as the timer events scheduled by the >!! operator mentioned above. An important consequence of this feature is that the monitor may signal the violation or satisfaction of a formula even when no event happens. For instance, when monitoring for a door left open more than time T during a Night slot using the formula *during(Door >!! T, Night)*, the satisfaction of the formula is signalled as soon as the delay T has elapsed since the door has been opened, without waiting for a new event to happen. In contrast, many existing monitors [1,2,6] wait for a next event, or rely on an artificial clock event to ensure reactivity. The problem in this case is that more the clock event is fine-grained, more the monitor is overloaded by processing these artificial events, decreasing its efficiency. For AllenRV, no such clock events are needed, and the monitor reacts as soon as it processes its timer events. In fact, our timer events may be considered as clock events generated on demand, without bloating the monitor with useless regular events. In practice, this strategy makes possible a reactivity of the order of 1 ms, currently unreachable by many other tools.

2.5   Input and Output

AllenRV is constituted by a compiler, called `allenc` and a virtual machine, called `allen`. The compiler takes a program adhering to the syntax in Fig. 2, expressing a set of named formulae to be monitored, and produces a compiled module. The virtual machine is designed as a Unix 'filter', that is, takes a log on standard input (which may come from a file or a pipe) containing the value changes of input signals, and produces a log of value changes of the output signals—one for each named formula.

Both the input and output are in CSV format (colon-separated values): each line is a triple containing a timestamp, a signal name, and a value. In the input log, signals commonly correspond to sensors, and timestamps are ordered in increasing order. Values having the same timestamp must correspond to different signals (recall that for each signal, the timestamps are strictly increasing) and are considered to happen simultaneously. Simultaneity is important in many Allen-logic operators such as meets(p,q), recognizing the situation when signal p falls at the same time when signal q is raising. In the output log, timestamps are not necessarily increasing, as output signals are de-correlated, and each value change is signalled immediately for maximal reactivity. This absence of sorting is similar to other recent monitors [1,2].

Timestamps may be either opaque integers (number of seconds or milliseconds since "the Epoch") or human-readable standard date-time timestamps.

2.6   Command-Line Options

The `allen` command offers, among others, options for:

- converting number-valued signals to boolean signals, by associating a threshold to a signal name (or a name pattern, to cover several signals)
- specifying symbolic values for a signal (e.g., OPEN/CLOSED) corresponding to 1 and 0
- debugging, e.g., by executing only one named formula in the specification, or by printing information about the computations performed at each event
- loading a library of operators extending the set of pre-defined operators

This last option is used, for instance, to extend the set of 4 native operators with the AllenRV library.

3   Applications

AllenRV has been successfully used for processing logs of real homes produced by different smart home projects. First, it has been used to simultaneously monitor more than 50 real AAL services on logs spanning one year from more than 100 homes of seniors living along, produced by the HomeAssist project [4]. It has also been used to simultaneously monitor 27 reals-size formulae on logs produced by the Orange4Home experiment [5], and to process logs of several weeks produced by the Amiqual4Home experiment [7]. All these examples are available with the AllenRV distribution, and can be reproduced easily by using the makefile in the examples subdirectory.

For instance, the Orange4Home example demonstrates on the corresponding dataset that AllenRV ensures close to real time processing with millisecond-class reactivity when processing the 27 AAL services simultaneously. These services include: infrastructure monitoring such as checking the correct functioning of light switches based on light sensors; recognizers for various activities in the home, such as showering, napping, or cooking; and meta-level rules built on top of the activity recognizers, such as alerting about unusual activity patterns, or about a potential danger when napping while cooking. The 'let' construct is especially useful in this context, when both activity and meta-activity rules are monitored. Without this construct, activity recognition formulae have to be computed many times, which, in this example, multiplies the total size of the monitored formulae by a factor of 4.3, and increases computation time by 63%.

4   Conclusion

Allen RV is a scalable and extensible tool for monitoring multiple complex specifications on discrete time boolean signals, scaling to arbitrarily fine-grain reactivity with no computation overhead. The system library demonstrates its smooth extensibility, but is only a starting point. The open platform constituted by the AllenRV opens the way to experiment with higher-level specifications abstractions in metric propositional temporal logic, driven by concrete practice. Although our previous practice was limited to the SH and AAL domains, we hope that this platform will be useful in other sensor-based applications in the IoT realm, for example.

References

1. Basin, D.A., Klaedtke, F., Zalinescu, E.: The MonPoly monitoring tool. In: RV-CuBES, pp. 19–28 (2017)
2. Basin, D.A., Krstic, S., Traytel, D.: Aerial: almost event-rate independent algorithms for monitoring metric regular properties. In: RV-CuBES, pp. 29–36 (2017)
3. Bauer, A., Leucker, M., Schallhart, C.: Runtime verification for LTL and TLTL. ACM Trans. Software Eng. Methodol. (TOSEM) 20(4), 14 (2011)
4. Consel, C., Dupuy, L., Sauzéon, H.: HomeAssist: an assisted living platform for aging in place based on an interdisciplinary approach. In: Duffy, V., Lightner, N. (eds.) AHFE 2017. AISC, vol. 590, pp. 129–140. Springer, Cham (2018). https://doi.org/10.1007/978-3-319-60483-1_14
5. Cumin, J., Lefebvre, G., Ramparany, F., Crowley, J.L.: A dataset of routine daily activities in an instrumented home. In: Ochoa, S.F., Singh, P., Bravo, J. (eds.) UCAmI 2017. LNCS, vol. 10586, pp. 413–425. Springer, Cham (2017). https://doi.org/10.1007/978-3-319-67585-5_43
6. El-Hokayem, A., Falcone, Y.: Bringing runtime verification home. In: Colombo, C., Leucker, M. (eds.) RV 2018. LNCS, vol. 11237, pp. 222–240. Springer, Cham (2018). https://doi.org/10.1007/978-3-030-03769-7_13
7. Lago, P., Lang, F., Roncancio, C., Jiménez-Guarín, C., Mateescu, R., Bonnefond, N.: The contextAct@A4H real-life dataset of daily-living activities. In: Brézillon, P., Turner, R., Penco, C. (eds.) CONTEXT 2017. LNCS (LNAI), vol. 10257, pp. 175–188. Springer, Cham (2017). https://doi.org/10.1007/978-3-319-57837-8_14
8. Letier, E., Kramer, J., Magee, J., Uchitel, S.: Fluent temporal logic for discrete-time event-based models. In: ACM SIGSOFT Software Engineering Notes, vol. 30, pp. 70–79. ACM (2005)
9. Thati, P., Roşu, G.: Monitoring algorithms for metric temporal logic specifications. Electron. Notes Theoret. Comput. Sci. 113, 145–162 (2005)
10. Volanschi, N., Serpette, B.: Scaling up RV-based activity detection (2019), submitted
11. Volanschi, N., Serpette, B., Carteron, A., Consel, C.: A language for online state processing of binary sensors, applied to ambient assisted living. Proc. ACM Interact. Mobile Wearable Ubiquit. Technol. 2(4), 192:1–192:26 (2018). https://doi.org/10.1145/3287070
12. Volanschi, N., Serpette, B., Consel, C.: Implementing a semi-causal domain-specific language for context detection over binary sensors. In: Proceedings of the 17th ACM SIGPLAN International Conference on Generative Programming: Concepts and Experiences, pp. 66–78. ACM (2018). https://doi.org/10.1145/3278122.3278134

Timescales: A Benchmark Generator for MTL Monitoring Tools

Dogan Ulus[✉]

Boston University, Boston, MA, USA
doganulus@gmail.com

Abstract. This article presents a benchmark generator, Timescales, which can be used to evaluate the performance and scalability of runtime verification tools using Metric Temporal Logic (MTL) formulas as their specifications. We mainly target runtime verification of cyber-physical systems and generate traces similar to the qualitative behavior of sensor readings and state variables of such systems that are observed/sampled continuously. Since such systems are composed of many heterogeneous components that work over very different time scales, it is crucial to measure the performance of the MTL monitoring tool for a wide range of timing parameters in specifications. Hence, Timescales supports the generation of benchmarks for 10 typical timed properties for any given trace length and timing parameters with several other useful features. Finally, we include some default benchmark suites generated by Timescales.

1 Introduction

Cyber physical systems (CPS) refer to large-scale interconnected control and communication systems that incorporate physical and computing components at various levels. Real-time decision making is the defining characteristic of cyber physical systems such that it does not only mean responding to soft and hard deadlines but also making decisions in a timely manner based on an ongoing interaction between the system and environment. The design of CPS often involves heterogeneous components that operate on different temporal scales and the correct operation requires a high level of coordination and cooperation among such components. Overall the design results in very complex artifacts to verify the correctness and evaluate the performance. Therefore, we usually resort to conventional simulation and model based testing methods for the analysis of CPS. Current research efforts include developing fast, scalable, and versatile runtime verification techniques and tools that handle complex timing requirements of CPS and provide an additional level of rigor and effectiveness over conventional testing methods.

Metric Temporal Logic (MTL) [6] is a popular formalism to specify temporal properties with timing constraints over the behavior of cyber physical systems. Several existing runtime verification (RV) tools support MTL as their specification and employ different techniques and algorithms to monitor MTL formulas over temporal behaviors (traces) [1,2,7–9]. From any MTL monitoring tool,

© Springer Nature Switzerland AG 2019
B. Finkbeiner and L. Mariani (Eds.): RV 2019, LNCS 11757, pp. 402–412, 2019.
https://doi.org/10.1007/978-3-030-32079-9_25

we typically expect a linear-time performance in both the length of the trace and the size of the formula. Furthermore, the insensitivity to the base time unit and numeric time values in formulas is a very much desired feature for MTL monitoring tools. This becomes especially crucial for CPS applications since we usually have to use small and large numerical constants in the same formula when specifying timing requirements of components that operate on different timescales. Hence, in this paper, we present Timescales benchmark generator, which can be used to evaluate the performance and scalability of MTL monitoring tools. In particular, Timescales generates temporal behaviors for a predefined set of MTL formulas with parameterized timing constraints. We consider the past and future fragments of MTL separately and our benchmarks consist of one trace file in the comma-separated values (CSV[1]) format and two (past and future) specification files in the YAML[2] format. Besides we provide ANTLR[3] grammar files to parse our MTL formulas. These file formats are widely supported and their implementations are already available for many programming languages.

Timescales is essentially developed to help measure the typical performance of MTL monitoring tools. Therefore, we, first and foremost, consider the most common types of timed properties encountered in real system designs. Such typical properties have been studied in the papers [4,5], which employs the template system developed by Dwyer et al. for untimed specifications [3]. In this template system, a property consists of (1) a pattern, which describes what must be observed, and (2) a scope, which describes the temporal extent of the pattern. Each property further contains one or two timing parameters, which can be controlled by the user. In Timescales, we support a total of 10 typical timed properties over 4 pattern (absence, universality, recurrence, response) and 4 temporal scopes (before, after, between, globally) for the benchmark generation. Then, the tool generates a discrete time behavior that satisfy the property for a given property, duration, and values of timing parameters. We also provide an option to generate dense time behaviors where the maximum density is controlled by the user. Since we usually want to generate a collection of benchmarks by varying all these parameters over a grid, we include some example scripts to generate such benchmark suites with some predefined values.

The structure of this paper is as follows. Section 2 overviews the syntax and semantics of MTL as used in this paper. In Sect. 3, we describe supported timed properties and corresponding MTL formulas for the benchmark generation. Section 4 explains the benchmark generation generally and gives further details about the implementation including trace generation, output formats, and default benchmark suites generated by Timescales.

---

[1] CSV is a common text-based data exchange format to store a sequence of data fields. (https://en.wikipedia.org/wiki/Comma-separated_values).

[2] YAML is a human-readable configuration file format. (https://yaml.org).

[3] ANTLR is a powerful parser generator tool. (https://www.antlr.org).

2 Metric Temporal Logic

Metric Temporal Logic (MTL) [6] is an extension of linear temporal logic (LTL) in which temporal operators are endowed with timing constraints. In this paper, we interpret MTL formulas over a bounded discrete time domain $\mathbb{T} = [1, N]$ of total duration N and use so-called non-strict (reflexive) semantics of temporal operators, *timed since* ($\mathcal{S}_I$) and *timed until* ($\mathcal{U}_I$). Given a finite set P of atomic propositions, the formulas of MTL are defined by the following grammar:

$$\varphi = p \mid \neg\varphi \mid \varphi_1 \vee \varphi_2 \mid \varphi_1 \mathcal{S}_I \varphi_2 \mid \varphi_1 \mathcal{U}_I \varphi_2$$

where $p \in P$ and $I \subseteq [0, \infty)$. Then the satisfaction relation $(w, t) \vDash \varphi$ indicates that the Boolean temporal behavior $w : \mathbb{T} \to \mathbb{B}^P$ satisfies the formula φ at the time point $t \in \mathbb{T}$ as follows.

$$
\begin{aligned}
(w, t) &\vDash p & &\leftrightarrow w_p(t) = \top \\
(w, t) &\vDash \neg\varphi & &\leftrightarrow (w, t) \nvDash \varphi \\
(w, t) &\vDash \varphi_1 \vee \varphi_2 & &\leftrightarrow (w, t) \vDash \varphi_1 \text{ or } (w, t) \vDash \varphi_2 \\
(w, t) &\vDash \varphi_1 \mathcal{S}_I \varphi_2 & &\leftrightarrow \exists t' \leq t. \ (w, t') \vDash \varphi_2 \text{ and} \\
& & &\qquad \forall t'' \in (t', t]. \ (w, t'') \vDash \varphi_1 \text{ and} \\
& & &\qquad t - t' \in I \\
(w, t) &\vDash \varphi_1 \mathcal{U}_I \varphi_2 & &\leftrightarrow \exists t' \geq t. \ (w, t') \vDash \varphi_2 \text{ and} \\
& & &\qquad \forall t'' \in [t, t'). \ (w, t'') \vDash \varphi_1 \text{ and} \\
& & &\qquad t' - t \in I
\end{aligned}
$$

where we use $w_p : \mathbb{T} \to \mathbb{B}$ to denote the projection of w onto its component p. Other timed modalities include time constrained variants of *sometime in the past* ($\blacklozenge_I$) and *always in the past* ($\blacksquare_I$) as well as *sometime in the future* ($\Diamond_I$) and *always in the future* ($\Box_I$). For any temporal operator, we usually omit the time bound if there is no constraint and call such an operator untimed. The past fragment of MTL, or past MTL in short, is defined as a restriction of MTL without the until operator. Similarly we do not use the since operator in the future fragment. In this paper, we write MTL formulas either in the past or future fragment of MTL.

3 Supported Properties

This section overviews supported timed properties in Timescales. By default a single benchmark consists of a logical formula that capture the property either in the past or future fragment of MTL and a temporal behavior that satisfies the formula. We select 10 typical timed properties for the benchmark generation and we cover in these properties all types of temporal operators and different types of intervals for timing constraints. Each timed property is parameterized with one or two timing parameters in order to generate benchmarks with different timing characteristics. Note that we do not claim or seek the logical equivalence between the past and future MTL formulas in the following but capture the intention in both fragments.

Bounded Absence After Q. This property has one timing parameter u. Intuitively it means that it is always the case that the event P does not occur at least for U time units after the event Q occurs. We capture this property by the formula

$$\blacksquare (\; \blacklozenge_{[0,u]}\; Q \longrightarrow (\neg P\; \mathcal{S}\; Q)) \tag{Past}$$

in the past fragment of MTL and by the formula

$$\square (\; Q \longrightarrow \square_{[0,u]} \neg P) \tag{Future}$$

in the future fragment of MTL.

Bounded Absence Before R. This property has one timing parameter u. Intuitively it means that it is always the case that the event P does not occur at least for u time units before the event R occurs. We capture this property by the formula

$$\blacksquare (\; R \longrightarrow \blacksquare_{[0,u]} \neg P) \tag{Past}$$

in the past fragment of MTL and by the formula

$$\square (\; \Diamond_{[0,u]}\; R \longrightarrow (\neg P\; \mathcal{U}\; R)) \tag{Future}$$

in the future fragment of MTL.

Bounded Absence Between Q and R. This property has two timing parameters l and u. Intuitively it means that it is always the case that the event P does not occur between events Q and R and the duration between Q and R is in l and u time units. We capture this property by the formula

$$\blacksquare (\; (R \wedge \neg Q \wedge \blacklozenge Q) \longrightarrow (\neg P\; \mathcal{S}_{[l,u]}\; Q)) \tag{Past}$$

in the past fragment of MTL and by the formula

$$\Box(\ (Q \land \neg R \land \Diamond R) \longrightarrow (\neg P\ \mathcal{U}_{[l,u]}\ R))$$ (Future)

in the future fragment of MTL.

Bounded Universality After Q. This property has one timing parameter u. Intuitively it means that it is always the case that the event P always occurs at least for u time units after the event Q occurs. We capture this property by the formula

$$\blacksquare(\ \blacklozenge_{[0,u]}\ Q \longrightarrow (P\ \mathcal{S}\ Q))$$ (Past)

in the past fragment of MTL and by the formula

$$\Box(\ Q \longrightarrow \Box_{[0,u]} P)$$ (Future)

in the future fragment of MTL.

Bounded Universality Before R. This property has one timing parameter u. Intuitively it means that it is always the case that the event P always occurs at least for u time units before the event R occurs. We capture this property by the formula

$$\blacksquare(\ R \longrightarrow \blacksquare_{[0,u]} P)$$ (Past)

in the past fragment of MTL and by the formula

$$\Box(\ \Diamond_{[0,u]}\ R \longrightarrow (P\ \mathcal{U}\ R))$$ (Future)

in the future fragment of MTL.

Bounded Universality Between Q and R. This property has two timing parameters l and u. Intuitively it means that it is always the case that the event P always occurs between events Q and R and the duration between Q and R is in l and u time units. We capture this property by the formula

$$\blacksquare(\ (R \land \neg Q \land \blacklozenge Q) \longrightarrow (P\ \mathcal{S}_{[l,u]}\ Q))$$ (Past)

in the past fragment of MTL and by the formula

$$\Box(\ (Q \land \neg R \land \Diamond R) \longrightarrow (P\ \mathcal{U}_{[l,u]}\ R))$$ (Future)

in the future fragment of MTL.

Bounded Recurrence Globally. This property has one timing parameter u. Intuitively it means that it is always the case that the event P occurs at least for every u time units. We capture this property by the formula

$$\blacksquare\blacklozenge_{[0,u]}P \qquad\qquad \text{(Past)}$$

in the past fragment of MTL and by the formula

$$\square\lozenge_{[0,u]}P \qquad\qquad \text{(Future)}$$

in the future fragment of MTL.

Bounded Recurrence Between Q and R. This property has one timing parameter u. Intuitively it means that it is always the case that the event P occurs at least for every u time units between events Q and R. We capture this property by the formula

$$\blacksquare(\ (R \wedge \neg Q \wedge \blacklozenge Q) \longrightarrow (\blacklozenge_{[0,u]}(P \vee Q)\ \mathcal{S}\ Q)) \qquad\qquad \text{(Past)}$$

in the past fragment of MTL and by the formula

$$\square(\ (Q \wedge \neg R \wedge \lozenge R) \longrightarrow (\lozenge_{[0,u]}(P \vee R)\ \mathcal{U}\ R)) \qquad\qquad \text{(Future)}$$

in the future fragment of MTL.

Bounded Response Globally. This property has two timing parameters l and u. Intuitively it means that it is always the case that the event S responds to the event P in l and u time units. We capture this property by the formula

$$\blacksquare((S \longrightarrow \blacklozenge_{[l,u]}P) \wedge \neg(\neg S\ \mathcal{S}_{[u,\infty)}\ P)) \qquad\qquad \text{(Past)}$$

in the past fragment of MTL and by the formula

$$\square(P \longrightarrow \lozenge_{[l,u]}S) \qquad\qquad \text{(Future)}$$

in the future fragment of MTL.

Bounded Response Between Q and R. This property has two timing parameters l and u. Intuitively it means that it is always the case that the event S responds to the event P in l and u time units between events Q and R. We capture this property by the formula

$$\blacksquare\Big((R \wedge \neg Q \wedge \blacklozenge Q) \longrightarrow ((S \longrightarrow \blacklozenge_{[l,u]} P) \wedge \neg(\neg S\ \mathcal{S}_{[u,\infty)} P))\Big) \qquad \text{(Past)}$$

in the past fragment of MTL and by the formula

$$\square\Big((Q \wedge \neg R \wedge \lozenge R) \longrightarrow (P \longrightarrow (\neg R\ \mathcal{U}_{[l,u]}(\neg R \wedge S))\ \mathcal{U}\ R)\Big) \qquad \text{(Future)}$$

in the future fragment of MTL.

4   Implementation

Timescales is an open source command line program[4] written in Python. For example, using Timescales, we generate a benchmark for the property bounded universality property between Q and R by executing the command

```
timescales always_bqr --lbound 300 --ubound 600 --duration 1000
```

where the argument specifies the duration of trace and arguments lbound and ubound specify the value for lower and upper timing parameters of the property, respectively. Then Timescales produces a concrete specification file, which contains an MTL formula, as a standard YAML file and a trace as a standard CSV file. These output formats are simple human-readable text files and very well supported in virtually all major programming languages. In the following, we give further details on the trace generation, output formats, and default benchmark suites.

4.1   Trace Generation

Given a timed property and parameter values, Timescales generate a temporal behavior in a periodic fashion where each period contains a sequence of propositional values that satisfies the property. For each period, we randomly determine actual timings of the sequence according to timing constraints specified by --lbound and --ubound arguments. Consequently, the duration of each period varies accordingly and we terminate the generation process once we exceed the total duration specified by the argument --duration. For example, suppose we want to generate a trace for the property always_bqr for $l = 300$ and $u = 600$. We start each period with a time point where Q holds and end with a time point where R holds. Then the actual number of time points where P holds between Q and R is randomly selected between 300 and 600. We repeat this procedure as many times as needed.

---

[4] https://github.com/doganulus/timescales.

```
usage: timescales [-h] [-d INT] [-l INT] [-u INT] [--min-
    recur INT] [--max-recur INT] [--name STRING] [--condense
    INT] [--failing-end] [--future] [--output-dir DIR]
    property

positional arguments:
property
    absent_aq                 UBOUND
    absent_br                 UBOUND
    absent_bqr      LBOUND UBOUND

    always_aq                 UBOUND
    always_br                 UBOUND
    always_bqr      LBOUND UBOUND

    recur_glb                 UBOUND
    recur_bqr                 UBOUND MIN_RECUR MAX_RECUR

    resp_glb        LBOUND UBOUND
    resp_bqr        LBOUND UBOUND MIN_RECUR MAX_RECUR
```

Fig. 1. Timescales command line interface

For benchmark generation, the command line interface of Timescales provides a few more customization options as shown in Fig. 1. First, properties that contain some kind of recurrence have additional parameters to specify the minimum and maximum number of recurrence inside a single period. By the arguments --min-recur and --max-recur , we can specify a range and actual number of recurrences is randomly selected to be within this range. Secondly, generated temporal behaviors may involve the repetition of the same value over long periods called stuttering periods. We provide an option to condense such behaviors by omitting a time point in the trace file if the next time point also has the same value. By the argument --condense, we can control the amount of condensation, which caps the duration of such omitted periods. Choosing a large value (such as larger than the total duration) would eliminate any stuttering in the trace file while choosing zero means there would be no condensation and the trace file explicitly includes every time point. Finally, we provide another option to append a sequence that makes the property fail at the end of the trace. This trick often serves a sanity check for that the monitoring algorithm does actually find an error (thus not silently fails) during the benchmarking. The option --failing-end enables this behavior.

4.2   Output Formats

Timescales produces a specification file in the standard YAML format and a temporal behavior in the standard CSV format as its output. These are simple human-readable text files and several implementations to read and write these formats already exist in virtually all major programming languages. Hence, Timescales can be used directly for RV tools that support these formats or else requires little implementation effort for the rest.

```
---
name : "always_bqr_300_600"
spec : "(r && !q && once q ) -> (p since[300:600] q)"
```

time,q,p,r		time,q,p,r		time,q,p,r
1, 0,0,0		1, 0,0,0		10, 0,0,0
2, 1,1,0		2, 1,1,0		11, 1,1,0
3, 0,1,0		6, 0,1,0		111, 0,1,0
4, 0,1,0		7, 0,1,1		211, 0,1,0
5, 0,1,0		16, 0,0,0		311, 0,1,0
6, 0,1,0		17, 1,0,0		411, 0,1,0
7, 0,1,1		18, 0,1,0		454, 0,1,0
8, 0,0,0		27, 0,1,1		455, 0,1,1
9, 0,0,0		29, 0,0,0		500, 0,0,0

Fig. 2. (Top) An example specification file generated for the property with timing values 300 and 600. (Bottom Left) An example discrete time behavior in CSV format. (Bottom Middle) A dense time behavior with limited 10. (Bottom Right) A dense time behavior with limited 100. Note that whitespaces in CSVs are for the aesthetics.

At the top of Fig. 2, we show an example specification file that we have generated using Timescales. The name attribute indicates the name of property, which can be overwritten via the command line, and the spec attribute denotes the actual MTL formula. We provide our MTL grammar as an ANTLR grammar file so that an ANTLR parser can be automatically generated to parse our MTL formulas. The bottom row of Fig. 2 demonstrates three example CSV files generated using Timescales. The leftmost CSV file contains a row of propositional values for each time point in the time domain and represents a discrete time behavior. The CSV file show a condensed trace where some time points are omitted in the file if the next time has the same value of propositions. Finally the rightmost CSV is generated with the option --condense 100 and therefore the duration of time jumps in the file is capped by 100 time units.

4.3   Default Benchmark Suites

In the source code distribution, we also include a Makefile script to generate three predefined sets of benchmarks named as small, large, and full suites using the generator. First, the small suite is intended for initial testing and demonstration purposes. It contains one benchmark for each supported property (10 in total) with small timing bounds over short traces with a duration of 1000 time units. Secondly, the large suite targets discrete time MTL monitoring tools and contains three benchmarks for each property (30 in total) with increasingly larger time bounds (1×, 10×, and 100×) over traces with a duration of one million time units. These numbers are often sufficient to check whether a runtime verification tool scales towards large time bounds in the specification. The total size of the large suite is about 400 MB and not included in the distribution. Finally, the full suite extends the large suite by varying the length of generated traces (10K, 100K, 1M) and the amount of condensation (1, 10, 100). These benchmarks can be used to check the scalability of the tool with respect to the trace length as well as compare discrete and dense time implementations if the tool supports both settings.

5   Conclusion

In this paper, we presented Timescales benchmark generator to help testing the performance and scalability of MTL monitoring tools over the most common types of timed properties encountered in real designs. In particular, we have been interested in checking such tools when the specification contains large values of timing constraints and ideally expect that large timing constraints do not deteriorate the performance. This is especially important in runtime verification of cyber-physical systems, which involves various cooperating components operating in different timescales. Hence, our main motivation has been to generate benchmarks of the same property with the varying timing constraints and measuring the performance of the tool over them. In our tool, we have considered 10 typical properties for the benchmark generation and provided various customization options, which can be accessed easily via the command line interface. We adhered standard file formats for the implementation and tried to conform current practices in runtime verification as much as possible.

References

1. Basin, D., Klaedtke, F., Zalinescu, E.: The MonPoly monitoring tool. In: Proceedings of the Workshop on Competitions, Usability, Benchmarks, Evaluation, and Standardisation for Runtime Verification Tools (RV-CuBES), vol. 3, pp. 19–28 (2017)
2. Basin, D., Krstíc, S., Traytel, D.: AERIAL: almost event-rate independent algorithms for monitoring metric regular properties. In: Proceedings of the Workshop on Competitions, Usability, Benchmarks, Evaluation, and Standardisation for Runtime Verification Tools (RV-CuBES), pp. 29–36 (2017)
3. Dwyer, M.B. Avrunin, G.S., Corbett, J.C.: Property specification patterns for finite-state verification. In: Proceedings of the Workshop on Formal Methods in Software Practice (FMSP), pp. 7–15 (1998)
4. Gruhn, V., Laue, R.: Patterns for timed property specifications. Electron. Notes Theor. Comput. Sci. **153**(2), 117–133 (2006)
5. Konrad, S., Cheng, B.H.C.: Real-time specification patterns. In: Proceedings of the International Conference on Software Engineering (ICSE), pp. 372–381 (2005)

6. Koymans, R.: Specifying real-time properties with metric temporal logic. Real-Time Syst. **2**(4), 255–299 (1990)
7. Ničković, D., Lebeltel, O., Maler, O., Ferrère, T., Ulus, D.: AMT 2.0: qualitative and quantitative trace analysis with extended signal temporal logic. In: Proceedings of the Conference on Tools and Algorithms for the Construction and Analysis of Systems (TACAS), pp. 303–319 (2018)
8. Schumann, J., Moosbrugger, P., Rozier, K.Y.: R2U2: monitoring and diagnosis of security threats for unmanned aerial systems. In: Bartocci, E., Majumdar, R. (eds.) RV 2015. LNCS, vol. 9333, pp. 233–249. Springer, Cham (2015). https://doi.org/10.1007/978-3-319-23820-3_15
9. Ulus, D.: Online monitoring of metric temporal logic using sequential networks. In: arXiv preprint arXiv:1901.00175 (2019)

Author Index

Printed in the United States
By Bookmasters